THE RELIGION
OF THE OCCIDENT

BY THE SAME AUTHOR:

    Milton and Servetus
    The Modernity of Milton
    The Theory of Logical Expression
    Plaster Saint
    Lady Sans Discretion

THE RELIGION
of
THE OCCIDENT

or

The Origin and Development
of the Essene-Christian Faith

BY

MARTIN A. LARSON

(Alfred)

PHILOSOPHICAL LIBRARY
New York

Andrew S. Thomas Memorial Library
Morris Harvey College, Charleston, W. Va.
38348

COPYRIGHT, 1959, *by* PHILOSOPHICAL LIBRARY, INC.
15 East 40th Street, New York, N. Y.

All rights reserved

Printed in the United States of America

To

My wife, Emma, who has shared with me from the beginning the experience of writing this book;

and

To all seekers for truth, wherever they may be.

. . . .truth is strong. . . .she needs no policies, nor stratagems, nor licensings to make her victorious; those are the shifts and the defences that error uses against her power.

MILTON

TABLE OF CONTENTS

Introduction, by Harry Elmer Barnes — xi

Foreword, by the Author — xv

PART ONE: THE PAGAN ORIGINS — xxi

Chapter

I	The Original Savior-God: Osiris	1
II	Adonis and Aphrodite	24
III	The Primitive Greek Dionysus	32
IV	Attis and Cybele	51
V	Demeter-Persephone	60
VI	The Orphean Reconstruction of Dionysus	72
VII	The Zoroastrians	83
VIII	Brahmanism	107
IX	Buddhism: Revolution in India	126
X	Pythagoras	155
XI	Isis and Serapis	177
XII	Mithraism	182

PART TWO: THE JEWISH SOURCES — 193

I	Judaism	195
II	The Essenes: The External Evidence	225
III	The Essenes: The Internal Evidence	247
IV	The Essenes: Analysis and Tradition	280

PART THREE:
THE INNER MEANING OF THE GOSPEL JESUS — 293

Prefatory:	Cultic Preparation for Christianity	295
I	The Historicity of Jesus	304
II	The Composition of the Synoptic Gospels	311
III	The Apotheosis of Jesus	316

IV	Jesus Rejected in Nazareth	319
V	Miracles in Galilee	322
VI	The Storm Clouds Gather	327
VII	Ethics: The Sermon on the Mount	332
VIII	Art Thou He That Should Come?	345
IX	Approaching Crisis in Galilee	347
X	The First Apocalypse	354
XI	Indecision and Reorientation	360
XII	Thou Art the Christ!	363
XIII	The Transformed Christ	367
XIV	Interlude at Bethany	370
XV	Many Are Called, but Few Are Chosen	375
XVI	The Kingdom of Heaven	381
XVII	At War with the Pharisees	389
XVIII	The Second Gospel Apocalypse	394
XIX	The Eucharistic Mystery	398
XX	Gethsemene	402
XXI	The Trial and Death of Jesus	404
XXII	Summary and Evaluation	411

PART FOUR:
REDEVELOPMENT IN THE PAGAN WORLD 423

I	The Earliest Christians	425
II	*The Didache*	434
III	Paul: Jew vs. Gentile	437
IV	The Catholic Epistles	453
V	The Great Synoptical Additions	456
VI	Revelation	471
VII	Christian Eschatology	480
VIII	The Fourth Gospel	492
IX	Primitive Christology	498
X	The Search for Authority	503
XI	Semitic Christianity	512
XII	Hellenic Gnosticism: Marcion	520
XIII	Mystical-Pythagorean Gnosticism	532
XIV	The Monarchians	539
XV	Manichaeism: The Great Gnostic Synthesis	545

XVI	The Trinitarian Controversy	562
XVII	Christological Heresies	583
XVIII	Persecution	595
XIX	St. Augustine	607
XX	Life under the Catholic Church	631
XXI	The Development of the Papacy	646
XXII	The Christian Mysteries	657

GLOSSARY 663

BIBLIOGRAPHY 667

NOTES 673

INDEX 695

INTRODUCTION

It is personal pleasure and a professional opportunity for me to write a commendatory introduction to Dr. Larson's learned, readable, and highly useful book. Ordinarily, in such an introduction, I would endeavor to state succinctly just what task he has set himself and how well he has performed it. Since, however, he has, in his own admirable Foreword done this far more effectively and authoritatively than I possibly could, it has seemed to me that it would be more appropriate for me to make the introduction something of a personal memoir which will indicate the manner in which I became acquainted with the field of knowledge which he has covered in so exhaustive and convincing a manner.

Dr. Larson's volume takes me back to one of my favorite branches of professional interest: intellectual history and, within that, the genesis of Christian doctrine. In my youth, I was subjected to the rather rigorous orthodoxy of the Disciples of Christ, known as the Campbellites. This was mitigated by the fact that my boyhood was spent in a town not far from Auburn, New York, the seat of a very prominent Presbyterian Theological Seminary, in which the father of John Foster Dulles was a member of the faculty. Our rural church profited by the fact that several able young ministers filled the pulpit with a minimum of salary in exchange for the privilege of studying at the Seminary. Their orthodoxy was tempered by their new intellectual adventure there.

About the time, however, that I had finished high school one of the more distinguished of the older ministers in the denomination came to our church to preach during his declining years. His orthodoxy was as thorough as his faith was sincere. His sermons were built around the conception of "the faith once for all delivered to the Saints," a text which constituted his favorite quotation from the Scriptures. This implied that Christianity is a unique religion which was rather abruptly revealed through Jesus Christ and his Apostles and had no relation to the pagan cults which preceded or surrounded it in the Mediterranean world.

Orthodox religion never "took" very deeply with me personally. Hence, I underwent no serious emotional upheaval when, at Syracuse University, the tenets of the faith were gradually undermined in my classes. The professors who were foremost in this salutary process of emancipation were Jesse Erwin Wrench, William R. P. Davey and Philip A. Parsons. Wrench had been a student at Cornell under George Lincoln Burr, our leading authority on toleration and a master of medieval religious thought. Wrench was also well informed on the oriental foundations of Judaism. Davey was a follower of the immensely erudite George Foot Moore of Harvard, one of our leading authorities on comparative religion. Davey handed out to us large doses of such unsettling works as Nathaniel Schmidt's *Prophet of Nazareth*. Parsons was fresh from taking his doctorate under Franklin Henry Giddings at Columbia and, for the first time, enabled me to gain some insight into the anthropological and sociological background of all religions, including Christianity. But it was not until I entered Columbia University as a graduate student that I gained any detailed and well organized knowledge concerning the actual nature of the origins and growth of the Christian Epic, as George Santayana designated it.

My graduate major was the history of thought and culture, and my outstanding professors were James Harvey Robinson and James Thomson Shotwell. No student in American higher education could have been more fortunate in securing stimulating instruction. In my first year, I elected Robinson's famous course on "the History of the Intellectual Class in Europe," and Shotwell's seminar on "Paganism and Christianity."

Shotwell had written his doctoral dissertation on the origins of the basic Christian rite, the Eucharist, or sacrament of the Mass, and had given special attention to the derivation of Christian doctrine from the general religious complex of the Mediterranean region. We were introduced to all stages of the evolution of religion from V. G. Bogoraz's famous study of the primitive religion of the Chukchee reindeer Eskimo of eastern Siberia to the synthesis of early Christianity in Augustine's *City of God*. We read such books as Emile Durkheim's *Elementary Forms of Religious Life,* which had been translated by Joseph Ward Swain, a member of the seminar; Robertson Smith's *Religion of the Semites;* Franz Cumont's *Oriental Religions in Roman Paganism;* Jane Harrison's works on Greek religion; Ward Fowler's *Religious Experience of the Roman People;* and Frederick Cornwallis Conybeare's *Myth, Magic, and Morals,* a brilliant survey of Christian origins. No intelligent and thoughtful member of this seminar could leave it without having a clear conception of the manner in which Christian doctrine and organization were forged over the centuries out of the religions that had grown up from primitive times onward, in the Levant and southern Europe.

In the relevant sector of his broader course, Robinson, with a unique combination of mature knowledge and subtle wit, provided a synthesis of both Christian beliefs and ecclesiastical organization as they took systematic form in the Roman Catholic international state of the Middle Ages. It was also my good fortune to attend courses given by Alexander Goldenweiser, the most brilliant lecturer among all of the products of Franz Boas's seminars, and a specialist in the anthropological foundations of religion. He and Shotwell agreed that the permanent and enduring raw material and basic impulse of religion is the emotional thrill derived from the contemplation of the mysterious.

One might inquire what this has to do with Dr. Larson's book. My answer is that in his single volume one can find a masterly synthesis of what I laboriously gathered over many years, reading numerous books and listening to many illuminating seminar reports and classroom lectures. Actually, the reader can obtain far more than this, for Dr. Larson has included new and vitally important material which was all but unknown in my student days; indeed, sensationally novel and immensely valuable data with which even scholars and specialists in religion were unfamiliar as recently as 1955. Notable here, are the *Dead Sea Scrolls*, with their precious information concerning the origin and nature of the Essene creed and ethics, which played so crucial a role in shaping the trends in Christian doctrine and guiding the career of Jesus.

In the volume now before us, we find a comprehensive synthesis of the facts most directly related to the genesis of the Christian Epic and its supporting organization. To encompass this knowledge in far less complete fashion required a considerable segment of all the reading I have ever done. Only those who have found their way slowly and laboriously through the vast field of complicated information which Dr. Larson has explored and digested, can fully appreciate the magnitude of his undertaking, the success with which he has accomplished his purpose, or the practical value of what he has achieved. He has earned, or at least deserves, the gratitude of all those who are seriously concerned with the nature and evolution of Christianity and its relevance for our nuclear age.

Dr. Larson makes it clear that any true realization of the vast intellectual and emotional debt of Christianity to other religions already hoary with age during the lifetime of Jesus must undermine the basis for all narrow sectarianism, dogmatic bigotry, and arrogant intolerance within the realm of Christian doctrine and practice. Many will go further and contend that few, if any, of the beliefs which contributed to the growth of Christianity can measure up to the tests of modern science in relevant fields. They will hold that those who seek a body of saving knowledge that can solve the problems of our critical nuclear era can only find it in such a secular program as Auguste Comte forecast a century ago in his "Religion of Humanity," and is now promoted by the Humanist movement of our day. But any prospect of notable success for this movement will depend upon that enlightenment and emancipation to which Dr. Larson's *Religion of the Occident* offers so notable a contribution.

HARRY ELMER BARNES.
Malibu, California

FOREWORD

The religious faith of the occident, or the western world, consists substantially of a synthesis of beliefs and doctrines which had their origin in many lands and among various peoples and which were combined and proclaimed in what we may call the Gospel Jesus, specifically those documents known as the Synoptics. The creeds, disciplines, and dogmas on which almost all the churches of Europe and the Americas and many of those in Asia are based purport to derive their authority from this Gospel; and all these multifarious communions proclaim that theirs is the religion established by Jesus, whom they revere as the Christ.

More than thirty years ago, this writer was first fascinated by the thought that the principal concepts of the Christian Gospels, which have played so crucial a role in occidental life, might be traced to their ultimate sources. Some six or seven years ago, leisure for such an elaborate project became possible: scores of modern books and hundreds of articles in encyclopaedias were first read by way of orientation; but, since recondite knowledge is to be had only by a minute study of the sources, this soon became an industry. More than four years were consumed in the intensive study of ancient Egyptian, Persian, Brahmana, Gaina, Buddhist, Judaistic, Essene, and Christian literature, most of which is listed at the close of this volume. Quotations totaling some two million words were copied and organized for easy reference. All the major streams of thought were then carefully analyzed. Important elements from various ancient cultures were discovered to have converged, first, in the Pythagorean *thiasoi* and then in the Essene Order, whence the Christian Gospel emerged, which, in turn, proceeded to penetrate the emotions and to achieve dominion over the Graeco-Roman world.

The Essenes, lately the object of so much attention,

play a central role in our drama. They were an extraordinary group of Jewish communist-celibates who, in their formative stage about 170 B. C., absorbed the metaphysics and the eschatology of the Zoroastrians, and then, some sixty-five years later, by becoming Pythagoreans, incorporated into their system much of the discipline and soteriology of the mystery-cults of Greece and Asia Minor. Upon all this, they engrafted a Christology which combined a Persian with a Messianic Judaic concept, which, in a period of crisis, they personalized in their martyred Teacher of Righteousness, whom they expected to return upon the clouds about 35-30 B. C., accompanied by myriads of angels to conduct the Last Judgment. It is our conclusion that Jesus was an Essene who, convinced that He was Himself the incarnate Christ destined to redeem and judge mankind, left the Order for the purpose of creating a mass-movement.

Our objective being to investigate the origin, the sources, the inner meaning, and the redevelopment of the religion of Jesus, this study falls naturally into four divisions: first, its pagan origins; second, its Jewish sources; third, an analysis of its inner meaning; and, fourth, its reconstitution in the pagan world.

The certainty finally emerges that Christianity was a highy composite doctrine which combined many of the age-old religious concepts first developed by Egyptians, Babylonians, Assyrians, Persians, Buddhists, and Greeks, as well as by Jews, Phrygians, Syrians, and other inhabitants of Asia Minor. It was congenitally related to all of these; and when any of them accepted Christianity, they were simply recovering what was, at least in part, originally their own.

We feel that the realization of this fact must induce among all sectarians a definite humility, which should in turn, contribute toward eliminating those doctrinal differences which divide our society into a multiplicity of groups shut off from each other by ideological barriers, as if we all lived in hermetically sealed compartments, incapable of fellowship or communion.

Mature Essenism taught and the Gospel Jesus elaborated the following concepts: that the human race is divided into two groups which are forever separated, the Elect and the unrighteous, the Children of Light and the Children of Darkness; that the former may be redeemed for everlasting glory in heaven, but only through divine intervention; that a god-man must appear as a human being on earth, and, in fact, had appeared, to bring salvation to humanity; that all of the Elect who accept him and become his disciples will be redeemed; that all others are doomed to suffer eternally in hell fire; that the Children of Light are made manifest through their celibacy, saintly brotherhood, and communal poverty and equalitarianism; that the god-man is the *soter*, i. e., the divine sacrifice who gives his life for many and whose flesh and blood are consumed by his communicants so that they too may become divine and immortal; that in his first manifestation the savior proclaims his revelation; that after his death, he returns to the Father for a period while his followers preach his gospel; that before the end of the then existing generation he would certainly return in a grand Parousia to judge all mankind and establish the kingdom of heaven.

This was the Essene-Christian faith, which is also the religion of the occident.

This gospel consists primarily of four basic elements: soteriology, eschatology, ethics, and the Messianic concept. And first we must consider the sources of its soteriology, that is to say, its doctrine concerning the incarnate godman who dies for humanity and whose body and blood must be consumed sacramentally so that the Elect may become divine and immortal. The trail leads us first to the Nile, where civilization and organized religion began in the dim reaches of the prehistoric past.

We present this study as the work of a searching Humanist; our objective is to understand the forces which have created our ideologies. And may we suggest that religion is neither sacrosanct nor simply a phenomenon of primitive culture: it is now, as it has been for thousands of years, a striving of the human spirit for security, consolation, peace of mind, and an abundant life; and also for unity with something greater than the self and for the realization of one's ultimate capacities. To ridicule religion is puerile; to use it as an authoritative bludgeon is criminal; to employ it as a means to stifle reason or freedom is the offense for which there must be no forgiveness.

And so we have searched wherever knowledge may be found; for thus only "ye shall know the truth; and the truth shall make you free."

MARTIN A. LARSON
Detroit, Michigan

ACKNOWLEDGMENTS

I wish to thank the Viking Press for its generous grant allowing me to quote from Millar Burrows' translations of original documents in his *Dead Sea Scrolls;* the Macmillan Company for the privilege of using a sentence by Mr. Dupont-Sommer in his *Dead Sea Scrolls;* and to Mr. Edmund Wilson for his personal and gracious permission to reproduce certain of his words as published in his *Scrolls from the Dead Sea.*

M. A. L.

The victorious Saoshyant . . . shall restore the world, which will thenceforth never grow old . . . the dead will rise . . . life and immortality will come . . . and the world will be restored.

                Zoroaster:
                    "Zamyad Yast" of the *Zend-Avesta*

Indeed, there was never any religion so barbarous and diabolical, but it was preferred before all others whatsoever, by them that did profess it. . . .

And why, say they, may not you be mistaken as well as we? Especially, when there is, at least, six to one against your Christian religion; all of which think that they serve God aright; and expect happiness thereby as well as you. . . . And hence it is that in my looking out for the truest religion, being conscious to myself how great an ascendent Christianity holds over me beyond the rest, as being that whereinto I was born and baptized, and that which my parents educated me in; that which every one I meet withal highly approves of, and which I myself have, by a long-continued profession, made almost natural to me: I am resolved to be more jealous and suspicious of this religion, than the rest. . . . That, therefore, I may make diligent and impartial enquiry into all religions and so be sure to find out the best, I shall for a time, look upon myself as one not at all interested in any particular religion whatsoever, much less in the Christian religion: but only as one who desires in general . . . to be made partaker of that happiness my nature is capable of.

                    Bishop Beveridge, 1636-1707:
                    Private Thoughts on Religion

PART ONE
THE PAGAN ORIGINS

CHAPTER I

THE ORIGINAL SAVIOR-GOD: OSIRIS

A. RELIGIOUS FOUNDATIONS

1. *Antiquity of Egypt.* Herodotus[1] and Diodorus Siculus[2] both point out that civilization as known to them originated in the valley of the Nile; and did so because there the annual inundation of the great river with its rich deposits of silt made possible an abundant agriculture, which provided ample sustenance with little effort. This not only caused the population to multiply: it also created leisure for many activities beyond those necessary for bare subsistence. Thus it was that thousands of years ago, the arts and sciences flourished in Egypt; cities were built and social classes established; and private property, economic exploitation, and glaring contrasts between wealth and poverty developed. Ruling classes consisting of priesthoods and political dynasties lived in luxury while the impoverished masses groaned under the yoke of their double servitude. Thus, the land which first yielded an abundance of physical wherewithal spawned also glaring inequities and gross injustice.

Egyptian civilization antedates all other Eurasian cultures except the Sumerian; but just how old it is, no one can say with certainty. We know that the great pyramids were built during the Fourth Dynasty about 2700 B. C.; and that Nilotic civilization was then already hoary with age. The First Dynasty dates back at least to 3000. But there was a pre-dynastic culture stretching back, perhaps, to 8,000.

2. *Preoccupation with the After-Life.* For some reason, the Egyptians believed in, and longed for, personal immortality in a manner unique among ancient peoples.

Perhaps the comparative ease of life in the Valley; the long periods of physical inactivity when the inundations made the cities and villages into isolated islands; the endless generations which, following one upon another, made each human life an infinitesimal speck in the vast corridors of time; and the fearful frustration resulting from class exploitation and social inequality—all these may have helped to turn the minds of men from this world to a better one of unlimited duration. Whatever the cause, we know that the Egyptians longed for, and therefore believed in, a blessed immortality beyond the grave: and the desire for it became ever stronger as one millennium succeeded another.

The Egyptians therefore invented an after-life replete with rewards dependent upon ethical and sacramental considerations in this life many centuries before any similar concept appeared elsewhere. The preparation for eternity became a vast industry requiring an elaborate priesthood and consuming a large proportion of all human energy. Cheops and Khafre, who built the two greatest pyramids, did so primarily in order to insure their own eternal triumph in the kingdom of Osiris. To build these required the labor of one hundred thousand men for sixty years and left the nation sullen and exhausted. And the bribe which drove these toilers on was the promise that they too might hope for immortality in the Elysian Fields. The savior-god Osiris was a creation of the ruling classes; but in time he became the supreme hope of an enslaved and tortured people, by them beloved more than wealth or freedom.

3. *The Pre-Osirian Theogony.* In the Egyptian theogony preceding Osiris, Tem or Ra was the God and Father of all, the ungenerated original of the universe. He it was who laid the egg in the chaotic waters from which he was himself reborn or evolved. We find a fairly detailed description of the creation in the Papyrus of Nesi Amsu, reproduced by Sir E. A. Wallis Budge.[3]

4. *The Emergence of Isis and Osiris.* Tem, Shu, and Tefnut were worshiped by the primitive and dark-skinned aborigines some six or seven thousand years ago. But

sometime before 3000 B. C., Egypt was invaded by a light-skinned race of Aryan-Sumerians who stormed out of Mesopotamia, conquered the natives, and engrafted new gods upon the older pantheon. These newcomers possessed metal in place of stone tools and weapons and a much superior culture and economy. Osiris was undoubtedly an early ruler of theirs, whom they deified in order to establish their supremacy and who, during his progress, gradually absorbed the characteristics of various indigenous gods.

5. *The Primitive Osirian Theogony.* The revised theogony of prehistoric Egypt may thus be summarized: in the beginning there was only darkness, chaos, and a watery waste; however, God, or Tem, was there, although as yet quiescent; but since he willed at a given point to evolve life and develop order in the universe, he reproduced himself from an egg into Ra or the sun-god, which is the creative power immanent in all existence. Ra evolved from himself, first, a daughter Maat, who is the principle of regularity or law in the cosmos; and, second, Thoth, who is the Word, or its creative agency.

Ra thereupon produced from himself by masturbation[4] the brother-sister divinities, Shu and Tefnut, who, in turn, gave birth to Seb or Keb, the earth-god, and to Nut, the sky-goddess, who became the wife of Ra. Tem, Ra, Thoth, Maat, Shu, Tefnut, Nut, and Keb—this was probably the Egyptian pantheon preceding the Sumerian conquest. At this point, the invaders engrafted their own divinities upon the indigenous theogony of the aborigines. They declared that Nut, seduced by Keb, bore premature quintuplets: Osiris, Horus, Set, Isis, and Nephthys. Isis bore the younger Horus to Osiris; and Nephthys became by the same father the mother of Anubis.

6. *The New Culture.* Along with their religion, the Sumerians established also their superior culture: they controlled the flood waters of the Nile by constructing canals and by dividing the fields for agriculture, a science they had already mastered in the Tigris-Euphrates valley; they introduced a much more stable and civilized diet; they sowed grain and made it into bread; they

brewed ale from barley; they forbade promiscuous cannibalism, especially the dismembering of the dead, who were now instead to be embalmed unviolated and buried in tombs built at great or considerable cost; they introduced a higher morality than was previously known; they practiced the arts of writing, brick-making, stone-cutting, and street paving; and they lengthened the year from 360 to 365 days. As these reforms could not be accomplished without supernatural sanction, they were attributed to the divine Osiris; he became the original god-man incarnate.

How Osiris and his brothers and sisters could be human although both their parents were gods, the naturalistic priests of ancient Egypt seem never to have explained. But divine they were and yet human no less. The age of the skeptic had not yet dawned.

7. *The Tribal Totem.* Foreigners often noted with contempt and disgust the variety of animals worshipped in Egypt: the cow, the bull, the cat, the dog, the snake, the ibis, the hawk, etc. But these simply bear testimony to the antiquity of its religion. The same phenomenon has been found among Indians and other aborigines, concerning whom Lewis H. Morgan wrote his *Ancient Society*. There can be little doubt that all these animals were primitive clan-totems, worshipped at one time as ancestral spirits and absorbed by the Osirian cult to maintain the allegiance of the superstitious natives. And when any of these were slain and eaten, this was the literal sacrifice of a deity, by which his devotees absorbed his powers.

8. *The Pre-Eminence of Osiris.* Over a period exceeding three thousand years, some half a billion Egyptians lived and died in devotion to Osiris; he was the beloved god of the people; and they had no conceivable hope higher than that they might in death become one with him in blissful immortality.

We possess a remarkable series of Egyptian tomb and papyri inscriptions written over a period of several thousand years and known as *The Book of the Dead*. These are funerary formulas addressed almost exclusively to Osiris; they were to be learned by a man when living or inscribed on his coffin so that when dead he might enter the blessed abodes. Although none of them tell the story of the god, all assume a minute knowledge of him. Osiris was venerated by all Egyptians and was at least as familiar to them as is Jesus Christ to the Christian world.5

B. THE RELIGION OF OSIRIS

1. *A Mystery-Cult.* Only those initiated into the Osirian cult could know its doctrines or ceremonials: for these were "an exceedingly great mystery . . . in the handwriting of the god himself. . . . And these things shall be done secretly."6

Like the Egyptians, the Greeks, who copied their rituals, declared it a sacrilege to reveal the rites or doctrines of their mysteries. Herodotus tells us, II 3, that what the Egyptian priests "told me concerning their religion, it is not my intention to repeat." Plutarch says that he must "leave undisturbed what may not be told."7 Pausanias declares: "as I was intending . . . to narrate all things appertaining to . . . the Eleusinians, a vision in the night checked me: but what it is lawful for me to write for everybody, to this will I turn."8 Once, when the Athenians believed that Aeschylus had revealed the Eleusinian ritual in a play, the audience stormed the stage, threatening to rend the dramatist limb from limb. It is therefore with some difficulty that we reconstruct these esoteric rites.

2. *The Osirian Myth.* The Osirian myth itself, however, is fully told in Plutarch;9 and this account, reinforced and elaborated by Diodorus Siculus,10 runs briefly as follows:

The sun-god Ra detected his wife Nut embracing Seb, the earth-god. He therefore decreed that her illegitimate offspring could not be born on any day of the year. Thoth, however, came to her aid; for, playing at draughts with the moon, he won from her a seventy-second portion of each day. By this means, five intercalated days were added to the year, effecting a much-needed reform in the calendar. The year had previously consisted of 360 days, but this wide disparity between the solar and the calendar year was constantly creating a wide divergence between the seasons; although the Osirian reform still left a disparity between the calendar and the solar year of about six hours, the seasons now receded much less rapidly; their retrogression created what is known as the Sothic year, consisting of one thousand four hundred and sixty-one solar years, after which the sun again coincided with the season.

By winning the five additional days, Thoth rescued Nut and her offspring, because on these the curse of Ra was ineffectual; and she gave birth to five children, one on each of the intercalated days. On the first, which became the 361st day of the year, Osiris was born; on the second, Horus; on the third, Set; on the fourth, Isis; and on the fifth, Nephthys. Osiris married Isis; and Set Nephthys, while Horus became the celibate and intellectual scribe. All were born of earth and heaven, and in them commingled the qualities of both. They were therefore equipped not only to understand but also to solve the problems of suffering humanity.

Osiris was crowned king of Egypt in his twenty-eighth year; according to another version he ruled during twenty-eight years. It is obvious that this number relates to the days of the lunar cycle. It was said that he established the people in settled communities, taught them the arts of war and peace, and prohibited the practice of cannibalism, especially the eating of dead relatives, which, up to this time, had been common practice. Above all, he was credited with conferring upon his people the culture of wheat and barley and thereby transforming them from virtual cannibals into cereal-eating, civilized men and women, who developed respect for each other and who came in time to abhor the eating of their parents and other relatives.

But Osiris was not content to confer his benefits upon Egypt alone. He therefore journeyed over the inhabited world to civilize all nations and peoples. Diodorus emphasized that he carried with him men and women highly skilled in music and dancing who taught these arts to less cultured peoples. It was necessary for him to kill and dismember the barbarian king Lycurgus, as well as others who resisted his reforms. In due time, he returned to Egypt, laden with gifts.

In his absence, Isis had governed Egypt justly and equitably; but the evil Set, who was violently in love with her, had been making illicit advances to her, which she had rejected. Set is depicted as the great serpent, and the Greeks called him Typhon; he symbolized the powers of darkness, storms, and all disturbances of nature. Jealous of Osiris because of the honors heaped upon him, Set conspired with seventy-two others to encompass his destruction. This indicates that Set was the leader of the old and now counter-revolutionary priesthood, who, proclaiming their 360-day year, attempted to overthrow the new dynasty and its reformed calendar.

Having measured Osiris, Set built a coffin in which he induced his brother to lie down; instantly he and his co-conspirators clamped the lid shut and welded it tight with molten lead, so that Osiris died of suffocation. They threw the coffer into the Nile, on which it floated out to sea and then across the Mediterranean until it came to rest at Byblus. This indicates a generic relationship between Egypt and Syria, which has been established. For excavations carried out at Byblus (modern Jebeil) in 1922 prove that in the third millennium B. C., this city was a magnificent Egyptian colony which approximated the religion and culture of the motherland. It has also been established that any floating object thrown into the Nile will eventually be carried to this port. Lastly, this city became in time the center of the great Adonis cult, which we will discuss in due course.

Now in imminent danger of her life, Isis fled into the delta swamps, where she gave birth to the younger Horus. But Set pursued, and killed the child; but the ever-beneficent Thoth instructed her in the use of magic and medicine, which enabled her to restore the child to life. Leaving the infant to be reared at Buto, she set out to find the body of her husband, which she finally discovered at Byblus encased in a pine tree and which, after various adventures, she brought to Egypt. But Set tore the corpse into fourteen parts (some accounts say sixteen) and buried them, one in each of the provinces of Egypt.

Isis thereupon began her celebrated search for the broken body; and whenever she found a portion, she pieced it together with others until she was able to reconstruct the whole. The male member alone she could not recover, because Set had thrown it into the Nile, where it had been eaten by the Oxyrhynchus (pike), which therefore became a sacred fish. Isis made images of the missing member out of balsam wood, and erected them as objects of adoration in all the temples. She also constructed wax figures of Osiris, gave one to the priests of each district, saying that they alone possessed the true god. Another account states that each temple received the portion of Osiris which was found in that province and which therefore became its sacred relic. The principal temples were established at Abydos, in Upper, and at Busiris, in Lower, Egypt, where the head and backbone (tet) had been recovered. In addition, Isis generously provided that the priests should receive one third of the produce from the land, promised them munificent yields of grain, and exempted them from all taxation.[11]

Isis breathed her own life into the nostrils of Osiris; and with the help of Thoth, and of Horus, who opened his mouth and gave him his eye to eat, she accomplished the resurrection of Osiris to a second and eternal life; and thus he became the first-fruits of them that slept, the first among humanity ever to rise from the dead. Upon rising from his bier, he instructed his son Horus in the arts of war and adjured him to revenge the foul deed done by Set. Thereupon Osiris departed to the world of the immortals in Khenti-Amenti, where he became judge of the dead and the ruler of the blessed.

In the meantime, Set had usurped the throne of Egypt; and when Horus claimed it, the wicked uncle accused Horus of illegitimacy and Isis of adultery. There was a trial before the gods, who determined that Isis was virtuous and that Horus was lawfully conceived and therefore entitled to the succession. A terrific battle now ensued between Set and Horus, who subdued his evil uncle and bound him in chains, himself sustaining a bruised heel. Finally, Horus crushed the serpent's head (see Genesis 3:15), and ruled Egypt happily for the remainder of his life. After a trial before the gods in Khenti-Amenti, annihilation by fire was inflicted upon Set, the diabolical Adversary.[12]

3. *The Growth of Horus and Isis.* During the ages when *The Book of the Dead* was written, a definite development took place. Horus gradually assumed expanded powers, and was identified with his father. The cultists began to identify themselves with Horus also; and with his growth came also a vast expansion in the worship of Isis. She it was who established the civil law while Osiris was traveling over the world; she taught men to transform the golden grain of Osiris into the bread of life; when Horus was slain, she gave him life again; she revivified and made possible the resurrection of Osiris; and she established his worship throughout Egypt. In short, without Isis there would have been no Horus, no resurrection, no mystery, and no hope of an after-life. She became the universal and infinite benefactress of humanity, the eternal protective mother, the queen of earth and heaven. Images of her and her son were sacred objects in every Egyptian household, resembling the Madonna and the Christ-child, both in appearance and in the veneration they elicited.

4. *Symbolism in the Osirian Myth.* The dynamic power of the Isis-Osiris myth lay in the fact that these deities symbolized abundant life and natural vitality in all their aspects: astronomical, sexual, and most of all agricultural. The sun was often identified with Osiris and the moon with Isis.[13] We know that at the time when the Osiris-cult was established, the dog-star appeared in the East just before sunrise in the month of June, which was also the time the Nile began to overflow. Osiris is called "the great one of Abydos . . . the morning star which appears in the eastern part of heaven."[14] The

Egyptians sometimes called it Sothis, the star of Isis, who was the goddess of love, and life, and motherhood, mourning for her departed lover and awakening him again to life. Isis was a dynastic reconstitution of the older Hathor, the goddess of love, identified with the cow. The dog-star was also the "star of Osiris,"[15] or Sirius, as it is still known. Thus, Isis and Osiris were the heavenly powers which regulated the seasons, caused the Nile to inundate the fields, and made the grain to grow.

We find that Osiris is also identified with the bull and Isis with the cow. Plutarch tells us that in Memphis the bull of "Apis is kept, being the image of the soul of Osiris."[16] At Sakkara, sacred, living bulls were worshipped for centuries and at death were buried in the Serapaeum in regal splendor, as if they were gods indeed. These animals may have been considered sacred because of their economic value; we believe, however, that this veneration depended even more upon astronomical symbolism. For when the cult was first fully established, some five thousand years ago, the precession of the equinoxes during the zodiacal year, which equals some twenty-six thousand solar revolutions and is known also as the Great or Platonic year, had reached the point at which the sun passes through Taurus, or the Sign of the Bull, at the summer solstice, when the Nile begins to overflow. The cow and the bull, therefore, were the animals identified with Isis and Osiris; they were believed to bring the inundation of the Nile and were consequently sacred and worshipped as gods. About four thousand years ago, this precession had so altered the position of the zodiac that the sun passed through the Ram at the summer solstice; and then this animal, or the lamb, gradually became sacred, although the change was neither immediate nor everywhere uniform. It was for this reason that in the old temple at Memphis, Osiris is represented as a bull; but in the later temples at Busiris and Philae, he is depicted as a Ram, which is there called the soul of Osiris incarnate.[17] The altered position of the zodiac is also reflected in the Jewish scriptures, in which we find that the calf and the bull of Genesis are eventually replaced by the lamb. And still later, when the sun had passed into Pisces, the fish became the sacred symbol of the Christians and is found everywhere inscribed in the Roman catacombs where they buried their dead.

Isis and Osiris were also the deities of generation; without them there could be no children and the human race would become extinct. We have seen that Isis set up an image of her husband's phallus in all the temples of Egypt; and we know that its worship was a characteristic not only of the Osirian cult but of others directly derived from it, as the Dionysian in Greece. Osiris, we are told, "is the Lord of the Phallus and the ravisher of women."[18] Isis became not only the symbol of motherhood, but also goddess of childbirth. Osiris gave men the power to impregnate, and Isis gave women the power to conceive and bear new life.

But the most important symbolism of the Isis-Osiris concept was agricultural: "When the Nile begins to rise, the Egyptians have a tradition that it is the tears of Isis which make the river rise and irrigate the fields."[19] Ancient writers knew that the dismembered body of Osiris buried in all the provinces of Egypt symbolized the grain which had been sown; and that his death and resurrection were symbols of the death and rebirth of the wheat and the barley. In countless representations of Osiris, we see the grain sprouting from his body: and in thousands of funerary inscriptions we are told that the sacred bread is the body of the god. At the annual Osirian celebrations, images of the god were made of wheat paste and eaten as a holy sacrament. And even as Osiris was the grain which was planted, died, and sprang to life again, so Isis symbolized the earth-mother who received it and in whom it was nurtured. "They regard both the cow and the earth as the image of Isis."[20]

5. *Egyptian Doctrines Concerning the Soul*. The hope of every Egyptian was to achieve immortality by being transformed into an Osiris and to obtain "a homestead forever in Sekhet-Aru" (the Elysian Fields) "with wheat and barley therefor."[21]

In order to understand the eschatology of the Egyptians,

we need to know their metaphysical concepts concerning themselves. The physical body was called the *Khat,* which was the foundation also for immaterial reality. In this, or rather in the heart of this, dwelt the *Ba,* the heart-soul, which was considered the essence of life, and the destruction of which meant annihilation. Now this *Ba* projected its *Khu,* which was its double, a sort of shadow being or spiritual duplicate, and which could come or go, having a being separate from, if not independent of, its original. At death, the *Khu* lived on, required food and drink, could visit the tomb or go abroad, and starved when the funerary offerings ceased; and if it had not entered Elysium by this time, it was reduced to eating human excrement, and, on this diet, withered into nothingness.

The *Khat* and the *Ba,* therefore, were always ephemeral. It was the *Khu,* only, a kind of celestial body, which possessed the potential of immortality. In order that a human being might be transformed into an Osiris and live eternally, it was necessary that this be endowed with incorruption; and this could be done only by uniting it to its *Sahu,* which was its spiritual essence.

6. *Reasons for Mummification.* And this brings us to the question of why the Egyptians made such an industry of embalming and mummifying their dead. In the first place, this was necessary because Isis, Horus, and Thoth had embalmed and swathed the body of Osiris before his resurrection; and in all things it was necessary, in order to become an Osiris, to duplicate his experiences. Before his cult was established, the dead had been eaten, and their dismembered bones cast helter-skelter about the tombs. But the new priesthood taught that immortality was impossible unless the deceased entered the after-life with his *Khat* inviolate. It was therefore imperative that the body be preserved intact so that, as a result of the magical incantations and ceremonies to be performed over it by properly qualified priests, the *Sahu* might germinate from it. If such corruption were only avoided, the *Khu* could be united with the *Sahu;* and if this, a new and wholly spiritual entity, was victorious in its

trial before Osiris, it would attain blessed immortality. Without preserving the *Khat* through mummification, then, there could be no immortality. The practice continued well into the period of Christianity and was only abolished about 350 A.D. when Antony and Athanasius assured their followers that at the resurrection Christ would give them celestial bodies even if their earthly ones had been consumed by worms.

7. *Prerequisites for Entry into Sekhet-Aaru.* It was no small achievement to become an Osiris. A man or woman must first be initiated into the exclusive cult of the god; he must be clean of hand and pure of heart; his essence must needs already have been transmuted into divinity by eating and drinking the sacred eucharist; the deceased must be properly embalmed; he had to be vindicated at a public trial before the funeral ceremonies could be performed; unless all his creditors were satisfied, he could not be buried; and the effectual incantations had to be recited by the official priests.

8. *The Hall of Judgment.* Once all these requirements were met, however, the deceased was to be ferried without delay across the Great Lake and into the Hall of Maat. Egyptian funerary literature teems with references to what the aspiring Osiris might there expect. One of the most important documents dealing with the subject is the judgment scene from the Papyrus of Ani, composed during the XVIIIth Dynasty, about 1550 B. C., in which we see the royal scribe Ani and his wife Thuthu approaching the great scales and Anubis weighing the heart of the suppliant against the feather of Maat. When it is found perfect, Thoth announces the result to the gods, who declare: "Osiris, the scribe Ani victorious, is holy and righteous. . . . It shall not be allowed to the devourer Amemet to prevail over him. Meat-offerings and entrance into the presence of the God Osiris shall be granted unto him, together with a homestead for ever in Sekhet-hetepu."

At the side of Thoth is seated the great monster Amemet or Apep, with crocodile-head, forebody lion-shaped, and with the rear of a hippopotamus ready to devour the heart and the heart-soul of those who are damned. But, as the Osiris Ani has emerged victorious from the weighing of the heart, by the records of Thoth, and by the consent of the company of the great gods, he is conducted into the august and awful presence of Osiris himself, seated on his throne, grasping the scepter, flail, and slave hook, wearing the tall white crown. His body is still encased as a mummy, and behind him stand Nephthys, who advises him, and the beloved Isis, who makes constant intercession for the deceased. Horus leads Ani before the throne, where he sinks to his knees; whereupon Horus, acting as mediator, prevails upon his father to admit the suppliant to his blessed realm. With this, the judgment is complete; and the victorious Osiris Ani enters the Elysian Fields.

The celebrated Chapter CXXV[22] of *The Book of the Dead* is an elaboration of the judgment scene just described. It consists of three parts: first, the addresses to Osiris by the scribe Osiris-Ani and by the Overseer of the Seal, Nu, triumphant; second, the well-known Negative Confession by the scribe Nebseni; and, third, the final address by Nu to the gods.

When Nu first enters the great hall, he does homage to the "Great God"; thence he proceeds to the hall of Maat, where he must face the gods of the forty-two Egyptian nomes. Since each of these is the avenger of a particular sin or crime, he must declare his innocence to all of them. The Negative Confession, therefore, consists of forty-two articles summarizing Egyptian ethics about 1600 B. C.: the deceased has not committed robbery, violence, theft, or murder; has not lied, deceived, cut measures, or purloined what belongs to God; has not slandered anyone, wasted the land, killed any sacred animals, pried into holy secrets, given way to wrath or terrified anyone; has never been guilty of adultery or sodomy; has not been deaf to the truth, stirred up strife, or caused any one to weep; has never abused anyone or judged hastily; has never scorned the god of the city or been irreverent to God; has never cursed the king, used too many words, made his voice haughty, been insolent, fouled the water, or increased his wealth unjustly.

The judgment before Osiris was not to be a mere formality. Osiris could search out the secret places of the heart, and before him no one could be perfect or even sufficient in his own right. Every aspirant to "Osiris-ship" knew that if the Law of Maat were strictly enforced, he could never enter the blessed abodes. Were it not for the advice of Nephthys, the intercession of Isis, the advocacy of Thoth, the mediation of Horus, and the mercy of Osiris himself, no one could see salvation. Nu therefore exclaims: "Do ye away with my evil deeds, and put ye away my sin which deserved stripes on earth, and destroy ye any evil whatsoever that belongeth unto me."[23]

In the third portion of Chapter CXXV, the suppliant elaborates his declaration of social morality: "bring ye not forward my wickedness . . . [for] I have given bread to the hungry man, and water to the thirsty man, and apparel to the naked man, and a boat to the shipwrecked mariner. I have made holy offerings to the gods. . . . Be ye then my deliverers, be ye then my protectors. . . . I am clean of mouth and clean of hands; therefore, let it be said unto me. . . . 'Come in peace; come in peace.'" For thousands of years, the initiates of the pagan mysteries were to repeat: "I am clean of hand and pure of heart."

9. *Annihilation.* In the Osirian eschatology, there was no waiting for judgment, no hell, no torture for the damned. The heart of the condemned was eaten by the great monster Apep or Amemet and thereby his heart-soul ceased to be; his body was then annihilated in the Lake of Fire.[24]

10. *The Elysian Fields.* Those who emerged triumphant from the judgment were admitted to the Elysian Fields, which are depicted as a land teeming with grain, wherein the blessed shall dwell forever in peace and abundance.[25] The scribe Nu declares: "the gates which are in Sekhem are opened unto me, and fields are awarded unto me, together with those of my flesh and bone."[26] The Osirian expected to be reunited with his family in the after-life and to rule over his servants as on earth.

Nebseni summarizes the aspirations of every ancient Egyptian: "May I become a *Khu* in Sekhet-Aaru, may I eat therein, may I reap therein, may I fight therein, may I make love therein, may my words be mighty therein, may I never be in a state of servitude therein, but may I be in authority therein."[27]

When a great personage died, his wives and servants, as well as captured enemy slaves, were executed and buried with him, so that they might serve him eternally. And so the happy *Khu*, made eternal by union with his *Sahu*, expected to continue during countless millenniums, sowing and reaping, eating the bread and drinking the ale of Osiris, occupying relatively the same material and economic status as on earth.

11. *Extension of the Osirian Hope.* During the early dynasties, those who might hope for happy immortality with Osiris must have been limited to the royal family, certain important officials, and members of the priesthood. But as time went on, democracy increased in religion; and Herodotus describes three methods of embalming,[28] one to suit every purse. Twenty-five hundred years after Cheops and Khafre, a small piece of papyrus, which was to be placed in the coffin and on which were inscribed a few words from *The Book of the Dead*, promised the same stupendous result as the pharaohs hoped to achieve by the building of the great pyramids. We find, for example, the following rubric: "If this chapter be known by the deceased on earth, or if it be done in writing upon his coffin, he shall come forth by day . . . in peace into *Sekhet-Aaru* . . . there shall he flourish as he did upon earth. . . for millions of years."[29]

12. *Identification with Osiris.* We have noted that every *Khu* seeking admission to *Sekhet-Aaru* called himself Osiris. Obviously all Egyptians who cherished the hope of resurrection and immortality believed themselves already transformed into the divine and immortal essence of their god. The Osiris Nu declares explicitly, "I am Osiris."[30] Being an Osiris, Ani expects a resurrection like that of the god, and therefore addresses himself as follows: "O thou . . . whose limbs cannot move, like unto

those of Osiris! Let not thy limbs be without movement; let them not suffer corruption; let them not pass away; let them not decay; and let them be fashioned for me as if I were myself Osiris."[31] The same aspirant continues: "The mighty *Khu* (Osiris) taketh possession of me . . . Behold, I am the god who is lord of the Tuat" (underworld).[32] And again: "I am the Great One, son of the Great One. . . . The head of Osiris was not taken from him, let not the head of Osiris Ani be taken from him. I have knit myself together; I have made myself whole and complete; I have renewed my youth; I am Osiris, the lord of eternity."[33]

13. *Public Ritual of Osiris.* Pagan authors wrote extensively concerning the "gloomy, solemn, and mournful sacrifices" of Osiris.[34] Plutarch tells us that the great mystery-festival, celebrated in two phases, began at Abydos on the 17th of Athyr, which is our 13th of November. This date commemorated the death of the god: and its significance is found in the fact that it was the very day on which the grain was placed in the ground. The death of the grain and the death of the god were one and the same: the cereal was identified with the god who came from heaven; he was the bread by which man lives. The resurrection of the god symbolized the rebirth of the grain.

The first phase of the festival consisted of a public drama, depicting the murder and dismemberment of Osiris, the search for and the finding of his body by Isis, his triumphal return as the resurrected god, and the battle in which Horus defeated Set, all presented by skilled actors as literal history; and this was a principal means of recruiting the membership. Julius Firmicus Maternus, a Latin Christian writer of the fourth century, declared: "In the sanctuaries of Osiris, his murder and dismemberment are annually commemorated with . . . great lamentations. His worshipers . . . beat their breasts and gash their shoulders. . . When . . . they pretend that the mutilated remains of the god have been found and rejoined . . . they turn from mourning to rejoicing."

They "say that the grain is the seed of Osiris, that Isis is the earth, and that Typhon is heat." [35]

We know that at all the temples of Osiris his Passion was re-enacted at his annual festivals. On a stele at Abydos erected in the XIIth Dynasty by one I-Kher-Nefert, a priest of Osiris during the reign of Usertsen III (Pharaoh Sesostris), about 1875 B. C., we find a description of the principal scenes in the Osiris mystery-drama. I-Kher-Nefert himself played the key role of Horus. In the first scene, Osiris is treacherously slain, and no one knows what has become of his body; thereupon all the onlookers weep, rend their hair, and beat their breasts. Isis and Nephthys recover the remnants, reconstitute the body, and return it to the temple. The next scene, in which Thoth, Horus, and Isis accomplish the revivification, undoubtedly occurs within the sacred precincts, and is therefore not witnessed by the populace. However, in due course the resurrected Osiris emerges at the head of his train; at this glorious consummation, the anguish and sorrow of the people are turned into uncontrollable rejoicing. Horus thereupon places his father in the solar boat so that he may, since he has already been born a second time, proceed as a living god into the eternal regions. This was the great "coming forth by day" of which we read so often in *The Book of the Dead*. The climax of the play was the great battle in which Horus defeated Set and which is described so vividly by Herodotus.[36]

14. *Esoteric Ritual.* Such was the public portion of the Osirian celebration. The esoteric phase consisted of ceremonials performed by the priests within the temples and witnessed only by the initiates. We learn something of these from various sources and are therefore able to reconstruct them. After saying that the festival of Osiris began on the 17th of Athyr, Plutarch continues: "On the nineteenth . . . the priests bring forth the sacred chest containing a small golden coffer, into which they pour some potable water . . . and a great shout arises from the company for joy that Osiris is found (or resurrected). Then they knead some fertile soil with the water . . . and

fashion therefrom a crescent-shaped figure, which they clothe and adorn, thus indicating that they regard these gods as the substance of Earth and Water."[37]

This summarizes the resurrection-ceremonial mentioned in the stele of I-Kher-Nefert. Fortunately, in the Osirian temple at Denderah, an inscription reveals what these secret rituals were.[38] Its first section deals with the making of models of each of the sixteen pieces into which Set hacked the body of Osiris. Each model was made of wheat paste, and sent to the town where that portion of Osiris had been found by Isis.

The second section describes the making of a figure of Osiris at Mendes. Wheat and paste were placed in a trough on the day of Osiris' murder, which was also that on which the grain was planted; and on this mixture water was poured for several days. A few days later, the contents of the trough were kneaded into a mold which was made into a figure of Osiris, taken to the temple, and buried. Other sections describe the process as carried on in other temples.

The fifth section describes how molds were made from the wood of a red tree in the form of the sixteen dismembered portions of Osiris; cakes of divine bread were then made from each mold, placed in a silver chest, and set near the head of the god. These are the mysterious and sacred cakes which are also "the inward parts of Osiris";[39] and these are the rites to which Plutarch refers when he says: "I pass over the cutting of the wood . . . and the libations that are offered, for the reason that many of their secret rites are involved therein."[40] This section also describes the Field of Osiris, adjacent to the temple, in which the grains, used in the sacred cakes, were grown. This sacramental food, which to the Osirian was literally the body of his god, could grow only in that holy field.

The sixth section describes the mysteries as practiced in the temple of Isis at Mendes. On the first day of the Festival of Ploughing, the goddess appeared in her shrine, where she was stripped naked. Paste made from the grain was placed in her bed and moistened with water. All this symbolized the great processes by which the human race is generated and food germinated from the earth. Osiris was the seed which fecundated Mother-Isis, who symbolized also the earth itself.

We see therefore that the publicly performed passion-play depicted the earthly career of Osiris; but the secret rites consisted of solemn ceremonies symbolizing the transfiguration of the grain into Osiris and of Osiris into the grain; and all this was climaxed by the eating of the sacramental god, the eucharist by which the celebrants were transformed, in their persuasion, into replicas of their god-man.

15. *The Osirian Sacrament.* We noted under B 7 some of the ethical and ceremonial prerequisites for becoming an Osiris. But none of these could avail at all without the miraculous power contained in the divine eucharist: there was power, there was power in the flesh and the blood of Osiris. He was the grain; and the bread made from it was the sacred food, the barley ale brewed from it the divine drink, literally believed to be the body and the blood of the god. Since the ancient Nilotics believed that human beings become whatever they eat, this Osirian sacrament was believed able to make them celestial and immortal.

The doctrine of the eucharist has its ultimate roots in prehistoric cannibalism: it was universally believed among savages that by eating other human beings or gods, their virtues and powers would be absorbed by the eaters. Such cannibalism, common among African tribes until very recently and still practiced among the most primitive, had this primary objective. Melville describes the same sacerdotal rite among the south sea islanders.[41]

One of the oldest of the Pyramid Texts is that of Unas from the VIth Dynasty, cir. 2500 B. C. This is of great importance because it shows that the original ideology of Egypt had commingled with the Osirian concepts. Although he is ultimately given high place in heaven by order of Osiris, Unas is represented as being at first an enemy of the gods and his ancestors, whom he hunts, lassoes, kills, cooks, and eats so that their powers and attributes may become his own. It is obvious that at the time this was written, the eating of parents and gods was considered a most laudable ceremonial; and it emphasizes how difficult it must have been for the Osirian priesthood to stamp out the older cannibalism: "The Akeru gods tremble, the Kenemu whirl, when they see Unas a risen Soul, in the form of a god who lives upon his fathers and feeds upon his mothers. . . . He eats men, he feeds on the gods . . . he cooks them in his fiery cauldrons. He eats their words of power, he swallows their spirits. . . What he finds on his path, he eats eagerly. . . . He eats the wisdom of every god, his period of life is eternity. . . . Their soul is in his body, their spirits are within him." Having partaken of this dynamic sacrament, Unas becomes an Osiris and is admitted to the company of the gods. A parallel passage is found in the Pyramid Text of Pepi II, who, it is said, "seizeth those who are in the following of Set . . . he breaketh their heads, he cutteth off their haunches, he teareth out their intestines, he diggeth out their hearts, he drinketh copiously of their blood!"[42]

Although crude, savage, and grotesque, this was the core of an overwhelming concept. The conviction that it was possible for humanity to achieve immortality by eating the body and drinking the blood of a god or of an immortal god-man who had died that mortals might have abundant and everlasting life, became a dominating obsession in the ancient world.

The cult of Osiris forbade the older cannibalism, but did not proscribe the dismemberment and eating of enemies; and it certainly practiced the bloody sacrifice of captives and the sacramental rending and eating of the sacred bovine, which symbolized Osiris.[43]

The moral elevation of the Osirian cult lay in its identification of bread with the flesh of its god and of barley ale with his blood. The partaker of this eucharist could now achieve a mystical transformation and become an Osiris by living on wheat and barley bread during his lifetime, by drinking and eating the sacred ale and cakes during the annual mysteries, and by enjoying the same sacred fare in *Sekhet-Aaru* once his *Khu* had joined his *Sahu* in the next world. By this simple metaphysical transposition, the bloody sacrament became symbolic, but no less effective. For Osiris was, to his believers, literally and with complete reality, the divine seed which came down from heaven and was reborn from the earth that men might have life and have it more abundantly; and all who ate of that bread might live forever, for it was the flesh of the god, which he gave for the life of humanity. Whosoever ate the flesh and drank the blood of Osiris had eternal life; for he would be resurrected beyond the grave. Whosoever ate that flesh and drank that blood dwelt in Osiris and Osiris dwelt in him.

This was the divine mystery which was given to the world by Egypt and which spread throughout the Mediterranean area in various cults; this concept originated only once, but it proliferated in all directions and became the dynamic force in every mystery-cult.

It was solely by means of this sacramental food that the corruptible of the deceased could be clothed with incorruption. This idea appears again and again in infinite variety. The scribe Nebseni implores: "And there in the celestial mansions of heaven which my divine father Tem hath established, let my hands lay hold upon the wheat and the barley which shall be given unto me therein in abundant measure."[44] This was the celestial eucharist without which the *Sahu* itself, the spiritual body, could not germinate from the mummy. Nu corroborates this fact by stating: "I am established, and the divine Sekhethetep is before me, I have eaten therein, I have become a spirit therein, I have abundance therein."[45] Again he declares; "I am the divine soul of Ra . . . which is god. . . I am the divine food which is not corrupted."[46] Nu identifies himself with Osiris and with Ra, who is called the divine, that is, the sacramental food. As we know, Horus was also frequently identified with his father; and we read: "Horus is both the divine food and the sacrifice."[47] We read that the bread and the ale of Osiris make the eater immortal,[48] an idea which is frequently elaborated. The Osirian "shall eat of that wheat and barley, and his limbs shall be nourished therewith, and his body shall become like unto the bodies of the gods."[49]

That the sacramental food which gave immortality was a very ancient concept we learn from the Pyramid Text of Teta, which dates from about 2600 B. C. and which embodies ideas far more ancient still. We read here that the Osiris Teta "receivest thy bread which decayeth not, and thy beer which perisheth not." In the Text of Pepi I we read: "All the gods give thee their flesh and their blood. . . . Thou shalt not die." In the Text of Pepi II, the aspirant prays for "thy bread of eternity, and thy beer of everlastingness."[50]

16. *The God-Man Osiris.* Such was the great godman Osiris: human, like us, and thus able to take upon himself all our sorrow, but also divine, and therefore able to confer divinity upon us. He brought the divine bread from heaven for mankind; he taught justice and practiced mercy; he died, was buried, and rose from the grave; he gave to all who became members of his mystical body his flesh to eat and his blood to drink so that this divine sacrament might then transfigure them into celestial gods; he went before to prepare mansions for his initiates in Elysium; and he was to be the just and merciful judge before whom men and women must appear beyond the grave.

17. *The Destruction of the Cult.* The Osiris-worship continued with little modification on the island of Philae in the Upper Nile for several centuries into our era and sacrifices of human enemies were performed there regularly as late as the sixth century. The edict of Theodosius that all pagan temples be destroyed and their worshipers forced to accept Christianity about 380 was there ignored. About 550, however, Justinian dispatched to Philae General Narses, who destroyed the great Osirian temples and sanctuaries, threw the priests into prison, and carried away the sacred images to Constantinople.

Thus died the cult of Osiris. But the soteriology which was its central feature had already assumed various forms which had long since proliferated far and wide in the ancient world.

CHAPTER II

ADONIS AND APHRODITE

A. BABYLONIAN-ASSYRIAN RELIGION

1. *The Semitic Empire.* Previous to about 2700 B. C., the Sumerians had ruled the Tigris-Euphrates valley; they were then conquered by a Semitic people, who established the first Babylonian Empire. This was succeeded about 1400 by the Assyrian, also Semitic and very warlike, with its capital at Nineveh, which was destroyed about 612. In 605, the center of power shifted again to the Valley, now ruled by Nebuchadnezzar from Babylon. This great city was captured by the Persian-Aryan Cyrus in 538; and this event marked the end of Semitic empire.

2. *Semitic Eschatology.* Assyrian religion and culture, derived from Babylonian, prevailed among all Semitic nations. There was a large pantheon of nature-deities, which were probably the first prototypes of the Hellenic, but there was no basic monotheism, as in Egypt. Babylonian-Assyrian concepts, themselves derived from the Sumerian, were the basic source of Greek and Jewish eschatology, until Buddhism, Zoroastrianism, and the mystery-cults effected their far-flung revolution. The Semites and the primitive Greeks alike believed that at death very nearly all souls pass into a cold, dark prison-house known as Sheol, Hades, or the House of the Dead, from which there could be no release and in which, for all alike, there was neither activity, joy, nor hope; above all, *there was no differentiation between the wicked and the righteous.* One might say that after death, the soul had an existence but no life. It was believed that unless the body was properly buried the spirit subsisted on dust and

mud, and, therefore angered, might do injury to the living.

3. *Ishtar.* The Babylonian-Assyrian religion does not fall within our province, since it did not exercise direct influence upon the Gospel Jesus. We concern ourselves only with Ishtar, the great Babylonian goddess, who grew and expanded over the centuries into the Queen of Heaven and the Mother of the Gods, who was adopted by the Assyrians and all the lesser Semitic nations as their greatest deity, and whose worship was absorbed, under various guises, by many Aryan nations as well. She appeared under many names, among which the most popular were Ashtoreth, Astarte, Mylitta, Cybele, Anaitis, Dindymeme, Aphrodite, and Venus; but her character remained substantially unaltered.

Ishtar was worshipped primarily as the goddess of generation and the source of life, whether vegetable, animal, or human. She ached with cosmic sex-desire; and without her influence, no creature could experience the same yearning, and hence no new life could come into being. According to ancient myth, she had taken a mortal lover, Tammuz, who had died and departed into his eternal underworld prison. She wept inconsolably, but could not retrieve him from the clutches of Allatu, mistress of the nether regions. To be with him again, she invaded the House of the Dead, where she was herself condemned by Allatu to perpetual imprisonment.

But now a terrible tragedy supervened upon earth. All the vegetation died, and could not grow green again; none of the wild beasts, the cattle, or even insects would copulate; and all sexual relationships ceased among the human race. In short, love was dead, and the world was doomed.

To meet this fearful emergency, there was a council of the great gods, who determined that Ishtar must be restored to earth. They therefore sent a delegation to Allatu, who reluctantly released her prisoner. But Ishtar could not endure life always separated from her beloved; and so, every fall, she went down into the underworld to be with him for six months, and every spring, on the 20th of June, when the star of Ashtoreth appeared in the

East, she came again into the upper world. With her return, the birds, the flowers, the trees, the grain sprang to life; the insects, the beasts, and the cattle copulated once more; and men and women, stirred by strong desire, hastened to embrace.

4. *The Ritual of Ishtar.* Every year, the passion of Ishtar was re-enacted at a great religious festival, at which the women wept for Tammuz, as we read in Ezekiel 8:14. Her ritual was consonant with her character. Close by her temples were her sacred groves, in which men and women performed her rites by uniting in the act which is symbolic of life and which was her sacrament. Herodotus declares that "the Babylonians have one most shameful custom."[1] Before marriage, every woman must "sit down in the precincts of Aphrodite" and wait for a stranger who will pay her a temple fee to have intercourse with her. "The woman goes with the first man who throws her money, and rejects no one." As soon as the man made his choice, he led the woman to the sacred grove, where they consummated the ritual. Thereupon, she returned to her home and never again submitted to the embrace of a stranger. Strabo describes[2] the same ceremonial at Byblus.

Wherever the orthodox Semites advanced, Astarte, together with her sacred prostitution, came with them. Not only were all women compelled to submit once to this pre-marital ceremony, but we know that the temples of the Queen of Heaven were staffed with professional priestesses, whose earnings swelled her coffers. Herodotus says that formerly Babylonians used to sell their daughters into slavery or wifehood to the highest bidder;[3] but now, to avoid such violence, they reared the damsels to become temple prostitutes in the service of Ashtoreth. We learn from Strabo that not only the Babylonian Ishtar, but also the Median Anaitis, offered the same service.[4]

Sir John G. Frazer suggests that Ishtar dates from an antiquity so remote that marriage was unknown or regarded as an immoral aggression against the communal rights of many women to many men;[5] Astarte and Aphrodite are therefore unmarried and unchaste. As monogamic marriage developed with private property, a relic of primitive communism lingered on in the ritual of Astarte: once in her life, each woman was compelled to surrender to men communally in the person of a single stranger; and we read that if women wished to preserve their chastity, they were required to sacrifice their hair in lieu thereof. The custom by which brothers or fathers married their sisters or daughters was also a relic of ancient communism, in which all property and the line of descent belonged to women alone. Only by marriages regarded as incestuous after private property was consolidated, could wealth be continued among the males of the same family.

B. THE CONJUNCTION OF ISHTAR AND OSIRIS

1. *A New Mystery-Cult.* The Semitic culture and religion spread all over Asia Minor to the Hellespont and the Mediterranean. We have already seen that ancient Byblus was a colony of Egypt four or five thousand years ago; and that the body of Osiris, later recovered by Isis, was said to have landed there. The story is told by Plutarch,[6] from whom we learn also that the chest containing the body of Osiris was enclosed in a great myrrh or heather tree; and that Isis poured perfume upon the wood, which was still, in the first century, preserved in her shrine at Byblus.

What actually occurred was something of far-reaching importance: for in Byblus, the religions of Babylonia and Egypt met and coalesced; and a new cult emerged, which bore a generic resemblance to both progenitors, but developed certain characteristics of its own. This was the first time that Osiris was exported; but the old religion he encountered here was so thoroughly established that it could not be displaced in its entirety. Ishtar, therefore, remained almost intact. Osiris, however, continued as the savior-god, and, in this character, drove Tammuz into oblivion. In this first mystery-synthesis, Ishtar and Osiris became Aphrodite and Adonis. Lucian notes the identity of these gods and declares that Adonis is Osiris.[7]

2. *The Myth as Known to the Greeks.* As known to

the Greeks, the myth runs as follows: the Ancient Syrian king Cinyras and his wife Astarte, who ruled both at Byblus and in Paphos, had a daughter, Myrrha, whom Aphrodite caused to become desperately enamored of her father, who unwittingly impregnated his own child when she replaced her mother in his bed; on discovering his impiety, he attempted to destroy her, but she escaped his wrath and the gods transformed her into a myrrh tree. After ten months, the tree burst asunder, and forth sprang the beautiful Adonis (*Adon*, in Syrian, means lord) who developed into a handsome youth with whom Aphrodite became hopelessly enamored. But before she could consummate her love, he was killed and his body mangled by a boar in a hunting accident.[8] The disconsolate goddess followed her beloved into Hades, whence she sought his return to the upper air; but Persephone had herself fallen so deeply in love with him that she would not permit his release. Aphrodite thereupon appealed the case to Zeus, who determined that Adonis should spend a portion of each year, four or six months, with Celestial Aphrodite and the remainder with Persephone. All this, of course, re-creates in main outline the myth of Ishtar and Tammuz; and as we shall see, it was reproduced in the Demeter-Persephone myth. Furthermore, the aromatic Isis and the myrrh tree of Adonis; Osiris and the child Adonis both enclosed in the tree—these are elements reflecting the congenital relationship between Osiris and Adonis.

From Byblus, the Adonis-cult spread far and wide; and Pausanias declares: "among the Athenians, her worship was instituted by Aegeus, thinking that he had no children . . . owing to the wrath of the Celestial One."[9]

The Greeks called Aphrodite a Cyprian, because her worship on Cyprus antedated Greek civilization; and they called her sea-born, because she came from across the Mediterranean. Her temple at Paphos, of which ruins are still extant, probably dates back to 1500 B. C.; but even this, according to Herodotus, was built in imitation of the more ancient one at Ascalon.[10] And that at Byblus was the oldest of all, and was said by the Phoenicians to have been built by the god El, the creator of the world.

3. *Ishtar and the Mystery-Cults.* The important question for us, however, is to discover the relationship between the Mother Goddess and the savior-cults; for her worship was never celebrated as a mystery in her original habitat. It became such only when Osiris, displacing Tammuz, became known as Adonis. In the new cult, this god was at least equal to the Great Mother: Tammuz, a vegetation-god, had died in the autumn, after which he descended to the underworld; but Adonis, like Osiris, died at seed-time because he was the god of resurrection who symbolized the grain quickened into a second life; and, even more significant, it was *his* passion and not that of the goddess which was celebrated. Tammuz, who remained forever in the underworld, was simply the lover of Ishtar; but Adonis, like Osiris, symbolized the grain which is placed in the earth and which dies and is reborn that mankind may have abundant life. During the winter months, Ishtar lived in the nether realm with Tammuz; but Adonis was the *soter* who ascended each spring from Hades to dwell during the summer with the celestial Astarte.

4. *The Ritual of Adonis.* The river Adonis empties into the Mediterranean below Byblus, where stood for centuries that stretched into millenniums the celebrated temple of Aphrodite. The worshipers believed that every spring their god was gored and slain by a cruel boar upon the jagged mountainside, and that his blood discolored the waters of the stream and caused a profusion of anemones to redden the earth.

We know that the great festival of Adonis, commemorating his death and resurrection, occurred at midsummer, because that is when the river Adonis runs red and the anemones bloom in Syria. We know this also from the fact that the great fleet fitted out by the Athenians against Syracuse left at just that time in 415 B. C.;[11] and the streets of Athens at the same moment were lined with the coffins of Adonis and with the women lamenting and bewailing their slain god.[12] When Emperor Julian arrived in Antioch in 362 A. D., the Festival of Adonis was in progress, and the people plunged in grief; for Venus, the Morning Star of Salvation, had just appeared in the East, the god had just died, but had not yet been resurrected.[13]

5. *Sex and Sacrament.* The ritual of Adonis as celebrated in Alexandria is described in the fifteenth *Idyll* of Theocritus. Couches were set up, on which figures of the god and the goddess reclined; their union was celebrated with music, recitations, and rejoicing; and there were altars laden with many fruits and cakes. The phallic Osiris and the lascivious Ishtar were represented by objects symbolizing the male and the female generative organs; and their union was celebrated as a holy mystery, which must be concealed from the uninitiated, but the details of which are described and excoriated by Clement of Alexandria.[14]

Each year at Byblus, Paphos, and other cities, the festival of Adonis was celebrated with a mystery-drama, even as was that of Osiris in Egypt. The time was spring or early summer, because that was the time of sowing in Syria, instead of autumn, as in Egypt. The god was slain by the wild-boar, and his rent and bleeding body crimsoned the earth and the river with his blood. At this fearful tragedy, the women-mourners filled the air with shrieks and lamentations. Yet they did not grieve like those who are without hope; for shortly thereafter, the Star of Venus appeared in the East; this was the goddess coming to rescue her lover from the nether regions, to resurrect him to life, as did Isis in Egypt. Thereupon, before their very eyes, Adonis rose before them and ascended into heaven to be again with his heavenly bride. This festival occurred annually about the twentieth of June.

In the Adonis-Aphrodite cult, there seems to have been no eucharist; there was only a thank-offering of fruits and grains. The sexual ritual seems to have taken the place of the sacred meal. There can be no doubt that each new initiate became a member of the cult through intimacy with the sacred temple personnel: female novitiates became Aphrodites by union with the priestly Adonis; and the men were similarly sanctified with the sacred prostitutes. Personal immortality through a eucharist was an idea so foreign to the Semitic mind that it could not be engrafted upon the worship of the Great Mother.

6. *The Sacrificial God.* There can be no doubt that in the primitive phases of the cult, a priest, impersonating Adonis, was ceremonially slain at each annual festival; as civilization advanced, however, this was replaced by a simulated sacrifice.

7. *Ishtar Among the Greeks.* Adonis never penetrated the pantheon of the Greeks; nor did the Adonis-Aphrodite cult progress far among them. As Aphrodite freed herself from Adonis, she became in time simply the goddess of beauty and of love and her cultic mysteries retreated from the peninsula. The reason was probably that her sacrament became progressively more repulsive as monogamy and private property became more and more firmly entrenched; it was therefore impossible for the Aphrodisiacs to compete successfully against the Eleusinians and the Dionysiacs, whom it now becomes our province to describe.

CHAPTER III

THE PRIMITIVE GREEK DIONYSUS

A. THE CIVILIZATION AND OFFICIAL RELIGION OF ANCIENT GREECE

1. *A Resourceful People.* Perhaps the most amazing phenomenon in world-culture is the emergence some twenty-six hundred years ago of the Greeks, a vigorous, intelligent, and freedom-loving people, descended from prehistoric Aryans who had emigrated from the Iranian plateau. Creative, original, and resourceful, they were the first who elevated human life into the sunlight of reason. They had appropriated the best elements of other cultures and devised from them new and superior forms. They adopted the Phoenician alphabet and made it more pliable; they accepted, modified, and expanded the Cretan pantheon; they learned agriculture and geometry from Egypt and astronomy from Chaldea. But whatever they acquired, they made their own and developed in a spirit of freedom. In the successive empires of the ancient world, such concepts as democracy, the integrity of the ordinary individual, and his right to ideological dissidence were entirely unknown: these were purely Hellenic innovations and constitute the glory of Greece.

2. *A Secularistic People.* The characteristic which placed them in sharp contrast with their contemporaries was their *secularism:* that is, their primary interest was *this* world and what they could do for themselves. Among all the nations and peoples whom the Greeks designated as barbarians, religion was an omnipresent and universal force which frustrated every innovation, since every new or variant idea was heresy and sacrilege. We have seen

that in Egypt it required a farflung revolution to reform the calendar; and the 365-day year could not be extended even by a few hours without another drastic upheaval.

The Greeks were the least priest-ridden of any ancient people. They were so exhilarated with the joy of living that they had no leisure for brooding upon eschatology. And they were so successful that they never seriously questioned the justice of providence. They conceived or developed almost every idea concerning art, logic, ethics, philosophy, and politics which has yet been formulated; they laid the foundation for modern science, mathematics, and political economy; and they achieved the highest development in sculpture, painting, drama, poetry, metaphysics, and architecture. Above all, it was they who created the secular way of life, by which alone progress is possible. They originated and the Romans expanded our civil law, which replaced the hieratical codes of Egypt, Persia, India, and Judaea, all arrogating to themselves the authority of divine revelation.

3. *Democracy.* In their political, as in their intellectual life, they practiced ultimate democracy. Army generals were elected or removed at sessions of the Areopagus. They were forever in disagreement and conflict with each other; nor could they establish national unity. But as a result of their freedom, they developed an unparalleled creative power; and when, for brief intervals, even a portion of them presented a united front against the vast Persian fleets and armies, they annihilated them with ease. The unappreciative Diodorus Siculus complained that his countrymen were forever "wrangling with each other over the most important matters of speculation . . . unable to believe anything at all with firm conviction, they simply wander in confusion."[1]

4. *No Sacred or Authoritarian Books.* Inseparable from their intellectual freedom was the fact that, whereas, among other ancient peoples, most writings purported to be divine revelations, among the Greeks very few fell into this category and none of these have survived. There were literally hundreds or even thousands of gifted authors whose works on every conceivable subject were com-

posed from about 800 B. C. to about 300 A. D. Many of these dealt with the gods or with religious subjects: but not one which is still extant was written by a priest or purported to possess revealed authority. In Iran and India as well as among the Jews, almost all writings claimed divine authority; but among the Greeks not even the law was considered sacerdotal. Diodorus rejected summarily the supernaturalistic claims of such lawgivers as Zoroaster, Zalmoxis, and Moses.[2] Strabo remarks that "Minas pretended to receive from Jupiter the decrees he promulgated." And he continues that Lycurgus learned both in Crete and in Egypt this trick by which to establish authority; and that, after returning to Sparta, he feigned the reception of divine revelations from the Delphian Oracle.[3]

In fact, while the Jews had an entire tribe whose duties were purely sacerdotal and while the priests of Osiris received one third or more of the national income and constituted a dominant caste, the Greeks had no formal priesthood at all. Even the shrine at Delphi was manned by only a few attendants and two or three priestesses.[4]

This neglect of religion was due to the self-reliance of the Greeks and to their emphasis upon the present life. The oracles were consulted only in regard to temporal interests or enterprises; and even then not so much to obtain favor as to discover whether fortune would be propitious. Whereas the Egyptians made the preparation for death a vast industry, the Greeks betrayed very little interest in it; it is not recorded that Apollo was even consulted on matters relating to the after-life. When Circe called up the shade of Achilles, he told Ulysses that he would rather be the meanest slave on earth than the ruler of the underworld.

The Greeks, therefore, have not left us one sacred book; yet they contributed vastly to Christianity, because the unlettered among them finally accepted Osiris under the name of Dionysus in their mystery-cults; and he became the universal savior-god and the prototype of Christ.

5. *The Official Religion of the Greeks.* It was not that the Greeks were without gods or religion; but their

official deities were only immortal men and women, subject to all the passions and most of the moral frailties of mankind. When people wanted something of immediate concern, they implored these Olympians for aid, and offered sacrifices as rewards or propitiations. The most informative Greek work dealing with the origin of these deities is the *Theogony* of Hesiod, which was probably composed about 750 B. C. and of which the following is a brief summary:

In the beginning was Chaos, and Earth, who conceived and bore Heaven, or Uranus, without "the sweet rites of love." And then in the bed of Uranus, she bore the Titans, including Hyperion, Iapetos, Rhea, Mnemosyne, and Cronus, who married Rhea and who, by her, became the father of Hestia, Demeter, Hera, Hades, Poseidon, and Zeus. As Cronus had been told that one of his children would overthrow him, he ate the first five at birth. This so saddened Rhea that she appealed to her parents for aid; "and they conveyed her . . . into the rich land of Crete, when she was about to bring forth . . . Zeus." She hid her child in a cave, and, swaddling a stone, gave it to Cronus, who ate it, never suspecting the imposition. When Zeus grew to manhood, he compelled his father to disgorge the stone and the five children he had devoured. After a fearful ten-year battle in which he defeated the Titans, Zeus became the king of the gods, the lord of the sky, the cloud-gatherer, and the master of the thunderbolt.

In the form of a golden shower, he seduced Danae, who bore Perseus; in the form of a bull, he abducted Europa, who bore Minos, Rhadamanthys, and Sarpedon. By various amours and marriages, he became the literal father of the Greek pantheon. And, last of all, Semele, daughter of Cadmus in Thebes, bore him Dionysus, the only child of a mortal ever to be recognized as an immortal god in the Greek pantheon. According to a later variant of the myth, Persephone was the first mother of Dionysus and Semele the second.

This anthropomorphic polytheism, which was the religion of Homer, was without a creator or a revealed law;

without a devil or a redeemer; without witches, spirits, or relics; without hell, heaven, punishment, or judgment in the after-life; without renunciation or a sense of guilt; without fear of the supernatural; without a sacrament or a system of ethics; without any post-mortem differentiation between the wicked and the righteous; and without a messianic hope.

We can with certainty trace this Olympian convocation to the Minoan civilization of Crete.[5] The celebrated Minos was an actual Cretan king who, long before Moses, sanctified his laws with divine authority, and who, with his brother Rhadamanthus, in a subsequent phase of the Dionysiac cult, became the judge of mortals in the underworld.

Cretan culture and mythology date back to at least 3000. The original settlers of the island probably came from the Iranian plateau. Certain it is that they developed a pantheon and an eschatology somewhat resembling the ancient Sumerian-Babylonian and that the Greeks appropriated these during the Mycenaean era, before 1500 B. C.

In the fifth century B. C., Herodotus evidently still believed that some prescience might reside in the Delphian Oracle. The great Epicurus, however, although neither an atheist nor an agnostic, declared about 300 B. C. that there is no providence and no life after death. About 70 B. C., the Latin materialist Lucretius[6] elaborated upon Protagoras and Leucippus by repudiating all religion. Strabo, writing about 1-10 A. D., states that "the temple at Delphi is now much neglected, although formerly held in great veneration."[7] Pausanias declares that at Thelpusa in Arcadia, there was a "temple of the twelve gods in ruins."[8] Plutarch states: "either silence or utter desolation has taken possession of"[9] Delphi, although every one consulted it at the time of the Persian War. In the second century, A. D., the brilliant Lucian subjected the old gods to condescending ridicule.[10] By that time, all real faith in them had long been dead.

In the Greek pantheon, three of the most important were not members of the original company, but pushed their way into it later. The first of these was probably Aphrodite. The second was Demeter, who was the Hellenic recreation of Isis and who became the great mystery-goddess of the upper classes in ancient Greece. The third was Dionysus, who finally became the most important of all: he was ubiquitous in the barbarian world before he penetrated Greece, and he was the last of the Greek gods. He obtained many devotees upon the peninsula itself among the lower classes, and particularly among women, before the Trojan War; and after that event, his cult underwent a series of reforms, divisions, and expansions. As the older gods faded, the mystery deities became progressively more powerful: and among these, the greatest was Dionysus.

That the mysteries were neither of Cretan origin nor a part of the original Greek religion is established by the fact that the initiatory rites as practiced among these islanders were open to everyone,[11] in contrast to the secret rituals of Byblus, Cyprus, Thrace, Samothrace, and Eleusis. The mystery, which originated in Egypt, was imported into Greece long after Zeus and his strange family had migrated from Mt. Ida to Mt. Olympus.

B. THE CULT OF DIONYSUS

1. *Complexity of the Subject.* The subject of Dionysus is complex and baffling. The problem is further complicated by the fact that he appears in at least four characters: first, as the respectable patron of the theatre and the arts; second, as the effeminate, yet fierce and phallic mystery-god of the bloodthirsty Maenads; third, as the mystic deity in the temples of Demeter; and, fourth, as the divine savior who died for mankind and whose body and blood were symbolically eaten and drunk in the eucharist of the Orphic-Pythagorean celibates. Beyond this, almost all barbarian nations had their own versions of Dionysus under many names.

And yet there is a simple explanation: Dionysus, Bromius, Sabazius, Attis, Adonis, Zalmoxis, Corybas, Serapis, and Orpheus himself are replicas of their grand prototype Osiris; and the variations which appear among them resulted from the transplantation of the god from one country to another, and reflect simply the specific needs of his multifarious worshipers.

2. *Sesostris.* The *Argonautica* glorifies Sesostris.[12] History and tradition alike bear witness to the greatness of this king, who ruled Egypt from 1980 to 1933. We know also that this period saw a great resurgence in the cult of Osiris. If we may trust the account given to Herodotus[13] by the Egyptian priests and confirmed by Diodorus,[14] Sesostris had a career so closely parallel to that attributed to Osiris that we conclude much of his history to have been incorporated into the Osiris-Dionysus myth. He is said to have led an army over all portions of Asia; and, passing into Europe, to have made himself master of Thrace and Scythia, where he left not only monuments but also soldiers for permanent colonization, which explains the widespread worship of Dionysus in these regions. According to this hypothesis, the mysteries of Osiris were established in Thrace about the twentieth century, perhaps five hundred years after the Astarte-Adonis cult was established at Byblus.

3. *Dionysus among the Barbarians.* Dionysus was entrenched among the barbarians and especially in Thrace long before he appeared in Greece. Although the widely-traveled Herodotus never mentions a single shrine or temple of this god in his own country, he found his cult officially established in many other lands. He mentions particularly the Smyrneans,[15] the Scythians,[16] the Byzantines,[17] the Budini,[18] the Getae,[19] and the Thracians themselves,[20] who had an oracle of the god with a priestess, similar to that of the Greeks at Delphi.[21]

4. *Osiris Becomes Dionysus.* When Osiris arrived in Thrace he became Dionysus, the god from Nysa. Herodotus uses the names interchangeably and declares: "Osiris is named Dionysus by the Greeks."[22] And he continues: "According to the Greek tradition, he was no sooner born than he was sewn up in Zeus's thigh, and carried off to Nysa, above Egypt, Ethiopia,"[23] where he was said to have been reared.

Many Greek cities claimed Dionysus, but almost all

admitted that he was reared at Nysa.[24] He was the only deity who could penetrate nation after nation, become truly an international savior-god, for he was the adored and beloved redeemer who promised resurrection and immortality. That Osiris had become universal by 125 A. D. is established by Plutarch, who declares that we should "identify Osiris with Dionysus . . . the god of all people in common . . . and this they who have participated in the holy rites well know."[25]

Ancient authorities had no doubt concerning the identity of Osiris and Dionysus. Even as the Latins adopted the entire Greek pantheon intact but gave its members new names, so the Greeks themselves as well as the barbarians at a much earlier time appropriated the gods of other nations, altered them to suit their own needs, and called them by new names. Diodorus, writing in the first century B. C., declares: "the rite of Osiris is the same as that of Dionysus and that of Isis very similar to that of Demeter, the names alone having been interchanged."[26] And again: "Osiris is the one whom the Greeks call Dionysus."[27] Plutarch reiterates that Osiris and Dionysus are identical,[28] and declares that the public ceremonies of Osiris in Egypt and those of Dionysus in Greece are one and the same.[29]

5. *Melampus.* The only possible explanation for the ubiquitous Dionysus is that between 3000 and 500 B. C. Osiris was exported from Egypt by foreign visitors and carried along the trade routes by Egyptian armies and commerce into many lands, whose people readily embraced a god who conferred such benefits in this life and promised such unparalleled rewards hereafter. Diodorus reflects the confusion in which Dionysus was inextricably involved, and explains that the myths concerning him do not agree; some say that there was only one, others that there were three, by that name; some believe that he never had a human birth at all; and others that he was simply the symbol of wine.[30]

No wonder that the classical historians found it impossible to convey a clear-cut history of Dionysus, or a single image of him: for, in addition to the multiple replicas which existed among the barbarians, we know that there were at least two major penetrations into Greece by his cult before 1200, and at least three far-reaching reforms of it between 1100 and 500. The cult was first introduced from Egypt by a priest named Melampus, celebrated for divination, possibly as early as 1300; the second invasion came directly from Thrace, may have occurred about 1200, and is credited to Orpheus, although it probably antedated this prophet. Then followed several reforms or reconstitutions of the worship, to which Herodotus alludes when he says that "various sages have since" the time of Melampus "carried his teaching to greater perfection."[31] The first of these revisions was the Orphean, which must have taken place between the eleventh and the ninth century, when also Dionysus became an integral portion of the Eleusinia; the second, was that of Onomacritus, which occurred in the sixth century; and the last was the Pythagorean, which occurred contemporaneously. In the present chapter, we are concerned only with that primitive *soter* who came from Egypt and from Thrace before recorded history began and who commanded such astonishing devotion from the mutinous women of Greece.

Melampus was a pre-Trojan hierophant mentioned by Homer[32] and well known among the legendary Greeks of the heroic age. The evidence indicates that he was the first who, as Diodorus declares, "brought from Egypt the rites which the Greeks celebrate in the name of Dionysus."[33] And again: "Isis thought the privates of Osiris worthy of divine honours . . . the Greeks, too, inasmuch as they received from the Egyptians the . . . festivals . . . of Dionysus, honour this member both in the mysteries and the initiatory rites and sacrifices of the god."[34]

That the Melampian cult was definitely phallic and that the great majority of its devotees were women is elaborated by Herodotus,[35] who calls Osiris Dionysus and states that in Egypt his "festival is celebrated almost exactly as Dionysiac festivals are in Greece . . . They use . . . images eighteen inches high, pulled by strings, which the women carry around the villages. These images have male members about the same size, also operated by strings."[36]

Apollodorus declares that Melampus and his brother Bios insisted upon and received as their fee for curing the daughters of Proetus, driven mad by Dionysus, not only two thirds of the kingdom, but also the hands of the rehabilitated damsels in marriage.37

6. *The Thracian-Hellenic Myth.* While the Dionysian cult as introduced by Melampus bears a strong congenital resemblance to its Thracian relative, we note also a certain divergence. While the former was distinguished by its phallic emphasis, the Thracian cult was characterized by wild orgies, sexual excesses, and feasts of raw flesh, especially that of infants. Both, however, obtained their following almost exclusively among women.

We note further that although the story of Dionysus' birth from Semele is credited to Orpheus, his reforms had certainly not been incorporated by that phase of the cult which was known to Herodotus and Euripides. We can only conclude that the Thracian Dionysus had penetrated Greece and that Semele had been made his mother before the Orphean reform. We need not be surprised that in so confused and composite a myth, Orpheus should be credited with elements older than himself. In the following, Diodorus describes the primitive Dionysus as accepted by the Greek cultists who remained unaffected by its Orphean reforms and who "was born in Boeotian Thebes of Zeus and Semele, the daughter of Cadmus . . . Zeus had become enamoured of . . .her, but Hera . . . assumed the form of one of the women who was an intimate of Semele's and . . . suggested to her that it was fitting that Zeus should lie with her while having the same majesty . . . as when he took Hera to his arms. . . . Consequently Zeus, at the request of Semele . . . appeared to her accompanied by thunder and lightning; but Semele, unable to endure the majesty of his grandeur, died and brought forth the babe before the appointed time. This babe Zeus . . . took and hid in his thigh, and afterwards . . . brought it to Nysa in Arabia. There the boy was reared by nymphs and was given the name Dionysus after his father (Dios) and the place (Nysa)." Arriving at manhood, he organized an army of thyrsus-bearing women, at whose head he appeared in various countries, where he established his mysteries.

Those who accused the god of incontinence or of establishing his ritual "that he might thereby seduce the wives of other men . . . were punished by him right speedily . . . either striking them with madness or causing them while still living to be torn limb from limb by the hands of the women. . . . Dionysus made over to Charops the kingdom of the Thracians and instructed him in the secret rites connected with the initiations; and Oeagrus, the son of Charops, then . . . handed down the rites" to his son "Orpheus," who "made so many changes in the practices . . . that the rites were also called 'Orphic.'"[38]

And so we see that Dionysus, like Osiris, was a premature child. This was the original Greek version of Dionysus, and the only one mentioned by Apollodorus, who elaborates the myth as follows: "On the death of Semele the other daughters of Cadmus spread the report that Semele had bedded with a mortal man, and had falsely accused Zeus, and that therefore she had been blasted by thunder . . . Zeus eluded the wrath of Hera by turning Dionysus into a kid, and Hermes took him and brought him to the nymphs who dwelt at Nysa in Asia. . . . Dionysus discovered the vine, and being driven mad by Hera he roamed about Egypt and Syria. At first he was received by Proteus, king of Egypt, but afterwards he arrived at Cybela in Phrygia. And there, after he had been purified by Rhea and learned the rites of initiation, he hastened through Thrace against the Indians. . . . Having traversed Thrace and the whole of India and set up pillars there, he came to Thebes, and forced the women to abandon their houses and rave in Bacchic frenzy on Cithaeron. . . . Thus men perceived that he was a god and honoured him; and having brought up his mother from Hades and named her Thyone, he ascended up with her to heaven."[39]

The primitive Dionysiac cult which embraced this myth went on for centuries, but its members were gradually softened and chastened by developing civilization. It was this branch of the Dionysia which Diodorus observed and described as follows in the first century before Christ: "The Boeotians and other Greeks and the Thracians . . . have established sacrifices every other year to Dionysus, and believe that at that time the god reveals himself. . . . Consequently, Bacchic bands of women gather, and it is lawful for the maidens to carry the thyrsus and to join in the frenzied revelry, crying out 'Evai!' while the matrons . . . celebrate his mysteries . . . acting the part of the Maenads who, as history relates, were of old the companions of the god."[40]

7. *Skepticism.* In another rendition, we read that Orpheus transferred the birth of Dionysus to the Greek Thebes, because Cadmus, who had emigrated from the Egyptian city of the same name, had a daughter, Semele, who was seduced by a stranger; and when, after seven months, she gave birth to a child who resembled the Egyptian Osiris, Cadmus attributed the fatherhood of the child to Zeus, "in this way magnifying Osiris and averting slander from his violated daughter. . . . Now at a later time Orpheus . . . was entertained . . . by the descendants of Cadmus . . . And since he had become conversant with the teachings of the Egyptians about the gods, he transferred the birth of the ancient Osiris to more recent times, and . . . instituted a new initiation, in the ritual of which the initiates were given the account that Dionysus had been born of Semele and Zeus. And the people observed these initiatory rites partly because they were deceived through their ignorance, partly because they were attracted to them through the trustworthiness of Orpheus and his reputation in such matters, and most of all because they were glad to receive the god as a Greek."[41]

This version must have been current among the intellectuals of the first century. But it indicates again, from beginning to end, how the Egyptian Osiris and the Greek Dionysus are conjoined by a multitude of congenital ties. Although the preponderance of evidence indicates that Dionysus was first worshipped in Thrace, there was much uncertainty on this point also; and Strabo points out that both Pindar and Euripides confuse the rites of Cybele,

Mother of the Gods in Phrygia, with those of Dionysus.[42] And this we can well understand; for the rituals of Attis, Adonis, Sabazius, and Dionysus all stemmed from those of Osiris. This is confirmed and emphasized by Pausanias.[43]

8. *Dionysus in Classical Literature.* That Dionysus was the latest of the Greek gods we know from Euripides and Herodotus; that he had become the most powerful by the beginning of our era is obvious from many later authors. But the growth of this soteriological interloper with many faces covered more than a thousand years.

There are references to Dionysus in Homer, where he is represented as having been driven, together with his Bacchantes, out of Nysa by Lycurgus.[44] From the twelfth to the eighth century, Dionysus was neither respectable nor an Olympian; he was not, however, to be ignored or abused, as many discovered to their sorrow. He was a fearsome divinity at the head of his intoxicated Maenads who filled the mountainsides with unseemly revelry while they searched for living victims to rend; from such a character, the dignified upperclass *Iliad* and *Odyssey* necessarily held aloof.

The Hymn to Demeter, also attributed to Homer and probably composed in the seventh century, declares that when Demeter beheld her daughter, she "rushed forth like a Maenad down a dark mountain woodland."[45] There are also two short Homeric hymns to Dionysus, in which he is glorified as the god of wine. During the centuries following the Trojan War, the Bacchantes were notorious; but insofar as Dionysus had penetrated more respectable circles, he was still no more than the god of song, of wine, of music, of dancing, of the theatre, and of agriculture.

Euripides, who was born some thirty years after Herodotus, has left a classic known as *The Bacchanals*, which describes the wild progress of the Dionysiac mystery into the heart of Greece, perhaps in the eleventh century. Led by the maddened Agave, mother of Pentheus, king of Thebes, the women of the city had become demented and roamed over the mountainsides, shouting "Evoe! Evoe!"

—44—

Pentheus had seized the delirious celebrants, bound them in fetters, and thrown them into his dungeon.

At this point, Dionysus himself arrives, not from Thrace, but from Phrygia, disguised as a mortal, to wreak vengeance upon those who had accused his mother of harlotry. It is significant that the Osirian cults of various barbarian nations were so similar that Greek classical writers were constantly mistaking one of them for another. The respectable Pentheus appears and deplores the fact that all the women of the city have abandoned their work, their homes, their children, their husbands, and all human decency to partake of these "fabled mysteries." And they followed "the god of yesterday . . . this womanly man . . . Dionysus, whosoe'er he be, with revels dishonorable. In the midst, stand the crowned goblets; and each stealing forth, This way and that, creeps to a lawless bed." Pentheus declares that "where 'mong women, The grape's sweet poison mingles with the feast, Nought holy may we augur of such worship." And now he learns to his consternation that all the Maenads have been miraculously released from their bonds and are leaping about "in their wild orgies," like converts at a nineteenth-century camp meeting. He espies Dionysus, whom he believes to be only an emissary of the god, and asks him what form his orgies take. "That," declares Dionysus, "is not uttered to the uninitiate." When Pentheus deplores the arrival of these new and violent rites, he is told that they are practiced and adored by all the barbarians.

A messenger now arrives who tells Pentheus how he and some of his companions were driving a herd of bovines over the mountainside when they were suddenly attacked by the Maenads and compelled to flee on pain of being torn limb from limb; and how the god-possessed women tore the calves and heifers asunder and flung the mangled remnants among the trees. Dionysus persuades Pentheus to dress himself in women's apparel, so that he can observe these orgies. Having complied, however, the king loses his mind; Dionysus seats him high in a tree, where he can be seen by the Bacchantes. When Agave spies him, she being also mad and thinking her son a beast, commands that he be seized so that he "might ne'er betray the mysteries of our god." The women bend the tree down and seize their victim: "His mother first began the sacrifice." Foaming at the mouth, she tears his arm out of his shoulder; and the other women, setting to with frenzy, rip him into many portions. Agave carries his head back to the city, thinking it that of a lion cub.

9. *The Dionysiac Sacrament.* That the Dionysiacs ate the raw flesh of a bovine, a human enemy, or an infant in order to become immortal Bacchoi or Dionysiacs is attested by incontrovertible evidence. Porphyrios reproduced the following from Euripides' *Cretans,* now lost: "Pure has my life been since that day when I became an initiate of Idaean Zeus and herdsman of night-wandering Zagreus; and having accomplished the raw feasts and held the torches aloft to the Mountain-Mother, yea torches of the Kuretes, I was raised to the holy estate and called a Bacchus."[46] Plutarch wrote of "the mysteries . . . in which the eating of raw flesh, and the tearing in pieces of victims . . . are in use . . . and the human sacrifices offered of old."[47]

Clemens Alexandrinus declares that "the Bacchanals hold their orgies in honour of the frenzied Dionysus . . . by the eating of raw flesh."[48] He also states that, according to Dosidas, the Lesbians offered human sacrifices to Dionysus.[49] And Arnobius describes the feasts of the "wild Bacchanalians, which are named in the Greek omophagia . . . in which with seeming frenzy and the loss of your senses, you twine snakes about you; and to show yourselves full of the divinity and majesty of the god, tear in pieces the flesh with gory mouths."[50]

Ovid relates the terrible experiences of the daughters of Minyas in Orchomenas.[51] When these dutiful imitators of the industrious Athena were determined to shun the mad revels of the Bacchanalians, Dionysus came into their midst, filled the air with wild beasts, drove the girls mad, and transformed them into bats. According to another version, they drew lots and devoured the infant child of one of their number, Leucippe. Herodotus confirms[52] the tale of Apollodorus concerning the daughters of Proetus to the effect that only by payment of a huge bribe to Melampus could the virgins and matrons of Arcadia be freed from their dementia, in which they "roamed over the whole Argive land . . . abandoned their houses, destroyed their children, and flocked to the desert."[53] In another passage, Apollodorus states that Dionysus drove the women of Argos mad because they would not honor him "and they on the mountains devoured the flesh of the infants whom they carried at their breasts."[54]

W. K. C. Guthrie reproduces the scene from a vase of the fourth century B. C., now in British Museum, showing the sacramental rending and eating of a child.[55] This depicts the ancient Dionysiac ritual, which the Orphean reform repudiated. We see Dionysus himself at the left looking on in dismay while a Thracian at the right is running away in horror. The central figure, who represents a primitive cultist, is holding an infant; he has just ripped out its arm and is conveying the bloody morsel to his lips. It is at least interesting to note that this is the very ritual which the pagans later attributed to the Christians and of which the Catholics accused their own Montanist sectarians.

10. *Analysis.* It is obvious that neither Herodotus nor Euripides understood the esoteric nature or the dynamic forces which lay at the root of the Dionysiac mystery. It is certain that such wild and passionate excesses must have grown from hopes and promises hitherto unknown and undreamed. It was a religion of the poor, of women, of the common herd; it gave them a sense of worth and significance and offered what seemed a priceless reward. At the very least, it was a romantic surcease from the continuous drudgery of a meaningless existence.

We believe that the Thracian Dionysus reflected the Osirian mystery in its crude and ancient form, preceding the era of Ani and Nebseni. It was more like the Osirianism of the Pyramid Texts, in which we find Unas eating gods and ancestors and Horus drinking copiously of the blood of his slain enemies. At that time human beings as well as animals were sacrificed by rending, and the raw flesh was eaten and the warm blood lapped up by the frenzied celebrants, to whom this gruesome sacrament was a precise and identical replica of their own dismembered Osiris. The somewhat more mature form of Osirianism imported by Melampus emphasized its phallic nature; but it, too, practised human *omophagia*.

The older Dionysiac mysteries which preceded the reforms of Orpheus were, therefore, definitely cannibalistic; except by rending and eating Osiris in the form of a divine substitute, which could be a bovine, a human enemy, or an infant, there could be no victory over death and the grave. These rites, orgies, and sacraments had a single purpose: to make the celebrants immortal by transforming them into an essence identical to that of Dionysus. The initiates were therefore called Bacchoi or Dionysiacs, which was no mere symbolism: it was understood as a literal fact. In the same manner, many centuries later, the followers of Christ were called Christians: they also believed themselves mystical members of His body and they became so by a process identical to that by which the devotees of Dionysus became Bacchantes.

11. *A Cult of Women.* Among the barbarians, both men and women seem to have joined the cult of Dionysus: but in Greece, it was peculiarly a religion of women. The reason for this we may surmise. Perhaps women were then, as some say they now are, more religious than men; but we believe rather that in the Dionysiac mystery women found the means to throw off the heavy domination of their husbands which had come with the end of primitive communism, the establishment of private property, monogamic marriage, and the concomitant requirement of chastity among wives, all of which was of such recent origin that the memory of their former freedom, economic independence, and social dominance was still vivid in their consciousness. There is no doubt that this mutiny even involved the murder of their own children, whom the husbands now desired as property-heirs. As additional acts of revenge, the frenzied women also indulged in *omophagia* and promiscuous sex-orgies under the direction of the Dionysiac priests.

Although these female Dionysiacs revolted against their husbands, they were without taint of celibacy: in fact, there has never been an authentic feminist celibate movement. Women have often mutinied against men, but have never rejected them; for it is the nature of women to desire children, and men are essential for their generation and support. The feminine Osirians and Dionysiacs worshiped the male generative organ in their processions; and at Memphis they displayed their genitals to the sacred bull Apis, or Osiris, so that they might absorb something of his virility.56 The Maenads did not repudiate sex; they simply rebelled against monoandric marriage until such time as they could gain equality with their husbands, or at least a better position in the home. The Amazons constituted another phase of the same revolt.

12. *Dionysus a Partial Osiris.* Plutarch, who repeats so often that Osiris and Dionysus are one and the same, tells of one Eudoxus, who objected that if these gods were identical, why did not Dionysus "cause the Nile to rise, or rule over the dead?"57 The answer is simple enough: all who embraced the worship of Osiris under one of his pseudonyms took of him what they required, and otherwise altered him to conform with their own needs. Since they had no Nile to rise, naturally he did not bring any flood in the mountains of Thrace or Phrygia, or upon the rain-blessed fields of Greece. We must also note that nowhere is Dionysus identified with the seed which is buried and which is resurrected in the grain. This, we believe, is the case because at the time he first came among the Thracians, cereal-agriculture was not sufficiently important to be identified as the bread that came down from heaven. However, since they possessed grapes in abundance, he became the god of wine, which now replaced the barley-ale as his blood. And since this eschatology was new to the Hellenes, we need not be surprised that they did not at once import with Dionysus all the Osirian doctrines concerning the after-life. It was enough for these primitive Thracians and Greeks to know that, like their god, they could be resurrected into im-

mortality by becoming one with him through his mystical sacrament.

Such was the god who pushed and elbowed his way into Greece during the second millennium. He was crude, gruesome, and in many respects repulsive; and before he could be widely accepted in a more refined age, it was necessary that he undergo a basic reformation. And this is precisely what happened in Orphism.

CHAPTER IV

ATTIS AND CYBELE

A. THE MYTH

1. *Exported from Thrace.* Attis was, as it were, a grandchild of Osiris, because he was a reconstituted Dionysus, joined also, like Adonis, to the Great Mother. What happened is clear: after the Thracians had absorbed the Egyptian mystery, they carried it with them, as Strabo declares,[1] first, into the island of Samothrace, and next into Phrygia, as they colonized both. In Asian Phrygia, Dionysus, like Osiris at Byblus, encountered the age-old Semitic Mother; and from their conjuncture issued a new and strange amalgam. We would guess that this cult preceded the Eleusinian, and probably dates back to 1800-1600.

2. *According to Samothracian Legend.* According to the myth current among the Samothracians, "the sacred rites of the Great Mother of the gods . . . together with cymbals and kettledrums and the instruments of her ritual"[2] had first been established there. It seems that Cybele became the mother of Corybas, to whom she bore a daughter, also named Cybele. We note here the similarity to the Cinyras-Aphrodite myth. Corybas gave the name Corybants to all who, in celebrating the sacred rites of his mother, acted like men possessed. Moving to the Asian mainland with their attendant Dardanus, they established the Cybele-Corybas ritual in Phrygia. It would thus appear that Corybas (or Attis) was at once the father, the lover, and the son of Cybele.

3. *The Phrygian Version.* The Phrygians themselves, however, had a variant version.[3] King Meison of Phrygia

had married Dindymeme—which often appears as one of the names of the goddess—and she bore a daughter, Cybele, whom he, thinking her illegitimate, exposed to die. She, however, suckled by wild beasts and adopted by herdsmen, grew into great beauty and was the first to devise the pipe of many reeds, the cymbal, and the kettledrum. Upon attaining womanhood, she fell in love with Attis, later called Pappa. She conceived a child by him shortly before her parents discovered that she was the royal princess and brought her back to the palace. When the king learned of her seduction, he executed not only her nurses but Attis also, whose body was cast forth unburied. Cybele, like Isis and Astarte, was disconsolate with grief; and she "became frenzied and rushed out of the palace into the countryside. And crying aloud and beating on a kettledrum she visited every country alone, with hair hanging free. . . . But a pestilence fell upon human beings throughout Phrygia and the land ceased to bear fruit, and when the unfortunate people inquired of the god how they might rid themselves of their ills, he commanded them, it is said, to bury the body of Attis and to honour Cybele as a goddess."[4]

4. *Another Version.* Arnobius relates a third version: The Great Mother, sleeping upon a mountain in Phrygia, was assailed by Jupiter but she repelled him; and so he spent his lust upon a stone, which brought forth Acdestis, a fierce and bloody creature. Dionysus made him drunk, and emasculated him; from the drops of his blood sprang a pomegranate tree; Nana, daughter of King Sangarius, placed some of the fruit in her bosom, and she conceived and bore a child, which her father exposed on the mountainside as illegitimate. When the Mother of the Gods beheld his beauty, she loved him exceedingly, as did the wickedly lustful Acdestis, who gave him gifts and forced an unnatural relationship upon him. King Midas of Pessinus, wishing to withdraw the prince from so disgraceful an intimacy, offered him his daughter in marriage. But the Mother Goddess, determined to free Attis forever both from shame and matrimony, filled him "with furious passion," so that he mutilated himself under a pine tree.

saying, "'Take these, Acdestis, for which you have stirred up so great and terribly perilous commotions.'" As his life ebbed away with his flowing blood, the Mother of the Gods gathered the parts and spread earth upon them. A violet sprang from the blood. Weeping, the Goddess carried the sacred pine tree to her cave, where "she beats and mutilates her breasts."[5]

5. *Salvation through Emasculation.* Such are the fragments which survive concerning the tragic fate of Attis. Again we have the beloved and mutilated youth as in the Adonis and Osiris myths; again we have the goddess lamenting his loss and searching for his dismembered body; again we have the image set up as its substitute. Again, we have the failure of the crops, as in the myths of Ishtar, Artemis, and Demeter. But now, instead of salvation through *omophagia,* as in the Dionysia, or through copulation, as in the Aphrodite-cult, we have a frenzy of emasculation: in short we find escape from sin and guilt and a highway to blessed immortality through celibacy and castration, the eradication of the sexual urge. And so, by a strange twist of irony, we have two bizarre conjunctures of the Osirian concept with the Mother Goddess of Asia: in the first, the mystery called for sacred sexual communion; in the second, the ritual consisted primarily in the castration of the male initiate and in the mutilation of the woman's breasts.

B. EXPANSION OF THE CULT

Although the Attis-cult never developed as extensively in Greece as did those of Dionysus, Demeter, and Isis, we learn from Strabo,[6] Pausanias,[7] and Pindar[8] that "the mighty Mother of the Gods" and her desexed lover were by no means unknown in Hellas. But it was among other less sensitive Mediterranean people that the Attis-cult made its greatest conquests: in Africa, Gaul, Spain, and Italy. Wondrous powers were attributed to the Phrygian goddess. And so it was that, in the year 204 B. C., while Rome was facing crop failures and imminent destruction at the hands of Hannibal, some one suggested

—53—

that Cybele could make the imperial city the mistress of
the world. Livy states that the Delphian Oracle had
once declared that should Italy ever be invaded by a
foreign foe, he could be driven out "if the Idaean Mother
should be brought from Pessinus to Rome."[9] Ambas-
sadors were therefore dispatched to Phrygia, who in due
time returned with a small black stone. Whatever may
have been its efficacy, it is certain that during the ensuing
season the crops were excellent and the hosts of Carthage
were defeated. Arnobius expresses a commendable skepticism concerning the powers of the diminutive stone and
the emasculated priests of Cybele; many, however, were
convinced of their puissance; for the cult was soon firmly
established, and the mystery-dramas, noisy processions,
and bloody rites of Cybele became familiar sights in the
streets of Rome; and her temple rose on the very site
where the basilica of St. Peter stands today.

C. THE PUBLIC ORGIES

1. *As Told by Apuleius.* Apuleius wrote that the
devotees of Cybele "went . . . forth, shouting and dancing . . . they bent down their necks and spun round so
that their hair flew out in a circle; they bit their own
flesh; finally, every one took his two-edged weapon and
wounded himself in divers places. Meanwhile, there was
one . . . who invented . . . a great lie, noisily . . . accusing himself, saying that he had displeased the divine
majesty of the goddess . . . wherefore he prayed that vengeance might be done to himself. And therewithal he took
a whip . . . and scourged his own body . . . so that you
might see the ground wet and defiled with the womanish
blood that issued forth abundantly."[10]

The celebrants thereupon brought in a youth whom
they had abducted and upon whom they inflicted some
form of sodomy. It is clear that the Phrygian mystery
reflects its Osirian origin; but it is also obvious that here
appeared for the first time that overwhelming sense of
guilt which was considered inseparable from the sexual
lust residing in our members and which must be con-

quered by beating, whipping, slashing, torture, and self-mutilation, but which, nevertheless, must needs seek relief through some vile and abnormal practice. Since the frenzied devotees of Attis identified their congenital corruption with erotic desire, they must needs renounce not merely all sexual consummation but sexuality itself before they could be united with their god. The climacteric of the mystery-ritual, therefore, consisted in the same emasculation once performed by Attis and Cybele.

2. *As Told by Arnobius.* Arnobius was one of those scholarly converts who rejected paganism more than they accepted Christianity. He flourished about 300, some five hundred years after the cult of Cybele had been introduced into Rome. There is no doubt that he had been outraged by witnessing the gruesome atrocities performed in the public dramas representing the passion of Attis. We gain a vivid impression of what these were like from his description of the emasculated priests, "the Galli, with disheveled hair, beating their breasts." They must, he surmised, "be involved in the infamy of some shameful deed. For who would believe that there is any honour in that which the worthless *Galli* perform, effeminate debauchees complete?"[11]

D. THE ESOTERIC RITUAL

1. *According to Hippolytus.* There is a long discussion in Hippolytus,[12] who wrote about 210 A. D., concerning the Naasenes, one of several Christian heresies deriving certain tenets from the Phrygian mystery. According to them, when Jesus declares that "there be eunuchs, which have made themselves eunuchs for the kingdom of heaven's sake," He was simply repeating an injunction which had been taught throughout Asia Minor by the cult of Attis for more than a thousand years. Hippolytus elaborates by adding that, according to the Naasenes, "the ineffable mystery of the Samothracians, which it is allowable" only for "the initiated to know" was precisely the same as that proclaimed by Christ when He declared, "If ye do not drink my blood, and eat my flesh,

ye will not enter the kingdom of heaven." This flesh-and-blood sacrament, states Hippolytus, is according to the Naasenes, called Corybas by Phrygians as well as by those "Thracians who dwell around Haemus." Hippolytus continues that Attis prohibited all sexual intercourse and quotes his Naasene source as follows: "Hail, Attis, gloomy mutilation of Rhea. Assyrians style thee thrice-longed-for Adonis, and the whole of Egypt calls thee Osiris . . .; Samothracians, venerable Adam; Haemonians, Corybas; and the Phrygians name thee at one time Pappa, at another time God . . ., or the Green Ear of Corn that has been reaped."[13]

All this establishes further the congenital relationship among the savior-cults; the identification of Attis with the seed that dies and is resurrected; and, most significant of all, that in Attis the *soter* appears at last as a eunuch who requires celibacy from his devotees. The fact is that although Osiris and Dionysus were gods of virility, the opposite characteristic was always immanent in them also. For the priests of Osiris had been mandatory celibates since time immemorial; and the images of Dionysus had for centuries resembled an hermaphrodite, a "womanly man," an effeminate god. In Attis, the repudiation of sex took its most drastic form.

2. *The Passion of Attis.* The annual festival of Cybele, which lasted four days, began on the 22nd of March, when the trunk of a pine tree was carried ceremonially into the temple. Wreathed with violets and swathed with woolen cloth, the tree stood in the midst of its worshipers; and to this the effigy of Attis was then affixed or impaled. On the second day, there were processions of overwrought mourners, bearing images upon their breasts, following the statue of the goddess through the streets; driven to the highest pitch of frenzy by the wild and discordant music of fifes, cymbals, tambourines and kettledrums, they screamed and whirled and leaped about like demented dervishes, and slashed themselves with knives and swords. On the next day, March 24, the bloody passion-drama reached its climax. As Sir J. G. Frazer notes, this was "the Day of Blood," on which

"the novices sacrificed their virility. Wrought to the highest pitch of religious excitement, they dashed the severed portions of themselves against the image of the cruel goddess."[14] Thus, while their god hung upon the pine tree, his initiates performed the same sacred mutilation upon themselves which he had undergone, so that they might share in his resurrection.

At the close of March 24, the priests reverently removed the sacred effigy from the tree, and laid it in the tomb. The older as well as the newly desexed initiates watched and fasted all through the long night, until the dawn of March 25. The tomb was then opened; and a great shout of joy went up from the assembled worshipers: for the tomb was empty; the god was not there! He had been resurrected from the grave into eternal life.

With the resurrection, the people gave themselves over to an unrestricted Saturnalia of joy, gaiety, and license. The festival ended with a procession bearing the sacred black stone to the river Almo, where it was washed and purified; after which it was returned amidst singing and rejoicing to its sacred place within the temple.

3. *Similarity to Easter Celebration.* The similarity between these rites and the pascha or Easter celebration in the Catholic Church is striking indeed. Like the devotees of Attis, the Christians mourned and watched all through the dreadful hours when their god hung upon the tree; but on resurrection morning, they too were filled with joy at the empty tomb. Ambrose in his sermon on "The Mystery of the Pascha" calls the day the real beginning of the year, in which nature revives after the long death of winter.[15]

4. *The Sacramental Eucharist and the Taurobolium.* The evidence supports the suspicion of Arnobius[16] that other and even more revolting ceremonies were performed: for there were secret rituals which only the emasculated initiates could witness. These consisted of a sacramental meal in which the novices ate out of a drum and drank from a cymbal.[17] And there was the great

initiatory sacrament known as the *taurobolium,* or baptismal blood bath, in which the newly-inducted member, wreathed with the violets of Attis, descended into a pit, covered with a grating, on which stood the sacred bull. This was ceremonially slain, so that his blood streamed copiously over the inductees below who, by this ritual, were literally *washed in the blood of the bull,* and thus born anew into everlasting life. Again, we see the generic relationship to Osirian symbolism. It is ironic to note that on the very spot where the Pope now presides, the initiates of another *Pappa* were saved by a more realistic sacrament than that which now prevails.

5. *The High Priests Originally Crucified.* There is no doubt that in the original ritual, an Archigallus, or desexed high priest, was annually impaled upon the pine tree; and that, during the era preceding recorded history, a thousand emasculated saviors had been crucified in Phrygia for the original sin of many and had died upon the tree so that others might have eternal life. This idea had become so deeply rooted in pagan consciousness that it was almost an obsession: the god-man must die and rise from the grave so that his devotees might also be resurrected into life immortal. However, as advancing civilization softened the manners of all races, this ceremony became an innocuous scene in a passion-play. And finally the living priest was simulated by a lifeless figure which was first impaled and then laid in his sacred tomb. The curse of Deuteronomy 21:23 against all who are hanged on a tree must have been directed at the crucified priests of Attis.

E. INFLUENCE OF ATTIS UPON CHRISTIANITY

Attis became one of the most potent savior-gods of the ancient world, and left his heavy imprint upon Christianity. The Gospel injunction commanding auto-emasculation, which was so widely practiced in the early Catholic Church, was derived primarily from the cult of Attis, since it is found nowhere else. Equally significant was its influence in the Easter celebration. We know that for centuries the date of the Christian crucifixion had caused the bitterest dispute; and, next to the Trinitarian controversy, this was the most serious issue which faced the First Ecumenical Council at Nicaea in 325. The Eastern Church had celebrated the resurrection on the 16th Nisan, in April, which was also the Jewish Passover, and which is certainly the time indicated in the Gospel narrative. In the West, however, this date had never been popular and we know from Irenaeus[18] that the question was already a burning issue before the end of the second century. At all events, Lactantius tells us categorically that Jesus was crucified on March 23,[19] which would place His resurrection on the 25th; and these are precisely the dates on which the death and resurrection of Attis had been celebrated for nearly two thousand years. To say that the final selection of these by the Catholic Church after several centuries of vacillation and bitter controversy was a mere coincidence places too heavy a burden upon credulity; the Christian Easter and the Passion of Christ simply incorporated into a new cult a date and a ritual which had been celebrated by the communicants of the Attis-Cybele mystery beyond the dimmest reaches of history.

CHAPTER V

DEMETER-PERSEPHONE

A. HISTORY

1. *Greek Adaptation of Isis.* After considering the mystery-cults which took form in Syria, Thrace, and Phrygia, one is inspired with a sense of serenity when turning to the stately Eleusinian ritual. In this, the gory, lustful, and violent elements which distinguish the primitive Dionysus are wholly absent; and the reasons for this are apparent: first, it appropriated a more benign aspect of the Egyptian religion than did the others; and, second, it developed among the Greeks after they had made enormous strides into civilization. It is probable that the Isis-worship, centered at Coptas in Egypt, had become more or less independent by 1600 B. C.; and it is certain that Demeter was Isis with a new name and in another habitat. The upper-class Athenians of 1500-1000 B. C. found the fierce and bloody Osiris repellent and revolting; but they took to their hearts his beneficent sister, altered her in a few details, gave her a daughter (Persephone), instead of a son or a brother-husband, to rescue from death and oblivion, and made of *them* their *soter*-substitutes.

2. *Demeter, the Imported Grain.* The Greeks were well aware that Demeter was not indigenous.[1] The Homeric *Hymn to Demeter* reveals her foreign origin: for, upon arriving at Eleusis, she declares: "hither have I come in my wandering, nor know I what land this is."

Plutarch tells us that Persephone was called the autumnal air which causes the dissolution of the crops;[2] that the grains cut by the reapers are "the limbs of Demeter"; and that "among the Greeks also many things are done which are similar to the Egyptian ceremonies in the shrines of Isis, and . . . at about the same time."[3] Diodorus Siculus declares that "Demeter was the discoverer of corn," who "also taught mankind how to prepare it for food"; and that she was known as Thesmophorus, because she taught men laws, which accustomed them "to the practice of justice."[4]

3. *Isis-Demeter at Eleusis.* We do not know just when the worship of Demeter was established at Eleusis; but we do know that she was venerated there during the Mycenaean period, probably as early as 1400. We know that the cult survived the edicts of Theodosius and continued without interruption until 396 A. D., when the Christian monks accompanying the Arian Alaric destroyed the shrine. Thus there was a continuous celebration of the Eleusinia for nearly two thousand years.

On a promontory at Eleusis facing the Gulf of Aegina some ten or twelve miles from Athens stood the courtyard and the magnificent temple of Demeter, which was built by the same Ictinus who also constructed the Parthenon at Athens.[5] The road between the two cities was known as the Sacred Way,[6] because it was trodden by thousands of pilgrims and initiates every autumn when they journeyed to Eleusis to celebrate the Greater Mysteries.

4. *Demeter the Upper-Class Soter.* The cult never aroused such hysterical ecstasy among its devotees as did Dionysus, the savior of the illiterate; Demeter was the refined *soter*-substitute of the cultured classes. It was therefore inevitable that she should pass away and that Dionysus should survive; because, as Frazer remarks, "while the higher forms of religious faith pass away like clouds, the lower stand firm and indestructible like rocks."[7]

5. *Held in Veneration.* That the Eleusinian mystery was held in the highest veneration by the ancients is amply witnessed. Hesiod tells us: "But do thou . . . work . . . that . . . worshipful Demeter of the fair crown love thee and fill thy barn with livelihood."[8] Diodorus relates that Hercules was initiated into the Eleusinian mystery at the time when Musaeus, son of Orpheus, was

— 61 —

said to have been in charge of the temple;[9] and it was believed that potency so acquired enabled the hero to drag the three-headed Cerberus into the light of day. Pausanias declares: "the Eleusinian mysteries and the Olympian Games seem to exhibit more than anything else the divine purpose."[10] A legend told by the same author[11] concerning the people of Phigalia in Arcadia illustrates the power attributed to Demeter. Her statue there had been destroyed and her festivals neglected. A great dearth came over the land and the people were in danger of reverting to cannibalism and a diet of acorns. But when her statue was replaced and her mysteries reinstated, all was well again.

6. *Promised Immortality*. The mysteries of Demeter promised blissful immortality. *The Hymn to Demeter* declares: "Happy is he among mortals who has beheld these things! and he that is uninitiate, and hath no lot in them, hath never equal lot in death beneath the murky gloom." Pindar, writing in the fifth century, declared that the happy survival of the soul is possible only for those who have "by good fortune, culled the fruit of the rite that releaseth from toil,"[12] that is, the Eleusinian, concerning which he continues: "Blessed is he who hath seen these things before he goeth beneath the hollow earth; for he understandeth the end of mortal life, and the beginning of a new life given of god."[13] Isocrates, 436-338, declared that Demeter enabled mankind to rise above the status of beasts by conferring "the fruits of the earth;" and that she instituted "the holy rite which inspires in those who partake of it sweeter hopes regarding both the end of life and all eternity."[14]

7. *Arrival of Isis to Sicily and Athens via Crete*. We conclude that the cult reached Crete from Egypt late in the Minoan period and from there spread to Sicily and Athens. It is true that various locales claimed to be the scene of the Rape of Persephone and proudly exhibited the cave from which Hades emerged and back through which he bore the terrified maiden. Pausanias describes the spot[15] where the Athenians said he ab-

ducted her; but Diodorus relates the myth as told by the Sicilians, which was the generally accepted version.¹⁶

B. THE MYTH

The myth, according to *The Hymn to Demeter* and other sources, is briefly as follows:

Persephone, the daughter of Zeus and Demeter, was picking flowers with Athena, Artemis, and other virgin goddesses: according to the very ancient Hymn, this was in the Nysian plain but, according to the Sicilians, it was in the Vale of Enna, near Syracuse. Thus we see that primitive tradition placed both Dionysus and Demeter at Nysa, a province near the Ethiopian border of Egypt, and therefore congenitally related to Isis and Osiris. At all events, Zeus had promised his brother Hades that Kore, or Persephone, should be his bride; and so he suddenly emerged in his chariot drawn by his fiery steeds, snatched the beautiful maiden, and bore her away, wailing from the depths of the sea.

From this incident grew a tale of mother-grief which embodies and surpasses the lament of Isis for Osiris, of Astarte for Adonis, of Cybele for Attis, of Orpheus for Eurydice, of Dionysus for Semele: all of these, of course, being variants of the same theme, symbolizing the grief and fear which crushed the heart of primitive humanity when the sun declined and winter killed the vegetation.

When her beloved daughter was nowhere to be found, Demeter, seeking her, sped like a bird over land and sea "for nine days . . . with torches burning in her hands," which according to the Sicilian version, had been kindled from the fires of Etna. From land to land she went, inquiring of all. Arriving at Eleusis in the form of an old woman seeking humble servitude, she was met by the handmaidens of Metaneira, wife of Celeus, and became the nurse of her son. While the fragrant deity was transforming the infant Demophoon into immortality by the application of fire, Metaneira surprised her in the act; the goddess thereupon angrily let the child fall, denounced the stupid intrusion, revealed herself as the goddess of the law, the seasons, and the grain, and stood before the trembling woman in all the terrors of her divine majesty. The fact that in all those details the Demeter-story coincides with that of Isis in Syria as told by Plutarch[17] proves that the Greek myth derives from the Egyptian. Demeter then commanded the people of Eleusis to build for her a "great temple and an altar thereby" on the jutting rock below the town; "the rites I myself will prescribe, that in time to come ye may pay them duly and appease my power."

The temple was forthwith built; but she sat apart "wasting away with desire for her deep-bosomed daughter." And, since she would not permit the grain to grow, famine ensued; and "now would the whole race of mortal men have perished utterly . . . if Zeus had not conceived a counsel within his heart."

That Demeter was not of the Olympian convocation is established by the myth that Zeus sent several gods one after another to her with precious gifts and with the offer of untold honors if she would permit the corn to grow again and accept her position among the gods. But she, brooding and sorrowing in her grief and wrath, sat still in stony silence. Now desperate, Zeus sent Hermes to the underworld to persuade Hades to release his bride so that mankind might not perish; and to this Aidoneus apparently gave willing consent. But as Persephone left, he gave her a pomegranate seed, which she, not suspecting his treachery, took and ate. Hermes placed Persephone in his flashing chariot and conveyed her to her mother's temple at Eleusis, where she revealed the fact that she had eaten the fatal seed; at this, the heart of Demeter was riven, for she knew that her daughter would therefore be compelled forever to spend four or six months annually in the underworld.

By this stratagem, Hades obtained a part-time bride, and Demeter finally agreed to a compromise in which she permitted the grain to grow again in return for her daughter's companionship during the summer months; and she took her place reluctantly among the Olympians. For it seems that Zeus could take Persephone away from her mother, but could neither compel the latter to obey his will nor cause the plants to grow. And thus, while the Demeter-mystery was incorporated into the official religion of Greece, and particularly at Athens, it remained always separate and distinct.

C. DEVELOPMENT OF THE CULT

1. *In Sicily.* The Sicilians celebrated two festivals to the Great Goddesses:[18] the first was in honor of Demeter, when the seed was laid in the ground; and the second to Kore, when the grain was harvested. This was the reverse of the Athenian order, in which the Thesmophoria, or the festival of Demeter, was celebrated at harvest-time. In both, however, the goddesses symbolize the grain in its successive phases as buried seed, waving stalks, and harvested cereal.

2. *Combined Egyptian and Babylonian Elements.* It is obvious that the Demeter-concept combines the salient features of Isis with the Astarte-Tammuz myth. The Egyptian Earth Mother who forbids the practice of cannibalism, who prevents the relapse of mankind into savagery, who is and gives the grain, who imparts the knowlege by which it can be made into civilized food, who teaches mankind to live in communities under just law, and who heals with magical drugs and confers immortality, here coalesces with the Great Mother of Semitic lands mourning for her lost lover-son, who symbolizes the vegetation withered by autumnal frost. Demeter herself, however, remains always the beneficent Isis and never becomes the lascivious Ishtar seeking to instill life by the mystery of sexual communion. Demeter remains the pure and tender mother; she is chaste and noble, determined and inflexible, but always loving and protective.

3. *Penetration by the Orphean Dionysus.* Sometime around 1000 B. C. the Orphean Dionysus penetrated the Demeter-Persephone mystery; and in the sixth century, this new element was completely reconstructed and remained thereafter the central soteriological feature of the

cult. This, however, belongs rather to Orphism than to the Eleusinia.

D. THE DEMETER-PERSEPHONE RITUAL

1. *Happiness Here and Hereafter.* By the time of Pausanias, cir. 120 A. D., all Hellas was filled with the statues, altars, and temples of Demeter; her festivals were celebrated everywhere; yet Eleusis remained always the center of her cult. Since it had been accepted since prehistoric times, there was no conflict between Demeter and Olympus; initiation into her ritual was, as it were, an extension of the prevailing religion. However, it was a complete and independent worship, and, once initiated into it, the votary required no other faith for time or eternity. Countless men and women, craving something more than the Olympians could offer, turned to Eleusis in their search for moral elevation as well as assurance of a better life beyond the grave. *Come,* said the hierophants of Demeter, as did those of Osiris in Egypt, *all those clean of hand and pure in heart, and receive the better life in this world and the hope of eternal happiness hereafter.*

2. *Soteriology.* The immortality expected through the Eleusinia was similar to the Homeric Elysium, which was formerly reserved for the greatest heroes or demigods or was conferred as a special boon of the gods; for example, we read that at death both Helen and Menelaus were rewarded with this supernal gift. But this was something totally beyond the reach of ordinary mortals: not even Achilles or Agamemnon was so rewarded, nor could anyone achieve such blessedness by any striving of his own. The Eleusinia, however, by initiation into the Greater Mysteries conferred upon many Athenians this ultimate Homeric hope. But this involved no special discipline or cataclysmic regeneration, and no organization of the initiates into separate communions or churches. There was no hint of Buddhist ethics, Brahmanic hell-torture, Zoroastrian eschatology, or an Osirian Judgment. It was only necessary to witness the holy

spectacles, partake of certain rites and sacraments, and undergo a mystic initiation, possessing a magical efficacy; the *mystagogue* could then return to his usual pursuits, live his life as before, and yet hope for blessed immortality, in contradistinction to the hopeless and bloodless shadow-existence which was the common lot of the Homeric dead. There was no creed to embrace, no theology to master, no special discipline to accept. Perhaps it was this ease of salvation which made the masses skeptical of its efficacy; and Diogenes the Cynic was reported to have jeered that, according to the Eleusinians, the initiated liar and hypocrite would go into Elysium before the hero Epaminondas. We can only say that the Eleusinian Mystery constituted Greek soteriology at an early stage of its development.

3. *The Purpose of the Lesser Mysteries.* We know that the Demeter-Persephone Mysteries were divided into the Lesser and the Greater,[19] and that the former were open even to strangers and were performed at Athens in honor of Persephone about the 21st of March to coincide with the vernal equinox; but to the Greater, which were performed at Eleusis, only Athenians were eligible and only after becoming initiated into the Lesser Mysteries.

Hippolytus discusses[20] the manner in which the Naasenes had absorbed various elements from the Eleusinian mystery. And from this we learn that the Lesser Mysteries, those of Kore or Persephone, were of an ethical nature, the sole purpose of which was to make the initiate just, noble, happy, and successful in the present life.

4. *The Greater Mysteries.* The Greater Mysteries, however, had a higher objective. Hippolytus says that the hierophant conducting the rite is not a eunuch like the priest of Cybele, but nevertheless a strict celibate "despising all carnal generation." This indicates that with the advent of the Orphic Neo-Dionysus at Eleusis, the cult had absorbed definite celibate characteristics previously unknown. And he says that at the height of

the ceremony, the initiates are shown "an ear of corn in silence reaped," which was the mystic eucharist.

This indicates that those who had achieved the good life in this world through the Lesser Mysteries might look heavenward to the ritual of Demeter. Still summarizing the doctrines of the Naasenes, Hippolytus declares that after initiation into the "inferior mysteries," the neophytes were admitted into the great and heavenly ones . . . . where no unclean person shall enter, nor one that is natural or carnal; but it is reserved for the spiritual only. And those who come hither . . . become all of them bridegrooms, emasculated through the virginal spirit."

Through the Greater Mysteries, the initiates were to live forever in heaven with the good deity, by becoming the bridegroom of the savior-goddess. This was the second spiritual birth, which probably involved a vow of perpetual chastity and a mystery-ritual in which the *mystae* were wedded to the beneficent Isis-Demeter. The Christian Church was centuries later to call itself the Bride of Christ; and to this day the nuns in the Catholic communion wear wedding rings and consider themselves the virginal brides of Jesus.

5. *The Esoteric Ritual.* Fortunately, in the Villa of the Mysteries at Pompeii was found a series of seven frescoes describing the Orphic liturgy of initiation;[21] and these establish the substantial accuracy of Hippolytus. In the first scene, we see the female initiate taking the veil and preparing to become a mystic bride; in the second, a priest reads the ritual; in the third, a priestess celebrates the lustral meal or sacrament at the altar table; in the fourth, the communion is celebrated, in which the kid, one of the symbols of Dionysus,[22] receives milk, the eucharist of Isis, from a virgin satyr; in the fifth, we have the annunciation, in which the death of the initiate to this world is proclaimed; in the sixth, she views the phallus, the symbol of the mystical marriage, and, in the presence of Dionysus and Kore, she suffers flagellation in order to repress or destroy her lower and Titanic elements; in the seventh, the initiate,

now reborn into the second and immortal life, is shown as a dancing Bacchante filled with Dionysiac ecstasy. It is obvious that in this ceremony, we have a synthesis of various ancient cultic elements.

When we realize that this was the rite celebrated by untold thousands of Greeks and Romans over a millennium beginning with the sixth century B.C., we see how closely Christianity resembled the mysteries out of which it grew. In these Pompeian frescoes, the bride is a woman being married to Dionysus; and we know that the mystery celebrated is the Orphic-Eleusinian because of the prominence of Kore and because of the flagellation which had its inception in the Zagreus-Titan myth. There were certainly similar wedding ceremonies in which male initiates became the mystical bridegrooms of Kore or Demeter. By the first century, their ritual had become thoroughly intertwined with the Orphic-Dionysiac.

That the secret and mysterious baskets, containing the Eleusinian sacrament, were well known to the ancient world, we learn from various sources. In *The Golden Ass* of Apuleius, Psyche invokes "the secrets of thy baskets" in her prayer to Demeter. Because early Christian writers converted from paganism sought to discredit the pagan mysteries, we sometimes learn more from them than from the reticent classical authors. "These mysteries are, in short," declares Clemens Alexandrinus contemptuously, "murders and funerals," [23] little realizing that the Passion of Christ was also a murder and a funeral. "Do you wish," demands Arnobius, "that we should reveal the mysteries and those ceremonies which are named by the Greeks Thesmophoria?" [24] He states pursuantly that the "cyceon" is a "wine thickened with spelt," [25] or barley. Thus we know that the sacred drink of the Eleusinians was a combination of the Osirian and the Dionysiac eucharist: which indicates that at Eleusis certain elements of the two cults had met and coalesced. Arnobius reproduces the sacred formula by which the *mystae* became full initiates: "I have fasted, and drunk the draught; I have taken out of the mystic cist, and put into the wicker basket; I have received again, and transferred to the little chest."²⁶ Clement of Alexandria, who lived about a century before Arnobius, describes the same ceremony with almost the same words.²⁷

Quite possibly Clement had himself been an Eleusinian. There is no doubt that he was describing the ritual depicted in the Pompeian frescoes by which the initiate believed himself transformed into the nature of divinity.

6. *The Greater Mysteries.* We know that every autumn the Greater Mysteries were celebrated at Athens and Eleusis; and, as nearly as we can now determine, the following agenda was observed: on the thirteenth of Boedromium (September), the priestesses proceeded from Athens to Eleusis, whence on the fourteenth, they conveyed the *sacra,* or the holy symbols, from the great temple back to Athens; on the fifteenth, the *mystae,* who had previously been, or were for the first time about to be, initiated into the Greater Mysteries, gathered at Athens, while the herald warned that no one defiled or impure, no murderer, traitor, or non-Greek, must approach. On the sixteenth, the *mystae* purified themselves by sacerdotal lustrations, or baptisms, in the sea. On the seventeenth the great soteriological sacrifice took place, in which a holy bull or heifer was ceremonially slain. On the eighteenth there were further but individual purifications, which concluded the preparations for the esoteric rituals at Eleusis.

Early on the morning of the nineteenth, with the statue of Iacchus (Bacchus or Dionysus) at the front, the great procession set forth along the Sacred Way. The *mystagogues,* carrying torches and crowned with myrtle wreaths, made many stops at shrines and altars which commemorated the various incidents in the passion of Demeter. When the journey was completed, the Great Eleusinia began: these were the secret rituals from which all but the initiates of the inner circle were strictly barred. The first night was devoted to the presentation of the sacred drama, in which the events of the Demeter-Persephone Passion were re-enacted. The final ceremony consisted in the celebration of the Great Sacrament: initiates not only repeated the acts once performed by the goddess herself, but they united themselves with her and with Dionysus in chaste and mystical wedlock.

After this rite, the *mystae*, filled with joyous exhilaration, purified by a moral catharsis, born again into eternal blessedness, and transfigured into divinity by these holy ceremonies, returned to Athens along the *Sacra Via*.

The extent to which the cult of Demeter had become an integral element of Athenian life is witnessed by the fact that as soon as the annual Mysteries were concluded, the senate always met in extraordinary session to determine whether any one had been guilty of profanation in connection with the celebration. We learn from Thucydides and from Plutarch that Alcibiades[28] was tried in absentia and condemned to death for such impiety; and we know that Aeschylus was convicted of revealing the secrets of the mystery and acquitted only when it was established that he was not an initiate in the cult.

The influence of the Eleusinia upon Catholic Christianity was great indeed; and to this we shall call further attention in the proper place.

CHAPTER VI

THE ORPHEAN RECONSTRUCTION OF DIONYSUS

A. THE MULTIPLE ORPHEUS

The available material concerning Orpheus bulks perhaps as large as that dealing with Dionysus himself; and again we are confronted with a difficult and composite personality. He and his even more elusive "son" Musaeus are the only names to whom the Greeks attributed sacred, authoritarian literature; to them were accredited the lost poems setting forth the history and ritual not only of Dionysus but of Demeter-Persephone as well. Successive layers of Orphic literature were ascribed to the legendary prophet, each expressing the theology of its own age.

Classical literature knows Orpheus as a Thracian; yet Pausanias relates that in a huge mural by Polygnotus "Orpheus' dress is Greek, no part of his attire being Thracian."[1] This indicates that although the cult of Dionysus was Thracian, its Orphean reform was certainly Greek.

We shall here attempt to reconstruct the Orphean development of the Dionysiac myth, subsequent to its original Thracian-Hellenic form, through two stages of the Eleusinia. Its final phase as an integral portion of Pythagoreanism belongs in a later chapter.

B. THE ORIGINAL ORPHEAN MYTH

The tragic tale of Orpheus was celebrated in song and story by many classical authors. The religious meaning of the legend, however, seems to have escaped them: and it is with this that we are concerned.

We have already seen that, according to Diodorus, Dionysus was said to have given Charops the rule over the Thracians and instructed him in secret rites; that Oeagrus, son of Charops, inherited both the kingdom and the mysteries; and that, finally, Orpheus, son of Oeagrus, learned these from his father, but made so many changes in them that they were thereafter called Orphic. Diodorus continues: "He journeyed to Egypt, where he further increased his knowledge and so became the greatest among the Greeks both for his knowledge of the gods and of their rites."[2] Pausanias declared that "Orpheus... attained to great influence as being thought to have invented the mysteries of the gods, and purification from unholy deeds, and cures for diseases and means of turning away the wrath of the gods. And they say the Thracian women laid plots against his life, because he persuaded their husbands to accompany him on his wanderings;" and "when they had primed themselves with wine, they carried out the atrocious deed. But some say that Orpheus died from being struck by lightning by the god because he taught men in the mysteries things they had not before heard of."[3]

C. THE HISTORICAL ORPHEUS

1. *As Known to Classical Authors.* With Orpheus we leave the realm of pure myth and deal at last with a kernel of historical fact. We are told in the *Argonautica*[4] that the prophet accompanied Jason in his quest for the Golden Fleece; and, as we have noted, Polygnotus placed him at the siege of Troy. Accordingly, Orpheus flourished about 1150. However, the oldest poems attributed to him and to Musaeus were probably composed in the tenth or the ninth century, and may have been written in a Mycenaean script which has not survived.

2. *Successive Orphean Phases.* Diodorus, Pausanias, and other writers of the first century could not distinguish between the original elements of the Orphean myth and theology and those which were engrafted upon

them in subsequent ages. They speak, therefore, as if the sixth-century *Hymns of Orpheus*, which were used in the Eleusinia and which are extant, belonged to the original Thracian prophet.

3. *The Historical Probability.* We conclude that Orpheus went to Thrace and there attempted to reform the cult of Dionysus. It is clear that the infuriated Bacchantes wreaked vengeance upon the innovator, either because he took their husbands from them or because he attempted to introduce doctrines considered subversive or impious. It is further obvious that he wished to transform the mystery from an orgiastic ritual practicing *omophagia,* especially of infants, into a more civilized religion, which would reject the Maenadic worship and seek instead its devotees among celibate men. We can easily see why the Thracian priests and their Maenads would rend this innovator: for he wished to deprive the former of their power and the latter of their beloved instrument of rebellion.

D. CHARACTERISTICS OF ORIGINAL ORPHISM

1. *Celibacy.* The Orpheans, embracing celibacy, rejected the rebellious women who wished to possess husbands while continuing as Bacchantes. To account for this bizarre repudiation of masculine duty, the touching myth of Eurydice was devised, which also incorporated elements of the age-old story of Ishtar and Tammuz in reverse, and which reflects the development of monogamy and private property. According to the tale, Orpheus loved his beautiful wife surpassingly; when she died, therefore, he was distraught and disconsolate, and, to regain her, descended into Hades where he persuaded Persephone to permit her to follow him into the upper world on condition that he would not look back. When their escape was almost accomplished, however, he cast a fleeting glance; and Eurydice, mingling with the bloodless shades, faded forever from his sight. Having loved Eurydice so passionately, Orpheus now forswore womankind forever, which brought upon him the wrath of the Bac-

chantes. Ovid describes in detail the lynching of Orpheus.[5]

So goes the myth, which was rejected by Diodorus and others. Its great age is obvious, since it bears all the earmarks of the ancient Dionysia, and since its eschatology is that of Homer; it includes none of those doctrinal or mythological elements introduced after 1100.

In the *Hippolytus* of Euripides we find the cult of Aphrodite in conflict with that of Orpheus. The Greek goddess of love, reconstructed from the Semitic Ishtar, is furious because the son of Theseus has forsworn the connubial rite; because he is, in short, a confirmed celibate. To avenge herself for this injury, she inspires his stepmother, Phaedra, with an irresistible passion for the young man; when he rebuffs her with scorn and contumely, she hangs herself, but leaves a note addressed to her husband in which she accuses his son of improper advances to her. This drives Theseus to condemn Hippolytus to exile and to call down upon him the wrath of Poseidon, who causes the young man's death in a chariot-accident. Although the Orphean religion is not endorsed by Euripides, the tone of the tragedy makes it plain that the doings of Aphrodite are considered highly reprehensible by the audience. As the Mycenaean period was drawing toward its close, private property and monogamy had won the victory in Greece over communal property and other forms of sex-relationship.

2. *A Prophet Who Arrived too Late.* Orpheus was a prophet with vast pretensions who arrived too late. Although he was credited with every experience and suffering usually prerequisite for apotheosis, he never achieved divinity. He was assigned a goddess-mother, Calliope: but this maternity was rejected;[6] he was torn into bloody remnants by the ferocious Maenads: but this never made him a successor to Osiris, Dionysus, or Attis; he went into the underworld seeking his wife: but this did not make him a savior-god capable of conferring a similar immortality and apotheosis upon his devotees. Orpheus arrived among the Hellenes after they had attained sophistication: he remained therefore only the great poet, musician,

theologian, and prophet, while Dionysus continued to grow as the universal savior-god.

E. TWO INVASIONS BY THE THRACIAN DIONYSUS INTO GREECE

1. *The Thracian God.* We noted that the primitive cult of Dionysus had invaded Greece both from Egypt and from Thrace before the Orphean reformation, which did not invent, but simply adopted, the version according to which the god was born in Thebes of Semele.

2. *The Orphean Dionysus.* There were, therefore, two Dionysiac invasions of Greece from Thrace: first, that which made Semele his mother in order to Hellenize the god but left him otherwise substantially unchanged; and, second, the Orphean, which established a new ritual, penetrated the Eleusinia, became the soteriological center of that mystery by means of a new myth, and was finally absorbed by the Pythagoreans.

F. ORPHEAN INNOVATIONS

1. *Transformation of the Sacrament.* The first Orphean innovation was the transformation of its sacrament. It repudiated the eating of the raw flesh of bovines, human enemies, or infants, and replaced it with a symbolic eucharist. Since wine was the gift and the blood of Dionysus even as the grain was his body, the red juice of the grape and the bread which is baked from flour became the bloodless sacrifice of the new dispensation, which, by means of mystical ceremonies, conferred immortality upon the initiates.

2. *Development of Dogmatic Theology.* In another basic innovation, Orphism based itself upon a dogmatic theology and upon a formal and elaborate set of doctrines, all of which were set forth in the oldest stratum of Orphic poetry and which was well known to Clemens Alexandrinus and other early church fathers; there were, however, no revolutionary ethics; and certainly no concepts of dualism, a last judgment, hell fire,

metempsychosis, or universal immortality. These poems, which were probably a century or so older than the Homeric, were composed by the priests of Eleusis, and were probably transmitted orally from one generation to the next, until they could be committed to classic writing late in the seventh century. Like the scriptures of the Brahmanas, the Zoroastrians, and the Jews, they purported to be divine revelations.

3. *Its Misogyny.* This ancient Orphism was not basically ascetic: its misogyny was of a nature quite different from that which we find among the Buddhists or the Pythagoreans. Clemens Alexandrinus quotes Orpheus as saying "nothing else is more shameless and wretched than woman,"[7] which we may accept simply as a reprimand for Bacchante excesses.

G. ORPHEAN PENETRATION OF THE ELEUSINIA

1. *Ancient Assumption of Direction.* We have seen that, according to the legend, Musaeus, son of Orpheus, inducted Hercules into the Eleusinian Mystery. That the Orphics very early assumed direction at Eleusis is indicated by Pausanias,[8] who implies that its ritual is explained in the Orphic poems; and Arnobius quotes passages of Orphic poetry which describe how Demeter drank the cyceon.[9]

2. *The Phanes-Theology.* The theogony of the original Orphic poems was that of Hesiod and Homer, except that it made certain significant additions and alterations, concerned primarily with the creation. We find that Dionysus becomes here a god similar to the Egyptian Tem or Ra, who, in a series of incarnations, was the creator, the father, and the savior of mankind, very much as in later Sabellianism. At the beginning, there was only Night; and from this, as in the Egyptian cosmogony, sprang the primeval egg, which contained Eros-Phanes, which was simply another name for Dionysus. When the egg burst, it separated into two elements, which became Heaven (Uranos) and Earth (Ge). These

copulated, as in the Hesiodic system, and gave birth to Cronos or Time, and to the other Titans; Cronos became the father of Rhea, Demeter, Mnemosyne, Hades, Poseidon and Zeus, who, by eating his own father, encompassed all creation. Zeus now copulated with Persephone, who gave birth to Zagreus, the incarnation of Phanes, or Dionysus reborn, who was the father-creator in the sixth generation; and to him he gave the sceptre and universal dominion. Father Phanes thus became Father Dionysus, or, as he was better known, Father Liber or Bacchus.

Exactly what existence the Orphic-Dionysus cult had independently of the Eleusinia we can only guess. Nor can we describe in detail the soteriological ritual of Dionysus within the Demeter-cult before 600 B. C. That such rites were well developed is certain; their exact forms we cannot know. There must have been at least a sacrament of bread and wine, which the communicants ate to be transformed into the essence of the god.

3. *The Zagreus-Titan Myth.* The foregoing was apparently the Orphean-Dionysiac theology prevailing within the Eleusinia until the sixth century. But around 500, another far-reaching alteration consisting in the addition of the Zagreus-Titan myth took place. According to this, the reincarnated god, while still a boy known as Zagreus, was killed, cooked, and eaten by the Titans, who, in turn, were thereupon, by the thunderbolts of Zeus, burned to ashes, from which the human race was generated. The whole tale is never told in its entirety by any single extant author; but it is possible to reconstruct it from passages in Firmicus Maternus, Clemens Alexandrinus, the voluminous writings of the Neo-Platonists, and a number of other sources.

We learn from Herodotus[10] of a certain Onomacritus, "an oraclemonger, and the same who set forth the prophecies of Musaeus in their order," and who was "banished from Athens by Hipparchus," because he was caught in the act of corrupting the older writings attributed to Musaeus. Pausanias declares that "Onomacritus borrowed the name of the Titans from Homer when he wrote his poem about the orgies of Dionysus and represented the Titans as contributing to the sufferings of Dionysus."[11]

Together with the Zagreus-Titan element, introduced by Onomacritus late in the sixth or early in the fifth century, additional elements of Egyptian myth and ritual were incorporated with the Greek Dionysus. Plutarch declares that "the tales regarding the Titans and the rites celebrated by night agree with the accounts of the dismemberment of Osiris and his revivification and re-genesis . . . and the Holy Ones offer a secret sacrifice in the shrine of Apollo whenever the devotees of Dionysus awaken the god of the Mystic Basket."[12] Thus the Titans finally took the place of Set and his co-conspirators; and the sacrament of Dionysus was eaten from a mystic basket, exactly as in the Osirian ritual.

Diodorus thus summarizes this sixth-century innovation, according to which "the Sons of Gaia tore to pieces the god, who was the son of Zeus and Demeter and boiled him, but his members were brought together again by Demeter and he experienced a new birth as if for the first time. . . . And with these stories, the teachings agree which are set forth in the Orphic poems and are introduced into their rites, but it is not lawful to recount them in detail to the uninitiated."[13]

Diodorus also recounts the version of those Eleusinians who, having first adopted the Phanes-theology, expanded this by means of the Zagreus-Titan myth and finally incorporated with it the older tale of Dionysus' virgin birth from Semele, his descent into Hades to recover her, and his subsequent apotheosis with her in heaven. In this fully-developed form, Dionysus appears as the creator of the world; reborn from Persephone as Zagreus, he suffered dismemberment and death; resurrected from his heart, he lived as a god in the celestial realms; his body, eaten by the Titans, from whose ashes mankind was created, became the divine spark in humanity; descending from the celestial mansions, he was reborn from the pure virgin Semele, whom he later rescued from the nether realm, and now sits forever at the right hand of God. And so being twice-born, Dionysus was called Dimetor.[14]

And so we know that about 500 B. C., there lived in Athens a clever priest by the name of Onomacritus, a notorious forger of oracles, who either composed or rewrote certain Orphic poems, and in this manner made the Zagreus-Titan myth an integral portion of the Dionysiac theology. It probably was he, who described the Titans in the Orphic hymn addressed to them as the "Fountains and principles from which began, The afflicted, miserable race of man."

The English Platonist, Thomas Taylor, has composed an inimitable summary of the Zagreus-Titan myth,[15] which runs briefly as follows: Phanes-Eros-Dionysus was reborn from Zeus and Persephone as Zagreus, upon whom, even as a boy, his father conferred the might and the glory of his kingdom. At this the wicked and materialistic Titans became jealous, and they killed, cooked, and ate the boy in a grisly but conventional, ancient Egyptian-type sacrament. Athena, however (or Demeter or Persephone), retrieved the heart, the seat of life, as in the Osirian system, and returned it to Zeus, who therefrom effected the regenesis of the God into his second birth. Zeus, blasting the Titans with his thunderbolts, reduced them to ashes, from which the human race was generated. At a much later date, this savior-Christ left the glory of his heavenly home, and deigned to be reborn of the virgin Semele, whom he raised from Hades as a token of his power. Humanity, therefore, generated from Titanic fragments, is prone to evil. However, since elements of Dionysus were also present in the Titanic ashes, there is a divine spark in all mankind, which makes it possible for us to escape our lower and achieve our higher destiny. In order to do this, we must mortify the body to set free the soul. There is, therefore, in this reformed Eleusinian Orphism a definite dualism, an enmity between the spiritual and the material, which could easily produce a completely celibate movement.

H. CONCLUSION

1. *Dionysus a Soter Only.* When Onomacritus in-

vented the Zagreus-Dionysus-Titan myth and combined this with the virgin birth from Semele, Orphism became a systematic soteriology designed to effect the salvation of a race otherwise irretrievably lost in sin and requiring regeneration because their souls are debased and imprisoned in sinful bodies. Throughout all those centuries, however, Dionysus remained a *soter only*. His worship embraced no distinctive economic, ethical, or eschatological doctrine; all such innovations were to be introduced by later Pythagoreans.

2. *The Original Eleusinia without a Soter.* Although the original Eleusinian ritual was both stately and exhilarating, it nevertheless was wanting in the most dynamic single element constituting the ancient mystery: the *soter*. For at its center was Demeter-Persephone, not Osiris-Dionysus, the god whose body and blood we must eat and drink in order to assume the incorruption of divinity.

3. *Dionysus at the Center of the Eleusinia.* That Dionysus was an inseparable element in the Demeter-Persephone cult long before the first century B. C. is confirmed by overwhelming evidence. Strabo sums up this development succinctly: "They call also Bacchus, Dionysus; and he is the chief Daemon of the mysteries of Ceres."[16] That Demeter (Latin, Ceres), Persephone (Proserpina), and Dionysus (Bacchus) were not only ubiquitous but also inseparably intertwined, we discover over and over. Pausanias declares, in a statement that could apply to almost any Greek city,[17] that in the temple of Eleusinian Demeter at Thelpusa were large statues of Demeter, Proserpina, and Dionysus. And so it was everywhere. The same author states: "and inside the grove are statues of Demeter, Prosymne, and Dionysus . . . but in another temple there is a wooden one of Dionysus the Savior."[18] This was a common situation: by the first century, Dionysus had become central in the Demeter-Persephone worship, but he had also a separate cult of his own in every community. And he was called *the Savior*.

4. *Only One Soter.* And so we see that although Osiris could not penetrate Greece under his own name, he did so repeatedly in the guise of Dionysus. History proves

over and over that nothing is easier for mankind than to copy and imitate; but, by the same token, nothing is more difficult than to invent or originate. Certain concepts, like that of a god, or the virgin birth, or the belief that theft and murder are wrong, were almost universal and are therefore indigenous to many people. But civilization itself, as well as various primitive specialized concepts, like that of a savior-god and his eucharist, of hell and heaven, of metempsychosis and Nirvana, of the Messiah and his Parousia—these originated only once and were either adopted by others or never found among them at all.

There has never been more than one Osiris; never more than one basic soteriological concept, however much and often translated and transfigured. The Dionysus who, in the end, became the chief demon in the Ceres-Proserpina ritual was substantially the same god to whom Unas and Pepi, Ani and Nebseni, and the wild mountaineers of Thrace and Phrygia had offered sacrifice in bygone ages and by whom they hoped for victory over death and the grave. In the end, the nurturing Demeter and her dread daughter Persephone proved insufficient: in order to survive, their cult was forced to incorporate their greatest competitor. By the first century, then, the Demeter- and the independent Dionysus-cult were both ubiquitous; and we suppose that the difference consisted chiefly in emphasis and appeal: the Eleusinian remained to the end more dignified, more suitable to the refined and educated; but in both the same deity was predominant. Possessing an aspect to suit every communicant, Dionysus became the universal savior-god of the ancient world. And there has never been another like unto him: the first to whom his attributes were accredited, we call Osiris; with the death of paganism, his central characteristics were assumed by Jesus Christ.

CHAPTER VII

THE ZOROASTRIANS

A. EXTERNAL HISTORY

1. *An Instrument of National Policy.* Zoroastrianism, named after the Persian prophet known also as Zaratust, Zathraustes, Zarathustra, etc., was for centuries embraced by those ancient Caucasians known as Aryans or Iranians; and it became for them an instrument of national policy in their bitter conflicts against surrounding nomadic tribes and Semitic nations, represented primarily by the "Turanians," Babylonians, Assyrians, Phoenicians, and Arabians. With the emergence of the first Persian Empire under Cyrus and its further expansion under Darius the Great Hystaspes, 521-486, the worship of Ahuramazda dominated twenty-three nations. These Iranians did more than drive the Semitic races into permanent eclipse: themselves descended from the older Sumerians, they were the prehistoric conquerors of Egypt and India as well as the progenitors of the Greeks, the Romans, and the Teutons: in short, they have ruled most of the civilized world for two and a half millenniums.

2. *Empire Succeeding Empire.* In that ancient world, one empire succeeded another, and throughout the domains of each, religious doctrines and ceremonials were carried from one country to another along the caravan routes. The Assyrian Empire with its capital at Nineveh, dominated Asia Minor from the twelfth century to about 612. After a brief resurgence of the Egyptian power, Nebuchadnezzar overwhelmed it in 605 and extended the Babylonian Empire from the African desert to the Persian

Gulf and the Caspian Sea. These Chaldeans, however, did not remain long in control; for in 538, Cyrus captured Babylon; and thirty years later Darius ruled an empire which stood astride the world from Libya and Greece to the center of India, a territory comprising two million square miles and including dozens of great and populous cities, of which Babylon was the most fabulous. This vast domain continued substantially intact until it toppled overnight before the fierce onslaught of the Macedonians around 330. About 250, Arsaces established the loose confederation known as the Parthian Empire, which continued for four hundred and seventy-five years and in which a modified form of Zoroastrianism was the prevailing religion.

3. *Development of Zoroastrian Mazdeism.* The history of Mazdeism—the worship of the sun and of fire out of which Zoroastrianism grew—spans some four thousand years. It began among the prehistoric Iranians, occupying an upland area between the Caspian Sea and the Persian Gulf. Although we cannot be sure just when Zoroaster lived, we need not doubt his historicity. The *Gathas*, which are psalm-like utterances, are full of personal references and were probably composed by the prophet himself. E. W. West, who translated the Pahlavi Texts, published in Max Muller's *Sacred Books of the East,* places the birth of Zoroaster in 660 and his death in 583. His teachings achieved a firm foundation with the conversion of King Vishtasp, which occurred when the prophet was forty-two. Zoroaster appeared as his people were emerging from a nomadic state into a settled agricultural economy; he exerted his utmost influence to accelerate this process and place upon it the stamp of divine approval.

4. *Zoroastrianism Triumphant.* After the conversion of Kai-Vishtasp, the Iranians became bolder and refused tribute to the northern "Turanians." A series of wars ensued in which the Persians were victorious, and during which the new faith was consolidated. With the advent of Cyrus and the fall of Babylon, it entered upon the stage of authentic history and became a preponderant world-force. Under the Achaemenides, the *Avesta* became

the world's foremost sacred book. The great fire-temples in time erected to the glory of Ahuramazda appeared everywhere and in them burned perpetually his sacred flame. A vast literature proliferated, and tradition records that Alexander the Great seized and destroyed two copies of the complete scriptures each written on twelve thousand cowhides.

The aggressive expansion of the Persian Empire, however, came to a sudden halt with three great defeats inflicted by the Greeks: Marathon, 490; Plataea, 479; and the decisive naval engagement at Salamis, 480. Had the Persians been victorious, Zoroastrianism would have conquered Europe, and it might conceivably have become the religion of mankind.

5. *Fall of Persia.* However, for better or for worse, this was not to be: and in 330, Alexander crushed the Persian power, and attempted to establish a new and unified world, in which race, creed, and nation were to be submerged and superseded by a universal brotherhood in which values would be determined, not by any supernatural revelation, but by the all-conquering force of Greek enlightenment. Had he lived the full span of human life, he might have succeeded in this grandiose objective; but he died at the age of thirty-three and his newly-born empire was split into four divisions by his generals who were soon at war with each other.

6. *Zoroastrian Scriptures.* The oldest portions of the Zoroastrian scriptures, known as the *Avesta,* were written in an ancient Persian dialect. Among them are the *Gathas* (psalms), *Vendidad* (laws), and the *Yasts* (liturgies). However, during the millennium preceding the Moslem conquest, another literature grew up, now known as the Pahlavi Texts, or commentaries on and elaborations of the *Avesta,* written in the Parthian dialect during the Arsacid and Sassanian dynasties. European scholars have mistakenly called the whole the *Zend-Avesta;* actually, the correct name is *Avesta* and *Zend,* which means revelation and commentary.

7. *The Zoroastrian Renaissance.* In 226 A. D., Zoroastrianism began its great renaissance. In that year, Ar-

dashir overthrew the Parthian Empire; this was the more remarkable, since this achievement forever eluded Roman arms. Ardashir established the Sassanian dynasty, which inaugurated the second Parthian Empire with its capital at Persepolis; and from 226 until 642 this included most of the countries over which Darius had once held sway. As soon as Ardashir came to power, he commanded the priests to compile and reconstitute the sacred scriptures. Although this was not entirely possible, the new documents were no doubt substantially the same as those used during the first Persian Empire.

8. *Conquest by Islam.* What no other conqueror had been able to do in twelve centuries was accomplished by the Moslems in ten years. Islam toppled the Sassanian Empire and replaced Zoroaster; the *Koran* became the sacred scripture in all the lands over which Darius had ruled, and remains so to this day.

9. *Escape to India.* A few of the Parsees, however, who would not renounce their ancient faith fled to India, where they settled in and around Bombay. About 100,000 of them still live in that land where, since the Buddhist revolution, every religion has been tolerated. They still revere the doctrines and practice the ceremonials of Zoroaster; they are monotheists; they are distinguished from the Hindus who surround them by their thrift, industry, prosperity, and complete freedom from caste.

10. *Anquetil-Duperron.* The manner in which the occident came into possession of the Zoroastrian literature is a romance in itself; for, having suffered persecution from European imperialists in India, the Parsees were suspicious of foreigners; and they had never forgotten the catastrophes visited upon them by Alexander and the Moslems. In 1755, a young French scholar, Anquetil-Duperron, arrived in Bombay, and, in due course, won the confidence of the Parsees. They gave him not only copies of their books but also the key by which to translate them; and in 1771, he published these to an incredulous world. Critics called the whole a monumental forgery; and it was not until the *Avesta,* thus translated, served to decipher

the inscriptions at Behistun that all doubt concerning the antiquity and genuineness of the documents ceased.

B. THE LIFE AND MYTH OF ZOROASTER

1. *Pre-Existence.* As with other great personalities, tradition recorded certain historical facts concerning Zoroaster; but around these there soon grew up a periphery of myth, the purpose of which was to establish his authority and divinity. We are told that the spiritual body of Zaratust was created by Ahuramazda some six thousand years before his earthly manifestation.[1] During this period of celestial pre-existence, he dwelt with the creator and the seven archangels. Fifteen years before his birth, this supreme glory, that is, the spiritual body of the prophet, entered the wife of Frahimrvana-zois, and by this miraculous conception, she gave virgin-birth to Dukdaub, the destined mother of Zaratust.[2]

2. *The Virgin-Birth.* Thus filled with supernatural glory, Dukdaub became so radiant that she aroused the hatred of the devas, who brought winter, pestilence, and marauders upon the district; and they caused the neighbors to accuse the divine maiden of witchcraft, so that she was banished.[3] Her father sent her to the home of Padiragtaraspo, father of Purushaspo, to whom she became betrothed.[4] At this juncture, Ahuramazda sent the archangels Vohu Manu and Ashavahisto into the world; they gave the sacred hom-juice to Purushaspo and caused two virgin cows to conceive. Dukdaub drew milk from these and gave it to her betrothed, who mixed it with the hom-juice. The nature of Zaratust's spiritual body was miraculously present in this divine mixture; and as Dukdaub drank of it, she conceived Zaratust, who was the fleshly incarnation of his own pre-existing spirit.[5] The immaculate conception of Mary became in due course the Catholic equivalent of the miraculous origin of Dukdaub.

3. *The Revelation of Zoroaster.* At the age of twenty, the young prophet became a wanderer, seeking "Who is the most desirous of righteousness and the nourishing of the poor;"[6] and is said to have journeyed as far as India

and China. And, like Jesus, at the age of thirty, he began his active ministry with a sacred baptism and "exaltation" in the waters of the Daitih.[7] Thus ordained for his great work, Vohu Mano led him into the presence of Ahuramazda and the archangels.[8] There were altogether seven such conferences and apocalyptic visions[9] during ten years,[10] in which Ahuramazda revealed the mysteries of time and eternity: the origin of the world, the dual nature of the cosmos, the primeval history of the race, the role of Angra Mainyu, the laws of the good religion, the future millennial saviors, the secrets of hell and heaven, the final resurrection and judgement, the ultimate salvation of mankind, and the cataclysmic renovation of the universe.[11]

All this, which Zaratust wrote down as he emerged from his successive trances, was therefore the unalterable word of God, which must stand for ever and ever.

4. *The Great Temptation.* Just as Zoroaster was approaching the period of his great ministry, he, like Buddha and Jesus, was subjected to his Great Temptation;[12] Angra Mainyu (Angry Spirit, or Aharman, or Ahriman, as he is known in the later documents) "the Maker of the Evil World," assailed the prophet with fearful terrors and tempted him with magnificent promises; he offered to make him "the ruler of the nations" if he would but "renounce the good religion." The holy man rejected the offer with scorn. "By whose word wilt thou strike, by whose word wilt thou repel . . . my creatures, who am Angra Mainyu?" Zaratust replied: "The sacred mortar, the sacred cup, the Haoma, the Word taught by Mazda, these are my weapons."

5. *Struggle for Converts.* Zaratust tried desperately to win converts, but he was rebuffed wherever he went; for all were wicked unbelievers and heretics, the ungodly, ruffianly, two-legged *ashemaogha*. But at last, in his fortieth year, he converted a relative and then Frashaostra, his future father-in-law; and then, two years later, King Vishtasp accepted the good religion and Zaratust became the first Zarathrostema, or high priest, of the faith. According to tradition, the prophet was slain at his own altar by the Turanians in his seventy-seventh year.[13]

C. NATURE OF ZOROASTRIANISM

1. *A Primitive Faith.* Zoroastrianism was a lusty, life-embracing cult, which sought and promised every physical and material advantage in this life. Although it was based upon a concept of cosmic metaphysical dualism, it taught also the freedom of the will: it was too primitive an ideology to draw ethical conclusions from speculative doctrines. That it *was* primitive is obvious: for it taught brother-sister marriage; it saw in every blessing of nature the dynamics of the Good Spirit, and in every suffering or calamity, in every weed or pest, in every natural disturbance, the direct intervention of Angra Mainyu.

2. *Water, Fire, and Holy Wind.* Since life and vegetation are impossible without water, this became sacred to a vigorous people living on upland plains and was regarded as the holy gift of Ahuramazda; and it was given divine personification in the goddess Ardvi Sura Anahita.[14] Water had the power to purify whatever it touched, and could cleanse the believer from a multitude of deva-impurities: it was therefore used as the sacrament of baptism. But even more sacred was living fire: for by its agency a higher culture became possible: food could be cooked, houses warmed, metals forged into tools and weapons. Fire was said to be the Son of Ahuramazda,[15] the supreme gift of the Creator. Before the sacred fire, the devas fled cowering. A woman about to give birth kept it always aflame in her chamber, as did the priests within their temples. And, since the gentle breeze was a welcome relief from the fierce summer heat of the upland plains, this came to be known as the Pure Wind, or the Holy Spirit of Ahuramazda. When John the Baptist declared[16] that he could baptize with water but that after him would come one who would baptize with fire and with the Holy Ghost, he was uttering words which came directly from the heart of Zoroastrianism.

3. *Other Holy Things.* In addition to water, fire, and pure wind, many other things were holy to Zoroaster: the earth, because food grew from it; the grain, because it was the source of strength; the horse, because of its

value in war; the ox and the cow, indispensable for labor and nourishment; the sheep, because it provided meat and clothing; the dog, because sheepherding was impossible without it.[17] Thus, all things were sacred in proportion as they conferred life, comfort, and security.

4. *Angra Mainyu.* Zoroaster regarded the nomadic tribes to the north as the especial enemies of Ahuramazda; everything from that direction was of Angra Mainyu, and to be ruthlessly destroyed. As a settled agricultural life only was sacred, it became the duty of those of the good religion to stamp out the roving and plundering nomads —creatures of sin and darkness. The cold north wind was a creation of the Evil One; in Zoroastrian mythology, the near-destruction of the human race had once occurred through the cold of Angra Mainyu, who killed all the crops with frost for seven years, and only a remnant had been saved by Yima, who had thus become, like the Babylonian Noah, a second progenitor of the race.[18] To the upland Iranians, cold was a destroyer; to the people living in the valley of the Tigris-Euphrates, it was the flood.

5. *Good and Evil Creation.* The Zoroastrians conceived of the world as a vast battleground on which the forces of good wage a fierce and constant struggle against the powers of darkness. Whenever the beneficent creator brought forth a good thing, Angra Mainyu counter-created an evil one. When Ahuramazda created the good and pleasant land, Iran, "thereupon Angra Mainyu, who is all death, counter created by his witchcraft the serpent in the river, and winter."[19] Ahuramazda created the plain, and the good land of Baktria in which to grow the golden grain; but Angra Mainyu created drought, frost, mice, locusts, ants, and other *khafstras* to destroy it; and among the human kind he sent sin, unbelief, grief, pride, unnatural intercourse, witchcraft, abnormal issues in women, etc. . . . Ahuramazda gave flocks and herds, but Angra Mainyu sent nomadic robbers to kill and plunder. Ahuramazda created the virtuous wife, Angra Mainyu the vile and wicked courtesan; to frustrate man's sexual virility and women's fecundity, Angra Mainyu created impo-

tence and frigidity; to offset the good dog, he made the wolf; to harrass the healthy, handsome man and the well-shaped, industrious woman, he devised 99,999 diseases. To counteract the work of the Mazdean priests, he filled the world with witches and sorcerers. To mislead and destroy humanity, he sowed abroad various false religions, which were later identified as Judaism, Christianity, Manichaeism, and Muhammedanism. To attack the pure worship of the invisible and spiritual Ahuramazda, he inspired men to become heretics and unbelievers and caused them to carve idol-statues and thereby to worship devas in their devil-temples.

Ahuramazda gave his people 10,000 plants, his sacred water, fire, and haoma-juice; he gave also his irresistible Word, the Ahuna-Vairya, the holy formula, by which to exorcise the foul fiend: "I confess myself the worshiper of Mazda, a follower of Zarathustra, one who hates the Daevas, and obeys the laws of Ahura."[20] This served exactly the same purpose as the Sign of the Cross among the Catholics.

The Zoroastrian world was literally alive with good and evil spirits. Whenever anything unpleasant happened to a Mazda-worshiper, this was the work of Aharman; and whenever anyone opposed the good religion, or accepted any other, this was conclusive proof that he was possessed by a deva. A thousand years later, the Roman popes were to proclaim a parallel doctrine.

D. LAWS AND CEREMONIALS

1. *Zoroaster the Universal Lawgiver*. Like the priests of Judaism, Brahmanism, and the Catholic Church, the Zoroastrian hieratics claimed the prerogative of universal legislation. The laws dictated by Ahuramazda to Zaratust and written down by him in the *Vendidad* cover not only all religious duties, but all civil relationships and ethical values as well. Zoroastrianism was thus a quasi-form of priest-state.

2. *Exorcising the Devas*. Since every physical ill was considered the result of direct interference by Angra

Mainyu or his princes of darkness, every case of human illness, including insanity, heresy, or any other aberration, indicated possession by a fiend. The problem was to separate the deva from the victim upon whom it had seized; and this could be accomplished only by superior spiritual power, by spells and exorcisms. This belief and practice are reflected in the Gospel Jesus and were absorbed by the Catholic Church, where vestiges of them still continue, even in the United States.

3. *The Hom-Eucharist.* The hom-tree and the haoma-juice had been regarded as divine many centuries before Zoroaster reorganized and reformed the Mazdean faith. "Every one who eats of it," declared the prophet, "becomes immortal."[21] The Haoma was an intoxicating drink, the predecessor of wine, which imparted a sense of exhilaration, mistaken by millions of primitive people for a divine afflatus. The Zoroastrians believed that it contained a supernatural essence which conferred immortality. At their sacrifices, they ate the sacred mortar, and drank the holy elixir, which were supposed to transform body and soul into eternal essences, suitable for the blessed life in the regions of celestial light.

In Zoroastrianism, there is no *soter;* that is, there is no god-man who dies for mankind and whose body and blood must be consumed in a holy sacrament. Yet we find in it another eucharist possessing a certain affinity to Osiris-Dionysus, yet entirely independent in origin. The same yearning for immortality in Egypt and in Persia produced in both a *modus vivendi* for achieving it: a ritual in which a divine food and drink were to confer eternal life. This was natural since primitive people in many lands believed that we become what we eat. We cannot study the Christian Gospel objectively without realizing that in it the religions of Iran and the Nile met and coalesced.

E. THEOLOGY

1. *A Monotheistic Nature-Worship.* Herodotus declared that the Persians had no images or altars, con-

sidered the gods to be supernal spirits, and worshiped the moon, sun, earth, fire, water, and wind.[22] We read that Ahuramazda is "all-ruling, all-knowing, and almighty ... a spirit even among spirits; and from his self-existence, single in unity, was the creation of the faithful."[23] At least insofar as the good world was concerned, the Zoroastrians were monotheists.

2. *A Cosmic Dualism.* However, their theology was inseparable from their dualist cosmology, in which we have, on the one hand, the entirely Good Creator, who dwells in the Endless Light; and, on the other, the Evil Creator, Angra Mainyu, who rose from the primeval darkness. It is true that the sacred literature emphasizes the ultimate superiority of Ahuramazda: for he alone has omniscience, prescience, and mercy.[24] Angra Mainyu did not even know that his opposite existed.[25] Ahuramazda, however, is neither omnipotent nor omnipresent; nor is he the creator of the entire universe since the vast realm of Aharman is not the production of the Good Spirit. These two are primordial and uncreated powers which stand opposed throughout what is known in Zoroastrian chronology as Time. Thus we have a gigantic dualism which governs every phase of nature and affects every thought, word, and deed of every human being.

3. *The Zoroastrian Chronology.* In the Zoroastrian system, Time consists of twelve thousand years, divided into four tri-millenniums. In the first of these, all creation lay in quiescence; during the second and third, Ormazd and Ahriman reigned successively; but during the fourth, the two contend for mastery, and at its conclusion in the year 2401, A. D., the God of Light is at last to be victorious.

4. *The Hierarchy.* Ahuramazda had created a whole hierarchy of assistants: first among these, whom he had created from his own splendor,[26] were the seven archangels, the Amesha-Spentas, and the Spirit of Wisdom, his active, creative agency in the universe: a concept startlingly similar to the logos of Zeno the Stoic, Philo Judaeus, and the Fourth Gospel. In the *Gathas,* the Holiest Spirit appears as the creator of the Ox, the

Waters, and all creatures.²⁷ Ahuramazda is called "the holy Father of this Spirit." ²⁸

5. *The Older Pantheon.* We find, beyond these, a whole pantheon of other divinities, probably inherited from a much older Mazdeism or Magianism, all "made by Ahuramazda": Mithra, symbolizing the sun, the god of flocks, herds, war, and contracts, and one of the judges who meet the dead at the Kinvad Bridge; Sraosha, the Incarnate Word, and the protector of the poor;²⁹ Ardvi Sura Anahita, the goddess of waters, who makes the seed of all males pure and enables females to bring forth in safety; and millions of good guardian angels. Angra Mainyu, however, also had his active agent, the opposite of the Spirit of Wisdom, who was a wicked fiend called Aeshm; he had also his seven archfiends; and he had millions of devas to oppose the guardian spirits at every turn. Finally, there was the great demon Azi-Dahak, the old Babylonian deity, overthrown by Fredun according to Zoroastrian myth when Persian arms conquered the Chaldeans. We find reflections of these supernatural beings in Jewish literature, beginning with Daniel.

6. *Zoroastrian Ditheism.* Zoroastrianism postulates a definite ditheism during twelve millenniums of Time, while the two great spirits stand opposed to each other; for it cannot be denied that Aharman was as unoriginate as Ahuramazda; he was, as it were, the evil and obverse twin of the God of Light.³⁰ And it is quite possible that, according to the Zoroastrian system, *with prescience,* the wicked spirit might ultimately have seized the upper regions, annihilated the Celestial Light, and reduced the universe to chaotic and Stygian darkness. Nevertheless, at the renovation of the world, Aharman and all his irredeemable creatures are to be annihilated, his realm of darkness is to be recovered for the universe of light, and God is to reign alone in the cosmos. Then "all things shall be subdued into him . . . that God may be all in all."³¹

7. *Explains the Origin of Evil.* This dualism has been impugned because it limits the omnipotence and omnipresence of the creator-god; but it furnishes a logical explanation for the existence of evil. A Zoroastrian author

of the ninth century castigates his Christian and Mohammedan opponents because they postulate a single supreme being.[32] He declares that they cannot escape the horns of an obvious dilemma: either their deity is impotent because He permits evil to exist; or else He is unjust and wicked because He punishes His own creatures for the wickedness which He Himself brings upon them. According to the Zoroastrian, it is idle to say that man has free will and is thus morally responsible; for God made him also susceptible to temptation and sent the devil to seduce and destroy him. Curiously enough, the Zoroastrian author quotes passages from the Gospels to prove that Jesus Himself embraced and taught the Zoroastrian doctrine of duality: for He told the Jews that they did the works of their father, the devil;[33] and, since He declared that every tree not sown by the Father must be cast into the fire, there must be another sower or creator.[34] The fact is, of course, that Essenism, which was the principal source of the Gospel, drew heavily upon Persian ideology.

8. *Zoroastrian Ahriman is Christian Devil.* The truth is also that Christianity adopted the Persian Aharman, who has no counterpart in authentic Jewish or any other primitive theology, and called him the devil. But it failed to grant him an independent or eternal origin, or to endow him with natural powers sufficient to wreak the devastation attributed to him. The Zoroastrians demanded: If your devil is only a creature fallen from grace, why does your supreme being permit him to persecute and murder the apostles of your Messiah? If your God is omniscient and prescient, He foreknew all this: why would He create such an evil race and so miserable a world? If the Christian God could by fiat create whatever He wished, then He must have ordained all the sin and misery which exist: He is therefore the author of evil. If a prescient and omnipotent God created Satan, He knew what he would do, and is therefore to blame for every wicked act he perpetrates. The Jewish-Christian God, therefore, must be either wicked or impotent.

9. *Ahuramazda Not Supreme during Time.* The Zo-

roastrians admitted candidly that the God of Light is neither omnipresent nor omnipotent and that evil exists because Ahuramazda can neither destroy the Evil One nor prevent his activity.[35] The Good Principle cannot destroy Aharman until the appointed ages have run their course. Nor is it possible for Ahuramazda to transform the nature of Aharman or to change darkness into light.[36] Actually, there can be no Supreme God until the renovation of the universe has occurred. Thus, evil is inextricably intermingled in the world and in the human soul, and can be extirpated only by degrees until the final consummation.[37]

10. *The Zoroastrian Chronology.* In order to understand history, past and present, as depicted in the Zoroastrian literature, it may be useful to present an outline of its chronology:

ZOROASTRIAN YEAR	EVENT	CHRISTIAN YEAR
1	Time began	9660 B.C.
3000	9000-Year Pact with Aharman	6660
3000-6000	Rule in universe by Ahuramazda	6660-3660
6000-9000	Rule in world by Aharman	3660-660
6300	Human race saved by Yima	3300
9000-12,027	Tri-millennium of contention	660 B.C. to 2398 A.D.
8970	Birth of Zoroaster	660 B. C.
9970	Birth of Hushedar	341 A. D.
10,001	Hushedar's ministry begins	371
10,971	Birth of Aushedar-Mah	1341
11,001	Aushedar-Mah's ministry begins	1371
11,941	Soshans born	2341
11,971	'Soshans' ministry begins	2371
11,998	Armageddon and Last Judgment	2398
12,000	New Heavens and New Earth Kingdom of Righteousness begins	2400

During the first tri-millennium of Time, the primary ideas of all good creations remained motionless and insensible. At its close, in 6660 B.C., Ahuramazda concluded his treaty with Aharman, as we learn from various documents.[38] He did so because the powerful Adversary, having wandered near the upper bounds of the dark domain and seen a gleam of light, conceived a violent desire to seize the celestial realm and so control the entire universe. In order to accomplish this end, he created a vast army of fiends, devas, wizards—all creatures of darkness, eternally evil—and prepared to attack, first, the sublunary world, and ultimately the regions of light.

Ahuramazda, unprepared to withstand such an onset, thereupon concluded the celebrated nine-thousand-year pact, under which the Good Principle would rule the world for three thousand years and the Evil One during the following tri-millennium; but during the last, the two antagonists would strive for mastery.

Through his prescience, however, Ahuramazda outwitted his adversary. He created the Primeval Ox, who represents the animal creation, and the Primeval Man, the progenitor of the human race, who remained peaceful and undisturbed during the first tri-millennium.

11. *Zaratust Created.* However, he took further steps to insure his own ultimate victory: first, he caused the archangels to fashion the spiritual body of Zaratust, the pre-existing savior, who then dwelt for six thousand years in the Supreme Heaven with the archangels; and, second, he built an impregnable rampart about the heavenly mansions, so that Aharman could never seize this ultimate bastion.

12. *The Tri-Millennium of Aharman.* In the year 6000 of Time, the tri-millennium of Aharman began. At the head of millions of fiends, he rushed into the material world, mixed smoke with fire, corrupted the waters, sowed thorns in the earth, covered the trees with bark, destroyed the vegetation, killed the Primeval Ox and distressed Gayomard, and created billions of noxious creatures such as ants, lice, locusts, and destructive beasts. He also dug a great hole in the earth and established there the infernal regions of hell and purgatory. He debased all mankind by filling them with evil thoughts and wicked desires; he made them vicious and corrupt. He filled the world with

misery; nature itself served his evil purpose, and generated storms, drouth, earthquakes, and devastating cold. The human race seemed destined only for suffering, extinction, and the everlasting fires of hell. At one time, Aharman sent continuous and murderous frost for seven years and almost succeeded in extirpating mankind. And had it not been that by means of the good Yima Aharumazda saved a remnant in a well-stocked cave, all would have died about the Zoroastrian year 6300, which corresponds to 3300 B. C.

13. *Zaratust Revealed in the Flesh.* The complete dominion of Aharman ended with his tri-millennium; for Ahuramazda had not merely fortified his mansions, but had, as we have noted, prepared the instrument by which the Enemy would ultimately be destroyed. Aharman could not know that a series of Christs would walk the earth, who would appear to be men among men but who would actually be supernatural incarnations. These he could not defeat; for they would win over the human race to the good religion and, as a consequence, reduce the fiend to impotence; and thus it would eventually be possible to crush and destroy the cosmic monster himself.

And so (in the Zoroastrian year 8970, which was 660 B. C. by our reckoning), Ahuramazda sent the great prophet, Zaratust, into the world. The tenth Zoroastrian millennium and its final tri-millennium began with the ministry of the great prophet, when he was thirty years old, in 630 B.C.

F. THE VISIONS OF ZARATUST

1. *The Three Millenniums.* One of the prophet's most celebrated visions is related in the first chapter of the *Bahman Yast*. Zoroaster was shown all that would happen during his millennium, that is, the period before the coming of the first Messiah, Hushedar, due A. D. 371. Zaratust saw a great tree with four branches, which symbolized the four ages of his millennium: that of gold, under King Vishtasp; those of silver, steel, and mixed iron under

successively degenerating regimes. In another vision[39] the tree had seven branches, which symbolized "the seven periods which will come." Again, the golden age, like that of Nebuchadnezzar in Daniel, was that of Vishtasp, when "Aharman and the demons rush back to darkness." Then follow the ages of silver, brass, copper, tin, steel, and iron, in which at last the world is again dominated by the fiends. The end of the tenth millennium was to be heralded by the coming of "myriads of demons with disheveled hair, the race of Wrath,"[40] who were later identified as the Christians. And by what token will men know that the end of the millennium is nigh and the appearance of Hushedar at hand? Ahuramazda declares that in the last days "all men will become deceivers" and affection will depart from the world; the father will hate the son, the son the father; brother will hate brother; "the son-in-law will become a beggar from his father-in-law, and the mother will be estranged from the daughter."[41] All the sacred ceremonials will be treated with contempt; wrath and avarice will take over; and apostasy will be all but universal.[42] In those terrible days the sun and the moon will show signs; there will be frightful storms;[43] there will be wars and rumors of wars, and earthquakes; there will be great battles, and so many soldiers will be slain that a thousand women will seek to kiss one man.[44] But Mitro will be victorious and will at last destroy the idol-temples and restore the good religion of Ahuramazda.[45] And then Hushedar will come.[46]

It is evident that the apocalyptic tribulations of Daniel and those described in the New Testament[47] are appropriated from the literature of the Zoroastrians, who, curiously enough, were persuaded that the conflicts and defeats which beset *them* about 350 as a result of Christian aggressions and Manichaean apostasy were the very ones which would precede the coming of their first Messiah, Hushedar, due in 371.

At the close of each of the last three millenniums of Time, a great savior was to appear, who would reconstitute the good religion; each of these was to be born through a virgin-birth from a maiden directly descended from Zaratust himself, and therefore of the divine spiritual body first produced by the archangels in the year 3000 of Time.

2. *Hushedar.* Thus, in the Zoroastrian year 9970, the virgin Shemig-abu, who, although of the ripe age of fifteen, has never known a man, "walks up to the holy water," and becomes pregnant with Hushedar, the first reincarnation of the Zoroastrian Messiah. At the age of thirty, in the year 10,001 of Time—which falls in A. D. 371 — the sun was to stand still for ten days and Hushedar was to ascend into the eternal light and confer with the archangels. He was then to return to the earth, re-establish the good religion, and one third of the human race was to be converted.[48]

3. *Aushedar-Mah.* As in the previous formula, in the year 10,971, which was A. D. 1341, the fifteen-year-old maiden Shapirabu, who "has not before associated with men; nor yet afterwards, when she becomes pregnant . . . walks up to the water"[49] and, through contact with this holy element, conceives Aushedar-Mah, upon whose arrival at the age of thirty, the sun was to stand still for twenty days; he too was to have conferences with the archangels, return to the earth, and so thoroughly establish the good religion that two thirds of the human race would become Mazda-worshipers.

4. *The Great Soshans.* Finally, in the year 11,001 of Time, which fell in A. D. 1371, the twelfth and final millennium was to begin. During this period, such great advances were to be made in medical science that no one would die of sickness or disease; and all wars would cease. During the progress of the millennium, all men and women were to become Mazda-worshipers. In the year 11,941 — A.D. 2341—the great Soshans (Saoshyant) would be born of the virgin Gobak-abu; she too would conceive by contact with the holy water and give birth to the great benefactor of mankind. At the age of thirty, he too is to have conferences with the archangels, and the sun is to stand still for thirty days. After his birth, there are to be "seventeen years of vegetable-eating, thirty years of water-diet, and ten years of spiritual food."[50] Thus the earthly

life of Soshans was to comprise fifty-seven years, and the end of Time was to occur in the Zoroastrian year 12,000, which would be 2400 A. D. During this period, iniquity is gradually to decrease on earth, disease and decrepitude are to disappear, death and persecution will not occur, and multitudes are to be united in the religion of Ahuramazda.[51]

5. *Armageddon.* Nevertheless, Aharman will be able to mobilize a vast army which will march upon Iran, the holy nation, where the great and final Armageddon will be fought. The slaughter is to be so great that the rivers of blood will reach the girths of the horses. Soshans smites the hordes of unbelievers and demons, and ushers in the kingdom of righteousness.[52] The great fiend Azi-Dahak, long since defeated by Fredun, and now in the infernal pit,[53] is released, as in Revelation 20:7, and rules for a year and a half with fearful devastation; he slays one third of mankind, and destroys one third of all cattle, sheep, and other creatures;[54] he smites the water, fire, and vegetation.[55]

6. *Resurrection and Final Judgment.* After this, comes the resurrection, the final judgment, and the renovation of the world, in which complete triumph is to be achieved by Soshans and Ahuramazda for the benefit of the faithful. That much older Zoroastrian prophecy is simply recreated in our Revelation, in which the Soshans becomes the Judaic Christ, should be sufficiently obvious.

G. ESCHATOLOGY

1. *Hell and Heaven.* We cannot be certain whether the Zoroastrians or the Brahmanas first developed the intense and highly personalized concepts of hell which permeated the Eurasian world centuries before the advent of Christianity; but we know that it was the former who conceived of an intermediate stage, *Hamestagna*, which became the Manichaean and Catholic purgatory.

2. *The Kinvad Bridge.* According to Zoroastrian doctrine, when a man or woman dies, the disembodied soul remains near the corpse for three days, after which the

good soul is approached by a beautiful maiden, who personifies its good conscience; the evil soul, on the contrary, by a fearfully ugly old woman, who symbolizes the evil perpetrated during life.[56] Each soul is conducted to the Kinvad Bridge, which separates this life from the next, where it is judged by Mithra, Sraosha, and Rashnu, according to its works of charity, even as in Matthew 25: 31-46. If the good thoughts, words, and deeds, outweigh the evil, by so much as "one filament of the hair of the eyelashes,"[57] the Kinvad Bridge becomes a broad highway, and the soul enters the position in heaven which it has earned: the greatest saints proceed to the realm of Endless Light, where they will sit on thrones.

If, however, its evil outweighs the good, the Kinvad Bridge becomes like a razor blade, and the hapless soul falls headlong into hell, which "is sunken, deep, and descending, most dark, most stinking, and most terrible . . . the place of demons and fiends. . .; in it are all stench, filth, pain, punishment, distress, profound evil, and torture," [58] which must continue until the Last Judgment.

But there is a third place, called *Hamestagna*, which is reserved for those in whom good and wicked works balance and who must remain in a place of considerable discomfort but without intense torture. Hell and *Hamestagna* are within the circumference of the earth, as in Dante.

3. *The Last Judgment.* The *Bundahis*[59] contains detailed exposition of Zoroastrian eschatology. We are told that during the fifty-seven years of the Soshans, all the dead are to be resurrected, righteous and wicked alike; each is roused on the spot where he died; earth and sea surrender their dead, who assume their former bodies. All are gathered before the great judgment seat of the Soshans in the assembly known as Sadvastaran: the wicked, as conspicuous as black sheep among white, are separated from the righteous, and cast into the depths of hell, where frightful punishment is inflicted upon them. As they depart to undergo this torture, they weep so that the tears run down to their legs,[60] and they upbraid their right-

eous brethren and friends who did not teach them the good religion during the earthly life.

4. *The Great Conflagration.* Then comes the great conflagration in which the world burns in fantastic holocaust. The earth becomes as it were a river of molten metal, like the Platonic Periphlegethon, and all men, righteous or wicked, must walk through this liquid fire. To the righteous it will be like a pleasant bath of warm milk, but to the wicked it will be indescribable torture. But "by that pre-eminent ablution, they are thoroughly purified from guilt and infamy . . . and become saintly."[61] "All men become of one voice and minister loud praise to Auharmazd and the archangels."[62]

The Soshans will prepare a hush, or eucharist, made from the fat of the ox and from white hom; this will be administered to all men, and make them immortal. In addition, each adult will assume a body of forty years, and all children one of fifteen. Each man will receive again his own wife and children, but there will, as in Mark 12:25, be no more begetting in the heavenly kingdom, in which all mankind become celestial spirits.[63] Thus we see that Zoroastrianism was the world's first universalist faith, for in the end all men were to be redeemed.

5. *Annihilation of the Fiends.* But the end is not yet: even when all men are safely in the supernal regions and human labor is necessary no more, Aharman and his first lieutenant, Azi-Dahak, though defeated, are still present in the sublunary world. Auharmazd and Saoshyant now attack them, and the seven archangels assail the seven archfiends;[64] all these creatures of darkness take refuge in the pit of hell,[65] where they and Aharman, the great serpent, are burned "in the melted metal, and the stench and pollution which were in hell are burned and hell becomes quite pure." Aharman and all his minions are annihilated at last and their like can never exist again.

6. *Renovation of the World.* Auharmazd now "brings the land of hell back for the enlargement of the world; the renovation of the universe arises at his will, and the world is immortal for ever and everlasting."[66] The earth at last becomes an iceless, slopeless plain; even the moun-

tain whose summit is the support of the Kinvad Bridge, "they keep down, and it will not exist."[67] Out of the final holocaust, arises a new earth, a renovated universe; in this, all evil is at last destroyed, and all men become blessed saints.

H. CONCLUSION

1. *Frustrated Expectations.* Such was the religion of the Zoroastrians. Their magnificent prophecies, their grandiose hopes, have suffered the same fate as every other religious expectation which has ever been proclaimed. Their Hushedar is now 1600 years overdue and Aushedar-Mah is tardy by 600 years. We find here the progenitors of all apocalyptic prophecy. It is true that later writers twisted dates and facts in an effort to make Ardashir into Hushedar; but all such attempts remained feeble and unconvincing. And certainly there has been no vestigial Aushedar-Mah.

2. *A World of Intolerant Unity.* From its very beginning, Zoroastrianism envisioned a nation and finally a world united in the worship of the Lord Mazda; to the inspired prophet it was inconceivable that any other cult should dare to advance its pretensions against the God of Light. Zoroastrianism did not seek simply redemption for single, sinful individuals, but the total transformation of the world and of the human race. All who opposed it were agents of Aharman, minions of the foul fiend, children of darkness, as in I Thess. 5:5. With such an orientation, the creed could not avoid extreme intolerance. Zaratust declares that he hates all who do not embrace his religion;[68] that to those who do not practice it "shall be woe at the end of life;"[69] and that there can be no well-being in any land where heretics exist, who must be "smitten to death on the spot."[70] Apostates, made by Aharman, must perish when the good religion is victorious;[71] all who adopt a foreign faith "are worthy of death."[72] Ahuramazda commands the prophet to curse all who do not accept the good religion.[73] And again: "There is no other creed through which it is possible for

one to obtain the treasure of the worldly and spiritual existences,"[74] which is thus paraphrased in Acts 4:12: "There is none other name under heaven given among men whereby we must be saved."

3. *Never International.* In its original form, Zoroastrianism could never be acceptable to anyone except an Iranian; for it was proud and without a guilt-complex, intensely nationalistic, an instrument of Persian policy, and could, therefore, never voice the needs of other races or nationalities. Furthermore, expressing, as it did, the interests of the dominant classes, it could never appeal to the poor, the defeated, the miserable, the exploited, the downtrodden, the frustrated, the propertiless, as did Buddhism and the Gospel Jesus, which directed their appeal to the great majority, who, having nothing and never expecting to be anybody in this world, were interested primarily in escaping the bonds of economic servitude.

4. *Contributions to Christianity.* The permanent contribution of Zoroastrianism to European life and culture has come to us through its enormous influence upon the Gospel Jesus via the Essenes. Among the basic elements which the Synoptics obtained from Zoroastrianism we may mention the following: the intensely personal and vivid concepts of hell and heaven; the use of water for baptism and spiritual purification; the savior born of a true virgin-mother; the belief in demons who make human beings impure and who must be exorcised; the Messiah of moral justice; the universal judgment, based upon good and evil works; the personal immortality and the single life of every human soul; the apocalyptic vision and prophecy; and the final tribulation before the Parousia.

In addition, Paul, Revelation, and the Fourth Gospel drew heavily upon Zoroastrianism for elements which are absent from the Synoptics: e. g., the doctrine of absolute metaphysical dualism, the Logos concept, transformation into celestial spirits, the millennial kingdom, Armageddon, the final conflagration, the defeat of Satan, the renovation of the universe, and the celestial city to be lowered from the Supreme Heaven to the earth.[75] In Revelation, as in Zoroastrianism, seven is a holy and mystical number,

Furthermore, we may note that until the middle of the third century, the Catholic Church shared with the Zoroastrians their horror for all idols, images, and altars. In the fifth century, the Church began accepting the doctrine of purgatory and early in the seventh this became established dogma.

And there were at least three other elements which Catholic Christianity drew from or shared with Zoroastrianism: first, an utter intolerance toward all other religions and the conviction that these were devil-cults; second, the demand on the part of the priesthood to be civil lawgivers as well as the masters of religious ritual and ceremonial; and, third, adoption of the Zoroastrian Aharman and his creatures as the Christian devil and his imps, wizards, witches, and werewolves. The Church took this infernal character to its heart and made of him the cornerstone of its speculative system.

CHAPTER VIII

BRAHMANISM

A. THE ANCIENT ARYANS OF INDIA

1. *Their Conquest of India.* Some four thousand years ago, a group of Aryans belonging to the same stock as those who later made Zoroastrianism their national creed burst into India, established themselves as the dominant race, and instituted the intricate system of sacerdotal law and discipline known as Brahmanism. Since the political problems of India were quite different from those of Egypt or Iran, religion developed along entirely different lines. India already possessed a teeming population, which had learned to wring subsistence from the soil by agriculture: the Aryans could, therefore, perpetuate their position, privileges, and sovereignty only by divine sanctions. Revelation became an instrument, not of *national,* but of *class* and *race* policy. As the conquerors swept eastward across the land, they established various codes, such as *The Laws of Manu,* who was said to have been the second progenitor of the human race after the flood; the *Institutes of Vishnu,* delivered, it was said, personally by the god; and many others, of which the *Apastamba,* the *Baudhayana,* and the *Vasishtha Darmasastra* are representative.

2. *Brahmanic Scriptures.* Nowhere else, except perhaps in Egypt, has a single religion controlled a national population so long. The oldest sacred book in the world is the *Rig-Veda.* Other canonical Vedas, also very ancient, are the *Yagur-Veda* and the *Sama-Veda.* There is also the later and uncanonical *Atharva-Veda,* consisting of magical spells and incantations. A theology, which made Brahman the creator of the universe and the father of mankind,

gradually evolved; and along with it a priesthood, known as the Brahmanas. This was reinforced by various codes of civil and ecclesiastical law devised by the hierarchy, as noted above. Finally came the *Upanishads,* the *Bhagavad Gita,* the *Anugita,* and other documents expounding the metaphysical doctrines of mature Brahmanism.

3. *The Vedas.* The *Rig-Veda* contains elements congenital with Zoroastrianism; we are reminded throughout of the fervid *Gathas.* The *Rig* consists of hymns or invocations written by ancient Aryan poets and filled with a lust for life; they know nothing of caste, purgatory, hell, heaven, eschatology, metempsychosis, introspection, metaphysics, monotheism, or renunciation.

4. *Relationship to Zoroastrianism.* The primitive Mazdeism of Iran was the parent of Zoroastrianism and of Brahmanism, both of which developed their own ideologies in Persia and India: but, as they did so, they carried with them certain common and congenital characteristics. Both had a similar sacred plant and drink: the Zoroastrian, the haoma, the Brahmana, the soma. The Indo-Aryans worshipped Mitra, the sun-god; Agni, the fire; and Vayu, the wind—just as did the Iranians; and with both, the sky, water, plants, and trees were holy.[1] In both, the cow was sacred; but since the people of India were not sheepherders, the dog became to them a worthless and unclean beast. The lovable Anahita, goddess of the waters and of domestic happiness, bears a close resemblance to Varuna in the *Rig.* By a curious inversion, the evil daevas of the Persians became the angels and inferior gods of India. In Persia, fire and water were so holy that no corpse could be brought near them; but in India, by another strange convolution, the dead body was consigned to them because they *were* holy. And this difference in practice stemmed naturally from the opposing metaphysics which developed with the passing centuries: whereas the Persians became absolute dualists, the Brahmanas became monists and pantheists; with the latter the world and everything in it were made by and *were* literally the one Supreme God. The late *Vedanta-Sutra* de-

clares: "the entire world forms the body of Brahman."[2] In such a metaphysical system, no cosmic evil could exist.

It is possible that the Brahmanas were the first to develop the concept of hell; and that the Zoroastrians elaborated their intricate eschatology independently or appropriated this one element of it from India. In any event, despite the common ancient source of the two religions, that of the Brahmanas and the Buddhists never had any dualism, cosmic warfare, prophecy, apocalypse, Messiah, resurrection, last judgment, final tribulation, universal holocaust, renewed earth and heaven, or personal immortality for every human soul.

5. *Later Doctrines Not Based on Vedas.* Brahmanism claimed authority from the *Vedas* and declared them to contain the ultimate revelations; but it established a theology and a social system unknown to the ancient rishis, or prophets. The simple nature gods of the *Rig* were replaced by a trinity consisting of the abstract Brahman, the Father, and creator of the world; and of the old and popular deities of the aborigines, Vishnu, the Preserver, and Siva, the Destroyer. This process of incorporation was similar to what happened in Egypt under the Sumerian conquerors. There were also some thirty other important deities, of whom the old Iranian gods Indra, Agni, Vayu, and Mitra ranked among the more important.

The Brahmanic creation-theory is similar to the Egyptian.[3] In the beginning, the universe existed only as darkness, immersed, as it were, in a deep sleep. Then he, the divine Self-Existent, placed a golden egg in the waters, from which he was himself reborn as Brahman, or Pragapati, the progenitor of the world, who produced all creatures from his own body.[4]

6. *The Brahmanas Triumphant.* The fundamental feature of Brahmanism, however, is the social system it developed, and enforced with such diabolical success that even Gandhi could never attack directly its basic and grotesque injustice. For centuries, the Brahmanas and the Kshatriyas, or nobles (kings, warriors), carried on a bitter struggle for supremacy, in which the former were finally victorious and were thus able to establish a priest-state.

They were successful in this objective because they monopolized learning, made all moral, religious, and civil decisions, issued all codes of law, appropriated nearly all social privileges, and gradually gathered most of the national wealth into their own coffers. The Brahmanic codes were designed to consolidate the supremacy of the priesthood and to maintain the racial purity of the upper castes.

B. THE CASTE SYSTEM

1. *The Four Social Orders.* We are told that Brahman created the four castes for the eternal security and prosperity of the world; that he produced the Brahmanas from his head, the Kshatriyas from his arms, the Vaisyas from his thighs, and the Sudras from his feet.[5] The duties of the Brahmanas are to conduct religious rituals, teach the *Vedas*, and accept gifts; of the Kshatriyas, to study the *Vedas*, bestow gifts on the Brahmanas, sacrifice to the gods, defend the nation in time of war, and administer the codes prepared by the Brahmanas; of the Vaisyas, to make gifts to Brahmanas and work at agriculture, trade, cattle-raising, etc.; of the Sudras, to serve the three other castes, especially the Brahmanas.[6] The Brahmanas and Kshatriyas, who are Aryans, maintain the world;[7] but of these, the former are superior.[8] The importance of the productive classes, who were the indigenous natives, was, however, not overlooked, for we read that should "these two castes swerve from their duties, they would throw this whole world into confusion."[9] They would indeed!

The three upper castes are "twice-born"; that is, in addition to their human origin, each experiences a second birth, after a prescribed course of study under a Guru, who is called a "father because he gives instruction in the Veda."[10] Sudras were of course excluded from the sacraments; and from all Vedic knowledge, as were women.[11]

Brahman, as the creator of mankind, was the Great Father; and the Brahmanas, as his primary creatures, his direct representatives, and the microcosmic replicas of God, were themselves actually gods or lesser Brahmans, that is, Fathers, in their own persons. It was this concept which inspired the clergy of the Catholic Church to designate themselves as the Holy Fathers.

2. *A Rigid Social Structure.* This caste system froze the social fabric into a rigid structure. The conquered natives and their descendants were thus divinely ordained to everlasting inferiority, ignorance, and servitude. The greatest possible sin was to cause confusion or blending among the castes. A twice-born man became ceremonially unclean merely by reciting a Vedic text in the hearing of a Sudra;[12] the child of a Brahmana and a Sudra woman was a Parasava, "as impure as a corpse";[13] and "a twice-born man who has eaten the food of a Sudra during impurity caused by death or a birth, will suffer dreadful punishment in hell and be born again as an animal."[14]

3. *Complicated Marriage Laws.* To maintain the caste system, it became necessary to classify all marriages according to quality; eight forms of wedlock were declared legitimate.[15] Of these, four were acceptable for Brahmanas: "the quality of the offspring depends on the quality of the marriage rite."[16] A Brahmana could have four wives, a Kshatriya three, a Vaisya two, a Sudra one only.[17] The law of the gods was that "Men of the three first castes, who through folly marry a woman of the lowest caste, quickly degrade their families and progeny to the state of Sudras."[18]

4. *The Untouchables.* Degraded as were the Sudras, however, they nevertheless had *caste,* and with it certain elementary rights. Below them were the unfortunates who had lost their social status entirely, i. e. had become *outcastes.* These were the untouchables, and especially the Parasavas and Khandalas, the offspring of Brahmanas or Brahmanis with Sudras. They were excommunicated from birth and compelled irrevocably to gain their livelihood through the most degrading servitude no matter what their virtues or natural capacities might be.

C. THE DOCTRINE OF METEMPSYCHOSIS

1. *Kharma.* The concept of *Kharma* was invented to account for and to justify the caste system. Naturally, those artifically excluded from social privilege or economic opportunity would point out that they were not inferior, either morally or mentally. To crush such sedition, the Brahmanas devised the doctrine of metempsychosis, or soul-transmigration, according to which all living creatures had an eternal generation, have already been born over and over, and will be born again and again. A soul inhabits every insect, fish, bird, animal, and human being; according to the Gainas, lichens, plants, trees, and particles of air or fire also possessed souls. The condition under which each soul re-enters the world is predetermined by its *kharma,* that is, by the quantity of virtue or wickedness, merit or demerit, which it has accumulated during former incarnations. Sudras are simply being punished for sins so perpetrated and Brahmanas rewarded for merits so earned; each may enjoy his privileges, or must endure his punishment in patience and resignation, for it is the decree of Brahman.

2. *Rebirth in Lower or Higher Forms.* Those who earn a higher place in the next birth are, upon death, rewarded with a temporary sojourn in heaven, after which they are reborn in a higher caste; those guilty of sins and crimes, go to hell, where they are tortured for an appropriate period, after which they become reincarnated in the form and condition they deserve: a lower caste, a beast of burden, a rat, an insect, or a plant. In addition to a miserable status, they will also often be marked by various diseases and deformities; the criminal will have leprosy; the drunkard, black teeth; the violator of a Guru's bed, skin disease; the malignant informer, stinking breath; the foodthief, dyspepsia; the incendiary, madness.[19] Thus, metempsychosis and the caste-system complemented each other. Not only did they account for evil and suffering in the world: they perfumed all human misery and injustice with the odor of sanctity.

D. CHARACTERISTICS OF BRAHMANIC SOCIETY

1. *Absolute Authority of Priesthood.* We read that all authority is vested in the *Vedas* as interpreted by tradition and by the Brahmanas,[20] a claim identical to that advanced later by the Catholic hierarchy; that the gods, who exist by the favor of the Brahmanas, will execute every curse or benediction uttered by them on earth,[21] which was the very power the Roman See arrogated to itself because Jesus gave Peter the power to loose and to bind. Even as the gods are the invisible, so are the Brahmanas the visible deities, who sustain the world.[22] We are overwhelmed by such modesty.

2. *Direct Revolt Impossible.* As the laws and traditions of the Brahmanas became sanctified in hoary antiquity, the difficulty of removing or even relieving the straightjacket of caste became more and more insuperable. All questioning or heresy was forbidden on pain of the most ferocious punishment. There was no learning or teaching except that of the Gurus, the teaching Brahmanas. There was no historical record or chronology: in short, any direct revolt by the lower classes was no more possible than among the American slaves.

3. *The Immunities of the Brahmanas.* It is most revealing to examine some of the practical characteristics of this society. Brahmanas were forever free of taxes, "for they pay taxes in the form of pious acts."[23] Though dying of want, "a king must not levy a tax on Srotriyas," i. e., learned Brahmanas. [24] No matter what crime a Brahman committed, he could never be fined. The worst that could happen to him was banishment, without violation to his wealth or his person.[25] He could not, we read, even be rebuked for the most revolting crimes committed against members of the lower castes.[26] Punishments for all derelictions were elaborately graduated; and were determined, not by the enormity of the act, but by the castes of the victim and the criminal.

4. *Penalties for Being a Sudra.* If a Sudra so much as listened to a recitation of a *Veda*, molten metal was

poured into his ears; if he recited Vedic texts, his tongue was cut out; if he remembered them, his body was cleft in twain.[27] If he approached a Brahmanic female, *without committing physical contact,* he "shall be tied up in Varuna grass and thrown into the fire."[28] If he "mentions the names and castes of the twice-born with contumely, an iron nail, ten fingers long, shall be thrust red hot into his mouth."[29] If he presumes to teach a Brahmana his duty, "hot oil shall be poured into his mouth and ears."[30] To accuse the Guru falsely or to claim a higher caste were crimes, when committed by a Sudra, of the same magnitude as murdering a Brahmana, and were punished by frightful death or twelve years of *abhisasta* penance.[31] The law provided that "With whatever limb an inferior insults or hurts his superior in caste, of that limb shall the king cause him to be deprived. If he places himself on the same seat with his superior, he shall be banished with a mark on his buttocks. If he spits on him, he shall lose both lips; if he breaks wind against him, his hindparts; if he uses abusive language, his tongue."[32]

The Sudra was substantially a slave; for we read: "A servant who abandons his work shall be flogged."[33] And thus the savage contradiction in Brahmanism was laid bare: for while no beast or insect might, because it contained a human soul, be pained or confined, a Sudra was subject to death by whipping on the smallest pretext.

A Brahmana could lawfully seize the property of any Sudra by fraud or force or from a rich Vaisya who neglected his religious duties.[34]

5. *Graduated Punishments.* There seem to have been two crimes which the Brahmanas feared with preternatural terror: violence to their beds and to their persons. These are therefore treated elaborately and condign punishments provided;[35] a man of lower caste who "has had connexion with a Guru's wife shall cut off his organ together with the testicles . . . and walk towards the south until he falls down dead. Or he may die embracing a heated metal image of a woman."[36] Nor was the Brahmani exempt: "A woman who commits adultery with a

man of lower caste, the king shall cause to be devoured by dogs in a public place."37

It is interesting to note that this practice was similar to that once inflicted in the South upon white women and their Negro paramours or assailants.

Murdering or attempting to murder a Brahmana made the perpetrator an *abhisasta*, who must erect his hut in the forest, carry the skull of his victim on a stick, and, proclaiming his deed wherever he went, starve or subsist by begging for twelve years, after which he was returned to caste.38 But if he had slain a Guru, the penance must continue throughout his life, and he could be purified only after death.39 For killing a Kshatriya a nine-year penance was sufficient; for a Vaisya, three; for a Sudra or a woman, one.40 One year was also required for slaying a crow, a chameleon, a peacock, a Hamsa, a vulture, a frog, a muskrat, or a dog.41 For killing a eunuch, the murderer must give his Brahmana a load of straw;42 for slaying a harlot, nothing at all.43

6. *Gifts for Brahmanas.* The Brahmanas provided munificent gifts for themselves at every turn: when a king became aware that his end was approaching, he was required to bestow on the Brahmanas all wealth he had accumulated from fines and then seek death in battle;44 and anyone who sought Nirvana through asceticism had first to bestow all his possessions upon them.45

E. SPECIAL FEATURES OF THE SOCIAL STRUCTURE

1. *The Position of Women.* Women were especially oppressed: like Sudras, they were excluded from all sacred learning.46 "In childhood, a female must be subject to her father, in youth to her husband; and when her lord is dead, to her sons; a woman must never be independent."47 "No matter how destitute of virtue . . . a husband must be constantly worshiped as a god by the faithful wife."48 If he dies, she must never take a second.49 So fearful was this crime of remarriage by a woman that even her son became an *abhisasta* outcast.50 When the husband

died, the good wife ascended the funeral pyre after him.[51]

2. *Trial by Ordeal.* One juridical development of Brahmanism was the Trial by Ordeal. However, it was specifically provided in revelation that no Brahmana could be made to risk *his* innocence by so desperate a chance.[52] No one else, however, was exempt: if water did not drown, if fire did not burn, and if poison did not kill, or upset the stomach, the accused was presumed guiltless.[53]

3. *Rules Governing Students.* Every student took the vow of poverty, chastity, and obedience. He must never touch a woman, "nor," as Jesus was to reiterate, "shall he desire her in his heart."[54] He must dwell at the Guru's house; must be his diligent, humble, and unpaid servant; must beg food and other necessities from virtuous and twice-born persons; must bring everything so obtained to his master; may eat a portion only of the food so collected after receiving permission from the Guru; and must avoid all frivolity during his years of studentship. If he is himself a Brahmana and continues as a student until death, he passes at once into Nirvana.[55]

In the Brahmanic system, there were four orders, any of which a twice-born man might choose after his Vedic studies were completed. He could continue as a student, or might become a householder, an ascetic, or a hermit.[56] But we are told that "the venerable teacher prescribes only . . . the order of householders,[57] because these alone produce wealth or children,[58] and because "all mendicants subsist through the protection afforded by householders."[59]

F. THEOLOGY AND RELIGIOUS PRACTICE UNDER MATURE BRAHMANISM

1. *Nirvana.* Thus we see that in addition to the four castes as well as the hordes of untouchables, two new religious orders sprang up within mature Brahmanic society. Just when ascetics and hermits became numerous, we cannot now know, but we may assume that it was at least six centuries before Christ. *Why* they arose is not difficult to comprehend; for in that heavily populated

land, priest-ridden and ignorant, full of misery and frustration, countless human hearts must have been bursting with pent-up despair. The joy of living reflected in the ancient *Rig* had long since departed; there was no hope or solace for the fettered millions, hemmed in on every side by rigid caste, denied all hope and pleasure in this world of frustration and despair. This life was a morass of slavery and starvation: and that beyond the grave was even more terrifying. Even if one were fortunate enough to achieve a brief stay in heaven, one would soon be born again into this vale of tears and suffering, repeat the same useless struggle, perhaps be plunged into hell, and be reborn a louse or a worm.

And so it was that someone in ancient India devised the doctrine of Nirvana, which was ultimate extinction for the personal entity, the end of conscious soul-existence, and its final union with the Self, the Universal Soul, the Brahman, the Atman, even as the river loses itself in the boundless ocean. To escape forever the Wheel of Life, the endless round of birth and death, became the fervent yearning of countless millions. Through the practice of yoga, the concentration upon the Self, in which the syllable *Ohm* was endlessly repeated, men hoped to enter the Universal Soul.[60] This desire was a complete negation of the primitive *Rig-Veda;* and the concept itself certainly did not exist in earlier Brahmanism. But, as it was an irresistible popular reaction to prevailing conditions, it became necessary for the reigning priesthood to incorporate asceticism into their system as a social safety valve, and to offer the achievement of Nirvana to those plunged into ultimate despair.

2. *Renunciation*. Since the burdens of supporting wife and children were almost intolerable to the poor, the conviction took root among them that celibacy would be rewarded eschatologically.[61] But before they could become hermits living alone in the forest, or ascetics begging their way from door to door, they must first undergo a long period of Vedic study and then remain always under the authority of the Brahmanas. That great numbers embraced even these stringent terms we know: for

all the Brahmanic codes detail the regulations governing the lives and the duties of both these religious orders. And so Mother India spawned the monster Renunciation, which has played so vast and spectacular a role in European and world history.

The ascetic hoped to attain Nirvana by rejecting all human relationships; by eliminating fear and desire from his soul; by complete indifference to pain, pleasure, hell, heaven, past, present, and future. He must seek the Universal Soul by fixing his gaze upon the eternal and becoming impervious to the evanescent;[62] he must realize that his body is a filthy, stinking sink of iniquity, the stay of carnal desire, wrath, greed, folly, pride, and selfishness. [63]

Such was the ancient ascetic of India, the prototypes of Sts. Antony and Simeon Stylites.

And so while the ruling Brahmanas and the privileged Kshatriyas took the cash and let the credit go, preferring money, power, women, and pleasure, millions of their less fortunate brethren found surcease from slavery and exploitation in renunciation. When the human spirit has undergone indescribable torture for centuries, it seeks refuge at last in irrevocable extinction.

Thus we see that the basic ideal of the ascetic was an utter individualism by which he sought his own salvation only. He was the first Existentialist. Even as the world had given him nothing, so would he give nothing to the world. He would undertake no project, do no work, concontribute nothing to the support or welfare of any one else: Nay more: he would not even lift a finger to provide his own most elementary necessities, but would live by begging, utterly indifferent alike to abuse or charity, to cold or heat, to life or death. He was the end-product of the Brahmanic system of degradation and suppression.

3. *Works of Holiness.* In the Brahmanic system, *works* of holiness played a large role. These were not, however, as one might surmise, labors of charity but rather ceremonial performances, such as saving the life of a cow or a Brahmana, bestowing gifts upon a priest, reciting the *Vedas,* bathing in holy water, journeying to sacred places,

or eating the five products of the cow (urine, dung, milk, sour milk, and clarified butter). All such activities were believed highly efficacious for removing guilt.

We read that "all mountains, all rivers, holy lakes, places of pilgrimage, the dwellings of rishis, cowpens, and temples of the gods are places which destroy sin."[64] At such sacred spots penances were extremely effective, and required only periods ranging from a single day to a year to obliterate a variety of sins, including the most revolting.[65] Most sacrosanct were various altars and shrines to which pilgrimages were made. Hundreds of thousands of pious persons journeyed long distances, particularly to the Ganges at Benares, so that their souls might attain heaven and a more fortunate incarnation in the next birth.

4. *Penance.* Under the priestly codes, elaborate formularies were devised by which sinners might free themselves from guilt. They must "always perform a penance, by the advice of a Brahmana."[66] Scarcely by accident, these penances were often very profitable to the Brahmanas: and they ranged anywhere from giving them a bundle of straw to committing suicide by fire or starvation. Although there is not the smallest vestige of all this in Buddhism, the Gospel Jesus, or in pristine Christianity, it became one of the characteristics of the Catholic Church in the fourth century and remains so to this day.

5. *Heaven and Hell.* The Brahmanic concepts of hell were used to reinforce the caste system and metempsychosis. In Brahmanic eschatology hell and heaven are places of reward for the obedient and further punishment for the wicked or heretical. While heaven remained vague and indefinite, hell became an elaborately developed concept with a multitude of graphic tortures appropriate for every type of miscreant.

We are told that there are twenty-three hells which are characterized by darkness, howling, burning, parching, stench, iron spikes, frying pans, a flaming river, sword-leaved trees, iron fetters, etc., in all of which the worst criminals are tortured successively.[67] Those who have committed a crime effecting loss of caste are tortured for a thousand years: they are dragged hither and yon upon rough roads, devoured by dogs and jackals, hawks and cranes, serpents and scorpions. They are scorched by blazing fire, pierced by thorns, divided by saws into parts, and tormented by thirst. They are agitated by hunger and fearful troops of tigers, and faint away because of foul stenches. They are boiled in oil, pounded with pestles, and ground in iron or stone vessels. They are compelled to eat vomit, pus, blood, and excrement. They are tormented by frost, suspended from trees, shot full of arrows and cut into pieces.[68] "After having suffered the torments inflicted in the hells, the evil-doers pass into animal bodies."[69] Several centuries later, concepts comparable to these reappeared in various Christian apocalypses.

6. *Excommunication*. As we have already noted, the Brahmanas insisted on controlling each and every member of society: no one could escape their rule and they made some kind of provision for every one. This, of course, is the fundamental characteristic of the priest-state: a hierarchy may or may not seek moral improvement, but it always insists on universal sway, heavy tribute from all, and the extirpation of every ideology except its own. It proclaims its prerogative to legislate for every phase of human activity, social, political, moral, domestic, civil, and religious, all by revealed and sacred authority. In such a society, no human being is permitted to live his own life, follow his own reason, or earn a living in his own way, asking merely to live at peace with his fellowmen. Anyone desiring such independence will be regarded as a dangerous subversive.

The fearful weapon always ready for use in the hands of the Brahmanas was *excommunication*. This was the punishment by which the heretic, the unbeliever, the independent individual, or anyone who did not adequately perform his religious obligations would be deprived of caste and degraded to the rank of Sudra or Khandala. Brahmanic law provided specifically that anyone "who does not worship standing in the morning, nor sitting in the evening, shall be excluded, just like a Sudra, from all the duties and rights of an Aryan."[70] And again: "He who divulges the Veda to persons not authorized to study it, he who sacrifices for Sudras, and all those who have fallen from the highest caste shall be excommunicated."[71] We must never "honour, even by a greeting, heretics . . . or logicians, arguing against the Veda."[72] And so we find that the principal thunderbolt of the Catholic clergy had been fully developed many centuries before in India. The fearful thing about excommunication was not that it cut the victim off from all religious associations, but that it sealed him away from all human contacts and made it impossible for him to earn a living. And where the priesthood had sufficient power, excommunication included also exile or death.

7. *Exclusive Salvation.* The Brahmanic codes were declared unalterable and everlasting, because they were ancient and based upon irrefragable authority: "All those doctrines differing from the Veda, which spring up and soon perish, are worthless and false, because they are of modern date."[73] This, of course, was aimed at such heretical innovations as Buddhism, which, because of recent origin, must soon perish.

8. *Pantheism.* The *Vedanta-Sutra,* the *Bhagavad Gita,* and the *Upanishads,* contain the most complete exposition of mature Brahmanic metaphysics. Brahmanism moved finally into a thorough-going pantheism, and prepared the way for Buddhism by developing a philosophy which denied that the *Vedas* were in themselves sufficient for salvation.

In the *Bhagavad-Gita,* the instructor is Krishna, one of the various terrestrial incarnations of Vishnu. He declares that "in this world there is a two-fold path,"[74] just as we shall find the Essenes and the primitive Christians declaring. The first is pursued by those who overcome passion and desire, a doctrine elaborated in the *Anugita;*[75] who repudiate family, sex, property, wealth, and all material things; who are indifferent to all things good or bad, here or hereafter; and who seek only the Self, that is, the union of the finite with the infinite Soul of the Universe, which is Brahman, Atman, Vishnu, Pragapati

—the Over-Soul, as Emerson calls it. Thus, they will be freed forever from the circle of birth and death, from the endless Wheel of Life. The second pathway is that of those who, deceived by their senses and driven hither and yon by their passions, crave property, family, and wealth. They are slaves of delusion, who must descend in the scale of life, be tortured in hell, and be reborn again and again only to repeat their pointless sufferings through endless eons.

According to the *Upanishads,* the universe is Brahman; he is also the Atman, the living, permeating life, which is the Infinite Soul. This divine power is called the Self. Every soul that is manifest in plant, tree, fish, insect, bird, beast, or man is a portion of this omnipresent spirit; and every such microcosm, as it were, may choose to undergo continued misery as an independent existence or rejoin the Universal Self, the macrocosm, become one with the infinite, lose consciousness and identity, and so escape forever the Wheel of Life.

G. CONCLUSION

1. *The Final Development of Hinduism.* To summarize: the *Vedas* were the original scriptures of the Aryan conquerors of India; but in time their descendants developed legal and ecclesiastical codes to establish their authority and give divine sanction to the caste system and the doctrine of transmigration. A vast hierarchy proliferated, which clamped its iron rule upon every human being and every phase of life. The despair and frustration which resulted among the masses made it necessary to devise the doctrine of renunciation and to provide for hermits and ascetics within the framework of that society. And lastly, the pantheistic doctrines of the *Upanishads* were developed,[76] which rejected the sufficiency of the *Vedas,* promulgated the concept of the Self and the Wheel of Life, and prepared the way for Buddhism.

In the seventh and eighth centuries of our era, Islam swept into India and conquered large territories; but their converts were taken rather from the Buddhists than from the Brahmanas. There are in India today some 80,000,000 Mohammedans and 260,000,000 Hindus; the Buddhists were long since driven from India and have never regained a foothold there.

2. *Influence of Brahmanism upon Christianity.* The influence of Brahmanism upon the Gospel Jesus was very slight, except insofar as its asceticism carried over into Buddhism; but upon the priesthood of the Catholic Church, especially after its political triumph, it became paramount. We may list the following practices, which were certainly derived from Brahmanism: trial by ordeal; use of excommunication; the prohibition against any conversation with heretics; encouragement of such religious "works" as pilgrimages to altars and shrines; severe sanctions against remarried women; the recognition of degrees of legality in marriages; the bestowal of unprecedented honors upon ascetics who tortured their bodies and lived a life of bizarre or fantastic physical hardship; the requirement that an ascetic, upon joining a religious order, bestow all his wealth upon the official priesthood; the acceptance of certain precise and vivid descriptions of torments in hell; the interpretation of the revealed scriptures by the official hierarchy alone; the ultimate authority of tradition; the vows of obedience, poverty, and chastity; the immunity of the priesthood from taxation or civil duties; the claim on the part of the hierarchy to establish all juridical codes; the doctrine that it is the function of kings to administer and enforce such codes; the use of confession and penance to expiate an intricate system of venal and mortal sins; the priestly monopoly over the training and education of youth; the denial of the sacred scriptures to the lower orders or the laity; and the use of spells and incantations (white magic) to defeat enemies, to be successful in love, business, etc., exactly as in the *Atharva-Veda.* All these characteristics, unknown both to the Gospel and to the Apostolic Church, became standard after 350 A. D. The priestly prerogative to legislate for every one in all fields of human conduct was common to Judaism, Zoroastrianism, and Brahmanism; and for their own parallel pretensions, the Catholics were

probably indebted equally to Jews and Brahmanas. Finally, we may be certain that Catholic reverence for and worship of sacred images (so horrifying to Jews, Zoroastrians, and early Christians alike) came at least as much from India as from Greek and Roman paganism.

3. *Endurance of Brahmanism.* The success of Brahmanism is attested by its permanence: the Greeks of Alexander could not conquer it; after several centuries, it expelled Buddhism from India, and, after certain alterations, reappeared as Hinduism; it withstood the fiercest assaults of the Mohammedans, and neither Christianity nor modern enlightenment have been able to make any serious inroads into its domains. Brahmanism or Hinduism is a religion, a social system, a way of life: and it still holds the destiny of some 300,000,000 communicants in its iron grip, frustrating every effort intended to emancipate its victims. It remains to be seen what such men as the Marxist Nehru and his British-educated colleagues can do to alter or transform this ancient ideology and social structure. The modern Hindu has shown that he can elect socialists to operate his government, but he has not shown that he can conquer his ancient superstitions or adopt a secularist or progressive way of life.

4. *Brahmanism and the Gospel Jesus.* We conclude this chapter with one curious item. We have noted why the Brahmanas called themselves Fathers.[77] We know, furthermore, that the Buddhist heresy repudiated the *Vedas,* the Brahmanas, and their title of father-gods. In Matt. 23:9, Jesus says, "And call no man your Father upon the earth: for one is your Father, which is in heaven." We suggest that this text can have only a single meaning: it reflected Buddhist influence and was a repudiation of all such priestly authority as the Brahmanas arrogated to themselves. The Catholic hierarchy, however, found Brahmanic ideology far more to its liking than it did the Gospel Jesus; and therefore it patterned itself in the image of the former. The Catholic Church re-established the very system which Buddhism and the Gospel Jesus repudiated. The Church became the counter-revolution which rejected the religion of Jesus. From Brahman-

ism, through Buddhism, apostolic Christianity and the Catholic Church, the wheel turned full circle. It was therefore no accident that the new clergy, in the fourth and fifth centuries, began to call themselves by the very name which their nominal Founder had so stringently forbidden. And it was also no accident that under their authority a social structure was erected in Europe which substantially reproduced that of India: they themselves became the Brahmanas; the feudal aristocracy, the Kshatriyas; the tradesmen and peasants, the Vaisyas; serfs and the slaves, the Sudras. And the heretics became the *outcastes*.

CHAPTER IX

BUDDHISM: REVOLUTION IN INDIA

A. THE DISINHERITED GO ON STRIKE

1. *Revolt Based on Brahmanic Doctrine.* It was scarcely possible that a large mass of humanity should submit forever to galling and artificial restraints, to irremediable inferiority and frustration. However, since the ruling classes were so thoroughly intrenched, no revolt could be successful unless based upon established doctrine. As it happened, the desired foundation existed in the *Upanishads* and in the asceticism already tolerated. Powerful movements, therefore, took shape in the sixth century to emancipate the disinherited. Both Gainaism and Buddhism grew out of Brahmanism and derived from it such concepts as transmigration, *kharma,* heaven and hell, the Wheel of Life, Nirvana, and renunciation. Mahavira, the founder of Gainaism, and Gautama, of Buddhism, were contemporaries; but the break of Mahavira with Brahmanism was less complete. We find, for example that Gaina ascetics, like the Brahmanic, were strict individualists, practicing self-mortification; they regarded filth as almost synonymous with holiness; among them, we hear nothing of *Samghas,* monasteries, or brotherhoods. Gaina teachers were even called Gurus.

2. *Central Doctrine of Revolt.* The revolt of the Gainas and the Buddhists centered upon revolutionary ideas which were everywhere rampant: that the Brahmanas were worldly, hypocritical, exploitive, and hopelessly enmeshed in passion, injustice, and greed for material wealth; that caste should be abolished; that position in society should be based, not upon the accident of birth, but on

moral excellence; that the *Vedas* should be discarded summarily; that men and women should be encouraged to become saints and renunciators while still in the prime of youth; that pacifism and non-violence should be established as the holiest of all principles; that religious teachers should not seek to control society-at-large, but should initiate only their own converts into a way of life calculated to achieve Nirvana; and, consequently, that religious and civil codes should be entirely separate. In short, they demanded the separation of church and state. Here was something new; for here were religious teachers who did not aspire to control anyone except their own voluntary disciples. They had no interest in worldly affairs, which they simply abandoned and repudiated. This was the great difference between Buddhism and Brahmanism: the latter insisted on totalitarian dominion over all; the former accepted only those who would submit to its code; the punishment for violation of discipline was expulsion only, with the consequent return to civil society.

3. *Doctrine of Universal Equality.* The doctrine of equality is poignantly illustrated by a curious story concerning the harlot Bindumati who lived in the great city of Pataliputra and who performed a great miracle. She explains that, when bought with gold, "free alike from fawning and dislike," she treats men of all castes as equals. "This . . . is the Act of Truth by the force of which I turned the Ganges back."[1]

Throughout the Buddhist scriptures as well as the Gospel Jesus, we find this ideal of universal human brotherhood, which expresses the profound yearning of the oppressed and the despised, the poor, and the ignorant for equality with their more successful brethren. Since the Sudras and the outcasts of India could not hope for priority, they sought first of all to escape the bitter exploitation under which they groaned. Through holy beggary, they might even achieve a humble parasitism of their own. But man cannot live by bread alone; he must have food also for his spirit, that is, he must have inspiration for his ego: he must believe that he is significant. The disinherited of

India, therefore, seized eagerly upon a doctrine by which they might escape unrequited toil and social degradation and at the same time attain stature as elect saints.

4. *The Repudiation of Labor.* Because it enabled the toiling masses to strike a blow against frustration and exploitation, Buddhism grew into a great and mighty force: less than three hundred years after its origin, it probably numbered more adherents than any other religious discipline in the world. The new preachers proclaimed the gospel: "Come unto me, all ye that labor and are heavy laden, and I will give you rest." All were welcome: slaves, Sudras, outcasts, women, harlots, thieves, murderers, on the same terms, all to be emancipated from the control of the Brahmanas. The way was revealed by which men might escape work: even if subjected to unlimited abuse, nakedness, and starvation, they would, whatever the cost, withhold their labor. They would renounce life, but they would not submit to involuntary servitude. Even if they should be beaten to death or compelled to subsist like beasts of the jungle, *they would perform no service under the old conditions.* This was the world's first great organized strike.

5. *An Extension of Brahmanic Asceticism.* The revolutionaries capitalized upon Brahmanic teachings and so made it impossible for the authorities to extirpate them. They extended to everyone the privileges which the Brahmanas had already conferred upon aged, twice-born ascetics. The nub of the heresy consisted in its demand for independence from Brahmanic authority and in its declaration of universal equality by which it invited the poor, the downtrodden, the criminals, the outcasts, from the byways and the hedges to come and receive salvation freely and without price. Other cults chose their saints with the most meticulous care; Buddhism and Christianity opened their arms in welcome to all the disinherited miscreants of the earth.

6. *Repudiation of Home and Family.* The American I. W. W., which flourished at the turn of this century, believed that workers could never free themselves from exploitation as long as they were involved in family rela-

tionships; it was a fervent portion of their faith that they must never marry or accept any social responsibility. This very doctrine was the foundation of the heresies of India. Unless we understand this simple fact, we can never comprehend such movements as Buddhism and Christianity: wife, children, home, all these, they believed, are the instruments by which the exploiters fasten slavery forever upon the necks of the poor; and thus the bondage is gilded over with a veneer of moral sanctity. For in every conservative society, such as in ours and in the Brahmanic, a man who abandons wife, children, parents, and home is regarded as the most despicable of all moral monsters. The Buddhists and the I. W. W. agreed that men are born into slavery, destined and condemned to a treadmill of useless and meaningless toil, not only to keep their economic lords in luxury, but also to feed, clothe, and house a domestic brood who give them nothing of value in return.

7. *Glorification of Celibacy.* In addition to this, India was heavily overpopulated and workers exceedingly numerous. For this, there was only one practical remedy: a sharp reduction in the available labor force. The poor must withdraw from the labor market and must cease to multiply. The core of the new religion, therefore, consisted in the repudiation of work and marriage and in the glorification of celibacy and idleness. Sex and sex-consummation became therefore the greatest and the most shameful evils which afflict mankind. Anything even distantly related to human generation became repulsive, unclean, and degrading in the sight of Buddhism; and even the most furtive reference to the organs of life was viewed with extreme abhorrence and disgust. Brahmanism had degraded women to the level of beasts, but it never belittled or rejected motherhood; the revolutionaries, on the contrary, honored women as human beings, but repudiated them as wives, sweethearts, or mothers. Women could become Arhats (saints); but if one of them aroused the smallest erotic disturbance in a man, she was a creature of Mara. Women were dreadfully dangerous,

because they seduced men into a relationship which made endless labor inescapable.

8. *Renunciation of Woman.* Erotic desire became, therefore, the most fearful of all sins: it was not so much the sexual act itself that must be avoided as the wish to commit it: whosoever looketh on a woman to lust after her hath committed adultery with her already in his heart. This became the basic article of the Buddhist faith.

Even a cursory examination of Gaina and Buddhist scripture reveals that Woman was the grand renunciation which Man must achieve: "So long as the love of man toward woman, even the smallest, is not destroyed, so long is he in bondage."² The Buddhist monks imagined themselves constantly tempted by seductive females, ready to smother them with affection and gifts; the pathway to Nirvana was forever beset by fragrant and voluptuous maidens who wished only to enjoy their masculinity; even the gods, forever jealous of the *Arhat's* superiority, appeared to them in the form of transcendently beautiful women to arouse in them that fatal desire. We are not to "desire women, those female demons . . . who continually change their mind, who entice men, and then make sport of them as slaves."³ It is better to "fall into the fierce tiger's mouth, or under the sharp knife of the executioner, than to . . . dwell with a woman . . . Better far with red-hot pins bore out both your eyes, than . . . look upon a woman's form with desire."⁴ Jesus proclaimed the same philosophy.

9. *Rejection of Parents and Children.* But it was not sufficient for the *Arhat* to renounce sex and marriage. He must also abhor and summarily reject all those things which accompany family life and require labor for their acquisition. He must thrust aside gold, money, clothing, comforts, land, cattle, houses. Since such *impedimenta* cannot be obtained without toil or wickedness, they must be renounced and all desire for them must be eradicated from the soul. Only those who abandoned father, mother, sister, brother, wife, children, lands, and house without regret could be disciples of Buddha or Mahavira. In return for such renunciation, they would gain knowledge,

peace of mind, cessation of desire, many brethren and sisters in the faith, the kingdom of righteousness, and, beyond all this, eternal salvation. This is precisely the reward promised also in Mark 10:29-30.

We are told that all the *Bodhisattvas* abandoned their wives and gave away their children, or sold them into slavery.[5] The devout wept at the heartrending tale of King Vessantara, who consigned his beloved children into slavery under an ogre-like Brahmana: "It is because what he did . . . was so difficult that the fame of this Bohisat was spread abroad among gods and men . . . and that the gods exalt him in heaven."[6] Such was the Buddhist reward for acts which, under our social-economy, bring infamy and imprisonment.

The monk was warned against the pressures from his family, who "will surround him and say: 'Child, we have brought you up, now support us! . . . Your father is an old man . . . Support your mother and your father . . . it is your duty in this world . . . Your sons . . . are very young; you have married a wife.' . . . These are the whirlpools which have been pointed out: . . . the wise keep clear of them, but the ignorant go down in them."[7]

And so we see that the revolutionary religions of India actually began as a strike by poor and weary men against the economic burdens imposed by masters, parents, sisters, wives, and children.

B. THE WEAPONS OF REVOLT

1. *Renunciation of the Brahmanas.* The revolutionaries in chorus denounced the Brahmanas as hypocrites and deceivers. Not by forms, ceremonies, or the accident of birth does one become a Brahmana or an outcast, but by deeds which bring their own reward or punishment.[8] We can well imagine the denunciations which the new ascetic heaped upon the corrupt and pleasure-loving Brahmanas, who, in their *Upanishads,* had taught an ethical system which they ignored, but which the Gainas and the Buddhists appropriated. The Brahmanas, like the Pharisees, were painted sepulchres "within whom there is

ravening desire" although "the outside they make clean."9 "These ignorant priests pretend to know the sacrifice..., they shroud themselves in study and penances, being like fire covered with ashes."10 Their sacrifices of animals and their recitations of the *Vedas* can never remove their evil *kharma*.11 They possess wealth and wives, lands and houses, are full of anger, malice, depravity, and passion; therefore, they will not escape the wrath to come.12 See Luke 3:7 and Matthew 3:7. They are vile creatures wallowing, like swine, in the filthy delights of the senses. Among all criminals, they are the worst: for they are hypocrites as well as exploiters. To robbers, harlots, and thieves, Gainas and Buddhists extended an easy forgiveness; for the impecunious are rarely injured by such as these.

We are told that since not even one of the ancient *rishis* had ever seen Brahman face to face,13 all this talk of *Vedas* composed by the god was nothing but nonsense; and to intone these verses precisely as handed down was sheer folly.

2. *The Reversion of Hell.* The Brahmanas had threatened all who violated their codes with torture after death. But the revolutionaries turned the tables, and made hell the inevitable portion of the rich, the comfortable, the powerful—in short, of all those who enjoyed the good things which the underprivileged could not obtain. Thus, for the first time, hell became the means of compensating for social injustice. The Buddhist told the Brahmana: "Verily, ye have had your reward"; and hereafter for them there would "be weeping and gnashing of teeth."

3. *Alliance Between Lower Classes and Kings.* It is significant that the founders of the heretical communions were reported to be Kshatriyas or Kings, who were considered far less tyrannical than the priests. The Gainas and the Buddhists sought to make allies of the secular rulers by offering to transfer the civil authority to them. They desired, in effect, to separate religion from politics, to remove the priesthood from control over temporal life, and to abolish the Brahmanic codes together with the caste system. They demanded the right to worship as they

pleased. Buddhism was an attempt to establish a free conscience.

4. *The Rights and Virtues of the Poor.* Buddhism emphasized the *rights* and the *virtues* of the poor; it considered poverty and sainthood synonymous; and proclaimed that, since wealth is wicked, the rich must give all they have to the indigent on pain of excruciating torture in hell. We are not to bestow gifts on those who will reciprocate! We must give only to those who can return nothing, and such must we entertain at our tables. This was also the ethic of Jesus, as declared in Luke 6:35: "lend, hoping for nothing again." This is a moral system dear to the hearts of all the penniless. Neither Buddhism nor the Gospel Jesus has one word of commendation for industry, thrift, self-reliance, domestic responsibility, or the hard-working man who produces the food, clothing, and shelter by which the world subsists. For religions are, like political creeds, instruments to attain the social and economic objectives of those who embrace them. It would indeed be unnatural for grossly underpaid toilers to glorify labor.

C. MAHAVIRA

1. *Myth and History.* The following sketch of Mahavira[14] indicates that the tradition concerning him mingled fact with myth, as is the case with so many outstanding personalities. Like all the Gainas who inherited his authority, he was said to have been conceived in an extraordinary virgin birth. He was a pre-existing god who at the proper moment assumed a human form for the purpose of saving humanity. First, he entered the body of Devananda, wife of a Brahmana; but, while still in embryonic state, he was transferred to that of Trisala, wife of a Kshatriya. The prophet was thus a member of both upper castes.

Many wonderful portents accompanied his birth: the whole universe was resplendent with gods and goddesses descending from and ascending to heaven; the king increased all weights and measures; customs, taxes, and confiscations were remitted; police officers were prohibited from entering and searching houses; fines and debts were canceled. We are reminded of the American Bill of Rights.

At the usual age of thirty, Mahavira began his active ministry; and when he entered upon his great work, the gods sang a song in which they hailed him as the savior of mankind.

2. *Discipline.* Of Mahavira, we read that he "gave up forever his claims in any property, just as a snake casts off its slough. His power and wealth, his friends, wives, sons, and relations, he gave up as he shook the dust from his feet. More than four months many sorts of living beings gathered on his body, crawled about it, and caused pain there. For a time, the Venerable One, giving up his robe, was a naked, world-relinquishing, houseless sage. Renouncing the female sex, . . . he meditated . . . . Giving up the company of all householders whomsoever, he meditated . . . he, to whom women were known as the causes of all sinful acts, saw the true state of the world."[15]

Like a Brahmana ascetic, but repudiating Brahmana control, he wandered from village to village, houseless and homeless, renouncing all human fellowship, naked and forlorn, indifferent to every hardship and misery, making converts, and teaching the pathway to Nirvana,[16] which he declared could be attained by any individual, regardless of age, caste, or Vedic knowledge, provided only he embraced the Gaina discipline.

3. *Central Doctrine.* The core of the Gaina teaching, as in the *Bhagavad-Gita,* was that men are divided into two classes, the wise and the fools. The wise renounce everything, but the fools heap up an evil *kharma,* which will plague them into hell, and which compels them to believe that they must "provide for a mother, for a father, for a sister, for a wife, for sons, for daughters" and must possess "different kinds of property . . . Longing for these objects, people work day and night . . . commit injuries and violent acts."[17]

4. *The Rich Fool.* While the wise ascetic who begged at his door goes to heaven, the rich fool goes to the tor-

ments of hell; "thus a fool doing evil deeds which benefit another will ignorantly thereby come to grief."[18] Again and again we are told that only fools lay by stores, where fire destroys and where thieves break in and steal. We must not hoard anything, not even so much as a speck of grease in a begging bowl.[19] We are to take no thought for the morrow, where we shall lodge, what we shall eat, or wherewithal we shall be clothed.

5. *Sowing Alms in Blessed Fields.* We are told the curious story of Harikesa, monk and sage, who came begging to a place where the Brahmanas had prepared a feast. Seeing the sage, they exclaimed in disgust: " 'Who are you, monster? . . . You miserable devil of a dirty man! Go, get away!' "[20] A good spirit, assuming the monk's voice, replied from a tree: "I am chaste . . . I have no property . . . I have come for food . . . The husbandmen throw the corn on high ground and on low ground, hoping for a return. For the like motive give unto me; I may be the field which will produce merit, as the return for your benevolence."[21] This is the Gaina version of the Parable of the Sower; here the seed symbolizes alms for holy men, which will bear fruit, that is, a good *kharma,* in abundance. The good spirit declares: "the Brahmanas are without pure birth and knowledge; they are very bad fields . . . The saints call at high and lowly houses; they are the blessed fields."[22] In short, gifts to the official priesthood would never reduce the giver's evil *kharma;* but alms to Gaina saints would bear fruit an hundredfold. Those who cast their bread upon the waters would receive it again after many days.

6. *The Three Talents or Capitals.* The allegory of the three merchants[23] is the original version of the Gospel parable of the three servants who received differing talents from their master; here the first loses his capital, symbolizing those who must go to hell at death, to be reborn in a worse condition; the second merely preserves it, symbolizing those who go to heaven, to reappear on earth as men; the third, who "gains much," symbolizes the ascetic, who achieves non-existence when this life ends. We read: of those who are to be "born again, evil doers go to hell;

the righteous go to heaven; those who are free from all wordly desire attain Nirvana."[24]

We are told that a man who once accepts the good life and then returns to wife, children, and property,[25] "returns to his vomit."[26]

7. *The Life of an Animal Existentialist*. The sage concludes: "A wild animal goes by itself to many places, lives in many places, and always gets its food . . . I shall imitate this life of the animals."[27] Verily, foxes have holes, and the birds of the air have nests; and the Gaina ascetic, like Jerome, seeking the life of an existentialist beast, declared: "Individually man is born, individually he dies, individually he falls from the state of existence, individually he rises to another."[28]

D. GAUTAMA

1. *Life and Myth*. Among Max Muller's *Sacred Books of the East* are the *Fo-Sho-Hing-Tsan-King* and the *Buddha-Karita*, which are purported biographies of Gautama and in which we find, as we might expect, a skeleton of fact heavily encrusted with myth. The fabulous founder of Buddhism was known by a variety of names: the Tathagata, the Bodhisattva, the Master, Lord, or Teacher, the Eye or the Light of the World, the Blessed or the Awakened One.

2. *Pre-Existence and Miraculous Birth*. The Bodhisattva had for ages been a heavenly spirit until in the fullness of time he entered the womb of Queen Maya, wife of the great King Sakya of the Gotama family in northern India. At his birth, the Devas, or angels, as in Luke 2:14, raised their voices in heavenly song.[29] But the Queen, his mother, overcome by the supernatural birth she had given, departed this life and ascended to heaven in a miraculous assumption very much like that later accorded to Mary. A venerable rishi came to the palace and foretold the destiny of the newborn savior.[30] The prophet declared that this child "will rule the world," and that he "shall give up his royal estate from the domain of the five

senses, with resolution and with diligence practise austerities, and, thus awakening, grasp the truth."[31]

We are told that the child's foot was marked with the Wheel of the Law.[32] The prophet-seer declares that "having forsaken his kingdom . . . He will proclaim the way of deliverance to those afflicted with sorrow . . . now overcome by misery, destitute of every refuge."[33] The fond father, revolving in his mind these disturbing prophecies, sealed his heir away from the world, surrounded him with every luxury, and in due time married him to the unblemished princess Yasodhara, who bore him a splendid son Rahula.[34]

3. *Gains Knowledge of the World.* Gautama, however, yearned to observe life outside the royal gardens; and the king was at last constrained to give consent. In spite of every precaution, the young man witnessed old age, disease, and death; and learned that these are inevitable for all. Upon his return, the saddened prince was not beguiled by the bevies of beautiful women with whom the king had surrounded him. All he could think of was that "youthful beauty soon fades, destroyed by old age, disease, and death . . . This is the great distress."[35]

Again, the young man ventured forth and discovered that men are born to weariness, poverty, suffering, and sorrow; and "anguish pierced his soul afresh, to see those laborers at their toil, struggling with painful work, their bodies bent, their hair disheveled, the dripping sweat upon their faces, their persons fouled with dust."[36]

4. *Abandons Home and Family.* At this point, now approaching the well-established thirtieth year, the prince decided he must become a mendicant-ascetic to seek escape from the Wheel of Life. And so he abandoned father, foster-mother, wife, son, relatives, houses, lands, and riches to seek the Kingdom of Righteousness.

5. *Studies the Doctrines of the Ascetics.* First, he came to the Wood of Austerities, the Painful Forest, in which six Brahmana ascetics practiced rigorous self-mortification. Gautama, however, found that all this hardship could, at best, lead only to a temporary sojourn in heaven; it could never lead to Nirvana, because it did not guarantee any

radical transformation of the moral nature. Turning his back, therefore, upon these men, he declared that he sought a higher law. All the religious teachers he had so far met were, he said, "like the man born blind, leading the blind man as a guide,[37] as in Matthew 15:14.

Arriving at the hermitage of the great Gaina sage Arada, Gautama listened intently while the renowned ascetic expounded his system, which, of course, rejected Brahmanism, here described as the way "of ignorance and doubt."[38] We must achieve that "inward rest and peace" by which "the idea of 'I' departs, and the objects of 'I'; clearly comprehending the non-existence of matter is the condition of immaterial life."[39]

But the metaphysical idealism, as well as the *Upanishad* theory of the universal soul, which lay at the base of the Gaina philosophy, left Gautama unconvinced. For he never believed that finite souls are mere particles of the Supreme Self which can subsist as isolated atoms. He sought instead a doctrine which would remold and reweld the bond of human fellowship shattered by Brahmanic divisiveness; and he sought, not the mastery *over* desire, but the complete emancipation *from* it, and from all objects of sense. And so the young saint rejected Arada's doctrines with respect, but with finality.[40]

6. *Rejects Asceticism*. With the celebrated, independent sage Gaya, Gautama then practiced abstinence for six years until his body was emaciated into skin and bones. He perceived, however, at last that ultimate happiness can never be attained by mortification, by isolation, or by self-denial. He concluded that true sinlessness has meaning only when it exists in one enjoying his full strength and in complete possession of his organs and his faculties.[41] The real saint would renounce only the duties and the obligations of the world, but none of its comforts or security. And so the great sage bathed, took food, and, thus refreshed, seated himself under the celebrated Bodhi tree; he resolved never to go thence until he comprehended fully the pathway to salvation.[42]

Later, when the ascetics of other breeds, like the disciples of the Baptist beholding Jesus, saw how the Tathagata conducted himself, "They said to one another, 'This is Gautama who has come hither, the ascetic who has abandoned self-control,' " who " ' wanders about now, greedy, of impure will and unstable.' "[43]

7. *The Great Temptation.* And now, in his still weakened condition, he was compelled to endure *his* great temptation. Mara, the god of this world and the Lord of desire, rebuked the Tathagata for rejecting the religion of his fathers; offered empire and wordly power; told the sage that he should perform his political duties when young, and become saintly in his old age. Mara's three daughters, Lust, Thirst, and Delight, lavished their wiles upon him in vain. They upbraided him for abandoning his duties toward parents, wife, children, home, as only the Evil One would do; they painted the life of the prosperous householder and virtuous king in the most glowing colors.[44] But the saint saw through all the stratagems of Mara, who, cowering in fear,[45] slunk at last ignominiously away, and left the Bodhisatva in triumphal peace.[46]

And now a great light burst upon Gautama: for he comprehended the Four Noble Truths and the Eight-Fold Path which lead to salvation. Sitting under the Bodhi-tree in ecstatic contemplation, the sage became the Buddha, the Enlightened One, "the Bhagavat, the Arhat, the King of the Law, the Tathagata . . . the Lord of all science."[47]

8. *First Converts.* The six Brahmanic Bhikkshus whom Gautama had met in the Painful Forest became his first convert-disciples. Next, he converted fifty-four Yasas, noble companions of his former days. He gave these sixty perfect *Arhats* their charge, exactly as another religious teacher was to do some six centuries later in Palestine. We read: "Go ye then through every country, convert those not yet converted."[48]

9. *King Bimbasara.* King Bimbasara, the first royal disciple, was followed by many others, who, renouncing everything, and equipped with orange robe and begging bowl, assumed the houseless state. It must have been a great inspiration to Sudras and Parasavas to know that, in

becoming ascetics, they were members of so glorious a fellowship!

10. *The Samgha*. And now the Buddha made a revolutionary innovation at about the same time that a parallel development was taking place in southern Italy under Pythagoras. Rejecting the Existentialism of the Gainas, Gautama founded holy brotherhoods and sisterhoods; and he provided communal homes, donated by wealthy converts, for their comfort and protection. Thus he restored the bond of human fellowship: men and women were no longer to be isolated atoms, living unto themselves alone. They became organized societies, sharing their property as well as their ministrations and aspirations. They forsook the world, but they no longer forsook each other; they rejected marriage, family, home, and labor, but they did not reject humanity. These Bhikkhus and Bhikkhunis were the prototypes of the monks and nuns who appeared some eight centuries later in Catholic Europe, Egypt, and Asia Minor.

11. *Conversion of His Father and Son*. The Buddha returned to his home, where his father was anguished to see his royal son begging for food. The Tathagata, like Jesus, was "moved with pity for the multitude,"[49] and performed miracles, which prompted the conversion of the king, together with all his household, including Yasodhara and Rahula: "the people all were filled with faith."[50] His aunt and foster-mother Gopiti became the head of a convent.

12. *Amrapali*. Buddha now made one of his great conquests by converting the celebrated courtesan Amrapali, who immediately donated her palace to his monks as a home of rest.[51]

13. *His Ministry*. And so for forty-five years Gautama trod the highways and the byways of India, making "millions of ascetics, disciples, Arhats, sages, mendicants, and fasters—and delivering from their ills the blind, the humpbacked, the lame, the insane, the maimed, as well as the destitute—and establishing many persons of the fourth caste in the true inactivity and inaction."[52]

And so the great prophet converted harlots, robbers,

and other criminals; he called unto himself the poor and the ignorant, women, children, slaves, Sudras, and outcastes. And in this religion all were glorified.

14. *Death of Gautama.* The Buddha declared:[53] "I shall not die until this pure religion of mine shall have . . . been well proclaimed among all men!"[54] At the age of eighty, he decided to leave this world, and enter his well-earned rest. When his soul passed, "the great earth quaked throughout" and "up to the heavenly mansions flames burst forth; the crash of thunder shook the heavens and earth, rolling along the mountains and valleys . . . The sun and moon withdrew their shining."[55] After all, an incarnate god, the savior of the world, could scarcely depart without some strange disturbances of nature![56]

E. BUDDHISM AS AN ESTABLISHED RELIGION

1. *Early Development.* Scholars believe that Gautama was born in or about 557 and died in 477. There is no doubt that the principal features of his religion—such as the Four Noble Truths, the Eight-Fold Path, and the organization of celibate orders—were established by the founder himself. Buddhism in time produced a large number of sacred books and, as is the case with all ancient religions, no one knows by whom or just when these were written. As there was no writing in India in the fifth century, B.C., such scriptures must have been transmitted orally from one Tathagata to another. We know that by the end of Gautama's life, his teaching had spread far and wide and he had a multitude of followers. In the year of his death, the First Council was held at Ragagriha under the leadership of Buddha's most important disciples, Kasyapa, Ananda, and Upali. Just a century later, the Second Council was held at Vesali.

2. *King Asoka.* During the subsequent period, Buddhism made enormous progress; and in 256 B. C. occurred the greatest single external event in its history, when King Asoka, ruler of the territory which now approximately comprises modern India, Afghanistan, and

Baluchistan, was converted; he made Buddhism the state religion; he erected temples, shrines, altars, and monuments throughout his realm; and he issued many edicts to establish the faith. In 242, he presided at the great Third Council held at Pataliputra, his capital, at which the Buddhist canon—thereafter accepted as divinely revealed—was established and closed; and various questions dealing with doctrine and discipline were resolved. The basic documents of Buddhism, therefore, derive from the third century, B. C.

3. *Missionary Activity.* Immediately after the great council at Pataliputra, an immense proselyting campaign was undertaken. Buddhist missionaries penetrated every portion of the then known world, including Greece, Egypt, Baktria, Asia Minor, and the Second Persian Empire. Palestine must have been permeated by Buddhist ideology during the first century. It would have been impossible for anyone to remain unaffected by its doctrine. However, the new faith won its most signal victories in the Far East. In 241, Mahendra went to Ceylon, and converted its political leaders. That country remains Buddhist to this day, and the faith is still widespread in Burma, Siam, Bangkok, Japan, China, and Tibet.

4. *The Golden Age of Buddhism.* The golden age of Buddhism, therefore, came in the third century, B. C. But its strength was also its weakness; it won adherents by revolutionary renunciation, but by the same token it cut off the source of wealth and, even worse, threatened *the continuity of the race.* Slowly, gradually, Brahmanism won back India; for, even though it was an onerous system, it demanded labor, and encouraged human propagation. It absorbed a good deal of the Buddhist philosophy, including toleration, and became Hinduism. Buddhism itself, however, expelled from India, was constrained to modify its pristine doctrines in order to survive.

5. *Doctrine.* The Four Noble Truths of Buddhism are those about sorrow; the cause of sorrow; the cessation of sorrow; and the path which leads to its cessation:

"When these noble truths are grasped and known, the craving for existence is rooted out . . . and there is no more birth."[57] The Eight-Fold Path consists of "Right Views; Right Aspirations; Right Speech; Right Conduct; Right Livelihood; Right Effort; Right Mindfulness; and Right Contemplation."[58] Buddha declared that these Noble Truths and this Eight Fold Path constitute the Middle Way to salvation, avoiding alike the worldliness of the Brahmanas and the harsh asceticism of the Gainas. "I, then," he said, "reject both these extremes; my heart keeps in the middle way."[59] The victorious Bhikkhu could even wear fine clothing, enjoy comfortable living quarters, and eat nourishing food without sin, so long as he did not *crave* these material things or *perform any labor to obtain them*.[60] His body must never be subjected to abuse, torture, or starvation. And so Buddhism became, in its maturity, the creed of idle and indigent voluptuaries.

The six-spoked Wheel of the Law remains to this day the symbol of Buddhism, as the Cross is that of Christianty; and it represents the victory of the Arhat over the six deadly sins, all of which originate in the body; any craving arising from sight, taste, smell, touch, hearing, or in the mind itself can only lead to pain, torture, and misery. The Wheel of the Law must therefore be implanted in the heart of man to stop forever the motion of the Wheel of Life.

Buddhism made salvation an internal, not an external, process. Again and again in history similar developments have taken place: any religion which, like Brahmanism, long enjoys exclusive power, creates a privileged priesthood and establishes forms, rituals, and ceremonies which have nothing to do with man's moral regeneration or the ethical inter-relationships of society. Buddhism declared: as man thinketh in his heart, so is he. "All that we are is the result of what we have thought: it is founded on our thoughts, it is made up of our thoughts."[61] Hatred and anger, resentment and hostility, must be replaced by tranquil love. A true conversion is the *sine qua non:* that is, the whole of life must be directed by new aspirations into new channels. In this, outward acts or religious rituals are without efficacy: "Neither the flesh of fish, nor fasting, nor nakedness, nor tonsure, nor matted hair, nor dirt, nor rough skins, nor the worshiping of the fire, nor the many immortal penances in the world, nor hymns, nor oblations, nor sacrifices, nor observances of the seasons, purify a mortal."[62] Thus the sacraments and ceremonials so dear to every priesthood were repudiated. The great battle must be fought out within the mind; the victory must be over the self: "If one man conquers only himself, he is the greatest of conquerors."[63]

The gospel of Buddha, like that of Jesus,[64] was offered to every one: "As the rays of the sun and moon descend alike on all men, good and bad . . . so the wisdom of the Tathagata shines like the sun . . . upon all."[65] Jesus repeated the very same idea in Matt. 5:45.

F. THE SAMGHA: THE HOLY BROTHERHOOD

1. *A Social Reconstitution.* As we have noted, Gautama organized his disciples into a new kind of community, intended at a single stroke to dissolve the bonds of tribe, clan, nation, city, village, and family, replace all these by voluntary associations of male and female celibates, dwelling together solely for meditation and spiritual edification.

2. *Barriers against Admission.* Instead of using persuasion to recruit membership, the *Samgha* erected barriers against admission; it established a rigorous discipline; and it expelled those who proved indocile. One can easily see why members would fear expulsion: for in addition to shipwreck in the life to come, this involved no small deprivation in the present. For many of the monks and nuns—often former Sudras, slaves, outcastes, and harlots—lived comfortably and with little or no effort in monasteries and convents which had formerly been the palaces of nobles, kings, or wealthy courtesans. Such gifts were a reasonable price from Kshatriyas to pay for political victory over the Brahmanas. The only exertion on the part of monks, we read, consisted in walking—a

very healthy and, we take it, necessary exercise for these quiescent saints. No wonder that the poor, the despised, the downtrodden, the disinherited of the earth came flocking to the Buddhist order by the thousands, where they could live, not only in comfort, but also in security and idleness.

Those considered worthy were admitted to the sacred circle. Taking the vow of poverty, chastity, and obedience, as Brahmana students had done since time immemorial, they assumed the yellow robe, and, turning their backs upon the world, entered the holy life of communist celibacy and equality.66

3. *Expulsion.* We read that any "Bhikkhu who is angry, and who bears enmity in his heart . . . remains without reverence for, and without delight in, the Teacher, the Dhamma [Doctrine], and the Samgha [Brotherhood], and does not fulfill the duties of the disciple."67 Such an evil person must be put away, removed, expelled. The same peremptory treatment must be applied to any one who is hypocritical, envious, jealous, crafty, treacherous, or who has "sinful desires and false beliefs; who is tarnished by love of worldly gain, devoted to getting and taking, for whom to renounce a thing is hard."67

4. *Elaborate rules of Conduct.* As time went on, codes almost as elaborate as the Brahmanic, accredited to Gautama himself, were developed to regulate offenses for which a Bhikkhu must be expelled: first, for having carnal knowledge of woman or beast; second, for committing theft; third, for inciting to suicide; and, fourth, for claiming knowledge which he does not possess."68

G. THE ETHICS OF BUDDHISM

1. *In Personal Relationships.* The ethical system of Buddhism is its most important feature; and especially so to us, since it reappears substantially unaltered in the Gospel Jesus. We must never be proud, nor harbor anger or resentment against any one. Whosoever exalts himself shall be degraded;69 harsh language must never be used to anyone.70 "Let a man overcome anger by love . . .

evil by good . . .; the greedy by liberality, the liar by truth!"[71] "Let us live happily, then, not hating those who hate us . . . among men who are greedy, let us dwell free from greed!"[72] We must not scrutinize the mote in another's eye, and fail to see the beam in our own.[73] No matter how unjustly one is attacked or abused, one must never strike back at an aggressor.[74] This was the Buddhist commandment to turn the other cheek.

2. *Communist Practice.* We are to live happily, calling nothing our own;[75] if we possess two garments, we must give one to a needy Bhikkhu who is less fortunate.[76] This was the same ideal which Jesus expressed when He said that if any one demands our coats, we should surrender our cloaks also.

3. *The Wickedness and Foolishness of Wealth.* The story of the rich man who goes to hell occurs in Buddhist as well as in Gaina literature. The man who is enslaved by wife, children, lands, and stores declares: "'Here shall I dwell . . . in winter and summer,' . . . and does not think of his death. Death comes and carries off that man, praised for his children, and flocks . . . as a flood carries off a sleeping village."[77] The cravings of ignorant and sensual men are insatiable; no quantity of wealth is ever sufficient. We read: "If the whole world and all treasures were yours, you would still not be satisfied, nor would all this be able to save you;"[78] which is also the message of Jesus.[79]

4. *Alms and Gifts.* Although the Buddhist *Arhat* despised the world, he was in no hurry to depart, nor did he scorn the good things therein. Alms or gifts to the saints are, therefore, always represented as of incomparable virtue.[80] The greatest virtue of laymen consisted in supplying Arhats with their every need.[81] And, most of all, they should provide them with monasteries or rest homes, complete with pleasant walks and gardens. It seems that the idle saints wished to live like royalty. We are told that anyone who gives a monastery to the *Arhats* will himself at death attain Nirvana;[82] and again, that even though the Blessed One could be attacked with impunity, had Mara attempted to prevent the giving of

alms to *Arhats,* his head would instantly have been split into a thousand pieces.[83] One of the principal objectives of Gautama was to divert the gifts of householders and Kshatriyas from the Brahmanas to his own disciples. And so he made asceticism comfortable and attractive.

5. *The Internal Contradictions.* And now we come upon the same contradiction which is implicit throughout the Gospel Jesus. For in this Buddha-teaching, which purports to radiate so much gentleness, mercy, non-violence, forgiveness, brotherhood, humanity, non-aggression, universal love, and benignity toward enemies, there blazes up suddenly a fierce and implacable hatred toward all those who abuse the brethren or reject the doctrines of the Master. For all these, the fires of hell blaze hot and long, and its tortures are elaborated with excruciating refinement.[84]

The step between condemning an opponent to hell and laying violent hands upon him in the here and now has, unfortunately, proved very short in the bloody history of religious persecution. If every heretic is possessed by the devil and must, at all events, burn in hell, why not give him a slight foretaste without delay? Buddha and Jesus inculcated love among the brethren and non-resistance to superior force; but there was little love or toleration for skeptics, Brahmanas, or Pharisees; that is, for religious opponents or for anyone who doubted the truth of their revelations.

6. *Monks Demand Privileges and Immunities.* In time, the Buddhist monks—although they never sought to control civil society as such—began to claim almost as many privileges and immunities as had once been the lot of the Brahmanas: "Those who scoff and hoot at monks . . . shall have their teeth broken and separated . . . disgusting lips, a flat nose, contorted hands and feet, squinting eyes, a putrid body covered with stinking boils, eruptions, scabs, and itch. If anyone speaks an unkind word concerning them, true or not true, . . . it must be considered a most heinous sin."[85] Even the most wicked monks must therefore be immune from criticism.

H. SUPERSTITIONS

Buddhism borrowed generously from Brahmanic supernaturalism and elaborated upon it. Various charms and spells were to be used by Buddhist missionaries; and when these were hurled against the creatures of darkness, "No one shall overpower or hurt such preachers: no goblin, giant, ghost, devil, imp, sorcerer, spectre, gnome."[86] If a person is bound in fetters, he has but to think of these mighty spells, "and the bonds shall be speedily loosened."[87] The pious monk was assured that "his body can never be hurt by weapons, fire, poison, sticks, or clods."[88] Buddhist propagandists were provided with ample protection: "I shall rouse, excite, and stimulate them, and give them spells whereby those preachers shall become inviolable, so that no being, either human or not human, shall be able to surprise them, and no woman able to beguile them. I will protect them . . . avert blows, and destroy poison." [89] This is also the promise of Mark 16: 17-18.

I. THE PARABLES OF BUDDHISM

1. *Purpose.* The literature of India proves that Jesus drew heavily upon Buddhism, directly or indirectly, to obtain not simply the content of His ethics, but the very form in which it was delivered. Both Gautama and Jesus found the parable effective, since it provided a necessary and convenient disguise through which "men of good understanding will . . . catch the meaning."[90]

2. *The Parable of the Jewel.* The Parable of the Jewel which a man finds in a field[91] was the recension of a Buddhist allegory: A certain man entertained a friend at his home and secreted a jewel within his robe, who "unaware of it, goes forth from that place and travels to another town. There he is befallen with misfortune and, as a miserable beggar, seeks his food in affliction. Under these circumstances he is seen by his old friend who . . . shows him the jewel within his robe," the value of which "is such that he becomes a very rich man, of great power

... In like manner, O Lord, we were unaware of our former aspirations laid in us by the Tathagata himself in previous existences from time immemorial."[92]

The revolutionary implication is unmistakable. The man who fell into misfortune symbolized the oppressed of India; the jewel was the gospel of Buddha which would accomplish his emancipation.

3. *The Parable of the Prodigal Son.* Most elaborate among Buddhist parables is that of the Prodigal Son,[93] which emphasizes the same theme and which was adapted in the Gospel Jesus for application to the Jewish-Gentile problem. By virtue of the Buddhist victory, "we have acquired a great heap of precious jewels such as we were not thinking of ... It is like the history of the young man who, seduced by foolish people, went away from his father and wandered to another country, far distant." Oppressed with sorrow, the father searches for his son; at last, he settles in a great city, where he becomes very rich. Becoming old, he yearns for his lost son, who bears an unmistakable similarity to the ascetics of India and who "is wandering from village to village, poor and miserable, seeking food and clothing ... his body vitiated with scabs and itch."

Arriving at his father's magnificent mansion, he fears forced labor and flees. The father recognizes his son, and sends messengers, whom the son fears as executioners. The father realizes that he must not reveal to his son at once his great destiny because he is so stupid and ignorant, as a result of long degradation; he therefore provides him with menial labor. Little by little he wins the son's confidence by allowing him to enter the house. When the son is sufficiently prepared, the father calls together all the neighbors, citizens, and members of his household and declares him his heir. "On a sudden today we have been seized with surprise, just as the poor man who acquired riches; now for the first time have we obtained the fruit under the rule of Buddha."

The father is the creator of the world; the great mansion is India; the foolish son represents the poor and downtrodden, who, by means of the new gospel, will again come into their own, overthrow the Brahmanas, take possession of the country, and again be rich and powerful. As the prophet declares: "We have no doubt, no uncertainty whatever, that we shall become supreme amongst men."[94]

And so this revolutionary and proselytizing religion, which began as a strike of poor men against the obligations of family and fatherhood, aspired to universal dominion.

4. *The Ethical Contradiction.* And we can scarcely fail to note that in the Buddhist as in our Gospel parables, normal values prevail: pleasure is desirable, and deprivation a calamity; poverty constitutes misery: and wealth is not only desirable, but highly laudable as well. Servants are often lazy, deceitful, and criminal, while kings are just, generous, virtuous, and beneficent. The parables betray the fact that in the eyes of the oppressed, luxury is an evil only because their enemies alone possess it; for in the imaginary realms which they construct for themselves, they revel in surfeit.

J. THE KINGDOM OF RIGHTEOUSNESS

1. *Twofold Meaning.* The Kingdom of Righteousness runs like a red thread through all the Buddhist scriptures, as does the Kingdom of Heaven in the Gospel Jesus; and in both evangels, it has a two-fold meaning: first, it is a moral entity, to be set up in the heart and the mind of the saint; and, second, a physical reality to be established one day on earth. In that glorious kingdom, in which the saints shall have achieved final victory, the renovated earth "will be filled with high edifices . . . monks will be exempt from . . . punishment and from womankind; . . . they will lead a spiritual life, have ideal bodies, be self-lighting, magical, moving in the firmament, strenuous, of good memory, wise, and possessed of gold-colored bodies."[95]

2. *Renunciation Abandoned.* As the Buddhists became socially and politically dominant, they cast off even the mild renunciation of their founder, and were no longer content with the prospect of Nirvana. Instead,

they anticipated personal immortality after death and residence in a great city of sensuous delight which was to have seven ramparts, made of gold, silver, crystal, beryl, agate, coral, and "one of all kinds of gems."[96] And in this wondrous city, the Great King of Glory will maintain the faithful in perpetual luxury.[97]

3. *The Essential Contradiction.* And so once again the essential contradiction of Buddhism lies starkly revealed: in heaven, the righteous will luxuriate precisely in those very things which it is the greatest infamy to possess in this life. As the rulers were rich and idle, and as the laborers were poor and weary, the mere possession of wealth and ease was the ineradicable badge of iniquity. In heaven, however, by a divine poetic justice, all things will be reversed: the Great King will give every material blessing to the poor of the earth, who become righteous because they renounce what they cannot obtain. And in heaven there need be no injustice or exploitation, because food, clothing, gold, palaces, jewels, etc., will all be produced by divine fiat, and there all will live eternally in blissful repose.

K. BUDDHISM TRIUMPHANT

1. *Nagasena.* We have already cited *The Questions of Melinda*, written in Ceylon about 100 B. C., where Buddhism had become the dominant faith. The hero of the piece is the sage Nagasena, who, like so many other religious teachers, came into the world through a virgin birth.[98] As a child, we are told, he learned the three canonical *Vedas* in one moment "by heart, could intone them correctly, understood their meaning . . . and grasped their mysteries;" but "he found no value in them;" they were worthless, "empty as chaff."[99]

We find in *The Questions* certain accretions to doctrine and practice, absent from the original Buddhist canon: for example, purgatory has now become an established eschatological feature, and bathing to purify from sin an essential ritual.[100]

2. *Unavoidable Contradictions.* The most significant

portions of the work deal with the problems which arose with the triumph of Buddhism. Since it was devised to escape the oppression of a ruthless and impregnably intrenched ruling class, its strength lay in its power to withdraw the labor on which the whole social superstructure rested; its weakness lay in the fact that, should its ideals be victorious, these must be remade or ignored, since they called for the extinction of the race. Many contradictions, therefore, had arisen which critics were quick to emphasize; and when King Melinda of Ceylon (called Menandrasa by Plutarch) was converted to Buddhism, no one but Nagasena could resolve his doubts, which he struggled valiantly to do, in a series of mythical conversations. For example, the king notes that "the Blessed One said: 'Doing no injury to anyone, dwell full of love and kindness in this world.' And on the other hand he said: 'Punish him who deserves punishment' . . . if the first injunction is right . . . the second must be wrong."[101]

To which the Venerable Nagasena replies: "The Blessed One . . . gave both commands you quote . . . But as to the second command . . . that is a special use of terms . . . The proud heart, great king, is to be subdued, and the lowly heart cultivated."[102]

In due course, the king inquires whether Nirvana can be attained otherwise than by living as a recluse and a celibate.[103] At great length, Nagasena explains that many millions of laymen who do not renounce the world are nevertheless *Arhats;* the puzzled king wonders "what purpose . . . these extra vows serve . . . if laymen, living at home and enjoying the pleasures of sense, can see Nirvana."[104]

There was a good question! And the prolixity of the reply indicates the incompatibility of Buddhism with life itself. The sage, however, finally devises a solution: anyone who, in his last incarnation, has rigidly observed the thirteen vows, achieves *Arhatship* in the present life.[105] No longer do the saints pass immediately into Nirvana upon death; for they "will be reborn only once more on earth."[106] And so the celibate of a former incarnation receives a double reward; for he appears once again on earth as a Vaisya- or Kshatriya-*Arhat,* enjoying once more the pleasure of sense[107] before eternal oblivion.

3. *Original Buddhism Swept Away.* This novel doctrine opened the door wide to almost everything that the founder of Buddhism had condemned so virulently. Now there could be millions of comfortable or wealthy laymen who, merely by giving verbal assent to the Buddhist philosophy and by persuading themselves that they had been ascetics in their previous existence, could marry, rear children, produce goods, own houses and stores, engage in business, manufacture, or agriculture, employ laborers at small wages, and still imagine themselves to be *Arhats* because of virtue acquired in a former incarnation. And so, in spite of all doctrine and discipline, men and women went on with their immemorial task of reproduction and of earning their livelihood. An almost precisely parallel development took place in Christianity once it took root. *As it was in the beginning, is now and ever shall be, world without end. Amen! Amen!*

L. INFLUENCE UPON CHRISTIANITY

We have noted that the Brahmanas became the models for the official Catholic clergy and that the Buddhist movement was incorporated into Christianity in the fourth century as monachism; and thus the Church took to its bosom both of the great and antagonistic religions of India.

Buddhism, however, exercised another and even greater influence upon Christianity: for much of its ethical system passed almost intact into its pristine Gospel, probably as an independent influence upon Jesus Himself, although much of this philosophy was almost identical to that held by the Pythagorean Essenes. In this morality, the following principles are dominant: we must practice brotherhood, charity, and communism among the Elect; before God, all humanity is equal; it is wicked to possess wealth; all property constitutes a moral contamination of which we can be purged only by giving it to the poor; only the indigent can be righteous; we must divest ourselves of the world and all its works; we must renounce sex, family, father, mother, sister, brother, child, and relations; we must give all that we possess to those poor who have renounced the world, who have not where to lay their heads; we must return love for hate, kindness for abuse; we must never retaliate against those who injure us; above all, we must rid the heart and mind utterly of all anger and resentment; sin consists not so much in outward acts, as in the desire to perpetrate them; there must be a cataclysmic moral transformation called conversion, by which we conquer the evil indwelling self, and create the kingdom of righteousness within ourselves. Jesus also agreed with Buddha that religion should be separate from the civil government and that religious men should obey the established secular laws which, in turn, should never dictate to the conscience. Buddhism made this ideology the common possession of the ancient world.

We said at the beginning that four basic elements constitute the Gospel Jesus: soteriology, ethics, eschatology, and the Messianic concept. The first, as we have seen, came from the mystery-cults, and the second from Zoroastrianism. And now we find that its ethics were derived, at least in part, from Buddhism.

We observe also that the doctrine of the Virgin Birth, without which no prophet or savior-god could be a divine incarnation, was so common among ancient cults that it was impossible for any religious founder to achieve acceptance without it. It was, indeed, unknown in Brahmanism or Judaism; but these exercised little or no influence on the Gospel Jesus. In the mystery-cult, in Zoroastrianism, and in Buddhism, all saviors, past, present, and future, were incarnate gods, born of human virgins; this was an idea which came so easily and so naturally to primitive priests in order to establish their own authority that it sprang up independently in many places; Jesus was simply accorded the same honor by universal demand after His cult began making converts in the pagan world.

CHAPTER X

PYTHAGORAS

A. HISTORICAL SKETCH

1. *A Universal Genius.* Many think of Pythagoras, cir. 580-500, only as a geometrician; but his activities included every field of knowledge. Diogenes Laertius declares that he did not "neglect medicine,"[1] and that he was the first who taught metempsychosis.[2] And he *was* the first who propagated this doctrine in the Graeco-Roman world, declaring that he could remember four previous incarnations.[3] He made important contributions to music and astronomy; he was a metaphysician, a natural philosopher, a social revolutionary, a political organizer, and the universal theologian. He was one of those all-embracing intellects which appear at rare intervals.

2. *Pythagoreanism in Italy.* Ancient literature teems with references to Pythagoras. From the beginning of his manhood, he was engaged in intense political activity; and he was driven from his native Samos in 529 by the tyrant Polycrates, who judged him subversive. He thereupon migrated to Italy, and at Croton established a school of philosophy where he lectured to classes consisting of six hundred students. He created also a political organization which exercised a very wide influence. This consisted of celibate brotherhoods whose objective was their own moral regeneration through a communist reorganization of society. The Pythagorean order was therefore at once economic, religious, and political. Although it must originally have been designed only as a community of dedicated saints, the astonishing fact is that the Pythagoreans in less than two decades became so

numerous and so powerful that they were able to assume the public power without any resort to force. Since this was a drastic reconstitution, which sought to halt the progress of society into private property, by reversion to communism, violent repercussions were inevitable. In 510, the tyrant Cylon attacked the revolutionaries and drove them out of Croton after which they reorganized at Metapontium, where Pythagoras met his death by an assassination concerning which various versions are extant. According to one, he was burned in a temple, like Zoroaster; according to another, he was murdered in a beanfield, because he would not cross it; according to a third, he starved himself to death as a protest against the prevailing luxury and gluttony.

3. *The Massacre of the Pythagoreans.* Following the death of Pythagoras, the brotherhoods again grew rapidly in what was known as Magna Grecia (southern Italy) until about 450, when the protagonists of private property and monogamic marriage assaulted the saints everywhere, murdered them indiscriminately, and sacked and burned their residences. There was particularly a House of Milo in Croton (a communal dwelling for the brethren), which was surprised, and in which fifty or sixty of them were slain. Diogenes Laertius says that many others were burned at the stake in mass executions. Thus, the world's first communist revolution (or counter-revolution) was drowned in its own blood. Everything indicates that the Pythagoreans, like the early Buddhists, practiced non-violence and non-resistance; for even though they were at one time in control of society, they neglected to provide themselves with arms; and they never raised their hands in self-defence. Their only weapons remained a fervent appeal to the moral sense, the threat of hell, and the promise of eternal bliss in heaven. There is a curious passage in St. Basil which illustrates their ethics by relating an incident in which Socrates took revenge on a drunken ruffian who mutilated his face only by writing on his own forehead: "This was so-and-so's doing."[4] The Buddhist-Pythagorean-Essene morality required of one smitten upon one cheek to turn the other also.

4. *Movement Becomes Solely a Religious Cult.* The massacres at Croton marked the end of Pythagoreanism as an overt political force. One of its outstanding protagonists, Lysis, escaped to Thebes, in Greece, where he became the tutor of the noble Epaminondas. Philolaus, one of the great expositors of Pythagorean philosophy, also lived and worked in Thebes at the end of the fifth century; but he was able to return to Italy with others of the brethren, including Archytas, where they established a great center at Tarentum. After 350, Pythagoreanism became far less a philosophical school than a purely religious cult; and as such it continued to attract devotees and exercise direct influence for at least seven or eight centuries. This we learn from many sources; and particularly interesting is a passage[5] in Justin Martyr which explains that when, as a youth, he eagerly sought enlightenment, he went first to a "very celebrated" Pythagorean; but when he was told that before he could be initiated into esoteric mysteries, he must first master music, geometry, and astronomy, he was discouraged and turned to the Platonists instead. Presumably, these also required too much; for shortly we find him a Christian lecturer in Rome.

We learn something of practical Pythagoreanism as it existed in the first century from *The Life of Apollonius of Tyana*,[6] according to which this prophet and wonderworker had a divine birth, absorbed the wisdom of Pythagoras, and practiced celibacy, vegetarianism, and voluntary poverty; he healed the sick, cured the halt and the blind, drove out devils, restored the dead to life, foretold the future, and taught the mysteries of religion. Finally, it was said that he never died, but went directly to heaven in a physical assumption.

B. GENERAL PHILOSOPHY OF PYTHAGORAS

1. *Monotheism.* The Pythagoreans were definite monotheists, as various Christian writers bear witness: "God is one; and He is not . . . outside of the frame of things, but within it; but, in all the entireness of His being, is

in the whole circle of existence . . . the mind and vital power of the whole world." [7] According to this pantheistic concept, God becomes a universal, spiritual force, an idea which the Stoics were to adopt. It is clear that no anthropomorphism could attach itself to such a theology; and the Pythagoreans naturally forbade any representation of the deity in pictures or statues,—in this respect resembling both the Jews and the Zoroastrians.

2. *Dualism.* A passage in Archelaus[8] attributes the dualism of Manes to Pythagoras, who was thus credited with originating the doctrines he borrowed from the Brahmanas and the Persians because he first proclaimed them in Greece. The Zoroastrian base of Pythagorean metaphysics is revealed in the doctrine that the soul, which is our higher principle, is imprisoned in this mortal body as in a tomb, and that the latter is governed by evil passions, which are our indwelling Furies.[9] We must not, declared Pythagoras, be the slaves of our own bodies;[10] and we can improve and save our souls by escaping from the domination of the flesh.

3. *Consequent Attitude Toward Sex.* As sexual consummation was considered the prime pandering to the indwelling Furies, every passion, in fact, every symbol related to it must be repudiated. We know that the Pythagoreans felt an overwhelming horror for beans; Diogenes Laertius says that this was, according to Aristotle, because they resemble the human testicles. Hippolytus declares that it was because, when they decay, they emit an odor similar to that of human seed; and when sprouting from the ground, they resemble the female genitals.[11]

4. *The Third Repudiation of Marriage.* And thus we find that by the sixth century B. C. there had already appeared three important movements in which men repudiated marriage: and for three quite different reasons. The primitive Orpheans did so because of what they considered the extreme misconduct of women; the Buddhists to escape Brahmanic exploitation; and the Pythagoreans because of metaphysical dualism, which made all sexual passion the mark of ultimate wickedness, the essence of original sin.

5. *The Master's Sojourn in Hell.* Perhaps the most important single element in the Pythagorean myth was the descent of the Master into hell and his seven-year residence there, which made him the final authority on this subject. In spite of the skepticism of Tertullian, Eusebius, and other Christian writers, the ancient pagans believed this tale just as implicitly as Christians accept the existence of heaven and hell, which, oddly enough, Pythagoras himself first introduced into the occident. Diogenes Laertius states that when Pythagoras returned from the nether world, he related that he had seen Homer and Hesiod suffering tortures because of their slanders against the gods; and he says that Hermippus had related that the great prophet "came up withered and looking like a skeleton, then went to the assembly and declared that he had been down to Hades . . . His disciples were so affected that they wept and wailed, looking upon him as divine."[12] Pythagoras assured all who did not embrace his doctrine and discipline that the tortures of this dreadful place were prepared especially for them, while mansions in heaven awaited his own elect. According to Eusebius, "Pythagoras . . . declared to the Italians that the doctrines which he had received . . . were a personal revelation to himself from God."[13]

6. *Literature.* Diogenes Laertius states that Pythagoras wrote three books,[14] of which none were extant in the third century, A. D. A book by Lysis, however, and others by Aston of Croton and by Philolaus, all credited to the Master, were still available. At the beginning, all Pythagorean teachings were reserved strictly for the initiated; but later, various documents were made available to the public explaining the less recondite aspects of the cult. The central mysteries, however, remained the sole possession of the Elect.

7. *The New Communism.* In order to comprehend Pythagoreanism, we must understand the great social forces at work in that extraordinary sixth century. Private property, class divisions, and economic exploitation had broken down the equalitarianism of the primitive community: it was therefore communism which was conservative or

reactionary, and private property which was dynamic and revolutionary, carrying within itself an intense individualism, constituting a new center of loyalty, which in time made the adhesions of communal society impossible. Pythagoreanism sought to re-estabish communism, but on a higher plane than that of primitive society, which was an automatic growth; the communism of Pythagoras was to be regulated by the strictest social control. It was intended to achieve the greatest possible good, but for a society consisting of, and acting in unison as, self-determining individuals. Pythagoreanism certainly did not succeed in its objective; but it did remold the ethical standards, the spiritual interests, the speculative doctrines, and the metaphysical concepts of the ancient Greek world. Had it not been for Pythagoras, the doctrines of hell and heaven might never have permeated the occident.

Not only did that sixth century consolidate the position of private property; it was also the first in which man became introspective and self-conscious. It was therefore a period of great religious upheaval throughout the world; men began asking the ultimate questions: what are we? whence came we? whither do we go? what is the mystery of life? In Persia it was Zoroaster who attempted to solve these conundrums; In India it was Gautama and Mahavira; in China it was Confucius; in Judea it was Ezekiel and Jeremiah; and in Greece it was Pythagoras, the greatest of them all.

C. THE PYTHAGOREAN ORPHEUS

1. *Appropriation of the Eleusinian Dionysus.* The third and last great revolution in Orphean theology occurred when it was taken over by Pythagoras late in the sixth century. He appropriated the *soter* of the Eleusinia, who was born as Zagreus from Zeus and Persephone, who was killed as a child and eaten by the Titans, who was reborn from Semele as Dionysus, and who became the savior of mankind. But we must separate the Orphism which Onomacritus engrafted upon the Eleusinia and that proclaimed by Pythagoras. The former contains not the

slightest hint of the Brahmanic metempsychosis, the Buddhist ethics, or the Persian dualism and eschatology with which Orphic-Pythagoreanism is surcharged. When Diodorus speaks of Orpheus' "fabulous account of his experiences in Hades and the punishments of the unrighteous . . .which are figments of the imagination,"[15] he was referring to a document written by Pythagoras or a Pythagorean, and, as usual, accredited to the Thracian prophet.

2. *Pythagoras Wrote New Orphic Poem.* When Pythagoras created his Neo-Orphic system, including its metempsychosis, eschatology, ascetic discipline, and communist brotherhoods, he set forth these innovations in "some poems of his own making" which he ascribed "to Orpheus."[16] Even as Onomacritus wrote Orphic poems describing the death of Zagreus and the origin of the human race, so Pythagoras wrote others embodying his own doctrines, which he, like his predecessors, ascribed to the original prophet.

3. *Pythagoras Absorbed All Existing Religions.* That Pythagoras absorbed the religions of Greece, Egypt, Persia, Chaldea, and India we learn from sources, of which the following are typical: "Pythagoras . . . had himself initiated into the rites and mysteries not only of Greece, but also of foreign countries . . . he learned Egyptian . . . journeyed among the Chaldeans and the Magi."[17] Clemens Alexandrinus declares that Pythagoras was a pupil of Zoroaster and a disciple of the Brahmanas.[18] Hippolytus states that "Pythagoras came to Zaratus the Chaldean, who explained to him that there are two original causes of things . . . two daemons, the one celestial, the other terrestrial."[19] A passage in Herodotus proves that even in 450 B. C. it was well known that the Orphic-Bacchic mystery was also Pythagorean and that its funerary customs were Egyptian.[20]

Pythagoras appropriated the ultimate Eleusinian savior, because he was the center of every mystery-cult. In the new synthesis, however, soteriology was only a single element: for now, at long last, eschatology and social or class ethics became equally fundamental in the doctrinal theology of Greece. By creating this amalgam, Pythagoras revolutionized the thinking and the morality of the western world in a way that still hangs heavily over our entire culture. The dying god-man was no longer sufficient for eternal blessedness, and, since this involved an elaborate system of ethical renunciation, religion ceased to consist merely in ceremonies, rituals, and festivals, or even in an elaborate and difficult theology: it became a radically transformed way of life, a rigorous and lifelong discipline.

D. PRE-PYTHAGOREAN ESCHATOLOGY

1. *Egyptian.* At this point, let us briefly recapitulate the eschatology from which Pythagoras drew in order to formulate his own. In Egypt, we found that only a small proportion of all souls ever reach the judgment seat; the rest simply fade into nothingness. Those fortunate enough to stand before Osiris and to be adjudged worthy by him, were admitted to the Elysian Fields, where they continued in very much the same manner as in their earthly lives. Those souls adjudged wicked were destroyed when the beast Apep ate the heart and when the *Khu* was thrown into the Lake of Fire. The concepts of metempsychosis, universal immortality, or a system of post-mortem punishments were unknown.

2. *Persians.* In Persia, the immortality of every human soul was assumed. But there was no metempsychosis: each birth involved the creation of a new soul which could belong to one human being only. At death, the righteous went to heaven, the wicked to hell, where terrible tortures were to be inflicted upon them until the renovation of the universe. For those who were neither wicked nor righteous, a third place, *Hamestagna,* was prepared, in which souls would be retained until the judgment. Finally, the Zoroastrians were universalists: at the renovation of the universe, all souls were to wade through a river of molten metal for three days, and, as a result of this purification, achieve everlasting blessedness.

3. *Brahmanism.* Again, we found that the eschatology of the Brahmanas was quite different: for, together with

the caste system, they devised the doctrine of transmigration and gave souls to every fish, fowl, insect, and beast. And to the caste system and to the doctrine of metempsychosis, they added a realistic concept of hell-torture, more detailed and ferocious than that of Persia. All of this was an instrument of class suppression and exploitation; but, as it turned out, the doctrine of hell was a two-edged sword: for the Gainas and Buddhists turned it against their enemies, the Brahmanas.

E. THE PYTHAGOREAN SYNTHESIS

1. *Greek Communism.* Neither Buddhism nor Gainaism had been established in India at the time when Pythagoras could have journeyed there; but the ideology of these movements was already rife, and the Samian sage could have absorbed them, as he certainly did. There was, however, an important difference: for the Pythagoreans did not repudiate labor; but instead of working for an exploiter or for self-aggrandizement, they were the first who established the principle: from each according to his ability, to each according to his need.

2. *The Amalgam.* Orphic-Pythagoreanism was the world's first great synthesis of religious components. We find, first, the Dionysiac sacrament, by which the devotees were believed to achieve divinity; second, the doctrine that souls transmigrate from age to age until, by Orphic initiation and life, they attain blessed immortality or, by outrageous sin and crime, are consigned to eternal hell-torture; third, the conviction that all humanity is metaphysically separated into the children of light and those of darkness, the Elect and the Reprobate, and that only the former have the power of adopting the Orphic way of life; fourth, the persuasion that the essence of righteousness consists in renouncing all carnal and material things, all the sensuous pleasures of this world; fifth, the conclusion that by adopting the celibate, communist, vegetarian, and equalitarian way of life, all aggressions will cease and salvation be assured.

Pythagoras imported into the Grecian world the metaphysics and eschatology of Persia, the metempsychosis of Brahmanism, the ethics of the *Upanishads,* and the funerary customs of Egypt, and united all these with the Orphic-Dionysiac soteriology. The only significant alterations made by him were, first, his institution of a perpetual hell for the incorrigibly wicked and his abolition of Nirvana in favor of eternal mansions in heaven for his Orphic saints; and, second, his rejection of an idle mendicant brotherhood in favor of one which was industrious and self-supporting and, therefore, proud and aloof, self-respecting, and independent. Buddhist monachism was adopted by the Catholic Church; the Pythagorean by the Essenes.

F. ORPHIC-PYTHAGOREAN TOMBS

We know that Orphic-Pythagoreanism was first established and flourished in southern Italy near Croton and in the valley of the river Crati. A few decades ago, a number of tombs in this region were excavated, each of which yielded a stone casket within which were the remains of a body covered with a white linen sheet; but most interesting were the golden tablets, inscribed with Orphic verses.[21] These had a purpose similar to the Papyri scrolls which Egyptians deposited in their coffins, and indicate that Pythagoras had adopted certain Osirian funerary customs, just as Herodotus and Diodorus declared. One of these scrolls, dating from the fourth century, reads:

"Thou shalt find to the left of the House of Hades
   a spring . . .
To this spring (Lethe) approach not near.
But thou shalt find another from the Lake of Memory...
Say, 'I am a child of Earth and starry Heaven:
But my race is of Heaven alone . . . Give me quickly
The cold water flowing forth from the Lake of Memory'
And of themselves they will give thee to drink of the
   holy spring,
And thereafter among the other heroes thou shalt have
   lordship."

One inscription states that the deceased has become a god because he has "suffered the suffering" while others declare:

"I am of your blessed race . . .
And I have paid the penalty for deeds of unrighteousness . . .
I have flown out of the sorrowful, weary circle,
I have passed with swift feet to the diadem desired. . . .
And now I come a suppliant to holy Persephoneia,
That of her grace she send me to the seats of the hallowed."

We find, therefore, first, that the newly departed soul is to discover two springs of water, one on the left, the other on the right. The former is the fountain of Lethe, of which it is to drink *after* each millennial sojourn in the ghostly realm. But that on the right is the fountain of Mnemosyne, or memory, that cool, refreshing river of life, of which it must quaff before entering the realms of eternal bliss, as in Revelation 21:6. Second, we find that the soul of the Orphic is a child of Earth and starry Heaven; which is to say that he was in part divine or spiritual and in part material and earthy, as predicated by the Zagreus-Titan myth. "But my race is of Heaven alone," the soul is to declare; for it has purged itself of its Titanic elements. And, therefore, after drinking of the waters of life and memory, it becomes a hero, that is, a deified soul. Third, we discover that the soul becomes divine through renunciatory suffering. Fourth, we note that the soul is of the blessed race, a child of light or spirit which has purged away its inborn and original sin; it has paid the penalty for deeds of unrighteousness committed by its ancestors, the Titans; its lower, Ahrimanic nature has been destroyed by the mortification of the flesh. Lastly, we discover that the Orphic was to escape the Wheel of Life, "the sorrowful, weary circle," and pass directly to his everlasting reward.

Orphic-Pythagoreanism introduced into Greece and Italy the doctrines of dualism, of original sin, of necessary suffering and renunciation, of metempsychosis, of hell and heaven, of judgment after death, and of escape into eternal bliss through sacramental initiation and communal brotherhood from an otherwise endless circle of miserable birth and death.

G. PYTHAGOREANISM IN CLASSICAL LITERATURE

We find here the ultimate manifestation of Osiris-Dionysus; yet even *this* split into two divisions: the philosophic or literary, and the definitely cultic. Such thinkers as Heraclitus, Empedocles, and Plato absorbed and adopted its dualism and eschatology by the fourth century B. C., even though they rejected it as a mystery-cult; and through Plato the Pythagorean eschatology became the common heritage of the Graeco-Roman world.

1. *Aristophanes.* Aristophanes, who was born some twenty years before Plato, wrote a rollicking satire called *The Frogs.* In this, the Eleusinian aspiration for immortality is treated with reverence, and Ceres (Demeter) is hailed as the "holy patroness." One passage, however, proves that Orphic-Pythagorean eschatology, although already familiar, was still a fit subject for ridicule among the upper classes. Since he had been in Hades and was therefore an authority concerning it, Hercules is made to declare:

> "There's an abyss of mire and floating filth,
> In which the damn'd lie wallowing and o'erwhelmed;
> The unjust, the cruel, and the inhospitable: . . .
> The perjurers, and assassins, and the wretches
> That wilfully and presumptuously transcribe
> Extracts and trash from Morsimus's plays."

Aristophanes made these new-fangled but already popular doctrines the butt of his satire. He did not, however, ridicule everything attributed to Orpheus; for later in the drama we find a serious passage which describes an older phase of Orphean mystery-religion and which refers

to the transformation of the Dionysiac *omophagia* into
a symbolic eucharist:

> "Orpheus instructed mankind in religion,
> Reclaimed them from bloodshed and barbarous rites;
> Musaeus delivered the doctrine of medicine,
> And warnings prophetic for ages to come."

2. *Plato.* We turn now to Plato, 427-347, who came at the peak of the Athenian renaissance. There is so much of Gospel doctrine in his writings that Justin Martyr never tired of reiterating that Plato must have been versed in Christian prophecy. It was common knowledge that he was a disciple of Pythagoras; and to this fact many ancient authorities bear witness.[22] As if to summarize all his predecessors, Eusebius declares: "Plato, more than any one else, shared in the philosophy of Pythagoras."[23] Indeed, the works of Plato teem with Pythagorean eschatology.

We may, then, expect to find the teachings of the Samian in the writings of Plato who was, however, a philosophic Pythagorean and never an Orphic cultist. He had only contempt for those who taught or believed that God could be persuaded or bribed to confer blessed immortality upon an initiate, merely because he performed special ceremonials, sacraments, and rituals, because he accepted certain doctrines or revelations, or even because he adopted a way of life involving ascetic renunciation. Plato believed that the moral law was fixed and immutable, that our fate depends upon our actions during life, and that each of us has the power to rise above his Titanic nature. He believed that only a virtuous life can lead to eternal happiness. In his *Laws,* he declares that there are three subversive ideas concerning the gods: first, that they do not exist; second, that although they exist, they do not care about mankind; and third, that although they exist and do care for us all, they can be bribed or propitiated by sacrifices or ceremonials.[24] Plato therefore excoriated as charlatans those Orphic prophets who promised salvation in return for a specific ritual and particularly those who offered to relieve a man's ancestors of hell-torture,[25] another doctrine first invented by the Brahmanas and adopted by the Catholics.

It was Plato's view that blessed immortality was to be achieved rather through a life of virtue and philosophy than through the rites of the mystery-cults: "true virtue . . . temperance, justice, fortitude, and wisdom itself, are a kind of initiatory purification. And those who instituted the mysteries . . . have intimated long since that whoever shall arrive in Hades unexpiated and uninitiated shall lie in mud, but he that arrives there purified and initiated, shall dwell with the gods. 'For there are,' say those who preside at the mysteries, 'many wand-bearers, but few Bacchoi.' These last, in my opinion, are no others than those who have pursued philosophy rightly."[26]

There is another significant passage in which Plato reveals his Orphic-Pythagorean dualism: "Now some say that the body [soma] is the sema [tomb] of the soul, as if it were buried in its present existence . . . the followers of Orpheus . . . hold . . . that the soul is undergoing punishment for some reason or another, and has this husk around it, like a prison, to keep it from running away."[27]

We find one Thrasymachus declaring that the unjust and wicked are most happy and fortunate because they can enjoy their ill-gotten gains throughout life and can, at death, through public gifts and charities, purchase the good opinion of their contemporaries.[28] "But," declares one Cephalus in reply, "be assured that after a man begins to think he is soon to die, he feels a fear . . . about . . . a future state . . . that the man who hath done injustice here must there be punished. . . . He becomes therefore full of suspicion and dread . . . and is awakened from sleep as children by repeated calls, is afraid and lives in miserable terror."[28]

In the *Gorgias* 523-4, Plato describes in great detail the scene of judgment in the grove of Persephone, reminiscent of the golden Orphic funerary inscriptions, and says that it will occur "in a meadow, where is the fork from which lead two roads, the one to the Islands of the Blest, the other to Tartarus." In still another passage, Plato summarizes the Orphic-Pythagorean eschatology, which declared "that vengeance for such acts" as murder "is exacted in Hades, and that those who return again to this earth are bound to pay the natural penalty,—each culprit the same, that is, which he inflicted on his victim,—and that their life on earth must end in their meeting a like fate at the hands of another."[29]

And so we see that in a little more than a century, the Pythagoreans had filled the Greek world with terror concerning future punishments formerly ridiculed or unknown. And now we turn again to *The Republic*,[30] where we find the most detailed exposition of Orphic-Pythagorean-Platonic eschatology. We are told that a Pamphylian whose name was Erus, having died in battle, sojourned in Hades for twelve days, after which he returned to his fleshly tenement and declared that "his soul . . . came to a certain region of spirits, where there were two gulphs in the earth . . . and other two openings in the heavens . . . and judges that sat between them. And . . . they commanded the just to go to the right hand, and upward through the heaven . . . but the unjust they commanded to the left, and downwards."

In Plato, as in Matthew, therefore, each is judged according to his deeds; the wicked stand on the left, the righteous on the right: "And he saw there, through the two openings, one of the heaven and one of the earth, the souls going away, after they were judged; and . . . he saw, rising through the earth, souls full of squalidness and dust; and he saw souls descending pure from heaven." All these "told one another" of their millennial sufferings below and "explained their enjoyments and spectacles of inexpressible beauty" in heaven. But for "whatever injustice any had committed . . . they were punished for all these separately and tenfold."

These were the ordinary souls returning for another earthly incarnation after their respective millennial sojourns in hell or heaven. However, even as Orphic saints never returned to earth, so there were others, egregious criminals, who, like one Aridaeus, could never escape the tortures of hell; as prototypes of the subsequent Christian devils, there were "fierce men and all of fire to look at" who "took . . . Aridaeus and the rest, binding their hands and their feet, and thrusting down their heads and pulling off their skin . . . tearing them on thorns, declaring . . . on what accounts they suffered these things, and that they were carrying them to be thrown into Tartarus."

Erus then describes the scene in which the souls who had spent their allotted time in the other world prepared to re-enter the earthly life. Many went into birds or wild beasts.

It may be pertinent to add that Plato was, like Pythagoras, a thorough-going communist, believing private property to be a divisive force which drives the crafty, the greedy, and the more capable members of society to countless acts of aggression against their fellow-men. There was, however, a sharp difference between Pythagoras and Plato in their attitude toward marriage; for while the former, as we have seen, repudiated the institution entirely in favor of celibacy, Plato, wishing the race to increase and multiply, or at least to continue in stable numbers, believed in the community of all husbands, wives, and children, since only under such a system would all men, in his opinion, love all children as their own.

3. *Philemon.* How widespread the Orphic-Pythagorean eschatology became shortly after Plato's time is indicated by a passage from the Greek dramatist Philemon, who flourished at Athens early in the third century B. C. "Think'st thou," he asks, that men "escape the notice of divinity?" If "good and bad" are without reward or punishment after death,

> "Then go thou, rob, steal, plunder at thy will,
> Do all the evil that to thee seems good.
> Yet be not thou deceived; for underneath
> There is a throne and place of punishment set,
> Which God the Lord of all shall occupy."[31]

To all the Orphic-Pythagoreans, including Plato, it was simply inconceivable that mankind could be governed by equitable moral principles without the fear of eschatological retribution.

4. *Vergil.* The Aeneid, written about 30 B. C., sets forth the Orphic-Pythagorean eschatology in detail. The poet tells us that all souls drink of the fountain of Lethe before reincarnation so that they will have no memory;[32] and that in all the universe there is "one universal, animating soul" from which proceed man, "beasts, and birds of air, And monsters that in marble ocean roll."[33] But human souls "in darkness and in chains" cannot attain the celestial realm until their "fleshly grossness and corporeal stains" are purged away.

> "Therefore are they wracked with pains,
> And schooled in all the discipline of woe:
> Each pays for ancient sin with punishment below."[34]

This original or inherited sin resembles the *kharma* of the Brahmanas and that Pauline sinfulness in our members, which so oppressed St. Augustine. It is not merely our own sin which must be purged away, but something ancient and inherent in our nature. The poet continues:

> "Some hang before the viewless winds to bleach;
> Some purge in fire or flood the deep decay
> And taint of wickedness. We suffer each
> Our ghostly penance; thence, the few who may,
> Seek the bright meadows of Elysian day,
> Till long, long years, when our allotted time
> Hath run its orbit, wear the stains away,
> And leave the aetherial sense, and spark sublime,
> Cleansed from the dross of earth, the cankering crust
>   of crime.

> "These, when a thousand rolling years are o'er,
> Called by the God, to Lethe's waves repair;
> There, reft of memory, to yearn once more
> For mortal bodies and the upper air."

We could cite other pagans such as Plutarch, who depicts the tortures of the damned;[35] but it is scarcely necessary to belabor the thesis further: by the first century B. C.

the Orphic-Pythagorean eschatology had penetrated every level of society in the Graeco-Roman world; and among the hopeless masses it had become an obsession.

H. THE PYTHAGOREAN BROTHERHOODS

1. *A Way of Life.* Since all the literature of the elusive Pythagorean brotherhoods has been lost, and since they provoked nothing but contempt from the great pagan writers, we are forced to glean our knowledge of them from fragmentary references. We find in them at a time even preceding Buddhist monachism, a religion which was not merely a mystery-cult, not simply a theology and an eschatology, but an all-embracing way of life. These tightly-knit groups of celibate men who renounced family and private property were called *thiasoi* and constitute one of the most astonishing phenomena of history. Their metaphysical and speculative doctrines were those of Plato and Vergil; but their discipline and their soteriology were something totally different.

2. *Initiates Became Bacchoi.* It is very doubtful that these brotherhoods possessed temples, or constituted religious congregations in the modern sense; but it is certain that they were bound together by the strictest vows and by the strongest moral, doctrinal, and emotional bonds. Euripides makes Theseus twit his son because he had turned bookworm and Orphic-Pythagorean, and was "so holy that no flesh where life hath been feeds thee who has Orpheus for thy king."[36] And in another passage from the same dramatist we are told that the initiate "is set free and named by name a Bacchus of the mailed priests, robed in pure white, clean from man's birth and coffined clay, while from his life is ever banished touch of meat where life hath been."[37]

3. *Vows, Discipline, and Sacraments.* All Pythagoreans were vegetarians who renounced sex, family, and private property. There were also societies of female celibates because we read that "the virgin daughter of Pythagoras was the head of a band of virgins and instructed them in chastity."[38] We are told that Pythagoras "distributed his

pupils into two orders, and called the one esoteric, but the other exoteric. And to the former he confided more advanced doctrines. . . . Whenever anyone repaired to him with a view of becoming his follower, the candidate-disciple was compelled to sell his possessions, and lodge the money with Pythagoras, and he continued in silence to undergo instruction, sometimes for three, but sometimes for five years. And on being accepted, he was permitted to associate with the rest; and remained as a disciple, and took his meals along with them; if otherwise, however, he received back his property, and was rejected. These persons, then, were styled Esoteric Pythagoristae."39

The Esoterics were the Elect who, at the end of life, would escape the circle of birth and death; the holy meals to which they were finally admitted were the daily sacrament in which they consumed the body of Dionysus symbolically and so became immortal Bacchoi. Initiation was an irrevocable step; once the hand was laid to the plough, there must be no turning back. Origen tells us that "the Pythagoreans used to erect a cenotaph to those who had apostasized from their system of philosophy, treating them as dead."40 Diogenes Laertius declares that the Pythagoreans practiced baptismal purification constantly41 to renew and maintain their sanctity, a ceremonial which the Jewish Essenes adopted from them.

4. *Teachings and Practices.* Laertius declares that Pythagoras forbade his disciples to pray for themselves; he enjoined chastity; he required them "to put all their possessions into one common stock;" he lectured to them for five years while they remained silent, after which, if they passed their examinations, they were permitted to speak to the Master and be initiated into the brotherhood. He forbade not only the eating but also the killing of any animal or other living creature, since all of these share with us the privilege of possessing a soul; his disciples ate uncooked food only and pure water was their drink. Their sacrifices or sacraments "were always inanimate." Together with his Esoterics, Pythagoras wore a spotless white robe of linen; wool was prohibited, since

it came from an animal. He prescribed the most intense ethical soul-searching as a daily discipline. He forbade all use of oaths, declaring that it is a man's duty "to make his own word carry conviction." He required his disciples to give honor and precedence to their elders in the order of their worth and seniority. He taught that we must regard nothing as our own private property, that we must support the established government, that we must never injure any living creature, that we must never give way to such emotions as fear, grief, or hatred. He believed that gods (divine agencies) and men are akin, that is, that they are emanations from the same universal soul, which is God. Providence is a divine fact, and constitutes that fate by which the world and every individual life is ordered. The soul is distinct from physical life, is alone immortal, and its essence is Reason, which is indestructible. "The most momentous thing in human life is the act of winning the soul to good," that is, of enabling it to escape this physical prison house and the power of the Furies which infest it. We must always pay divine worship to God, in reverent silence, in white robes, after daily purification, which is to be had by cleansing and lustration, by avoiding contact with death and birth and all pollution, by abstention from the meat of animals, and by performing the mystical rites of the cult.

5. *Communist Brotherhood.* We must also emphasize that, according to the Pythagoreans, the practice of communist brotherhood was the minimum prerequisite for blessed immortality, since only under such a system can ethical purity be attained or injury to our fellow-men be avoided. Aggression and exploitation are not, according to Pythagoras, the only crimes: the mere enjoyment of comfort or personal wealth while others suffer want is a sin for which there can be no forgiveness and cries for vengeance to the throne of God.

6. *Emotional Basis of Communism.* The ethical foundation of Pythagoreanism was simply that, since it is impossible to obtain private wealth except through social injustice, and more important, since all members of the human race are blood brethren and therefore equally

worthy, it is impious for any one of them to possess more than any other. This is the overwhelming fact which all the Elect will realize and the principle by which they will reconstruct their lives. Under this morality, it becomes the inescapable duty of the capable and the industrious to support those who cannot or do not work. It is obvious that this can never be a rational principle: it belongs in the realm of emotion.

I. SPREAD OF PYTHAGOREANISM

1. *Fervent Missionaries.* In Pythagoreanism we have the first great fusion of almost all the basic elements which constitute the Gospel Jesus; and we know that the ancient world was filled with erudite and fervent missionaries who preached these doctrines in a manner similar to that later described in the Christian *Didache*. It was these propagandists whom Plato regarded with such loathing and contempt. "Mendicant prophets," he declared, "go to rich men's doors and persuade them that they have a power committed to them by the Gods of making an atonement for a man's own or his ancestor's sins by sacrifices or charms . . . binding heaven, as they say, to execute their will. And they produce a host of books written by Musaeus and Orpheus . . . according to which they perform their ritual, and persuade not only individuals, but whole cities, that expiations and atonements for sin may be made by sacrifices . . . which . . . are equally at the service of the living and the dead; the latter sort they call mysteries, which they say redeem us from the pains of hell, but if we neglect them we shall incur the most dreadful doom."[42]

Such were these Orphic prophets who claimed the power to bind and to loose in heaven; who performed mysterious rituals, sacrifices, or sacraments intended to save the soul from hell; who claimed authority and power to relieve the tortures of the damned; who based their preaching upon scriptures said to be divinely revealed; and who promised to redeem their disciples from their personal as well as their original sin.

2. *Continuity of the Thiasoi.* We know from a passage in Plato that in his day the Pythagorean societies were well known: "Even in this day such as denominate themselves from the Pythagorean manner of life appear to be somehow eminent beyond others."[43] Although we possess only scant information concerning the *thiasoi* after the fourth century B. C., there is little doubt that they continued at least to the time of Josephus; for he declares that the Essenes "live the same kind of life as do those whom the Greeks call Pythagoreans,"[44] which proves that both of these disciplines still flourished during his lifetime.

CHAPTER XI

ISIS AND SERAPIS

A. ISIS

1. *Her Independent Cult.* The worship of Isis probably became an independent Egyptian cult near the close of the Middle Kingdom, which was concluded by the XVIIth Dynasty in 1580. And during the succeeding millennium under the New Kingdom, her shrines and temples spread into every corner of the land. Statues of Isis suckling her infant son were familiar to all; in this characteristic pose, she became the venerated madonna of the pre-Christian world. For centuries, Catholics mistook these images for Mary-Jesus. Sometimes, Osiris was depicted with his wife and child; and the three became the type of the Holy Family.

2. *Spread of Cult.* The cult of Isis appeared in Syria about the 7th century B. C. It was not, however, until the Hellenistic period beginning in 333 that it began spreading rapidly; in that year, a temple was erected for the goddess at Piraeus. During the reign of Ptolomy I Soter, 323-285, she became so popular in Greece that a great temple was built for her at the foot of the Acropolis; and in the ensuing centuries, as we learn from Pausanias, almost every Greek city and village had its Isis-temple.

Her cult, introduced into Italy in the second century B.C., was even more successful in the West. By 58 B.C. it had altars on the Capitoline and fifty-three chapels in Rome alone. In spite of sporadic persecution, in 43 the triumvirs ordered the erection of a temple to Isis and Serapis. In the first century of our era, the cult possessed several fine temples in Rome.

3. *Conflict with Christianity.* In the second century A. D., the Isis-cult became a bitter and effective antagonist of Christianity and numbered among its initiates many outstanding Romans. With the accession of Constantine, the shrines and temples of Isis were everywhere razed. It was not, however, until the time of Justinian, about 560, that the last remnants of her worship at Philae were extirpated. The independent cult of Isis, therefore, enjoyed a continuous existence exceeding two thousand years.

4. *A Composite Goddess.* The cult of Isis possessed such vigor and longevity because she encompassed within herself the virtues and attractions of all her competitors; her ceremonials were elaborate and solemn; her dramatic presentations convincing and fascinating; her promises scarcely to be outdone; and her discipline delightful to souls burdened with sin and guilt.

5. *Sacraments and Festivals.* The eucharist of Isis consisted of the bread which she had given mankind and the milk which flowed from her bosom; the chalice from which the initiate drank this sacred potion was a cup formed in the shape of a woman's breast.

We know also that Isis, like Demeter, had two great festivals, one in the spring and another in the fall: the former coincided with the Egyptian harvest, and was celebrated at the vernal equinox, March 20. The autumnal celebration, however, was the greater, and consisted of a passion play which continued for four days; although the date varied in different places, it usually began on October 31, and ended on November 3. On the first day, actors impersonating Isis, Nephthys, Anubis, Horus, etc., searched for the body of Osiris; weeping and wailing, they manifested all the signs of grief. On the two days following, the portions of Osiris were found, reconstituted, and resurrected. This was the central element in the myth, for if Osiris could regain life and become immortal through the power of Isis, then all her devotees could do the same. The fourth day of the festival was called the *Hilaria* and was given over to the most unrestrained rejoicing since the god, now risen into immortality, would

be the kindly judge of all who had become divine by
drinking the milk of Isis. And there could be little doubt
concerning the future felicity of those who put their trust
in her; for assuredly, Osiris would not deny mercy to
those for whom Isis made intercession when they appeared
before his awful throne.

6. *Veneration for Chaste Mother Goddess.* There was
one important element in the Isis-cult which made it
unique: the veneration of the chaste and beneficent Mother-
Goddess. Fortunately, a classic called *The Golden Ass*
written in the second century A. D. by Lucius Apuleius
gives us a great deal of information concerning the cult.
In this celebrated tale, the author, drinking the potion
of a witch, was turned into an ass, and could regain his
normal shape only by eating roses. At last, the glorious
Isis appears to him in a dream, informing him how to
find the necessary flowers; and he addresses her as the
"blessed Queen of Heaven . . . the Dame Ceres . . .
motherly nurse of all fruitful things on earth." In reply,
Isis declares herself "nature's mother, mistress of all the
elements, the first-begotten offspring of all the ages, of
deities mightiest, queen of the dead. . . . The Phrygians,
first-born of men, call me the mother of the gods that
dwell at Pessinus; the Athenians, sprung from the soil
they till, know me as Cecropian Minerva; the wave-beaten
Cyprians style me Venus of Paphos; the Archer-Cretans,
Diana of the hunter's net; the Sicilians, with their three-
fold speech, Stygian Proserpine; the Eleusinians, the ancient goddess Ceres. Others call me . . . by my true
name, Isis the Queen."

Isis had become the symbol and the synthesis of all the
great goddesses of love, protection, creative life, and
maternal nourishment which the world had ever known.

Apuleius is at last initiated into the order and becomes
a priest; he dares not reveal the secrets of the mystery,
but the experience itself he preserves in the following
dithyramb: "I drew nigh to the confines of death . . . I
approached the gods above, the gods below, and worshiped them face to face."

In the author's hallucinations, the deity appeared as the

"Holy and eternal protectress of the human race" who "tendest the mischances of miserable men with a sweet mother's love . . . givest the light to the sun, guidest the universe, and tramplest under foot the powers of hell . . . At thy word, the winds blow, the clouds give increase, the seeds spring to birth, and the buds burgeon . . . My voice is too poor in utterance to tell what I feel concerning thy majesty. Nay, had I a thousand tongues, and everlasting continuance of unwearied speech, it would be all too little."

7. *Mary Becomes Isis.* When the Gospel Jesus first emerged, it was devoid of a mother-goddess. However, since the ancient world was permeated with the cults of Demeter, Cybele, and Isis, it was impossible for Christianity to conquer without filling the void created by their departure. And in this, as in everything else, the Catholic Church demonstrated the accuracy of its name: it was indeed all-inclusive. As the need for the protective and beneficent goddess of chaste, maternal love was imperative, the Virgin Mary gradually grew from the woman to whom Jesus would not even speak into the magnificent replica of Isis, Queen of Heaven.

B. THE CULT OF SERAPIS

1. *Growth in the Graeco-Roman World.* The name Serapis was formed by combining Osiris with Apis, the bull; and this god was the Hellenized version of his Egyptian prototype, in which his functions were combined with those of the somewhat parallel Greek deity, Hades or Aidoneus. It is certain that the ithyphallic aspects of Osiris were heavily emphasized and that Serapis was related to Priapus, son of Dionysus and Aphrodite, who symbolized the generative principle. The worship of Serapis came into wide vogue after the conquests of Alexander, first in Egypt and then throughout the Graeco-Roman world; although he certainly retained some of the characteristics of the ancient Osiris as well as some congenital relationship with Isis, his cult seems to have become independent in the third century B. C. We

read in Socrates Scholasticus that even in the fourth century A. D. the Egyptians believed that if Serapis were offended, the Nile would not overflow.[1] The center of the worship was in Alexandria, where a Serapeum was built during the Ptolemaic dynasty; like all the other mysteries, its esoteric doctrines and practices were jealously guarded secrets, known only to its mystics.

2. *Destruction by the Christians*. In 390, Bishop Theophilus, with the aid of Emperor Theodosius, razed the Serapeum of Alexandria. "And he had the phalli of Priapus carried through the midst of the Forum . . . the governor of Alexandria and the commander-in-chief of the troops of Egypt assisted Theophilus in demolishing the heathen temples . . . All the images were accordingly broken in pieces, except one statue of the god before mentioned, which Theophilus preserved and set up in a public place; 'Lest,' said he, 'at a future time the heathen should deny that they ever worshipped such gods.' "[2]

3. *Pagan World Moving to Destruction*. And so, in that pagan world of freedom and diversity, each could choose whatever religion he liked best; but analysis reveals that mankind was plunging headlong into a general disaster for which no solution could be found and as a result of which some international and intolerant religion was inevitable to administer a fantastic soporific, to offer the masses hope and consolation, and to expunge by universal ruin the ineradicable frustration created by the Roman Empire.

CHAPTER XII

MITHRAISM

A. A ZOROASTRIAN SYNTHESIS

1. *Combined with Other Elements.* The worship of Mithra had been carried to completion under the Arsacids, whose language was Pahlavi, whose religion was Zoroastrian, and who founded the Parthian Empire in 248 B. C. Mithraism issued from the heart of Zoroastrianism, but absorbed various Chaldean characteristics, including much zodiacal and astrological symbolism, and was profoundly influenced by the ubiquitous mystery-cults of Asia Minor, particularly that of Attis-Cybele, which, as we have seen, flourished in Phrygia, a territory in the domain of the Arsacidae. When Christianity arose two centuries later, it did so independently of Mithraism; yet the two cults were astonishingly similar, because they were composed of elements which were the common possession of Asia Minor. Renan declared that had Christianity not conquered, Mithraism would have emerged victorious; our own opinion is that the child of Mithraism known as Manichaeism would have become the faith of the ancient world.

2. *Opinions of the Christian Fathers.* Here then we have the world's second great religious synthesis. Because of its similarity to Christianity, the fathers could only declare that the devil had established Mithraism for the sole purpose of sowing confusion. Justin Martyr declared: "Jesus took bread, and . . . said, 'This do ye in remembrance of me, this is my body'; and, after the same manner, having taken the cup and given thanks, He said, 'This is my blood'; and gave it to them . . . Which the wicked devils have imitated in the mysteries of Mithra, command-

ing the same thing to be done."¹ Tertullian was certain that all rival cults were the devil's handiwork: "Washing is the channel through which they are initiated into the sacred rites of some notorious Isis or Mithras; . . . at the . . . Eleusinia they are baptized" to achieve "regeneration, and the remission of" their sins. "Which fact being acknowledged, we recognize here also the zeal of the devil rivalling the things of God, while we find him, too, practicing baptism."²

Tertullian states that Mithra "in the kingdom of Satan, sets his marks on the forehead of his soldiers; celebrates also the oblation of bread, and introduces an image of resurrection. . . . What also must one say to Satan's limiting his chief priest to a single marriage? He, too, has his virgins; he, too, his proficients in continence. . . . Satan has shown such emulation in . . . administration of Christ's sacraments" that he has "succeeded in adapting to his profane and rival creed the very documents of divine things and of the Christian saints."³

And again: "Blush . . . to be condemned by some soldier of Mithras. . . . Let us take note of the devices of the devil, who is wont to ape some of God's things with no other design than, by the faithfulness of his servants, to put us to shame."⁴

3. *Close Parallel to Christianity*. The fact is that the parallel between Mithraism and apostolic Christianity was actually far more extensive than any of the early Fathers implied. Both taught almost identical doctrines concerning heaven and hell, the last judgment, and the immortality of the soul. Both practiced the same sacraments, those of baptism and the communion of bread and wine. Regeneration through the second birth was a basic doctrine of both, and each had the same conception concerning the inter-relationship of their members,—that all were mystical brethren. Each believed that its founder was mediator between God and man, that through him alone was salvation possible, and that he would be the final judge of all. Both taught the doctrine of primitive revelation. Both emphasized the constant war-

fare between good and evil, required abstinence and self-control, and accorded the highest honor to celibacy.

We need not be surprised at these similarities, since we know that Mithraism and Christianity were alike based upon ubiquitous doctrines and practices already hoary with age before these cults appeared.

4. *Later Christian Debt to Mithraism.* Christianity borrowed significant elements from Mithraism *after* they had become active competitors: Justin Martyr declared that "in a certain cave near Bethlehem ... Mary brought forth the Christ ... those who presided over the mysteries of Mithras were stirred up by the devil to say that in a place called among them a cave, they were initiated by him."[5] The Christians, in time, made Sunday, which the apostolic Church had never observed but which had always been sacred to the Mithraists, their holy day. And, after several centuries, they made the 25th of December, which had always been celebrated as the birthday of Mithra, that of Christ also. Until the fourth century, and in some eastern churches as late as the sixth, the Christians celebrated Epiphany, or January 6, both as the date on which Jesus was born and that on which He was anointed into Christhood at His baptism. It is interesting to note that this was the very day which for centuries had been hallowed by the Egyptian cult of Persephone as that on which she gave birth to Dionysus, known as the aeon. The ancient Mazdeans had glorified December 25 as the day when the sun-god was reborn, for then it was apparent that the days were growing longer and that life would again revive. During the preceding night, the devotees of Mithra kept vigil; and when the dawn fringed the earth with its first gleam of light, the priest emerged from the temple to announce triumphantly: "The God is born!" And so when the Christians made December 25 the birthday of their savior also, they made as great a concession to the Mithraists as they had previously made to the Attis-Cybele cult when they accepted March 22-25 as the date of Christ's passion.

B. HISTORICAL SKETCH

1. *Rapid Dissemination under the Roman Empire.* Although Mithraism does not seem to have made much progress among the Greeks, it spread rapidly among the Romans and the barbarians. We learn from Plutarch[6] that the cult was introduced into the Roman Empire in 67 B. C. by pirates. It was attractive to the emperors and the nobles, because it taught that kingly authority is granted by Ormazd: it counted Nero, Commodus, Aurelian, Diocletian, Galerius, Licinius, Julian, and many senators among its devotees. Since Mithra was the invincible god of battle, soldiers were his particular favorites; and, with his cross branded upon their foreheads, they carried his cult to the farthest limits of the Empire. Since Mithra taught the necessity of stable government, civil servants were among his ardent supporters. And, since he thundered against social injustice and preached the brotherhood of man, the poor, the exploited, and the slaves embraced his worship by myriads, prepared to die for the faith. Mithraism, then, encouraged by the state, spread among the poor, through the army, and everywhere in the civil service. Hundreds of Mithraeums were established along the trading routes of Africa, Italy, Gaul, Spain, Germany, Britain, and the Orient. Slaves from the Middle East, transported to Rome and the provinces, sang hymns to Mithra from the Indian Ocean to points beyond the Pillars of Hercules.

2. *Strength and Weakness.* The power of Mithraism lay in its syncretism, its flexibility, its universality, its attractiveness to various classes. Its weakness lay in the fact that it could not point to an historical god-man savior, that it abandoned the Messianic concept, and that, instead of making any provision for women, it regarded them, since they were the cause of erotic desire, as the instrument of the Evil One.

C. THE ORIGINAL MITHRA

Mithraism elevated the most dynamic deity of the Zoroastrian pantheon into a position of pre-eminence. Mithra was a very ancient deity; and, since he appears in the oldest myths of both Persia and India, we know that he antedated 2000 B. C. Although he was not an Ameshaspenta, that is, one of the original seven divine powers, he was one of the greatest creations; and he must have grown progressively with the imperial expansion under Cyrus and the Achaemenides. He was the lord of heavenly light always identified with the sun; he was the god of truth, cattle, agriculture, and the wide pastures; he was also the god of battle, the protector of the good men of Ahuramazda, and one of the judges who met all souls at the Kinvad Bridge. He was, finally, the power or agency by which Ahuramazda created mankind and all other good creatures which live upon the earth; he became the Logos, for he is called "the incarnate Word."[7] Mithra became so great that he was at last substantially equal to Ahuramazda himself; and we read in the sacred scriptures of Zoroaster: "We sacrifice unto Mithra, the lord of all countries, whom Ahuramazda made the most glorious of all the heavenly gods. So may Mithra and Ahura, the two great gods, come and give us help!"[8]

Mithra granted every benefit to the righteous and visited the wicked with condign punishment;[9] he was "victory-making, army-possessing, and all-knowing;"[10] he smote all his adversaries, the unbelievers, the creatures of Ahriman;[11] he was the just and merciful god "whom the poor man, who follows the good law, when wronged and deprived of his rights, invokes for help, with hands uplifted;"[12] he was the god who kept and protected his devotees in this world and gave them salvation in the next;[13] he required sacrifices from the faithful, who must first prepare themselves with lustrations and penitential stripes;[14] he was the god of immortality, who confers everlasting mansions upon the true believers.

Such was the Mithra of Zoroaster.

D. MITHRAIC MYTH AND DOCTRINE

1. *Rejection by the Zoroastrians.* The new mystery-cult retained Ormazd and Ahriman, but abandoned the old

Ameshaspentas and Yazatas; it accentuated the metaphysical dualism of Zoroastrianism, emphasized and re-oriented its eschatology, and absorbed a variety of foreign elements. Thus panoplied, it set forth to win dominion over the human mind.

As no Mithraic scriptures or documents are extant, our analysis of the cult must be based upon fragmentary references and upon sculptures, inscriptions, and bas-reliefs. All this material has been gathered into a single monumental work,[15] from which the following reconstruction emerges.

2. *The Mithraic Myth.* The new Mithra was born miraculously, in a cave, on the 25th of December; this event was witnessed only by some shepherds, who brought gifts and adored the new-born god, a mythology reproduced in Luke 2:8-20. Having grown into a sturdy youth, he set out to become the master of the earth. First he made the sun subject to his will and was therefore associated with this luminary; he was also identified with the bull, or ox, of Zoroastrianism, which it became his duty to capture and slay. He did this reluctantly, since it was the pristine creation of the good god; but the sacrifice was imperative, because from the soul of the bull arose all the celestial spheres and from his body sprang all the life of earth, including man. From the carcass of the bull grew all useful herbs; from its spinal marrow, wheat; from its blood, the grape, which furnished the wine used in the mysteries; and from its seminal fluid issued all animals serviceable to mankind. In many of the reliefs depicting the slaying of the bull, ears of grain sprout either from its body or from the wound, somewhat as was the case with the slain Osiris; and we find Mithra holding a drinking horn in his left hand and receiving a bunch of grapes from the sun-god. The bull was sacrificed that mankind might have the bread of life, and Mithra drank his wine-blood eucharist.

Through identification with the slain bull, therefore, Mithra became the creator of all good creatures, and of all the beneficent things that grow upon the earth, as well as the progenitor and savior of man. But now Ahriman entered upon his role as the Great Adversary; and Mithra became the protector of all good men, of all useful creatures and herbage, as well as the mediator between Ormazd and the human race. When Ahriman sent a terrible drought that would have destroyed mankind, Mithra saved it by shooting an arrow into a rock from which copious streams of water emerged. When Ahriman sent a great flood, and later a great fire, Mithra enabled the human race to survive. His work now complete, Mithra celebrated ceremonially a Last Supper and returned to Ormazd; but continued from the celestial mansions to protect and encourage his devotees.

3. *Mithraism Retains Dualism.* Mithraism retained the basic cosmogony and metaphysics of Zoroastrianism; that is, it conceived of the material world as the domain of Ahriman, which Mithra had invaded to reclaim it for Ormazd. The soul of man comes from the celestial sphere, but his body from darkness. All that is physical is of Ahriman, all that is spiritual of Ormazd. All useful creatures and beneficent forces are the gifts of the latter through the agency of Mithra; all those which bring disaster or destruction are the counter-creations of Ahriman.

4. *Mithra the Soter.* The central element in the Mithraic myth is the slaying of the bull, which is replete with Osirian soteriology; this made of it a mystery-cult and of Mithra a savior-god. The event is depicted in countless friezes and bas-reliefs which have been found in the ruins of Mithraeums. Mithra is represented as a powerful youth thrusting his sword into the side of the sacred bull; the scorpion and the serpent, creatures of Ahriman, are depicted as attacking and attempting to drink the blood of the animal and thus to prevent the birth of mankind.

5. *Ceaseless Warfare Between Good and Evil.* In the Mithraic system, as in the Zoroastrian, there is a constant struggle between good and evil, light and darkness, the spiritual and the physical. In this bitter war, man can hope for victory only by the ceaseless aid of Mithra, and

by suppressing and mortifying his Ahrimanic nature; he must employ constantly the sacraments of baptism, lustration, and the communion of bread and wine to achieve mystical union with the god. As the slaying of the bull was the central element in the soteriology of the cult, it practiced the *taurobolium* in the same manner as the cult of Cybele. Initiates were placed under a grating, above which the sacred animal was ceremonially slain; thus incarnadined, the newly-inducted member was drenched and so saved in the blood of the bull.

E. MITHRAIC ORGANIZATION AND WORSHIP

1. *The Congregations.* The Mithraic congregations were not communal groups like the Pythagorean *thiasoi;* except that they contained no female communicants, they were quite similar to modern church congregations. Each was small, comprising perhaps a hundred members; as the number of converts increased, new units were established. Since Mithra was born in a cave, the "churches" themselves were built underground, or at least so as to simulate subterranean conditions.

2. *The Orders.* Jerome informs us that the Mithraic mystic passed through seven degrees or orders,[16] which reflect Chaldean influence. They succeeded one another as follows: Corax, or Raven, signifying a messenger; Cryphius, or Hidden, indicating esoteric; Miles, or soldier, symbolizing the warfare of good against evil; Leo, the Lion, representing fire; and then in order, Perses, Heliodromus, and Pater, or Father, which consisted of the order of priesthood.

3. *The Initiation.* Actual initiation into the order, however, began with the degree of Miles, when the member was branded in the forehead with the figure of a cross. Thereafter, the communicant was inducted into the higher mysteries: he took an oath never to reveal the secrets of the order and he underwent frequent purificatory lustrations. When inducted into the degree of Leo, he was purified with honey, and baptized, not with water, but with fire, as John the Baptist declared that his suc-

cessor would baptize. After this second baptism, initiates were considered *participants,* and they received the sacrament of bread and wine commemorating Mithra's banquet at the conclusion of his labors.

F. SPECULATIVE DOCTRINES

1. *The Soul.* Mithraism, like Platonism, taught that all souls pre-exist in the ethereal regions. At the birth of each new human being, one of these descends into a human body and by this process a portion of Ormazd is imprisoned in the coffin-clay of Ahriman. Only the human body, the material prison-house, perishes at death.

2. *Metaphysical Dualism.* At birth begins for every human being the great struggle between spirit and matter, light and darkness, good and evil, soul and body, the indwelling Ormazd and Ahriman, which must go on until death. Those members of mankind in whom the lower elements prevail are Children of Darkness; those in whom the higher are victorious, the Children of Light. This is the same metaphysical dualism which permeated Pythagoreanism, Essenism, and the Pauline theology, all of which called for the suppression of material, carnal, or worldly desires; in short, for an asceticism based not upon economic but upon metaphysical imperatives.

3. *Eschatology.* The eschatology of Mithraism was in part similar to but also in part different from that of Zoroastrianism. Neither had an eternal hell: but Mithraism was not universalist: again, its doctrine in this respect was that of Paul. At death, the elect souls are sent by Mithra direct to heaven; others are consigned to a condition of sleep until the final consummation, when Mithra will appear to reawaken them. A great and wonderful bull, like that pristine bovine, will appear; Mithra will separate the good from the bad, judge all according to the deeds they have done, slay the sacrificial bull, serve to the redeemed a final and immortalizing eucharist prepared from this animal, and send these fortunate ones to reside forever with the Elect. The terrestrial universe will then be consumed by a great conflagration in which all the

wicked, including Ahriman and his demons, will be annihilated.

Mithraism, therefore, divided the human race into three classes: first, the spiritual, the Elect, the higher initiates into that cult, who were to be admitted to heaven immediately upon death; second, the wicked, the evildoers, the incorrigibly material, who will be destroyed in the final holocaust; and, third, the lesser Mithraists, who strive for the higher things but succeed only in part, and those essentially good members of mankind who have not participated in the communion. The souls of these will sleep during the ages which intervene between death and the final consummation (a doctrine later known as soul-sleeping); their grossness will then be purged away and blessed immortality conferred upon them by the ultimate eucharist.

G. DESTRUCTION OF MITHRAISM BY CHRISTIANITY

That Mithraism was a virulent competitor of Christianity is proved by the hatred which the latter exhibited toward it and the terrible persecution which it perpetrated against it after the accession of Constantine. The followers of Mithra were hounded with such pertinacity that no one even dared to look at the sun, and farmers and sailors dared not observe the stars for fear of being accused of the heresy. Julian attempted to re-establish the cult; but after his untimely murder, the onslaught of the Christians became more furious than ever. Nevertheless, Mithraism was not easily extirpated: its temples were numerous from India to Scotland, and it numbered sincere devotees among slaves, laborers, merchants, soldiers, and senators, who were alike inspired by the ethical elevation of its teachings and the assurance of the immortality which it promised. But the persecution was persistent, sanguinary, and indiscriminate; the great Mithraeum at Alexandria was razed by the Arian George in 358;[17] Theodosius took the most extreme measures against the cult after his accession in 379;[18] and after the fourth century, it seems to have had no organized existence.

Since it was exclusive, Mithraism was not equipped to do battle against a priest-state; it accepted only the dedicated and the Elect who would consecrate their lives to virtue and devotion. Since its objective was not to control the government, it was tolerant of other creeds and disciplines. It invited all men, but persuaded no one, to reject the temptations of the world. The struggle between Catholicism on the one hand and the esoteric mystery-cults on the other proved once and for all that any religion which becomes the state will most certainly destroy all its competitors and, at the same time, every vestige of freedom. And one of the first to fall before the Church Trimphant was the cult of Mithra, to which Christianity owed so much.

H. ORIGINATORS OF CULT UNKNOWN

That such an effective and elaborate synthesis could have been developed only by a religious genius or by a very resourceful group of priests is obvious; but, since the cult glorified Mithra alone and sought to invest the new creation with primordial authority, the founder or originators remained forever unknown. And this was one of the basic weaknesses of Mithraism: it had no historical founder. Manichaeism, its child, had no reputedly divine originator: and it paid Christianity the ultimate tribute by incorporating into its system both its Jesus and His Gospel, without which it could never have mounted its assault upon the ramparts of the Catholic Church.

PART TWO
THE JEWISH SOURCES

I saw the mansions of the elect and the mansions of the holy.

The Book of Enoch xli

Be hopeful; for . . . ye shall shine and the portals of heaven shall be opened to you. . . . Ye shall not have to hide on the day of the great judgment. . . . And now fear not, ye righteous, when ye see sinners growing strong and prospering in their ways: be not companions with them, but keep afar from their violence; for ye shall become companions of the hosts of heaven.

The Book of Enoch civ

And a man who reneweth the law in the power of the Most High, ye shall call a deceiver; and at last ye shall rush upon him to slay him, not knowing his dignity, taking innocent blood through wickedness upon your heads . . . And ye shall . . . be a curse among the Gentiles . . . until he shall again visit you, and in pity shall receive you through faith and water.

Testaments: "Levi" IV 27-29

In thee shall be fulfilled the prophecy of heaven concerning the Lamb of God and the Saviour of the world . . . that a blameless one shall be delivered up for lawless men, and a sinless one shall die for ungodly men in the blood of the covenant, for the salvation of the Gentiles and of Israel, and shall destroy Beliar and his servants.

Testaments: "Benjamin" I 21

The King of heaven . . . appeared upon earth in the form of a man in humanity. And as many as believe on Him on the earth shall rejoice with Him. Then also shall all men rise, some unto glory and some unto shame. And the Lord shall judge Israel first, for their unrighteousness; for when He appeared as God in the flesh to deliver them, they believed Him not.

Testaments: "Benjamin" II 18-21

CHAPTER I

JUDAISM

A. JEWISH DEDICATION TO RELIGION

1. *Dependence upon Yahweh.* Although there were various major religions in the ancient world, it remained for the small and despised Jewish nation to cradle the Essene cult, which would create an ideology capable of conquering the occident. We believe that this was possible because the Jews were dedicated to religion in a manner elsewhere unknown. Among other people, dependence upon the supernatural was only a single phase of life: but the Jews considered themselves the chosen of Yahweh and attributed to Him their every victory, defeat, or chastisement. If historical religion may be defined as a system of beliefs, doctrines, or rituals designed to please or placate the unseen powers, then the Jews were religious *par excellence*.

Philostratus, agreeing with classical writers generally, declares that "the Jews have long been in revolt not only against the Romans but against humanity"; and that they are "a race . . . apart and irreconcilable." [1] This separation stemmed from, and then intensified, the Jewish faith. At least half a dozen times in three thousand years, their annihilation has been decreed; and it was partially executed by Sennacherib of Assyria, Ahasuerus (Artaxerxes?) of Babylon, Antiochus Epiphanes, Titus, Hadrian, the Inquisition, and Hitler. It was experiences such as these which enabled the Hebrew genius to create a savior-cult which could defeat all others.

2. *The Messianic Expectation.* The cherished records of the Jews amply reveal their own aspirations. The doc-

trine is repeated *ad infinitum*: "The Lord hath chosen thee to be a peculiar people unto Himself, above all the nations that are upon the earth."2 "And it shall come to pass, if thou shalt hearken diligently unto the voice of the Lord thy God to observe and to do all his commandments which I command thee this day, that the Lord thy God will set thee on high above all the nations of the earth."3 And again: "Thou shalt reign over many nations, but they shall not reign over thee." 4 No other people has ever been so conscious of ultimate primacy through supernatural intervention. This has given them cohesion and courage to persevere in the face of persecution and decimation. The conviction that every Jew will one day share in his divine destiny as a member of the world's ruling race has made him proud and has enabled him to survive unassimilated among the nations of the earth. At the Passover meal, Jews still place wine upon their tables and leave their doors ajar, so that Elijah, who is to precede the Messiah, may enter and drink; and then they repeat this devout prayer: "May the Merciful One cause us to inherit a day which is all good. May the Merciful One permit us to live unto the days of the Messiah!"5

The Jewish Messianic concept may have arisen even earlier than the Zoroastrian, was certainly original with them, and differed fundamentally from the Persian.

3. *No Need for Self-Reliance.* The ancient Jews did not deem it necessary to bestir themselves overmuch to master the arts of war or peace. Yahweh would do everything for them: at the command of Joshua, the sun stood still; at the sound of trumpets, the walls of Jericho fell; under the outstretched hand of Moses the waters of the Red Sea parted. As long as the Israelites were obedient to Yahweh, all was well; but when the people worshiped strange gods, Yahweh turned His face away, rain ceased to fall, pests devastated their fields, enemies defeated them, and universal desolation ensued. The Assyrians and the Babylonians were simply the instruments by which God chastised His disobedient children. Even though Yahweh would never destroy the Jewish race utterly, He would, because of their disobedience, visit upon them every pun-

ishment, including humiliation, captivity, slavery, poverty, dispersion, persecution, and reduction to a despised remnant. So thundered the Yahweh prophets. It was indeed a Judaeo-centric world.

B. THE RELIGION OF IKHNATON

1. *Egyptian Prototype of Yahweh.* We believe that the Jews obtained their concept of Yahweh from Egypt: indeed nothing could have been more natural. For we know that a great Egyptian school of philosophic theology flourished under Amenhotep IV, known as Ikhnaton; and that this gave to monotheism its first full expression. The abortive revolution of this young Pharaoh, who came to the throne in 1375 as a very young man and who died only seventeen years later, was overthrown at his death by the reactionary priests of Amen in coalition with the wealthy and imperialist elements of the nation; nor were his drastic reforms attractive even to the poor and ignorant; for they were incapable of comprehending their own welfare. But if Egypt rejected his grandiose and humanitarian principles, they were, we believe, absorbed in part by the Jews, who transmitted a distorted copy of his concept through their scriptures to the modern world.

2. *Amenhotep IV.* The conception of the sun-god had arisen during the reign of Amenhotep III, father of Ikhnaton. Egypt had just established a great and stable empire; and men had begun to think in universal terms. Amenhotep IV proclaimed himself the high priest of Aton, who was, however, something far more than the material sun and whose symbol was "a disk from which diverging rays radiated downward, each ray terminating in a human hand."[6] It was as if the creator were clasping his children, all the inhabitants of the earth, in His protecting power. The plural "gods" and the name *Amen* were expunged from all public monuments; and Aton was proclaimed the benevolent father of all mankind, no matter of what speech, race, or color. He was the creator of the natural world and was "actively concerned for the

daily maintenance of all his creatures, even the meanest."[7]

3. *A Profound Revolution.* This religion actually entailed a profound revolution. It called for a "naturalism" in art and living which attempted to throw off at a single stroke the traditions of two thousand years. Ikhnaton freed the slaves and released the convicts from the prison-mines; he confiscated the huge landed estates of the Amen priesthood and gave them to the peasant-serfs in the form of freeholds; he attempted to establish schools, wherein all were to learn to read and write. And this was to be only the beginning.

4. *A Frenzied Reaction.* The Osirian-Amenite priesthood lived in wealth, luxury, power, and ease; they were in possession of huge and magnificent temples, great treasure houses, and enormous influence among all classes of the people. Imagine, then, their frenzied rage when the new Pharaoh decreed the division of their lands, the confiscation of their wealth, the revocation of their income, and the dissolution of their order!

Ikhnaton attempted to banish the worship of Isis, Osiris, and Horus by discrediting the eschatology of their faith, which, as we have seen, was its central article and which, as it turned out, the people loved more than secular well-being.

5. *The Dissolution of the Empire.* Furthermore, Ikhnaton's program called for the dissolution of the Empire. If God is the universal father who loves all His creatures equally, irrespective of speech, color, or nationality, how can it be just for one nation to send soldiers to kill and oppress, and to collect tribute from another? As a result of this philosophy, the imperial armies received scant appropriations, and the empire withered away.

6. *Israelites in Egypt.* We cannot know with certitude just when the Israelites arrived in Egypt, or when they left. We know, however, that before their coming the Egyptians had been invaded by a nation of shepherds or Hyksos, who were "an abomination to the Egyptians."[8] After their expulsion, the land they had occupied was in

part tilled by the Hebrews, who, for a time, were probably well treated. But this situation did not long endure, for we learn that they were reduced to slavery,[9] probably under Rameses II, 1292-1225. His son Merneptah was forced to repel a horde of Libyans in 1221; and it is quite possible that during this disturbance the Israelites made good their escape.

It is also credible that the beneficent principles of Ikhnaton should have taken some root among the Israelites; and even more likely that various Egyptians of noble ideals continued to cherish his doctrines. It is likely that Moses was a royal Egyptian who, banished and ostracized from his own country, found in the Jews a people whose leader, lawgiver, and emancipator he could become.

7. *The God of Ikhnaton Altered.* It was natural enough that the Israelites should reconstruct the god of Ikhnaton according to their own needs. He remained the God of all the earth, but not equally of all men. He was the Creator, more powerful than other gods; but the children of Jacob alone were His chosen race. He was infinitely solicitous concerning Hebrew welfare, but indifferent to that of the Gentiles. The Chosen People were to bind themselves together by bonds of mutual solidarity, but all others they might deceive and exploit at will. To another Hebrew who was "waxen poor," monies must be loaned without interest; but "unto a stranger mayest thou lend upon usury."[10] Aton was the father of all living creatures and he cared for all alike; but when Yahweh commanded, "Thou shalt love thy neighbor as thyself," this was intended to apply only to "the children of their people."[11] After the destruction of Jerusalem by Titus, the Jew continued no less conscious of his magnificent destiny, which caused the fervent author of *Fourth Esdras* to exclaim: "as for the rest of the nations which are sprung from Adam, you have said that they are nothing and are like spittle. . . . And now, Lord, behold, these nations . . . rule over us and devour us. But we, your people, whom you called your first-born, only-begotten, chosen, and beloved, are delivered into their hands. If it was for

our sakes that the world was created, why do we not possess it as our inheritance?"

In one respect, however, Judaism remained the child of its parent: it was a one-world, nominally monotheistic religion, with no interest in the hereafter, no concept of hell or heaven, no system of rewards or punishments after death. In this respect, it was also similar to all Semitic religions, notably those of Assyria and Babylonia.

Inspired by a great leader who organized their escape, the Jews later attributed to him their Law, which differs from other ancient codes principally by certain distinctive customs and by its great emphasis upon the worship of Yahweh. Many of its features, however, were reminiscent of Ikhnaton. For example, all debts were to be canceled and all Hebrew slaves freed in the sabbatical year;[12] no usury was to be exacted from Hebrews; and land was to be returned to the family of the original owner at the close of each jubilee.[13] Even though these provisions were never honored, we may believe that the original lawgiver was actuated by such ideals.

C. CALAMITY IN ISRAEL

1. *Pretensions of Israel.* We may say that Israelite history from David to Bar-Cochba was little else than a series of national disasters; these are of the utmost importance because through these the Jewish race developed characteristics which enabled it to re-create a religion of ultimate renunciation.

The descendants of Jacob burst into Palestine about the beginning of the twelfth century, declaring that God had given them the land and had also commanded them to extirpate its inhabitants. Not only had they persuaded themselves that they were justified in robbing, killing, and expropriating: to them it was impious to refrain from so doing.[14] And so the Jews lived precariously in the midst of Philistines, Canaanites, Ammonites, Moabites, Amalekites, Jebusites, and Edomites, virtually in a state of perpetual warfare.

2. *David and Solomon.* David finally gave his people

a brief period of peace, glory, and national unity under a people's government; and the outward tranquillity continued under Solomon, the most crafty, splendid, and opportunistic king ever to rule over Israel. He had a seraglio of seven hundred wives and three hundred concubines; he imposed crushing tax-burdens throughout the empire; every social injustice began to flourish; and he built many altars to heathen gods.

3. *The Division of the Kingdom.* At his death, the submerged resentment flared above the surface. The Ten Tribes sent Jeroboam to plead with Rehoboam, the heir of Solomon, for a reduction in their taxes. But Rehoboam "answered the people roughly . . . and spake. . . . My father made your yoke heavy, but I will add to your yoke: my father also chastised you with whips, but I will chastise you with scorpions."[15] As a result, the nation divided into the northern kingdom of Israel, comprising the Ten Tribes with their capital at Samaria, and the smaller southern state, including only Judah and Benjamin, with headquarters at Jerusalem. From that day forward, there was almost continuous war between these two divisions of the descendants of Jacob,[16] and each was constantly making alliances with heathen nations against the other. This continued until the destruction and disappearance of Israel in 721.

4. *Continuous Calamity.* Between 950 and 745, both Judah and Israel paid constant tribute to Egypt, Syria, or Assyria; and both nations suffered invasions, wars, lootings, and destruction so many times and to such a degree that one becomes sick at heart merely in perusing the sanguinary record. There was a major catastrophe in almost every decade. The Assyrians laid siege to and captured Damascus in 742, carried away many into captivity, scattered them through Media and Mesopotamia, and replaced them with Assyrians. The Israelites, nevertheless, refused to humble themselves; Shalmaneser and Sargon II therefore besieged Samaria, 724-721; and, after a fearful struggle, captured King Hoshea, utterly destroyed the city, and resettled the population in Media.[17] Thus ended the kingdom of Israel; the Ten Tribes were

scattered and forever lost. They intermarried with their new neighbors, forgot their ancestor Jacob, and disappeared from the stage of history. In the villages and the countryside of Galilee, however, some of the Chosen People continued for centuries; and it was from these that Jesus and His disciples were born.

5. *Under the Assyrian Heel.* Judah, the sole organized remnant of Yahweh's people after 720, escaped extinction through abject submission and the payment of heavy and constant tribute to Assyria. About 607 Pharaoh-Necho invaded Judah and slew the "good" King Josiah at the battle of Megiddo, put upon the throne his puppet-son, Jehoiakim, and required ruinous tribute.[18]

6. *Destruction by the Babylonians.* When the Babylonians defeated the Egyptians at the decisive battle of Carchemish in 605, the Jews fell prey to a new empire. Nebuchadnezzar reduced Jerusalem and exacted heavy tribute.[19] At the end of three years, in 598, the Jews rebelled; Nebuchadnezzar took the capital a second time, looted the treasure houses, and carried away several thousand captives. When the puppet-king Zedekiah revolted ten years later, the Babylonians in 586 took the city,[20] razed not only the Temple but the city generally and carried away the whole population, except a remnant who were left to till the soil as peasants.[21] This was and remains the most overwhelming catastrophe in Jewish history.

7. *Subservience to Persia.* After the return from Babylon, the Jews continued in subservience to the Persians, whose religion they began to absorb; when the Greeks arrived in 333, tribute was paid to them; when the Seleucidae were established at Antioch about 313, the Jews became at times their tributaries and at intervals groaned under the heel of the Egyptian Ptolemies.

8. *Under the Greek Empire.* And now a new threat to Judaism appeared, different from any that had preceded, but certainly no less potent. This was Greek culture, which penetrated and conquered almost everywhere. And perhaps it was only an accident that it was not victorious among the Jews also; for we learn from the *First Book*

of the Maccabees that a great many Jews had begun to despise their own Law, and we know that Hebrew Hellenization was proceeding apace.

9. *Desecration of the Temple by Antiochus Epiphanes.* In 175, the eighth Seleucid king, the fanatical Antiochus IV Epiphanes, came to the throne. In 167, he took Jerusalem, looted and desecrated the Temple, established the Dionysiac-Eleusinian sacrifice there for three years, and systematically depopulated the city of all Jews who rejected Hellenic culture. This aroused the faithful more against their own apostates than against the foreign foe; and the Maccabaean wars, which resulted, continued with almost unabated fury for thirty years, when victory, peace, and unity, finally established under Simon in 142, gave the nation its second brief interval of independence.

10. *Secularization under the Asmoneans.* When the Maccabees began their revolt, they were imbued with a strong religious and crusading fervor. But as they succeeded beyond the expectation or aims of the pietistic Chasidim, who gave impetus to Mattathias and his five sons, known as the Asmoneans, their government became more materialistic and political, and no longer coincided with the interests of the Pharisees, who had, in the meanwhile, developed from the Chasidim.

11. *Fierce Internecine Conflict.* It was during the reign of John Hyrcanus, 134-104, that a profound change occurred. Quite suddenly, about 109, he shifted allegiance from the party of the Pharisees to that of the Sadducees. This must have reflected the cooling of the Asmonean fervor for Yahweh in favor of material progress. At all events, in spite of Pharisaic popularity,[22] the new development reached its climax under Alexander Jannaeus, 103-76. So bitter was the struggle between the rich and secularist Sadducees on the one hand and the primarily pietistic Pharisees on the other that the strife so engendered resulted in acts of unbelievable barbarism: "Alexander . . . ordered eight hundred [Pharisees] to be hung upon crosses in the midst of the city; he had the throats of their wives and children cut before their eyes; and these executions he saw as he was drinking and lying

down with his concubines."²³ Such were the atrocities committed by the Jews upon each other only a few years after they had been freed from Syrian tyranny.

12. *Under the Roman Heel.* Shortly after the death of Alexander Jannaeus, we find his two sons, Hyrcanus II and Aristobulus II, rivals not only for the throne of Judah but also for the favor of Pompey; but when Aristobulus, first favored by the Roman, dealt doubly with him, Pompey entered Jerusalem in 63 B. C., plundered the Temple, and desecrated the Holy of Holies. Thus ended the brief Asmonean dynasty and the Jews became tributaries of Rome.

13. *Messianic Hysteria.* The Jewish cup of sorrow now ran over; and the Messianic utterances of many centuries became the principal element in the national consciousness. No longer could the fervent hopes of Israel be limited to silent yearning or prophetic announcements. The land was a boiling cauldron of Messianic expectation, and many were daily awaiting the Son of Man arriving upon the clouds and surrounded by myriads of angels, coming to establish the "everlasting kingdom."

14. *Herod the Great.* In 37 B. C., Herod the Great came to the throne and ruled for thirty-three years. In the eyes of the Hebrew, he was *persona non grata* partly because he was half Idumean and only half Jew, and even more because he ruled by the grace of the Roman overlord. But he suppressed the ubiquitous robbers, maintained tranquillity, and rebuilt the Temple on lines exceeding the magnificence of Solomon. However, at his death, in 4 B. C., open disturbances again erupted. Josephus declares that "Judaea was full of robberies; and, whenever the several companies of the seditious found any one to lead them, he was created a king immediately. . . . Varus . . . crucified on this account two thousand."²⁴

In 7 A. D. Judas the Gaulonite, the originator of the fourth Jewish sect known as the Zealots, "whose doctrines infected the nation to an incredible degree,"²⁵ led an insurrection, which was crushed. But his movement only went underground. About 44 A. D., came a number of "such men as deceived and deluded the people under pretense of divine inspiration"[26] including one Theudas the Egyptian, who led thousands into the wilderness and who was expected to march straight through the Jordan dry shod after the manner of Joshua.[27] But these uprisings were drowned in Jewish blood. [28]

15. *The Revolt against Rome.* Palestine was filled with robbers, and no man's life was secure. Any wild-eyed seditionist could procure a following through extravagant promises. The activities of the Zealots were supplemented by those of the Sicarii, a secret society of assassins who mingled with the multitude in the crowded streets especially during feast and holy days, and struck down their victims with daggers. The High Priest Jonathan was one of the first to fall. Life had become a species of universal terrorism.[29]

Josephus describes a succession of greedy and unscrupulous Roman procurators, of whom Florus was the worst; he licensed bandits to steal, murder, and plunder, on condition that he receive a share of the loot.[30] Tension continued to mount, and, in 66 A. D., it could no longer be suppressed. The sorrow of the Jews approached a crescendo; like a tragedy of terrifying immensity, striding toward its denouement, came the war with Rome. As Tacitus observes,[31] Roman indignation was aroused since the Jews alone were rebellious. In due course, Vespasian reduced Galilee, marched into Judaea, and laid siege to Jerusalem, overflowing with its Passover throngs. Called away to accept the royal purple in Rome, he left his son Titus to prosecute the siege, in which three claimants to the Messiahship, John of Gischala, Eleazor the Zealot, and Simon of Gioras, conducted a triple war: first, against the rich Jews; second, against each other; and, third, against the Romans.

16. *Civil War.* The narrative of Josephus reveals the social content of the conflict as well as the mutual ferocity of the Jewish leaders. Their uncompromising hatred suggests that each was certain of divine election and feared no human opposition. The three generals were leaders of various outlaw elements, all of whom took exquisite delight in murdering wealthy Jews. The enmity they ex-

hibited toward the prosperous could have been born only of the fiercest ideological antagonism. Any Jew of means who so much as looked sorrowful when his dearest ones were murdered was himself put to the sword and his possessions were confiscated.

At the outset of the revolt, conservative Jews sent both to Agrippa (Jewish puppet king) and to Florus for help in suppressing the revolutionaries; [32] but they "set fire to the house of Ananias, the high-priest, and to the palace of Agrippa and Berenice; after which they carried the fire to the place where the archives were reposited, and made haste to burn the contracts belonging to their creditors, and thereby to dissolve their obligations for paying their debts; and this was done to gain the multitude of those who had been debtors and that they might persuade the poorer sort to join in their insurrection with safety against the more wealthy."[33]

Again and again Titus offered generous terms for capitulation, which were scornfully rejected by men hourly awaiting the apocalyptic Messiah. Instead of uniting in a common defense, the warring factions within the city burned each other's food supplies, and so brought on a famine in which cow's dung became a delicacy and mothers cooked and devoured their infant children.

The Jews defended themselves behind their triple wall for nearly eight months; but in the end their courage was unavailing. Titus burned the Temple and the Cloisters, demolished the Antonia, and, in general, destroyed the city. According to Josephus, nearly 1,350,000 Jews were killed, or died of starvation, and several hundred thousand more were carried away into captivity or sold into slavery.

Thus perished the Jewish state: but not utterly or finally.

17. *Bar Cochba.* In 132, under Hadrian, Bar Cochba, declared by the Rabbi Akiba to be the Star of Jacob, foretold in Numbers 24:17, began the final revolt of the Jews against the Roman power. The bitter war continued for three years, after which Jerusalem was razed and Jews forbidden to approach the site again.

18. *Israel in Constant Turmoil and Chaos.* From Solomon to Bar-Cochba more than ten centuries elapsed; during this immense period, the Jewish state enjoyed peace, unity, internal tranquillity, and independence less than a total of fifty years. In one millennium, Jerusalem was taken, looted, or destroyed twenty times; and it was saved from the same fate on many other occasions by abject surrender and heavy tribute. Had the kingdom of Israel not split about 975, had there been less enmity between them and their neighbors, had the Hebrews been able to live in harmony with themselves, and had they not looked so entirely to Yahweh for aid, they could have enjoyed centuries of prosperity, tranquillity, and independence. But then there would have been no apocalyptists, and there would never have been a Gospel Jesus.

D. THE TRIUMPH OF THE YAHWEH-CULT

1. *A Prolonged Struggle.* The cult of Yahweh was proclaimed over a millennium from Samuel through Zechariah and Malachi by a succession of prophets who claimed divine inspiration, declaimed against social injustice, and proclaimed the inevitable supremacy of Israel or Judah. The triumph of this movement, consummated about 450, is of definite importance in the study of Christianity, because Jesus considered Himself in direct line with these prophets and because substantial elements of His teaching seem closely in accord with theirs.

The Jews were not easily unified under the novel monotheism of Moses. For centuries they were deeply contaminated by the neighboring cults, which were those common to the Semitic world. The prophets thundered against this debasement of the Yahweh worship, which even so became triumphant only after making enormous concessions to heathen rituals.

2. *The Prophets.* In the books of Samuel, we first begin hearing a good deal about the *prophets*. Exactly who they were or what was their economic base remain obscure problems; but that they were poor and crude, hysterical and fanatical, and, at times, numerous and

influential, is certain.³⁴ According to Isaiah 20:2, they were clad in rough raiment or went "naked and barefoot." They spoke for the humble, the oppressed, the exploited, the outcast, as did the Buddhists of India; they hated the prosperous, the proud, the powerful. In fact, they may have been roving bands of robbers, from whom David recruited his following: "every one that was in distress and every one that was in debt, and every one that was discontented, gathered themselves unto him; and he became captain over them."³⁵

We gain a vivid view of the prophets from I Samuel 19:20-24. The devotees of Yahweh were pariahs and malcontents who conducted frenzied religious rites known as prophesying. It was they who overthrew the judges, who anointed Saul, and who, when he became reactionary, replaced him with David. During peace and prosperity, they were driven back into their caves; but during periods of enslavement, captivity, and degradation they came into their own. For then the people listened to their fulminations against the rich and the wicked, and believed that their misfortunes resulted from disobedience to Yahweh. Ezekiel 6:9 declares that in captivity will Judah return to the Lord: and Jeremiah states³⁶ that in the days of her affliction will Jerusalem remember.

3. *Under David and Solomon.* David drew his initial strength from these fanatics and outlaws; and the chief "prophets," who were their leaders, held a quasi-legal status throughout his reign. Such men as Gad and Nathan continued to denounce him whenever he strayed from strict obedience to Yahweh and they relayed to him the threats and promises of the deity. With the advent of Solomon, however, the conservatives resumed power, and the Israelites returned to the immemorial worship of the agricultural god Baal and to that of the great Ashtoreth, Queen of Heaven.

4. *Elijah.* When the next great battle for Yahweh occurs, the scene has shifted northward from Judah and Jerusalem to Israel and Samaria. The leader of the Yahweh cult was Elijah, "an hairy man, and girt with a girdle of

leather about his loins."[37] We are told[38] that the wicked Queen Jezebel had 450 prophets of Baal and 400 of the grove, or Ashtoreth, who ate at her table, and that Elijah was the sole remaining prophet of the Lord.[39] Nor were conditions much better in Judah, for, concerning Manasseh, we read that "he reared up altars for Baal, and made a grove, as did Ahab king of Israel. . . . And he built altars for all the host of heaven in the two courts of the house of the Lord."[40] It is clear that the priesthoods of Baal and Ashtoreth converted Solomon's Temple to their own use for centuries. Idolatry in Judah was nearly, but not quite, complete, down to about 700. And in the kingdom of Israel, conditions were even more deplorable; for there the worship of Yahweh had never really taken any root at all. That was the reason the Ten Tribes disintegrated and were lost when Tiglath-Pileser III and Sargon II carried them into captivity in 742 and 721. They had never become deeply conscious of being the Lord's especial and chosen people.

5. *The "Good" Hezekiah.* It is however reasonable to believe that the destruction of the Ten Tribes exercised a powerful emotional influence upon Judah. For Hezekiah, who came to the throne in 726, with the ruin of Samaria before his eyes and with Sennacherib's army at his gates about 704, not only humbled himself before Assyria and paid enormous tribute,[41] but he also "removed the high places, and broke down the images, and cut down the groves. . . . He trusted in the Lord God of Israel."[42]

Here was a tremendous event in the history of the Jews; at last and for the first time, about 700, the worship of Yahweh was officially and publicly triumphant in Jerusalem. However, that worship was neither pure nor undefiled; for Jeremiah[43] and other prophets[44] declaimed against the iniquity of blood sacrifices borrowed from the heathen. Isaiah, 1:11, exclaimed indignantly: "I am full of the blood offerings of rams. . . . I delight not in the blood of bullocks, or of lambs, or of he-goats." The prophets continued to denounce the kings and the official priesthood with a ferocity similar to that once employed against the Baalim.

The Old Testament contains at least forty passages in which the Yahweh prophets denounce the temple groves of Ashtoreth (Ishtar) with their sacred prostitution; and it is obvious that the Israelites celebrated her ritual almost universally until the middle of the seventh century. It was her ubiquitous worship that Hezekiah removed when he "cut down the groves," and which his son Manasseh restored. It was because of this prostitution that the Mosaic Law specifically outlawed harlots and excluded money earned by them from the Temple.[45]

6. *Priests Consolidate Their Position.* As soon as the priests of Yahweh seized control of the Temple ritual, they set out to consolidate their position. This required the commitment of their history, ceremonials, and sacerdotal law to writing. Thus it was that about 630 "Hilkiah the high priest . . . found the book of the law in the house of the Lord."[46] Its complete novelty was emphasized by King Josiah when he heard its words read by Shaphan, because "he rent his clothes."[47] The reaction of Jeremiah,[48] however, was quite different; for he made clear his conviction that the document of Hilkiah was a forgery from "the false pen of the scribes," or at least a corruption of the Mosaic Law. Nevertheless, all the vestiges of idolatry remaining from the days of Hezekiah were now destroyed by Josiah, who "brake in pieces and made dust of" the molten images.[49]

7. *The Mosaic Law Becomes Supreme.* From that day forward, the authority of the Mosaic Law was supreme among the Jews, whose unity was consolidated during the Babylonian captivity. Despite the *Diaspora* they remained thenceforth a separate race. Empires rose and fell, civilizations came and went, but the Jew continued his changeless way.

8. *Scriptures Assume Definitive Form.* It was not until well after the return from the Captivity and the rebuilding of the Temple that the scriptures assumed their definitive form around 450. We are told that Ezra, or Esdras, was sent from Babylon to be governor of Jerusalem;[50] much of the work of writing, assembling, and editing the sacred writings must be attributed to him.

9. *The Priest-State*. When the Jews returned to Palestine about 545, they established a theocracy, or priest-state. Judah was from that time on as much a church as a nation.

10. *Racial Purity*. The story of Ezra's horror at the intermarriage of the Hebrews with the neighboring heathen is related in Ezra 9, and is told in the apocryphal *First Book of Esdras*. Whereas in the days preceding the Captivity, the greatest crimes had been idolatry and social injustice, now we find that violation of racial purity had become the most heinous of all offenses. This was another great milestone in Jewish progress toward ultimate isolation.

11. *Prophecy Forbidden*. And something else also happened. When the Mosaic Law at last became the law of life, prophecy was forbidden. The new priesthood, with their symbols, their scrolls, their learned jargon, their ephods, their special costumes, their goodly incomes, their authority and power, their altars and their Temple, made short shrift of independent prophets claiming divine inspiration. The priests now possessed the Written Word, attributed to Moses himself: and this was to be the sole and final authority to be interpreted by the established priesthood and by none other. Prophecy was no longer to be tolerated: "When any shall yet prophesy, then his father and his mother that begat him shall say unto him, Thou shalt not live; for thou speakest lies in the name of the Lord; and his father and his mother . . . shall thrust him through when he prophesieth . . . neither shall they wear a rough garment to deceive."[51]

This was the culminating act by which the religion of Yahweh was congealed into its final form. The prophets made prophecy a mortal offense.

12. *The Advent of the Apocalypse*. Once it was established that prophecy was blasphemy, Jewish dissidents were forced into a novel expedient: in order to promulgate their ideology, they presented it as the vision of some ancient Hebrew. Such literature is known as the *pseudepigrapha* because the purported author had

long been dead, and it commonly took the form of the *apocalypse*.

E. OPPRESSION AND REVOLT IN ISRAEL

1. *Inseparable from Messianic Concept.* We must recognize revolt among the Israelites as of decisive importance because it is inextricably intertwined with the Gospel Jesus. Out of internecine strife, frequent defeat, and constant frustration germinated their Messianic aspirations, which were their peculiar contribution to Christian ideology.

2. *Breaking the Brotherhood.* The religion of Yahweh proclaimed the brotherhood of all Israelites; but this idea, which appealed to all during periods of universal slavery, became instead a divisive force when they were organized as an independent state. For, as such, they soon developed antagonistic social classes; and with the normal operation of these, the equalitarianism of the Yahweh prophets was incompatible. An irreconcilable struggle therefore developed and continued to the very end. When successful Jews could exploit no one except others of their own race, the bond of solidarity was broken; as a result, there was always a revolutionary movement, until all were scattered in the Diaspora. Jesus considered Himself one in the line of these revolutionary prophets; and had it not been for this long tradition of social revolt, the Gospel Jesus could never have developed in Galilee and Judaea.

3. *The Revolution of Jehu.* About 880, Jehu, aided and abetted by Elijah and Elisha, led a revolt against the landowners in the northern or Samarian division of Israel. Ahab and his aggressive Baal-worshiping wife, Jezebel, had been dispossessing the small operators of their freeholds, which they consolidated into large estates. Such prophets as Amos, Joel, and Micah thundered against the injustice of this development. Micah declared that they "eat the flesh of my people, and flay their skin from off them. . . . They build up Zion with blood, and Jerusalem shall become heaps."[52]

After the second capture of Jerusalem by Nebuchadnezzar in 598 the Jews, in sudden burst of piety, set free their slaves in accordance with the provision of the recently published Mosaic Law; however, the masters immediately repossessed their servants.53 This enormity elicited a fierce denunciation from Jeremiah in which he declared that because of this iniquity, the Lord would "proclaim a liberty for you . . . to the sword, to the pestilence, and to the famine; and I will make you to be removed into all the kingdoms of the earth."54

As we have seen, usury from Hebrews was strictly forbidden by the Mosaic Law. Jeremiah righteously avers, 15:10, that he neither gave nor accepted usury; but Ezekiel, 22:15, declares that God will scatter and destroy Israel for their many mortal sins, among which was this, 22:12 that "thou hast taken usury and increase, and thou hast greedily gained of thy neighbors by extortion, and hast forgotten me, saith the Lord."

4. *Slavery among the Jews.* We may add that the permanent enslavement of Hebrews by Hebrews was a common practice even after the revolt of Bar Cochba.55 It is somewhat disconcerting to learn that when they returned from the Babylonian captivity, they carried with them 7,337 Hebrew slaves.56 No wonder the prophets were unpopular among the wealthy Jews. And we know from the edict of Gregory the Great that, at the end of the sixth century, the Jews were still holding their brethren in slavery, because this prelate was constantly attempting to entice these bondmen to Christianity by offering them their freedom in return for apostacy from the faith of their fathers.

5. *Jesus and the Prophets.* The sayings of Jesus are replete with echoes and quotations from the Psalms and the prophets. Although His social and ethical doctrines were in reality those of Buddha and Pythagoras, He thought of Himself with some justification as one inspired by the Jewish prophets.

F. ESCHATOLOGY

1. *Orthodox.* In Psalm 49:12, we read that man is like the beasts that perish; in 103:16, that his days are as the grass; in 115:17, that the dead cannot praise the Lord; and in 143:3, that they dwell in darkness.

The Sadducaic Ecclesiastes treats the subject with gloomy finality: men are like beasts—"as one dieth, so dieth the other"; man "hath no pre-eminence above a beast"; "all go into one place; all are of the dust, and all turn to dust again," 3:19-20. We read also, 9:5, that the living know that they shall die, "but the dead know not anything, neither have they any more a reward." All the dead, in short, have only an identical and semi-conscious existence.

Even so late a composition as Job, dealing as it does with the problem of good, evil, suffering, and undeserved punishment, never once surmises that there will be compensation hereafter for the inequities of this life. Quite the contrary: for Job emphasizes the inscrutability of God's way, and declares that there is no life beyond the present; men, 6:18, "go to nothing, and perish"; "so he that goeth down to the grave shall come up no more," 7:9.

The orthodox Jewish eschatology was similar to the Homeric and modeled upon the Babylonian. The dead are bloodless shades which inhabit Sheol; among them there is neither vitality nor differentiation, neither any reward for the good nor punishment for the wicked. Yet they have an existence; for the witch of Endor was able to summon the reluctant ghost of Samuel.[57] Euripides tells us that "The soul of the deceased, although it live no longer, yet doth still retain a consciousness which lasts forever."[58] But, since nothing could be done to achieve happiness in the after life, the Jews, like the Homeric Greeks, evinced little concern over man's eternal and individual destiny.

2. *Zoroastrian Penetration.* However, during the Seleucid and the Asmonean periods, under Greek and Persian influence, a new eschatology began to develop among

the Jews. In the second or possibly the third century B. C., the Zoroastrian-Pythagorean doctrines of immortality, resurrection, supernatural judgment, hell, heaven, and punishment hereafter, began to penetrate a segment of Jewish consciousness. The Sadducees certainly had a legitimate argument when they declared, as they must have done, that if all these things are realities, Yahweh would have revealed them through Moses, or at least through the Psalms and the ancient prophets; surely, He would not have left the Great Lawgiver, together with Isaiah, and Ezekiel, in complete ignorance!

The book of Isaiah, however, was composed over several centuries; and it is true that a late interpolation, 26:19, expresses a vague belief in a resurrection: "Thy dead men shall live, together with my dead body shall they arise. Awake and sing, ye that dwell in dust: for thy dew is as the dew of herbs, and the earth shall cast out the dead."

But the celebrated declaration of Daniel 12:2 is more definite: "And many of them that sleep in the dust of the earth shall awake, some to everlasting life, and some to shame and everlasting contempt." Compare these passages: the first, probably written in the third century, simply implies that there will be a resurrection of Jews. The second, written in 163 B. C., declares that many — not all—who have died, shall arise: some to eternal life, others to endless punishment. This is the oldest declaration of this concept in the Bible: there are, according to Daniel, three classes among the dead: first, those who will remain unconscious in the dust; second, those who will ascend to heaven; and, third, those who will be consigned to endless shame.

Let us note that while the Sadducees remained adamant in rejecting the new eschatology, the Pharisees did not remain immune; concerning this, Josephus is our principal authority, and a competent one, since he belonged to their sect. He states that, according to them, "all souls are incorruptible . . . the souls of good men only are removed into other bodies, but . . . the souls of bad men are subject to eternal punishment." [59] Josephus himself seems to have embraced this Brahmanic-Pythagorean doctrine, since he expresses the same theory in a speech to his soldiers at Jotopata to dissuade them from suicide while facing imminent death at the hands of the Romans.[60] In another passage, he elaborates that, according to the Pharisees, all souls are immortal and subject to rewards and everlasting punishments after death; that the good "shall have power to revive and live again; on account of which doctrine, they are able greatly to persuade the body of the people."[61]

The rabbis, who became the successors to the Pharisees, abandoned this Zoroastrian-Pythagorean eschatology, and returned to that of the Old Testament, possibly in part because of the conflict with Christianity. It is interesting to note that a Jewish colony, discovered in China about 1800, which had lived there in complete isolation since the first century, still believed in "Purgatory, Hell, Paradise, the Resurrection, and the Last Judgment."[62] Thus we know that at least some of the Pharisees had embraced the Zoroastrian doctrine of purgatory six centuries before it appeared as a dogma in the Catholic Church.

G. THE OLD TESTAMENT MESSIAHS

1. *Forces Which Created the Messianic Concept.* No disinterested scholar will deny that the surrender and frustration created among their subject peoples by the long Roman oppression prepared them for a religion of renunciation. Likewise, we believe that the innumerable sorrows and catastrophes suffered by the Jews over many centuries created the climate in which apocalyptic hope took precedence over every other. Out of these experiences grew the Messianic concepts of the Jews.

2. *Intense Jewish Faith in the Messiah.* The Messianic hope has been a major preoccupation of the Jewish mind for twenty-five centuries. Maimonides, 1135-1204, declared that belief in the expected Messiah was mandatory; after eighteen centuries in China, the small Jewish colony there was still awaiting its Messiah.[62] Under a dateline of March 13, 1954, a news item released from Jerusalem and

printed in the world-press, told of a Jewish sect in Palestine which declared that the Messiah would appear within three months of that time. A detailed history of modern or late medieval "Messiahs," many of whom got large followings and some of whom amassed fortunes, would fill a volume in itself. All these, however, were only pale imitations of the Messianic expectation existing just before and after the destruction of Jerusalem, when the Jews, in frenzied excitement, lived in daily anticipation of apocalyptic catastrophe and salvation. The Romans recognized that this hope was a political force with which they must reckon; and that the recalcitrancy of the Jews stemmed from their anticipation of a supernaturally endowed Messiah who would crush and destroy their masters.63 For this reason, they executed any Jew professing Messianic pretenses.

3. *Variety of Messianic Concepts.* Among the Jews, in different periods and among different groups, we find three principal Messianic concepts. The first had been prevalent since the eighth century B. C.; it envisioned a great human leader, a descendant of David, a kind of second Moses,64 who, supported by divine approval and perhaps by supernatural intervention, would gather the children of the twelve tribes into Judea, reconstitute them into a unified kingdom, and make Israel the center of a world-empire, to which all the Gentiles would offer allegiance and the religion of which all nations would at last embrace. The second concept was more overwhelming: it conceived of the Messiah as an all-powerful, supernatural being; Daniel called Him the Son of Man and saw Him in a vision surrounded by thousands of thousands of His ministers, coming to defeat and destroy the enemies of Israel, call the dead from their graves, conduct the last judgment, and establish the Jews in their everlasting kingdom. The third concept retained the supernatural and apocalyptic Messiah coming on the clouds with glory and surrounded by multitudes of saints; but it transformed Him into the almighty moral judge of all mankind, who would establish the kingdom of righteousness on earth. This concept made the Messiah

impartially international; it is not found in the Old Testament, which is consistently Judaistic; it occurs only among the Essenes and in the Gospel Jesus.

4. *The Primitive Messianic Concept.* Perhaps the oldest expression of the primitive Messianic idea is found in Joel, where we find that agricultural pests and Gentiles would both be destroyed by supernatural intervention. But it is in the sonorous and majestic poetry of Isaiah that we find the first fully-developed Messianic concept, which was the prophet's reaction to the final destruction of Samaria and Israel in 721 and the imminent dangers surrounding Jerusalem and Judah.

The first twenty-three chapters of Isaiah were composed in the eighth century and portray the kingdom of a purely human Messiah, under which the nations "shall beat their swords into plowshares, and their spears into pruninghooks: nation shall not lift up sword against nation, neither shall they learn war any more."[65] We are told of the young woman who, though still a virgin, is soon to conceive and bear a child;[66] and before this child is old enough "to cry, My father, my mother, the riches of Damascus and the spoil of Samaria shall be taken away by the king of Assyria."[67] This, of course, was actual history, then recently consummated; the following genuine prophecy, however, like most of chapters 13-23, was never to be fulfilled: "For unto us a child is born . . . a son is given; and the government shall be upon his shoulders; and his name shall be called Wonderful, Counsellor, the Mighty God, the Everlasting Father, the Prince of Peace. Of the increase of his government and peace there shall be no end, upon the throne of David . . . henceforth even for ever."[68]

Before this child could become the warrior-king of Israel, Judah and Jerusalem must suffer great tribulation.[69] Yet a remnant would return;[70] the reconstituted tribes would become mighty; "and he shall set up an ensign for the nations, and shall assemble the outcasts of Israel, and gather together the dispersed of Judah from the four corners of the earth."[71] Some have thought that this wonder-child was Hezekiah; but this is impossible, since the Messiah-to-be was still an infant in 721 when Samaria fell, and Hezekiah was born about 740 and became king of Judah in 726. Isaiah indeed calls him his own child, Mahershalalhashbaz,[72] born of a prophetess.

Micah is celebrated because of the prophecy concerning Bethlehem, which "though thou be little among the thousands of Judah, yet out of thee shall he come forth unto me that is to be ruler of Israel."[73] This mighty Messiah king, "the root of Jesse," shall lay his enemies prostrate before him,[74] create the Jewish kingdom,[75] and establish the Gentiles in the worship of Yahweh.[76]

Zechariah reflects an elaborate ideology in which the Messiah is to be a priest-king;[77] he will bring the scattered Israelites from all nations back to Jerusaem;[78] many of the Gentiles will embrace the religion of Yahweh;[79] the Jewish Empire will extend to the ends of the earth;[80] there will be a great tribulation in which the heathen will sack Jerusalem;[81] but then the Messiah will appear and destroy all his enemies in a final Armageddon and all their wealth will become the spoil of Israel;[82] and finally the whole world will be organized under the Jewish theocracy.[83] This conception continued substantially unchanged through Revelation and other Jewish apocalypses written as late as 100 A. D.

As we have seen, prophets had been proscribed. Henceforth, only one more could appear: Elijah, the harbinger. Generation after generation, the Jews awaited his appearance: no one could impersonate him with impunity, since he would be permitted only a brief ministry before the Messiah himself must be made manifest. And from *him* no mean accomplishments would be required: he would have to recall the scattered children of Israel from the four corners of the earth; establish a powerful and united government; defeat all the enemies of his people; bring the whole world under the rule of Jerusalem; attract all the Gentiles as proselytes to the worship of Yahweh; and establish universal peace and prosperity. Failing to accomplish all these objectives, he would be revealed as an imposter and a blasphemer, and his punishment would be death forthwith by stoning, as provided in Leviticus.[84]

5. *The Suffering Servant and the Atoning Messiah.*
One of the most pathetic and poignant concepts of the
Jewish Messiah is that of the Suffering Servant of Isaiah
53, which may have been this prophet himself. This was,
furthermore, the model upon which Jesus consciously
patterned His own career: "despised and rejected of men:
a man of sorrows, and acquainted with grief . . . wounded
for our transgressions . . . bruised for our iniquities . . .
the Lord laid on him the iniquity of us all. . . . He was
oppressed and . . . afflicted, yet he opened not his mouth."

Ezekiel saw strange visions and imagined the twelve
tribes re-established in Palestine under a new covenant.
He even saw the vision of a new and glorious temple; and
his prophecy closes with a description of the New Jerusalem, which prefigures the Holy City in Revelation. The
most vital portions of Ezekiel, however, consist in his
conception of himself as a sacrifice and atonement for the
iniquity of Israel. He calls himself "Son of Man" ninety-four times. And this Son of Man (a title which Jesus was
to apply to Himself almost exclusively) was made a
prophet, a teacher, and the vicarious savior of his people.

6. *The Supernatural Judaistic Messiah.* In addition
to these concepts, there grew up under Persian influence
in the period following the Captivity a new and fearful
idea: a Messiah modeled upon the Zoroastrian Soshans,
who would be a supernatural manifestation of infinite
power and effulgence, who would appear suddenly in the
dreadful day of the Lord surrounded by myriads of angels,
and who would judge the wicked, destroy the enemies of
Israel, and establish the kingdom of the righteous saints.

a. *Deutero-Isaiah.* We turn, now, to Deutero-Isaiah,
comprising chapters 40-55. The world-power is no longer
Assyria; even Babylon has faded, and is now merely staked
out for vengeance. Cyrus, who is called God's Anointed,[85]
and Persia, now loom large. The probable date is about
536. Elijah, who will be succeeded by the Messiah himself, is about to appear as "The voice of him that crieth
in the wilderness, Prepare ye the way of the Lord, make
straight in the desert a highway for our God;" after which
"the glory of the Lord shall be revealed, and all flesh

shall see it together."[86] This Messiah shall bring judgment upon the Gentiles and they shall become the slaves of Judah: "the labour of Egypt, and the merchandise of Ethiopia and of the Sabeans, men of stature, shall come over unto thee, and they shall be thine: they shall come after thee; in chains shall they come over, and they shall fall down unto thee, and they shall make supplication unto thee."[87]

b. *Trito-Isaiah.* Trito-Isaiah, consisting of chapters 56-66 probably composed in the fifth century, contains the oldest fully developed concept of the apocalyptic Messiah. There can be little doubt that this, like Daniel, reflects Zoroastrian influence; for there is to be a new heaven and a new earth. And no longer will the savior of Judah be a man, no matter how divinely endowed or supported; instead, he will be God Himself.[88] And to house, as it were, this Messianic kingdom, "behold, I create new heavens and a new earth: and the former shall not be remembered."[89] In this blessed new Jerusalem, there shall be universal peace,[90] and blood sacrifices will be abolished forever.[91] And God shall be the light and glory of the Holy City, even as in the Persian heaven;[92] and "the Gentiles shall come to thy light. And the sons of strangers shall build up thy walls, and their kings minister unto thee. . . . For the nation and kingdom that will not serve thee shall perish."[93]

c. *Daniel.* Josephus marveled at the accuracy of Daniel's "prophecies,"[94] which describe the events of several centuries, and adds that herein we have a refutation of the Epicureans, who deny the existence of providence. He noted however that some of Daniel's predictions remained unfulfilled. But modern scholarship has established that the first chapters of Daniel were written about 238; and the last six in 164-163, or nearly four hundred years after the purported date. This afforded the author a long period of history to present as prophecy.

The book as a whole uses the standard method of apocalyptical revelation, which came into common usage in the second century B. C. Some personage was chosen from Hebrew tradition—Enoch, Abraham, Moses, Isaiah,

Ezra, Baruch, etc.—and a vision was attributed to him. In this, history is accurately portrayed as prophecy down to the moment of writing; at that point, it passes abruptly from the known to the unknown, and, with the authority established by previous authenticity, seeks to gain credence for actual predictions, never to be fulfilled.

Although certain portions of Daniel remain obscure, the references for the most part are clear enough. For example, we can guess but cannot establish just who were the ten horns or kings preceding the "little horn,"[95] who was Antiochus IV Epiphanes. Nor is it possible with certainty to unravel the mystery of the seventy weeks.[96] On the other hand, the kingdoms referred to in dreams or visions are unmistakable; it is obvious that the northern and the southern kingdoms, the wars of which are discussed at such length in chapter 11, are those of the early second-century Seleucids and Ptolemies. There are at least eight specific references to Antiochus, who was the great enemy of Israel from 171 to his death in 163, and these run like a red thread through the last six chapters.

We note that the author has a much more accurate knowledge of Seleucid history than of Babylonian. First, there was never a king Belshazzar; second, Babylon was taken, not under Darius, but under Cyrus; third, Darius succeeded Cyrus, not vice-versa; fourth, history knows no Ahasuerus, and if Artaxerxes is meant, Darius was not his son, but his grandfather; and, fifth, had Daniel lived into the reign of Darius Hystaspes, he must have been well over a hundred years of age when the Great King set him "over the whole realm."[97]

We must also point out that Daniel departs so sharply from his Hebrew predecessors that he is, in reality, only semi-Judaic; he represents a thoroughgoing amalgamation of Jewish aspirations with Zoroastrian eschatology. In him, for the first time, we hear of archangels, immortality, a general resurrection, a last judgment, a book in which the names of the redeemed are written, a system of rewards and punishments after death, and eternal regions of bliss and shame. The Messiah, too, is transformed and becomes much more like the Saoshyant than the descendant of David who is to occupy a temporal throne. In fact the Son of Man is a supernatural agency of the Supreme God, who has very little resemblance to Yahweh; there is not the slightest indication that the Messiah has any human ancestry or relationship; he is not of the root of Jesse, but the effulgent Word of God. Daniel rejects the whole Judaic concept of the Messiah, but retains the conviction that the Jews are the saints and the Chosen People. He reflects the first great penetration of paganism into Jewish theology and this document stands midway between the most ancient Isaiah and the Gospel Jesus.

In the second chapter, Daniel interprets Nebuchadnezzar's dream of the Great Image, of which the head was gold, the breast silver, the belly brass, the legs iron, and the feet partly clay and partly iron. As we know, this was a common Zoroastrian metaphor. Finally, all these, which represent the Babylonian, the Median-Persian, the Greek, and the Seleucid-Ptolemaic empires, down to 240 B.C., are to be swept away as dust, to be followed immediately by the Messianic Jewish kingdom, which is to be like a great mountain, or as a stone "cut out without hands,"[98] and which will destroy and replace all the preceding empires.[99]

As to the time of fulfillment, there is no evasion. The eternal kingdom of the Messiah is to be established "in the days of these kings,"[100] that is, of the Seleucids and the Ptolemies of the third century, B. C.

Beginning with chapter 7, we have a series of true apocalyptic visions of the highest and most elaborate category. In December, 167, Antiochus Epiphanes, as we have noted, desecrated the Temple and established there the Eleusinian ritual. The second portion of Daniel was written immediately after the restoration of the Jewish worship in December, 164, but probably before the death of Antiochus, April, 163.

The eighth chapter describes the ram with the two horns, Media and Persia, which was overcome by the rough goat, Grecia. This beast had a great horn, who was Alexander; when this was broken, four kingdoms arose in its place, headed by his four generals, who divided the

Empire. In due time, there comes "a king of fierce countenance, and understanding dark sentences."[101] This king (Antiochus) shall vent his fury upon the holy covenant, shall enter into league with the apostate Jews, shall bring tribulation upon the saints, shall desecrate the sanctuary, and "shall place the abomination that maketh desolate" for three and a half years.[102] This is the fearful tribulation which must precede the Saoshyant, the resurrection, and the Last Judgment. [103]

There is an elaborate vision which culminates in the accession of the Son of Man, and in which we find a variant version of the four empires.[104] In order passed before him the Lion (the Babylonian Empire), the Bear (the Median-Assyrian Empire), the Leopard (the Persian Empire), and then "a fourth beast, dreadful and terrible," with "great iron teeth," which was the Greek Empire. And from this had issued ten horns, or kings, and the eleventh, "another little horn," who was Antiochus Epiphanes, presently to be destroyed and consigned to the burning flame.[105] The Ancient of Days now appears on His throne, and He gives the Son eternal dominion over the saints: "I beheld one like the Son of Man" who "came with the clouds of heaven . . . to the Ancient of Days. . . . And there was given him dominion, and glory, and a kingdom that all people, nations, and languages, should serve him," whose "dominion is . . . everlasting . . .But the saints of the most High shall take the kingdom, and possess the kingdom forever, even for ever and ever."[106]

And when shall all this come to pass? "From the time that the daily sacrifice shall be taken away, and the abomination that maketh desolate set up, there shall be a thousand two hundred and ninety days."[107] Thus, 1290 days were to elapse between the beginning of the desecration and the establishment of the Messianic kingdom, which according to this computation, was due in July or August, 163. The desolation itself actually endured for a period of 1095 days; there were, therefore, to remain some six months between the restoration of the worship and the advent of the Soshans. The apocalypse was due in less than a year after the second half of Daniel was composed.

7. *The Messiah of Universal and Moral Judgment.* Among the earlier prophets we find everywhere the orthodox Jewish concept of a purely human Messiah, which was never accepted by Jesus Himself, but which often intrudes in the New Testament and from which His original disciples could never free themselves. This was the age-old idea inseparable from Jewish tradition, but with the advent of Zoroastrian influence, the Messiah became a supernatural power; and out of this, when absorbed by Jewish theology, grew the doctrine of the Parousia.

One great Messianic doctrine remains to be developed: that the final judgment shall be on ethical and not on Jewish national or racial lines; that the Messianic kingdom will be international, will be based on moral regeneration, and will not simply constitute a division of humanity into saintly Jews and Jewish proselytes on the one hand and wicked Gentiles on the other.

We shall see how this concept was completed by the Essenes and appropriated by the Gospel Jesus.

CHAPTER II

THE ESSENES: THE EXTERNAL EVIDENCE

A. IDENTIFICATION

1. *Discovery of the Dead Sea Scrolls.* With the discovery of the Dead Sea Scrolls, the relationship between Essenism and the Gospel Jesus has become a subject of consuming interest. The evidence now coming to light confirms what various scholars have long surmised: namely, that it is impossible to evaluate pristine Christianity correctly except through an understanding of the Essenes.

Old prejudices die hard; but since that day in 1947, when a Bedouin goatherd stumbled into a cave in which the Essenes had secreted their manuscripts just before they fled before the Roman armies in 68 or 69 A. D., it is scarcely possible any longer to deny their direct influence upon Christianity. A few cautious scholars have questioned whether the Covenanters who lived at the Qumran Monastery were actually those Essenes described by Pliny, Philo, and Josephus. Others have argued that the Scrolls are medieval forgeries[1] or were composed by Jewish Christians of the third or fourth century.[2] Such arguments, of course, serve merely to accentuate the generic relationship between the Covenanters and the Gospel Jesus; otherwise it would be impossible to maintain that documents unquestionably composed in the second or first century before Christ were composed by Christians several centuries later.

2. *Authenticity.* Space does not permit us to reproduce the archeological, paleographical, and other evidence which proves that the Dead Sea Scrolls were composed between 170 and 60 B. C. by a Jewish cult which flour-

ished until 69 A. D. This material is carefully reviewed by Millar Burrows in his *Dead Sea Scrolls*. Professor W. F. Libby of the University of Chicago subjected a piece of linen wrapping which covered one of the MSS. to the Carbon-14 Process and found that its date of origin was approximately 33 A. D. Suffice it to say that today no competent scholar doubts that the latest possible date on which any of the Scrolls could have been copied was 68 A. D. This, of course, does not determine the date of composition, which could have occurred at any time during several preceding centuries and which must be determined from internal evidence.

There can be no dispute concerning the authenticity of the Scrolls, which, in addition to several previously unknown and complete documents, now translated and published, include two MSS. of Isaiah and literally thousands of fragments found in various caves. Among these are portions of practically every book of the Old Testament.

3. *Literature of the Covenanters.* In addition to the Old Testament scriptures, the celibates of Qumran had a sacred literature of their own. Of documents previously known, fragments have been found of the *Book of Enoch, The Book of the Jubilees,* and *The Testaments of the Twelve Patriarchs.* In addition, a complete manuscript of *The Damascus Document* was discovered. We know, therefore, that these writings, long known but never correctly evaluated, must be identified with the Dead Sea Covenanters. Finally, other complete works were also found; these have now been translated and they cast a brilliant light upon the cult: *The Manual of Discipline, The Habakkuk Commentary, The War of the Sons of Light with the Sons of Darkness,* and *The Thanksgiving Psalms.*

4. *Covenanters and Essenes Identical.* We agree with Mr. A. Dupont-Sommer that the Essenes and the Qumran Covenanters were most certainly one and the same. It is simply incredible that Khirbet-Qumran and its occupants could be anything other than the monastery and the cult described by Pliny, who wrote about 60 A. D.: 'Lying on the west of Asphaltites [Dead Sea], and sufficiently distant to escape its noxious exhalations, are the

Esseni, a people that live apart from the world, and marvellous beyond all others . . . for they have no women among them; to sexual desire they are strangers; money they have none. . . . Day after day, however, their numbers are fully recruited by multitudes of strangers that report to them, driven thither to adopt their usage by the tempests of fortune, and wearied with the miseries of life."[3]

Whether or not Pliny had seen the Qumran monastery, it is certain that his information was accurate: the ascetics who lived there were known to him as Essenes; and, since not the slightest vestige of any other remotely similar group has ever been discovered and since the words of Pliny are reinforced and elaborated not only by Philo and Josephus but also by the Dead Sea Scrolls, we must conclude that they and the Covenanters were identical. *Essenes* means "holy ones"; this was a nickname used only by outsiders, and never by the cultists themselves.

B. CHARACTERISTICS

1. *Practices.* This unique order existed for more than two centuries. Only their inner circle knew their esoteric doctrines. The organization consisted almost entirely of male celibates, of whom there were some four thousand. A small percentage of them lived in the Dead Sea Monastery; the remainder, residing in special communal houses scattered throughout Judaea, worked full time at some regular occupation, and were to be found in every walk of life; and so great were the compensations of membership that the Order flourished, even though unaugmented by the birth of children.

2. *Essenes Were Pythagoreans.* The Essenes were in no wise mendicants, like the Buddhists; nor were they monks, except perhaps the specially selected brethren who lived at Khirbet-Qumran; in fact, there was apparently little external difference between them and other Jews. They did not renounce *work;* they simply rejected the individualism of the world, its acquisitive ways, the ob-

ligations of family and relatives, and the sensual appetites common to humanity.

We have already noted the statement of Josephus that the Essenes had adopted the Pythagorean way of life.[4] And indeed the parallels between the two were many and striking: both were organized into celibate *thiasoi*, or communal communities; both rejected animal sacrifices; both practiced daily baptismal purification and ate common sacramental meals; both rejected the use of oaths; both were organized on the basis of strict precedence and priority; both taught similar doctrines concerning atonement, predestination, and redemption. Even their eschatology had much in common. The leaders of both were regarded with such veneration that their names must not be uttered; and they were believed to have received revelations directly from God. New members were required to undergo an initiation of several years; novices, having sold all their possessions and placed the money in escrow with the treasurer of the Order, received this back if they were finally rejected, but if accepted it became a part of the communal treasury. The Essenes, however, never adopted the Pythagorean doctrine of metempsychosis: on this one point they remained closer to Zoroastrianism, which as we have seen, had already made deep penetration into Judaic thought. We may say that mature Essenism was seventy per cent Pythagorean, fifteen per cent Zoroastrian, and fifteen per cent Judaistic, which element, however, was pertinent only in relation to its external forms.

3. *The Solution of the Ethical Problem*. To their own satisfaction, the Essenes had delivered the definitive answer to the ethical problem of Job. No longer need the saints be perturbed over the misery of the righteous and the prosperity of the wicked, for now they had an eschatology which would right all wrongs in an everlasting existence after death. To achieve the bliss of heaven and escape the eternal torments of hell, God's Elect will love Him and do His will in the present life. To that end, they will combine into communal societies, where all will contribute according to their ability and receive accord-

ing to their need; by achieving this perfect brotherhood now, the righteous are made fit for the apocalyptic kingdom of God on earth and for a blessed eternity thereafter in heaven.

C. HISTORICAL SKETCH OF THE ESSENES

1. *The Zadokites and the Chasidim.* During the period preceding the desecration of the Temple by Antiochus Epiphanes, apostasy to Hellenism had become rampant; and, to combat it, a group had arisen known as the Zadokites and later as the Chasidim (Hasidim, Assidaeans). Zadok had been the high priest in the time of David. We must realize that these patriots of 185-160 underwent a complex evolution and division into parties during the ensuing decades. The old name continued as a badge of honor; and therefore we find both the Essenes and the antithetical Sadducees calling themselves the Sons of Zadok as late as 60 B.C. The latter were the nobles, the wealthy, the educated, who composed the dominant class. They rejected the Zoroastrian-Pythagorean eschatology, and were totally unaware of any social injustice.

2. *The Three Jewish Parties.* During the early Maccabaean campaigns, the original Sons of Zodok, who were simply intensely Judaistic, split into two divisions: the political nationalists, or Sadducees; and the religious enthusiasts, or the Chasidim, who absorbed the Zoroastrian eschatology, remade the Jewish Messiah in the image of the Saoshyant, and engrafted the doctrines of hell, heaven, immortality, resurrection, and the last judgment upon the traditional Judaism. It was a Chasid who wrote the last six chapters of Daniel, which became the model for Revelation. The older portions of *The Book of Enoch* were composed by Chasids, as were other documents ever after held sacred by the Essenes.

While discussing the reign of Jonathan, 160-143, who became also high priest in 152, Josephus declares that during this period (about 145) the three great religious sects, which were really political parties, became established among the Jews. He declares that the Sadducees, like the Epicureans, denied the existence of providence and believed in free will; the Pharisees, like the Stoics, believed in determinism; but the Essenes, like the Pythagoreans, taught the doctrine of necessity or fate.[5] What happened was this: the Sadducees became more conservative economically and politically, but less religious; the Chasidim split into two divisions, the Pharisees and the Essenes. As the last two matured between 145 and 100, their divergence, in spite of their common Zoroastrianism, became wider and deeper. Whereas the Essenes more and more abandoned the temporal, the Pharisees, becoming worldly, sought power, wealth, and popular influence. The latter became the spokesmen for the people, and the former the depository of extreme religious fervor. The Pharisees envisioned a world in which the Jews would rule over a great empire to be established by their Messiah, the son of David; the Essenes considered themselves the Elect Ones of the Supreme God, chosen by Him to rule over an apocalyptic kingdom of saints to be inaugurated by the supernatural Messiah of Moral Judgment. The Pharisees accepted and developed the Temple worship, while the Essenes, rejecting the ritual of blood-sacrifice, established a severe and all-encompassing discipline based upon faith, sacraments, and holy works. While the Pharisees externalized religion into an elaborately formalized discipline, the Essenes made it a way of life, requiring profound moral regeneration intended to govern every overt act and secret thought. That many of these characteristics already existed by the time of John Hyrcanus in 134, we can scarcely doubt. Josephus declares that the "Pharisees have delivered to the people a great many observances . . . which are not written in the laws of Moses and" which "the Sadducees reject," who "are able to persuade none but the rich," while "the Pharisees have the multitude on their side."[6] Eventually, the latter elaborated thirty-nine classes of labor forbidden on the Sabbath, and made endless subdivisions under each. Various schools of casuistry arose, which debated the finest points of interpretation. For example, a woman could untie certain knots on the Sabbath, but only if she could do it with one hand. A light might be extinguished to exorcise an evil spirit, but not for the sake of thrift. And so it went.

3. *The Essenes Become Pythagoreans.* Shortly before the year 100, a revolutionary development took place among the Essenes. A great leader arose among them, who, perhaps, like Zoroaster and Pythagoras traveled abroad and absorbed the religions of Persia, Egypt, and Greece; certain it is that he mastered Pythagoreanism; upon the Zoroastrianized Judaism which already constituted Essene ideology, he engrafted the discipline and the mysteries of the Orphic-Pythagoreans. It is also certain that he claimed a divine power by which to interpret the prophets. It is likely that he composed an additional revelation in the name of Enoch; that he wrote *The Manual of Discipline;* and that he interpreted various ancient prophecies as descriptions of current catastrophes. He transformed Essenism into a doctrine of social revolt, in which the possession of wealth or property became criminal *per se*. Under his leadership, the cult abandoned Judaism more than ever before and embraced much broader ideas concerning race and salvation: the Messiah, no longer a mere moral judge nor simply an avenger of the Jews, as in Daniel and Isaiah, became an international Saoshyant. In short, under the new dispensation, the Essenes were transformed substantially into Pythagoreans.

4. *Essenes Retain Their Jewish Integument.* The Essenes, however, even while abandoning Judaism in reality, never surrendered the discipline of the Mosaic Law, for which they remained sticklers to the end. Nor did they surrender the Jewish scriptures, especially the prophets; for they saw in these fervent denunciators of wealth and idolatry their own true brethren and forerunners. In order to establish their peculiar doctrine, they composed documents which they attributed to Enoch and the Patriarchs, men whose antiquity did, and whose authority might, exceed that credited to the Torah itself. After adopting the eschatology of Zoroastrianism and the discipline and soteriology of the Pythagoreans, what remained of Judaism was a mere husk, as it were, to support the

concepts derived from Persia, India, Greece, and Asia Minor. Thus was formed the great Jewish synthesis which was contemporaneous with Mithraism but which followed Pythagoras by four centuries.

5. *Excavations at Khirbet-Qumran.* From February 9 to April 24, 1954, an expedition worked to uncover the ruins of Khirbet-Qumran, which include a principal building 111x90 feet and several smaller ones. From coins, pottery, and other evidence, found there, we know that the monastery was first used about 104; and this original occupation continued to about 31 B. C., when the structure was seriously injured by an earthquake. It was then abandoned until 4 B. C., when the building was repaired and reoccupied as before, until 68-69 A. D., when it was gutted by fire. It was again used in 132-135 by Bar Cochba, and then abandoned forever to the shifting sands. We know, consequently, that Khirbet-Qumran was the headquarters of the Essenes from about 104 to 31 B. C. and from 4 B.C. to 68-69.

The construction of the building establishes that it was a community center; it contained a large upper room (see Mark 14:15) in which the eucharistic feasts were celebrated; it had a scriptorium, equipped with seats and benches, in which the scrolls were studied and copied; it had a commissary in which the common goods were stored; and just outside stood the cistern in which the daily baptismal baths were taken. It is obvious that the main building contained no living quarters; the residents, who may have numbered some two hundred at any given time, lived in caves or tents nearby. The cemetery, which lies to the east of the building, contains about two thousand graves, of which a small percentage have been excavated.

6. *Cleavage in Jewish Society.* We know that John Hyrcanus, 134-104—the first who assumed the triple crown of ruler, high priest, and prophet[7] — carried out various military expeditions against his neighbors. The Asmoneans, having achieved independence, immediately sought to establish a savage imperialism upon the Samarians, Edomites, Moabites, Ammonites, and others. Nor were

they content with tribute: they gave their neighbors the short shrift of accepting Judaism, being driven from their homes, or suffering death at the point of the sword.[8] About 109, however, an event occurred which was fraught with fearful consequences for the Jewish nation: Hyrcanus went over to the Sadducees, and embarked upon a career of domestic persecution.

7. *The Master of Righteousness.* It was undoubtedly soon after this that the Essenes reorganized themselves into their *thiasoi* under their current Master of Justice or Teacher of Righteousness.. Thereafter, the fierce struggles between the Pharisees and the Sadducees became a matter of indifference to the Essenes, who withdrew from all such conflicts among the Sons of Darkness and dedicated themselves to meditation concerning the impending apocalyptic catastrophe. Considering this ephemeral existence quite inconsequential, they gave formal allegiance to whatever civil power happened to exercise authority at the moment; but their esoteric religious documents and doctrines became profound secrets, to be shared only by their tried and trusted comrades.

Thus, under the leadership of their Master, the Essenes lived their submerged life for something like forty years preceding Pompey's capture of Jerusalem, which, at a single stroke, put an end to the Asmonean dynasty and the political independence of the Jews.

Authentic history knows even less concerning the Teacher of Righteousness than it does of Jesus. And is this so strange? The Essenes were sworn to absolute secrecy. Since their doctrines were revolutionary, the publication of these would have brought condign punishment upon them. Even as Pythagoras and his followers were ruthlessly slaughtered, so the Essenes had good reason to fear at all times bloody assault and general destruction. We can only say that the Teacher was venerated by the community, but that his identity was little known beyond its pale.

8. *The Teacher Executed.* Nevertheless, in spite of their secrecy and their apparently innocuous activity, the Essenes must have incurred suspicion and enmity. They

refused to take any oath; they were pacifists; their holy days were different from those of the orthodox; they ignored the Temple worship; they rejected marriage and private property: all this must have been generally known, even though their scriptures were effectively concealed. It is possible that Aristobulus II, the last Asmonean king, had learned their secrets from spies planted within their ranks. At all events, it is certain that shortly before Pompey rent the veil of the Temple, the Teacher of Righteousness was arrested, tried, condemned to death, and executed. Some have surmised that this was the "Onias, a righteous man . . . and beloved of God," who was stoned to death by "wicked Jews,"9 about 65. However, the evidence is too fragile to establish such a conclusion.

9. *The Teacher Becomes the Expected Messiah.* Thereupon the conviction took hold upon his followers that the Teacher had risen from the dead, had ascended to heaven, and would shortly return as the all-powerful Son of Man, surrounded by myriads of angels; and that he would conduct the last judgment, establish the kingdom of heaven upon earth, and send all sinners—that is, all who love material things, indulge in marriage, and reject the communal life—to an eternal flaming hell. The Teacher of Righteousness became thus, in his first appearance, a divine incarnation, who, in his second, was to be a reconstituted Danielic Son of Man who would also be the Messiah of Moral Judgment, actuated by Buddhist-Pythagorean ethical principles. Precisely when his Parousia was expected we cannot now declare with certainty; but we know that the delay was to be brief. Those who had seen his execution expected also to witness his return in glory.

Had the Asmonean dynasty continued in power after the execution of the Teacher, the Essenes in general would probably have suffered a similar fate. But with the advent of Roman sovereignty in Jerusalem, such extirpation could no longer be carried out. The Essenes, therefore, more secretive than ever retired to their monastery and to their various *thiasoi* throughout the land, to practice their communal living, study their mysterious scriptures, and await their Messiah.

10. *Absence from the Monastery.* We have noted that the monastery at Khirbet-Qumran remained unoccupied after the earthquake of 31 until 4 B. C. What was the reason for this? We believe that a passage in Josephus supplies the key.[10] While Herod was very young, the Essene Manahem had prophesied that he would one day be king; and, therefore, "he continued to honour all the Essenes." Because of the constant conspiracies against him, Herod required oaths of allegiance. "The Essenes," however, "were excused from this imposition."[10] We believe that during the reign of Herod, they enjoyed such favor and immunity that they abandoned their headquarters in the desert.

11. *The Messiah Fails to Return.* By 25 A. D. the Essene Messiah was more than half a century overdue. Nevertheless, the air was electric with expectation. At this juncture, John the Baptist, believing himself the incarnate Elijah and the harbinger of the Messiah, appeared suddenly in the wilderness off the shore of Jordan in Judea declaring that the kingdom of heaven was at hand. Whether he was an Essene who had left the Order or whether he was simply an individual prophet attempting to establish a cult of his own, we cannot now determine. Like Jesus, he despised and hated Pharisee and Sadducee alike, whom he characterized as "a generation of vipers."

We doubt that the careers of John or of Jesus Himself provoked more than a passing ripple within the Essene community. Their Messiah had already completed his earthly career, and, even if his return was inexplicably delayed, there could certainly be no other. And so the Essenes gazed skyward and waited. Their dreams, however, were crushed in the general catastrophe which destroyed the Jewish state in 70 A. D. We know only that the Romans burned the Khirbet-Qumran monastery and we conclude that the Essenes were scattered to the winds.

D. DESCRIPTIONS BY CONTEMPORARIES

1. *Philo Judaeus.* It is indeed fortunate that we possess detailed descriptions of the Essenes from the pens of two

great Jewish writers, Josephus and Philo Judaeus. The second of these was an Alexandrian, who made himself the master of Hellenic philosophy, especially that of Plato, Pythagoras, and the Stoics, and who had attempted a union of Greek metaphysics with Judaic theology. He it was who first gave the Logos doctrine, previously enunciated by Zeno, its final formulation. Since Philo was an earnest inquirer who lived a long life which ended about 40 A. D., he must have known intimately all the elements constituting Jewish life during the half century preceding his death. His testimony, therefore, must be accepted as authentic. We read that their leader had "trained to"[11]

community of living many thousands of disciples, who are called Essens, because of their holiness. . . . They dwell in many cities of Judaea and many villages, and in large and populous societies. . . . And their mode of life is our evidence of their liberty; none ventures to acquire any private property at all, no house or slave, or farm cattle, or any of the other things which procure or minister to wealth; but they deposit them all in public together, and enjoy the benefit of all in common. And they dwell together in one place, forming clubs and messes in companies, and they pass their whole time in managing every kind of business in the public good. But different members have different occupations, to which they strenuously devote themselves, and toil on with unwearied patience, making no excuses of cold or heat or any change of weather. . . .

Of the men, then, who thus differ in occupations, every one on receiving his wages gives them to one person who is the appointed steward: and he, on receiving them, immediately purchases the necessary provisions, and supplies abundance of food and other things of which men's life is in need. And they who live together and share the same table are content with the same things every day, being lovers of frugality . . . Not only have they a common table, but also common raiment; for they are supplied in winter with thick coats, and in summer with cheap tunics, so that every one, who will, may easily take whichever he likes, since what belongs to one is considered to belong to all, and the property of all to be, on the other hand, the property of each one.

Moreover, if any of them should fall sick, he is medically treated out of the common resources. . . . And so the old men if they happen to be childless, are wont to end their lives on a very happy and bright old age, inasmuch as they are blest with sons both many and good. . . .

Further, then, as they saw with keen discernment the thing which alone, or most of all, was likely to dissolve their community, they repudiated marriage and also practiced continence in an eminent degree. For no Essene takes to himself a wife, because woman is immoderately selfish and jealous . . . For the man who is either ensnared by the charms of a wife, or induced by natural affection to make his children his first care, is no longer the same toward others, but has unconsciously become changed from a free man into a slave.

A second passage from Philo contains complementary information:[12]

There are . . . Essenes, in number something more than four thousand . . . not sacrificing living animals, but studying rather to preserve their minds in a state of holiness and purity. These men . . . not storing up treasures of silver and gold, nor acquiring vast sections of the earth out of a desire for ample revenues . . . are nevertheless accounted very rich, judging contentment and frugality to be great abundance, as in truth they are.

Among these men you will find no makers of arrows, or javelines, or swords, or helmets, or breastplates, or shields; no makers of arms or military engines; no one, in short, attending to any employment whatever connected with war, or even to any of those [ordinary] occupations even in peace which are easily perverted to wicked purposes; . . . they repudiate and keep aloof from everything which can possibly afford any inducement to covetousness; and there is not a single slave among them, but they are all free, aiding one another with a reciprocal interchange of good offices; and they condemn masters, not only as unjust, inasmuch as they corrupt the very principle of equality, but likewise as impious, because they destroy the ordinances of nature, which generated them all equally.

But in their view this natural relationship of all men to one another has been thrown into disorder by designing covetousness, continually wishing to surpass others in good fortune, and which has therefore engendered alienation instead of affection, and hatred instead of friendship; and leaving the logical part of philosophy . . . they devote all their attention to the moral part. . . .

Now these laws they are taught at other times, indeed, but most especially on the seventh day, for the seventh day is accounted sacred, on which they abstain from all other employments . . . a great many precepts are delivered in enigmatical modes of expression, and allegorically. . . .

In the first place, then, there is no one who has a home so adequately his own private property, that it does not in some sense also belong to every one: for besides that they all dwell together in companies, the house is open to all those of the same notions, who come to them from other quarters; . . . and they cherish respect for their elders, and honour them and care for them, just as parents are honoured and cared for by their lawful children; being supported by them in all abundance both by their personal exertions, and by innumerable contrivances.

2. *Josephus.* We turn now to Josephus, who was born about 37 and died about 100. He was a general in the Jewish army of insurrection during 68-69, but earned the clemency and favor of the Romans after he decided

the war was hopeless. In his *Life,* he tells us that at the age of sixteen he became an Essene neophyte and dwelt for three years in the wilderness with a teacher named Banus, who bathed constantly in cold water to curb his libido, who, like John the Baptist, lived on uncooked food that grew wild, and who wore only such clothing as could be procured from trees. We conclude that this discipline lost its attraction, because presently Josephus joined the Pharisees, "which is of kin to the sect of the Stoics."[13] Although he was never admitted to the inner circle of the Essenes, he certainly knew more about them than any other extant witness; and he has left us several descriptions of them. In one passage he declares:[14]

> The doctrines of the Essens is this: That all things are best ascribed to God. They teach the immortality of souls, and esteem the rewards of righteousness are to be earnestly striven for; and when they send what they have dedicated to God into the temple, they do not offer sacrifices there, because they have more pure lustrations of their own; on which account they are excluded from the common court of the temple, but offer their sacrifices themselves; yet is their course of life better than that of other men; and they entirely addict themselves to husbandry. It also deserves our admiration, how much they exceed all other men that addict themselves to virtue. . . . This is demonstrated by that institution of theirs which will not suffer anything to hinder them from having all things in common, so that a rich man enjoys no more of his own wealth than he who hath nothing at all. There are about four thousand men that live in this way, and neither marry wives, nor are desirous to keep servants; as thinking the latter tempts men to be unjust, and the former gives the handle to domestic quarrels; but as they live by themselves, they minister to one another. They also appoint certain stewards to receive the incomes of their revenues, and of the fruits of the ground; such as are good men and

priests, who are to get their corn and their food ready for them. They none of them differ from others of the Essens in their way of living.

We find that the Essenes, like the Buddhists and the Pythagoreans, sought personal freedom and independence by rejecting marriage, together with all family ties and responsibilities; and they mortified "the body of this death," by renouncing sex-consummation, which has appeared to ascetics of all ages as the ultimate triumph over our lower nature.

The following is our most detailed account:[15]

> For there are three philosophical sects among the Jews . . . the third sect, which pretends to a severer discipline, are called Essens. These last are Jews by birth, and seem to have a greater affection for one another than the other sects have. These Essens reject pleasures as an evil, but esteem continence, and the conquest over our passions, to be virtue. They neglect wedlock, but choose out other persons' children while they are pliable, and form them according to their own manners. . . .
> 3. These men are despisers of riches. . . Nor is there any one to be found among them who hath more than another; for it is a law among them that those who come to them must let what they have be common to the whole order, insomuch that among them all there is no appearance of poverty, or excess of riches, but every one's possessions are intermingled with every other's possession, and so there is, as it were, one patrimony among all the brethren. . . .
> 4. They have no certain city, but many of them dwell in every city; and if any of their sect come from other places, what they have lies open to them, just as if it were their own, and they go into such as they never knew before, as if they had been ever so long acquainted with them. For which reason they carry nothing at all with them when they travel into

remote parts, though still they take their weapons with them for fear of thieves. Accordingly, there is, in every city where they live, one appointed particularly to take care of strangers, and to provide garments and other necessaries for them. . . . Nor do they allow of the change of garments, or of shoes, till they be first entirely torn to pieces, or worn out by time. Nor do they either buy or sell anything to one another, but every one of them gives what he hath to him that wanteth it, and receives from him again in lieu of it what may be convenient for himself; and although there be no requital made, they are fully allowed to take what they want of whomsoever they please.

5. . . . .every one of them are sent away by their curators to exercise some of those arts wherein they are skilled, in which they labor with great diligence till the fifth hour. After which they assemble themselves together again into one place, and when they have clothed themselves in white veils, they then bathe their bodies in cold water. And after this purification is over, they every one meet together in an apartment of their own, into which it is not permitted to any of another sect to enter; while they go, after a pure manner, into the diningroom, as into a certain holy temple, and quietly set themselves down; upon which the baker lays them loaves in order; the cook also brings a single plate of one sort of food, and sets it before every one of them; but a priest says grace before meat, and it is unlawful for any one to taste of the food before grace be said. The same priest, when he hath dined, says grace again after meat, and when they begin, and when they end, they praise God, as he that bestows their food upon them; after which they lay aside their white garments, and betake themselves to their labours again till the evening. . . .

6. And truly, as for other things, they do nothing but according to the injunctions of their curators; only these two things are done among them

at every one's own free will, which are to assist those that want it and to show mercy; for they are permitted of their own accord to afford succour to such as deserve it, when they stand in need of it, and to bestow food on those that are in distress; but they cannot give anything to their kindred without the curators. They dispense their anger after a just manner, and restrain their passion. They are eminent for fidelity, and are the ministers of peace; whatsoever they say also is firmer than an oath; but swearing is avoided by them, and they esteem it worse than perjury; for they say that he who cannot be believed, without swearing by God, is already condemned. They also take great pains in studying the writings of the ancients, and choose out of them what is most for the advantage of their soul and body, and they inquire after such roots and medicinal stones as may cure their distempers.

7. But now, if any one hath a mind to come over to their sect, he is not immediately admitted, but he is prescribed the same method of living which they use for a year, while he continues excluded, and they give him also a small hatchet, and the forementioned girdle, and the white garment. And when he hath evidence, during that time, that he can observe their continence, he approaches nearer to their way of living, and is made a partaker of the waters of purification; yet is he not even now admitted to live with them; for after this demonstration of his fortitude, his temper is tried two more years, and if he appear to be worthy, they then admit him into their society. And before he is allowed to touch their common food, he is obliged to take tremendous oaths that, in the first place, he will exercise piety towards God; and then that he will observe justice towards men, and that he will do no harm to any one, either of his own accord or by the command of others; that he will always hate the wicked and be assistant to the righteous; that he will ever show fidelity to all men,

and especially to those in authority; because no one obtains the government without God's assistance; and that if he be in authority, he will at no time whatever abuse his authority, nor endeavour to outshine his subjects, either in his garments or any other finery; that he will be perpetually a lover of truth and propose to himself to reprove those that tell lies; that he will keep his hands clear from theft, and his soul from unlawful gains; and that he will neither conceal anything from those of his own sect, nor discover any of their doctrines to others, no, not though any one should compel him so to do at the hazard of his life. Moreover, he swears to communicate their doctrines to no one any otherwise than as he received them himself; that he will abstain from robbery, and will equally preserve the books belonging to their sect, and the names of the angels (or messengers). These are the oaths by which they secure their proselytes to themselves.

8. But for those that are caught in any heinous sins they cast them out of their society, and he who is thus separated from them does often die after a miserable manner; for as he is bound by the oath he hath taken, and by the customs he hath been engaged in, he is not at liberty to partake of that food that he meets with elsewhere, but is forced to eat grass, and to famish his body with hunger, till he perish. . . .

9. . . . . Moreover, they are stricter than any other of the Jews, in resting from their labour on the seventh day; for they not only get their food ready the day before, that they may not be obliged to kindle a fire on that day, but they will not remove any vessel out of its place, nor go to stool thereon. Nay, on other days . . . covering themselves round with their garment, that they may not affront the divine rays of light, they ease themselves. . . .

10. Now after the time of their preparatory trial is over, they are parted into four classes; and so far are the juniors inferior to the seniors, that if the seniors should be touched by the juniors, they must

wash themselves, as if they had intermixed themselves with the company of a foreigner. They are long-lived also, insomuch that many of them live above a hundred years, by means of the simplicity of their diet, nay, as I think, by means of the regular course of life they observe also. They contemn the miseries of life, and are above pain, by the generosity of their mind. And as for death, if it will be to their glory, they esteem it better than living always; and indeed our war with the Romans gave abundant evidence what great souls they had in their trials, wherein, although they were tortured and distorted, burnt and torn to pieces, and went through all kinds of instruments of torment that they might be forced either to blaspheme their legislator or to eat what was forbidden them, yet they could not be made to do either of them, nor once to flatter their tormentors, or to shed a tear; but they smiled in their very pains, and laughed those to scorn who inflicted the torments upon them, and resigned up their souls with great alacrity, as expecting to receive them again.

11. For their doctrine is this, that bodies are corruptible ... but that the souls are immortal, and continue for ever and that they come out of the most subtile air, and are united to their bodies as to prisons, into which they are drawn by a certain natural enticement; but that when they are set free from the bond of the flesh, they then, as released from long bondage, rejoice and mount upward ... and thence are those exhortations to virtue, and dehortations from wickedness collected, whereby good men are bettered in the conduct of their life by the hope they have of reward after their death, and whereby the vehement inclinations of bad men to vice are restrained, by the fear and expectation they are in, that although they should lie concealed in this life, they should suffer immortal punishment after their death. These are the divine doctrines of the Essens about the soul. which lay an unavoidable bait for such as have once had a taste of their philosophy.

12. There are also those among them who undertake to foretell things to come, by reading the holy books, and using several sorts of purifications. . . .

13. Moreover, there is another order of Essenes, who agree with the rest as to their way of living, and customs, and laws, but differ from them in the point of marriage, as thinking that by not marrying they cut off the principal part of human life, which is the prospect of succession; nay rather, that if all men should be of the same opinion, the whole race of mankind would fail. . . . But they do not use to accompany with their wives when they are with child, as a demonstration that they do not marry out of regard to pleasure, but for the sake of posterity. . . .

3. *Summary*. Instead of consuming the space necessary to analyze these quotations, we ask the reader to re-read and carefully consider every statement, for each is weighted with far-reaching implications. We proceed now to an analysis of several Essene documents, which corroborate fully the statements of Philo and Josephus, but which, in addition, reveal a great many facts and doctrines entirely unknown, or not attributed with assurance to the Essenes, before the discovery of the Dead Sea Scrolls.

CHAPTER III

THE ESSENES: THE INTERNAL EVIDENCE

A. GENERAL CONSIDERATIONS

The Essene scriptures were, as Philo remarked, "delivered in enigmatical modes of expression, and allegorically," which would, nevertheless, be plain enough to the esoterics for whom they were intended. Since some of the personalities and incidents discussed are now obscure, definitive interpretations are sometimes impossible. Yet, every now and then, there is an unmistakable reference, which places a whole sequence in its historical setting.

Since the Jewish canon as organized by Ezra about 450 knew nothing of the novel doctrines later absorbed by the Chasid-Zadokite priests, it became mandatory for them to devise an entirely new corpus of sacred literature, nearly all of which exhibits certain common characteristics, among which we may note the Zoroastrian eschatology, the attribution of all earthly sin to the Watchers, the unquestioned authority of Enoch and his priority over Moses, the inscription of the Law upon "the heavenly tablets," and the insistence upon the 364-day year, which was in conflict not only with the 365¼-day Greek year but also with that of official Jewry as well.

In the ensuing pages, we use Millar Burrows' translation of *The Damascus Document, The Habakkuk Commentary, The Manual of Discipline, The War of the Sons of Light,* and the *Thanksgiving Psalms.*

B. THE DAMASCUS DOCUMENT

The *Damascus Document,* also known as *A Zadokite Fragment,* was found in Egypt in the Genizah (storehouse for discarded documents) of a Karaite monastery late in the nineteenth century and published in 1910. It represents a stage in the development of the Essene cult long preceding its reorganization into a communist society; and we can only conclude that it was produced by a segment of the developing Chasidim who had broken away from the main body of the older Zadokites because the religious fervor of these was insufficient and because they rejected the new eschatology.

Its first section provides a clue to its date of composition. Pursuant to the three hundred and ninety days (years) of tribulation prophesied in Ezekiel 4:5, the author infers that this punishment was to begin with the destruction of Jerusalem by Nebuchadnezzar in 586. This brings us to 196 when God "caused to sprout from Israel and Aaron a root of planting to inherit the land." This must have been the movement organized by the Sons of Zadok who "were like men blind and groping for the way for twenty years." This carries us to 176. At this point, God "raised up for them a teacher of righteousness to lead them in the way of his heart." Note that this was not *the* but *a* teacher of righteousness; the reference must have been to the Damascus leader, elsewhere called the Unique Teacher and the Star of Jacob.

The Damascus Document belongs to an early phase of the Essene movement; it breathes fiercely of Judaism; its Zoroastrian eschatology is rudimentary; the concepts of Pythagoras are unknown; there is no communism; Hebrew slaves are permitted; members are encouraged to marry; and blood sacrifices are required.

The Zadokites of Damascus were exiles who had established their residence in Syria: "The well is the law, and those who dig it are the captivity of Israel, who went out from the land of Judah and sojourned in the land of Damascus."[1] We learn that these exiles had a great leader called "the Star," who was also "the interpreter of the law who came to Damascus, as it is written, 'A Star shall come forth out of Jacob, and a sceptre shall rise out of Israel.' The sceptre is the prince of the whole congregation."[2] But we learn also that this "interpreter of the law" was in no sense regarded as the Messiah, nor was he expected to return. Rather he is called the Unique Teacher, between whose death, or "gathering," and the coming of the Messiah, a period of "about forty years" is to intervene. This is a projected fulfillment of Ezekiel 4:6. We hear much concerning the Man of the Lie, who may have been one of the Hellenizing high priests; and we learn that there were deserters from the Damascus Covenanters, and that these were to be cursed, expelled from the congregation, and have no "share in the house of the law."[3]

Assuming that the *Damascus Document* was composed about 170-165, and that the Unique Teacher was "gathered in" about 170, the Messiah and the annihilation of the wicked were due about 130. These forty years are called the "whole period of wickedness."

That the Damascus enthusiasts were a tightly organized group we learn in detail.[4] They lived in camps, or at least had their headquarters there. Groups could be set up in any community with not less than ten members, of whom at least one must be a priest or a Levite. They practiced purification by water and took their sacramental meals in common; and offenses were punished by separation from the sacred food or by excommunication and expulsion exactly as with the later Essenes. To bear a grudge against a brother was a very serious matter; and, precisely as among the Essenes and in the Gospel Jesus, an erring brother must first be rebuked in private, then before witnesses, and finally before the whole congregation. Those of the Covenant could not transact "business with the sons of the pit. . . . And no man shall make an agreement for buying and selling unless he has told the superintendent who is in the camp."

Admission at this time required no novitiate; but it was a very serious matter: oaths and examinations were prerequisite and non-members were denied knowledge concerning the ordinances of the group.[5] Membership was divided into four classes, who were seated in order at "the session of all the camps. . . . The priests first, the Levites second, the sons of Israel third, and the proselytes fourth."[6] It was provided that every member must donate for charity "at least . . . the wages of two days every month . . . and they shall put it into the hand of the superintendent."7 Between all this and the equality, celibacy, and communism of full-blown Essenism, there remained a wide gulf; yet the road from the one to the other was direct and unbroken.

The Covenanters must "separate from the sons of the pit; and keep away from the unclean wealth of wickedness."8 They must not "rob the poor"; they must separate the clean from the unclean and "keep the Sabbath day according to its explanation, and the festivals and the day of the fast according to the decision of those who entered into the covenant in the land of Damascus."8 This would indicate that a new calendar, of which we shall hear more, was devised at this time. Each covenanter is "to love his brother as himself"; and each is "to rebuke his brother according to the commandment, and not bear a grudge from day to day."8 These principles were carried over into mature Essenism and the Gospel Jesus.

C. THE WAR OF THE SONS OF LIGHT WITH THE SONS OF DARKNESS

1. *The Sons of Darkness Identified.* This book reflects a high degree of Zoroastrian influence. We are shown a world in which the Sons of Light, who are loyal children of Israel, are locked in a vast battle against the Sons of Darkness, or the army of Belial, which, we are told specifically, consists of "the troop of Edom and Moab and the sons of Ammon . . . the people of Philistia . . . the troops of the Kittim of Assyria (Syria), and with them as helpers the violaters of the covenant,"9 that is, the apostate or Hellenizing Jews.

2. *Date.* We believe that *The War* was composed soon after *The Damascus Document*, perhaps about 165-163, or soon after Antiochus retreated from his African campaign. For we are told that there would be war between the Kittim of Egypt and the king of the north (Syria); "and his wrath shall destroy and cut off the horn of his strength."10

3. *The Sons of Light.* When *The War* was written, the Damascus exiles must have returned to rejoin the main body of the Jews in their current wars; they now gave the Maccabees the support they had withdrawn from the Zadokites. After listing the Sons of Darkness, the author declares that the sons of Levi, Judah, and Benjamin and "the exiles of the desert, shall fight against them and their forces with all their troops, when the exiles of the sons of light return from the desert . . . And the dominion of the Kittim [the Syrians] shall come to an end . . . and there shall be no survivor of the sons of darkness."[11]

We remember that according to *The Damascus Document* forty years remained before the Messiah was due; in *The War* we read that "thirty-three years . . . are left the men of renown."[12] This can only signify that *The War* was written seven years after the *Document*. The Messiah was still due about the year 130 B. C.

4. *The Holy War.* The author is depicting a holy war as conducted by the Maccabees; but it is neither apocalyptic nor Messianic; it is to be fought by the Jewish saints according to ordinary tactics. The writer has exact knowledge concerning the organization and strategy of current warfare: the array of battle, the number of men and chariots involved, the qualifications of horses and soldiers, the precise role of the priests.

With overweening confidence, the author outlines a series of victorious wars which the saints will wage during a ten-year period against Egypt, Mesopotamia, Lud, Syria, Uz, Hul, "Tozar and Mashsha, who are across the Euphrates"; against Arpachshad, Assyria, Persia, "and the people of the east as far as the great desert;" and finally against Elam, Ishmael, Keturah, and the sons of Ham.[13] In short, the saints are to conquer all nations and establish a world-empire surpassing that of Alexander.

D. THE BOOK OF THE JUBILEES

1. *Purpose.* The purpose of *The Book of the Jubilees*, which was a drastic revision and elaboration of Genesis and which was written during the reign of Hyr-

canus, was to establish the ultimate authority of *Enoch;*[14] to introduce Zoroastrian eschatology;[15] and to supply divine sanction for the 364-day year, consisting of four 91-day seasons.[16] In addition, it confers patriarchal blessings upon Levi and Judah, and prefigures the descendants of these as the ultimate rulers of Israel and the source of the Messiah.[17] This is another characteristic of Essene ideology during this stage of its development and is particularly emphasized in the ground-stratum of *The Testaments of the Twelve Patriarchs.* Unlike the older Jewish prophets, these Essenes had no expectation of reconstituting the twelve tribes.

2. *Excoriation of Jewish Persecution.* The author begins by condemning the Jewish leaders for persecuting the true prophets. In a strain almost identical to various statements of Jesus, we read that God will send them witnesses, whom they will slay; and that they will persecute those who seek the law. . . . And they will go astray as to new moons, and sabbaths, and festivals, and jubilees, and ordinances."[18]

This reflects the suppression suffered by the Essenes and the continuing conflict over the calendar and diverging dates for holy days.

E. THE THANKSGIVING PSALMS

The *Thanksgiving Psalms* breathe the aspirations of early Essenism, but, since they are devoid of historical allusion, they cannot be placed in a particular decade. They reflect Zoroastrian metaphysics and eschatology; in this they differ from the Davidic psalms. Since they are not concerned with any specific temporal conflict, they are totally different from the Pharisaic *Psalms of Solomon,* which are filled with terrible imprecations against the Asmoneans and the Sadducees and relate graphically the capture of Jerusalem and the desecration of the Temple by Pompey, who is even more fiercely condemned.

F. THE BOOK OF ENOCH

1. *The Principal Essene Document.* The Book of Enoch is unique, since its various portions represent every formative period of the cult; since it was its principal independent scripture; and since it contains most of its novel doctrines. It consists of a series of revelations produced one after another between cir. 180 and about 95-70. In the older portions, we find a commingling of Zoroastrianism with Judaism, somewhat as in the last six chapters of Daniel. The later sections, however, reflect a fundamental development; and this was inevitable, since they were composed after the Essenes became Pythagoreans and express, therefore, a communist and celibate philosophy.

It is pertinent to note that in *Enoch* we find the first precise formulation of Christian eschatology, according to which all souls are immortal individuals who, at death, pass either into eternal bliss or everlasting torture. This, and the concept of the Parousia, according to which the god-man prophet is both the sacrificial deity and the Messiah who rises from the grave later to return for the purpose of conducting the Last Judgment and establishing on earth the kingdom of the saints, were the specific, original contributions of the Essenes to world-religion.

An Ethiopic MS. of the book was first discovered by Bryce in Abyssinia in 1773. Since then, others have been found. Although *The Book of Enoch* is quoted directly in Jude 14-15 and was widely known and used in the early Church, it gradually fell into disuse and no copy of it was known in Europe for more than twelve hundred years.

2. *Division by Chronology and Sequence.* As the nine parts into which the book is formally divided do not coincide with its real divisions, and as their sequence does not conform with the chronological order of composition, we present the following analysis:

FIRST PORTION: Before 170 B.C.

PART I   Chapters i-v   There is here no Messiah or Son of Man,

PART II   Chapters vi-xi   but a God, known as
                                    the Holy Great One, who
PART III   Chapters xii-xxxvi   conducts the last judg-
                                    ment, condemns the
                                    Watchers to the abyss
                                    of fire, and establishes
                                    the Messianic Kingdom.

SECOND PORTION (Fourth in Sequence): 161 B.C.

PART VIII Chapters lxxxiii-xc   In this apocalypse, Jud-
                                as Maccabaeus inaugur-
                                ates the Messianic King-
                                dom, which the Messiah
                                later takes over, and
                                from which he is to rule
                                over all nations in Jeru-
                                salem. This portion of
                                Enoch is a completely
                                nationalistic Jewish con-
                                ception, probably written
                                by a Chasid, and it re-
                                flects the ideology of *The
                                War.*

THIRD PORTION (Also Third in Sequence): 140 B C.

PART VII   Chapters lxxii-lxxxii This is a treatise on
                                    Astronomy, explaining in
                                    detail the 364-day year
                                    and its division into four
                                    seasons, as also estab-
                                    lished in the *Jubilees.*

FOURTH PORTION (Fifth in Sequence): 105-95 B.C.

PART IX   Chapters xci-cv   This is a highly devel-
                                       oped apocalypse, com-
BOOK OF NOAH: Chs. cvi-cviii   posed after the Essenes
                                       became Pythagoreans, in

which the desire for riches and power is condemned as the proof of unrighteousness, and in which sainthood appears as union with God and his Son, evidenced by love for mankind and the renunciation of all things worldly.

FIFTH PORTION (Second in Sequence): 95-70 B.C.

PART IV	Chapters xxxvii-lix	An elaborate Zoroastrian-Pythagorean synthesis. The Lord of Spirits commissions the Son of Man, who now appears under that title for the first time in *Enoch*, chosen before the world was created, to judge sinners and righteous. The Elect are those who have a congenital compulsion toward righteousness, which causes them to abhor the things of this world, and to love God and their fellowmen; thus, they achieve sainthood and will be called to everlasting glory.
PART V	Chapters lx-lxxi	

3. *Analysis of First Portion.* This purports to be a vision of Enoch describing a remote future, which was to be the last age and was actually that in which the real author lived. It is the most primitive of all extant Jewish documents permeated by Zoroastrianism, and it

is certainly older than the second half of Daniel. There is no Messiah or supernatural agency separate from God Himself, who is called The Holy Great One or The Great Glory. The author is filled with wrath against the wicked and unrighteous, who seem to be simply the Jewish ruling class. The Watchers, that is, the evil angels who introduced luxuries and weapons of war among men, are sentenced to everlasting torture; and their leader, Semjaza, is bound in chains and cast into eternal hell-fire. The righteous Elect are shortly to be established as the perpetual rulers in the Messianic kingdom. God Himself will appear upon earth to conduct the last judgment and to institute His government amidst disturbances of nature.

God commands Raphael, one of the seven archangels or Ameshaspentas appropriated from Persian angelology, to "bind Azazel," that is Satan or the devil, "hand and foot, and cast him into the darkness . . . and on the day of the great judgment, he shall be cast into the fire,"[19] precisely as happens in Zoroastrianism and in the Christian Revelation. It is pertinent to note that the Satan or devil-concept is completely absent in the purely Jewish scriptures, since these were based on Semitic ideology, which was entirely devoid of metaphysical dualism.

That early Essenism was untinged by Pythagorean philosophy is established by its desire to "beget thousands of children."

Enoch is conducted by the archangels Uriel and Raphael to the end of the universe, where he finds that souls are kept in three "hollow places," under the earth;[20] it is obvious that we have here a re-creation of the Zoroastrian concept according to which the righteous, the wicked, and the neutral souls remain in separate and appropriate regions within the earth until the judgment day.

There is a curious blending of Persian with Chaldean-Jewish myth.[21] At the Zoroastrian judgment, as in the Mithraic, immortality is to be conferred upon purified souls by the administration of a last eucharist; and we find that a similar result is to be achieved in *Enoch* by eating of the tree of life, the fruit of which was forbidden in the Garden of Eden. Thus the Zoroastrian Haoma is identified with a Genesis-concept.

4. *Second Portion.* The second apocalypse is also comparatively primitive, but reveals a distinct development. Like *The War,* it is very belligerent and intensely Judaic. God Himself is still called The Holy Great One, who again conducts the last judgment. The destruction of the earth is foretold, according to Zoroastrian prophecy, and there is to be a new and glorious Jerusalem.

The vision consists largely of allegory relating the events of Genesis and Jewish history down to Judas Maccabaeus, at which point the end of Time and the last judgment are to occur. Under a transparent veneer, the *dramatis personae* of Old Testament history parade before us as bulls, heifers, wolves, asses, eagles, kites, ravens, etc.

There is a long passage devoted to the seventy shepherds who slew and destroyed more sheep (Jews) than they were commanded by the Lord. These are the kings and high priests who misruled Israel between Solomon and the Maccabees.

After the Babylonian exile, "I saw until that twenty-three had undertaken the pasturing and completed in their several periods fifty-eight times."[22] Now, if a time is a seven-year period, we subtract 416 from 586; and this brings us very aptly to the year 170. At this time, a new era of righteousness began, because "behold, lambs [Chasids] were borne by these white sheep [Jews], and they began to open their eyes and to see, and to cry to these sheep. Yea, they cried to them, but they did not harken to what they said."[22]

This reminds us of a passage in *The Damascus Document* in which we read that "they were like blind men and groping for the way for twenty years." But God "raised up for them a teacher of righteousness to lead them in the way of his heart." The wicked Jews, however, "banded together against the life of the righteous, and all who walked uprightly their soul abhorred."

Returning to *Enoch,* we read: "I saw in the vision how the ravens [Syrians] flew upon those lambs and took one of those lambs [Mattathias], and dashed those sheep [the

Chasids] in pieces and devoured them. And I saw . . . till there sprouted a great horn [Judas Maccabaeus] from one of those sheep, and their eyes were opened. . . . And those ravens fought and battled with it and sought to lay its horn low, but they had no power over it." History now passes into prophecy; the battle continues without decision until the God of the sheep destroys all their enemies, who "were swallowed up in the earth."[22] God now sets up His throne "in the pleasant land," (Palestine); the archangel who has kept the record opens the sealed books; and the Last Judgment supervenes.[22] The fallen angels known as the Watchers, the wicked Jewish rulers called shepherds, and the apostates known as "blinded sheep" are cast into the fiery abyss. The supernaturally constructed Jerusalem appears; and the Messianic kingdom in which the Chasid saints are the rulers is established by the Holy Great One. The Gentiles are now transformed into "white bulls," that is, they become regenerate, and submit to the universal dominion of the Chasidim. From the bosom of this enlightened world-community, the Messiah emerges at last, who is, presumably, to rule forever; "the first among them became a lamb, and that lamb became a great animal . . . and the Lord of the sheep rejoiced over it and over all the oxen."[22]

Thus, for the first time, the Messiah is called a lamb.

5. *Third Portion*. This is *Enoch's* revelation concerning astronomy, important because the calendar was determined by it, together with the number of days in the year, and the sequence of sabbaths, feast days, and holy days. It is clear that the Chasid-Essene year of 364 days was an attempt to correct the older Jewish year of 360 by intercalating four days, one at the end of each season. Confusion became worse confounded when Antiochus Epiphanes in 165 attempted to establish the Hellenic year of 365¼ days, as indicated in Daniel 7:25. Enoch assumes that the Chasid year had existed from time immemorial and that the intercalary days had been eliminated only of late; and it attributes recent crop failures to this official repudiation of the true calendar and the obligations of the jubilees.

6. *Fourth Portion*. With this section, which contains the third apocalyptic vision, we find a new and different *Enoch:* for we have now entered the Pythagorean period of Essenism. The holy and righteous are those who have separated themselves from the world, and the possession of wealth has become the badge of damnation; those who acquire lands and money must burn in the everlasting fires of hell. World history is divided into ten weeks, in the sixth of which the Babylonian Captivity occurs. Then "in the seventh week, shall an apostate generation arise . . . And at its close shall be elected The elect righteous."[23] The apostates consisted of the Hellenizers, the Sadducees and the later Asmoneans. The close of the week was the second century, when the Essenes, "The Community of God," would arise, which would receive the revelation of Enoch and constitute "the eternal plant of righteousness." The eighth week was then to follow, in which the Messianic kingdom would be established and in which the saints would "acquire houses through their righteousness" and "sinners shall be delivered into the hands of the righteous."

This was written about 100: and the writer believed the apocalyptic kingdom he was describing was to come immediately. And his promise was the same as that contained in the Gospel Jesus, in which we read that the meek shall inherit the earth and that those who forsake family, lands, and houses are to be reimbursed a hundredfold as soon as the wicked are consigned to hell; for then the saints will occupy their houses and their lands and the universe will be renewed, as in all Zoroastrian eschatology.

This portion of *Enoch* burns with fierce hatred toward those who have acquired wealth and oppress the poor; the author is persuaded that private possessions can be obtained only through social crime: "Woe to you, ye rich. . . . Ye have committed blasphemy and unrighteousness, And have become ready for the day of slaughter and . . . judgment."[24]

The following, itself similar to an ancient Buddhist parable, is the original of the Lazarus-rich-man story of

Luke:[25] "Woe to you who acquire silver and gold . . . and say: 'We have become rich . . . and have possessions. . . . And now let us do what we purposed; For we have gathered silver. . . . And our granaries are . . . full. Yes, and your riches shall not abide . . . For ye have acquired it all in unrighteousness and ye shall be given over to a great curse."[26]

Those whose luxury derives from the labor of others are bitterly denounced: "Woe to you who build your houses through the grievous toil of others, All your building materials are the bricks and stones of sin. . . . In blazing flames worse than fire shall ye burn. Ye sinners, who are content to eat and drink, and rob and sin, and strip men naked, and acquire wealth and see good days . . . ye shall have no peace."[27]

7. *Fifth Portion*. This is the latest, longest, and most elaborate of the visions. God is now called the Lord of Spirits; the Messiah is a distinctly separate agency called the Son of Man, as in Daniel; the fierce hatred of the author is concentrated upon the mighty of the earth, probably the Asmoneans, represented by Alexander Jannaeus; there is also a change in eschatology, for the blessed dead now dwell before the throne of God while awaiting the Messianic kingdom, as in the *Bundahis*, the *Dinkard*, the *Bahman Yast*, and in Revelation. But the most significant alteration is in the Messiah Himself: He is now, like the Soshans, a spiritual and pre-existing power, to be seated on the throne of his glory at the inauguration of his kingdom. The coming of this Son of Man is to be a sudden manifestation, at which time "Mine Elect One shall sit on his throne of glory. . . . And I will transform the heaven. . . . And I will transform the earth and make it a blessing: And I will cause Mine Elect Ones to dwell upon it: But the sinners and evil-doers shall not set foot thereon . . . I shall destroy them from the face of the earth."[28] The Essenes lived in happy anticipation of the Last Judgment, when they would behold their enemies burning "as straw in the fire . . . The name of the Lord of Spirits be blessed!"[29] Obviously, this is Ahuramazda, not Yahweh.

The revelation concerning the Son of Man had as yet been made only to the Elect; the congregation of the righteous was gradually being created;[30] on the Great Day, these would be glorified and their oppressors, "the kings and the mighty . . . who rule the earth" would be delivered up to vengeance, "because they have oppressed his children and his elect . . . and they shall be a spectacle for the righteous," who "shall rejoice . . . because" the sword of the "Lord of Spirits . . . is drunk with their blood."[31]

The Sons of Light are the Elect Ones, predestined to glory.

G. THE MANUAL OF DISCIPLINE

1. *A Code of Conduct. The Manual of Discipline* sets forth the practical rules and regulations of the Pythagoreanized Essene community.

2. *Cult Universalized.* With the adoption of Pythagoreanism, the cult became universalized near the end of the second century: no longer are the Sons of Light identified as the children of Jacob, and the Sons of Darkness as their current political enemies. Now, instead, it is the poor who are the righteous, because they practice community, are pitted against those who are guilty of social injustice or economic exploitation. In this newly discovered division of humanity into saints and sinners, race is no longer a determining or even an important factor.

3. *Membership in the Community.* Our copy of *The Manual* begins by listing the duties of the members. They are to seek God; do what "he has commanded through the prophets and Moses; . . . love all the sons of light, each according to his lot in the counsel of God, and hate all the sons of darkness, each according to his guilt."

Josephus declares that one of the solemn oaths taken by an Essene was "that he will always hate the wicked and be assistant to the righteous." Actually, this hatred was a duty quite as sacred as his love for the brethren. *The Manual* explains that those who enter the covenant must practice community of goods, and must never seek to alter the established calendar. Members must never swerve from the pathway of community "because of any dread or terror or trial or fright in the dominion of Belial," that is, from fear of those who remain outside the holy Order. "The Levites shall recount the iniquities of the sons of Israel and all their transgressions and sin in the dominion of Belial." In a dramatic repudiation of orthodox Judaism, the Essenes declared upon entering the community: " 'We have committed iniquity . . . we and our fathers before us.' . . . Then the priest shall bless all the men of God's lot . . . And the Levites shall curse all the men of Belial's lot and shall answer and say: 'Accursed may you be in all your wicked, guilty works . . . and may you suffer wrath in the deep darkness of eternal fire . . .' And all who are passing over into the covenant shall say after those who bless and those who curse, 'Amen! Amen!' "

In *The Damascus Document* we found that there were four classes, which agrees with Josephus. *The Manual*, however, speaks only of three: priests, Levites, and lay members. The novices must have been the fourth division. After the cult was communized, no distinction was recognized bewteen Jews and proselytes.

We are told that until the coming of the Messiah, there must be an annual convocation in which each covenanter shall take his position according to established rank. This confirms the statement of Josephus concerning the manner in which the Essenes arranged themselves in order of precedence and seniority. It is interesting to note Jesus declaration that the first should be last and the last first which was obviously part of His revolt against the rigid system of Essene priority, and constituted a democratic invitation to mass-membership along Buddhist lines.

No rituals could bring salvation outside the Order whoever "refuses to enter God's covenant . . . with the upright he will not be reckoned. His knowledge and his strength and his wealth shall not come into the council of the community . . . He will not be purified by atonement offerings, and he will not be made clean with an water . . .; Unclean, unclean he will be all the days that he rejects the ordinance of God."

4. *Doctrine of Metaphysical Dualism*. We have already seen that the Zoroastrian concept of the universe and of every human being was based upon a cosmic dualism in which the two primordial powers carry on perpetual warfare in the macrocosm of the universe, and within every human organism, which is the microcosm. This metaphysical system flowed from Zoroastrianism into Pythagoreanism, and became the basis for its celibacy; it entered Platonism in modified form, making the body the prisonhouse of the soul. Finally, *via* Essenism, it became the philosophical basis for the Gospel Jesus. This dualism is expressed categorically in the *Gathas*,[32] the ideology of which is reproduced in *The Manual,* which attempts to engraft these Zoroastrian concepts upon Judaism. In the new synthesis, however, the Evil One is not recognized as unoriginated, but becomes, as in Christianity, a creation of God, who, we are told, "created man . . . and made for him . . . the spirits of truth and error. In the abode of light are the origins of truth, and from the source of darkness are the origins of error. In the hand of the prince of light is dominion over all the sons of righteousness; in the ways of light they walk. And in the hand of the angel of darkness, is all dominion over the sons of error; and in the ways of darkness they walk . . . In the ways of the two spirits men walk. And all . . . their works are in their two divisions, according to each man's inheritance . . . for all periods of eternity. For God has . . . put eternal enmity between their divisions . . . God . . . has ordained" the ultimate destruction "of error. . . . And he will make the upright perceive the knowledge of the Most High. . . . For God has chosen them for an eternal covenant, and theirs is all the glory of man. . . .

"Thus far the spirits of truth and error struggle in the heart of man . . . and according to each man's inheritance in truth he does right, and so he hates error but according to his possession in the lot of error he does wickedly, and so he abhors truth. For in equal measure God has established the two spirits until the period which has been decreed for the making new."³³

Here we have a faithful rendition of Zoroastrian ethics, metaphysics, and eschatology, except that in this version the wicked spirit was created by God, which certainly makes Him responsible for the origin and the existence of evil. As in Persian ideology, the human race is divided into two camps or armies, the Sons of Light and the Sons of Darkness. The God of knowledge, or prescience, who is here called the God of Israel, gives to some the power to be guided by the Spirit of Light, but to others falls the lot of darkness; every destiny, therefore, is controlled by fate and subject to eternal predestination. Those chosen by God for His eternal covenant are the Elect, who cannot fail to be redeemed. All others must inevitably be plunged into the eternal fires of hell.

The Sons of Darkness are easily recognized because they strive for money and wealth, own property, marry and rear families, and are always concerned over material things; the Children of Light, on the contrary, sell all that they have, combine this with the possessions of the poor, embrace the holy, communist, celibate life, enter the Community of God, and devote their lives to the praise and adoration of the Lord of Spirits. We know that this dualism was well established among the Essenes even before they became Pythagoreans.³⁴

5. *Admission, Novitiate, and Discipline.* "And this is the order for the men of the community . . . to become a community in law and in wealth, answering when asked by the sons of Zadok."³⁵ Members must, *The Manual* observes, "take it upon themselves in the covenant to be separated from all the men of error who walk in the way of wickedness."³⁵ And it continues: "unless they have turned from their evil," that is, unless there has been thorough moral regeneration, "they shall not enter the water, in order to touch the sacred food of the holy men. First, there must be an inner transformation; second there is purification by baptism; and, third, the member is admitted to the sacramental meals, a procedure confirmed by Josephus. The men of the community must

never be united with unholy men in work or in wealth; "and no man . . . of the community shall answer when asked by them regarding any law or ordinance."³⁵ As Josephus declared, the member "swears to communicate their doctrines to no one any otherwise than as he received them himself." The same relationships as those enjoined in the early Christian community were operative: "One shall not speak to his brother in anger or in resentment . . . a man shall not bring against his brother a word before the masters without having rebuked him before witnesses. . . . In these ways they shall walk in all their dwellings. . . . Together they shall eat, together they shall worship, and together they shall counsel."³⁵

The next paragraph makes it plain, as both Philo and Josephus indicate, that these Essene societies existed in many places; for it provides that whenever "there are ten men of the council of the community there shall not be absent from them a priest. . . ." This was the same ordinance as in *The Damascus Document*. "And when they set the table to eat, or the wine to drink, the priest shall stretch out his hand first to pronounce a blessing with the first portion of the bread and the wine." This was the daily sacrament which Josephus described and without which the Essene life would have been meaningless.

In explaining how admission to the Order was achieved, *The Manual* tallies exactly with Josephus. This was similar to that practiced in the original Pythagorean societies. The applicant was questioned by the masters, who rejected him, or accepted him as a probationer for one year, while he submitted to the discipline of the order without enjoying its benefits or fellowship. At the end of this period, if he passed the examinations then imposed, he received baptismal purification and was admitted to the novitiate. At the end of an additional year, there were further examinations, which, if passed, admitted him to the sacred food; his wealth and his wages, which, up to this time had simply been held in escrow, were now mingled with the wealth of the community. However, a third year and the most rigid examinations still remained before he could become a full-fledged brother; if these were successfully met, he was admitted to the holiest sacrament, the eucharistic wine, and to full counsel in the Assembly.

The punishment for concealing private assets was somewhat less drastic than in the case of Ananias and Sapphira: "If there is found among them a man who lies about his wealth, he shall be excluded from the sacred food of the masters for a year, and he shall be deprived of a fourth of his food ration."[35]

Offenses with their appropriate punishments are now listed: for minor infractions the penalty was exclusion from the sacraments and reduction of the food ration for periods ranging from ten days to two years. For major offenses, the penalty was excommunication and expulsion. For calling a brother a fool, the penalty was three months; for interrupting a neighbor, ten days; for gossiping about the brethren, one year; for murmuring against the community, expulsion; for turning traitor against and leaving the Order, irrevocable expulsion.

It may be difficult for us to realize how terrible these punishments were: exclusion from the sacred food and wine meant temporary spiritual death; reduction in the food ration meant serious undernourishment; and expulsion from the Order meant death from starvation, because, as a result of the terrible oaths they had sworn and the discipline to which they had become accustomed, the Essenes could not eat of any except the consecrated food: expelled members simply lay down and died in the desert. We are told by Josephus that rather than eat any "forbidden food," presumably that provided by the Romans, they died under fearful tortures. If such conduct seems irrational to us, we have simply failed to comprehend the fierce motivations of these cultists.

There is a section dealing specifically with the establisment of the Khirbet-Qumran. We are told that after the Order of the Community has been established in Israel, certain elect members will be chosen for a sacred mission "to make atonement for the land. . . . When these men have been prepared in the foundation of the community, for two years with blameless conduct, they shall be separated in holiness in the midst of the council of the men of the community."³⁵ These especially chosen holy men will establish a place of God in "the wilderness to prepare there the way of the Lord."

And so we see that the Essenes established a holy headquarters in the desert to study the law and to prepare for the arrival of the Messiah. The great majority continued in the various *thiasoi* in their regular employment; but those at the monastery must have been professionals of a kind, certainly not wholly self-supporting.

H. THE HABAKKUK COMMENTARY

The *Habakkuk Commentary* has occasioned more controversy than any other among the Dead Sea Scrolls. Mr. A. Dupont-Sommer, in a masterly analysis, has established in his *Jewish Sect of Qumran* II, that the Kittim are the Romans and that the date of composition is shortly after 63 B. C.

The method of the Essene author is to quote a passage from Habakkuk and then to interpret it as a prophecy of current events. What was actually written about the Chaldeans, he applies to the Romans. Should these interpretations seem far-fetched to us, they are certainly much more reasonable than those of modern preachers who profess to find prophecies in the Bible of events yet to come.

The principal characters appearing in *The Commentary* are "the teacher of righteousness," who was the great leader of the Essenes executed just before Pompey desecrated Jerusalem in 63; and "the wicked priest" or "the man of the lie," who was Aristobulus II, the last of the Asmonean kings.

We have already seen that the leader of the Damascus exiles was called the Unique Teacher, the Star of Jacob, and "a teacher of righteousness"; and we pointed out that there must have been such a leader who reorganized the Essenes as Pythagoreans late in the reign of John Hyrcanus. This must have been the usual title of successive cultic leaders; the one executed by Aristobulus and thereafter declared the Messiah simply became the greatest of these "teachers."

The Teacher of Righteousness was an actual individual, believed to possess divine powers by which to interpret the scriptures. And so where Habakkuk reads "'that he may run who reads it,' this meant the teacher of righteousness, to whom God made known all the mysteries of the words of his servants the prophets."[36] When Habakkuk states "'Look among the nations and see; wonder and be astounded'. . . . This means those who acted treacherously together with the man of the lie, for they did not heed the words of the teacher of righteousness from the mouth of God . . . at the end of days: that is, those who are ruthless against the covenant, who do not believe . . . all the things that are coming upon the last generation from the mouth of the priest into whose heart God put wisdom to explain all the words of his servants the prophets."[36] In short, the Teacher of Righteousness possessed divine power to interpret the prophecies. But the Pharisees and the Asmoneans rejected his message when he told them that they were then "at the end of days"; and they persecuted him and were ruthless against the members of the Covenant.

Now follows a passage in which the Romans are described in unmistakable detail, after which Hab. 1:13 is interpreted thus: "Why do ye look on faithless men, but thou art silent at the swallowing by the wicked men of one more righteous than he? This means the house of Absalom and the men of their party, who kept silence at the chastisement of the teacher of the righteousness, and did not help him against the man of the lie, who rejected the law in the midst of the whole congregation."[37]

We believe that "the house of Absalom" were the Pharisees, who, in spite of their own bitter conflict with the Asmoneans and all they had in common with the Essenes, nevertheless kept silence at the trial and "chastisement" of the Essene prophet. The *Commentary* continues "'But the righteous shall live by faith.' This means all the doers of the law in Judah, whom god will rescue from the house of judgment because of their labor, and their faith in the teacher of righteousness."[38] The *Commentary* then quotes Hab. 2:5-6, which condemns greed: "This means the wicked priest, who was named according to the truth when he first took office; but when he had begun to rule in Israel . . . he forsook God and betrayed the statutes because of wealth. . . . He plundered . . . the wealth of the peoples, adding to himself iniquity and guilt; and ways of abomination he wrought in all impurity of uncleanness."[39]

The wicked priest is here the whole Asmonean dynasty. We know that during the beginning of his reign the Essenes regarded Hyrcanus, who was the first to assume the triple crown of king, priest, and prophet,[40] as well as his Maccabaean predecessors with favor. We therefore read that he "was named according to the truth when he first took office . . . but he forsook God and betrayed the statutes." During his maturity, Hyrcanus went over to the Sadducees, fought with his neighbors, placed them under tribute, confiscated their wealth, and forced Judaism upon them. During this fierce crisis, the gulf between Essene and Pharisee was accentuated; for no matter how much the latter hated the Sadducees and the "Apostate" Asmoneans, they always remained throughout thoroughly Judaistic and abhorred the Edomites, Syrians, and other Gentiles even more. The *Commentary* finds in Hab. 2:8 a prophecy which concerns Alexander Jannaeus and Aristobulus II: " 'Because you have plundered many nations, all the remnant of peoples will plunder you'; this means the last priests of Jerusalem, who assembled wealth and booty from the spoil of the peoples, but at the end of days their wealth with their spoil will be delivered into the hand of the army of the Kittim, for they are the remainder of the peoples. 'For the blood of men and violence to the earth . . .:' this means the wicked priest, whom, for the wrong done to the teacher of righteousness and the men of his party, God delivered into the hands of his enemies, afflicting him with a destroying scourge, in bitterness of soul, because he acted wickedly against his elect."[41] The "wicked one," we are told, inflicted "his scourge with judgments of wickedness, and horrors of sore disease they wrought, in him, and vengeance in his body of flesh."[42]

Because the Asmonean "last high priests" had plundered their neighbors, the Jewish people were now being ravaged by the Kittim; and, because the "wicked priest" did wrong to the Teacher of Righteousness and to the men of his party, "God delivered him into the hands of his enemies." The Romans were simply instruments used by God to inflict richly-deserved punishment. Josephus states laconically that when Pompey took Jerusalem, "Of the Jews there fell twelve thousand, but of the Romans very few; . . . He also carried bound along with him Aristobulus and his children."[43] This is confirmed by Plutarch in his *Life of Pompey*.[44]

The *Commentary* proceeds: "'Woe to him who makes his neighbors drink, who pours out his wrath; yea, he has made them drunk, to gaze on their festivals!' This means the wicked priest, who persecuted the teacher of righteousness, wishing to banish him; and at the . . . day of atonement, he appeared to them to confound them . . . on the day of fasting, their Sabbath of rest."[45]

Here we discover the occasion of the Essene leader's execution. Aristobulus, having determined to exile him, had summoned him for inquisition and trial. But the Teacher of Righteousness turned the tables: on the day of Passover or atonement, which, because of the differing calendars used by the official priesthood and the Essene cult, fell on different days, he appeared boldly before the priests of Aristobulus, challenged their calendar, and made "them stumble." The prophet was arrested, tried, condemned, scourged, and executed during the Passover Festival.

And now at last the Essenes possessed that most precious of all religious treasures, without which any broad soteriological conquest over mankind in the Graeco-Roman world would have been impossible; they had their sacrificial god-man, who had given his life for the salvation of many. How the Teacher of Righteousness was transfigured by the imagination of the Essenes in the years following his death we learn from *The Testaments of the*

Twelve Patriarchs, which together with the revelations of *Enoch,* became the basic scriptures of the cult.

I. THE TESTAMENTS OF THE TWELVE PATRIARCHS

1. *Introduction.* In *The Testaments* each of the twelve sons of Jacob delivers to his children a death-bed monologue including ethical instructions, and prophetical revelations concerning "the last times," which, of course, were always those of the actual writer.

The book presents certain difficulties: for its original stratum was composed in the reign of Hyrcanus; but after the fall of Aristobulus II various passages were added and this era became "the end of the ages." Finally, to add to the confusion, we find a very few minor Christian revisions, belonging probably to the first century. What happened was this: the book was first composed about 130-120, before the brotherhood became communist and celibate; then, about the year 60, a number of interpolations were made in which the Teacher appears as the "savior of the world." These reflect a conception so similar to that of the Gospel Jesus that the early Catholics accepted *The Testaments* as Christian revelation. Copies of it were therefore multiplied: by the third century, however, theologians began to doubt its authenticity, and, like *The Book of Enoch,* its authority declined.

The interpolations of 60-50 are almost as distinctive as if they were printed in red ink. Three of the monologues have none; in five, they consist of only from two to seven verses; in two, they comprise from fifteen to twenty; the testaments of Judah and Levi contain the most elaborate additions, which was quite natural, since these were the only tribes which survived.

The Testaments have always been extant. The editors of the *Ante-Nicene Library* included the document among early Christian literature and stated confidently in 1871 that it was written in the second century of our era. R. H. Charles and other scholars, however, established that it was a Jewish composition of the second century

B. C., but interpolated with passages written shortly after the conquest of Jerusalem by Pompey. The conclusions of Charles have now been proved, because fragments of *The Testaments* have been found among the Dead Sea Scrolls. What scholars once believed could only refer to Jesus we now know to have been written about the Essene prophet.

The citations here used are from the translation in *The Lost Books of the Bible,* issued by the World Publishing Company.

2. *Glorification of Hyrcanus.* In their original form, *The Testaments* consisted simply of homilies in which the reader is warned against lying, resentment, hatred, jealousy, intoxication, lust, fornication, greed, covetousness, and the wiles of designing women. Their basic thesis is the primacy of Judah and Levi: from Judah is to arise the king, who is to exercise temporal sovereignty, and from Levi the priest, who is to rule over matters spiritual.[46] Since ancient tradition declared that the Messiah would arise from Judah and be of the stem of Jesse, a new revelation was now necessary to satisfy the Levite Asmoneans. We read that Levi shall be the high priest until the consummation, and that he must be obeyed;[47] the pretensions of John Hyrcanus to his triple office and authority are confirmed.[48]

3. *Altered Attitude toward Asmoneans.* In the interpolations, however, we find a profound change in the attitude toward the Asmoneans. That these additions were made after the capture of Jerusalem by Pompey is established by various passages. We read that "the veil of the temple shall be rent,"[49] as happened for the first and only time when Pompey desecrated the sanctuary; and that "among men of another race shall my kingdom come to an end."[50] This can refer only to the termination of Jewish independence which occurred when Pompey made Israel a tributary in 63. We have, however, a more detailed and decisive passage which expresses the final Essene attitude toward the Asmoneans and which also proves that the interpolations were made immediately

after 63 B. C., since this was the *terminus ad quem* of the author's historical knowledge:[51]

> In each Jubilee there shall be a priesthood.
> 2. And in the first jubilee, the first who is anointed to the priesthood shall be great, and shall speak to God as to a father.
> 4. In the second jubilee, he that is anointed shall be conceived in sorrow of beloved ones; and his priesthood shall be honored and shall be glorified by all.
> 5. And the third priest shall be taken hold of by sorrow.
> 6. And the fourth shall be in pain, because unrighteousness shall gather itself against him exceedingly, and all Israel shall hate each one his neighbor.
> 7. The fifth shall be taken hold of by darkness. Likewise also the sixth and the seventh.
> 8. And in the seventh shall be such pollution as I cannot express before men, for they shall know it who do those things.
> 9. Therefore they shall be taken captive and become a prey; and their land and their substance shall be destroyed.
> 10. And in the fifth week they shall return to their desolate country, and shall renew the house of the Lord.
> 11. And in the seventh week shall come priests, who are idolaters, adulterers, lovers of money, proud, lawless, lascivious, abusers of children and of beasts.
> 12. And after their punishment shall have come from the Lord, the priesthood shall fail.

The first of these seven priests is Judas Maccabaeus, 165-160;[52] the second, Jonathan, 160-143; the third Simon, 143-34; the fourth, Hyrcanus, 134-104; the fifth, Aristobulus I, 104-103; the sixth, Alexander Jannaeus, 103-76; and the seventh, Aristobulus II, 76-63. The whole thumbnail sketch is drawn with rare accuracy.

The estimate of the Asmoneans here and in *The Haba-*

kkuk Commentary is identical. In the time of Hyrcanus, the great sorrow and the final iniquity of Israel began: for then it was that the Jews, split into hostile factions, began to hate each other. The short reign of Aristobulus I is laconically characterized as one of darkness, and it is interesting to note that this agrees precisely with the judgment of Josephus.[53] The reign of Alexander Jannaeus, who crucified the eight hundred Pharisees, and that of Aristobulus II, which was marked by cruelty and profligacy, are likewise condemned. The latter is the "wicked priest" of the *Habakkuk Commentary* in whose reign "shall be such pollution as I cannot express." Therefore, continues our author grimly, "they shall be taken captive and become a prey, and their land and their substance shall be destroyed."

In the verses cited above, the time of each priesthood is called a jubilee; but in verse 10, it is called by the variant metaphor of a week, even though the periods were not equal nor do any of them consist of fifty or of seven years. The fifth week is the reign of Aristobulus I, 104-103, in which "they shall return to their desolate country, and shall renew the house of the Lord." This can only refer to the establishment of the monastery of Khirbet-Qumran, and the previous desolate sojourn may be a reminiscence of the Damascus exile. Verse 11 refers to the wild excesses of Aristobulus II, and verse 12 simply announces the end of the Asmonean and the Jewish kingdom.

4. *The God-Man Savior.* In the *Habakkuk Commentary*, written very soon after the Essene prophet was executed, he is called the Teacher of Righteousness. In *The Testament* interpolations, however, this Teacher has undergone a vast development; he is now regarded as God incarnate, who, appearing upon earth, had walked humbly among men, who had been slain as an atonement for sinners, and who would return in glory shortly. Thus, almost by accident the doctrine of the Parousia was devised and engrafted upon mystery soteriology.

The *Testament* passages which embody this concept

could not have been written by a Christian, because the apostolic Church never taught that Jesus was *God* or that He belonged to the tribe of Levi; it was, however, established among the Essenes that the ultimate judge of mankind would be both. We read, therefore: "God hath taken a body and eaten with men and saved men ... the Lord shall raise up from Levi as it were a High Priest, and from Judah as it were a king, God and Man; He shall save Gentiles and the race of Israel."[54] Priority belongs to Judah and Levi: "charge your children that they be united to Levi and Judah. ... For through their tribes shall God appear dwelling among men on earth."[55]

This priest-king, walking as a man among men, born of Levi and Judah, was the Teacher of Righteousness; but he was also God incarnate: "And ye shall be set at naught in the dispersion. ... Until the Most High shall have visited the earth, coming Himself as a man, with men eating and drinking. ... He shall save Israel and the Gentiles, God speaking in the person of a man." [56]

Again we read: "There shall arise unto you the Lord Himself. ... And ye shall see Him in Jerusalem. ... But again through your wickedness shall ye provoke Him to anger, and ye shall be cast away by Him unto the time of consummation."[57] And so we find that "the Lord Himself," who was the Essene Teacher, would be seen by the Jews in Jerusalem. But they would provoke Him to anger by their wickedness and would be cast away until His second coming.

5. *The Murder of the Savior.* And so the god-man savior had appeared in Jerusalem, where he had been murdered by the Jews. The patriarch Levi is made to purge himself of the crimes to be committed by Aristobulus against the Essenes: "I am clear of all your ... transgressions which ye shall do in the end of the ages against the Savior of the world. ... And ye shall deal lawlessly in Israel, so that Jerusalem shall not endure your wickedness; but the veil of the temple shall be rent, so as not

to cover your shame. And ye shall be scattered as captives amongst the heathen, and shall be for a reproach and for a curse, and for trampling under foot."[58]

And Levi continues: "And a blessing shall be given thee and to all thy seed, until the Lord shall visit all the heathen in [his] *the* tender mercies of *His Son,* even for ever. *Nevertheless, thy sons shall lay hands upon Him to crucify Him;* and therefore have counsel and understanding been given thee, that thou mightest instruct thy sons concerning Him, because he that blesseth Him shall be blessed, but they that curse Him shall perish."[59]

The words here italicized do not occur in the version used by R. H. Charles; and they may constitute a Christian revision in their entirety. The phrase *of His Son* could not have been Essene, for the cult never believed the Teacher to be the *Son of God,* but the Lord of Spirits Himself, incarnate. Should future discoveries reveal the second group of words in italics to be pre-Christian, we will know that the Teacher of Righteousness was also crucified.

Over and over we read of the crime against this prophet: "I have learned that at the end of the ages . . . the chief priests . . . shall lay their hands upon the Savior of the World." And again: "A man who reneweth the law, in the power of the Most High, ye shall call a deceiver; and at last ye shall rush upon him to slay him, not knowing his dignity, taking innocent blood through wickedness upon your heads. And your holy places shall be laid waste . . . because of him. And ye shall . . . be among the Gentiles a curse and a dispersion until He shall again visit you, and in pity receive you through faith and water."[60]

The Essenes called their revolutionary reconstitution a renewal of the law; but the reigning priesthood called it a deception. The sorrows of the Jews are depicted as a punishment from God because they slew the Teacher, the "man who reneweth the law." In due course, the Christians were to call the razing of Jerusalem a divine retribution upon the Jews for crucifying Jesus. Of utmost significance is the statement that the slain renewer of the law would return, and that only then could there be salvation for Israel in the Essene-Zoroastrian sacrament of baptism. So here we have the doctrine of the incarnate god-man, the dogma of the dual manifestation of the Messiah, and the proclamation of the Parousia, the three elements which constitute the core of the Gospel Jesus, two of which were first devised by the Essenes, who, about 60-50 B. C., were in a state of hysterical fervency, awaiting the Second Coming. And it is impossible that the savior here slain could be Jesus, because he is executed by a priest whose priesthood thereupon fails and who is "taken captive." Had the executed prophet been Jesus, it is simply incredible that the role of the Romans could have been ignored nor could he have been called God, or of the tribe of Levi. Furthermore, Caiaphas, Annas, and their confederates neither slew Jesus nor were they punished for their part in His death. They were neither taken captive nor did their office fail, as was the case with Aristobulus II. That the Teacher of Righteousness was judiciously murdered by Jewish priests who were the rulers of an independent state is obvious. Similar as were his execution and that of Jesus in certain fundamentals, it is clear that we are dealing with two separate events. Finally, we know that the whole group of interpolations describing the momentous event was written immediately after 63 B. C., because the writer's knowledge of history terminates at that point.

We have already seen that, according to *The Book of Enoch,* the Messiah was to be known as the Lamb of God. In "Benjamin," the Teacher of Righteousness is identified with this "Lamb of God, and Savior of the world . . . a sinless one" who "shall die for ungodly men in the blood of the covenant."[61] The Christian Church adopted precisely the same concept concerning Jesus: in John 1:29 we read: "Behold the Lamb of God, which taketh away the sin of the world."

6. *The Apocalyptic Parousia.* The "prophecies" in *The Testaments* concerning the god-man savior who

would be slain had already been fulfilled when they were written and served to induce credence for predictions concerning his second manifestation. During the years following Pompey's conquest of Judaea, the Essenes, in their Dead Sea Monastery and their various *thiasoi,* fervently awaited the return of the Messiah in power, surrounded by thousands of thousands of angels. This Parousia is described in various *Testament* interpolations. There would, as in Paul,[62] first be a resurrection of those who shall have died in the faith, as also in Revelation 20:5-6; the kingdom of God would then be established, after which the general resurrection would occur: "Then shall we also rise . . . worshipping the King of heaven, who appeared upon earth in the form of a man in humanity. And as many as believe on Him on earth shall rejoice with Him. Then also shall all men rise, some unto glory and some unto shame. And the Lord shall judge Israel first, for their unrighteousness; for when He appeared as God in the flesh to deliver them, they believed Him not. And then shall He judge all the Gentiles. . . . And He shall convict Israel through the chosen ones of the Gentiles."[63]

Precisely as Jesus was to do, therefore, the Essenes promised glory to those who accepted their Messiah before his second manifestation and the Elect from among the Gentiles would judge the children of the promise. The Parousia, the dual resurrection, and the Last Judgment of the Essenes are identical to those of the New Testament.

There is a detailed description of the late Asmonean period, the destruction of the Jewish nation, and the Messianic kingdom.[64] The prophet declares consolingly that "they who have died in grief shall arise in joy, and they who were poor for the Lord's sake shall be made rich, and they who are put to death for the Lord's sake shall awaken to life."[65]

We recall the passage which describes the seven Asmonean high priests, the enormities under Aristobulus II, and the end of the era.[66] The author then recapitulates Jewish history a second time, and describes briefly the Essene prophet in his first manifestation;[67] at this point we pass from history to prophecy, from completed fact to the expected denouement, which never came to pass; "he shall execute righteous judgment . . . and there shall be peace in all the earth. . . . And in his priesthood the Gentiles shall be enlightened . . . through the grace of our Lord. In his priesthood shall sin come to an end, and the lawless shall cease to do evil. And he shall open the gates of paradise and . . . give to the saints to eat from the tree of life . . . And Belial shall be bound by him, and he shall give power to His children to tread upon evil spirits."[68]

Thus would the Teacher of Righteousness establish the kingdom of heaven upon earth. The entire concept is parallel to that which Jesus entertained concerning Himself. Immediately upon returning to the earth in power, the Teacher was to conduct the Last Judgment and become the head and ruler of the new kingdom; the Gentiles would be enlightened by him, accept his gospel, and become regenerate; the heavenly mansions would also be opened to the saints, where eternal life would be conferred upon them through the mystical eucharist of which we have already heard in Zoroastrianism and *The Book of Enoch;* the Son of Man would bind Satan or Belial and cast him into the everlasting flames; and would give his children power over the evil spirits, as in Mark 16:17.

Here is further proof that the *soter* of *The Testaments* is not Jesus but the Essene Teacher; for the ultimate Zoroastrian eucharist of *Enoch* is unknown in the New Testament.

CHAPTER IV

THE ESSENES: ANALYSIS AND TRADITION

A. IMPLIED DOCTRINES

1. *The Risen Savior.* In the Essene documents at our disposal, we find no specific statement that the Teacher had risen from the grave and ascended to heaven; however, the doctrine of his Parousia implies his resurrection.

2. *The Sacrificial God-Man.* We have traced from its source the evolution of the central doctrine of Christianity, which is that the savior-god who dies that men may live and become immortal is himself the eucharistic bread and wine by which this miraculous transformation occurs. Now, whence did the Gospel Jesus derive this concept? Among the Jews, no one but the Essenes practiced this sacrament before the advent of Christianity; and Buddhism, which could have provided the only discernible elements in the Gospel not derived from Essenism, had no *soter* whatever. While they were appropriating so much else from the Pythagoreans about 105 B. C., it is unreasonable to believe that the Essenes should have failed to adopt the heart of the mystery. In some way, they must have identified their food with a concept of the sacrificed deity.

3. *The Sacraments.* However, the eucharist among the early Essenes must have been of an impersonal nature; for we can find no evidence that before 63 B. C. they had any specific savior-god; and this would indeed have been incongruous in a cult established upon Jewish tradition. Nothing could be more difficult than to engraft the *soter* upon Judaism. Before that date, the bread and wine they took so reverently must have been considered primarily as a consecrated gift.

4. *The New Soteriology.* The death of the Teacher, however, must have effected an almost immediate revolution in their soteriology. We learn specifically that he was "the Savior of the World . . . the sinless one who shall die for ungodly men in the blood of the covenant." He was God, the King of Heaven, appearing in the form of a man, who walked humbly among men and was seen in Jerusalem. The electrifying effect of this doctrine cannot be overstated: for instantly the age-old concepts which had grown up around Osiris-Adonis-Dionysus and the Persian Saoshyant crystallized themselves about this new god-man who had also suffered the very fate of his divine predecessors. There is even a cryptic passage in which a virgin-birth seems attributed to him: "And I saw that from Judah was born a virgin wearing a linen garment, and from her was born a Lamb, without spot."[1]

We believe that after the death of the Teacher, the sacramental meal of the Essenes took on a new and more potent symbolism and became for them mystically the blood and the body of their savior-god. He became their heavenly bread and the gift of everlasting life.

B. THE JEWISH LEGEND OF PANDERA AND YESHU

Throughout the middle ages, the legend of Pandera and Yeshu, considered by most scholars a Jewish invention, continued to persist. The tale, however, is extremely ancient, for it was known, long before the Christians had the power to persecute, to the Greek Neo-Platonist Celsus, who flourished 175-180. Origen, 185-254, quotes the Greek as having said, concerning the mother of Jesus, that "when she was pregnant she was turned out of doors by the carpenter to whom she had been betrothed, as having been guilty of adultery, and that she bore a child to a certain soldier named Panthera."[2]

Knowledge now available concerning the Teacher of Righteousness has thrown an entirely new light on this Pandera-legend, which is related in detail by Morris Goldstein and which, in brief, runs as follows:[3]

There lived in the days of King Jannaeus, 103-76, in Bethlehem, a certain disreputable young man whose name was Joseph Pandera. He seduced the chaste and lovely Miriam by pretending to be her betrothed husband, Johanan; and the result was a son, Yeshoshua, or Yeshu. When it became known that Yeshu was illegitimate, he fled to Galilee, where he practiced magic by learning the letters of the Ineffable Name and where he declared that he was born miraculously of a virgin, according to the prophecy of Isaiah, 7:14. Yeshu, thereupon, declared himself the Messiah, and produced various texts from the prophets, which he said applied to him. The Jewish sages then brought Yeshu before Queen Helene (probably the wife of Aristobulus II) and accused him of sorcery. A corpse was brought in, and when Yeshu restored it to life, the queen became his devotee. The sages now selected a man called Judah Iskarito and taught him also the letters of the Ineffable Name, by which he too could practice magic. In a trial before the queen, both Yeshu and Iskarito lost their memory of the Name and fell down powerless.

Yeshu was now seized and beaten, was given vinegar to drink, and a crown of thorns was placed upon his head at Tiberias. There was a struggle among the people, and Yeshu escaped with some of his fellow-conspirators to Antioch or Egypt, where they remained until the Passover, at which time Yeshu went to Jerusalem to relearn the letters of the Ineffable Name in the Temple. Riding into Jerusalem on an ass, he fulfilled the prophecy of Zechariah. Identified by Iskarito as the false prophet, Yeshu was seized, and put to death on the eve of the Passover Sabbath. If Yeshu was born near the beginning of Alexander Jannaeus' reign, he would have been in his thirties at the time of his execution.

The bold followers of Yeshu now came to Queen Helene with the report that he was not in his tomb, but had ascended to heaven as he had prophesied. Since his body could not be found, she demanded of the sages that they produce it within three days. It so happened, however, that the gardener, foreseeing conspiracies by the followers of Yeshu, had taken the body from the tomb and buried it in the garden; and when he learned of the queen's ultimatum, he told the sages where it lay. They seized it, tied it to the tail of a horse, and dragged it before Helene, who thereupon renounced the false prophet, commended the sages for their wisdom, and derided those who had been deluded by the sorcerer.

The story concludes with a resumé of how the followers of Yeshu sought to overthrow Judaism by re-dating their feast days and their holy celebrations and by repudiating their rituals and their dietary laws; and how they caused a great commotion among the Jews for thirty years by declaring that their prophet was now sitting at the right hand of God and would return as the almighty Messiah to condemn all unbelievers to the eternal fires of hell.

This ancient legend prompts theories which, to say the least, are quite fascinating. We know that the Essenes made a fundamental issue over their divergent calendar, which placed their feasts and celebrations on days other than those observed by the orthodox; and we have seen that it was a dispute over this which precipitated the trial and execution of the Teacher. This squares with the Pandera story but could have no reference to Jesus. There are other reasons for believing this an authentic tradition concerning the Teacher rather than of Jesus: for we are told that the "bold" followers of Yeshu came to Queen Helene declaring that he had ascended to heaven; this was an act quite understandable on the part of well-established Essenes whose leader had already been accepted by the reigning queen, but quite impossible for the cowering disciples of Jesus, who had not the slightest expectation of any resurrection and who had gone into concealment to hide their terrible humiliation. Even more decisive is the fact that the Romans are totally absent from the traditions concerning both Yeshu and the Teacher. And certainly there was no Queen Helene in the days of Pontius Pilate. Furthermore, the thirty-year commotion caused by the followers of Yeshu is entirely consonant with *The Testament* interpolations.

We conclude, therefore, that the Pandera-story was the popular-orthodox Jewish version of the life and death of the Essene prophet and had nothing to do with Jesus. If their careers seem parallel in tradition, this fact stems from their historical similarity. The Christian Judas Iscariot was perhaps a purely ideological re-creation of an historical namesake. We consider it likely that Jesus designed His course of action so that He would die in Jerusalem at the time of the Passover, not only because great crowds would be present, but also because the Teacher had died there during that festival; and that He rode into Jerusalem on an ass partly for the same reason. Even the gardener appears in the fourth canonical Gospel in an enigmatic role. And who can fail to notice the similarity of the empty tombs! Finally, it is entirely possible that a virgin-birth was attributed to Jesus in the second century, partly because this too was an element of the Yeshu-story.

C. ESSENE, CHRISTIAN, PYTHAGOREAN, AND BUDDHIST DOCTRINE

We believe that we can demonstrate the relationship of Christianity to other faiths by an itemized analysis. We exclude the Sadducees since they were antithetical to the Essenes and the Gospel Jesus on every point of doctrine and practice; nor do we include the Pharisees, who were similar to the Essenes only in Sabbath observation and partially in certain eschatological concepts, which their successors, the rabbis, soon abandoned. We do, however, include the Buddhists, who were the source of several important elements found in the Synoptics; and also the Pythagoreans, who were the direct progenitors of the Essenes, as were the latter of the Gospel Jesus.

ESSENE DOCTRINE OR PRACTICE	WAS THERE SIMILARITY IN GOSPEL JESUS OR EARLY CHURCH?	AMONG PYTHAGOREANS?	AMONG BUDDHISTS?
1. Long Novitiates	No	Yes	No
2. Tremendous oaths	No	Yes	No

3.	A secret order	No	Yes	No
4.	Differing classes among members	No	Yes	No
5.	Condemnation of slavery	No	Yes	No
6.	Industry required	No	Yes	No
8.	Sabbath observation	No	No	No
7.	Self-supporting communism	No	Yes	No
9.	Each candidate's property sold and	Yes	Yes	Yes
10.	Money deposited with steward	Yes	Yes	Yes
11.	Communal table	Yes	Yes	Yes
12.	Earthly riches despised	Yes	Yes	Yes
13.	Cultic brotherhood fostered	Yes	Yes	Yes
14.	Sex desire condemned	Yes	Yes	Yes
15.	Marriage repudiated	Yes	Yes	Yes
16.	All relatives rejected	Yes	Yes	Yes
17.	Dualism and predestination taught	Yes	Yes	No
18.	No animal sacrifices	Yes	Yes	Yes
19.	Extreme frugality	Yes?	Yes	No
20.	Equality of dress, etc.	Yes	Yes	Yes
21.	Civil obedience on principle	Yes	Yes	Yes
22.	Bread-wine eucharist	Yes	Yes	No
23.	Grace at meals	Yes	?	No
24.	Intense ethical soul-searching	No	Yes	No
25.	Pacifism	Yes	Yes	Yes
26.	Prophetic power claim	Yes	Yes	No
27.	Use of allegories and parables	Yes	No	Yes
28.	Initiation by baptism	Yes	Yes	No
29.	Use of white garments	Yes	Yes	No
30.	Practice of healing	Yes	Yes	Yes
31.	Ordinary oaths forbidden	Yes	Yes	No
32.	Joy at death	?	Yes	No
33.	Use of apocalypse	Yes	No	No
34.	One immortality for every soul	Yes	No	No
35.	Eternal torment or bliss for all	Yes	No	No
36.	Same salvation for Jews, Gentiles, etc.	Yes	Yes	Yes
37.	Worship of sacrificed god-man	Yes	Yes	No
38.	Chief prophet also *soter*	Yes	No	No
39.	Dual manifestation of *soter*	Yes	No	No
40.	Imminent Parousia	Yes	No	No
41.	*Soter* also final judge	Yes	No	No
42.	Founder to rule earthly kingdom	Yes	No	No

43. This kingdom imminent	Yes	No	No
44. Jews punished for killing god-man	Yes	No	No

We find, accordingly, that Essene doctrine or practice reproduced the Pythagorean under thirty-one of these forty-four headings and that the Gospel Jesus or the early Church, in turn, reproduced thirty-four of them. We discover also that under fifteen of them the ideology of Buddhism recurs in the Gospel; and finally that the Essenes reproduced Zoroastrian doctrine under five or possibly six headings.

But we must emphasize that the Gospel Jesus contains certain specific Buddhist elements: among these are the repudiation of the Sabbath, the establishment of democracy, and the abolition of oaths, secrecy, classes, and the novitiate. Most important are the doctrines, stated or implied, that the poor are holy *per se,* that thrift, industry, and self-reliance are of little value or actually criminal, that the indigent are entitled to alms, and that a mendicant society should replace the self-supporting communist brotherhood. In all these respects Jesus was a Buddhist rather than an Essene-Pythagorean.

Finally, we must note a complex of doctrines found only among the Essenes and in the Gospel Jesus: these deal with eschatology, the *soter,* the Messiah, and the Parousia. The Essenes were the first who taught the doctrine of irrevocable hell-torture for every unbeliever; who combined the concept of the *soter* with that of the Messiah; and who proclaimed the Parousia. All of these were reproduced intact in the Gospel and became the basic doctrines of Christianity.

When Jesus repudiated the fanatical Sabbath observation so holy to the Essenes, He revealed His Buddhist internationalism most dramatically. Other Buddhistic divergencies developed in part from the pressure of the situation: when He began His ministry, He was convinced that the kingdom of God was immediately at hand. The time was short: He was under the fearful compulsion of creating a mass-movement immediately. Instead of making it difficult to join, He invited everyone; oaths and initiations were consequently impractical; disciples were not forbidden to divulge His doctrines, but encouraged to do so; in His democratic following, there was room neither for seniority nor distinction; and He did not find it expedient to make an issue of economic exploitation. After all, in the kingdom now imminent, all the saints would be equal forever.

And we should note that although the Essenes were fanatics in their observation of the Sabbath, they did not follow the entire Mosaic Law. It is almost certain that they were vegetarians; and nothing indicates that they believed in circumcision. We know that they repudiated the Temple worship and sacrifices, and much else which was sacred to the reigning priesthood. The seeds of a classless and international philosophy were present in their ideology; Jesus simply went far beyond them.

D. JESUS AND THE ESSENES

1. *Several Hypotheses.* It may be interesting to note that the Essene-Christian relationship has long fascinated New Testament scholars, among whom several Germans developed intriguing rationalist theories. Bahrdt, 1784-1792, Venturini, 1800, Gförer, 1831-38, Hennel, 1840, and von der Alm, 1863, published disquisitions in which Jesus was represented as trained or controlled by the Essenes, who, in several of the hypotheses, staged His crucifixion with or without the co-operation of the Romans, revived Him after the ordeal, and so created the myth that He had risen from the grave.

About 1830, Thomas de Quincey wrote an essay[4] in which he contends that no such group as Essenes ever existed, that Josephus merely mistook the Christians—whom he never mentions even once!—for these strange persons, who were certainly not then known by that name. He argues that to assume the prior existence of a large and tightly organized group of men with teachings identical to those of the Christians would be a deadly offense against the faith: "If the Essenes were not the early Christians in disguise, then was Christianity, as a knowledge, taught independently of Christ; nay, in opposition to Christ," [5] which, he implies, is impossible and therefore a blasphemous opinion.

The significant fact is that all these and many others recognized the substantial identity of Essenism with the Gospel Jesus long before the discovery of the Dead Sea Scrolls.

Since 1947, more realistic theories have appeared. Mr. Dupont-Sommer declares: "The Galilean Master, as he is represented to us in the writings of the New Testament, appears in many respects as an astonishing reincarnation of the Master of Justice." [6] Mr. Edmund Wilson says, concerning the monastery at Kirbet-Qumran: "this structure that endures, between the bitter waters and precipitous cliffs, with its oven and its inkwell, its mill and its cesspool, its constellations of sacred fonts and unadorned graves of its dead, is perhaps, more than Bethlehem or Nazareth, the cradle of Christianity." [7]

2. *Jesus Not Sponsored by the Essenes.* In spite of the detailed parallelism existing between Essenism and the Gospel of Jesus, it would be a serious error to believe that He could have been a commissioned spokesman for the Order, a mistake which various German scholars made; for His divergencies were quite drastic. The revelation of Himself as the Messiah would necessarily have been a monstrous blasphemy in Essene eyes, probably as much as in Pharisaic. And the greatest treason of all would have consisted in the simple publication of their esoteric doctrines, and the application of them to Himself.

3. *Buddhist Elements.* And beyond all this we must note again that certain elements in the Gospel are Buddhist and not Essene-Pythagorean at all, of which the most important was the substitution of mendicant communism for the self-dependent community. We know that Asia Minor teemed with Buddhist proselytizers in the first century; and that almost no one could have been immune from their propaganda. We know also that the Pythagorean societies differed from the Buddhist primarily in that the former were organizations of working and self-reliant communists while the latter, living in idleness, de-

pended upon gifts and beggary. The Buddhists therefore emphasized the importance of charity, of giving to the poor, whose rights and virtues they always proclaimed. In all this, the Gospel Jesus is far more Buddhist than Essene.

Once we admit that this element in the Gospel is Buddhist, other problems are also solved. Whereas the Essenes were a secret order with a tightly knit membership, regimented into classes, who imparted their doctrines to initiates only after prolonged discipline, the Buddhists broadcast theirs to all who would listen: and they offered to heal the sick, the halt, the lame, and the blind, and to establish a universal kingdom in which private wealth, poverty, and exploitation would be abolished forever. Christians, like Buddhists, had no barriers to membership, no oaths, no novitiates, no distinct orders among themselves, and no rule against divulging their doctrines. In all this also the Gospel Jesus was patterned upon Buddhist rather than Essene antecedents.

However, it is also indisputable that the Gospel, by and large, is not Buddhist, but Essene; that many aspects of Buddhism were present in Pythagoreanism from the beginning and could thus have been transmitted to the Essenes indirectly; and that, finally, many elements are therefore common to Buddhism, Pythagoreanism, Essenism, and the Gospel Jesus, such as communism, rejection of marriage and family, and the glorification of personal poverty.

4. *A revolutionary Movement.* We must realize that Essenism as well as the Gospel Jesus belong among those movements of social revolt which have agitated mankind some three thousand years, the appeal of which has been to the poor and the unsuccessful and which were designed to ameliorate the sufferings of, and supply consolation to, the exploited and the downtrodden. Their ultimate source was Buddhism, which sanctified idleness and mendicancy as the holy pathway to Nirvana, and which renounced labor, property, sex, and family as the only practical means by which to escape the frustration of unrequited toil. All such movements tend to repudiate

the nationalist ideal in favor of a classless, international communion of the poor and the exploited. The philosophy proclaimed by Gautama, however, was so altered by the Pythagoreans as to make themselves self-supporting; but they still refused to surrender any of their labor to parents, brothers, sisters, wives, children, or relatives, and very little, if any, to the state. Such movements have always been distinguished by a fervently proclaimed brotherhood among the oppressed and a violent hatred for the wealthy and the powerful.

5. *Doctrines Parallel to the Christian*. We have, we believe, demonstrated that *The Book of Enoch, The Testaments of the Twelve Patriarchs,* and other Essene documents written before or immediately after the death of the last Teacher contain a whole galaxy of concepts central to the Synoptics. Among these we may list the doctrines of everlasting torture in hell for the damned and eternal bliss in heaven for the saints, a dogma previously unknown in that precise form; the doctrine of the Last Judgment; the concept of the god-man prophet who appears as a man in the flesh, who has been resurrected from the grave, and who combines the functions of the Greek *soter* with those of the Persian Saoshyant; the concept of the Son of Man as the universal Messiah of Moral Judgment; the conviction that the possession of property is incompatible with righteousness; the certainty that those who seek material wealth or who profit by the labor of others must spend eternity in hell fire; the persuasion that only by practicing communal brotherhood on earth is it possible for human beings to achieve eternal salvation; the principle of non-violence even under the most extreme provocation since we know that sinners will be punished amply in the hereafter; the teaching that the righteous will come into possession of the lands and houses of the wicked when these are dragged away to the everlasting flames; and the belief that the kingdom of the saints is to be established in a renewed and renovated earthly and heavenly kingdom by the savior at his second and imminent appearance.

Before 63 B. C., the Essenes had no savior-god; but the

execution of their most celebrated Teacher, as we have seen, provided them with this crucial necessity, precisely as the crucifixion of Jesus served the same purpose in the Christian Church. After 60 B. C., therefore, the Essenes projected their second basic and original doctrine which reappeared in the Gospel Jesus: that of the incarnate god man who dies sacrificially for the sins of the world, is resurrected from the dead, ascends to heaven, where he sits at the right hand of God, whence He is to return in a final parousia to judge the quick and the dead and establish the kingdom of heaven.

6. *World Significance.* The importance of the Essenes in the history of the occident can scarcely be overstated. Had they never existed, there would have been no Christianity and therefore no Catholic Church. In that event one of the rationalistic, scientific, and exclusive cults of Persia would have become dominant in the Graeco-Roman world: possibly Mithraism, but much more probably Manichaeism. We are convinced that had either of these defeated all its rivals, Greek enlightenment would have prevailed after a bitter struggle and the civilization of the ensuing centuries as well as the life of every human being in the western world would have been totally different from what it has been during the last sixteen hundred years.

7. *Our Hypothesis.* Our hypothesis concerning Jesus, is, then, that He had for some years been a member of the Essene community, but had developed serious doubts concerning the validity of its Judaic discipline, and, even more significantly, had become convinced that He, instead of the long overdue Teacher, was the true incarnate Messiah in his human manifestation. During this period of reorientation, He may well have come under the influence of a Buddhist proselytizer, from whom He could have adopted the missionary methods of Gautama. But since He had no following and probably no pre-eminence among the Essenes, He could not possibly reorganize the Community, which had become thoroughly fixed in its doctrines. His only alternative was, therefore, either to live and die in complete obscurity as an obedi-

ent member of the Order, or, combining the Essene synthesis with certain Buddhist concepts, to go forth as an individual, broadcasting the seditious tenets of the sect, proclaiming the acceptable year of the Lord, and hinting broadly that He was Himself the Messiah. In doing this, He would, of course, be repudiated by the Order; He would place His life in constant jeopardy, and His very survival from day to day would depend upon the utmost caution. In any event, He could not long continue in such a perilous undertaking. We believe that He consciously re-created the career of the Teacher of Righteousness and pursued by design a course of action which would lead inevitably to His sacrificial and spectacular death as an atonement for the sins of mankind, persuaded that in this way but in no other could He establish the kingdom of heaven.

Once dead, His teaching, which was a closely-knit synthesis of already-established pagan doctrine, began to take hold; in His repudiation of Judaism, He possessed an immense advantage among the Greeks over His predecessor, the Essene Teacher; through His absorption of Buddhist techniques and appeal, He laid the foundations for a mass-movement. And when a few zealous missionaries began proclaiming the Risen Christ, His Gospel spread like wildfire in the Graeco-Roman world, which was already athirst for just this elixir of life.

PART THREE
THE INNER MEANING OF THE GOSPEL JESUS

The Soteriology:

Verily. verily I say unto you, Except ye eat the flesh of the Son of man and drink his blood, ye have no life in you. . . .

Whoso eateth my flesh, and drinketh my blood, hath eternal life; and I will raise him up at the last day.
John 6:53-54

The Ethics:

He said unto him, Yet lackest thou one thing: sell all that thou hast, and distribute to the poor, and then shalt thou have treasure in heaven: and come, and follow me.
Luke 18:22

Verily I say unto you, There is no man that hath left houses, or brethen, or sisters, or father, or mother, or wife, or children, or lands for my sake and the gospel's, But he shall receive an hundredfold now in this time, houses, and brethren, and sisters, and mothers, and children, and lands with persecution; and in the world to come eternal life.
Mark 10:29-30

The Eschatology:

Then shall the king say unto them on his right hand, Come, Ye blessed of my Father, inherit the kingdom prepared for you from the foundation of the world. . . .

Then shall he say also unto them on the left hand, Depart from me, ye cursed, into everlasting fire, prepared for the devil and his angels.
Matthew 25:34-41

The Kingdom:

And then shall they see the Son of man coming in the clouds with great power and glory. . . .

Verily I say unto you, that this generation shall not pass, till all these things be done.
Mark 13:26,30

The Promises:

Come unto me all ye that labor and are heavy laden, and I will give you rest.
Matthew 11:28

Well done, thou good and faithful servant . . . enter thou into the joy of thy Lord.
Matthew 25:21

PREFATORY

CULTIC PREPARATION FOR CHRISTIANITY

A. ELEMENTS IN CHRISTIANITY

1. *Four Primary Components.* As we have noted, the Gospel Jesus consists of four basic components: soteriology, which came from the mystery-cults; ethics, which came primarily from India; eschatology, largely derived from Persia; and the supernatural Messianic concept, which was an Essene adaptation of a Zoroastrian doctrine. The history of Christianity over eighteen centuries has proved conclusively that its devotees can take or leave the last three of these; some have embraced, others have rejected, one or more of them. But the one central hope which remains constant, the essential element which gives vitality to the religion of Jesus Christ, is the faith in Him as the *soter,* that is, the god-man who sacrificed Himself for us, whose eucharist makes us divine, and who confers upon us resurrection and blessed immortality.

2. *Soteriology of Paramount Importance.* We regard these two conclusions as inescapable: first, that the ancient world had been thoroughly prepared for Christianity by the god-man mystery-cults; and, second, that without this preparation it could never have made any important headway. We note that great as was the debt of the Gospel Jesus to Buddhist and Essene ethics and to Zoroastrian metaphysics and eschatology, neither Persia nor India had ever known a *soter* and therefore to this day Christianity is able to win very few converts in these lands. The same held true of the Jews, the Arabians, the Iranians, the Japanese, the Chinese, and such primitive people as the

American Indians. Among the peoples who had risen above barbarism, only those who had already accepted Osiris, Dionysus, Attis, Adonis, or Mithra could accept Jesus as their savior-god.

3. *Source of Christian Appeal.* Christianity was successful because of its similarity to other religions which had already permeated the Graeco-Roman world. Its advantage was twofold: first, it was the creation of a people, the Jews, more dedicated to religion than any other; and second, it possessed an historical founder to whom was attributed almost every quality and achievement with which the mystery-cults had endowed their own originators.

4. *Why Pagans Accepted Christianity.* The gods of the pagan cults were shadowy figures, which their followers exchanged for a savior so real and so human that they could almost grasp His hand, or at least a hand which had lain in His. Christianity recruited its converts from the ranks of the mysteries by giving a new name to the doctrines and rituals which had been practiced since before the dawn of history. And this is the reason why Justin Martyr could say that "the Jews, in truth, who had the prophecies and always looked for the coming of Christ, not only did not recognize Him, but . . . even mistreated Him. But the Gentiles, who had never even heard of Christ until His apostles went from Jerusalem and preached about Him and gave them the prophecies, were filled with joy and faith, and turned away from their idols, and dedicated themselves to the Unbegotten God through Christ." [1]

This writer, however, was not quite so naïve as these words would indicate, for many passages in his works betray his acute awareness of the fact that, although the Greeks had never heard of Jesus, they were certainly familiar with older, similar *soters*.

5. *Many Messianic Pretenders.* Origen reproduces a significant quotation from the Greek philosopher, Celsus: " 'There are many,' he says, 'who . . . assume the motions and gestures of inspired persons. . . . These are accustomed to say, each for himself, "I am God; I am the Son of God"; or "I am the Divine Spirit; I have

come because the world is perishing for your iniquities. But I wish to save you, and you shall see me returning again with heavenly power. Blessed is he who now does me homage. On all the rest I will send down eternal fire, both on cities and on countries. And those who know not the punishments which await them shall repent and grieve in vain; while those who are faithful to me I will preserve eternally." ' "[2]

Such hierophants must have been numerous in the first century.

B. THE EXPLANATION OF THE FATHERS

1. *Pagan Mysteries Invented by the Devil.* Other elements in the pagan cults provoked the bitter denunciation of the Fathers. We have noted how Tertullian and Justin Martyr explained the similarities between Christianity and Mithraism; and in the following the latter elaborates a favorite thesis: "We . . . demonstrate that the myths have been" invented by "the wicked demons, to deceive and lead astray the human race. For having heard it proclaimed through the prophets that the Christ was to come, and that the ungodly among men were to be punished by fire, they put forward many to be called sons of Jupiter . . . to produce in men the idea that things which were said with regard to Christ were marvellous tales like the things said by the poets."[3]

And again: "For when they tell that Bacchus, son of Jupiter was begotten by . . . intercourse with Semele . . . and . . . relate that, being torn in pieces and having died, he rose again, and ascended to heaven; and when they introduce wine into his mysteries, do I not perceive that the devil has imitated the prophecy announced by the partiarch Jacob . . . [Gen. 49:10]? . . . And when the devil brings forward Aesculapius as the raiser of the dead and healer of all diseases, may I not say that in this matter likewise he has imitated the prophecies of Christ? . . And when I hear . . . that Perseus was begotten of a virgin, I understand that the deceiving serpent counterfeited also this."[4]

The devil, therefore, invented the cult of Dionysus

thousands of years before the advent of Christ so that when men should find the Christian mystery similar to his, they would reject both as poetic fables. Justin continues: "Plato stated that Rhadamanthus and Minos would punish the wicked who came before them. We declare the very same thing will take place, but that it will be Christ who will assign the punishment to sinners." [5]

Because he was intensely aware that various pagan cults performed sacramental rituals more or less identical to the Christian, Paul wrote: "But I say that the things which the Gentiles sacrifice, they sacrifice to devils, and not to God: and I would not that ye should have fellowship with devils. Ye cannot drink of the cup of the Lord, and the cup of devils: ye cannot be partakers of the Lord's table, and of the table of devils." [6]

2. *Christians Accused of Omophagia and Sensuality*. Christianity was so similar to the cult of Dionysus that in the first and second centuries the former was commonly charged with the same infanticide, *omophagia*, and sexual orgies, which had certainly at one time been practiced by the latter. Justin demands: "Do you also . . . believe that we eat human flesh and that after our banquets we extinguish the lights and indulge in unbridled sensuality?" [7]

Theophilus of Antioch, writing about 170, also found it necessary to defend the Christians against the charge of promiscuity and *omophagia*.[8] Communal sharing, however, was their boast; for Tertullian declares: "One in mind and soul, we do not hesitate to share our earthly goods with one another. All things are common among us but our wives." [9] The charges made in the time of Justin Martyr had in no wise abated when Tertullian wrote; he therefore states: "We are accused of observing a holy rite in which we kill a little child and then eat it" and in which "after the feast, we practise incest . . . This is what is constantly laid to our charge." [10]

It is obvious that these charges were leveled against the Christians because they were so similar to the Dionysiacs

3. *The Virgin Birth*. Another matter which intrigued Justin was the Virgin Birth. He did not know that both Zoroaster and his mother Dukdaub were said to have been

born supernaturally, and that the three expected Messiahs of that religion were all to come into the world through virgin births; or that Buddha, Mahavira, and other prophets of India were credited with the same miraculous birth. Justin must, however, have known that Plato was the reputed son of Apollo, as we learn from Origen,[11] and from Jerome,[12] who declares further that "mighty Rome cannot taunt us as though we had invented the story of the birth of our Lord and Saviour from a virgin; for the Romans believe that the founders of their city and race were the offspring of the virgin Ilia and of Mars." [13]

The Christians were indeed not the inventors of the virgin birth! And Justin was acutely aware of the parallel which existed between the origin of Dionysus, Hercules, Theseus, and countless other pagan demi-gods; and, like Origen and Jerome, seemingly oblivious to the fatal implications of this fact, he found justification therein: "When, indeed, we assert that the Word, our Teacher Jesus Christ, who is the first-begotten of God the Father, was not born as the result of sexual relations, and that he was crucified, died, arose from the dead, and ascended to heaven, we propose nothing new or different from what you say about the so-called sons of Jupiter." [13]

Tertullian also sought to justify the doctrine of the Virgin Birth on the basis of its pagan antecedents: "Your philosophers, too, regard the Logos—that is, the Word and Reason—as the Creator of the universe. For Zeno lays it down that he is the Creator ... This ray of God .. descending into a certain virgin, and made flesh ... is in His birth God and man united ... Receive, meanwhile, this fable, if you choose to call it so—it is like some of your own—while we go on to show ... by whom such fables have been set agoing to overthrow the truth." [14]

4. *The Claim of Christian Priority.* Tertullian wrote some fifty or sixty years after Justin Martyr; and it would seem that by this later date the theory that the devil had prepared his mysteries in advance merely to discredit Christianity was no longer considered tenable. With rare contempt for historical sequence, Tertullian declared that the Christian mysteries preceded the pagan and must

therefore be the superior original. As we cannot doubt his sincerity, we must attribute his blindness to a kind of psychosis. For he must certainly have known that doctrines concerning "a reservoir of secret fire under the earth," "the judgment seat in the realms below," "the Elysian Fields," and "Paradise," [15] are entirely absent from the Old Testament; and that they had been widely accepted among the pagans for centuries before the New Testament was written. Yet he declares blandly that all these were taken by the poets and the philosophers "from our religion . . . from our sacred writings, which are of earlier date . . . For never does the shadow precede the body which casts it, or the image the reality." [15]

Never, indeed!

C. PROLIFERATION OF THE PAGAN MYSTERY-CULTS

1. *Pausanias.* Early in the second century A. D., just as Christianity was beginning to penetrate the Roman Empire, there was an erudite and observing traveler, by name Pausanias. Notebook in hand, he visited every province, city, and village; and he left a detailed catalogue of the temples, altars, shrines, and religious statues which he found. For example, he declares that in Elis the temple of Dionysus stood adjacent to his theater, and that the people of the city honored him above all other gods.[16] In Heraea, there were two temples of Dionysus and a separate building in which his orgies were celebrated.[17] And so it was all over Greece. In the minute detail of this reporter, we find ample confirmation of the boast of Tertullian that the temples of the official gods were empty; as the African father declared, those deities were the laughing stock of the philosophers;[18] and Isis, Serapis, and Bacchus, once banished from the capital, had now become powerful gods in Rome.[19] Christians, he declared, now "fill every place ... cities, islands, the palace, the senate, the forum; we have left you nothing but the temples of your gods." [20] The fact is, however, that the Christians were only one among many cults which had subverted the people from the ancient

gods of the Cretan-Olympic pantheon. For the pages of Pausanias bear ample witness that by 100 A.D. every city, village, and countryside teemed with the temples, altars, and shrines of Dionysus, Demeter, Persephone, Cybele, Adonis, Diana, Isis, Serapis, Hecate, Mithras, and others of a congenial nature. Long before Christianity appeared, the battle between the mysteries and the official religion for dominion over the common mind had been concluded. The former were in complete control, so far as the masses were concerned, by the time of Caesar Augustus.

2. *The Religion of the Poor.* This conquest was the result of a long and gradual development which received its greatest impetus from the Pythagoreans, and thereafter became an irresistible tide which swept onward and upward until it engulfed almost the whole of society. It was, as we might expect, among the lower classes that the savior-cults assumed their more virulent and fanatical forms; for it was the poor, the disinherited, the exploited who craved at any price the consolation offered, and who found in the promise of salvation, resurrection, and immortality by mystical union with the *soter* the realization of their frustrated dreams. These cults were also often revolutionary, because, overtly or by implication, they promised economic emancipation to the masses, or at least some relief from the intolerable conditions under which they groaned. But the rich, the fortunate, and the powerful, doomed to destruction, went on their way blissfully unheeding, little realizing that the world under their feet was crumbling away. Even by 200 B.C., the official religion in Rome was falling into contempt, and the burgeoning mysteries had gained domination over the populace. Livy declares that the "Roman ritual was growing into disuse not only in secret, and in private houses; even . . . in the Forum and the Capitol, crowds of women were to be seen who were offering neither prayers nor sacrifices in accordance with ancient usage . . . Unauthorized sacrifices and diviners had got into possession of men's minds and the numbers of their dupes were swelled by the crowds of country people whom poverty or fear had driven into the City, and whose fields had lain untilled owing to the length of the [Punic] War

or had been desolated by the enemy. These imposters everywhere practiced their calling with as much effrontery as if they had been duly authorized by the State. Respectable citizens protested in private against the state of things, and ultimately the matter became a public scandal and formal complaint was made to the Senate. The aediles and commissioners of police were severely reprimanded by the Senate for not preventing these abuses, but when they attempted to remove the crowds from the Forum and destroy the altars and other preparations for their rites, they narrowly escaped being roughly handled." [21] The Senate then passed a resolution that all who had in their possession any of the manuals of these mystery-cults must surrender them to the city praetor; but the women, the peasants, and the poor in general had already fallen so deeply in love with these new religions that they preferred them above all they could hope for in this life, and were prepared to defend them to the death.

3. *The Role of the Roman Empire.* As the Roman power increased in the ancient world, more and more millions were reduced to slavery; and, for the first time, appeared the *proletariat,* a free but propertiless class of laborers, who often had no work and no function and who raised the futile cry, "Bread and the circus!" Nor were these developments the greatest cause of frustration: for, in spite of the generally equitable nature of Roman rule, it reduced the more capable among the conquered into nonentities; and, because the Empire gave them no scope for the exercise of their abilities, they too were prepared to embrace a religion of renunciation and revolt in which they could assume their place in the sun.

Christianity conquered the masses of the Roman Empire by giving them a totally new and different center of loyalty, by replacing the old mystery-cults with a more inclusive amalgam based upon them, and by uniting the people under a single, intolerant discipline and authority. It attracted powerful but frustrated personalities who found in the new cult a novel highway to power and domination.

Having now traced those religious concepts which entered into, and finally constituted, the Christian synthesis, from their original sources in Egypt, Persia, India, Greece, and Asia Minor, as well as from Judaism and Essenism, we are now ready to analyze the authentic Gospel Jesus itself: this begins with the baptism and ends with the empty tomb.

CHAPTER I

THE HISTORICITY OF JESUS

A. WHY IT HAS BEEN QUESTIONED

1. *The Gospel Narrative a Myth?* This study is not so much an interpretation of the Synoptics as an attempt to discover what they actually say. We simply ask the reader to scan the record with us and to consider carefully what Jesus was doing and what His words must have meant to those who heard them from His own lips.

Various scholars have striven to disprove the historicity of Jesus; especially interesting are studies by Edward Carpenter [1] and Georg Brandes,[2] who elaborated a thesis advanced earlier by Bruno Bauer and John M. Robertson. It is true that a case can be made for their point of view, since (1) there is no contemporary independent proof of such historicity; (2) the parallels between Jesus and other savior-gods are numerous and striking; (3) His teaching is obviously a combination of disparate if not contradictory elements; and (4) He could conceivably have been created ideologically, as were Demeter and Mithra.

2. *Silence of Justus and Josephus.* Like Josephus, Justus of Tiberias was a native of Galilee; he lived and wrote there immediately after the death of Jesus. His works include a *Jewish War* and a *Chronicle of the Jewish Kings from Moses to Agrippa II*. We know that his histories were extant at least until 891, because Photius, Patriarch of Constantinople, read them and expressed amazement that they contained not one word concerning Jesus.[3]

In Josephus we have three passages, one about Jesus, a second about the Baptist, and a third concerning the stoning of James the Just, "the brother of Jesus," at Jerusalem.

In the first, we read that "there was about this time Jesus, a wise man, if it be lawful to call him a man, for he was a doer of wonderful works, a teacher of such men as receive the truth with pleasure. He drew over to him both many of the Jews, and many of the Gentiles. He was Christ. And when Pilate, at the suggestion of the principal amongst us, had condemned him to the cross, those that loved him at the first did not forsake him; for he appeared to them alive again at the third day; as the divine prophets had foretold these and ten thousand other wonderful things concerning him. And the tribe of the Christians, so named after him, are not extinct at this day." [4]

The first reference to this occurs in Eusebius about 324 [5] and thereafter it was quoted everywhere by churchmen as important evidence, not of the historicity of Jesus, which no one had questioned, but of His divinity. However, there is not one scholar in the world today who believes the passage genuine. First, it is obvious that section 4 is intended to follow directly after section 2 in the text; second, Christian writers had been using Josephus for almost two centuries without once citing this text; and, third, only a Christian could have written it, which Josephus was not.

The passage referring to John the Baptist [6] was first cited by Origen [7] about 240. It is simply another forgery.

3. *Bruno Bauer.* Misled and overwhelmed by such evidence, Bruno Bauer about 1840 became the first to maintain the non-historicity of Jesus. Ironically, his career in Biblical criticism began with a fierce attack upon David Friedrich Strauss for his denial of any supernatural element in *Das Leben Jesu.* But Bauer soon veered far to the left; and his ultimate conclusions were foreshadowed in studies of the Fourth Gospel and Synoptics. In time he declared that Jesus Himself was only a myth. When his opponents marshaled evidence to the contrary, he was eventually forced into the position that the Christian religion originated during the reign of Marcus Aurelius, 175 A.D.; that all its primary documents were forged by a group of unknown conspirators; that Peter, Paul, Clement, Ignatius, Papias, Justin Martyr, Marcion, etc., were invented by them; that all documents attributed to these writers

were likewise forgeries, concocted late in the second century; that all references to Christianity in Josephus, Tacitus, Suetonius, and Pliny, and all mention of early Christian authors in Tertullian, Clemens Alexandrinus, Irenaeus, etc., were interpolations. The historicity of Paul, of course, if accepted, establishes that of Peter and Jesus also; for Paul teems with historical detail and refers often to them; and in Gal. 1:18 he states categorically that he dwelt fifteen days with Peter in Jerusalem. Certainly no Christian would have invented the bitter feud between Peter and Paul. Bauer might almost as logically have denied the historicity of the Roman Empire.

B. EVIDENCE IN SUPPORT OF HISTORICITY

1. *In Josephus.* The third passage in Josephus, referred to above, however, is certainly genuine. It implies no belief in Christianity; it belongs in the context; the references to James and Jesus are worked in as minor details; and the important element to the author is the unprincipled seizure of power by the High Priest, Ananus. It bears every mark of authenticity and constitutes conclusive evidence that by 62 there were in Jerusalem organized Christians who had aroused the implacable hatred of the Sanhedrin. After the death of Festus, Caesar appointed Albinus procurator of Judaea; but, states Josephus, before his arrival, the high priest Ananus, "a bold man . . . and very insolent . . . assembled the sanhedrin of judges, and brought before them the brother of Jesus, who was called the Christ, whose name was James, and some others; and when he had formed an accusation against them as breakers of the law, he delivered them to be stoned; but . . . those who seemed the most equitable of the citizens . . . went to meet Albinus . . . and informed him that it was unlawful for Ananus to assemble a sanhedrin without his consent. Whereupon Albinus complied with what they said, and wrote in anger to Ananus, and . . . king Agrippa took the high-priesthood from him." [8]

There are two similar references in Origen to this passage, one of which is combined with that dealing with

John the Baptist and noted above. The second of these reads: "And to so great a reputation among the people for righteousness did this James rise, that Flavius Josephus . . . wishing to exhibit the cause why the people suffered so great misfortunes that even the temple was razed to the ground, said, 'these things happened to them in accordance with the wrath of God in consequence of the things which they had dared to do against James the brother of Jesus who is called Christ'." [9]

This proves that sometime before 240 the Christians had corrupted Josephus to make him declare that the destruction of Jerusalem resulted from God's wrath against the Jews for stoning James the Just. It is fortunate that this corruption did not survive as the standard text of Josephus, since the correct reading provides evidence, first, that forgery was common among the early Christians; second, that Christianity was well established in Jerusalem by 62; and, third, that it was common knowledge that the founder of the new cult was one Jesus, known as the Christ. Before the time of Origen, some one had interpolated the passage concerning John the Baptist and had rewritten that concerning James the Just.

2. *Tacitus.* Once the authenticity of the above passage in Josephus is admitted, there is no difficulty in accepting as genuine the celebrated passage in Tacitus, written soon after 100: "Nero fastened the guilt" for the burning of Rome "on a class hated for their abominations, called Christians by the populace. Christus, from whom the name had its origin, suffered the extreme penalty during the reign of Tiberius at the hands of one of our procurators, Pontius Pilate; and a most mischievous superstition, thus checked for the moment, again broke out not only in Judaea . . . but even in Rome, where all things hideous and shameful from every part of the world find their centre and become popular." [10]

This is not the kind of forgery that a Christian, or, for that matter, any one else would have composed; it is simply what we would expect from the pen of any educated Roman like Tacitus. We must, therefore, believe that Christians were numerous both in Jerusalem and in Rome between 60 and 65; that it was common knowledge that a certain Jesus, also known as the Christ or Christos, executed by Pilate, was their founder; and that they were generally regarded as abominable and contemptible wretches, who, like the Jews, were distinguished by "their hatred of mankind." [10]

3. *Other Classical Evidence.* Nor is the passage in Tacitus our only early classical reference to Christianity. Pliny the Younger, in a letter to Trajan dated about 111, concerning the Christians of Bithynia, calls their religion "an absurd and extravagant superstition," [11] which had already been flourishing more than twenty years in that province. Suetonius, after detailing the enormities of which Nero was guilty, lists among his good works that he "inflicted punishment on the Christians, a class of men given to a new and mischievous superstition." [12]

For all practical purposes, these meager texts exhaust our authentic independent testimony; yet they prove that there were organized Christian movements in Jerusalem and in Rome before 65, and that, according to common knowledge, their founder was a certain Jesus, who was called the Christ and who suffered at the hands of the Roman procurator Pilate. The authenticity of all this cannot successfully be assailed.

4. *External Evidence.* Whoever comprehends the nature of *evidence* will know that Gautama, Mahavira, Zoroaster, John the Baptist, Simon Magus, and Manes were actual individuals, just as certainly as were Julius Caesar or George Washington; for we know certain definite facts about them in their historical setting which would never have been created mythologically. By the same token, we know also that Athena, Aphrodite, Mithra, Dionysus, Attis, Bromius, Demeter, Persephone, and Priapus were myths only, that is, purely ideological creations. Concerning Jesus, the evidence is much stronger than with older prophets or saviors, for when He came written records were well kept and His life is definitely fixed in the framework of current history. If we deny His historicity, we must also deny that of Peter, of Paul, of Clement of Rome, of Ignatius, of Papias, and of many others, which

few indeed have ventured to do; and we must devise a sound theory to explain their writings, which bear every earmark of authenticity. We cannot deny that there were many Christians in Rome and Jerusalem by 62, nor can we doubt that the leaders of the cult at that time proclaimed their personal acquaintance with Jesus. It is simply inconceivable that such a Gospel could have developed in thirty years without some historical basis.

The fact is that when certain modern rationalists discovered that Jesus shared various characteristics with the great pagan *soters,* they leaped gleefully but irrationally to the conclusion that He was no more historical than Dionysus or Attis. Actually, the non-historicity of Jesus is an infinitely far-fetched hypothesis, and even John M. Robertson dared not maintain it categorically.[13] If Jesus was a myth, there is nothing faintly comparable in all history; and those who believe that He was such, should produce parallel instances, replete with similar literature and authentic propagandists.

5. *Internal Evidence.* The internal evidence favoring the historicity of Jesus is even more decisive; it is far more conclusive than that concerning the Essene Teacher, which no one doubts. Not only is the Synoptic story between the baptism and the empty tomb forthright and consistent: it is also filled with details and elements which would never have been found in a myth. We shall call further attention to these as we proceed; we note here only that, according to the Gospel narrative, Jesus was driven from Nazareth as a blasphemer by the people who knew Him intimately; that His brothers and His mother, to whom He would not even speak, sought to drag Him home under duress; that He was supported by certain women; that He fled in terror from the Pharisees of Galilee; that when He was asked by them to reveal some evidence to support His pretensions, He answered only with abuse; that He traveled clandestinely by night so that He might not be apprehended; that He died in utter despair, believing that God had abandoned him; that He announced His imminent Parousia at the middle of His career and so proved Himself a false prophet. We must accept Matt.

10:23 as genuine, since no believer would, at a later date, have invented a prophecy which proved false almost with its utterance. Nor would writers of many years later have made Jesus promise a Parousia during His own generation. The fact that all this and more, which is so very human, appears in the Synoptics establishes the historicity of Jesus. All such material is deleted from the Gospel as revised in John, where the authentic Jesus disappears entirely.

C. HOW EXPLAIN THE SILENCE OF JUSTUS AND JOSEPHUS?

We find no great mystery in the silence of Justus and Josephus. There were probably several self-proclaimed prophets in Galilee and Judea, none of whom commanded much more attention than some orator in London's Hyde Park; such persons do not receive mention in the tomes of serious historians. And it is altogether unlikely that Jesus had seventy or even twelve disciples: these were simply standard numbers in common use among the Jews. The likelihood is that four or five devoted women, together with Peter, James, John, Andrew, and Matthew, constituted His following; they alone are given definite characterizations and only they, of the original disciples, play any role in the founding of the Church. It is very doubtful that His influence extended far beyond this circle until the first missionaries began to preach the resurrected Christ who would shortly return upon the clouds with power.

CHAPTER II

THE COMPOSITION OF THE SYNOPTIC GOSPELS

A. THE CANONICAL GOSPELS

1. *Our Sole Source of Knowledge.* As source-material concerning the ministry and teachings of Jesus, we must depend upon the Synoptics, that is, Matthew, Mark, and Luke; for this reason, the ensuing analysis is based almost exclusively upon them.

2. *Priority of Mark.* Mark is the oldest; its priority was recognized in the 18th and early 19th century by various German scholars preceding Christian Herman Weisse who, in 1838, published the first fully-developed Marcan Hypothesis, which is generally accepted today and which may be summarized as follows: of the 661 verses contained in the authentic Mark, 600 are reproduced in Matthew and 350 in Luke; only 31 fail to appear in either; the agreement between Mark and the other two is much more exact than the agreement of Luke and Matthew with each other; the actual order in Mark is almost always reproduced either in Luke or Matthew, and sometimes in both, which in this respect also differ from each other far more than they do from Mark. It is therefore incontrovertible that both used Mark as a source.

3. *Date of Synoptics.* Mark, except 16:9-20, which was a later addition, was written between 60 and 70; however, the resurrection story, here related, had been accepted much earlier. And we may add that the miracles also were an integral portion of the earliest tradition. Luke and our version of Matthew, except the introductory material, were probably written a few years after the siege of Jerusalem. The genealogies were probably interpolated be-

fore 100; the elements establishing the Virgin Birth were incorporated early in the second century.

4. *Source Materials for Synoptics.* The Gospel of Mark is primarily *narration,* and discloses the principal events in the life of Jesus. Long ago, however, it was discovered that Luke and Matthew drew heavily from another common source, frequently quoted verbatim, and called by the German scholars *Qvelle,* or sources. We know that there was a primary document known as the *Sayings of Jesus.* [1]Although Mark reveals no knowledge of this, Paul was familiar with it. Matthew in particular drew heavily upon these *Logia* especially in chapters 5 to 7, comprising the Sermon on the Mount; chapter 10, which constitutes the charge of Jesus to His disciples; and chapters 18-19, which include much of His ethics and theology. Luke scatters much of this material throughout his version.

Finally, it may be regarded as certain that our Greek Matthew is a recension of an earlier Matthew in Aramaic, which may have been older than Mark, which went out of its way to tie the Gospel to Old-Testament Judaism, and which was used by Jewish Christians for centuries.

5. *None Written by Eye-Witnesses.* None of our Gospels was written by an eye-witness; all were composed in Greek; and none, except that of Mark, who was an assistant to Peter, could have been written by the purported author. They were not composed until the Church had become Gentile. The Gospel of John could not have been earlier than 120. The Gospel of Luke 1:1-4 claims only to be a written rendition of common belief and tradition, and disclaims specifically the authority of first-hand knowledge. The canonical Matthew was not written by the apostle; it is probable, however, that our version was in part a recension of the original *Gospel to the Hebrews,* which may have been written by Matthew himself.

Mark is thus our basic source. Concerning him, Eusebius quotes Papias, a second-century prelate, as follows: "he had not heard the Lord, nor had he followed him, but later on, as I said, followed Peter, who used to give teaching as necessity demanded."[2] It is obvious that this wide gulf between the historical fact and its rendition permitted ample margin for myth and elaboration.

6. *Summary.* Several facts may therefore be regarded as established. Mark was written about 60-67, the author relying upon Peter and general tradition for his information. All parallel passages in Luke and Matthew were copied from it more or less verbatim. The Greek Matthew exhibits many similarities, absent from Mark and Luke, to an original Jewish gospel, as we shall note further in the proper place. We know also that both Luke and Matthew included substantial portions from the then current *Sayings of Jesus*. At an early date, the genealogies were added to make Jesus a Judaic Messiah; and later the totally contradictory pagan material concerning the Virgin Birth was incorporated after contact with the Hellenic world. The Gospel of John, which presents a divergent chronology and locale for the ministry of Jesus, came about fifty years later: and it was written to retain Christian converts on an entirely new basis; to transform a Jewish revolutionary into a Greek mystery *soter;* to make a God out of Jesus, a concept totally foreign to the Synoptics; and to proclaim the Logos doctrine, which was borrowed from the Stoics and which was, in time, to develop into the doctrine of the Trinity.

7. *Observations.* Even a casual examination reveals three facts: first, that between the Fourth Gospel on the one hand and the three Synoptics on the other, there is almost no agreement; second, that in the Synoptics themselves there is no agreement in the genealogies or in the stories concerning the birth and the resurrection of Jesus; third, that between the baptism and the empty tomb the Gospel narratives contain no fundamental discrepancy; and, fourth, that the most complete agreement among the four Gospels occurs in the narrative dealing with the arrest, trial, abuse, and crucifixion of Jesus. The fast-moving scenes, occurring as they do without transition, have all the earmarks of a scenario to be used for a drama or a pageant, such as had been enacted at the Osirian or Eleusinian mysteries for thousands of years.

8. *Conclusions.* We conclude, then, that the Fourth

Gospel was simply a propaganda document; that the narratives concerning the birth, genealogy, and resurrection of Jesus were invented solely for their dogmatic and theological value; and that the Synoptic rendition of the life and teachings of Jesus reflect an authentic tradition, constitute an idealization of historical reality, and contain a solid kernel of fact.

9. *Our Four-Column Version.* In preparation for our analysis, we laid out a four-column version of the Gospels, in which the parallel passages from all stand in juxtaposition. In general, we follow the sequence of Luke, since it is the longest and most specific; but whenever Matthew is more detailed and complete, as is the case with the *Logia*, especially the Sermon on the Mount, that Gospel is used as the pilot.

10. *Duration of Ministry.* We believe that the ministry of Jesus lasted less than a year. He completed His career at Jerusalem during the time of the Passover; there is no evidence that any other such festival occurred between His baptism and His death; and it is scarcely likely that a celebration of such importance to all Jews would have remained unmentioned. Furthermore, it would be difficult indeed to stretch out the career of Jesus to a period exceeding ten or twelve months, for it can be reconstructed, almost on a day-to-day basis, from the Synoptic record.

B. PRIMITIVE JEWISH GOSPELS

1. *Christianity Abandons the Jews.* During the earliest years, Christianity was entirely Jewish, and it had no thought of basing its future upon the Gentile world. But it soon became bitterly obvious that no substantial progress could be made among the Jews. The new church therefore turned to the Gentiles, and, with Paul as its leading protagonist, entered a road quite different from that envisioned by the first missionaries.

2. *Christian Jewish Scriptures Lost.* The meager fragments of the Jewish gospels consist of a few quotations found among the Fathers. These scriptures were eventually lost, because Jewish Christianity did not survive, and

its Aramaic compositions, which were of great antiquity, were destroyed by the Gentiles. However, the early Church was well acquainted with two Jewish gospels, which were extant for centuries. At least down to the time of Jerome, cir. 400, we find occasional mention of a *Gospel According to the Hebrews* (often named after Matthew), and another *Gospel According to the Ebionites*. The former was so similar to the canonical Matthew that sometimes the latter was mistaken for a translation of its Jewish counterpart.

We learn from Irenaeus that the Ebionites practiced circumcision and all other Judaistic observances, used only the *Gospel According to Matthew,* rejected the miraculous birth of Jesus, and repudiated Paul as an apostate from the Mosaic Law.[3] Even as the canonical Matthew is studded with purported prophecies of Jesus from the Old Testament, so the Hebrew gospel built the new faith firmly on the same foundation. And we learn from Epiphanius that this gospel contained the genealogy of Jesus from Abraham to Christ, exactly as does our Matthew.[4] The same author declares that the Ebionites were vegetarians and that they rejected the doctrine of the Virgin Birth.

With this preliminary, we are ready to scan the Synoptics. What precedes the baptism and follows the empty tomb belongs in PART FOUR.

CHAPTER III

THE APOTHEOSIS OF JESUS

A. JOHN THE BAPTIST

1. *His Essene Ideology.* Suddenly, about the thirtieth year of our era or slightly earlier, an extraordinary figure exploded into the Messiah-drenched atmosphere of Palestine. John the Baptist, filled with Essene ideology and doctrine, thundered his message of doom. As we have seen, all prophecy had been forbidden among the Jews except that of the reincarnate Elijah and of the Messiah whom he would immediately precede and proclaim. The Baptist appeared, therefore, according to prophecies in Malachi 3:1 and Isaiah 40:3 as the voice of one crying in the wilderness to prepare the way for the Lord. And he baptized all who came, after the manner of the Essenes and the Zoroastrians, that they might experience moral regeneration. There is no record of any Jewish prophet during the preceding centuries, and no such doctrine as John's had ever been publicly preached in Judaea.

2. *Essene Doctrine.* Luke develops the Baptist-narrative, revealing the Essene eschatology, communism, and Messianic concepts of John. The Jews were not to expect any special consideration because they were the children of Abraham;[1] the axe is now laid to the root, and the end of time is near; he who hath two coats should give one to him who hath none for soon will come one "the latchet of whose shoes I am not worthy to unloose ... and he will thoroughly purge his floor, and will gather his wheat into his garner; but the chaff he will burn with fire unquenchable."[2] Quite possibly, this expected judge was still the Essene Teacher; or John may have meant himself, in a second manifestation.

And so, for the first time, these Essene-Zoroastrian doctrines were hurled at the Jewish populace. John spoke with fierce urgency: there was no time to lose, the end was at hand; although he could not identify the Messiah, he would certainly come at once; there was no time left for buying and selling and begetting. We must prepare instantly for the Kingdom of God.

B. THE APPEARANCE OF JESUS

1. *His Baptism.* As John was preaching at the Jordan, there appeared suddenly an intense and fateful man who apparently had long brooded over His own mission. Capitalizing upon the message of John, He presented himself for baptism. We are told that during the ritual the Spirit of God descended upon Jesus in the form of a dove.[3] This, according to the Christian-Jewish concept, was His apotheosis, which transformed Him mystically into the Son of God.

2. *The Original Doctrine.* This is one of the most crucial incidents of the Synoptics. We read that at the completion of the ceremony, a voice from heaven declared: "This is my beloved son, in whom I am well pleased."[4] We find an almost identical wording in Mark[5] and Luke.[6] However, we learn from Epiphanius that the Ebionites had a different rendition, according to which the "voice from heaven" declared: "Thou art my beloved Son, in thee I am well pleased; and again: This day have I begotten thee."[7]

When the words *This day have I begotten thee* were deleted from the Christian Gospels, a Hellenization to conform with the pagan doctrine of the Virgin Birth was accomplished. We do not know when the alteration occurred in Mark and Luke, but concerning Matthew we have definite information: for Justin Martyr quotes Matthew 3:17 specifically,[8] using the same wording as Epiphanius attributes to the Ebionite gospel. And we know, finally, that even as late as 400 this text in Matthew had not yet been corrupted; for we learn from St. Augustine that the Manichaeans stated that according to Matthew the Son of God was begotten on the day of His baptism; and, since Augustine does not deny the allegation, we know that it must be correct. Faustus declared: "Matthew tells us that the . . . voice was heard saying . . . :'Thou art my beloved Son, this day have I begotten Thee.' It appears from this that what was born of Mary thirty years before, was not the Son of God, but was afterward made so by baptism . . . This is what Matthew says, if Matthew is the real author . . . and if you believe this doctrine, you must be called a Matthaean, for you will no longer be a Catholic."[9]

We know, therefore, that Matthew was finally made to conform with Catholic dogma simply by striking the words *This day have I begotten Thee* from the text. This must have required the concerted effort of the entire hierarchy, occurring, as it did, after 400, when there were already many hundreds of copies in circulation. The fact that this extraordinary feat was accomplished at all serves as a yardstick to measure the influence of the Ebionites, the Marcionites, and the Manichees, as well as others, all of whom denied the Virgin Birth and who could be defeated only by this drastic expedient.

3. *Inner Conviction of Jesus.* Although Jesus did not publicly and overtly announce His divinity immediately, there can be no doubt that beginning with His baptism all misgiving concerning it vanished from His consciousness. In His own mind, He was the Christ, the Son of God; and when He called Himself the Son of Man He did so because this was the title by which the Messiah of universal judgment was known in Daniel and in *The Book of Enoch.*

CHAPTER IV

JESUS REJECTED IN NAZARETH

A. FINAL PREPARATION FOR MINISTRY

1. *Forty Days in the Wilderness.* Mark 1:12-13 tells us simply that after His baptism, Jesus was driven immediately by the spirit into the wilderness, where He was tempted by Satan for forty days. This was an experience based upon a synthesis of religious tradition. We have already noted the Great Temptations of Zoroaster and Gautama. And we may add that in the *Apocalypse of Abraham* we find that this patriarch was similarly tempted by Azazel. It was therefore natural and inevitable that Jesus also should retire into solitude to gain victory over the adversary, to wrestle with His own soul, and to cleanse His emotions of all fears and doubts before entering upon His fateful career.

2. *Ministry Begins.* Galilee teemed with fanatics, including Essenes, Pharisees, and Zealots, as well as Herodians, who believed Herod was himself the Christ;[1] and into this welter of sects and ideologies, Jesus strode alone, convinced of His high destiny. A confluence of forces enabled Him to present a synthesis of threats, promises, hopes, doctrines, and aspirations that had never been so conjoined before. He declared: "The time is fulfilled, and the kingdom of God is at hand: repent ye, and believe the Gospel."[2] Such was His incisive message: the end of the world was very, very near; all must repent and receive the Gospel at once, or be thrown into everlasting hell fire.

3. *Chooses His First Disciples.* Now follows the scene by the Sea of Galilee in which Jesus chooses four of His disciples, Andrew, Peter, James, and John,[3] of whom the

last three were to constitute the inner circle. According to John, He calls also Philip, who goes to Nathanael, "and saith unto him, We have found him, of whom Moses in the law, and the prophets, did write, Jesus of Nazareth, the son of Joseph."[4] Here we see that later editors often failed to alter the wording of the original Gospel to conform with later doctrine for here we are told plainly that Joseph was the father of Jesus; and Nathanael recognized Jesus as the human Messiah, who was to restore the Jewish kingdom. It was ever to be the same: His disciples were always to regard Jesus as the temporal Messiah who, however, was to have command over the heavenly hosts: "Verily, verily I say unto you, Hereafter ye shall see heaven open, and the angels of God ascending and descending upon the Son of man."[5]

B. ATTEMPTED CONQUEST OF NAZARETH

1. *Declares Himself in Synagogue.* The next incident occurs in the synagogue at Nazareth, most fully related in Luke.[6] Here on the Sabbath, Jesus revealed Himself as the Messiah described in Isaiah. The people were astonished at His doctrine and told each other that He was only the son of the carpenter Joseph: and well might they be so, for He was the first, except John, to broadcast the esoteric teachings of the Essenes. He spoke with an authority born of the conviction that He was Himself the long-awaited Messiah. Turning to Isaiah 61:1-2, he read the passage which was to Him His commission to preach the Kingdom and "the acceptable year of the Lord."[7]

As He finished, all eyes were turned upon Him; and He continued intrepidly: "This day is this scripture fulfilled in your ears."[8] Thus Jesus announced His Messiahship to the people who had known Him since childhood.

2. *Nazarene Reaction.* When Jesus saw His auditors filled with doubt and skepticism, as the members of any modern congregation would be under similar circumstances, He declared that no prophet is accepted in his own country. And Mark tells us that "He marvelled because of their unbelief";[9] He was so certain of His own mission

that any doubt of it was to Him simply incomprehensible.

At this point, Jesus reveals for the first time His predestinarian doctrine. [10] He told His fellow-townsmen that salvation comes only to the chosen, who are often the little ones, or outsiders. He pointed out that there were many widows in Israel in the days of Elias, but the prophet came only to one of them; and there were many lepers at the time of Eliseus, but only Naaman the Syrian was cleansed. Jesus could scarcely have thrown a more bitter insult into the teeth of these Jews. Their lineage, their honorable lives, their immemorial Hebrew ancestry meant nothing. He did not urge them to accept His salvation: He merely warned them of the dire consequences if they did not. This was more than they could endure: and "they rose up, and thrust him out of the city, and led him unto the brow of the hill whereon the city was built, that they might cast him down headlong. But he passing through the midst of them went his way."[11]

The worst part of this experience was the fact that in Nazareth Jesus was rejected, not by the priests nor at their instigation, but spontaneously by the people. Mark tells us that here He could "do no mighty work."

3. *Jesus Offers Salvation to the Other Galileans.* The disappointment, however, did not reduce His fervency: His mission could not wait. Having revealed His message, His duty was performed. Those who doubted or rejected it were simply reprobates, predestined to eternal damnation. And He left His boyhood home, never to return, and set out to preach the Gospel in the other villages of Galilee.

CHAPTER V

MIRACLES IN GALILEE

A. ORIGIN OF BELIEF IN MIRACLES

1. *Myth-Making Propensity.* When David Friedrich Strauss published *Das Leben Jesu* in 1831, he established a revolutionary approach to New Testament study. Perhaps his greatest contribution consisted in his analysis of the Gospel miracles. He concluded that among the unlettered and superstitious followers of Jesus, it was inevitable that the myth-making faculty inherent in human beings would soon credit the founder of their cult with many acts and powers which had only a limited basis in fact.

2. *Limited Basis in Fact.* And let us stress this point: a limited, but a *real,* basis in fact. We know that the Essenes practiced the healing arts; and that the majority of Galileans were desperately poor, plagued by every species of bodily ailment, or filled with driving and agonizing fantasies. Among these wretches, a little mental and physical therapy could easily create a reputation for supernatural power. And certainly the Essene Jesus could easily have acquired this ordinary human skill. Actually the accomplishments attributed to Him seem quite modest. The Greek Aesculapius was said to have raised so many from the dead that the infernal regions were in danger of depopulation. Gautama was said to have healed untold numbers. Nor need we depend upon ancient mythology; for the Catholics claim that the shrines of Lourdes, Brother Joseph, and St. Anne de Beaupre have countless miraculous cures to their credit. Modern Christian Science claims a thousand times more healings than are mentioned in the

Gospel; Aimee Semple McPherson did likewise; various current religious cults do the same; and a contemporary evangelist, Oral Roberts, declares that through faith in Jesus he has accomplished countless cures beyond the reach of medical science. Millions believe in these "miracles" today; the wonder, therefore, is not that so many were accredited to Jesus, but rather that they were so few. And there is no doubt that many of His cures were authentic enough; for a whole host of diseases are mental or psychosomatic and for these He might often have afforded genuine relief, even without elementary medication.

There are serious scholars who maintain that physical cures, beyond the understanding of medical science, have taken place as a result of an overwhelming faith or emotional experience. Psychoanalysis has proved that people become lame, blind, bedridden, or will suffer heart trouble, dizziness, and many other ailments as a result of neuroses, and that the symptoms will vanish when the emotional pressure causing them is relieved. Is it then very difficult to believe that the man cured of palsy was simply a neurotic, long paralyzed by his inner conflicts?

And the same reasoning applies even more to the casting out of devils, that is, giving peace of mind to the mentally distraught. There can be no doubt that the calm and powerful gaze of Jesus, reflecting a mind certain of its power, could act as a restorative to broken personalities. Especially would this be true, once His reputation as a healer began to spread among the poor.

3. *Character of Galilean Poor*. Traveling through what was ancient Galilee in 1867, Mark Twain saw people who were probably quite similar to those who heard the Gospel of Jesus. In the cavalcade of the author was a doctor, who, when he administered a little free healing to one of these pitiful creatures, caused such a furore that the Americans were almost mobbed: "they all came trooping out—old men and old women, boys and girls, the blind, the crazy, and the crippled, all in ragged, soiled, and scanty raiment, and all abject beggars by nature, instinct, and education. How the vermin-tortured vagabonds did warm! How they showed their sores and scars, and pite-

ously pointed to their maimed and crooked limbs, and begged with their pleading eyes for charity!"[1] This sight moved Mark Twain to exclaim: "How it must have surprised these people to hear the way of salvation offered to them without money and without price." Unless we understand that the Gospel was proclaimed to and intended for just such hopeless outcasts, overwhelmed in filth, poverty, crime, disease, insanity, injustice, and indescribable misery, its language and its promises remain forever a volume sealed with seven seals.

4. *Heals the Sick and Proclaims the Kingdom.* It was to such as these that Jesus, like Gautama, carried His message. For this world, He offered economic equality and the strictly equal distribution of goods and income among all on the basis of need. He promised to heal the sick, the lame, the halt, the blind, the palsied, and the leprous. He promised to rid them of tormenting devils and demons, to give them peace of mind. All this for the present: and for the future there would be everlasting happiness and glory in the Kingdom of God. Everything was to be had without money; however, not without condition, for the Gospel must be accepted without question or reservation: all the things of this world, especially family and wealth and property, must be irrevocably renounced. This would entail little sacrifice for the toiling poor: and it was to them that Jesus addressed Himself. But those who enjoyed any of this world's goods must have looked askance upon this strange revolutionary who preached universal brotherhood, the community of goods, and salvation by mystical regeneration; and who repudiated marriage and family, announced an impending world-end, promised the Kingdom of Heaven to the Elect, and threatened everlasting hell fire for those who did not accept Him as the Christ.

B. THE GALILEAN MINISTRY

1. *Miracles in Capernaum.* The first of Jesus' "great works" was performed in the synagogue at Capernaum, another "city of Galilee," where He cast out a devil.[2] Next He entered the house of Simon Peter and his broth-

er Andrew. There He found Peter's mother-in-law ill of a fever and He cured her at a touch of His hand.[3] From this we know that Simon was married, the only one of the disciples, it seems, so encumbered. However, there is no doubt that Peter soon abandoned wife and family, according to the oft-proclaimed Essene principle of Jesus.

And so, to gain relief, "all the city was gathered together at the door."[4] Like those described by Mark Twain, they all had ailments, all were in desperate need. We are told that He healed many and cast out devils. He gave the people of Capernaum His message; He demonstrated His power; He offered those who could receive it their chance for salvation. But the time was short and He must hurry on. "Let us go unto the next towns, that I may preach there also: for therefore came I forth."[5]

2. *Jesus Forgives Sin.* After a tour of Galilee, Jesus returned briefly to Capernaum, where the poor and the diseased again thronged about Him.[6] One suffering from palsy was lowered through the roof. At this, Jesus took a long stride forward: instead of speaking to the man's physical needs, He addressed His moral and eternal necessities. "Son," He said, "thy sins be forgiven thee."[7] Jesus went directly to the core of His mission, which was to unite the human soul with God, to bring about moral regeneration, to create a totally new set of values, needs, and desires in the votary which would make him fit for the Kingdom of Heaven. Up to this point, Jesus had engaged in works calculated to create confidence in Him among His disciples and acceptance among the populace. Now He assumed a higher role, and spoke with authority: the body is temporal, but the soul, being immortal, is of infinite consequence, just as the Essenes also declared.

3. *Arouses Hostility of the Pharisees.* Jesus had already awakened the hostility of the ordinary Nazarenes; but now for the first time, He made new and more dangerous enemies. When He said to the palsied man that his sins were forgiven, the Pharisees correctly sensed in Him a mortal enemy, whom they considered a blasphemer of the Mosaic Law.

C. THE CALLING OF MATTHEW

As Jesus went forth from the house in Capernaum where this incident occurred, He met Levi, the publican, who was called Matthew and who was the son of Alpheus.[8] Matthew must have been one of the Elect, for when Jesus said "Follow me," "he left all, rose up, and followed him."[9]

And so ended the first phase of the ministry of Jesus; and the second began, in which He was brought face to face with the growing hostility of the reigning priesthood.

CHAPTER VI

THE STORM CLOUDS GATHER

A. CONFLICT OVER DOCTRINE

1. *On the Offensive.* We now find Jesus in an ever-deepening and inevitable conflict with the priesthood.[1] Certainly one reason why the Essenes concealed their teachings so meticulously was that had their doctrines been known they, like the original Pythagoreans, would undoubtedly have met the same sanguinary fate. And now a single individual strode forth proclaiming a doctrine that went even beyond theirs. For Jesus flouted the ceremonials and observances of the Mosaic Law; and He denounced the Pharisees in the most scathing terms. He made Himself as offensive as possible to the orthodox and the respectable. He preferred the society of the poor, of harlots, of simple workingmen, with whom He conversed on terms of familiarity. When the Pharisees saw this, "they said unto his disciples, How is it that he eateth and drinketh with publicans and sinners?"[2]

2. *Jesus Rejects Pharisaic Formalism.* To this He replied that mercy was greater than sacrifice and that He had "not come to call the righteous, but sinners to repentance."[3] By this reference to the prophets,[4] Jesus proclaimed that outward observances or formal respectability would mean nothing in His Kingdom; that social justice is worth more than religious ceremonials; and that hypocrisy is the ultimate sin.

3. *Jesus Rejects Extreme Asceticism.* We learn that a competing sect had grown up around the imprisoned Baptist,[5] whose disciples wished to know why they and the Pharisees often fasted, whereas Jesus and His disciples did

not. Jesus here appears like a Buddhist in contrast to a Gaina monk. His reply was that His followers should not fast as long as the bridegroom was with them; and now, for the first time, He declared that He would leave them for a time,[6] during which they would fast and mourn while awaiting His reappearance.

4. *New Forms for New Doctrines.* Jesus continued with His first recorded parable: we do not sew a piece of new cloth on an old garment; and we do not put new wine in old bottles.[7] That is, the new religion could not be contained within the old forms or implemented by the old observances, but must be clothed in accordance with its revolutionary content. Fasting, sacrifice, tithing, circumcision, the maintainence of racial purity, meticulous Sabbath observation and dietary regulations do not constitute the road to salvation, for these can never accomplish moral regeneration.

5. *Jesus Challenges the Pharisees.* Two incidents now occur[8] which cast into bold relief the conflict between Jesus and the Pharisees concerning the Sabbath. The Mosaic Law provided for six days of labor and a seventh of rest.[9] The original meaning of this is evident: the Sabbath was to be dedicated to the Lord and serve as surcease from otherwise endless toil; but concerning this a mass of hair-splitting controversy had arisen; and, what was worse from the standpoint of Jesus, these externalized observances were regarded as *in themselves efficient for salvation*. It was against this concept that Jesus rebelled, for God wants mercy, charity, kindness, brotherhood, the sharing of all our material possessions with those in need. First, we must love God with heart and soul and then our brethren as ourselves.

As any church or institution consolidates its position, its original fervor dies away, and emphasis shifts to creed and ceremonials. This had happened among the Jews; and Jesus sought to destroy the form as well as the content of the Pharisaic ritual.

The first sharp clash came when the disciples plucked food on the Sabbath as they walked through a field of grain. This was not labor in the formal sense, and Jesus could discern no desecration in the act; but, according to the Pharisaic interpretation, it was work, and therefore a flagrant violation of the Law. Jesus justified the act by saying that David took and ate the shewbread when he was hungry: His answer seems a justification for pilfering as much as for Sabbath violation. He declared also that the Sabbath was made for man and not man for the Sabbath, in other words, human welfare transcends every law: the hungry must be fed, the naked must be clothed, the homeless must be housed, and brotherhood must be established. The rights of the destitute take precedence over those whose toil has produced the grain. This was a Buddhist concept.

6. *Healing on the Sabbath*. And then, in a second clash, Jesus revealed the warrant by which He spoke. It was an authority vested in Himself alone, for He was the Son of Man and the Lord of the Sabbath; God had commissioned Him to abolish the outworn ceremonials of the Pharisees. It is hard to see how He could have offended them more decisively.

According to the Pharisaic interpretation of the Law, it was permissible to administer aid to man or beast on the Sabbath only in a mortal emergency. As if to bring His own morality into sharp relief, Jesus made a public spectacle on the Sabbath in the synagogue of healing a man with a withered hand. Before He did so, He challenged His enemies openly: "Is it unlawful to do good on the sabbath days, or to do evil? to save life, or to kill?"[10] Jesus had baited his hook carefully: If we may save the life of a beast on the Sabbath, why is it unlawful to heal a withered hand? He struck at the weakest link in their armor; and the Pharisees could not devise an effective retort. But they "went forth, and straightway took counsel with the Herodians against Him, how they might destroy Him."

3. CONFLICT WITH FRIENDS AND FAMILY

1. *Commissions His Disciples*. Thereupon, Luke tells us[11] that Jesus went up into a mountain to pray; and

Mark states[12] that He ordained His disciples there, prepared them to preach, and endowed them with power to heal the sick and cast out devils. Whatever the real number of these, Peter, James, and John were always to constitute the inner circle.

2. *Friends Seek to Bind Him as Insane.* At this point, two informative incidents occur. "And when His friends heard of it, they went out to lay hold on him for they said, He is beside Himself."[13] In other words, when the Nazarene friends of Jesus heard how He had commissioned disciples to heal the sick and cast out devils, they became convinced that He was insane and took steps to place Him under duress, very much as any one who, today, doing the same, would be placed in an asylum.

3. *Mother and Brethren Attempt to End Career.* And when they were prevented from doing this, presumably by the people surrounding Jesus, another attempt was made to end His unconventional career, and to compel His return to Nazareth and industrious citizenship. "There came then His brethren and his mother, and, standing without, sent unto Him, calling Him. And the multitude sat about Him, and they said unto Him, Behold, thy mother and thy brethren without seek for thee."[14]

Jesus knew only too well that their purpose was to terminate His ministry; and so He refused to speak with or even to see His mother or His brothers. He had nothing in common with them. They did not accept Him as the Christ or believe His doctrine. He rejected His family, declaring that only those who joined in His communion could be united with Him. The far-reaching significance of this act consists in its identity to the age-old practice of Buddhists, Pythagoreans, and Essenes, and it indicates that Jesus was a child of them: "Who is my mother, or my brethren?" He asked. "And he looked around about him on them which sat about him, and said, Behold my mother and my brethren! For whosoever shall do the will of God the same is my brother, and my sister, and my mother."[1

4. *The Authenticity of Mark.* Thus Jesus sundered forever the last ties which joined Him to Nazareth and to His family. From them He had received nothing but r

jection and contumely. This thoroughly convincing human drama would never have been invented. Had the Synoptics been mythological fabrications, they would, like the *Fo-Sho-Hing-Tsan-King,* have told a sentimental tale in which all the relatives of Jesus, especially His mother, were converted. When the Fourth Gospel placed her at the foot of the cross, precisely such a myth was launched, and it continued to proliferate for centuries.

C. REBUKES AN OVER-ZEALOUS ADMIRER

We are told that a great many thronged about Jesus when He descended to the seaside;[16] but when one in the crowd called Him the Son of God,[17] He rebuked him sharply, and charged him not to make this known. Jesus wished all to believe Him divine, but knew that such a claim would be condemned as blasphemous, and would bring immediate reprisal or destruction. His career had just begun; it was imperative that He have time to sow the seed.

And so we approach the Sermon on the Mount, which expounds in detail the ethics of Jesus, which are an amalgam of Buddhist and Essene morality.

CHAPTER VII

ETHICS: THE SERMON ON THE MOUNT

A. INTRODUCTORY

One of the most celebrated portions of the Gospel consists of Matthew 5-7, known as the Sermon on the Mount.

Albert Schweitzer believed the Gospel ethics to be entirely eschatological, that is, intended only as an interim rule of conduct for the Elect awaiting the Kingdom of God. But if such were the case, it is difficult to understand how Schweitzer could have discovered there the inspiration which he certainly found.

It is true that many of its precepts cannot be practiced in an economy based upon competition, private property, and the monogamic family. This, however, is precisely the point: they were never intended for such a society, but were, on the contrary, devised specifically to abolish it. The fact is that the ethics of Jesus had been practiced by Pythagoreans and Essenes for centuries, and by millions of Buddhists in the Far East; and that Plato had advocated them in part in *The Republic* as the basis for a self-perpetuating society simply by substituting community marriage for celibacy.

Of the Sermon on the Mount there is almost nothing in Mark; of the one hundred and eleven verses which comprise it in Matthew, some sixty are reproduced in Luke, but widely scattered. Not so much as an echo of all this reappears in John: by the time the Fourth Gospel was written, about 120-140, the Greek Church wanted no more truck with communism or social revolution.

B. THE BEATITUDES

1. *Eschatological Meaning.* The Sermon begins with the nine Beatitudes, which declare that those who seem most miserable in this life are really the most blessed. Jesus did not, however, mean that poverty, mourning, meekness, persecution, hunger, thirst, etc., are in themselves desirable; He simply emphasized that all these are the lot of the righteous, since they must live among evil and selfish men, but cannot, like them, commit acts of aggression. By renouncing material things now, the Elect will be rewarded by a superabundance of these hereafter when they may be obtained without social injustice. The miseries of the righteous, therefore, constitute blessedness, since they are inseparable from the life which leads to everlasting glory. Those who exploit and rob their fellowmen get a little out of this brief existence; on the other hand, those who are indigent, hungry, thirsty, meek, merciful, pacifist, and poor in spirit, shall have eternal rewards which make every moment of renunciation a matter of infinite profit.

2. *Affluence for Renunciation.* The Beatitudes would have been empty words unless Jesus had clearly indicated and His auditors had definitely understood that this life of sacrifice, sorrow, and persecution was to be very brief and to be succeeded by the new kingdom from which all the unregenerate, that is, all the powerful, all owners of private property, all who continued in the married state, were to be banished forever into hell and in which the Elect would enjoy indefinitely the lands, the money, and the houses expropriated from them. "Blessed are the meek: for they shall inherit the earth," and all the wealth that therein is. This was precisely the doctrine taught by the Essenes.

3. *Poor Filled with Excitement and Hope.* Such generous prospects must have filled the poor with wild excitement. Soon and without labor or conflict, they would possess all earthly wealth, not to mention the blessed immortality which was to follow.

There is a passage in Luke which belongs with the

Sermon, but which, oddly enough, is not found in Matthew. It begins: "woe unto ye that are rich! For ye have received your consolation. Woe unto ye that are full! for ye shall hunger . . ."[1] It is obvious from this and other texts that to be poor and to suffer on earth was considered almost tantamount to election; and that in the ethics of Jesus no righteous person can be rich or even an owner of any property whatever. Being well fed or comfortable are mortal sins *per se*. For any one to possess plenty while any among his fellows are in want is the ultimate crime; and, since the poor are with us always, no one can ever have the right to live well. The Elect, therefore, never acquire wealth; and if they inherit it, they give it to the poor. In the promulgation of this Buddhist-Pythagorean-Essene doctrine, Jesus was always consistent.

C. THE RECONSTITUTION OF THE MOSAIC LAW

1. *Our Matthew a Recension*. Jesus now delivers a series of re-interpretations of the Mosaic Law.[2] Since it is a recension of the *Gospel According to the Hebrews*, Matthew exhibits a close dependence upon Jewish antecedents, which is absent from the other Gospels: and this is the reason we read: "Think not I am come to destroy the law, or the prophets: I am not come to destroy, but to fulfill."

Matthew also represents Jesus as the Christ who came only to the "lost sheep of the house of Israel," [3] and who considers the Mosaic Law sacred. In the original Hebrew version, Gentiles were required to accept the Mosaic Law and submit to its discipline as prerequisites for membership in the Christian communion, although there is nothing to indicate that Jesus Himself ever established such a requirement; nevertheless, apostolic Jewish Christianity certainly did. At any rate, our Matthew, being a Hellenized revision of a Hebrew text, retains many earmarks of its original; and therefore in it Jesus appears, not as a revolutionary who wishes to overthrow the Mosaic Law, but as a reformer who desires to humanize and fulfill it. "Till heaven and earth pass, one jot or one tittle shall in no wise pass from the law, till all be fulfilled." In other words, the Law as interpreted by Jesus would obtain during the present dispensation; but when the Kingdom of Heaven is established following the Parousia, it will be superseded by the Law of Love.

2. *Enmity Banned.* Jesus continues: It was commanded in the olden time, *Thou shalt not kill;* but under the new construction, mere hostility against a brother is ground for judgment; one who says *raca* deserves arraignment before the Council but one who calls another a fool is in danger of hell fire. That this is an exact replica of Essene discipline is obvious; and we find here also that the real offense is not the commission of an evil deed, but rather the impulse to commit it: for if we are to eradicate sin and aggression, we must first extirpate from every human heart the emotions which cause them. These were the age-old ethics of the Buddhists and the Pythagoreans.

3. *On Concessions.* Jesus declares: "Agree with thine adversary quickly, whiles thou art in the way with him . . . ."4 In other words, whenever you find yourself in dispute with another, concede him more than is due: for the sake of peace, accept less than a judge would award. You will avoid bitterness and conflict.

4. *Adultery and Divorce.* Jesus now propounds His teaching concerning adultery and divorce. All of this is meaningless except in the light of the philosophic celibacy taught and practiced by Buddhists, Pythagoreans, and Essenes. Even as the whole ethical system of Jesus is based upon the principle that not the actual sin, but rather the desire or impulse to commit it, is the real offense, so we read: "Whosoever looketh on a woman to lust after her hath committed adultery with her already in his heart."

The Buddhists understood that as long as the desire for Woman remains in the heart of a man, so long is he hourly in danger of falling victim to his sex-desire. We remember that Banus bathed thrice daily in cold water to repress his *libido* even in the wilderness where assuredly no temptress dwelt. Celibacy was not sufficient: every vestige of the erotic impulse had to be eradicated, for this was in itself the adultery committed in the heart. In this precept, there was no difference between infatuation with a harlot and sexual consummation with a virtuous wife. Since marriage and family must be avoided at any cost, there could be no infallible protection against these except in the complete extirpation of desire.

Jesus now declares that it were better to pluck out an eye or to cut off a hand than by their possession to place the whole body in jeopardy of hell fire. He is here developing the doctrine that "there be eunuchs, which have made themselves eunuchs for the kingdom of heaven's sake. He that is able to receive it, let him receive it."[5] Even the hand or the eye must be removed, if concupiscence is transmitted through these; but He spoke specifically of those members in which sex-desire is concentrated. He means that if a man cannot free himself from the erotic need, he must commit auto-castration. Let those who can, follow this precept: Origen and thousands of other Christians did so during the early centuries of the Church.

In regard to divorce and remarriage, Jesus makes the Mosaic Law far more severe. Unless the precepts here ascribed to Him are interpolations, we find that He presumed to dictate the rules under which the unregenerate must live, while He commanded His own disciples to abandon wives, children, parents, and all other relatives. And so we find Him saying in Matthew that a wife may be put away only for fornication; and anyone who marries such a woman commits the same offense.[6] In fact, all except those who master celibacy with absolute absence of desire are adulterers and fornicators in the difficult moral system of Jesus.

5. *Prohibition against Oaths.* Like a true Essene-Pythagorean, Jesus forbids the use of oaths,[7] quite in contradiction to all Jewish tradition or practice.

6. *Ethics of Defenseless Revolutionaries.* And now we find those Gospel teachings which become rational only when we understand that they express the revolutionary needs of defenseless outcasts; and that they are the doctrines of a communist brotherhood of elect saints who have renounced the world and taken refuge in equalitarian se-

curity and poverty. In short, these are the ethics of the Buddhists and the Essenes and constitute the *modus vivendi* by which they emancipated themselves from their social and economic obligations. When the ancient ascetics of India went on strike against family and employer, we know that they were subjected to the most outrageous verbal and physical abuse. Had they retaliated in kind, they would have been slaughtered without mercy; and the same economic imperative operated in the Gospel of Jesus. Not knowing the basis of its precepts, Trypho tells Justin Martyr that the teachings of the Christians are such "that no one can keep them."[8]

Should we assume, however, that the Elect intended to practice these principles in their contacts with the Children of Darkness once they obtained political dominion, we should be in serious error. During the interim, the Christians were to organize into tight, communistic societies, where their contacts would be almost entirely with each other, and where the evil world could not enter and destroy. Their non-resistance was their means of survival in a hostile world; and their love was reserved for each other.

7. *Non-Resistance.* In these renunciatory principles, which were the reverse of the cautious self-protection and thrifty industry enjoined by Hesiod and the Jewish wisdom literature, Jesus is certainly not fulfilling but abrogating the Mosaic Law. In place of the ancient *Lex Talionis,* He commands peaceful non-resistance: if any one smite thee on one cheek, turn the other unto him; if any one sue you at law to take your coat, give him your cloak also; and if any one seek to borrow, never withhold the loan. Now to a member of an Essene community, to a monk in a Trappist monastery, or to one so poor that he has neither food nor raiment, these commandments could be nothing but the road to profit. But to a citizen living in a society based upon private property and working hard to save a competence for his family or his own old age, such a code must necessarily lead directly to ruin. The Essenes, acutely aware that the world is full of ruthless and predatory men, escaped them by retiring to their own houses or communities; and there, while renouncing their

wealth individually, they continued to enjoy it communally: for there was no limit to the riches which the Order might possess.

8. *Loving Our Enemies.* Jesus turns now to the ethics of human relationships. Since we are all the children of the same Father, as the Essenes taught, we are equally worthy, must love one another, and establish universal brotherhood. It is not sufficient to love those who do good unto us: even sinners and publicans do the same. We must love our enemies, bless them that curse us. Here Jesus goes far beyond the Golden Rule, which had been taught in various forms in many countries for centuries. This commandment to return good for evil is a bizarre morality; and all such commandments were intended primarily to shame or force the enemies of Buddhists, Pythagoreans, Essenes, and Christians into a policy of religious toleration.

9. *Never Practiced by Proponents.* The proof of sincerity comes by practical test: and we know of no one who has ever practiced such self-abnegation. The Essenes, as we have seen, considered their fierce hatred for the Children of Darkness quite as essential as their love for each other. And certainly Jesus never followed His own precepts in respect to the scribes and Pharisees, whom He denounced in a manner that would have made an Essene proud. Nor did Jesus exhibit much love for the money-changers of the Temple court. When He was ejected from Nazareth, He expressed no love for the doomed of His boyhood home. When He left Galilee, He invoked divine vengeance upon Bethsaida, Chorazin, and Capernanum. He repeatedly referred to His contemporaries as a "wicked and adulterous generation," because they rejected His message. We will search in vain through the vast expanses of literature for denunciations so vitriolic or so bristling with hatred as were His own, when directed against his cultic opponents, the Pharisees. James and John Boanerges wished to call down fire upon the Samaritans because they did not accept the Gospel.[9] There must have been inherent in Christianity an enormous potential for hatred; otherwise, the Catholic Church could not, beginning with the

day it achieved power, have been guilty of more sanguinary persecution than any other institution which has ever appeared upon this earth. Actually, this violence was the expression of long-suppressed hostility, cloaked under the strange doctrine of turning the other cheek. Since anyone who assumes unnatural virtues may always be expected to commit unnatural crimes, we may be sure that those who affect a self-abnegating pacifism will become fierce persecutors the moment they come to power; and this is especially true if they have adopted the doctrine of exclusive salvation.

The changeless fact is that self-preservation and non-aggression are the highest practical principles of human conduct. We may even add that the ethics of Jesus are in a real sense highly immoral since they cannot be proclaimed sincerely[10] and, except as a means by which helpless revolutionaries may escape immediate destruction, would normally constitute a species of suicidal insanity.

The Christians have never loved their enemies nor have they done good to those who injured them. Are we then to consider this passage totally fatuous? Not at all: for this morality was established, first, to govern their interrelationships while they remained a persecuted minority or continued as a celibate-communist community; second, to regulate their contacts with those among the unregenerate who might still be redeemed; and, third, to enable them to survive among all-powerful enemies intent upon their destruction. As for those who refused to accept the Gospel, or who, far worse, sought to refute, subvert, or expose it, *they* were in an entirely different category. They were like the political criminals in a modern communist state; they were the Children of Darkness, and, like the Essenes and the Buddhists, the Christians hated their ideological opponents with a true proselytizing wrath, based upon the conviction that they were the minions of Satan seeking to destroy the one true faith. Compared with such enemies, burglars, harlots, and murderers were venial offenders. It is never recorded that Jesus had one word of commendation for thrift, industry, or inventiveness; or that He ever criticized the shiftless, the lazy, or those who live by theft or pauperism. All of these were pardoned out of hand by Jesus as the innocent victims of a wicked social system.

D. RELATIONSHIP WITH THE CREATOR

Jesus declares that the relationship between man and his creator should be holy, secret, and intensely personal. It must exist for its own sake, and must never be a public function. In brief, there must be nothing external or formal about our religious worship; it must never be used to impress others with our virtue or piety.

The section closes with the Lord's Prayer, which certainly did not originate with Jesus. It was probably of Essene origin, and may have been used in a form similar to that given in the Gospel for centuries.

The Prayer pleads for such morality among men as exists in heaven, in order that God's kingdom among men may become possible. The daily bread is the holy sacrament, a fact clearly established by *The Didache*. The only morality commanded is that we forgive everyone his debts and remain free from animosity; for this is the basis of that brotherhood which Jesus everywhere proclaims. When Jesus speaks of "debts," there is no doubt that He means money or other borrowed material treasure, which should never be expected in return, since, in a communist world, no one possesses individual wealth and all "debts" are automatically canceled among the brethren. Under such conditions, we may be sure that lenders would be few indeed; these are the ethics of those who possess nothing, but hope to borrow, or receive gifts, without returning anything. We have seen how the poor of Jerusalem forgave themselves their debts during the Roman siege by the simple expedient of burning the public records.

Finally, the Prayer pleads that God may not lead us into temptation, which expressed the hope that we are not predestined to hell.

E. THE PRACTICE OF RENUNCIATION

1. *Individual Accumulation Forbidden.* Like the Buddhists, the Pythagoreans, and the Essenes, the Christian

were not to lay up treasures individually on earth, where moth and rust corrupt, and where thieves break through and steal. Instead, we should lay up treasures in heaven: for where our treasure is, there will our hearts be also.

2. *The Good and the Evil.* Jesus again draws a sharp line between the wicked and the righteous,[11] as He always does. Every human being is a Child of Light or a Child of Darkness. No man can serve two masters: either we will love material things, and pursue them as our principal objective in life, and in so doing will necessarily lie, cheat, circumvent, and exploit; or we will renounce all these hollow and transitory benefits, love God with heart and soul, and practice renunciation and communist brotherhood. These are the two ways expounded in the *Manual of Discipline, The Testaments,* and *The Didache,* for which the metaphysical and ethical foundation is to be found in Zoroastrianism and in Pythagoreanism.

3. *"Take No Thought for Your Life."* Jesus proposes a morality[12] which must be recognized as completely impractical in any individualistic society, but possible in a communal group: we are to take no thought for our lives—what we shall eat, drink, or clothe ourselves withal. In a society based upon private property, men following such dictates would soon betake themselves to the gutter: nor would they be very popular as husbands or fathers. But in a prison, an asylum, or a communist-celibate order, there are no husbands who must provide for the morrow. For them, "sufficient for the day is the evil thereof."

We must note that when the Essenes gave their wealth to the poor, they were themselves those "poor," whose storehouses were amply stocked. What they surrendered as individuals, they regained as members of the group, which might possess unlimited wealth. Thus, their communism was a device by which to escape the sinfulness and contamination of private property without foregoing its blessings and benefits. It is interesting to note that one of the Dead Sea Scrolls proves that the Essene monastery possessed vast quantities of hidden gold and silver.

The fact is, of course, that the early Christian communities modeled themselves upon these doctrines: and several hundred modern Christian sects have done the same, notably the Mormons and the Doukhobors. This writer once spent a day in the Trappist monastery at Bardstown, Kentucky. The residents are similar to the ancient Essenes in various respects: they are celibates, serve novitiates, take severe vows, repudiate their families, renounce private property, and live in permanent and equalitarian poverty. They take no thought for the morrow. They differ from the Essenes chiefly in that they have abandoned normal occupations and economic self-reliance, and thus resemble rather the Buddhist monks.

4. *Judge Not.* The injunction against judging, or finding fault with, our brethren was part and parcel of Jesus' teaching concerning brotherhood. Since no one is without fault in the eyes of his Maker, how can anyone judge a brother? All that we receive is from God, who gives us freely, and without merit of our own. How much more, then, does it behoove us to display the same charity toward our brethren.

5. *Avoiding the Reprobate.* But now the tone suddenly changes: for Jesus is speaking of the reprobate: "Give not that which is holy unto the dogs, neither cast ye your pearls before swine."[13] In the original *Gospel to the Hebrews,* the dogs and swine are explicitly identified as Gentiles who refuse to accept the discipline of Judaism; but in our Hellenized recension, they become simply those reprobates who do not accept or who openly oppose the Gospel. They are like the gluttonous or violent beasts who think only of their bellies or who will turn and rend their would-be benefactors. They are strictly to be avoided.

6. *The Elect Shall Receive.* "Ask, and it shall be given you; seek, and ye shall find." The Elect will not need to hear the Gospel a second time: nay, they need not hear it even once. As soon as they are aware of its promulgation, they will seek it out and the Kingdom of Heaven will be theirs.

Elaborating on the above, Jesus compares His heavenly Father to an earthly one. Who is so harsh as to give his child a stone when he asks for bread? Likewise, the Elect, impelled by their inner urge toward regeneration, will beg for salvation with such persistence and intensity that God will in no wise refuse to grant their prayers.

Jesus again expresses the Essene doctrine of election and predestination.[14] Many are called to the Kingdom, but few are they who shall enter. Only a small fraction of all those created can pass the strait and narrow gate. The great majority love godless things, broad is their way, and many be they who walk this highway to destruction.

7. *Mere Verbal Acceptance Useless.* After warning against false prophets, Jesus reaches His peroration with a discourse differentiating between outward conformity and the inner regeneration which alone can lead to salvation. It is even possible to perform miracles or to prophesy in the name of Christ, and yet be reprobate. There must be a mystical transformation of the moral impulses. Merely to give verbal assent to the Gospel teaching by saying, "Lord, Lord!" is useless. But the auditor who hears and builds his life in accord with them, *he* has a house builded upon a rock, which neither rain, nor storm, nor flood, can threaten: it is secure for time, for the Kingdom, and for eternity.

F. ESSENCE OF THE GOSPEL ETHICS

These ethics were indubitably loaded with meaning as an interim morality for believers awaiting the Parousia. It is equally certain, however, that this system seemed practical enough to a tightly organized community of religious revolutionaries who had turned their backs forever upon an acquisitive society.

Although Jesus advocated principles which neither He nor any follower of His has ever practiced, He nevertheless expressed the hopes and the aspirations of the lost and the downtrodden. It is curious to note that, in spite of the love for both brethren and enemies, which Jesus so often proclaims, the pagans universally considered the hatred which Christians felt both toward each other and mankind their outstanding characteristic. The power of the Gospel lay in the fact that it declared the inalienable rights of the poor: rights which their more clever, thrifty, industrious, intelligent, and capable brethren can ignore or deny only at their peril; Jesus proclaimed the ethical concept of universal brotherhood which has today permeated every portion and level of human consciousness; and His message, therefore, transcends all political and religious boundaries and barriers. He preached a dynamic synthesis of Buddhist-Pythagorean-Essene morality which no reaction has ever been able to silence utterly.

CHAPTER VIII

ART THOU HE THAT SHOULD COME?

A. INTERLUDE

1. *The Gentile Gospel.* At this point we meet the Roman soldier whose servant was "ready to die." This episode, which does not occur in Mark, differs in Luke and Matthew, and even more in John, and seems, therefore, like other important miracles, to be an addition to the authentic tradition. Jesus, much impressed by the faith and humility of the centurion, declares that "many shall come from the east and the west, and shall sit down with Abraham, and Isaac, and Jacob, in the Kingdom of heaven. But the children of the kingdom shall be cast out into the outer darkness: there shall be weeping and gnashing of teeth."[1] The Jews are the children of the Kingdom, and to them it is offered first. But their response has been disappointing, and they have no monopoly in the inheritance. Even as in *The Testaments of the Twelve Patriarchs*, regenerate Gentiles coming from East and West will judge the chosen people and share immortality with Abraham at the imminent Parousia in Palestine (a destiny quite unknown in the Hebrew scriptures) while the unbelieving Jews are to be cast forth into everlasting torment and darkness. In this drastic repudiation of Judaism, the Elect are all those in whom, regardless of race, the grace of God works its miraculous transformation, because they were predestined to such glory from the foundation of the world.

2. *Miracle-Myth.* The raising from the dead of the son of the widow of Nain is told only in Luke.[2] We recall that the resurrection of Lazarus is related only in John.

The more extraordinary miracles remain unrecorded in Mark, which was nearest to the sources.

B. THE BAPTIST SENDS MISSIONARIES

1. *A Cryptic Reply.* The still imprisoned Baptist,[3] unable to decide whether Jesus was the expected Christ, sent two of his disciples to elicit from Jesus a categorical declaration of identity, who, avoiding the issue, replied that the sick were being healed, and the Gospel preached to the poor; and added "blessed is he whosoever shall not be offended in me." In short, Jesus implied a divinity which He would not openly proclaim. Incidentally, this episode is in contradiction with others, notably in the Fourth Gospel, where the Baptist openly proclaims the Christhood of Jesus.

2. *Elaborates the Greatness of John.* At the departure of John's emissaries, Jesus turned abruptly to His disciples and elaborated His cryptic reply. John was not merely a prophet, but more than a prophet. He was the messenger, the voice in the wilderness, foretold in Isaiah[4] and Malachi,[5] who would prepare the way for the Lord. Among all those born of woman there was never a greater; nevertheless, the Elect of the Kingdom are all to take precedence over him: in short, not even the Baptist would be redeemed, since he did not accept Jesus as the Christ-Messiah.

3. *Jesus Is the Christ.* And so, once again, Jesus avoided an explicit answer to the crucial question: Are you, or are you not, the Christ, that is, the Anointed One? But He emphasized the divine mission of John, which was to precede the Messiah. And so Jesus almost, but not quite, proclaimed Himself. He closed with the enigmatic formula, which the Elect would understand but which the wicked could not use to destroy Him: "He that hath ears to hear, let him hear."

CHAPTER IX

APPROACHING CRISIS IN GALILEE

A. THE PARABLES

1. *Why Used.* It was becoming more and more imperative that Jesus reveal Himself as the Christ; but He was deterred from making such a momentous declaration by enemies awaiting the first pretext to destroy Him. By proclaiming His Messiahship, He would risk immediate execution for blasphemy and sedition. To categorical interrogation, therefore, He replied enigmatically in the affirmative. When finally at Caesarea Philippi He declared Himself explicitly to His inner circle, He also enjoined the strictest secrecy. In the meantime, He continued to reveal Himself through parables to those who had eyes to see and ears to hear. The Buddhists and the Essenes had always used the same method of concealing their revolutionary doctrines.

2. *The Two Creditors.* After a brief discourse in which Jesus compares His generation to discontented children[1] who rejected John because He was ascetic and Jesus because He ate and drank, we have the incident related in Luke only[2] in which He took meat at the house of Simon the Pharisee. A woman of ill repute anointed the feet of Jesus with costly oil. In the eyes of the Pharisees, it was disgraceful that so sinful a person should touch a prophet. This incident establishes that Jesus was accepted almost at His own appraisal by some of the Pharisees. When He became aware of Simon's thought, He propounded the Parable of the Two Creditors, one of whom (the sinful woman) owed ten times as much as the other (Simon) but both of whom were forgiven. The woman earned forgiveness by her sincere contrition.

3. *Exposition.* This incident is charged with soteriological implications. Past iniquity is never a bar to redemption: persons who have been sinners, publicans, thieves, harlots, murderers may still be members of the Elect. On the other hand, a man's life may outwardly be most exemplary, yet this in no wise indicates that he has been chosen for salvation. The crucial question is this: *how does he react to the Gospel?* If he reject it, or if, accepting it formally, he fails to achieve moral regeneration, he is of the reprobate. The greater a man's sinfulness, the more extraordinary will be his transformation. Some of those who followed Him, especially among the women, had been abandoned creatures. We are told that Jesus cast devils out of them, which we may take to mean that they had been guilty of scandalous immorality.

4. *The Imminent Kingdom.* We read that "he went throughout every city and village, preaching and showing the glad tidings of the kingdom of God."[3] Jesus was convinced that He was offering a treasure so incomparable that to refuse could only indicate a species of insanity or the most incorrigible wickedness. No one was to have a second opportunity to reject Him. He was proclaiming that His Kingdom would soon be established and that, under His rule, pain, fear, toil, injustice, sickness, and poverty would be abolished; that the poor would reign with Him and that all the rich would be forever banished and their property given to those who had never owned anything. All this was to happen within a few weeks, or months at most.

5. *The Women Who Followed Jesus.* And now we find another passage which accentuates the historicity of Jesus. Besides His disciples, there were with Him "certain women, which had been healed of evil spirits and infirmities, Mary called Magdalene, out of whom went seven devils, and Joanna the wife of Chusa Herod's steward, and Susanna, and many others, which ministered unto Him of their substance."[4] Like other prophets in various eras, Jesus was adored and attended by women who also supplied Him with the necessities of life. And what was it that commanded such devotion? We believe it was the doc-

trine of celibacy, which they now adopted to assuage a burning sense of guilt. They had probably been harlots or adulteresses driven by conscience to the verge of madness. After Jesus gave them peace of mind by assuring them that their sins were forgiven, they became His dedicated vestals.

6. *The Parable of the Sower*. And now Jesus re-creates the ancient Gaina-Buddhist parable of the sower,[5] perhaps the most famous of His allegories, elaborated also in the other Synoptics. The sower went forth to sow: some of the seed fell by the wayside, and was devoured by the fowls of the air; some, fallen upon stony ground, sprang up quickly, but soon died in the dry, hot sun; some fell upon fertile ground, and bore a munificent harvest. Jesus explains that "unto them that are without, all these things are done in parables . . . lest at any time they should be converted, and their sins be forgiven them."[6]

This states categorically that certain conversions were undesirable. Did Jesus really mean that? If one is converted, is one not then also regenerate? The answer is *no*: and again we encounter the doctrine of predestination. Even as it is possible to prophesy and perform miracles in the name of Jesus and yet be unregenerate, even so one may perform the outward gestures which go with conversion. A person may receive baptism, consume the eucharist, and be accorded forgiveness; but if the convert is not of the Elect, there can be no spiritual transfiguration and no sonship to God. It is therefore extremely important that only the Elect respond to the Gospel.

The Sower is Jesus Himself and the Gospel is the seed. It makes various impressions upon those who hear it: some, like the hardened Pharisees and Sadducees, reject it altogether; some receive it for the moment, but soon forget it; some have so many other interests that it is choked to death; but, finally, there are a few, the Elect, who respond wholeheartedly to it and are transformed by it; and in them it bears abundant fruit.

And then Jesus declares this much-quoted dictum: "For he that hath, to him shall be given: and he that hath not, from him shall be taken even that which he hath." At first blush, this seems contradictory: for generally it is the poor who shall receive munificently and the rich who shall be stripped of all. But here the reference is not to material wealth but to the gift of grace. Those who are elected to the Kingdom shall receive also the power to achieve it. And what is that little which the unregenerate now possess but shall lose? This consists of the material things now treasured so highly by the wicked but which will soon be transferred to the Elect.

The reinterpretation which Jesus gives this ancient parable of India proves that His basic orientation was Essene-Zoroastrian rather than Buddhist, in which the seed consisted of gifts to mendicant saints, who were themselves the good fields, and who are therefore contrasted to the Brahmanas, who are the worthless fields, which can produce no improvement in the donor's *kharma*. Buddhism knew nothing of predestination, which was central in Essene soteriology and which is reflected in the Gospel Parable of the Sower; and the overriding desire for alms among the Buddhists is replaced in the Gospel by the hope for cataclysmic conversion by the preaching of the Word.

7. *Tares among the Wheat.* The Parable of the Tares among the Wheat is found only in Matthew.[7] The Son of Man has sowed good seed in His field; but while men slept, His enemy came and planted tares. The good seed are the converted Elect. The tares are the reprobates who have apparently been converted and who, having entered the holy community by "violence,"[8] remain unregenerate. These cannot be removed until the Parousia, when "the Son of man . . . shall cast them into a furnace of fire: there shall be wailing and gnashing of teeth."[9]

Jesus here declares Himself the Messiah of Moral Judgment, who, on the dreadful last day, will pluck out from the congregation of the righteous all the hypocrites, all the wolves in sheep's clothing, who have infiltrated the society of the just but whose sins are not of that overt variety which bring immediate detection and expulsion from the congregation. It is impossible for the reprobate to live a regenerate life, for their nature impels them to evil thoughts and deeds, and in the end they must be damned.

8. *The Kingdom of Heaven a Dual Concept.* The Kingdom of Heaven is a dual concept: first, it exists as a communion of the Elect under present conditions, and this is what Jesus meant when He said, "the kingdom of God is within you";[10] following the Parousia, however, it was to comprise the entire earthly community. This Kingdom, which was to continue for an indeterminate period, would be inaugurated with a judgment by which all the wicked would be consigned to perdition. The Kingdom itself is like a treasure, hid in a field;[11] when a man hears of it, he tells all his friends of his wonderful discovery. Or, it is like a pearl of such great price that when a merchant finds it, he sells all his possessions and buys this single jewel.[12] Again, it is like a net,[13] which captures good and bad. And, just as the fisherman discards the worthless fish, "So shall it be at the end of the world: the angels shall come forth, and sever the wicked from among the just, And shall cast them into the furnace of fire: there shall be wailing and gnashing of teeth."[14]

Thus heaven beckons to the few and hell yawns for the many. In one hand, Jesus carries a magnificent promise, in the other, a fearful threat. All the wicked must suffer eternal torture: those of the Elect who are not fortunate enough to hear the Gospel as well as the unregenerate who force themselves into the Kingdom are to suffer the same lugubrious fate.

B. CLIMACTERIC IN GALILEE

1. *Three Miracles.* In rapid succession, Jesus is credited with three celebrated miracles. First He stills the tempest threatening to overturn the boat in which His disciples are journeying and in which He lies asleep.[15] Second, He casts out a legion of devils from a maniac tomb-dweller in the land of the Gadarenes.[16] And, third, He raises from the dead the daughter of a Roman centurion.[17] This incident seems to be another version of that in which the centurion's servant was sick unto death. The devils which

had possessed the man at once recognize Jesus as the Son of God, and plead to be left alone. When Jesus commands them to come out, they receive permission to enter a herd of swine, who thereupon rush over a precipice and are drowned. Anxious to have His fame broadcast, at least among the Gadarenes, Jesus urges the man to tell all that the Lord has done for him.

2. *Doctrinal Teachings Authentic.* While the miracles of Jesus could easily be created and multiplied by the credulity of His followers, they could never have devised ethical, speculative, or soteriological doctrines, which, although in no instance original, presented new combinations of established religious concepts and ethical principles. The Pythagorean philosophy, already uniting, as we have seen, the ethics, soteriology, and eschatology of Persia, Egypt, Greece, India, and Asia Minor, was absorbed by the Essenes, who combined all this with the teachings of the Hebrew prophets and transformed the whole into a synthesis of their own. Jesus reformulated this vast accumulation of emotional experience in a Gospel infused with His own genius. The miracle-stories were simply a vehicle to emphasize His ethics and His soteriology, and served to procure His initial audience.

3. *Demand for Faith.* We note that at this point the Synoptics begin to stress the necessity for faith, which serves to resuscitate the daughter of Jairus, and which later became the cornerstone of the Fourth Gospel. This suggests that many were skeptical because Jesus did not resolve their questions or because they witnessed no works sufficient to support His grandiose claims. And it seems rather peculiar that, after commanding the former madman to broadcast his cure, Jesus should "charge them straitly that no man should know" that He had raised the daughter of Jairus from the dead. Such a prohibition would indicate that this "miracle" would not bear close scrutiny.

4. *Galilean Ministry Concluded.* At all events, another important phase in the ministry of Jesus was now concluded. He must not repeat Himself; He must not cover the same ground twice; His mission must proceed in an ever-increasing crescendo to its ultimate climax. He had made

stupendous claims which must soon be established in glory or exposed in obloquy. Since He had now covered Galilee once (a small territory containing only small villages) nothing more was to be accomplished there. The response to His message had been bitterly disappointing and the future was veiled in doubt. His own family and friends considered Him a madman, and wished to drag Him home in bonds. The Pharisees and Herodians were poised to seize Him and inflict upon Him the fate suffered by the Baptist. He had now arrived at an impasse: something drastic must happen soon.

What would it be?

CHAPTER X

THE FIRST APOCALYPSE

A. PAROUSIA WITHOUT DEATH

1. *The First Climacteric.* And now we again abandon the sequence of Luke and follow the tenth chapter of Matthew, of which there is nothing in Mark. Here we find the first climacteric in the career of Jesus consisting of the first apocalypse and His charge to the Twelve (and to seventy others also, according to Luke) as He sent them out to preach the Gospel in Judaea. We may regard these numbers as largely imaginary.

2. *Gospel Is for Jews Only.* Jesus was persuaded that the end of the age was immediately upon Him. He therefore assembled the disciples, confirmed their power to cast out devils and heal the sick, and commanded them to go two by two, without script or purse, into all the cities of Israel: "Go not into the way of Gentiles, and into any city of the Samaritans enter ye not: But go rather to the lost sheep of the house of Israel. And as ye go, preach, saying, The Kingdom of Heaven is at hand."[1]

Reflecting its Judaistic base, the Gospel of Matthew considers the Jews the only children of the Kingdom, from which Gentiles and Samaritans are to be explicitly barred.

3. *Tribulation and Persecution.* Jesus was certain that the hour of tribulation, persecution, and sorrow preceding the coming of the Messiah was now upon them. The disciples would be haled before the councils and scourged in the synagogues, according to well established Zoroastrian and Buddhist precedents: "And the brother shall deliver up the brother unto death, and father the child: and . . . ye shall be hated of all men for my name's sake; but . . . when they persecute you in this city flee ye into another:

for verily I say unto you, Ye shall not have gone over the cities of Israel, till the Son of man be come."[2]

Certainly, if we seek proof of the historicity of Jesus, here it is. No myth would have attributed to its god-man a prophecy which was almost immediately proved false. Let us visualize the scene and the situation: Jesus had completed His basic work in Galilee; although the Kingdom of Heaven was at hand, it must first be offered to all the lost sheep of Israel; the disciples must hurry forth with their eschatological message. For they were never again to see the Master in His manifestation as the Suffering Servant: before they could complete their circuit of Israel, He would be made manifest in power as the Son of Man. He would then conduct the Last Judgment;[3] would sentence to the fires of hell all who had not in the meantime accepted His Gospel; and would establish the Kingdom of Heaven without delay in Palestine. The whole concept was parallel to that erected by the Essenes concerning the Teacher of Righteousness a century before.

4. *Death Unnecessary.* At this time, Jesus had no realization that He must suffer and die; instead, He envisioned an almost immediate assumption of supernatural power, declaring categorically that He would appear as the almighty Son of Man before the disciples could complete their brief mission.

5. *Bitterness against Galileans.* And now Jesus betrayed a fierce bitterness against the people of Galilee because of His rejection: "I say unto you, That it shall be more tolerable for the land of Sodom in the day of judgment, than for thee."[4] We must realize that this catastrophe was to come perhaps in a month and that Jesus in His character as the Son of Man was himself to be the judge. The Gospel writers did not comprehend His words; they simply wrote down verbatim what they heard.

Jesus declared that His missionaries would be in constant danger of abuse, persecution, and death. But they should not fear those who have the power to kill the body: "rather fear Him which is able to destroy both soul and body in hell."[5]

B. THE SOTERIOLOGICAL ETHICS OF JESUS

1. *An Apostle of Discord.* And now we find one of the celebrated passages in which Jesus contradicts His usually pacifist philosophy: "Think not that I am come to send peace on earth: I came not to send peace, but a sword."[6]

To resolve such apparent contradictions, which moved John MacKinnon Robertson to say that there are several Christs in the Gospels, we need only a simple key. Jesus was infinitely tolerant and merciful toward all who violated laws of private property. But for skeptics who threatened His mission He had neither kindness nor mercy, but imprecations, and threats of everlasting hell fire. It was His set purpose to sow social discord everywhere, to plant immedicable enmity between blood relatives, to rend families asunder: "Suppose ye, that I am come to give peace on earth? I tell you, Nay: but rather divisions: For from henceforth there shall be five in one house divided, three against two and two against three."[7]

There could be no compromise in matters relating to the Kingdom: either one is of it or one is not, in which case there must be hostility to the death. Thus we know the ethics of Jesus are never intended to apply as between the Elect and the reprobate. Like the Essenes, the followers of Jesus were to love their brethren in the faith, but to hate all unbelievers and avoid them like the plague, especially those of their own family.

2. *Dual Ethical System.* How, then, are we to explain the injunctions of Jesus to love those who despitefully use us, etc.? Can it be possible that even among the Elect there could be hostility? Yes, even that was possible: for there were always intruders, the tares among the wheat, who were guilty of hatred and resentment. But even these wolves in sheep's clothing we must love, and forgive them seventy times seven times.

But beyond these, there will also be powerful enemies who will seek to destroy the new cult by provoking its members into acts of violence, which would serve as the pretext for further persecution and complete suppression. Toward these, therefore, the disciples of Jesus, like the Buddhists, must practise non-resistance, and pray for their conversion. Such conduct, intended only as a means of self-preservation, might seem like love for an enemy. The only true test of its sincerity would come when the new creed achieved not only tolerance but domination.

We become aware, however, more and more, that Jesus has two systems of ethics: one for the unregenerate and another for the Elect. For the former divorce is prohibited and parents must be supported; the Elect, however, must desert brethren, parents, children, wives, and husbands, and cleave only to the members of the communion.

3. *Repudiation of Marriage and Family.* Jesus now develops His repudiation of marriage and family, and their replacement by the elect brotherhood. "He that loveth father or mother . . . son or daughter more than me is not worthy of me."[8] The doctrine is fully elaborated: "Verily, I say unto you, That . . . every one that hath forsaken houses, or brethren, or sisters, or father, or mother, or wife, or children, or lands, for my name's sake, shall receive an hundredfold, and shall inherit everlasting life."[9] Luke is even more emphatic: "If any man come to me, and hate not his father, and mother, and wife, and children, and brethren, and sisters . . . he cannot be my disciple."[10] Since these texts run counter to the morality which was developed by the Greeks under private property and on which our own social order is based, they are glossed over and ignored in modern churches. However, they are not incidental to the Gospel: they are its very center, pith, and essence. This celibate mandate is repeatedly enjoined: "The children of this world marry, and are given in marriage: But they which shall be accounted worthy to obtain that world and the resurrection from the dead, neither marry nor are given in marriage."[11]

Are we to accept this summary repudiation of family and marriage as the literal meaning of the Gospel? The facts are (1) that such texts are entirely consistent with the Gospel as a whole; and (2) that this was exactly the doctrine and the practice of the Buddhists, the Pythagoreans, and the Essenes. It was possible to become an Elect One, a disciple of Jesus, and to achieve the Kingdom of Heaven only by embracing celibacy and by abandoning every blood and family tie. This was a fundamental condition for redemption.

C. DEFEAT AND FRUSTATION

1. *All Predictions Prove False.* What Jesus was doing while His disciples were absent on their missionary journey, the record does not reveal. He must have been eagerly anticipating His imminent assumption of power. At all events, we know that He never expected His disciples to meet Him again in His guise of Suffering Servant.

But the event was soon to disprove His prophecies. We learn that the "disciples returned with joy, saying, Lord, even the devils are subject unto us through thy name." [12] There had been no tribulation, no persecution, no scourging, no social upheaval, no advent of the Son of Man. Perhaps, being more desirous of impressing the Master than of preaching the Gospel, they had proclaimed the Kingdom quite dilatorily.

This was a crushing defeat. Could it be that Jesus was mistaken concerning Himself and His mission, that He was suffering from delusions, that He was neither prophet nor Christ? Could His family and Nazarene friends have been correct in believing Him insane? Heaven forbid! The career He had begun must continue; it must not dwindle away into ignominious and shameful obscurity which would make of Him a mockery to the very urchins on the streets of Nazareth and a shaking of the head to the sneering Pharisees.

2. *What Next?* When the disciples returned, Jesus greeted them strangely. He had neither ethics nor eschatology to impart; He had neither threats nor miracles. Instead, He declared, in part, somewhat contemptuous of recorded fact: "I beheld Satan as lightning fall from heaven."[13]

Thus ineffectually ended the first apocalypse of Jesus. Fortunately for Him and His movement, the disciples had not comprehended His predictions, and were therefore neither frustrated in their work nor shaken in their faith. He was now compelled to reorient His ministry and develop a new concept concerning Himself.

CHAPTER XI

INDECISION AND REORIENTATION

A. JESUS ABANDONS GALILEE

The first great phase in the ministry of Jesus had now ended in crushing defeat. Up to this point, His entire activity, with the exception of the brief episode involving the swine at Gergesa, had taken place in Galilee, which, at the death of Herod the Great in 4 B.C., had become a Roman political subdivision under his son, Herod Antipas, who was made tetrarch or king by Caesar Augustus and who continued in this capacity until 37.

When the disciples returned from their missionary journey, Jesus abandoned His Galilean ministry. Among other reasons for this, we may note that Herod had executed John the Baptist,[1] who had stirred up sentiment against Herod for violating Lev. 18:16 by marrying his niece Herodias, divorced wife of his living brother Philip. John had thus incurred the mortal enmity of this influential woman. However, we may also believe that Herod regarded the Baptist as a truculent agitator, much better out of the way. If such were the case, certainly this would apply even more to Jesus. Constantly fed by streams of propaganda from the Pharisees and from his wife, Herod might suspect Jesus of being another Judas the Gaulonite, whose rebellion had been so ruthlessly suppressed in the year 7 We know that the Pharisees had been conspiring with the Herodians to destroy Jesus. And we read that the superstitious Herod believed Jesus to be the reincarnated Baptist.[2]

And so, to seek new fields and more receptive auditors to forget His defeats and disappointments, and to escap from His family and the lethal wrath of Herod, Jesus abandoned Galilee.

B. JESUS FORGES A NEW DECISION

1. *Escape from Herod.* We are told that when the disciples returned from their journey to Capernaum, Jesus took them by boat across the Sea of Galilee to the security of a desert place outside Bethsaida, which was a town in Gaulonitis, beyond the power of Herod.[3] Leaving them there, He sought solitude to think and pray.

But the hungry, wretched people, seeking food and medication, followed Him around the seashore and besieged Him and His disciples in their retreat.[4] It was here that the celebrated miracle of the loaves and fishes occurred.

2. *He Sends the Disciples Away.* The decision of Jesus to retire being thus frustrated, He now adopted a more drastic course: He sent His disciples back to Capernaum. Whether it was His intention at this point to sever permanently His relationship with them and to complete His mission alone, the record does not reveal. As for Himself, "He went up into a mountain apart to pray: and when the evening was come, he was there alone."[5] That He was undergoing fearful emotional stress is certain.

3. *Walks on Water.* The separation, however, was to be of short duration; for when a storm threatened to destroy the boat in which the disciples were returning to Galilee, Jesus was said to have stilled the wind and the waves and to have walked across the water to be reunited with them.[6] After this episode, they returned together to Gaulonitis where, going about the towns and villages, they preached the Kingdom and healed the sick.[7]

C. JESUS SEEKS CONFLICT WITH PHARISEES

And now, for the first time, we find Jesus lashing out savagely against the Pharisees.[8] In Galilee, He had evaded their legalistic traps and dilemmas by cautious counter-queries. But here, freed from the fear of Herod, He embarked on a deliberate campaign to arouse their utmost wrath. And so, when they criticized His disciples rather in surprise than with animosity for eating without first washing their hands ceremonially, He ignored the charge, as if too insignificant to notice, but unloosed instead a flood of denunciation upon the Pharisees because they limited their virtue to external observances. While they washed their hands, He accused them of permitting their indigent brethren to suffer want by declaring their property *Corban,* that is, religiously consecrated, and therefore exempt under the Mosaic Law:[9] "and many such like things ye do . . . Full well ye reject the commandments of God, that ye may keep your own tradition."

Again, we are forced to note that these Pharisees could have become the disciples of Jesus only by abandoning their parents entirely. It would seem that the unregenerate must observe certain duties and obligations which the Elect must repudiate with even greater emphasis. Jesus thereupon elaborates His Buddhistic teaching for the benefit of the disciples: rituals, ceremonies, and special foods are of no efficacy for salvation. It is not what a man receives into his belly that defiles;[10] it is rather the evil moral impulses which inspire all manner of sinful thoughts and deeds. To eat with washed or unwashed hands, to observe or violate the Sabbath, are equally matters of indifference: but a vile or evil desire will consign the one who is possessed by it to the lake of eternal fire and brimstone.

With this Buddhist-Essene concept, Jesus made a frontal assault upon the ceremonials of Judaism. And now seeking, instead of avoiding, the ultimate conflict with the Pharisees in a province where they lacked the immediate power to destroy Him, Jesus was carefully laying the groundwork for His own sacrificial destruction as the atoning savior of mankind.

CHAPTER XII

THOU ART THE CHRIST!

A. JESUS JOURNEYS BEYOND GALILEE

1. *His New Conception Takes Form.* When Jesus returned from the mountain to His disciples, He began to reveal the altered concept of His destiny.

2. *Goes Into Syria Alone.* As if to orient Himself to this new condition, Jesus went alone into Syria, to the borders of Tyre and Sidon,[1] where the principal incident was the casting out of a devil from the daughter of a Syro-Phoenician woman, with which we shall deal in a later chapter.

3. *Avoids Galilee.* He thereupon turned southward to Decapolis in Perea,[2] east of Lake Genessaret, thus avoiding Galilee.

B. JESUS DEFEATED BY THE PHARISEES

Now for the last time and very briefly, Jesus made a public appearance in eastern Galilee, at Dalmanutha,[3] a few miles south of Capernaum, where He rejoined His disciples. Scarcely had He set foot on the western shore of Lake Genessaret, when He was confronted by a delegation of well-primed Pharisees,[4] who demanded that He provide an authentic sign to prove His messiahship. To this, He only sighed and declared:[5] "Why doth this generation seek after a sign? Verily I say unto you, There shall be no sign." Here, in the tetrarchy of Herod, Jesus dared not challenge or denounce the reigning priesthood. We are told that He re-entered the ship and departed to the other side of the lake.[6] His Galilean ministry was forever concluded.

Convincing details like these stamp the Gospel narrative with the signet of authenticity. The myth-making faculty could easily invent the story of the seven loaves and the fishes, but never a reverse like this. Had this story been mythical, Jesus would have raised His hand, and His persecutors would have been destroyed by a thunderbolt or struck lame with palsy. This Synoptic incident disappears in John, like so much else.

C. JESUS DECLARES HIS CHRISTHOOD AT CAESAREA PHILIPPI

Fleeing precipitately with His disciples, Jesus took ship again to Bethsaida. They then journeyed northward into Gaulonitis about twenty-five miles to Caesarea Philippi,[7] where a very important event occurred. Here, far from the prying and hostile eyes of Jewish enemies, Jesus finally declared explicitly that He was indeed the Christ. On various occasions, He had revealed Himself darkly, in parables; He had also permitted others to call Him the Son of God. But now He broached the subject Himself: "Whom say ye that I am? And Simon Peter answered and said, Thou art the Christ, the Son of the living God. And Jesus answered and said unto him, Blessed art thou, Simon Bar-Jona: for flesh and blood hath not revealed it unto thee, but my Father which is in heaven."[8]

Here follows the charge and the commission to Peter, the rock upon which the church was built. This is the text used later by the Roman See as the principal foundation for its claim to authority. "Then charged he his disciples that they should tell no man that he was Jesus the Christ." Even in Gaulonitis, secrecy was still imperative; even here, He dared reveal Himself only to the inner circle.

D. THE NEW MESSIANIC CONCEPT

1. *Plans Revealed to the Disciples.* Jesus had now formulated His course of action; He began "to show unto his disciples, how that he must go unto Jerusalem . . .

and be killed, and be raised again on the third day."⁹ This was the new destiny which Jesus had developed concerning Himself. Like the Paschal Lamb of the Jewish Passover, like Osiris, Attis, and Zagreus, He must die to accomplish His atonement. He knew that He need only announce His Christhood in the stronghold of the enemy to bring upon Himself the persecution, the rejection, and martyrdom He sought. Thus He could become the Suffering Servant of Isaiah manifest in Jerusalem; thus He would repeat the sacrificial death of the Essene Teacher of Righteousness. In this new concept of His mission, Jesus extended the period that yet remained from a few scant weeks or months to a period of years following His death during which the disciples could announce the message of salvation to every Gentile nation.

2. *Peter Seeks to Restrain the Master.* When Jesus declared that He must die in Jerusalem, the impetuous Peter sought to restrain Him.[10] But Jesus could not turn back; He must not pause or listen to the siren words of those who counseled safety: "Get thee behind me, Satan: thou art an offense unto me: for thou savorest not the things that be of God, but those that be of men."

3. *Time of Parousia Proclaimed.* And now Jesus declared that "the Son of man would come in the glory of his father with his angels: and then he shall reward every man according to his works."[11] And just when would this tremendous consummation take place? "Verily, I say unto you, That there be some of them that stand here, which shall not taste of death, till they have seen the kingdom of God come with power."[12]

These words, simply incapable of misinterpretation, are confirmed by other passages of equal integrity and constitute the central meaning of the Gospel. Jesus promised definitely to return with power to establish His kingdom during the earthly lifetime of those who stood before Him and heard this announcement with their own ears.

And so Jesus molded His career according to this new conception. He would proceed to Jerusalem where He would denounce the Elders and the Pharisees in order to provoke their mortal hostility. There He would die His sacrificial death, to be followed in some miraculous way by translation into glory, where He would remain for a short, but indefinite, period, during which His disciples would preach the Gospel; finally, at the Parousia, He would return and establish the Kingdom of Heaven on earth before those then listening to His words should taste of death, before the then existing generation should pass away.

4. *Conventional Eschatology a Fraud and a Delusion.* This was the eschatology of Jesus. Without it, there would never have been any Christian church; for this doctrine was the dynamic force inherent in its original evangel. It was still its vital core well into the second century; and this is the reason why these eschatological passages were never deleted. By the time the Church was ready to abandon and repudiate the chiliastic kingdom, the texts which proclaimed it had become so thoroughly embedded into the scripture that they could not be removed.

The modern church ignores or misinterprets these texts. Schweitzer declares that the history of Christianity has consisted in evading the Gospel eschatology and postponing the Parousia of Jesus. And he adds: "It should be noted that the non-fulfillment of Matt. X 23 marks the first postponement of the Parousia." [13] And so thoroughly acclimatized had the thinking of all men become to these perversions that only in comparatively recent years has it dawned even upon the most acute scholars that Jesus meant what He explicitly declared. Even the acute Deists of the eighteenth century, who wrote whole libraries of higher criticism, failed entirely to notice that the imminent Parousia was one of the central doctrines of the Gospel.

CHAPTER XIII

THE TRANSFORMED CHRIST

A. THE MOUNTAIN VISION

On a mount north of Caesarea Philippi another climacteric in the career of Jesus occurred shortly after the declaration of His Christhood. Accompanied by the inner circle, He "leadeth them up into a high mountain, apart by themselves: and he was transfigured before them." [1] They were in a state of extreme exaltation; and we need not be astonished that Peter, John, and James saw also Elias and Moses; and that they heard again the voice from heaven which declared, "This is my beloved Son: hear him." [2] Suddenly, their intense emotional pitch subsided, and the vision vanished. And, as they descended, Jesus charged them not to reveal what they had seen "till the Son of man were risen from the dead." [3]

B. DEPARTURE FOR JERUSALEM

1. *Jesus Angry.* Returning to the other disciples, Jesus found them under questioning by the scribes. The disciples had been trying to cast out a stubborn devil, but could not. At this failure, Jesus, violating one of His own fundamental precepts, exclaimed angrily: "O faithless generation, how long shall I be with you? how long shall I suffer you?" [4] He was losing patience because His disciples had not developed the faith He expected.

2. *Clandestine Passage Through Galilee.* Leaving Caesarea Philippi "they departed thence and passed through Galilee; and he would not that any man should know it. For he taught his disciples, and said unto them, The Son of man is delivered unto the hands of men, and they

shall kill him; and after that he is killed, he shall rise the third day." [5]

When Jesus left Galilee, He fled from the Pharisees. And now, since it was imperative that He die at Jerusalem at the Passover, He must pass through Galilee unobserved by Pharisees or Herodians, who might arrest Him, and destroy Him in obscurity. It was crucial for His purpose that He die, not as an enemy of the temporal power, but as a divine sacrifice for the sins of humanity. This could be accomplished only in Jerusalem, never in some Galilean dungeon, where the Baptist came to his end. In Jerusalem at Passover several hundred thousand persons from every section of the country would be assembled, and there His sacrifice might be proclaimed to all. And, more to the point, before that vast concourse, God would make His Son manifest by signs and wonders in the hour of His destiny; and on the third day He would be elevated to His celestial throne. Such was the persuasion of Jesus.

3. *Disciples Quarrel over Priority.* After a journey of some thirty miles, Jesus arrived quietly with His disciples in Capernaum. There, behind closed doors, the latter were disputing heatedly the most burning, practical issue of the hour: who among them should be the greatest in the Kingdom of Heaven? [6] But Jesus threw cold water on their competitive aspirations: He told them that to enjoy priority there, they must first become the servants of all.

4. *Attitude toward Interim Temporal Authority.* At this point, in Matthew only,[7] Jesus expresses His Essene-Pythagorean compromise with instituted temporal authority, which made possible the survival of Christianity until its assumption of power. Since all ruling agencies come into existence by the will of God, it is the duty of all to live in obedience to them and to pay whatever tribute they demand. Thus, when the tax-collector asks Peter whether Jesus had paid His head-tax, he replies in the affirmative. Since Jesus was of course penniless, He directed the disciple to go catch a fish, in the mouth of which the necessary coin would be found. No matter how impractical this expedient may be for Christians in general, it established the general principle of civil obedience.

5. *Charity for the Brethren.* After declaring that those who are not against us are actually for us, Jesus repeats the basic ethics of the Sermon on the Mount.[8] Whosoever shall perform the smallest act of charity toward a believer or in the name of Christ, great shall be his reward; but if anyone injures one of those who have accepted the Gospel, "one of these little ones," it were "better for him that a millstone were hanged about his neck, and he were cast into the sea." Gautama had taught an almost identical doctrine.

6. *Threats of Hell and Hopes of Paradise.* Jesus here repeats the doctrine that any offensive member of the body may plunge the soul into hell fire: "And if thy foot offend thee, cut it off; it is better for thee to enter halt into life, than having two feet to be cast into hell, into the fire that never shall be quenched. Where their worm dieth not, and the fire is not quenched." [9]

And so the last words of Jesus as he left Galilee to meet His fate in Jerusalem bristled with threats of that hell fire which shall never be quenched and in which the soul of the sinner can never die.

CHAPTER XIV

INTERLUDE AT BETHANY

A. ON THE ROAD

1. *Jesus in Samaria.* Jesus and His disciples continued their journey through Samaria: "And it came to pass, when the time was come that he should be received up, he steadfastly set his face to go to Jerusalem." [1] The disciples understood that Jesus was to achieve power and glory, but not that He must suffer and die. And, like Zoroastrian saints, they imagined themselves sitting on thrones, judging the twelve tribes of Israel.

It was with great anticipation, therefore, that they set out on the eighty- or ninety-mile journey. Jesus was overcome with gratitude because the Father had revealed the mysteries of the Kingdom to babes such as His disciples, and concealed it from the wise and the prudent, like the scribes and the Pharisees.[2] The Kingdom was for the poor, the toiling, the ignorant, and the oppressed: it was not for the rich, the successful, the educated, the influential, and the powerful. "Come unto me, all ye that labour and are heavy laden, and I will give you rest. Take my yoke upon you, and learn of me; for I am meek and lowly in heart: and ye shall find rest unto your souls." [3]

2. *Parable of the Good Samaritan.* With the apparent purpose of attracting local converts, Jesus expounded His Parable of the Good Samaritan.[4] Since this was critical of Judaism, it does not appear in Matthew, or even in Mark. A lawyer, who wishes to tempt Jesus, asks Him what he should do to inherit eternal life. Jesus inquires what is written in the Law. The lawyer replies that one must love God with all one's heart and soul, and one's neighbor as

oneself. But then the crucial question arises: who is my neighbor? For according to the Mosaic Law, only a brother Hebrew is also a neighbor, and others remain beyond the pale. To drive home the universalism of Luke, Jesus tells the celebrated Parable of the Merciful Samaritan, who ministered to the wounded traveller left to die by a priest and a Levite. The Elect of the Kingdom, who will be found among all races and nations, will give aid selflessly to any stranger in want or distress. This love, which renders one fit to inherit the Kingdom, is diffused throughout mankind.

B. WITH MARTHA AND MARY

1. *Importance of the Elect.* Even as Jesus had depended upon devoted women in Galilee for His sustenance, so in Bethany He had the spinster sisters, Mary and Martha, who ministered to His wants.[5] And to them He expounded His predestinarian doctrine in one of its manifold forms: if we knock on the door of a friend at midnight, asking for a loaf of bread, he may at first refuse; but if we entreat with sufficient perseverance, he will rise at last and grant our request. So is it with the Elect: once they know that redemption is available, they will press forward with irresistible pertinacity until they achieve communion.

2. *Son of David.* When Jesus cast out a devil, the people cried: "Is not this the Son of David?"[6] Here for the first time we find a direct reference to Jesus as the temporal Jewish Messiah: He neither denied nor affirmed the implications of the title.

3. *Fierce Denunciations against the Pharisees.* And again, as in Dalmanutha, the scribes and Pharisees came to Jesus and demanded a sign. Repeating His previous answer, He added a prediction of His own death and resurrection: "For as Jonas was three days and three nights in the whale's belly, so shall the Son of man be three days and three nights in the heart of the earth."[7] In Bethany, Jesus did not need to retreat before the Pharisees; for here He enjoyed the protection of the

Roman procurator, and there were no Herodians who could fling Him into a dungeon. He therefore denounced the Pharisees at will, and they were reduced to retaliating by calling Him a servant of Beelzebub, a madman, and a charlatan.

And now Jesus became bold and reckless: His denunciations rose into vitriolic crescendos.[8] Even as He had previously condemned Capernaum and Bethsaida for rejecting His Gospel, now He attacked the people of Judaea for the same reason. The Queen of Egypt and the people of Nineve were less hardened than the Jews: for they listened to Solomon and to Jonas, and a greater than either had now come!

An incident similar to one in Mark[9] now occurred in Bethany; and this indicates the savage fury of Jesus, which erupted without apparent provocation. A friendly Pharisee, entertaining Him at dinner, marveled that He did not wash His hands. Jesus replied with a fierce diatribe against all Pharisees: "Woe unto you, scribes and Pharisees, hypocrites! for ye devour widow's houses, and for a pretense make long prayers: therefore ye shall receive the greater damnation . . . Woe unto you, scribes and Pharisees, hypocrites! for ye pay tithe of anise and cummin and have omitted the weightier matters of the law, judgment, mercy, and faith . . . Ye make clean the outside of the platter, but within ye are full of extortion and excess."

"Woe unto you! for ye build the sepulchres of the prophets, and your fathers killed them . . . From the blood of Abel unto the blood of Zecharias . . . verily I say unto you, It shall be required of this generation."

"Ye serpents, ye generation of vipers, how can ye escape the damnation of hell?" [10]

His enemies now "began to urge" Jesus "vehemently . . . seeking to catch something out of his mouth, that they might accuse him." [11] But He contented Himself for the moment with violent condemnation, which was wholly in the Buddhist and Essene tradition. And we wonder why the Jews should be held responsible for the death of Abel and what documents Jesus had at His disposal which related the death of so many prophets and the murder of

Zecharias, "which perished between the altar and the temple."

4. *The Wickedness of Wealth.* A man came to Jesus and asked Him to divide his inheritance with his brother,[12] but received instead a warning against covetousness. Jesus continues by relating the story of the Rich Man Who Died (of whom we read also in *The Book of Enoch*), and who had said to his soul: "Thou hast much goods laid up for many years; take thine ease, eat, drink, and be merry."[13]

This was the immemorial challenge of Buddhists and Pythagoreans alike. We are not to gather perishable wealth, but rather "Sell that ye have, and give alms; provide yourselves . . . a treasure in the heavens that faileth not, where no thief approacheth, neither moth corrupteth."[14]

This was comparable to the Buddhist doctrine that those who were wealthy and who gave their mansions to the holy monks would attain Nirvana at death.

5. *Eternal Vigilance for Parousia.* Jesus then delivered a sermon dealing with ethics and eschatology. Instead of riches, we are to seek the Kingdom of God: "and all these things shall be added unto you"; that is to say, after the Parousia, when the righteous have come into possession of the lands and the houses of the wicked, the Elect will enjoy a sheer surfeit of material wealth. Sell what you have, give alms, and lay up your treasure in heaven. And blessed are those who are watching and waiting when the Son of Man shall come to judge mankind: "that hour knoweth no man, no, not the angels which are in heaven, neither the Son, but the Father . . . For the Son of man is as a man taking a far journey, who left his house, and gave authority to his servants."[15]

Jesus would soon depart to dwell with His Father. Exactly how long He would be absent, that is, how long He would delegate "authority to his servants," i. e., the disciples, to build His church, no one could know, not the angels, not even the Son Himself, but only the Father. But the Parousia was certain, and it would come during the lifetime of those who heard His words. "Verily, I say unto you that this generation shall not pass till all these things be done."[16] This was His oft-repeated message, the basic promise and dogma of the Gospel. The disciples must continue in the faith, they must be ever active, they must preach the Kingdom day and night.

6. *The Faith of Skeptics.* In the Parable of the Faithful and the Unfaithful Servants, Jesus warned that during His approaching sojourn with the Father, there would be skeptics who would say in their hearts, "My Lord delayeth his coming." [17] But such a servant the Lord "will cut in sunder and appoint him his portion with the unbelievers," in the everlasting flames of hell.

Jesus declared that even sinners could predict the weather: why then could they not understand that the generation then existing was the last before the Parousia? To Him it was simply incredible and incomprehensible that everyone did not share His own conviction concerning eschatology and Himself.

CHAPTER XV

MANY ARE CALLED, BUT FEW ARE CHOSEN

A. THE LAST JOURNEY

1. *To Galilee and Back.* The initial ministry of Jesus in Judaea was now completed. We may well assume that the time was late winter, which was a mild season in that semi-tropical land, and that some eight or nine months had elapsed since His baptism. Since His consummation could not come before the Passover, His restless zeal drove Him forth into the countryside; and from the Gospel narrative we can reconstruct His last itinerary.

From Bethany, He proceeded north to Bethabara, which lay at a point close to the juncture of Galilee, Decapolis, and Perea. It was as if He must appear once more in his own province, even if He dared not traverse it openly. The Gospels do not make clear just where all the incidents of this journey occur, but we learn that, on His return, He took a route through Judaea beyond the Jordan by way of Jericho back to Bethany, whence He went to Jerusalem to complete the career He had so carefully formulated.

2. *Challenge to Pharisees.* Whenever Jesus encountered the orthodox priests, He seems to have taken an especial delight in flouting them by Sabbath-healings in the synagogue; and when one of them condemned Him for curing a woman who had been bowed down for eighteen years with an infirmity,[1] He called His adversary a hypocrite and declared that if an ass may be untied and led to water, certainly a woman may be loosed from her bonds of illness on the Sabbath!

3. *Gospel for the Gentiles.* Jesus again declares the universality of the Gospel;[2] but those who do not accept

it immediately will find themselves excluded from the Kingdom and ejected into that awful outer darkness where "shall be weeping and gnashing of teeth." Among the redeemed, we will find, not only Abraham, Isaac, and Jacob, but also many Gentiles from every nation of the earth.

4. *Warned by Pharisees.* We read: "The same day there came certain of the Pharisees saying unto him, Get thee out, and depart hence: for Herod will kill thee." [3] To this timely warning, Jesus replied: "Go ye and tell that fox, Behold I cast out devils, and I do cures today and tomorrow, and the third day I shall be perfected." The idea that His resurrection and assumption would occur the third day after His death was an obsession. We remember that Yeshu was also said to have risen from the dead on the third day. Finally, we must note that everywhere some of the Pharisees were friendly toward Jesus: otherwise, they would not have entertained Him in their homes or warned Him of impending danger, as they did repeatedly. In the light of this frequently manifested beneficence, His fiercely consistent hatred for them seems strangely incongruous.

5. *Announces Parousia Again.* And now, setting His face once more toward Jerusalem, Jesus addresses the Galileans for the last time: "I must walk . . . for it cannot be that a prophet perish out of Jerusalem . . . which killest the prophets . . . Ye shall not see me, until the time when ye shall say, Blessed is he that cometh in the name of the Lord." [4] And so, even as He announced His approaching death, Jesus proclaimed also His imminent Parousia when He would be seen returning on the clouds by those who now stood before Him.

6. *Heals on the Sabbath.* On the road to Jerusalem, Jesus healed another man on the Sabbath in the house of a chief Pharisee, which again suggests His close relationship with members of this sect, whom He could always discomfit by pointing out that their own interpretation of the Mosaic Law permitted emergency care for an ass or an ox on the Sabbath: how much more, then, should we

do good on the same day to humanity! "And they could not answer him again to these things."

7. *Parable of the Wedding Feast.* We are told the Parable[5] of the King who invites his friends to the wedding feast of his son. But instead of receiving the call with rejoicing, "the remnant took his servants . . . and slew them." If the children of the promise, the remnant, the Jews, will not accept the Kingdom, God will receive instead strangers, i. e., Gentiles. The invitation goes forth and the servants of the king "gathered together as many as they found, both good and bad: and the wedding was furnished with guests." If the Jews would not accept His Gospel, Jesus would offer it to the world-at-large.

The Kingdom of Heaven thus finds its Elect among all nations and peoples. When the guests are assembled, the king comes into the banquet chamber, where he finds one without a wedding garment; that is, one who has gone through the external routine of conversion, but has not achieved the requisite moral rehabilitation. This intruder is one of the tares in the Parable of the Wheat Field. Concerning him the king commands, "Bind him hand and foot, and take him away, and cast him into outer darkness; there shall be weeping and gnashing of teeth."

We could scarcely find stronger evidence to prove the universality of the authentic Gospel, because this parable occurs in Matthew, which is for the most part surcharged with Judaism but which here declares explicitly that "they which were bidden," i. e., the Jews, "were not worthy." The Judaistic elements in Matthew, therefore, reflect, not the authentic Gospel of Jesus Himself, but only the personal predilections of the author, who was probably of Pharisaic background.

8. *Predestination and Regeneration.* Jesus continues by declaring[6] His predestinarian doctrine in classic form: "For many are called, but few are chosen." Note that many, not *all*, are even called. To hear the Gospel is to receive the call; but among those called, only the Elect Ones, as they are named in *Enoch,* can enter the Kingdom. They do not accomplish their own salvation; they are "chosen"

for it; and they constitute a very small minority, since "few are chosen."

In a series of three parables,[7] Jesus elaborates His doctrine that no matter how utterly worthless, debased, or degenerate a human being may have become, this in no sense indicates that He is not of the Elect. What a man is now is unimportant; his potential capacity is everything; if he is one of the Elect, his acceptance of the Gospel is certain to work regeneration, and the most depraved sinner may become the greatest saint. The Gospel Jesus proclaims its power to transfigure human character.

B. THE PARABLES CONCERNING ELECTION

1. *The Prodigal Son.* Jesus tells of the man with a hundred sheep who lost one, and who rejoices more over that one when found than over the ninety and nine that never went astray. The same principle applies to the woman who loses a single piece of silver. And He concludes with the celebrated Parable of the Prodigal Son, which was an adaptation, as we have noted, of an ancient Buddhist allegory. Certainly, this wastrel had committed every possible sin and indiscretion; and assuredly the other son, who toiled usefully every day, was a model of filial virtue and civic excellence. But to emphasize all this is to miss the central teaching of the Gospel. The prodigal son was one of the Elect, and when he heard the call of the Gospel, he responded and was chosen for the Kingdom. He could achieve moral regeneration, which was beyond the power of the discreet, thrifty, and respectable brother, who committed the sin for which there is no forgiveness when he permitted envy and resentment to rule his heart.

Significantly, this allegory is found only in Luke, the most Hellenized of the Synoptics. We are justified in believing that the older brother represents the Jewish nation, so smug and correct in its adherence to the Mosaic Law, and that the wastrel represents the Gentiles, ultimate heirs of the Kingdom. Curiously enough, the ultra-Hellenic Marcionites rejected this parable, because of its assumption that the Gospel was ever intended for the Jews at all.

2. *The Dishonest Steward.* Jesus now elaborates His ethical-theological doctrine in the Parable of the Dishonest Steward,[8] who was being discharged for wasting his master's goods, and who, in order to place his employer's debtors under obligation to himself, reduces their just debts. For this "the Lord commended the unjust steward, because he had done wisely: for the children of this world are in their generation wiser than the children of light." In other words, Jesus tells the children of Ahriman, since they are destined for eternal hell fire anyway, to get all of this world's goods they can in the present, which is "their generation." Actually, the Children of Darkness are wiser in this world than are the Elect; for they know how to gain material possessions. In the Kingdom, however, the Elect will possess an abundance of material wealth in common without exploiting one another, and therefore no sin will be attached to the equal enjoyment of those treasures. Since, in the Kingdom of Christ, each will contribute according to his ability and will receive according to his need, wealth will at last be divorced from wickedness. Such was the Pythagorean-Essene-Gospel dream. It was also the dream of Plato, More, Bacon, Marx, and Lenin. How it operates in practice has now been illuminated by history.

3. *The Elect and the Reprobate.* However, Jesus never believed that more than a small fraction of mankind would ever be capable of such co-operation as He demanded. In the meantime, the majority cloak themselves in hypocrisy; they may even possess many reliable and social virtues. But these are the ethics of prudence glorified by Hesiod, Ecclesiastes, and Benjamin Franklin, and are primarily intended only as a protection for those who are successful, and who own property. For such as these, Jesus had only contempt and denunciation. As for the present, Jesus tells the reprobate to be wise according to "their generation," that is, the prevailing philosophy based on private property; they should get all they can, live as well as possible, enjoy this life to the hilt. The Elect Ones are the foolish of this world; but soon comes the Parousia when they will emerge

as the supremely wise, for theirs will be the Kingdom, to be enjoyed without toil, conflict, or aggression; and the wicked, who now seem so wise, will be the foolish, for they will be plunged into everlasting perdition.

4. *The Good and the Wicked.* All mankind are congenitally divided into two great classes: one of these seeks to serve the Lord of Spirits and the other wishes only to serve Ahriman: "No servant can serve two masters: for either he will hate the one and love the other; or else he will hold to the one, and despise the other. Ye cannot serve God and Mammon." [9]

As in the Zoroastrian system, there are no intermediate stages between the Elect and the reprobate: the human race is divided forever between the Children of Light and the Children of Darkness.

CHAPTER XVI

THE KINGDOM OF HEAVEN

A. RETURN TO JUDAEA

The journey from Galilee through trans-Jordanic Judaea by way of Jericho to Bethany is told in detail.[1] Jesus utilizes this period to instruct His disciples in the mysteries of the Kingdom.

His year of public activity was drawing to a close. The month Nisan, corresponding to the period from about March 16 to April 16, but varying in different years, lay not far ahead. This, the first month of the Jewish ecclesiastical year, included the Passover, a period of such potential commotion as to require additional Roman troops in the capital.

B. ETHICAL DOCTRINES REITERATED

1. *Divorce and Remarriage.* We now find the Pharisees tempting Jesus on the question of divorce.[2] Jesus repeats[3] the doctrine of the Sermon on the Mount, declaring that any man who divorces his wife for any cause other than fornication commits adultery when he remarries, and that any one who marries a woman so divorced is equally guilty. Note that the offense occurs, not in the divorce, but in the remarriage. Realizing the hard implications of this doctrine, the disciples ventured that it would be better never to marry. And this, of course, was the point: for Jesus was thinking in terms of Essene philosophy, which repudiated marriage unconditionally. And He continued: "All men cannot receive this saying, save they to whom it is given. For there are some eunuchs, which were so born from their mother's womb; and there are

some eunuchs which were made eunuchs of men: and there be eunuchs, which have made themselves eunuchs for the kingdom of heaven's sake. He that is able to receive it, let him receive it." [4] The Elect, that is, "they to whom it is given" to comprehend this commandment, knowing that celibacy without desire is a prerequisite for election, commit auto-castration. "He that is able to receive it, let him receive it." And we know that many did.

In both Mark and Matthew we find the text declaring that husband and wife, being a single flesh, joined by God, must not be put asunder by man. Since this is in fundamental contradiction to the whole teaching of Jesus, it must be stamped as a forgery. Luke, quite significantly, which reproduces more faithfully the celibate doctrine of Jesus, does not include this passage.

2. *Wealth Leads to Hell Fire.* Jesus now tells the story of the rich man and Lazarus,[5] which is an elaboration of that concerning the Rich Man Who Died, and which was well known in Buddhist and Essene scriptures. Again we find that Luke alone reflects the authentic celibate-communist principles of Jesus. The only wickedness of this rich man consists in the fact that he fares sumptuously and is clothed in purple and fine linen while the beggar Lazarus, full of sores, begs at his gate. We are not told that the beggar was a cripple; nor is this, as a matter of fact, of the slightest import; he was poor, and that made him holy.

Both men die: Lazarus ascends to the bosom of Abraham and the rich man necessarily goes down into the flames of hell, where, in the extremity of his agony, he begs a drop of water to cool his burning tongue. But any such relief would be a denial of the divine poetic justice, because "thou in thy lifetime receivedst thy good things, and likewise Lazarus evil things: but now he is comforted, and thou art tormented." The story of the rich man and Lazarus is completely meaningless except to establish the ethical necessity of practicing communism on earth in order to escape hell hereafter.

3. *Resentment and Forgiveness.* Jesus now elaborate further His omnipresent doctrine concerning forgivenes

of brethren.[6] We must never bear a grudge: a brother must be forgiven seven times seventy times; "Let not the sun go down upon your wrath." [7] For this inner poison contaminates the moral nature and makes us unfit for the Kingdom. Therefore, even as in Essene practice, if a brother trespass against you, tell him his fault in private; if he will not listen, procure witnesses; and if he finally refuse to hear you even so, he has proved himself a wolf in sheep's clothing, who, after trial before the congregation, must be expelled. Thus evicted, he will also be excluded from the Kingdom of Heaven, for "Whatsoever ye shall bind on earth shall be bound in heaven; and whatsoever ye loose on earth shall be loosed in heaven." All this proves conclusively that overt sinners are summarily to be expelled from all Christian congregations and that the tares are simply the unregenerate who cannot be detected by the Elect themselves.

4. *The Samaritan Leper.* On the road to Jerusalem,[8] Jesus met ten lepers, and healed them all; but only one, a Samaritan, gave thanks. Again we find Luke only making the appeal for Samaritan converts and no mention of this extraordinary miracle in Mark or Matthew.

C. THE ATTAINMENT OF THE KINGDOM

1. *Its Manifestation Described.* The Pharisees now demanded of Jesus when the Kingdom of God was to come.[9] His reply, however, was only intended to confuse these skeptics, for He declared: "the kingdom of God is within you." Turning then to His disciples, He warned them against pretenders who might attempt to impersonate Him in the future. There would be many false Christs exhibiting signs and wonders, which would "seduce, if it were possible, even the elect," who, since they are Children of Light, can never see damnation, once they have been redeemed. But such imposters need receive no credence, for the true Christ will appear "as the lightning, that lighteneth out of the one part under heaven, showeth unto the other part of heaven." [10] In His second manifestation, the Son of Man is suddenly

to brighten the sky from horizon to horizon. As in the days of Noe and of Lot, men would be eating and drinking and taking wives and planting and building. The Parousia would come as unexpectedly as the destruction of Sodom upon a sinful land.[11]

2. *Consciousness of Sin.* Jesus now contrasts a Pharisee who lists his virtues and thanks God he is better than others with a publican who smites himself on the forehead and cries, "God, be merciful to me a sinner."[12] The humility and repentance of the latter place him on the road to moral regeneration.

3. *Simple Faith Required.* Jesus blesses the little children, and declares that of such is the Kingdom of Heaven;[13] in short, we must accept the Gospel without doubt or skepticism.

4. *Renunciation.* A sincere but wealthy young man comes to Jesus and inquires: "Good Master, what shall I do that I may inherit eternal life?"[14] Jesus cites the Mosaic commandments; and the young man replies, "Master, all these have I observed from my youth." Then "Jesus ... said unto him, One thing thou lackest: go thy way, sell whatsoever thou hast, and give to the poor, and thou shalt have treasure in heaven; and come, take up the cross, and follow me."[15]

This was a hard commandment, as it would be for the average church member today, who would probably react in the same manner if he were faced with the alternative of being ejected from his communion or selling all his possessions and giving the money to the poor. At any rate, the young man "was sad at that saying, and went away grieved: for he had great possessions."[16]

Turning then to His disciples, Jesus declared that it i easier for a camel to go through the eye of a needle, thar for a rich man to enter the Kingdom of God. When th disciples were astonished at this, He added, "With men i is impossible, but not with God."[17]

This passage is usually misinterpreted. It means simpl that no human motivation or persuasion could be sufficier to compel a rich heir to surrender his wealth voluntaril but if he were one of the Elect, he would be compelled b a divine, inner compulsion to renounce his worldly goods. To believe that Jesus meant that the young man could keep his wealth and also inherit the Kingdom is preposterous. Yet this is precisely what the Christian Church has reiterated ever since Clemens Alexandrinus wrote his meretricious *Who Is the Rich Man That Shall Be Saved?*, according to which the riches to be renounced consist simply of spiritual pride.

5. *Peter Demands His Reward.* As soon as the rich young man left in sorrow, Peter exclaimed impulsively: "Behold, we have forsaken all, and followed thee; what shall we have therefor?" [18] He considered his own a comparable sacrifice although he had actually forsaken only his odorous fish nets, and a life of bitter poverty and hardship. Jesus did not rebuke him; for He never questioned the validity of a desire for ultimate wealth or personal advantage: He simply insisted that the Kingdom of Heaven is the paramount good; that only the Elect can enter it; and that in it they will be compensated materially a hundredfold for all temporary renunciation. Jesus therefore promised His disciples that they would "sit upon twelve thrones, judging the twelve tribes of Israel." [19] Mark elaborates the theme: "Verily, I say unto you, There is no man that hath left house, or brethren, or sisters, or father, or mother, or wife, or children, or lands, for my sake, and the gospel's, But he shall receive an hundredfold now in this time, houses, and brethren, and sisters, and mothers, and children, and lands, with persecutions; and in the world to come eternal life." [20] For abandoned wives, there is to be no replacement; but, even under the present dispensation and while persecution continues, for every father, mother, brother, sister, or child forsaken, for houses or lands renounced and lost, each who is of the Elect will receive a hundredfold; for all the members of the society will pool their goods and become a single family and common brethren. And then will come the Parousia, and the Kingdom of Heaven, in which the property of all the sinners also will fall to the Elect so that their possessions will be increased immeasurably. And finally, when the Kingdom has reached its apogée, the saints will begin their

eternal and celestial existence. This is precisely the doctrine of *Enoch*.

Jesus thus offered to His followers *for the future* the very things which the wicked strive so earnestly to attain in the present, the difference being that the unrighteous get them by labor or aggression while the Elect will obtain them by divine confiscation and will enjoy them cooperatively, each seeking sincerely the welfare of all.

D. THE DELAYED PAROUSIA

1. *Jesus Must Die*. And now, on this last journey toward Jerusalem, Jesus tells His diciples explicitly[21] that the Son of Man must be delivered to the scribes and the priests to be condemned, mocked, scourged, and put to death; and then will rise again on the third day. And yet, we read: "they understood none of these things: and the saying was hid from them." This proves that the disciples were not Essenes, for had they been so they would have recognized in this a re-enactment of the career of the Teacher of Righteousness.

2. *The Son of David*. When Jesus arrived in Jericho, He was hailed as the Son of David by the blind beggar Bartimeus.[22] This indicates that some among the populace had already begun to regard Jesus as the political Messiah who would lead the Jews to military victory. The disciples therefore charged the blind man to hold his peace, but Jesus did not rebuke him. Instead, He gave him his sight.

3. *Identical Rewards*. At this point, Jesus sets forth the Parable of the Unequal Labors.[23] A master hired workmen in the first hour to toil the whole day for a penny; at each succeeding hour, he employed others. But at the close of the day, when all received the same compensation, those who had labored longest murmured at this apparent inequity. The workers were the missionaries who would spread the Gospel during the ensuing years; and this was an assurance to those who should enter His service immediately preceding the impending Parousia that they would receive exactly the same reward as those who had toiled on from the beginning.

4. *The Partial Sacrifice of Zaccheus.* The incident involving Zaccheus occurred while Jesus was passing through Jericho.[24] This man was a publican and a sinner; but the leaven of moral regeneration was active within him, insomuch that he longed to see Jesus, was already giving *half* of his possessions to the poor, and was returning fourfold to any one he had wronged. Even if this may be a compromise with strict communist principle, Jesus accepted it as evidence of conversion and election.

5. *Disciples Could not Understand.* Jesus found it necessary to emphasize to His disciples that His second coming would be delayed, "because they thought that the kingdom of God should immediately appear." [25] They were so inflamed with expectation of immediate power and glory that their condition approached hysterical exaltation; and they could not apprehend the fact that He must first suffer and die, then leave them for an indeterminate period, during which they must preach the Kingdom without His visible presence, after which He would return upon the clouds surrounded by myriads of angel-servitors.

6. *Necessity for Explanation.* Only after Jesus was dead, were the disciples to remember how explicitly He had taught them that the Parousia would come only years later, but with certainty during their lifetime. Had He not done so, there would never have been any Christianity. Thus, they had time, perhaps twenty or thirty years, to carry the Gospel into every country comprising the Roman Empire and to construct the church militant, which, once in existence, would find the means of perpetuating itself when its original impulse had ceased to operate.

7. *The Parable of the Man Who Travels to a Far Country.* To emphasize His absence and Parousia, Jesus told His disciples the parable, based upon Buddhist sources, of the man (Jesus) who travels to a far country (goes to heaven for a space), and turns over all his goods and business (His ministry) to his servants (the disciples); and to each he gives a certain number of talents (abilities and duties).[26] "After a long time the lord of these servants cometh, and reckoneth with them." Some double the

treasure entrusted to them by the Master, but one hides it in the ground and shows no increase. In this manner, Jesus promised, that on the day of His return, He would meet his workers face to face and reward or punish each according to his production for the Kingdom. Those who had made no converts would be consigned to eternal hell fire. Such were His final injunctions. And so we find that, in order to fire the zeal of His disciples, Jesus sometimes offered them graduated and sometimes identical rewards.

All preparations were now complete; and Jesus was ready for His entry into Jerusalem.

CHAPTER XVII

AT WAR WITH THE PHARISEES

A. ENTRY INTO JERUSALEM

1. *Conforms to Old Testament Prophecy.* It is obvious that Jesus formulated His career so that it would conform with certain prophetic conceptions, especially those in Isaiah, Ezekiel, Daniel, and *The Book of Enoch.* Likewise, to fulfill the prophecy of Zechariah 9:9, in which the Messiah is represented as a meek and lowly king, just and having salvation, riding upon an ass, Jesus made the arrangements necessary for His triumphal entry into Jerusalem.[1] The disciples spread their garments before Him, strewed branches in His way, and cried: "Hosanna to the son of David: Blessed is he that cometh in the name of the Lord; Hosanna in the highest." [2]

2. *Hailed as the Son of David.* Because they were so steeped in Jewish tradition, the disciples could not comprehend the nature of Jesus' Kingdom. They thought of Him only as the temporal Messiah foretold by the prophets who would inaugurate a Jewish empire. Perhaps He permitted the misdirected enthusiasm of His disciples because it contributed to His own destruction. And again, we are confronted with the much-maligned but obviously friendly Pharisees who warn Him. "Master," they said, not comprehending His ultimate purpose, "rebuke thy disciples." [3] But "he answered and said unto them, I tell you that, if these should hold their peace, the stones would immediately cry out."

B. BAITING THE JEWISH PRIESTHOOD

One day soon after this carefully-staged entry, Jesus rushed into the Temple court,[4] whence He expelled the moneychangers and the dove-venders. The Temple, He declared, should be a house of prayer, and not a den of thieves. He could scarcely have made more bitter enemies out of the Temple personnel; and they "sought how they might destroy him." [5] Since it would be absurd to believe that He could have accomplished such an action single-handed, we must conclude that He was supported by a mob of Zealots.

The next morning, Jesus went again to the Temple; and now the priests had prepared questions to provoke Him into seditious or blasphemous utterances. We can visualize the scene in which these stern and forbidding men with their long beards and angry looks surveyed the young agitator. Hoping to entrap Him, they "say unto him, By what authority doest thou these things?" [6] But Jesus was not yet ready to provide His enemies with the means to destroy Him; so He evaded the baited hook. He promised to answer them if they would tell Him whether the baptism of John was of heaven or of men. Since they dared not condemn the popular Baptist, they had no answer. Incidentally, this also explains why the Christ-cult leaned so heavily upon the baptizing prophet.

After insulting the Pharisees by saying, "Verily I say unto you, That the publicans and harlots go into the kingdom of God before you," [7] He intensified this affront by relating the Parable of the Evil Husbandmen.[8] A certain man (God) planted a vineyard (the Jewish nation), gave it every manner of protection (the Mosaic Law, etc.), let it out to husbandmen (the orthodox priesthood), and went into a far country. The man then sent a servant (a prophet such as Isaiah), but the husbandmen beat him and drove him away. Again the man sent other servants but they also were wounded, stoned, mishandled, and shamefully evicted; and some were killed outright. Finally, the man sent his only son (Jesus), thinking the husbandmen would surely reverence Him. But they at once conspired among themselves, saying, if they killed the heir, they could seize the inheritance for themselves. "And so they took him, and killed him, and cast him out of the vineyard."

"What therefore shall the lord of the vineyard do?" Jesus demands; and replies: "He will come and destroy the husbandmen, and will give the vineyard unto others." In short, the Jewish nation would be taken from the reigning priesthood and given to the communion of Jesus, who declared that He was the stone which the builders (the Pharisees) had rejected, but which would become the head of the corner (the founder of the new religion). In His plan to infuriate His enemies, Jesus was successful; for "when the chief priests and Pharisees had heard his parables, they perceived that he spoke of them. But when they sought to lay hands on him, they feared the multitude." [9]

It was therefore imperative that the priests deprive Jesus of popular support. Since the Zealots desired a military leader, but were not looking for a soteriological redeemer, there can be little doubt that had Jesus openly declared Himself the incarnate Christ, the mob would have torn Him to pieces. He wished to die as a martyr, but only through the machinations of the reactionary priesthood and by the direct agency of the foreign tyrant. Thus only could He become the atoning savior of the poor.

C. JESUS LOSES THE JEWISH POPULACE

Seeking to entrap Jesus in blasphemy, sedition, or anti-Judaism, the Pharisees conspired with the ubiquitous Herodians.[10] With unctuous words, they inquired whether it was lawful to pay tribute to Caesar.[11] Thus they suspended Jesus between the horns of a dilemma: for should He declare that it was not, He would be guilty of sedition against Rome; but should He declare it lawful, He would discredit Himself with the Jews, especially with the Zealots and their sympathizers. When Jesus looked at the small coin and found Caesar's image upon it, He declared that we should render unto Caesar what is Caesar's, and unto God the things that are His. In this reply, He was guilty neither of evasion nor of cowardice: He expressed simply His own and the Essene-Pythagorean philosophy, according to which every civil government must be obeyed since it rules by the consent of God. However, by these simple words, which negated the Jewish concept of a priest-state and repudiated all ambition to establish a Judaic empire or even independence, He lost the Jewish populace, who now believed Him to be indifferent to their fate, or possibly an actual traitor in the service of imperialist Rome. It now remained for the priests only to convict Him of blasphemy by proving that He claimed to be the Christ; and of sedition by showing that He laid claim to the throne of David.

D. FINAL PUBLIC TEACHING OF JESUS

1. *Marriage and Heaven.* Next, the Sadducees, who denied any existence hereafter, tempted Jesus on the question of Levirate marriage.[12] They assumed the case of seven brothers, of whom the eldest dies childless. The second brother then marries his widow, and dies likewise; then the third, and so on; and finally the seventh also marries her and dies. Which of these is to be her husband in heaven? The answers attributed to Jesus in Mark [13] and Matthew [14] must be subtle corruptions of the authentic Gospel; but in Luke we read the true Essene doctrine, which is in basic harmony with the teachings of Jesus and on which the Marcionites relied to establish a celibate communion: "The children of this world marry, and are given in marriage. But they which shall be accounted worthy to obtain that world, and the resurrection from the dead, neither marry, nor are given in marriage."[15] This means simply that marriage occurs only among the children of perdition; that elect men, once redeemed, never take wives and that elect women never give themselves in marriage; that none of those who remain in that condition after hearing the Gospel can possibly be resurrected into the Kingdom of Heaven. Any dispute, therefore, as to which of these brothers will claim the wife in heaven is entirely fatuous, since none of them can possibly enter the Kingdom at all.

2. *Jesus Expounds His Christhood.* Jesus now declares that Christ could not be a descendant, i. e., "the Son o

David," since he had himself called the expected Messiah "my Lord." [16] The Messiah will neither be a temporal sovereign, nor of the stem of Jesse; instead, he is a spiritual power sitting on the right hand of God; and, as such, He is the lord of David as of all others. This text, which is undoubtedly genuine, invalidates the genealogies of Luke and Matthew and proves that these are fabrications.

3. *Final Excoriation of the Pharisees.* In His Jerusalem valedictory, Jesus launched once again into an unprovoked and vitriolic attack upon the scribes and Pharisees sitting in the seat of Moses. To the multitude, he declared that they "devour widow's houses, and for a pretense make long prayers: these shall receive the greater damnation." [17] And He exclaimed: "they bind heavy burdens and grievous to be borne, and lay them on men's shoulders; but they themselves will not move them with one of their fingers." [18]

4. *Execution Now Inevitable.* Thus ended the public ministry of Jesus. The mortal offense He had given His powerful enemies was working like a leaven; His implied claim to Christhood was known; His arrival in Jerusalem to the cries of "Hosanna to the Son of David" must have engendered suspicion of treason against Rome. He would die as the Lamb of God, despised and persecuted, a spotless sacrifice who would not even rebuke those who insulted and tortured, tormented and murdered Him. In His hour of agony and death, God would assuredly manifest some great and universal sign to seal His Christhood that all men might know that He was indeed the Son of God.

CHAPTER XVIII

THE SECOND GOSPEL APOCALYPSE

A. THE PREPARATION

1. *The First Apocalypse.* The first apocalypse of Jesus occurs, as we have noted, in the tenth chapter of Matthew, where His objectives embraced only Palestine and the chosen race; nor had it yet dawned upon Him that He must first suffer and die. But when He became convinced that the Jews would reject him, He not only sought His Elect elsewhere but He also universalized His doctrine; He commissioned the disciples to carry His Gospel into all lands; and He proclaimed, in His final eschatology, only that the Parousia would come sometime in that generation.[1]

2. *Disciples Demand Categorical Certainty.* Sitting at the feet of Jesus on the Mount of Olives, the members of the inner circle demanded: "When shall these things be? and what sign will there be when these things shall come to pass?"[2] Without definite assurance, the disciples could not preach the Gospel with requisite zeal. They had been disappointed in their Messianic hopes.[3] Now at last they understood that an altered destiny awaited them: but what would it be?

B. THE APOCALYPTIC KINGDOM

1. *The Great Tribulation.* Without evasion, Jesus prepared them for their mission, which was to build the community of the Elect before the Parousia. There would be many false Christs, and many would be deceived; there would be wars, and rumors of war, earthquakes, famine, and persecution; brother would rise up against brother,

and children against their parents; but the end would not be yet. Even though the Kingdom would not appear as soon as the disciples hoped and expected, He counseled, "In your patience, possess ye your souls."

2. *The Abomination of Desolation.* And then He declared: "But when ye shall see the abomination of Desolation, spoken of by Daniel the prophet, standing where it ought not, (let him that readeth understand,) then let them that be in Judaea flee to the mountains." [4] This passage proves that Mark was written *before* the destruction of Jerusalem. Jesus believed Himself to be the Son of Man depicted in Daniel; He did not, therefore, predict the siege of Jerusalem or the destruction of the Temple, but simply its *desecration*, which was the abomination of desolation committed by Epiphanes and described in Daniel. But since this Gospel prophecy was never fulfilled, we know that it preceded the siege of the city and the burning of the Temple by Titus.[5] The Temple desecration, then, was to be the final sign of the impending Parousia.[6]

The disciples were therefore assured of two great events, exactly as described in Daniel: first, the Temple would be desecrated, that is, used for pagan worship; and, second, they would then immediately "see the Son of man coming in the clouds," who would "gather together his elect from the four winds" and establish the Kingdom of Heaven. How long must they wait for this grandiose event? The answer, which is categorical, is found in all the Synoptics: "Verily I say unto you that this generation shall not pass, till all these things be fulfilled." [7]

And so, lest any one should have forgotten the words at Caesarea Philippi in which Jesus declared that those then standing before Him would never taste of death until the Kingdom of God should come, He repeated that His return would certainly occur during the then existing generation. "But of that day and that hour knoweth no man, no, not the angels in heaven, but my Father only." The assurance was only that "that hour" would come unexpectedly and during the lifetime of the disciples.

3. *A New Heaven and a New Earth.* As in *Enoch* and Zoroastrian literature, there was to be a new heaven and

a new earth; but these would come only *after* the establishment of the Kingdom of Heaven.

4. *The Wise and the Foolish Virgins.* We read now the Parable of the Five Wise and the Five Foolish Virgins.[8] The bridegroom (Jesus) tarries a while (returns to heaven) before claiming His brides (the Elect of the new communion), so reminiscent of the brides of Dionysus. These will stand ready day and night, joyfully awaiting the bridegroom; but the slothful ones who join the Church without complete regeneration are not ready to meet the groom when He comes at midnight. By the time these careless brides procure the necessary oil, the wedding (the Kingdom of Heaven) has already begun (been established); and when they knock at the door, the groom declares, "Verily, I say unto you, I know you not." This parable emphasizes the imminence of the Kingdom; Jesus could scarcely have meant that His converts were to sit awake every hour awaiting His return for more than nineteen hundred years!

5. *The Judgment.* In the Last Judgment,[9] which follows the Parousia without delay, all mankind is to be marshaled before the Son of Man, who "shall set the sheep on his right hand, but the goats on the left," as in Orphic-Pythagorean eschatology. Those on the right shall inherit the Kingdom because of their works of charity to the helpless, but those on the left "shall go away into everlasting punishment,"[10] because they never showed mercy to the Son of Man, as personalized in the naked, the sick, the hungry, and the imprisoned. Let the sinners beware. Their days are growing few. Soon, soon, Christ, like the Soshans, will appear in the heavens, surrounded by all His holy angels, an almighty police force which will bring before His throne the Elect from every corner of the earth and from every race and nation. But the wicked also, who will always believe themselves virtuous, will be haled before that awful judge: they too will come from every portion of the world and will consist of those who will have rejected the message of the Gospel missionaries about to set forth on their journeys. And the line of demarcation which will separate the righteous from the reprobate will be that

congenital moral nature which in the one case flowers into unselfish, uncalculated, and spontaneous acts of kindness and charity toward "the least of these, my brethren," the weak, the lowly, the oppressed, the unfortunate victims of social injustice. The meaning of the Gospel is simply that those who have worked and saved must give their possessions to those who have nothing or suffer eternal torture in hell.

6. *The Essence of This Morality.* Although the ethics of Jesus are here definitely Buddhist, He appears in the character of the Zoroastrian Soshans. And this is natural, since Christianity was an international synthesis. We cannot escape the conclusion that according to Jesus the unfortunate and underprivileged of this earth constitute a sacred international order. To love these and minister to their physical needs is an act which contributes to the union of all humanity. The poor and those who suffer are all of them Christ Himself in disguise.

7. *No Resurrection Preceding the Kingdom.* We find here also another important eschatological element. There are, it is true, various references in the Gospel to the resurrection; and, as we have seen, there were, according to Enoch, to be two reawakenings of the dead. There can be no doubt that Jesus believed in a general resurrection at some time; but it is also certain that Mark 13, Luke 21, and Matthew 25 envision no such event. The judgment which is to inaugurate the Kingdom applies only to those living at the Second Coming; there is no provision for such saints as may die during the interim; it seems scarcely to have occurred to Jesus that His return could be so long delayed.

CHAPTER XIX

THE EUCHARISTIC MYSTERY

A. THE BETRAYAL

1. *The Priests Conspire against Jesus.* After this revelation, Jesus told His disciples plainly that He must die during the impending Passover; and, indeed, the scribes, priests, and elders were busily plotting His destruction.[1] As yet, however, they did not have the witnesses necessary to support a mortal accusation; in fact, they were not sure just what charges to prefer.

2. *Judas Turns Informer.* An important incident, surrounded by obscurity, now occurred: "And Judas Iscariot, one of the twelve, went unto the chief priests, to betray him unto them. And when they heard it, they were glad, and promised to give him money." [2] We note that the pronoun *it* has no antecedent; what did the priests hear with such joy? Obviously that Jesus believed Himself the Christ and that He never denied being the Son of David, the temporal Messiah. If the first charge could be supported, Jesus would be convicted of blasphemy; and if the second could likewise be maintained, the Roman procurator would be compelled to inflict the death penalty. The enemies of Jesus now had the knowledge they desired; but in order to implement their purpose, they must have an additional witness. Upon what basis, then, was the money to be given? Undoubtedly on condition that Judas would procure another to corroborate his accusation or that his charge would persuade Jesus to confess His guilt on both these counts in open court, which would make further evidence superfluous.

3. *Jesus the Son of David.* Now we see why Jesus did

not deny being the *Son of David* when so accosted: He
wished to create a basis for the charge that He sought a
temporal throne, thereby to accomplish His martyrdom.
He also knew that should He claim openly to be the Christ,
the maddened populace would stone Him. So it was necessary to contrive His own death by treading a narrow line
between open proclamation and careful concealment. He
wished the poor to believe that He had been put to death
by the rich Jews in alliance with imperialist Rome because
He was the prophet of the communal kingdom; only
gradually were they to learn that He was actually the Son
of Man shortly to reappear as the all-powerful Messiah of
Moral Judgment.

4. *The Crucial Role of Judas.* In all this, Judas, who
plays no part in the previous Gospel narrative, was the
crucial figure, without whom the denouement was impossible. We have already seen that in the story of Yeshu,
Judah Iskarito was a rival magician; and it is reasonable
to conclude that our Gospel presents only an idealized
re-creation of the Essene Teacher's adversary. It is certain
that some one, possibly under direct orders from Jesus,
went to the priests to lay the necessary mortal accusations
against Him; otherwise, His execution could not have
taken place. Luke 22:22 implies as much: "And truly the
Son of man goeth, as it was determined; but woe unto
that man by whom he is betrayed!"

B. THE INSTITUTION OF THE EUCHARIST

1. *A Replica of the Essene Ritual.* We have now one
of the most important events of the entire Gospel: the institution of the eucharist.[3] Jesus had made arrangements to
use an Upper Room, reminiscent of that used by the
Essenes at Khirbet-Qumran, in which He and His disciples
would partake of a holy feast behind closed doors. Although such a sacrament or eucharist was unknown to the
Jews, the Essenes, having absorbed it from Pythogorean-
ism, had practiced it for more than a century; and it was a
central element in Christianity from the beginning. Jesus
was simply establishing for His disciples and followers for-

ever this Osirian-Dionysiac-Essene-Mithraic ritual by which mortals were to achieve divinity and immortality by a mystical pagan rite which had been celebrated since time immemorial.

2. *Incomprehensible to the Jews.* The Passover meal celebrated an atonement, but was fundamentally different from the Essene sacrament. It was over this ritual, perhaps more than on anything else, that the Essenes parted company with their racial brethren; but it was one of the reasons why Christianity spread with such facility among the pagans.

3. *The Eucharist in John.* We turn now to John for texts re-creating the Orphic mystery in which Jesus assumes the ancient role of Osiris and Dionysus and in which He declares Himself "the bread of God . . . which cometh down from heaven, and giveth life unto the world . . . he that cometh to me shall never hunger . . . if any man eat of this bread, he shall live for ever, and the bread I will give is my flesh, which I will give for the life of the world."[4] And again: "Whoso eateth my flesh and drinketh my blood hath eternal life."[5]

This concept, which was the core of the pagan mysteries, was an abomination to the Jews, who "therefore strove among themselves, saying, How can this man give us his flesh to eat?"[5] And some of them called it "a hard saying" and "went back, and walked no more with him."

The Synoptics place the institution of the sacrament at the Passover; but John completes its paganization by elaborating the doctrine, and separating the ritual from Jewish tradition.

4. *The Synoptic Version.* In the Synoptics, there is not a word concerning the eucharist until the Last Supper, at which, even according to Luke,[6] Jesus attempts to Judaize this Orphic ritual by calling it a Passover. Conversely, even Matthew reflects the pagan nature of the ceremonial: "Jesus took bread, and . . . said, Take, eat: this is my body. And he took the cup . . . saying, Drink ye all of it; For this is my blood of the new testament, which is shed for many for the remission of sins."[7]

The eucharist established by Jesus was therefore a pagan ritual encased within an Essene-Judaic integument.

5. *The Christian Mystery*. We know from the *Didache* that the eucharist was of paramount importance from the beginning in the church, since by partaking of it all its members believed themselves to be united incorruptibly and mystically in the body of Christ.

C. FINAL HOURS WITH THE DISCIPLES

This historic feast completed, we are given another interesting insight into the psychology of the disciples, who seem to have been actuated by other than purely altruistic motives. The mother of James and John came to Jesus and asked that her sons be seated on His right and on His left when He should come to the throne of His Kingdom; "And when the ten heard it, they were moved with indignation against the two brethren." [8] But Jesus, knowing that years of cruel hardship and suffering lay ahead, asked them whether they could drink of His cup and be baptized with His baptism. When they declared that they could, He assured them that such priority was not His to confer, but that "whosoever will be great among you, shall be your minister."

Since Jesus knew that His impending defeat would try the disciples sorely, He declared, "All ye shall be offended because of me this night." At this, the impulsive Peter, as usual, came forward and declared that he, at least, would never prove unfaithful.[9] Jesus told him that before the cock should crow, he would deny Him thrice. Yet Jesus inferred that Peter's faith was by far the strongest, for He declared: "when thou art converted, strengthen thy brethren."[10] Even Peter, therefore, was not yet actually converted, that is to say, not even he had experienced a cataclysmic moral transformation or arrived at a complete comprehension concerning the Christhood of Jesus and the nature of His mystical regeneration. This would come only after the crucifixion, when the disciples would gradually recall and comprehend the teachings of the Master concerning the atonement, the eucharist, and the Parousia.

CHAPTER XX

GETHSEMANE

A. FINAL INNER CONFLICT

And now Jesus faced the crisis for which He had prepared since Caesarea Philippi. Thoroughly aware that death was imperative, He yet recoiled from its terrors. Wrestling with Himself, He groaned: "My soul is exceeding sorrowful unto death . . . And he went forward a little, and fell on the ground, and prayed that, if it were possible, the hour might pass from him." [1] He wished that He might become the savior of the otherwise lost Elect by some less terrible ordeal. Perhaps God would answer His prayer with some supernatural sign, in the absence of which He would understand that He must undergo His full measure of humiliation and suffering: "And being in agony he prayed more earnestly: and his sweat was as it were great drops of blood falling down to the ground." [2]

While Jesus was undergoing this fearful struggle for decision, His disciples slept uncomprehending and unperturbed. In reality, however, He had long since determined what He must do: the decision had been made on a mountainside in Gaulonitis. Now He stood at the threshold of victory; another day or two, and His work would be completed, His sacrifice and atonement for Elect sinners consummated.

A third time He found John, James, and Peter immersed in sleep. But now He had summoned reserves of courage from His inner self; He had conquered His ultimate fears and doubts. Assured that He was indeed the Christ who must first die but who would soon reappear as the Son of Man coming with Power, He spoke calmly to His slumbering disciples: "Sleep on now, and take your rest: it is enough, the hour is come; behold, the Son of man is betrayed into the hands of sinners." 3

B. ARREST OF JESUS

Perhaps, as He spoke, Jesus heard the Jews, headed by Judas, approaching. The renegade disciple identified Jesus with a kiss, and the minions of the priests laid hold upon Him. One of the disciples struck an ear from one of the priestly retainers with his sword. But Jesus, according to Matthew, declared that although He could command twelve legions of angels, He would submit, in order to fulfill the scripture. To the high priests and the elders He declared that this was their hour, and that of darkness (or Ahriman).

Thus Jesus was bound and led away.

What a devastating climax for all the high hopes and dreams of the disciples! In spite of all that Jesus had said, it never occurred to them that He would be arrested in the middle of the night, bound, and carried away like a common malefactor without protest or heavenly sign.

This seemed the end, indeed. Instead of a great Jewish king, Jesus now appeared as a petty criminal; instead of the Messiah of Moral Judgment, He resembled a crackpot agitator, led away to deserving chastisement for attempting to mislead the poor, the unstable, and the ignorant. All His vast pretensions and promises had now collapsed in an instant, and the dreamed-of thrones of the disciples had vanished into nightmare darkness. And, as Jesus was dragged away, all the disciples, except Judas and Peter, scurried into concealment.

CHAPTER XXI

THE TRIAL AND DEATH OF JESUS

A. JESUS BEFORE THE BAR OF JUSTICE

1. *Confession to the Sanhedrin.* Jesus was at once haled before an emergency night session of the Sanhedrin (the Council of the Seventy Elders) called to convict Him of blasphemy. Not believing that He would testify against Himself, the Jews sought avidly for witnesses. But since their evidence was contradictory and inconclusive, Caiaphas finally demanded: "I adjure thee by the living God, that thou tell us whether thou be the Christ, the Son of God." [1] In Luke, Jesus evades the issue, and gives a noncommittal reply, as He had done on many previous occasions. But in Mark and Matthew, He is forthright: "I am: and ye shall see the Son of man sitting on the right hand of power, and coming in the clouds of heaven." [2] Insofar as revealed in the record, this was His only categorical declaration of Christhood; and Jesus made it in open court before His deadliest enemies.

2. *Guilty of Blasphemy.* In the eyes of His judges, this was ultimate blasphemy; and, not content with this definitive reply, Jesus added that His Parousia would occur during the lifetime of those now presuming to sit as His judges. Overwhelmed, Caiaphas "rent his clothes, and saith, What need we any further witnesses? Ye have heard the blasphemy: what think ye? And they all condemned him to be guilty of death." [3]

3. *Jesus Self-Condemned.* And so Jesus deliberately took another step toward Golgotha. He could have stood mute, or answered with a parable, an evasion, a fierce denunciation, or a discourse on ethics, as He had done so

often before. Why, then, did He take this suicidal course? There is only one rational answer: certain of His Christhood, He was also convinced that God had ordained this Passion as a preparation for His coming glory and power.

4. *The Denial of Peter.* Word soon trickled out that Jesus had proclaimed Himself the Christ. He was thus a self-convicted blasphemer. The Essenes must have repudiated Him from the beginning; He had lost the Zealotic extremists when He said that taxes should be paid to the Romans; and now the moderate, orthodox Jews must have turned against Him to the last man. Of the disciples, only the trembling Peter had followed Him. One of the palace maids recognized him as an intimate of the accused, and said, "thou also was with Jesus of Nazareth." Three times she made the charge, and thrice he denied that he knew Him.[4]

5. *Jews Could not Execute.* As far as the Jews were concerned, the mortal guilt of Jesus was now certified. Had the trial taken place in the days of Jewish independence, He would at once have been transported to some appropriate place and stoned. This, as we have seen, actually happened to the Essene Master; and later also to James, during a period of imperial instability. But since the Roman law did not permit the Jews to inflict the extreme penalty, it was necessary to hale Jesus before the procurator.

6. *Confesses to Non-Existent Guilt.* When the Jews dragged their victim to Pilate's palace,[5] thy made a variety of accusations, even charging Him with "forbidding to give tribute to Caesar." [6] Since only subversion, however, was of consequence to the Roman, he asked: "Art thou the king of the Jews?" To mockery and abuse, Jesus made no reply; but to this question, He declared: "Thou sayest it." He uttered the precise words which Pilate could ignore only at his own extreme peril. Had Jesus taken any other course, He would have been released. Again, He was the only effective witness against Himself. Never before had He declared Himself king of the Jews; by accusing Himself falsely, He compelled Pilate to execute Him.

7. *Almost Acquitted.* Even so, Jesus barely missed acquittal, for Pilate sensed something unauthentic in His

confession; he felt that the dispute between Jesus and the Sanhedrin concerned only the Jewish religion and with that he had no concern; he may even have known that the accusers of Jesus were perjurers. But he sensed more: he realized that before Him stood an incomprehensible man who, for some fantastic motive, wished to become a sacrificial martyr; and he wanted no such blood upon his hands. He even tried to turn the prisoner over to Herod,[7] who was in Jerusalem for the Passover, but who had no jurisdiction outside Galilee.

8. *Pilate Yields to Jewish Pressure.* We know from another incident, in which Pilate attempted to introduce Caesar's effigies into Jerusalem,[8] that this administrator was susceptible to popular pressure. And when Herod sent Jesus back to him with a horde of reviling Jews at His heels, Pilate ordered the execution of the Galilean agitator,[9] albeit against his better judgment. Pilate was in a delicate position; there had been one Messianic seditionist after another in Judaea, all of whom had been put to death. But it was obvious, despite His completely voluntary confession, that Jesus was no such incendiary. He had no armed men; He had made no denunciations against the government; no reliable witnesses could be found to testify that He had political aspirations or entertained ideas hostile to the Roman Empire. Quite the reverse. Why, then, should He be put to death? There were only two reasons: first, His own confession; and, second, Pilate's desire to preserve tranquillity.

B. THE EXECUTION

1. *The Road to Golgotha.* And now the Jews were in a frenzy of excitement. They stripped Jesus, smote and mocked Him, dressed Him in purple, and pressed a crown of thorns into His head. Since He was too frail to bear the cross Himself, the soldiers impressed one Simon of Cyrenia to carry it, while the maddened populace jeered close behind, striking the condemned with whips and staves, while He walked the terrible road in uncomplaining silence.

2. *Isaiah Fulfilled.* Thus Isaiah 53:2 ff. reads almost like a description of the Passion. With the artistry of genius, Jesus had determined that it should be so. The various so-called prophecies cited by Matthew are without validity; but Zechariah 9:9 and the Suffering Servant of Isaiah became contrived fulfillments. Jesus molded the climax of His career around a concept written centuries before by some fervent Jew. If some of the details do not apply, as in the first part of verse 12, the whole comes very close.

3. *No Supernatural Sign.* Above Him, the Roman executioners placed the warning superscription: THIS IS THE KING OF THE JEWS. Only this set Him apart from the two crucified thieves, between whom He hung. The Jews mocked and derided Him, demanding a supernatural sign. We may discount the brief texts in which such events as the rending of the Temple veil are related. Such were the standard accompaniments to the births and deaths of all the great Buddhist saints and saviors. Mark does not even mention the eclipse of the sun; nor the earthquake and the resurrection of some long dead, as does Matthew only.

4. *The Final Despair of Jesus.* The most significant detail is the cry of desperation uttered by Jesus before His death and quoted from a Davidic Psalm: "My God, my God, why hast thou forsaken me?"[10] The later "forgive them; for they know not what they do" of Luke, and the story of Jesus' mother at the cross, related by John, are Hellenistic elaborations. The irrefragable fact is that Jesus died in utter despair, certain that God had forsaken Him, that His sacrificial death was futile, and that His whole ministry was a delusion. For He had been utterly certain since that day on the mountain north of Caesarea Philippi that God would make Him manifest before the whole world as the Christ, the Son of God, and would therefore transfigure Him during His ultimate agony. Hour after hour of inexpressible suffering went by; but there was no sign of any kind. With consummate skill, Jesus had encompassed His own death according to plan; but the denouement failed to occur.

He had declared[11] that more than twelve legions of angels awaited His command; perhaps He had now summoned them,—in vain. And so with a cry of ultimate and elemental despair, He heaved a body-wracking sigh, and cried in His agony: "My God, my God, why hast thou forsaken me?"

C. THE BURIAL

1. *All the Disciples Deserted.* All the disciples, including Peter, fled into silence and concealment; only some women remained faithful, and, in the toleration accorded their sex, dared to stay close enough to watch their beloved Master undergoing the throes of death. There was Mary Magdalene, and Mary the mother of James the Lesser, Salome, and some others who had followed from Galilee.

2. *Joseph of Arimithea.* And now we hear of Joseph of Arimithea, "which also waited for the kingdom of God." [12] In other words, he, like Simeon and Anna,[13] was expecting not the political Jewish Messiah, but the Messiah of Moral Judgment, i. e., the Essene Teacher of Righteousness, or a facsimile of him. We are told in the Fourth Gospel only that Joseph was a disciple of Jesus: but we know that this cannot be accurate if for no other reason than that he still retained his wealth. Like others, living on the fringe of the Essene movement, he occupied an important position in Jewish life, was a "councilor," that is, a member of the Sanhedrin. He went to Pilate, and, obtaining permission to bury the crucified prophet, he did so in a new tomb. There is nothing to indicate that Joseph expected any miraculous resurrection; he wished merely to give Jesus such decent obsequies as might be fitting for an ex-member of the Order, who, unfortunately, had been led astray by an obsessive delusion.

3. *The Empty Tomb.* Wrapping the body in linen, according to Pythagorean antecedents, Joseph laid it in a newly-hewn sepulchre. And the two Marys observed where it was laid.[14]

We are told that on the following morning Peter and

John came to the tomb and found it open and the body gone.¹⁵ This incident seems so well confirmed by tradition that we can scarcely doubt it. Again, we find the career of the Essene Master repeated. But who took the body? Many scholars have thought that Joseph removed it in order to establish popular belief in the resurrection, or that he engineered a simulated death from which Jesus was restored by Essene medical science. All such theories, however, rest upon highly improbable assumptions. The disciples themselves were certainly too confused and defeated to carry out such a bold, conspiratorial deed. Nor could the Romans have had any motive for such an act.

4. *Pharisees Fear a Second Resurrection Hoax*. There is a significant passage¹⁶ in the Judaistic Matthew only, according to which the priests and Pharisees went to Pilate demanding that a watch be set so that the disciples might not steal the body and claim that He had risen from the dead; for "so the last error shall be worse than the first." ¹⁷ It is easy to see why the Pharisees should be so concerned: for this was precisely the cause of the first error, that is, the one which had continued for thirty years following the execution of the Teacher of Righteousness and during which *his* followers were proclaiming *his* Parousia together with the inauguration of the Kingdom of Righteousness by him in Palestine about the year 33 B. C. And now this battle was perhaps to be fought all over again! No wonder the Pharisees took precautions to prevent such a catastrophe.

5. *World Career of Christ*. And so ended the career of Jesus. And so began the unique personality of Christ. We must marvel that this lonely individual, alone among the countless men who have claimed to be divine incarnations, was able to make the world accept Him as the Son of God even though, while living, He made little impression upon those who saw Him, and failed to bolster His claim with one shred of evidence beyond His own, for the most part, evasive declarations. In this our twentieth century, His real or nominal followers comprise almost one third of the human species; all other *soters* have long since vanished from the hearts and the aspirations of mankind;

Buddha, His only remaining god-man competitor of any stature, who was also His ethical instructor, commands the allegiance of a bare hundred million devotees scattered among the outposts of civilized life.

During the nineteen hundred years which have elapsed since Jesus died, more has been said and written about Him than about any other personality. Pierre van Paasen is said to have had seven thousand different volumes in his private library about Him. Millions of ministers, writers, missionaries, and other functionaries have made a profession and a living from the propagation of His doctrines, or what purport to be such, and in organizing churches and movements founded in His name. Tens of thousands have become fabulously wealthy through His church; millions of others have lived and died in poverty or have perished by violence rather than surrender one iota of what they understood to be His teaching. Every Sunday the air waves reverberate with voices attempting to explain Him. Recorded history knows no comparable phenomenon.

CHAPTER XXII

SUMMARY AND EVALUATION

A. ESSENCE OF THE GOSPEL

We may thus summarize the basic teachings of Jesus, none of which were original with Him.

1. That He was the Christ, the Son of Man, now appearing as the Suffering Servant of Atonement, who would reappear, in a magnificent Parousia before the end of the generation then living, as the Messiah of Moral Judgment, as portrayed in *The Book of Enoch*.

2. That He would then establish the redeemed Elect in His earthly Kingdom, and banish all sinners to everlasting torture. This was an Essene concept, adapted from Zoroastrian sources.

3. That every human soul is immortal and will spend eternity either in hell or in heaven. Precisely this eschatology was first completed by the Essenes, and it was a revision of Persian antecedents.

4. That only the Elect can achieve salvation, following cataclysmic conversion by the Gospel. This was an established Pythagorean concept, completed by the Essenes.

5. That the Elect are those of any nation or language in whom there is a congenital compulsion toward righteousness, because of which they will instantly embrace the Gospel when they hear it. This was a Pythagorean doctrine, elaborated by the Essenes.

6. That this compulsion expresses itself in the rejection of all material possessions, in the establishment of a communal brotherhood, and in a selflessness which compels each devotee to sell all he has and give it to the poor, i. e., turn it over to the steward of the society. This

was an Essene-Pythagorean practice transmitted to the Gospel Jesus.

7. That it is a cardinal sin to live in comfort or luxury while any fellow-man suffers want: this was a moral concept derived from Buddhism, and is not found in that precise form either in Pythagoreanism or Essenism, both of which permitted the society to own unlimited wealth and which inculcated self-reliance and required their members to be self-supporting through their own labor.

8. That the Elect will never marry or be given in marriage; and that they will abandon wife or husband, children and parents, brothers and sisters, relatives and friends, and join the larger family of the Elect upon conversion. Christian communities were thus to be constructed upon Buddhist, Essene, and Pythagorean models.

9. That each will contribute according to his abilities and receive according to his need. This was Essene practice, derived from the Pythagorean *thiasoi*.

10. That, to become sons of God, the Elect must partake of the holy eucharist, which is the symbolic body and blood of Christ. This was a pagan doctrine taken by the Essenes from Pythagoreanism, which, in turn, derived it ultimately from Osirianism.

11. That the Elect must be initiated into the new communion by the rite of baptism. This was another Essene ritual, derived by them originally from Zoroastrianism, and later modified by their Pythagoreanism.

12. That Jesus the Christ must die the death of a despised martyr in order to accomplish a mystical atonement. This mystery is efficacious for the Elect only, i. e., for "many." This has some formal similarity to various Old Testament concepts, but it derives essentially from the Orphic-Pythagorean mystery.

13. That during the few years still to intervene between the sacrificial death and the Parousia of Christ, every one of the Elect must spread the Gospel with untiring devotion and energy; for at the Second Coming, each is to be rewarded according to His works. This concept originated with the Essenes, who developed it concerning their Teacher of Righteousness.

14. That, after an indeterminate period, there would be a new heaven and a new earth, and then the saints would be transferred to an eternal life in the celestial regions. This eschatology is never fully developed by Jesus; it is drawn primarily from *The Book of Enoch*, which derived it from Zoroastrian sources.

15. That the underlying force for good in the world is that congenital compulsion toward righteousness which activates the Elect and finds expression in natural deeds of kindness and charity toward all brethren, regardless of race or nation. This innate goodness, conferred by God upon certain persons only, renders them fit for redemption and ultimate divinity. However, this compulsion becomes operative only upon contact with the Gospel and can never by itself effectuate salvation. This concept was developed by the Essenes from Pythagorean sources.

This was the Essene-Christian faith.

B. REASONS FOR JEWISH REJECTION

That the Gospel Jesus was infinitely more Zoroastrian, Buddhist, and Pythagorean than Judaic must be obvious. In spite of His reverence for Moses and the prophets, Jesus had little in common with their basic ideology. Since no nation with a well-developed culture will accept any speculative doctrines which contradict those it already holds, there were many reasons why the Jews could never embrace the Gospel Jesus, among which we may note the following:

1. The idea of any actual sonship to God, even if only mystical, violated the fundamental concept of His spirituality, unity, and universality.

2. The doctrine of the Virgin Birth, which came later, and which had many counterparts among Greeks, Buddhists, and Persians, was an abomination to the Jews, since, for them, it reduced the deity into a vulgar and polytheistic concept.

3. The pagan doctrine of the eucharist could only excite repugnance among the Jews. And Zoroastrian baptism was nearly as flagrant a violation of Mosaic ideals.

4. After the Persian influence receded among the Pharisees, the Jews as a whole rejected the Zoroastrian eschatology of Jesus *in toto* and re-embraced that of Moses and the prophets, which knew nothing of hell or heaven, of rewards, punishment, or judgment after death.

5. The universalism of Jesus called for the merging of the Jews among the Gentiles around them, and the consequent destruction of the old, exclusive Judaism. No offense could have been greater than this.

6. No one could have been more different from the Messiah expected by the orthodox Jews than was Jesus; and furthermore, neither the disciples nor other early Jewish Christians expected a Messiah of Universal Moral Judgment during the years following the crucifixion. How, then, could the ordinary Jew accept the Greek mystery-concept of a savior-god?

7. The Jews had believed for centuries that when their Messiah appeared, He would perform feats of great political and military prowess. When the Jews asked Jesus for a sign, He answered them with abuse and denunciation, and provided no shred of acceptable evidence to support His Messianic claims.

8. Jesus' repudiation of family and marriage must have been extremely repugnant to the Jews. And His mandate that those who could not practice celibacy without desire should commit auto-castration must have appeared as nothing less than insanity, especially to a people who believed that they must increase and multiply until they became as the sands on the seashore.

9. The ethical teachings of Jesus, which required all persons with property to sell the same and give the money to the poor, and which made it a cardinal sin to enjoy any comfort or luxury not equally enjoyed by all, were quite beyond the comprehension of the Jews, who could only consider them completely subversive.

10. When Jesus repudiated the Judaic Sabbath, the Temple sacrifices, and other ceremonials, He became a criminal in the eyes of all pious Jews, little better than the historic monster, Antiochus Epiphanes.

C. THE DYNAMICS OF HIS OWN DIVINITY

1. *Jesus Convinced of His Own Divinity.* What, then, can we say of Jesus Himself, His personality, His permanent position, and His potential influence upon thoughtful people who cannot accept the supernatural elements of His Gospel?

He was distinguished by the sincerity of His own claim to Christhood. He sought no earthly advantage for Himself; He staked everything on His conviction that God would make Him manifest as the Christ during His hours of agony on the cross; and that in a few years He would send Him to judge mankind and establish the Kingdom of Heaven. He certainly never believed that without glory in death and without the fulfillment of His oft-promised Parousia, He could yet become the founder of a world-religion.

2. *Humanity Accepts Whatever It Desires.* The mind and the spirit of man are strange indeed: in this delicate complex, reason and knowledge are weak and frail, but desire and emotion are paramount. Jesus offered a world sick at heart a set of promises and hopes, an appeal to the poor and the heavy-laden, which could not be denied, because it was the very thing which the hungry and weary millions, almost wild with fear, craved with elemental desire. He offered them a communal system in this life, in which all the Elect who possessed wealth would sell the same and share it with the poor; after the Parousia, He offered them the Kingdom of Heaven on earth, which would endure an indefinite period and in which they would enjoy the wealth left behind by the wicked; and finally He offered celestial immortality in heavenly mansions as a reward for those who practiced communal brotherhood in this life.

3. *Accepted by the Pagan Masses.* This was the Gospel which Jesus commissioned His disciples to preach first to the Jews and then to all nations. Since the pagans were already familiar with Zoroastrian eschatology, Buddhist ethics, Pythagorean communism, and mystery-cult soteriology, they drank of this new gospel as if it were water

from the spring of Mnemosyne. Like a mustard seed, the tiny group of original disciples grew and expanded until they converted Constantine and transformed the pagan colossus into an international ecclesiastical empire.

4. *Could Any Competitor Have Survived?* We believe that, had there been no Christianity, Greek enlightment would, after a fierce struggle with Mithraism and its offspring Manichaeism, have emerged victorious. There would then have been no Dark Ages. With the exception of the cults of Simon Magus and John the Baptist, Christianity was the only significant savior-religion with an historical founder, or one who claimed Christhood or its equivalent; most other competitors were simple savior-cults, with little ethical or economic content. We believe that only a well-rounded synthesis enunciated by an historical god-man *soter* could conquer and survive. Buddhism could not prevail in Greece or Asia Minor because it was devoid of soteriology. Even without a known founder, Mithraism proved the most powerful early opponent of Christianity, precisely because it was a similar synthesis. It went down to defeat because it had no historical founder, was without a profound ethical message for the poor, and made no provision for women communicants. Manichaeism was far more potent than Mithraism, because it was, like Christianity, a much broader synthesis; yet, even so, since Manes never claimed to be a divine incarnation, his cult was forced to absorb the Christian God-man and His Gospel in order to wage its terrific battle for conquest or survival. Official Judaism still exists after more than twenty-five centuries, but it embraces only a few million people and lives by virtue of its exclusiveness.

5. *Evolution of Ideology.* And so we see that Egypt gave the world the god-man savior, who was several times reconstituted in the Greek and barbarian mysteries. Persia filled the world with fears of hell, with hopes of paradise, with the concept of the Last Judgment, and with the expectation of a renovated universe. The Jews and the Brahmanas gave us the priest-state. The Buddhists gave us renunciation, which made sex, family, wealth, labor, and comfort into crimes and which made of idle communism

and holy parasitism the saintly way of life. The Greeks gave us democracy and private property, which Pythagoras attempted to replace with a celibate but self-reliant communism. He also popularized the Zoroastrian metaphysics, the Brahmanic-Buddhist eschatology, and the Egyptian-Dionysiac soteriology in the Graeco-Roman world. Plato absorbed the communism, anthropology, and eschatology of Pythagoras, but rejected his celibacy and his soteriology, as well as his concept of religion as a mystery-cult. Aristotle rejected the features of Pythagoreanism which Plato accepted, and embraced the concepts of private property and the secular life, in this respect returning to the ideology of Hesiod. The Essenes were Pythagoreans who encased their pagan religious synthesis, which Jesus absorbed, in a Jewish integument, which He rejected, although He considered Himself one of the prophets of Yahweh; but He also incorporated a definitely Buddhist element, not found among the Essenes. In the Gospel, therefore, we find a synthesis of Osirian-Dionysiac soteriology, Zoroastrian eschatology, Buddhist ethics and renunciation, Pythagorean communism, and the Essenic Parousia. Since all this is in fundamental contradiction with private property or enterprise and since it is the reverse of the secular way of life which we have developed out of Greek originals, the modern individual who accepts the Christian synthesis as written exists in a state of duality: for he gives lip service to a philosophy of life which is diametrically opposed to his actual manner of existence. And for this reason, countless millions read their Gospel without the faintest realization of its true meaning. Should they understand and obey, they would necessarily become Buddhist-Pythagoreans. A number of individuals, like Count Leo Tolstoy, and some two hundred modern religious sects, have attempted to obey the Gospel in part by adopting its communist precepts; among these, the Amish, the Mennonites, the Mormons, the Doweyites, the Hutterites, and the Doukhobors may be listed as notable.

D. WORLD-PENETRATION BY COMMUNIST IDEOLOGY

1. *The American Surrender.* Let no one suppose that the social principles of Ikhnaton, Buddha, Pythagoras, and Jesus, re-created in modern terminology by Thomas Paine and Karl Marx, have failed to make enormous inroads upon modern life. These principles are, in brief, that all men are equally worthy in a moral sense, regardless of race, color, industry, thrift, nationality, intellectual endowment, ambition, or economic status; and that all must, therefore, share their material surplus with their less fortunate brethren. We need not travel to Europe, Russia, China, or India to discover the amazing penetration which these ideas have achieved; we need simply look at our own country, that last citadel of free enterprise. The principle that all men are their brothers' keepers has now progressed so far that the Republicans of the fifties look like the Socialists of the twenties. To deny that a multitude of laws, now considered integral in our way of life, are thoroughly communistic is absurd. What is left of American free enterprise has been saved only by adopting a goodly half of the principles of Karl Marx. Among these, we may mention powerful labor unions, the steeply graduated income tax, unemployment and old age security, and the extraordinary progress of the Negro race.

2. *Brotherhood by Compulsion.* We need only point out that whenever the welfare state takes the fruit of their labor from the industrious and the ambitious and gives it to the weak, the idle, the unfortunate, the improvident, or the parasitical, it is simply providing for human beings on the communist-Buddhist-Gospel principle that society as a whole is under an inescapable obligation to its poor and that each is to receive, not according to his merit or production, but according to his need. And since the wealth of the very rich would prove infinitesimal even if all of it were divided among all the needy, it is not the affluent, but the industrious of modest income who must support a sort of social brotherhood by compulsion, forced upon the more crafty, capable, and

industrious by their less successful or acquisitive brethren.

E. WHAT IS PERMANENT IN THE GOSPEL

1. *Wide Appeal.* After two millenniums, the Man of Galilee emerges as the sole creator of a religion which is permanent, universal in appeal, and infinitely various in manifestation. It was, as we have pointed out, a synthesis of human experience drawn from many cultures; and only by placing that Gospel in its proper perspective, can we accept it humbly yet critically for what it is. In one of its aspects, it is the expression of a profound humanism, since it implies that human beings are the ultimate jewels of the universe; but, on the whole, it is anti-humanist, since it seeks victory in renunciation and fixes its hope in a kingdom which never comes.

2. *The Gospel Dynamic.* The true ethical message of Jesus must remain meaningless to any one who seeks primarily the redemption of his own soul or who believes that salvation can come from the rituals or ministrations of a priest. To derive from the Gospel Jesus its permanent and irrefragable treasure we must understand that "He that loseth his life for my sake shall find it." In other words, those who give themselves in a life of service shall realize their utmost potential and shall, as a by-product, achieve the satisfaction which comes from the realization of self.

Many have found a vast regenerative power in that Gospel. Jesus means that no one can be happy or secure, or at peace with himself, so long as moral injustice flourishes in the world; that we can never be free from a guilty conscience so long as we profit by economic exploitation; that we cannot achieve righteousness so long as involuntary want exists alongside luxurious idleness. The Gospel Jesus has contributed to the creation of a world-conscience, which drives millions of comfortable people to read books on peace of mind to assuage their sense of guilt. Jesus teaches that only in service, only in losing ourselves for others, only by offering ourselves wholeheartedly to a purpose beyond the self, can we gain essential happiness. To achieve this was the objective of the schools of Greek philosophy also; and many great men have found their peace in them. A much greater number of simple and honest men and women, however, have achieved the same result as an unsought by-product of the Gospel Jesus; and many complex personalities have found the key to a life of meaning in the same inspiration.

And we discern a greater horizon beyond: for the world is not an aggregation of individuals so much as a communion of nations, which themselves consist of mutually antagonistic economic groups or classes. We believe that the Gospel Jesus has so penetrated the world that the exploitation of one nation or of one economic group by another is today approaching universal outlawry. Few privileged groups any longer dare to justify their advantages except by claiming service to society as a whole. Pearl Buck in *My Several Worlds* notes that the Chinese were perfectly aware of the revolutionary and humanitarian content of the Gospel Jesus which the indoctrinated missionaries who preached it failed to comprehend. Not only has a national conscience arisen, but a world-conscience as well. This requires that men everywhere shall regard all others, regardless of race, color, or nation, as substantially their brothers; and that any act of aggression committed anywhere must be considered an assault upon ourselves. It implies also that the humblest worker of factory, mine, or farm, has an inalienable right to whatever decency or security his national economy can provide.

3. *The Voice of Conscience.* Before the Essenes, only the Pythagoreans and the Buddhists had taught any such doctrine. Judaism was a racial cult which had as its purpose its own aggrandizement. The mystery-cults did not stress social ethics, but sought primarily immortality for their communicants. The official nature-religions sought little else than success in worldly enterprise. Zoroastrianism was a fiercely nationalistic creed. The Greek ethical schools explored every conceivable avenue by which to attain happiness and peace of mind by human reason and conduct: but they remained distant and intellectual, unable to thrill the heartstrings of the desperate masses. Mohammedanism

was from the beginning an assertive creed which appealed to the aggressive rather than the gentler emotions. It would indeed have been wonderful had so exalted and rational a philosophy as Epicureanism become the ethical code of mankind two thousand years ago: but an elementary understanding of history and psychology will reveal the impossibility of such a development.

Jesus proclaimed the universal conscience, that still small voice which never dies, which can never be exorcised or extinguished; and which, in spite of every obstacle, has permeated the world. The task of the Humanist is to absorb from the Gospel those elements which contribute to a religion of humanity based upon all the lofty ideals which have appeared during the long passage of mankind up from barbarism; a religion without creed and without a system of supernatural redemption; a religion which centers its ideal in the highest potential of mankind.

4. *Summary*. And so we find that the gospel of Jesus achieved acceptance by offering to heal the physically ill; give peace of mind to the mentally distraught; divide the wealth of the rich equally among the poor; confer divinity and immortality upon the Elect through the mystical eucharist; and establish the kingdom of the saints within twenty-five or thirty years when the Parousia and the last judgment would occur. All these benefits were obtainable without money and without price: the only condition was childlike belief and implicit acceptance. The reward was to be an eternity in heaven: the punishment for skepticism and rejection would be everlasting torture in hell.

Such modern cults as the Irvingites, the Adventists, the Mormons, and the Jehovah's Witnesses attained success by precisely the same methods. No religion can rise to power quickly without vast promises, fierce threats, and the doctrine of imminent catastrophe.

PART FOUR

REDEVELOPMENT IN THE PAGAN WORLD

Men go to hell for this reason, that they do not submit their persons to priestly control.

Shayast La-Shayast I xvii 8

Give me the liberty to know, to utter, and to argue freely according to conscience, above all liberties . . . Let truth and falsehood grapple. Who ever knew truth put to the worse in a fair and open encounter?

Milton: *Areopagitica*

It would be unfair to the generality of our kind to ascribe wholly to their intellectual and moral weakness the gradual divergence of Buddhism and Christianity from their primitive patterns. For it should never be forgotten that by their glorification of poverty and celibacy, both these religions struck straight at the root not merely of civil society but of human existence. The blow was parried by the wisdom or the folly of the majority of mankind, who refused to purchase a chance of saving their souls with the certainty of extinguishing the species.

Sir J. G. Frazer:
The Golden Bough IV:II vi

CHAPTER I

THE EARLIEST CHRISTIANS

A. JESUS AS THE FOUNDER OF A JEWISH EMPIRE

Let us visualize the Christ-cult in its earliest phase. At the death of their leader, the disciples were cowed and scattered; but the belief very soon took hold among them that He, like the Essene Master, about whom the whole model for early Christianity had already grown up, had risen from the grave and had ascended into heaven, where He sat on the right hand of God. We may assume that as soon as they were convinced of this, they also recalled His teachings concerning the Parousia, the Elect, and the sacraments, and His commandment to preach the Kingdom of Heaven. Faith in the resurrection was the spark which, under the leadership of Peter, ignited the new movement. "And with great power gave the apostles witness of the resurrection of the Lord Jesus." [1]

Acts is our principal source concerning the apostolic Church; the earlier chapters deal largely with the ministry of Peter, and the later almost exclusively with that of Paul. Of the original disciples, only Peter seems to have left any serious imprint; and, ironically enough, it was left for a fierce but sincere and intellectual Pharisee, Saul of Tarsus, to remold the Gospel Jesus, carry its message to the Gentiles, and create the Christian communion, which was first called by that name in Antioch.[2]

We know that the original disciples failed to comprehend that Jesus had offered His Gospel on terms of equality to all races and nations. To them, Jesus was indeed to reappear as the Messiah of Moral Judgment: but this

Christ was to resemble the Son of Man in Daniel more than the same personage in *Enoch*. The saints to be gathered from every corner of the earth at His Parousia were the Jews of the Diaspora; the Gentiles were to have no portion in this glorious adventure. The Kingdom of God would be the empire of Israel, which the Gentiles might share only by first becoming Jewish proselytes; and it was in this sense only that Christ was called a light unto the Gentiles. This concept differed so little from that then held by many Pharisees that their documents could scarcely be differentiated from the Christian. The *Apocalypse of Baruch* and the authentic portions of *Fourth Esdras*, both entirely Judaic, differ from Revelation so little that all three were incorporated into the Catholic scriptures.

We know from their activity as well as their recorded words that the disciples of Jesus had no comprehension of His universality. Cleopas says: "We trusted that it had been he which should have redeemed Israel." [3] The disciples "thought that the kingdom of God should immediately appear"; [4] and they asked, "Lord, wilt thou at this time restore again the kingdom of Israel?" [5] They could scarcely reconcile themselves to the slightest delay.

The first Christians proclaimed that Gentiles could embrace the religion of Jesus upon Mosaic terms only; and that, at His imminent return, He would inaugurate an Israeli empire. As long as it was possible to convince Jews that He would accomplish all this, converts could be made among them. When this could no longer be done, Jewish Christianity withered and died.

B. PROSELYTING VIRULENCE

The primary characteristic of pristine Christianity was its intense proselyting fervor. In this, it was similar to modern communism and to such religious sects as Jehovah' Witnesses, all distinguished by various common traits First, while they proclaim certain popular economic ethical, or soteriological doctrines, they are also intensel political, desire primarily to replace the current ruler and seek passionately to control the lives of all; second they direct their appeal to the poor, the downtrodden, the disinherited, who are filled with fierce resentment toward those superior to them socially, intellectually, and economically; third, they are based upon fantastic promulgations which the missionaries themselves could never believe, were they not emotionally unbalanced; fourth, through absurd and impossible promises, they awaken false hopes and delusions in their converts, which can only lead to a new enslavement; fifth, the zeal of the prophet as well as the acceptance of his message by the convert derives from the mental and moral insufficiency of both; sixth, the basic drive to proselyte stems from a preternatural craving for power in those who cannot succeed in any legitimate enterprise; seventh, whenever these prophets achieve power, they quickly wallow in the very luxury which they previously condemned so fiercely, and they reduce their proclaimed beneficiaries to servitude; eighth, since they are fanatically convinced that none except themselves possess any truth, they are immeasurably dogmatic and intolerant, cannot endure the existence of any other opinion, and insist on the extirpation of every deviation and deviationist; and ninth, through their fanaticism, they provoke persecution while they remain in a minority, but when and if they achieve power, they inflict it universally and ferociously upon all who do not conform to their doctrines or bend to their will. No well-balanced personality will, therefore, have the urge to proselytize; and no one who does will ever have a message that can withstand analysis. Its appeal will always be to the most primitive emotions.

The original apostles were nobodies who would have lived and died in obscurity had they not become propagandists for a new faith based upon three overriding postulates: first, that Jesus was the Christ, the Son of God; second, that He was the universal *soter,* risen from the dead; and, third, that He would return during the generation then existing to establish His kingdom and condemn to everlasting hell fire all those who failed to accept Him in the meantime.

The Seventh-Day Adventists, the Mormons, the English

Catholic Apostolic Church, and the Russelites, now known as Jehovah's Witnesses, all built their communions with the same propaganda: all promised an imminent Parousia in which they would reign on earth with Christ. The Witnesses still teach this doctrine with unabated virulence; and this is the source of their fanaticism and their power.

C. THE FIRST CHRISTIAN COMMUNITY

1. *Patterned after the Essene.* And so the first church of Jesus came into existence in Jerusalem. We know that it baptized, celebrated the eucharist, and practiced the laying on of hands to impart the Holy Ghost and exorcise demons, all non-Jewish rituals. We have every reason to believe that they insisted on celibacy and vegetarianism; and we know that they organized themselves into a communist society. In short, the new communion was patterned upon the Essene.

2. *Mass Conversions.* We read that Peter addressed the Jews declaring that Jesus was now "both Lord and Christ";[6] that three thousand souls were baptized into the new community; and that "all that believed were together, and had all things in common; and sold their possessions and goods and parted to all men, as every man had need."

The author continues: "Neither was there any among them that lacked: for as many as were possessors of lands or houses sold them, and brought the prices of the things that were sold, And laid them at the apostles' feet: and distribution was made unto every man according as he had need. And Joses . . . having land, sold it and brought the money, and laid it at the apostles' feet."[7]

3. *The Serpent in Paradise.* This idyllic situation however, was of brief duration; for these were not the Essenes, who chose their members meticulously, initiated them slowly, required them to assume burdens far in excess of their personal needs, and cared for their aged member graciously. Here, instead, was a mass movement, offering salvation to all: men, women, married couples, entire families. The spirit of God was to effect a profound regeneration in each and every one. Alas! this was not to be

and soon there was corruption in the Kingdom; the wealthy did not long continue to provide the wherewithal for the hordes of indigent to consume. Ananias and his wife Sapphira, upon joining the Elect, had sold their property and, according to the requirements of the society, had brought in the money to the apostles. But Peter learned that these two wolves in sheep's clothing, these tares among the wheat, were trying to defraud God and His saints by withholding for their personal use a portion of their own wealth. The punishment was swift and condign: both were struck dead (so the story goes) on the spot. We can only conclude that others were similarly guilty, for "great fear came upon all the church, and upon as many as heard these things." [8] So fierce was the desire of the have-nots for the material wealth of the haves.

4. *Communism Abandoned.* However, this Gospel-communism was of brief duration. The original stores must soon have been exhausted and few indeed with large substance were so aflame with the Messianic expectation that they would destroy their own temporal security. Many, who might have been converted upon less drastic terms, turned, no doubt, like the rich young man, sorrowing away. And so we read of Tabitha, who was "full of good works and almsdeeds;" [9] and concerning Cornelius, "a devout man, and one that feared God with all his house, which gave much alms."[10] No longer did the saints live communally, turn their wealth over to a steward, or draw from a common storehouse.

5. *Greek Infiltration.* We find also that conflict soon arose concerning the equitable distribution of charity. For we read that "there arose a murmuring of the Grecians against the Hebrews, because their widows were neglected in the daily ministrations."[11] Seven men, therefore, were appointed to investigate the complaint, of whom five bear Greek names.

And so we learn several facts: first, not only was communism soon abandoned, but charity was limited to needy widows, and given even to them insufficiently; second, bitterness arose over the racial allocation of this relief; and, third, the majority of the new converts were Greeks even while the acceptance and practice of the Mosaic Law was a prerequisite for membership. In short, Judaism was less repulsive to the Greeks than was the Orphic-Pythagorean mystery to the Jews.

D. JEW VS. GENTILE

1. *Explosion Inevitable.* It was unthinkable that the rapidly-growing Hellenic majority should long submit to Jewish discipline in the Christian community; and the strife inherent in the situation must soon explode into irreconcilable conflict. At least during the later phase of His ministry, Jesus understood that if His religion was to become universal, it would have to break the shackles of the Mosaic code; for its acceptance implied not only the primacy of the Jew and the inferiority of the Greek: it meant also that justification was to be achieved through ceremonials and not by moral regeneration.

2. *The Murder of Stephen.* Paul says[12] that he was commissioned to carry the Gospel to the uncircumcision, while Peter carried it to the Jews. Very early in the development of the new church, the problem of Jew vs. Gentile became a burning issue; and it erupted into violence in the case of Stephen, who "full of faith and power, did great wonders and miracles among the people."[13] We read that jealous disputants defeated by Stephen in debate "suborned men, which said, We have heard him speak blasphemous words against Moses, and against God . . . and the law . . . For we have heard him say, that this Jesus of Nazareth shall . . . change the customs which Moses delivered us."[14]

There we have it. Stephen was an earlier Paul, who had arisen just a little too soon. He too had comprehended the universality of the Gospel, and the necessity of breaking the fetters of the Law. The text declares that he was accused by suborned witnesses; but this was a gratuitous assumption, since Stephen did not deny the charges; he replied that his enemies were identical to those who had betrayed Moses, killed the prophets, and crucified Christ. He wished to base the new communion upon the Gospel doctrine that moral regeneration and not the Mosaic Law is the highway to redemption and that the Elect will come equally from all races and nations.

We are told that Stephen was brought before the Council (Sanhedrin)[15] and stoned by the people.[16] This is highly improbable: such an event could not have happened under Pilate or during any period of stability. It is far more likely that Stephen was privately condemned and lynched by the Judaizing faction of the Church.

3. *Paul Tries Vainly to Bridge the Gulf.* The gulf between Jewish and Gentile Christianity was simply impassable. The saviors projected by the two were utterly different. Only a dedicated, fiery genius like Paul, half Jew and half Gentile, at once Hebrew and Roman, could carry the Orphic-Essene message of Jesus to the Gentiles. But even He could not carry it to the Jews also. During the early years of his ministry, he always tried first to win the Jews wherever he went, but was invariably rebuffed. He was finally constrained to declare: "It was necessary that the word of God should first have been spoken to you: but seeing that you put it from you, and judge yourselves unworthy of everlasting life, lo, we turn to the Gentiles."[17] This was the inevitable result, because Paul re-created correctly so much of the Pagan Gospel Jesus. But among the Gentiles, he was extraordinarily successful. Both Jew and Gentile accepted only what had already long been his own.

4. *The Concessions of Peter.* Even before the meteoric success of Paul, Peter had been compelled to make definite concessions to the Hellenes.[18] In Caesarea there was a certain Cornelius, a Roman, who had a vision in which he was told to send to Joppa for Peter. Just before his emissaries arrived, the apostle also had a vision, in which a voice commanded him to kill and eat all manner of four-footed beasts, and creeping things, and fowls of the air. When Peter demurred, saying he had never eaten anything common or unclean, the voice replied: "What God hath cleansed, that call not thou common,"[19] which simply signified that Gentiles might accept the Gospel

without being subject to the Jewish ceremonial or dietary laws.

This version implies that Peter was the first who advocated concessions to the Gentiles; this, however, Paul angrily denied, and accused Peter of outright hypocrisy[20] because while alone with the Gentiles he ate as one of them, yet when other Jews were present, he compelled Gentile Christians to live as Jews. Paul declares that his Greek friend Titus entered the communion without submitting to circumcision.[21] After hot and acrimonious debate in Jerusalem, it was determined that Gentile converts should be required only to "abstain from meats offered to idols, and from blood, and from things strangled, and from fornication."[22]

5. *The Precarious Compromise.* And so a precarious compromise was concluded to exorcise the murderous strife. There were, in effect, to be two communions, one Jewish, the other Gentile, both based upon the same Gospel. On this issue, Paul and Barnabas, who had previously collaborated, became bitterly opposed. We read that "the contention was so sharp between them, that they departed asunder";[23] Barnabas, who was the famous Joses of Acts 4:36, took Mark to Cyprus, while Paul took Silas to Syria and Cilicia.

The question was now squarely posed: could the same Jesus be the Christ of two such disparate churches? The Hebrew Christians believed this was possible; Paul, on the other hand, saw clearly that it was not, and therefore advocated the abandonment of Judaism; when the Jews refused to heed him, he turned exclusively to the Gentiles.

6. *The Jewish Wing.* Jewish Christianity, always characterized by certain unmistakable traits, lingered on for centuries under various names, such as Nazarenes, Ebionites, and Cerinthians: it emphasized good works and human brotherhood; the condemnation of wealth and exploitation; a strict unitarianism, which rejected the Virgin Birth; a New Testament consisting of Revelation, the Catholic epistles, and the highly Judaistic version of Matthew; and an overwhelming emphasis upon the Messianic role of Jesus as head of the chiliastic kingdom.

7. *The Gentile Form.* Since the Gospel Jesus derived almost entirely from non-Jewish sources, it was easy for the Gentiles to accept it and eventually to add to it the Virgin Birth, the Logos Doctrine, the Trinity, Mariolatry, etc. When Greek Christianity assumed its ultimate form, little was left of the Jewish-Essene contribution except the Parousia, which was officially suppressed during the Montanist controversy at the close of the second century.

Let us now consider *The Didache*, which is perhaps the oldest extant document of the Christian movement.

CHAPTER II

THE DIDACHE

1. *Discovery*. In 1878, the prelate Bryennios called attention to a document in the Patriarchal Library at Constantinople called *The Didache* or *The Teaching of the Twelve Apostles,* a manual used by the earliest Christians and also known as *The Two Ways.* Known to scholars for some time, the MS. itself, nearly a thousand years old, was a copy of another probably completed about 100; while this, in turn, was a recension of a Hebrew composition, which may date back to 40-55. *The Didache* reproduces in part the Essene *Manual of Discipline* and contains quotations from the *Logia* or the *Sayings of Jesus.*

2. *Gospel Ethics.* The book begins with a discourse containing definite quotations from an already well-known document: "The way of life is this: 'First, thou shalt love the God who made thee, secondly, thy neighbor as thyself; and whatsoever thou wouldst not have done to thyself, do not thou to another. Bless those that curse you, and pray for your enemies, and fast for those that persecute you. For what credit is it to you if you love those that love you? Do not even the heathen the same? . . . If any man smite thee on the right cheek, turn to him the other cheek also,' and then thou wilt be perfect. 'If any man impress thee to go with him one mile, go with him two. If any man take from thee what is thine, refuse it not . . . he who receives alms without need shall be tried as to why he took and for what, and being in prison he shall be examined . . . . and he shall not come out thence until he pay the last farthring.'"

The Sermon on the Mount is simply an elaboration of *The Didache,* which continues: "Thou shalt not turn away the needy, but shalt share everything with thy brother, and shalt not say that it is thine own, for if you are sharers in the imperishable, how much more in the things which perish?"

Thus we find that while entire passages are couched in the very words of the Sermon, *The Didache* is closer to Buddhist communism than is Matthew; and yet it also falls short, because neither slavery nor the family is repudiated. After several admonitions concerning proper family relationships and those which should exist between masters and slaves, the first portion concludes with the words, "This is the way of life."

3. *The Way of Death*. The document now proceeds to expound the Way of Death, in which the author admits that much of the Gospel ethics is too hard to observe, for he says: "If thou canst bear the whole yoke of the Lord, thou wilt be perfect; but if not, do what thou canst."

4. *Baptism*. We now find directions for baptism "in the name of the Father, Son and Holy Spirit," a rite prerequisite to the eucharist; for we should "give not that which is holy to the dogs." The Lord's Prayer is then repeated as in Matthew.

5. *The Eucharist*. What had already become the most important ritual of the Church, the eucharist, is now explained. This, as among the Pythagoreans, was a full meal: "As this broken bread was scattered upon the mountains, but was brought together and became one, so let thy church be gathered together from the ends of the earth into thy kingdom, for thine is the glory and the power through Jesus Christ forever."

This passage is highly revelatory, for it hearkens back to the Dionysiac mysteries. According to the ancient myth, as we have noted, the Titans had killed and eaten Zagreus, and in vengeance his father Zeus had slain the murderers with his thunderbolts and scattered their ashes upon the mountains. The Bacchanals also dismembered their living victims upon the mountainsides. And now we find that through Jesus Christ the Elect would eat of the "broken bread that was scattered upon the mountains" so that they might be "brought together and become one" in the kingdom.

6. *No Pecuniary Compensation.* Since at that time there were neither bishops nor presbyters, *The Didache* continues with rules governing the ministers of the cult, known as apostles and prophets. The former were a lower order, and must never be given food or shelter more than two days in any one place. Not only are riches condemned: all ministers are forbidden to accept the smallest pecuniary recompense. Prophets could remain longer and were authorized to administer the eucharist, but must never receive any personal reward. When *The Didache* was written, a paid or a resident priesthood was an abomination. Several decades must have elapsed before such personages as bishops, presbyters, and deacons, unheard of in the Gospel, began to appear, near the end of the first century.

7. *Tribulations and Parousia.* The author expected the Parousia during his own lifetime. Just before its occurrence, as in Mark 13, there were to be terrible commotions and universal hatred; and Anti-Christ, "the deceiver of the world" shall appear "as a Son of God, and . . . he shall commit iniquities which have never been . . . And then shall appear the sign of . . . the trumpets, and thirdly, the resurrection of the dead; but not of all the dead, but as it is said, 'The Lord shall come and all his saints with Him.' Then shall the world 'see the Lord coming on the clouds of heaven.' "

We shall find a similar ideology in many later Christian writers, and it is parallel to that of Mark and Paul.

So here in this primitive *Didache,* we find in brief scope the ethics, the economics, the sacraments, the discipline, the organization, and the eschatology of the pristine Church as these had evolved from Essenism into the apostolic communions.

CHAPTER III

PAUL: JEW vs. GENTILE

A. THE PAULINE PROBLEM

1. *To Determine Authenticity.* The problem concerning the Pauline literature consists in determining the exact manner in which it was altered, rewritten, and expanded before it was accepted by the Catholic Church. For, oddly enough, although it preceded all other portions of the New Testament, it was the last to achieve authority; and not only are several of the epistles wholly spurious, but those which are genuine were drastically revised.

2. *Cerdo and Marcion.* It is interesting to note that Cerdo and Marcion agreed very closely with modern scholarship. They accepted "neither all the epistles, nor in their integrity."[1] We know that they rejected Titus and the Timothies. Precisely which passages in the other epistles they condemned, we are not told; but these are not difficult to identify.

3. *The Apostle of the Gnostics.* Few facts concerning early Christianity are more conclusively established than that Paul was accepted by the Platonic Gnostics from the beginning; and that these were heretical because they denied the virgin birth, the validity of Judaism and the Old Testament prophecies of Christ, the earthly kingdom of saints, the last judgment, and torture in hell; and because they proclaimed celibacy, predestination, the Logos doctrine, the docetic Christ, the resurrection of the soul only, and the uniqueness of the Christ-revelation. When Paul declares that the Jews "have a zeal of God, but not according to knowledge,"[2] he means simply that they did not accept Christ as an unforseen revelation; and Paul thus

— 437 —

specifically declared himself a Gnostic. He states categorically that the mystery of Christ "was kept a secret since the world began";[3] but that now He "is made manifest to his saints."[4] This can mean only that there are no prophecies of Christ in the Old Testament. In this, as in so much else, Paul was bitterly opposed to Peter, who represented Jesus as the Christ foretold by Moses and the Jewish prophets.[5]

4. *Paul Revised and Expanded.* There can be no doubt that the Pauline literature used by the Cerdonites and Marcionites was in meticulous agreement with their doctrines. We know also that the three spurious epistles contain the most complete repudiation of Gnostic ideology. The only question remaining is whether the non-Gnostic elements in the other ten had been deleted by Cerdo or whether they were added by the Catholics. The only reasonable conclusion is that, since Paul was the great Gnostic spokesman more than fifty years before his writings became orthodox, these were revised and expanded by a process of Catholic forgery.

5. *Many Christianities.* For we must realize that, in addition to numberless heretical versions of Christianity, there are several variants which have been syncretized in the accepted norms. The Gospel of the Synoptics has been most honored in the breach. The Jewish form ran into a stone wall in the Gentile world, even as the Jews rejected the basic Gospel and even more its pagan innovations. The Gnostic Christianity of Paul, as reconstructed in the second century and as restated in the Fourth Gospel, became the basis of the Gentile Church and particularly of the Protestant Reformation.

6. *Paul Easily Corrupted.* It was particularly easy for the Catholics to revise and expand the Pauline literature since it was used very little outside the heretical communions until after 170. The situation here was quite different from that pertaining to the Synoptics, of which copies had greatly multiplied after 80 and which, therefore, could be altered only with the greatest difficulty. Once the epistles of Paul became so popular that they could no longer be denied, it was a comparatively simple matter for the lead-

ing bishops to agree upon certain revisions as the true Pauline version. Since few variant copies could have been in the possession of the orthodox congregations, this would occasion very little confusion.

7. *Pauline Literature.* The genuine epistles are the two Thessalonians, the two Corinthians, Galatians, Romans, Philippians, Colossians, Ephesians, and Philemon. Titus and the two Timothies were not written until the second century, and must have been composed by a Pauline ideologist within the orthodox movement. At some point during the century-long struggle to include the works of Paul in the sacred Catholic literature, his genuine epistles were revised so as to exclude his celibacy and partially to conceal many of his Gnostic doctrines.

8. *The Gnostic Paul.* In II 5 of the Gnostic *Acts of Paul and Thecla*, which enjoyed a high reputation among early Christians, the apostle proclaims a whole series of celibate beatitudes: "Blessed . . . are the continent, for unto them shall God speak . . . Blessed are they that possess their wives as though they had them not, for they shall inherit God." Even our canonical Paul repeats this doctrine.

9. *Catholic Revisions.* The pristine Church taught celibacy; and Paul was the most celebrated proponent of the doctrine. By the middle of the second century, however, this ideology had become completely unacceptable in Catholic circles. As a preliminary, therefore, to Paul's elevation, long passages were inserted in First Corinthians and elsewhere to permit the connubial relationship among Christians. And so we read that "it is good for a man not to touch a woman."[6] Yet "to avoid fornication, let every man have his own wife";[7] and "it is better to marry than to burn."[8] If you are bound to a wife or a husband, seek not freedom. If you become a widow or a widower, remain so: yet if you remarry, it is no sin. Although the genuine Paul states that we must never remain yoked with an unbeliever,[9] the interpolation commands that if one is married to such a person, one must not abandon or divorce him; but if he leaves of his own accord, let him go.[10] To give in marriage is well, but not to do so is

better.[11] Celibacy thus became a state holier than matrimony, but marriage, properly contracted, ceased to be an abomination. Quite contrary to earlier practice and to later ecclesiastical law, widows might remarry with the approbation of the Church.[12] And so Paul was made to repudiate not only the Gospel Jesus but himself also and to establish the Church on its practical and permanent basis.

The several elaborate texts in which Paul proclaims the subjection and inferiority of women and especially of wives may be authentic. The Gnostics did not demand that connubial mates divorce, or even separate from, each other: only that they desist forever from physical intimacy. They were to possess each other "as though they had none."[13] Thus, under the Pauline-Gnostic discipline, wives could continue formally as such and still be subject to the authority of their husbands.

10. *Paul's Negation.* Since it was certainly impractical to make Paul repudiate himself completely by the simple process of revision, three new epistles were concocted. It is only necessary to glance through Titus and the Timothies to realize what a gulf separates them from pristine Christianity and even more from Pauline Gnosticism. The Synoptic genealogies, which did not exist during Paul's lifetime, are condemned;[14] whereas only unpaid apostles, prophets, and evangelists ministered in the days of Paul[15] and *The Didache,* we find now that bishops, deacons, and presbyters, ecclesiastics who sprang up only in the second century, play a large role;[16] not only are these officials permitted to marry, but are told how they should govern their households;[17] the basic Pauline doctrine of predestination is denied;[18] Paul is now made to pontificate like a Catholic prelate and addresses his co-worker Timothy condescendingly as his "son";[19] the Gnostic resurrection as depicted in Corinthians and Thessalonians gives way to a Matthaean kingdom and last judgment;[20] conventional morality is endorsed in a declaration that those who do not provide for their own house are worse than infidels;[21] Gnosticism as such is specifically repudiated;[22] and the whole celibate tradi

tion is categorically abandoned: old women are now to teach the young ones how to be good wives;[23] woman shall be saved in child-bearing;[24] the young women should marry, bear children, and guard the house;[25] and forbidding to marry has so soon become the doctrine of devils.[26]

11. *Our Analysis.* In our analysis of Paul, therefore, we assume that all Gnostic elements are genuine; that these may not always be fully expressed, since it must have been the chief purpose of the revisionists to conceal them; and that obviously non- or anti-Gnostic texts must be alterations or sheer forgeries.

B. GENERAL ESTIMATE OF PAUL

1. *Preceded the Synoptics.* The ten genuine Pauline epistles were probably composed between 45 and 62. Although these reflect no knowledge of any other New Testament document, they prove that Paul had read the *Logia,* or *The Sayings of Jesus.*[27]

2. *The Mission of Paul.* Paul is of paramount importance. He believed fiercely in himself as the peculiarly commissioned teacher, who had received his mandate from the celestial Christ Himself;[28] and he never doubted that he was divinely empowered to establish the Church. He had once been equally intent upon the destruction of the Christ-cult;[29] but, upon conversion, he became its most fervent missionary. He spoke proudly of his hardships and sufferings, including five floggings from the Jews;[30] but he was careful to avoid martyrdom.[31] Although thoroughly sincere in his desire to spread the Gospel, he was also the supreme opportunist. He declared "I am all things to all men, that I might by all means save some."[32]

3. *Jew, Roman, and Stoic.* It was indeed fortunate for the new religion that the Roman Empire had welded much of the civilized world into a single political unity; that the government of this colossus was tolerant of all religious ideologies; and that it found such a protagonist as Paul, who, being both Jew and Roman, could carry the

Gospel successfully into every corner of the Empire. Nurtured in the school of Zeno the Stoic, he comprehended the universality of the Gospel and the spiritual regeneration it offered. Thus, he sought to win the Jews, not on their terms, but on those of Christ's new law.

4. *Roman Toleration and Jewish Persecution.* When Paul was brought before Festus, he listened patiently while the evangelist unfolded his doctrine, which he, like Pliny, considered not subversive but fantastic.[33] When Paul was brought to Rome, the Jews, as usual, rejected his teachings;[34] but he dwelt there two years preaching freely, "no man forbidding him."[35] Under such conditions, Christianity spread rapidly in the Gentile world.

For the Jews, Paul had little toleration and few kind words. They had "killed the Lord Jesus, and their own prophets, and have persecuted us; and they please not God, and are contrary to all men."[36] One of their worst crimes was that they, and this means the Jewish Christians, forbade Paul to "speak to the Gentiles that they might be saved."[37] The curse of Paul was particularly directed against the Jews: "If any man love not the Lord Jesus Christ, let him be anathema."[38]

C. RUPTURE WITH JUDAISM

1. *Universalist Premise.* The universality of the Gospel is the dynamic principle of Paul, and is repeated in endless variety. We read that "there is no respect of persons with God."[39] For "by one spirit are we all baptized into one body."[40] And again: "there is neither Greek nor Jew, circumcision nor uncircumcision, Barbarian, Scythian, bond nor free; Christ is all, and all in all."[41] It is needless to multiply such citations; but that a vast abyss separated this ideology from Jewish Christianity is obvious.

2. *Disciplined by Judaizers.* We are told in Acts that at first the disciples preached the Gospel to Jews only. And we read that later certain men, arriving in Antioch, "which came down from Judaea taught . . . . Except ye be circumcised after the manner of Moses, ye cannot be

saved."⁴² No wonder, then, that when Paul came to Jerusalem, he was subjected to drastic discipline; for the brethren, who "are all zealous of the law . . . are informed of thee, that thou teachest all the Jews which are among the Gentiles to forsake Moses, saying that they ought not to circumcise their children, neither to walk after the customs."⁴³

And so, ironically enough, we find the Jewish Christians ordering this reconstructed Pharisee to observe the last jot and tittle of the Mosaic Law; and we read that more than forty Jews were sworn to murder him,⁴⁴ probably in the same manner as Stephen had suffered; but he, more docile than his predecessor, escaped death in the citadel of his enemies by abject, if temporary, submission.⁴⁵

3. *Paul Driven Out by the Jews.* Peter, John, and various other missionaries among the Jews, proclaiming the necessity of the Law, met with moderate success. But from the beginning, Paul taught that rituals are insignificant, and that only a cataclysmic transformation of the inner nature, a moral regeneration in Christ, is efficacious for salvation.⁴⁶ When Paul preached in the synagogue at Antioch, the Jews were outraged, but the Gentiles were delighted.⁴⁷ The Jews were so moved with hatred that they drove him and Barnabas from the city.⁴⁸ In Lycaonia, they stoned him;⁴⁹ and in the synagogue at Corinth, the Jews "opposed themselves, and blasphemed; and he shook his raiment, and said unto them, Your blood be upon your heads; I am clean: from henceforth I will go unto the Gentiles."⁵⁰

4. *No Compromise on Paramount Issue.* Paul had tried desperately to convince the Jews that the Christ he preached was the power and wisdom of God,⁵¹ whose function it was to abrogate the Mosaic Law by the institution of a new covenant. Had not Paul insisted upon this doctrine and upon the universality of the new revelation, he would not have been so rejected by the Jews. However, had he done otherwise, his message would have fallen upon deaf ears in the Gentile world. The fundamental issue was whether Christianity should be a tem-

porary Jewish cult or a permanent Gentile religion. And on this, Paul was never an opportunist. Instead of approaching compromise with the Jews, he drew further away. He taught that the Jewish Law and the Gospel of Christ were not simply contradictory but mutually exclusive also.

5. *Moves Toward Complete Break.* Step by step, Paul followed his logic to its conclusion. He states that the Law was intended for the Jews only;[52] and "we conclude that a man is justified by faith without the deeds of the law. Is he the God of the Jews only? is he not of the Gentiles? Yea, of the Gentiles, also."[53]

Paul declares that "now we are delivered from the law";[54] that there is no difference between Jew and Greek;[55] that diets and ceremonials have no efficacy;[56] that Jewish customs are now abolished;[57] that the Elect may even eat meat sacrificed to idols, unless doing so offends the weaker brethren;[58] and that there is nothing inherently unclean in any kind of food.[59] He emphasized that the Sabbath may be observed or ignored at will;[60] which proves that in the first century the Christians had no holy day. And we know that when they established one, it was not the Sabbath (Saturday) of the Jews, but the Sunday of the Mithraists.

6. *The Law vs. Gospel Regeneration.* In Galatians, the conflict with Judaism reaches its climax. In this epistle, addressed to a congregation which wished to return to the Mosaic discipline,[61] Paul accuses Peter and Barnabas of outright treachery;[62] and he declares that before Christ came, we were under the Law as under a schoolmaster,[63] which kept us in bondage; but the covenant of Christ is the promise which gives us freedom.[64] He declared that the Jews will remain blind until the "fullness of the Gentile be come in," when at last "all Israel shall be saved."[65]

He continues that salvation is impossible for those who observe the circumcision, i. e., the Law.[66] He could scarcely go further; to practice the Law is to seek justification therein; but when this is done, Christ is nothing. This became the doctrine of the Gentile Church; and no

Jew could thereafter be accepted into its communion unless he first repudiated the immemorial customs of his people. Thus the first decisive development in Greek Christianity placed a complete ban upon every vestige of Judaism.

D. PAULINE ETHICS

1. *Inferiority of Women.* Whereas Jesus honored women and found in them His most devoted followers, Paul never tires of proclaiming their inferiority. He declares that even as God is the head of Christ, and as Christ is the head of man, so is man the head of woman;[67] and she must always submit to his will. Like the Mithraists, Paul regarded woman as the source of lust and temptation, a concept which was to bear bitter fruit during the ensuing centuries.

2. *The Pauline Ethics.* Paul follows Gospel ethics in part: we are to obey the civil authorities;[68] settle differences with a brother-Christian without recourse to a public court;[69] put hot coals on the heads of our enemies by returning them good for evil;[70] and bless those who revile and persecute us.[71] But in many ways, he repudiates the Synoptics. Whereas the Essenes and the Gospel proclaimed equality among the brethren, Paul repeatedly declares that Christian slaves and servants must be honest and diligent, and faithful toward their masters.[72] There is no Buddhism or Pythagoreanism in Paul: at a single stroke, he removed from Christianity its revolutionary social content. Although he was constantly protesting that he earned his own living and received no compensation for his missionary labors,[73] he nevertheless thought "that they which preach the Gospel should live by the Gospel";[74] and thus justification was found in him for the opulent ecclesiastical orders which, in the second century, began to supersede the mendicant and itinerant prophets and apostles of pristine Christianity. There is no reason to consider the passage spurious in which Paul declares that those who will not work shall also not eat.[75]

3. *Marriage and Celibacy.* Since there can be no

doubt that all Pauline texts which condone the connubial relationship or repudiate celibacy must be corruptions or forgeries, it is necessary to examine the epistles closely to see what they say on these subjects. In spite of the drastic revision and corruption of the genuine epistles, Paul's Gnostic celibacy is obvious; and is most pronounced in such early works as Corinthians and Thessalonians. Paul declares that we must possess our vessel in sanctification, abstain from fornication, and free ourselves from "the lust of concupiscence."[76] This can only mean sexual desire, the satisfaction of which is the badge of sin, whether encompassed through wife or harlot. Paul eloquently emphasizes his metaphysical dualism in a text[77] which is quite meaningless except as a command to abstain from all sexual consummation: "to be carnally minded is death . . . but if ye through the Spirit do mortify the deeds of the body, ye shall live."[78]

It is, however, in the Corinthians that we find the most explicit celibate declarations. Paul states that he has espoused his converts to one husband "that I may present you as a chaste virgin to Christ."[79] When Paul condemned fornication, he meant not simply illicit but all sexual intimacy. "Now the body," he says. "is not for fornication, but for the Lord."[80] Therefore "Flee fornication . . . know ye not that your body is the temple of the Holy Ghost . . . ?"[81] Deeply embedded in long interpolated passages which permit marriage, we find this genuine Gnostic gem: "But this I say, brethren, the time is short: it remaineth that . . . they that have wives be as though they had none . . . and they that buy as though they possessed not . . . . for the fashion of this world passeth away . . . He that is unmarried careth for the things that belong to the Lord . . . But he that is married careth for the things of this world."[82] In short, Paul believed the Parousia extremely imminent; there was no time for buying, selling, or marriage; only in a state of holy celibacy could the Elect remain pure while awaiting their Christ in the air.

To doubt that this was the true doctrine of Paul is sheer absurdity.

4. *Charity Replaces Communism.* It is in the spurious Paul that the Gospel ethics are most completely repudiated. By the time these forgeries were written, the Church had become practical; it realized that the strait gate which leads to salvation must be widened a little.[83] We read that "the love of money is the root of all evil";[84] but Jesus had taught that its *possession* was that root. Under these ethics, a man may possess much, so long as he does not value the filthy lucre too highly and continues "rich in good works, ready to distribute."[85]

However, the genuine and celebrated thirteenth chapter of First Corinthians also renounces communism in favor of charity as a pathway to moral regeneration: "And though I bestow all my goods to feed the poor, and though I give my body to be burned, and have not charity, it profiteth me nothing." And so the authentic Paul removed one of the great stumbling-blocks in the Gospel: communism, which the Greeks had long outgrown. His and the Gospel celibacy, the second stumbling-block, which had led to a crime so abhorrent that even the Greeks had no name for it, "that one should have his father's wife,"[86] was repudiated in the Pauline revisions and forgeries.

E. THE PAULINE SPECULATIVE DOCTRINES

1. *Metaphysical Dualism.* Paul's metaphysical dualism, deriving ultimately from Zoroastrianism, assumes that every human being consists of two antithetical natures: the one, being spiritual, draws us toward redemption; the other, being material, drags us into damnation because it is subject to the "rulers of darkness."[87] "The flesh lusteth against the Spirit and the Spirit against the flesh: and these are contrary the one to the other."[88] And, since one or the other must predominate, each and every one of us is either a child of darkness or one of light.[89] Our spiritual nature must carry on an unending struggle with the lower and physical: "I know that in me (that is in my flesh) dwelleth no good thing."[90] And again: "I delight in the law of God after the inward

man: But I see another law in my members, warring against the law of my mind, and bringing me into captivity to the law of sin which is in my members. O wretched man that I am! who shall deliver me from the body of this death?"[91] We must therefore mortify our members;[92] Paul boasts: "I keep under my body, and bring it into subjection";[93] and he declares: "they that are Christ's have crucified the flesh with the affections and lusts."[94]

Thus frail and sinful man is hopelessly lost, except through divine intervention. Only through the atonement of Christ is it possible for the higher aspect of man to triumph over his lower.[95] Here we have a doctrine not found in the Gospel. Jesus did not repudiate marriage on metaphysical grounds, but, like the Buddhists, rather on economic and eudaemonistic: for He condemned the whole family relationship in the same manner. With Paul it was something else altogether; with him the body as such, its every desire and impulse, especially the sexual, was congenitally evil with a wickedness that could never be wholly eradicated: it could only be beaten down, subdued, mortified, and finally crushed. Paul was a Stoic-Zoroastrian.

2. *Paul the Predestinarian.* Paul's predestinarianism was more explicit and philosophical than that of the Gospel: "For whom God did foreknow, he also did predestinate to be conformed to the image of his Son . . . Moreover, whom he did predestinate, them also he called: and whom he called, them he also justified: and whom he justified, them he also glorified."[96] No man can possess any merit whatever.

Who are we to ask, "Why hast thou formed me thus?" For the potter has power over the clay, and some lumps he makes unto honor, and others unto shame.[97] Some human beings are vessels of wrath, prepared, since the world began, for destruction: while others are vessels of mercy, prepared for everlasting glory.[98]

The Elect are those whom God has chosen and appointed from all eternity; the humble and the foolish are very often those destined for such glory;[99] the brethren are assured of this election,[100] since "God hath not appointed us to wrath, but to obtain salvation by our Lord Jesus Christ."[101]

3. *Christology.* Paul declared the pre-existence of Christ[102] some sixty or seventy years before the Fourth Gospel proclaimed the Logos doctrine. Since he never mentions the Virgin Birth, it is certain that he had never heard of it; and since his epistles were used by all Gnostic sects, the authentic Pauline Christ must also have been Gnostic. There were, however, several such Christologies, some of which simply placed the supernal Christ in the mortal Jesus at His baptism. And this was probably the Pauline theory, since he states that Jesus was of the seed of David[103] made of woman.[104] Romans 8:3, however, certainly implies a purely docetic Christ who was the Son of God "in the likeness of sinful flesh." The mystery of the Pauline resurrection was that in our immortal condition we are to have bodies like that of the celestial Christ, not like the one He occupied temporarily on earth: "henceforth know we no man after the flesh: yea though we have known Christ after the flesh, yet now henceforth know we him no more."[105]

The Christ of Paul was the eternally pre-existing Son of God; the human Jesus was only "declared to be the Son of God with power" through His resurrection.[106] By this means He became "the first fruits of them that slept."[107] This, according to Hippolytus, was also the doctrine of Theodotus,[108] and it became the foundation for various Adoptionist Christologies.

4. *The Eucharist.* Paul transformed the eucharist into the mystical core of the Christ-cult. He says that "we are members of" Christ's "body, of his flesh, and of his bones."[109] And "The bread which we break, is it not the communion of the body of Christ? For we being many are one bread, and one body: for we are all partakers of that one bread."[110] By partaking of the bread which is Christ, the Elect become a single mystical body, which is miraculously[111] identical in essence with Christ Himself. This process is described repeatedly and in detail.[112]

5. *Eschatology*. During the thirty years of Paul's ministry, during which he tried desperately to carry the Gospel to every section of the Roman Empire, the expectation of the imminent Parousia was at fever height and is reflected most intensely in the Thessalonians and the Corinthians. There are at least twenty distinct references to the Parousia in the epistles of Paul; and that he expected to meet Christ in the air without ever experiencing death is certain. He declares: "Now is our salvation nearer than when we believed. The night is far spent, the day is at hand."[113] His trenchant message was that "the time is short."[114]

The Pauline eschatology, which is a drastic revision of the Synoptical Last Judgment and eternal torture in hell, declares that at the instant of the Parousia all the Elect, whether living or dead, shall be translated into glorious and immortal bodies: "flesh and blood cannot inherit the kingdom of God . . . . Behold, I shew you a mystery: We shall not all sleep, but we shall all be changed, In a moment, in the twinkling of an eye, at the last trump: for the trumpet shall sound, and the dead shall be raised incorruptible and we shall all be changed. For the corruptible must put on incorruption, and this mortal must put on immortality."[115] According to the metaphysical dualism of Paul, it was inconceivable that "the body of this death" should inherit immortality. At the Parousia, the vile bodies of all the saints, whether living or dead, will be transformed by Jesus Christ "like unto his glorious body."[116]

Paul repudiated the chiliastic concept entirely. He could not imagine a kingdom of saints on earth, or any communion of theirs under mundane conditions after the Parousia.

There is no doubt that during his early ministry, Paul believed with Jesus that the Parousia would occur before any of the saints should die. That was the reason why he declared that many an apparent Christian had fallen sick or had died because, eating the body of Christ unworthily, he had caused "damnation to himself."[117] At the inception of his ministry, Paul must have believed that anyone of the Elect who partook of the eucharist would never descend into the grave.

In the Gospel Jesus, as we have seen, there is no provision for the saints who should die before the Second Coming. This matter became, therefore, a burning issue; and the mature Paul proclaimed the resurrection of the righteous.[118] It was imperative for the brethren to know that all who had died in faith would be resurrected in glory.[119] Even as Jesus is risen into immortality, so also will His Elect rise from the dust. Like those who remain alive at the Great Day, the brethren who have died will also meet Christ in the air: "the Lord himself shall descend from heaven . . . and the dead in Christ shall rise first: Then we which are alive and remain shall be caught up together with them in the clouds to meet the Lord in the air: and so shall we ever be with the Lord."[120]

It is obvious that Paul considered the Parousia so near "that we which are alive" are to "remain unto the coming of the Lord." Many of the Elect then living would never die. And we note further: the Last Judgment of Matt. 25, in which the saints were to be separated from the sinners and sent to their opposite eternal destinies has quite vanished from the Pauline eschatology. The fact is that hell and damnation have also disappeared; if Paul has any belief in punishment after death, he never betrays it. In this also he was a Gnostic. Like the Marcionites, he believed that the wicked would simply be annihilated and that the Elect, both the living and the dead, with glorified bodies, would rise to meet Christ in the air and be with Him forever in the celestial realms.

We read that at the impending Parousia "Jesus shall be revealed from heaven with his mighty angels, In flaming fire taking vengeance on them that know not God and obey not the Gospel of our Lord Jesus Christ: Who shall be punished with everlasting destruction . . . when he shall come to be glorified with his saints." This means simply that at His Second Coming, Christ would glorify His Elect with celestial bodies and reduce all others with fire into extinction.

The same old question, however, still haunted Paul:

exactly when would all this come to pass? Like *The Didache,* he declares: "That day shall not come except there come a falling away first, and that man of sin be revealed, the son of perdition." [121] And so we find that the Parousia is to be preceded by a general backsliding among Christians and by the appearance of the Antichrist, "who opposeth and exalteth himself above all that is called God, or that is worshipped: so that he as God sitteth in the temple of God, shewing himself that he is God." [122] When, therefore, a wicked man sets himself up as God in the Jewish temple, we will know that the Parousia is at hand.

This proves that Paul as well as Mark wrote before the destruction of Jerusalem. According to the latter,[123] the Temple was to be desecrated as it had been by Antiochus Epiphanes, for it was inconceivable to him that Daniel's "prophecies" were already completed history. According to Paul's non-Gospel concept, a wicked man, probably a Jew, would set himself up there as God just before the return of Christ.

CHAPTER IV

THE CATHOLIC EPISTLES

1. *Ebionite Christology.* Beginning with Hebrews and ending with Jude, we find a series of Judaizing documents known as the Catholic epistles and written by unknown authors for Jewish Christians. Hebrews, incorrectly attributed to Paul, is filled with Jewish imagery and ideology; it proceeds entirely from the Old Testament to the New; it is addressed solely to Jews, and declares that the Gospel of Christ is simply the new covenant foretold by Jeremiah and written into the hearts of believers. Christ is the new priest after the order of Melchizedek.

Extremely interesting are 1:5 and 5:5: "Thou art my son, this day have I begotten thee." This proves that the author was in accord with the *Gospel According to the Ebionites:* for these were the very words carried over from this gospel into our canonical Matthew and deleted after 400.

2. *James.* The Epistle of James is another Judaizing document, addressed to "the twelve tribes which are scattered abroad." It was written primarily to refute the Pauline doctrine of justification by faith. The controversy swirled around the Mosaic Law; according to James, its works are imperative, and "faith, if it hath not works, is dead." Even Rahab the harlot was justified by her works!

James reminds us of the ancient prophets, of *Enoch*, and of the Gospels: "Let the brother of low degree rejoice that he is exalted. But the rich, in that he is made low." [1] The wealthy are to rejoice in renunciation; masters are condemned *per se*,[2] according to the manner of the Essenes; and there is a terrific denunciation of the rich.[3]

The Epistle of James must have been written near the

end of the first century, because the saints were obviously beginning to lose faith in the Parousia: "Be patient, therefore, brethren . . . for the coming of the Lord draweth nigh." [4]

3. *The Petrine Epistles.* The two epistles attributed to Peter are also intensely Jewish: to the author, even the eucharist is based on the Mosaic ritual described in Exodus; [5] and Christ is "a lamb without blemish and without spot." [6] To Jewish Christians, Christ was an atonement and never a sacrament; anything in the Gospel which did not derive from Jewish sources was incomprehensible and therefore repulsive. The new Christians were simply a chosen generation, a royal priesthood, a holy nation, and a peculiar people who are called out of darkness into light, as the Israelites were called out of Egypt.[7] Every image, idea, aspiration, and doctrine found here could have been produced only by a Jew and could be attractive only to other Jews.

The first Epistle of Peter declares: "The end of all things is at hand; be ye therefore sober, and watch unto prayer." [8] We can only conclude that the Second Epistle was by a later author, written after Peter had been for some time dead. For its principal purpose was to assure the wavering brethren that even though long delayed, the Parousia would one day certainly arrive, in spite of the scoffers, who "shall come in the last days" and say, "Where is the Promise of his coming?" But the author assures us that "one day is with the Lord as a thousand years, and a thousand years as one day." [9] Thus we find again a totally different concept. No more is there to be a great tribulation, a desecration of the Temple (which no longer existed), an antichrist, or a Last Judgment. But suddenly the Lord will come as a thief in the night and burn up the world in one vast Zoroastrian holocaust.[9] We can only conclude from the expression "since our fathers fell asleep," that the entire first generation of Christians had now passed away. The writer therefore declares consolingly that a thousand years with God are as a single day and that Christ will come when He is least expected.

4. *Paul as the Antichrist.* From the Epistles of John

we learn that various unidentified teachers had gone forth from the Jewish Christian community teaching false doctrines and denying the Christ; these were, therefore, antichrists. We may well believe that these were Pauline propagandists, who declared that Jesus was to reappear, not as the Messiah of the Jews, but rather as the universal savior who would transfigure the saints of all nations, living or dead, by providing them with celestial bodies and an immediate translation into the heavenly mansions. There would therefore be no earthly or chiliastic kingdom, no Last Judgment, and no condemnation to hell. It must have been some such controversy as this which caused the Asian, that is, the Jewish, churches to repudiate Paul as an apostate, as we know they did.[10] And it is more than likely that these churches considered Paul the False Prophet, who plays so large a role in Revelation.

CHAPTER V

THE GREAT SYNOPTICAL ADDITIONS

A. THREE INTERPOLATED ELEMENTS

The Synoptic narrative beginning with the baptism and ending with the empty tomb is, as we have noted, undoubtedly founded upon authentic tradition, and, though much embellished by popular mythologizing, is in substantial agreement. However, we are immediately confronted by three very important but extraneous and interpolated elements which bristle with contradictions: the resurrection story, the genealogies, and the narratives dealing with the births of John and Jesus. These became necessary as the cult developed, and each had its specific purpose: belief in the resurrection, which became current before there were any written Gospels, proclaimed the power of Jesus to make His devotees immortal; the genealogies, added at an early date, were forged by Judaizers intent on making of Jesus the long-awaited Jewish Messiah; and the Virgin Birth, interpolated early in the second century, was invented to make of Jesus a Christ whom the pagan world could accept. These two mythical personalities, one created by Jews and the other by Hellenizers, were, of course, antithetical not only to each other but also to the authentic Synoptical Jesus; and they reflect the irreconcilable conflict existing in the pristine Church. There is no historical Jesus preceding the baptism.

B. THE RESURRECTION

1. *At the Tomb*. The Gospels agree that certain women followed the body of Jesus and saw its interment; and a

four state that early on the ensuing first-day one or more of them returned to the tomb. At this point, however, all agreement ceases. In Matthew there are two women, in Mark three, in Luke an indefinite number, in John Mary Magdalene only. In Matthew only, there is an earthquake which occurs after the women arrive and during which "the angel of the Lord descended from heaven, and came and rolled back the stone from the door and sat upon it." [1] The keepers become as dead, and the angel declares that Christ is risen and will precede the disciples into Galilee. Strangely enough, even here it is not recorded that any one witnessed the actual resurrection. Why the stone should be rolled away *after* this miracle remains obscure. In all the other versions, the tomb stands open and the soldiers are gone when the women arrive.

According to Mark, three women with spices came to anoint the body; how they expected to do this, in view of the existing watch, stone, seal, and closed tomb, we cannot tell. However, there is no earthquake, no guard, and no descending angel; instead, the stone has already been rolled away, and a young man is sitting inside the otherwise empty tomb. He tells them to declare the great news to Peter and the others, who are to proceed to Galilee. In Luke there are two men in the tomb; and there is no Galilean appointment in either Luke or John.

2. *Telling His Disciples.* According to Matthew, the women run at once to inform the disciples; according to Mark, they tell no one; according to Luke, they tell everyone; John has a totally different version.

3. *Final Scene in Mark.* We have already noted that the concluding verses of Mark are a later addition.[2] According to these, Mary Magdalene learns, not from the young man sitting in the sepulchre, but from Jesus Himself, that He is risen; she thereupon goes to the disciples, but they "believed not." The disciples do not go into Galilee at all, as commanded by the angel in a preceding verse of the same Gospel.[3] Instead we find that Jesus "appeared in another form unto two of" the disciples, who tell the rest, who, however, still refuse to believe. It is obvious

that none of them expected any resurrection. Jesus then appears to the eleven as they sit at meat, upbraids them for their unbelief, gives them their final charge, and is then "received up into heaven" where He "sat at the right hand of God." [4]

4. *Final Scene in Matthew.* According to Matthew, Jesus meets the women on their way to impart the glad news to the disciples,[5] and repeats the command of the angel that they proceed to Galilee, where they meet Jesus on a mountainside, "but some still doubt." [6] He gives them their final charge, but nothing is said concerning an assumption.

5. *Final Scene in Luke.* According to Luke, the women tell their story to the disciples,[7] who do not believe; but Peter, arriving at the tomb, stands "wondering in himself at that which was come to pass." [8] Two of the disciples go to Emmaus, a few miles outside Jerusalem, where they fall in with Jesus, whom they mistake for a complete stranger and who expounds the scriptures to prove that He had been foretold by Moses and the prophets.[9] When He breaks bread with them, they recognize Him at last; [10] and He vanishes. Thereupon they return to Jerusalem, where they find the eleven, who are saying that the Master had appeared to Simon, an event not previously recorded. But at that very instant, Jesus appears in their midst; they think Him an apparition, and He is at great pains to prove that He has a physical body, which He demonstrates by eating solid food. He gives them His final promise, telling them to remain in Jerusalem until "ye be endued with power from on high." [11] He then leads them out to Bethany, whence He ascends to heaven.[12] This, of course, is in complete contradiction with the versions which command the disciples to go to Galilee.

6. *Contradictions.* According to Luke, therefore, the assumption takes place in Bethany; according to Mark, from a room, presumably in Jerusalem; according to Matthew, the final scene occurs on a mountainside in Galilee; according to John, on the shore of Lake Tiberias. According to Mark and Matthew, the disciples are commanded to go to Galilee, which they do only in the latter; but accord-

ing to Luke, they are told to remain in Jerusalem. The Assumption itself is dismissed with half a dozen words. Such cursory treatment and fantastic contradictions prove that the whole story was a garbled invention.

7. *According to John.* The version of John is elaborate, theological, and totally different from the Synoptics. Mary Magdalene, finding the tomb empty, runs to Peter and John, who return with her, but who, finding no one, go away. Mary remains, and sees two angels in the sepulchre, who ask her why she weeps; and, turning, she sees Jesus Himself, but mistakes Him for the gardener, whom she believes to have hidden the body of her Lord, just as happened in the case of Yeshu. But when Jesus calls her Mary, she recognizes Him at last.[13]

During this period, the disciples are meeting furtively behind locked doors in Jerusalem; and periodically the apparitional Jesus floats into their midst. It is on one of these occasions that Doubting Thomas is shown the prints of the nails and the wound of the spear so that all future skeptics may be convinced.[14]

Now the scene shifts to the Sea of Galilee (Tiberias), where Peter and several other disciples have returned to their old trade. They catch nothing, however, until a stranger arrives, who tells them to throw their nets out on the right side, where they catch 153 great fishes, symbolizing all the peoples and nations to whom the Gospel is to be preached. Even after Jesus invites them to a eucharist of bread and fish, He still remains incognito. He is known only after He has tested Peter thrice and commanded him to feed His sheep.[15]

8. *An Impersonator?* Following the empty tomb, the one constant element in the resurrection narrative is the fact that in almost all of His appearances, Jesus is unrecognizable even to His disciples and to the faithful women. This suggests an impersonator. We know that Jesus recreated consciously Isaiah's Suffering Servant and the prophecy of Zechariah. We know also that He was convinced that God would raise Him from the grave after three days; but we cannot establish that He expected a physical resurrection. Knowing how frail was their faith,

He may well have arranged a means to strengthen it. Nor would such a supposition impugn His sincerity: for He never promised to return as He was before. When He promised to meet His disciples in Galilee, it is entirely possible that He had already groomed some one who resembled Him slightly to act as His substitute; and that, when the disciples were so terrified that they hid themselves in Jerusalem, this man was compelled to seek them out there to convey to them the astounding news of the resurrection.

9. *Who Took the Body?* It is obvious that some highly interested persons, friends or enemies, took the body from the tomb. We believe that Matthew points to the solution.[16] We find first that, according to this Gospel only, the Pharisees secured the tomb so that the disciples might not abscond with the corpse and so declare that Jesus was risen; for this was precisely what happened when Yeshu's body disappeared, a century before. According to Matthew, therefore, the Jewish priests later bribed the Roman soldiers to say that the disciples had stolen the body during the night.[17] We may be sure that they said this only to cover their own guilt; because the record proves that the disciples had no expectation of any resurrection; and, further, that they were too weak, disorganized, and terrified to accomplish so bold a deed.

Who, then, had the requisite motive and power? Why, the members of the Sanhedrin! They were aware that Jesus had foretold His own resurrection; and they knew what commotion the followers of the Teacher of Righteousness had caused in an exactly parallel situation. If they had possession of the body, they could expose the disciples as frauds when, on the third day, they announced that their prophet had risen.

The Jewish priests, however, were defeated because the terrified disciples had gone into hiding. The furtive evidence that Jesus had risen was whispered only among the faithful. Paul says indeed that on one occasion Christ was seen by more than five hundred persons,[18] but this could have been no more than an unconfirmed rumor, since it is nowhere supported in Acts or in the Synoptics. When Peter announced publicly that Christ had ascended to the

Father, the body which the Pharisees were holding had fallen prey to corruption.

There are two other possible theories: first, that Joseph of Arimathea was part of a conspiracy to remove the body: but this assumes that He and other powerful men were devout followers of Jesus, which they certainly were not; or, second, that Jesus pre-arranged the removal of His own body, which assumes influence on His part in high places which He did not possess.

The only hypothesis which stands analysis is that by removing the body the Pharisees overreached themselves and brought on the very development they dreaded most, viz., that future generations would believe Jesus risen from the dead, that "last error" which would "be worse than the first." And so, once more, the Essene Teacher inspired the act which made Christianity possible.

C. THE GENEALOGIES

1. *Contradictions.* There are two genealogies: first, that of Matt. 1:1-17; and, second, that of Luke 3:23-38. The former traces the ancestry of Jesus through his father Joseph to Abraham; the latter carries it back to Adam and God. Between David and Jesus there are forty-two generations in Luke, but only twenty-eight in Matthew; only three names occur in both. Thus, each descendant in the chain of Matthew was born of fathers who had reached the advanced age of thirty-nine, while, according to Luke, they would be twenty-five, which, in itself, constitutes an incredible disparity.

2. *Impossible to Delete.* Epiphanius declares that the Nazarenes "have the Gospel according to Matthew quite complete in Hebrew . . . I do not know if they have even removed the genealogy from Abraham to Christ." [19] This proves first that the Gospel of Matthew used by the Jews included the same genealogy we find in ours; and, second, that such Greeks as Epiphanius considered this spurious and believed that it should be eliminated. Yet both genealogies had become so firmly established that they could not be removed in spite of their contradictions with each

other and their common repudiation of the Virgin Birth.

3. *Paul Repudiates the Genealogies.* Not only Paul but his Catholic revisionists also rejected the "fables and endless genealogies"[20] of the Judaizers. Although he thought of Jesus as descended from the seed of David,[21] he rejected any doctrine intended to make of him a Jewish Messiah. According to his Gnostic-Zoroastrian concept, Christ was the eternally pre-existing Power and Wisdom of the Supreme God[22] who became incarnate in the human Jesus at the baptism.

4. *Who Invented These Fables?* The genealogies must have been devised by two separate Jewish sects intent on making Jesus into their earthly Messiah. Neither could have been part of an original Gospel, but each was added later and independently of the other; for the Synoptics repudiate any authority deriving from Davidic descent.[23]

5. *The Concept of the Disciples.* In spite of Jesus' specific denials, His disciples consistently thought of Him as the Jewish Messiah; and when they preached "to the circumcision," they presented Him as the Christ who, at His impending Parousia, would establish a kingdom of Hebrew saints. It was therefore unthinkable that He would be other than of the root of Jesse. And so, by a strange quirk of fate, the Catholic theologians were saddled with the irreconcilable contradiction of a supernatural Christ who was born of Mary and descended from David through Joseph, but who yet had no human father.

D. THE BIRTHS OF JOHN AND JESUS

1. *Jewish and Pagan Concepts of Christ.* In the authentic Gospels, the anointing or apotheosis of Jesus to Christhood occurred at His baptism when the Holy Ghost came upon Him in the form of a dove. This concept satisfied the Hebrews, to whom any more literal sonship to God was a profanation. But to the pagans, conditioned to polytheism and universally familiar with the concept of divine sonship, this Hebrew concept was far from sufficient. They could not accept any savior who was less than the literal

offspring of God Himself, born, like Dionysus, of a human virgin.

2. *Controversy Concerning Legitimate Birth of Jesus.* In the authentic portions of the Synoptics and in the Pauline literature there is not a single allusion to the Virgin Birth; had it been accepted doctrine when these were written, they would have contained dozens of texts reflecting or proclaiming it, as is the case with all Christian literature subsequent to 150. Why, then, and when was the Virgin Birth invented?

We have noted that an illegitimate birth was attributed to Yeshu by legend and that Celsus imputed the same to Jesus. And we learn from a document of great antiquity, the apocryphal *Acts of Pilate,* which Justin Martyr frequently cited and deemed of far higher authority than the Synoptics, that during the earliest period of Christianity, the controversy was not whether Jesus was born of Joseph or of the Holy Ghost, but whether He was born in wedlock or of fornication.[24] This establishes not only that the Virgin Birth was unknown to the earliest Christians but that the Jewish disciples of Jesus, so far from claiming divine parentage for Him, were desperately zealous to establish his human legitimacy. It is clear from Epiphanius that after the doctrine of the Virgin Birth became prevalent among the Gentiles, the Jewish Christians denied it more vigorously than ever.[25]

3. *The Problem of Reconciliation.* To reconcile the genealogies with the Virgin Birth became an exceedingly thorny problem for the ancient Church. Eusebius preserves a letter by Africanus[26] in which he attempts to explain Joseph's two genealogic fathers through the operation of the Levirate Law, under which, if a man died without an heir, his brother married the widow to raise up seed for him. This hypothesis, however, falls to the ground, because under it Joseph would still have the same grandfather, great-grandfather, etc., unless we are to accept the fantastic and gratuitous assumption of Africanus that the Heli of Luke and the Jacob of Matthew were foster-brothers of different Davidic descents who married the same woman, which would still leave unex-

plained the enormous disparity in the number of generations in the two genealogies.

Various church writers have surmised that Joseph is called the father of Jesus simply because he was married to His mother and therefore performed the protective function of a male parent. But this ignores the necessity of blood descent from David.

4. *The Manichaean Critique.* Various theologians struggled without success to solve the conundrum; and in the fourth century, the orthodox were compelled to meet the determined assault of the rationalist Manichaeans. We have already noted the comments of Faustus on Matt. 3:17, who, turning to the genealogies, declares that this son of Mary cannot possibly be the son of David unless it be ascertained that He was begotten by Joseph.[27] Since both genealogies trace the ancestry of Jesus through him, it follows either that Joseph was actually His father or else that Jesus was not of the seed of David. "To begin with calling Jesus the son of David, and then go on to tell of His being born of Mary before the consummation of her marriage with Joseph, is pure madness." Furthermore, continues Faustus, Mary herself was not of the tribe of Judah, for her father was Joachim, a Levite, as stated in the *Protevangelium,* another document held in high esteem by the ancient church; nor does Joachim's name occur in the genealogies. It is therefore impossible to place Mary in the line of descent from David. The son of Mary could not be the son of David unless she be either the daughter of Joseph or the mother of his child.

5. *Augustine's Answer.* Evidently realizing the untenability of Africanus' hypothesis, Augustine attempted to refute Faustus by offering another solution.[28] Since adoption was very common among the Jews, the Jacob of Matthew could be the real father of Joseph and the Heli of Luke the adoptive. "With two fathers, why not two grandfathers, and two great-grandfathers, and so on, up to David?"

This hypothesis, of course, is as absurd as that of Africanus. Not only is this far-fetched assumption without basis in the record, but it too fails to explain the disparity in the generations and ignores the crucial point: for if there was no blood-relationship, then was neither Joseph nor Jesus of the stem of Jesse, and it is absurd to include Joseph in the genealogy at all. The plain fact is that both Matthew and Luke contain two contradictory concepts of Christ, the Jewish and the pagan; after the Greek theologians had committed themselves to the latter, they could not openly repudiate the already established Jewish Christology of the Gospels and they were compelled to reconcile it with the new theology by whatever means they could.

Augustine concludes his argument by declaring that inasmuch as the scriptures declare that Jesus is descended from David and that He was begotten, not by Joseph, but of the Holy Ghost, we must believe, no matter what may be shown by other evidence, that He was born of the Virgin Mary and that she was of the line of David. "Otherwise, not a single page" of scripture "will be left for the guidance of human fallibility."[29] Obvious contradictions must be mere delusions.

6. *The Major Contradictions.* A single careful reading of the two first chapters of Matthew and Luke reveal that they are in complete contradiction, not only with each other but also with the authentic portions of the Gospels and with the known facts of history. We have, in fact, four conflicting renditions of the birth of Jesus: the first, told in Matthew 2:1-23; the second, in the second chapter of Luke; the third, in the first; and the fourth, in Matt. 1:18-25. Each of the four authors had a different concept of the birth, and was expressing the tenets of his own peculiar sect. And we are not dealing with simple discrepancies, for the versions are mutually exclusive: if any one of them is true, the others must be false.

According to Matthew, Joseph was a permanent resident of Bethlehem, and Jesus was born and remained in a *house* there, where the Wise Men came to see Him, following the star; according to Luke, Joseph was a resident of Nazareth, who went to Bethlehem to register, and Jesus was born in a stable, where, not Wise Men, but shepherds, as in Mithraism, came to pay Him homage.[30] According to the once authoritative *Protevangelium*, Jesus, like Mithra, was born in a cave, and this was what Justin Martyr believed.[31] Origen declares that this cave was still being shown to travelers in 230.[32] According to Matthew, Jesus was born before the death of Herod, which occurred in 4 B.C.; Luke contradicts him by stating that He was born during the registration under Cyrenius in 7 A.D. According to Matthew, Joseph fled to Egypt with Mary and Jesus, whence he returned after an indefinite sojourn at the death of Herod, which, as we have noted, occurred in 4 B.C.; and moved then to Nazareth to fulfill another Old Testament prophecy, which no one can find. In Luke, however, there is no journey to Egypt; Joseph and Mary remain in Bethlehem and Jerusalem for the period of a woman's purification, which was forty days, and then "returned into Galilee, to their own city Nazareth."[33]

7. *The Version of Matthew*. According to Matthew 2, Jesus was born of parents who resided in Bethlehem. In due course, the Wise Men, inquiring for the king of the Jews, came to Herod, who commands them to seek the Christ in Bethlehem, and, upon finding Him, to report back. They follow an incredibly low-hanging star until it stops above Joseph's home, which, it would seem, Herod's spies could have done just as easily. However, the Magi are warned by a dream not to return to Herod. Joseph is likewise warned and flees to Egypt, so that another prophecy,[34] predicting a leader who would deliver Israel from the no longer threatening Philstines might be fulfilled; whereupon Herod murders all children up to the age of two years, which implies that Jesus had been living in Bethlehem at least during this period of time.

It is obvious that this version must have been written by a Judaizer who was under Zoroastrian influence, for the Wise Men are Persian sages. And, although this legend is totally different from that of Luke, both represent Jesus as the temporal king of the Jews, "a governor, that shall rule my people Israel,"[35] born in Bethlehem and descended from David; that is, He was to be the temporal Messiah envisioned in the Old Testament.

8. *The Primitive Version of Luke.* Let us now consider the primitive version of Luke, which comprises the second chapter and which contains not one word concerning dreams, annunciations, or a supernatural birth. There could have been no legal reasons why Joseph should travel from Nazareth to Bethlehem to register his property; and certainly none for bringing the delicate Mary on such a long and hazardous journey. Furthermore, the decree of Augustus, according to which "all the world should be taxed,"[36] is unknown in Roman history. The registration ordered by Cyrenius occurred eleven years after the death of Herod, in whose lifetime Jesus was born, according to Matthew.

Most notable in this version of Luke is the fact that neither Joseph nor Mary have any premonition concerning the destiny of Jesus. When the shepherds tell them of their vision, "they wondered . . . But Mary kept all these things and pondered them in her heart."[37] Had she received the annunciation from Gabriel as stated in the preceding chapter[38] and had she prophesied concerning Jesus as she is represented as doing,[39] she would certainly have had small cause to wonder. It is obvious that the author of Chapter 2 had no knowledge of Chapter 1, which was added later. In Chapter 2, we find a whole series of events which predicate a great future for Jesus; but at all of these, Mary is surprised and amazed: when Simeon waxes prophetic at the Temple circumcision, "his mother marvelled";[40] when, at the age of twelve, Jesus disputes with the doctors at Jerusalem, His parents are astonished and amazed and they reprove Him for causing them worry; and when He says, " ' Wist ye not that I must be about my Father's business?' . . . . they understood not . . . but his mother kept all these sayings in her heart."[41]

At the circumcision of Jesus, we find Simeon and Anna "waiting for the consolation of Israel."[42] The Christ *they* expected was not a temporal ruler, nor a military leader, but one who would offer redemption through moral regeneration; "this child is set for the fall and rising again of many in Israel; and for a sign which shall be spoken against,"[43] all of which reminds us of the Teacher of Righteousness. These passages seem actuated by Essene philosophy.

9. *The Second Version of Luke.* Let us now examine Luke, chapter 1, which is its final version. In this we find that John, by whom Israel would at last "be saved from our enemies,"[44] looms almost as large as Jesus Himself; and, oddly enough, the author of this false prophecy was at once a fanatical Judaizer, a social revolutionary, and a believer in the pagan doctrine of the Virgin Birth, which shows that this interpolation occurred much later than chapter 2; it must have been added in the second century, and was the work of a Hellenized Jewish sectarian. That there were two Ebionite sects, one of which accepted the Virgin Birth, we learn from Origen;[45] and that another existed, even as late as the fifth century, known as the Nazarenes or the Minei, holding the same tenet, we learn from Jerome.[46] In Luke 1, the Virgin Birth is not an interpolation, but an integral portion of a second-century Christology which is set forth in the entire chapter. The genealogy in Luke 3, which made Jesus a descendant of David, was the first interpolation; the second chapter, which previews the Messianic greatness of Jesus but makes no claim to divinity, was the second; Luke 1, which contains the annunciations concerning John and Jesus and which makes a god of the latter, was the last.

Beginning with Luke 1:5, we are told of the annunciations by Gabriel to Zecharias in his old age; next, of the parallel announcement to Mary of her virginal motherhood.[47] Mary travels then some ninety miles, presumably alone, from Nazareth to Bethlehem to visit with her cousins. When she arrives at their house, Elizabeth cries out: "Blessed art thou . . . And whence is this . . . that the mother of my Lord should come to me?"[48] This, of course, expresses a highly developed theology unknown in the Synoptics. And now let us note the kind of Messiah envisioned: "the Lord God shall give unto him the throne of his father David: And he shall reign over the house of Jacob for ever."[49]

In other words, Jesus was to have become the perpetual earthly ruler of the Jews. And He would give mercy to those who fear Him; scatter the proud; put down the mighty from their seats; exalt those of low degree; and send the rich empty away.[50] In short, He would accomplish a social revolution, according to the ideals of the ancient prophets of Yahweh.

And so we see that, according to Luke, Mary made two hazardous and entirely unnecessary journeys to Judea during her pregnancy, once alone.

10. *The Second Version of Matthew*. At the conclusion of Matthew's genealogy, we find a passage announcing the Virgin Birth. That this is a later interpolation is obvious from the fact that the next chapter relates an entirely different version of the same event more in accordance with the primitive concepts of Luke 2. Matthew 1:18-25 was added by a Greek or by a Hellenized Jew early in the second century.

When Matt. 1:23 used Isaiah 7:14 as a prophecy of the Virgin Birth, a maelstrom of controversy was unleashed. It soon became necessary for the orthodox to defend themselves against Ebionite and Gnostic opponents. Analysis of Isaiah 7:1-25 and 8:1-4 reveals that this passage refers to a Jewish Messiah-king who was expected soon after 721 B.C. But the interpolator of Matt. 1:18-25 found the word *virgin* in Isaiah, and pounced upon it like a hawk.

That Isaiah 7:14 could have no reference to Jesus is obvious from *ib*. 8:4, in which it is stated that while the child is yet an infant, the riches of Damascus and Samaria shall be carried away by the king of Assyria: events which actually happened in 742 and 721. To evade these facts, Justin Martyr declared that Isaiah "foretold that the power of the evil demon that dwelt in Damascus should be overcome by Christ . . . For the Magi, who were held in bondage for the commission of all evil deeds through the power of that demon, by coming to worship Christ, show that they have revolted from that dominion which . . . the Scripture has showed us to reside in Damascus."[51]

11. *What Happened?* What actually happened is obvious enough: at an early date, Judaizers interpolated passages designed to make Jesus the Messiah who would establish a Jewish empire at His Parousia; but then, about 115-125, since it had become impossible to remove these interpolations, certain Hellenizers simply superimposed Matt. 1:18-25 and Luke 1 upon them, which provided Jesus with a Virgin Birth and made of Him a savior generically similar to Dionysus and therefore acceptable in the pagan world.

CHAPTER VI

REVELATION

A. GENERAL CHARACTERISTICS

1. *Jewish-Zoroastrian.* Like Daniel, Revelation is intensely Judaistic, but it also reflects the Persian influence; it rejects Old Testament ideology; it reflects little knowledge of the Gospel Jesus; it harbors no toleration for Gentile Christianity; and its seven spirits are the Zoroastrian Amesha-Spentas. It is an expression of Jewish Gnostic Christianity, which was actuated by the bitterest hostility, not only toward its Hellenic counterpart, but also toward traditional Judaism. The Jesus of Revelation was a human being of the line of David; but the supernatural Christ who was temporarily conjoined with Him was simply the Word, the Power, the Wisdom of the Supreme God. Whoever the author of Revelation may have been, his Christology was Cerinthian (see IV:XI A); and it is not hard to understand why so many of the Fathers rejected the document. It is often confusing because the prophecy turns back upon itself and the metaphors are often inconsistent.

2. *Why Rome Is Denounced.* Who is the Antichrist of Revelation? The intensely Jewish nature of the book gives us the necessary clue. The writer was not concerned over the persecution of Gentile Christians by Nero: what aroused in him such frenetic wrath was the Roman attack upon Judaea, supplemented by popular and bloody assaults upon the Jewish communities in cities throughout the Middle East, which occurred simultaneously. Antichrist is Vespasian.

3. *A Pressing Urgency.* Throughout, we are aware of

a pressing urgency, for the Parousia is regarded as very, very near: "the time is at hand"; "surely, I come quickly."[1] And we are told specifically that those "which pierced him"[1] shall also see Him return. The book presents a panorama of events which were to be completed within forty-two months, or 1260 days; and these were believed to be the fulfillment of Daniel, whose "abomination that maketh desolate"[2] had been re-prophesied in Mark.[3]

4. *Addressed to Jews.* The vision of things shortly to be[4] is addressed to the Jews of the seven Asian churches, which had repudiated Paul. As in Daniel,[5] the Messiah appears "Like unto the Son of man, clothed with a garment down to the foot . . . His head and His hairs were white like wool, as white as snow; and his eyes were as a flame of fire."[6]

5. *The Pauline Blasphemy.* The first three chapters constitute the message of Christ to the seven churches. He is deeply outraged by "the blasphemy of them which say they are Jews, but are not, but are of the synagogue of Satan."[7] These and similar denunciations point to Paul and his school, against whom the Jewish Christians were embittered to a degree which passes all comprehension.

6. *Author in Heaven.* Chapter 4 begins with an invitation to the apocalyptist to come up to heaven to see the "things which must be hereafter." God, resembling a vision out of Daniel or Ezekiel,[8] sits on his throne, about which stand the four beasts and the twenty-four elders. Since seven is a mystical Zoroastrian number, God holds in His hand a book sealed with seven seals. No one could open the book except "the Lion of the tribe of Juda, the Root of David," who was "a Lamb as it had been slain."[9] We are told that the Jewish saints will reign on earth with their Christ-Messiah over the Gentiles at the institution of the Messianic kingdom; and every saint is to be a priest-king.[10] As in Daniel, "ten thousand times ten thousand" angels surround the throne.[11]

B. THE VISION

1. *The Plagues Begin.* In the scene which inaugurates the final tribulation, the Lamb opens six seals, each

unloosing its ferocious plague, symbolic of Jewish hatred against the Gentiles. Meantime, the martyred saints at the throne of God cry for vengeance.[12]

2. *The Celibate and Other Saints.* The Holiest servants of God, who total 144,000,[13] twelve thousand from each tribe of Israel, are now sealed in their foreheads, as in Ezekiel.[14] As soon as this is done, the apocalyptist "beheld, and lo, a great multitude, which no man could number out of all nations, and kindreds, and people, and tongues, stood before the throne, and before the Lamb, clothed with white robes, and palms in their hands."[15] Many have thought that these must be the Gentiles; but the writer is careful to state that these are "out of," not members of, all "nations, kindreds, and people." This text is parallel to 5:7-10, where we read of the "elders," the great men of Israel, who are "redeemed . . . by thy blood out of every kindred, and tongue, and people, and nation," and who "as kings and priests . . . shall reign in the earth." The "great multitude" are simply the secondary Jewish saints, those not beatified by celibacy, gathered out of the *Diaspora*. There are no Gentiles in this kingdom, except those proselytes who have first become Jews by embracing the Mosaic Law, including circumcision.

3. *The End of Time.* At last the seventh seal is broken, and seven angels appear; as six of these sound their trumpets, terrible woes are unloosed. A mighty angel now declares that the end of Time is approaching, as indicated by the current siege of Jerusalem: "the holy city shall they tread under foot for forty and two months."[16] (The siege lasted eight months.) Revelation must, therefore, have been composed between January and September, 70, which was the period of the siege, because the Roman army was encamped before Jerusalem while this passage was written. Otherwise, such a grotesque error concerning its duration could not have been committed; nor would the destruction of the city and the Temple have been left unrecorded. But, since the author was persuaded that Daniel 12:11 was now in process of fulfillment, he could only re-prophesy a desecration of forty-two months, as occurred under Antiochus Epiphanes.

4. *The Messianic Empire and Judgment.* At this point, the vision passes abruptly from history to prophecy. The seventh angel sounds his trumpet and great voices in heaven are heard, saying, "The kingdoms of this world are become the kingdoms of our Lord, and of his Christ; and he shall reign for ever and ever."[17] In short, all the Gentile kingdoms were shortly to be incorporated into one great empire in which the Messiah-Christ and His Jewish priest-saints would rule forever. After this, the Great Judgment was due immediately, at which the still-living wicked would be condemned,[18] as in Daniel.[19]

5. *The Jewish Christ.* And now appears in heaven a woman clothed with the sun (the Christianized Jewish nation), with the moon under her feet (her earthly empire), and upon her head a crown of twelve stars (the twelve tribes);[20] and she, being with child (about to establish the Messianic kingdom) is opposed by the great red dragon with seven heads, ten horns, and seven crowns (Rome built upon seven hills, in league with ten co-operating kings, and having had seven emperors). The dragon "stood before the woman . . . to devour her child as soon as it was born."[21] The Roman armies in Judaea are attempting to destroy the new theocracy at its very inception. But she had already "brought forth a manchild, who was to rule all nations with a rod of iron and her child was caught up unto God, and to his throne. And the woman fled into the wilderness, where she hath a place prepared of God, that they should feed her a thousand two hundred and sixty days:"[22] which means simply that the Jewish nation had given birth to the Christ, who had been "caught up unto God" and was now sitting on His right hand. Just before Vespasian ringed Jerusalem, the Jewish Christians had fled to Pella, where, according to Revelation, they were to remain for 1260 days, at the end of which the Parousia was to occur. At His reappearance, Christ would rule all nations with a rod of iron, as the Jewish prophets had said of their Messiah a thousand times. These words must have been written during the siege, for the tense shifts, as if unconsciously, to the present in 12:6, where

we are told that the woman *hath* a place where she can remain.

6. *Satan on Earth*. Michael now casts Satan down to the earth where he stirs up the dragon, Rome, to persecute the saints; but "to the woman were given two wings . . . that she might fly into the wilderness . . . where she is nourished for a time, times, and half a time from the face of the serpent." [23] The serpent is the army currently besieging Jerusalem, for again the tense shifts: wings *were* given to the woman, but now she *is nourished*. The woman, of course, is the Jewish Christian Church which has taken refuge in the wilderness.

7. *Daniel and Revelation*. As we have noted, Revelation finds in Daniel a prophecy of the current situation, and predicts a Messiah as near at hand as that prophet had believed him to be two hundred and thirty-three years before.[24] The method used is that of the Essene *Commentary on Habakkuk*.

8. *Galba*. In 13:1 Rome is called a beast with seven heads and ten horns rising from the sea. The heads are emperors, and the horns are kings in league with Rome. One of the heads was wounded to death, but was healed, and all the world wondered. This was Galba, whose execution was ordered by Nero in the spring of 68, but who became emperor and was the seventh in succession.

9. *Vespasian the Antichrist*. "And I beheld another beast coming up out of the earth; and he had two horns like a lamb, and he spake as a dragon,"[25] i. e., an emperor. This fits Vespasian perfectly; for he began the siege of Jerusalem, had two sons, and was offered the imperial purple by the troops late in 69. Since the Christians fled to Pella in the autumn of that year, and since they were to remain there 1260 days, the Parousia was due early in 72.

We are told that the number of the beast is 666.[26] Since this spells out Neron in Hebrew letters, many have thought that the reference is to Nero, in spite of the fact that he had already been dead two years when this was written. In some copies, however, the number is

616, which simply spells Antichrist. The one in the mind of the author was Vespasian, who became emperor in December, 69, and who brought the fiercest Jewish hatred upon himself during his campaign in Galilee and by pressing the siege of Jerusalem under the generalship of his son.

10. *The Parousia.* At this point, the vision again passes abruptly from fact to fantasy. The apocalyptist sees the Lamb standing on Mt. Sion with His 144,000 primary saints "which were not defiled with women; for they are virgins."[27] An angel goes forth bringing the everlasting Gospel to all nations; a second follows who declares that Babylon (Rome) is now fallen (not destroyed); a third proclaims that any one who continues to worship the beast (the Roman emperor) "shall be tormented with fire and brimstone."[28]

And now, at long last, the Parousia supervenes: "And I looked, and behold a white cloud, and upon the cloud one sat like unto the Son of man."[29] Meanwhile, the final, dreadful plagues are unloosed by seven angels upon those who have taken the mark of the beast (i. e., all who have accepted Gentile Christianity or the rule of Rome). And just before the last vial is emptied, the dragon (Satan) causes the Gentile kings to make war against Sion at Armageddon.

11. *The Roman Emperors.* With the seventh vial, a great voice cries, "It is done."[30] One of the angels tells the apocalyptist that he will see the judgment "of the great whore . . . with whom the kings of the earth have committed fornication."[31] Again the metaphor changes[32] and Rome becomes a woman sitting upon a scarlet-colored beast, full of blasphemy, having seven heads and ten horns, and "drunken with the blood of the saints."[33]

The ensuing vision is in part historical, in part prophetic: the period 68-69 is presented as if it were in the future. We are told that the seven heads are the seven mountains on which the woman sits; that she has had seven kings, of which five are fallen, one *now* is, that is the sixth, or Nero, and the seventh, Galba, is not yet come, "and when he cometh he must continu a short space."[34] And the eighth beast, Vespasian, was, and is not, and yet is: that is, he was proclaimed emperor by his troops in Judaea and in Alexandria in July, 69; his claim to the throne was contested by Otho and Vitellius; but he finally came to power in December, 69 ". . , he is the eighth, and is of the seven, and goeth into perdition."[35] He is to be the last ruler of Rome; he is the man of sin, the Antichrist who will be destroyed by the Jewish Christ.

We are told that the sixth king, Nero, who died in June, 68, now *is*. But the reign of Galba, which began immediately and ended in January, 69, is clearly delineated, as is the accession of Vespasian. We know furthermore that the siege of Jerusalem began late in January and ended on September 8, 70. Revelation was, therefore, written during this period. The author knew of the accession of Vespasian, but not of the termination of the siege of Jerusalem. In order to give himself two years of history to depict as prophecy, the writer pretended that Nero was still living.

12. *Vespasian Defeated*. We are told that the ten horns shall hold "power as kings one hour with the beast."[36] And "These shall make war with the Lamb, and the Lamb shall overcome them: for he is the Lord of Lords, and King of Kings."[37] The Christ-Messiah with his Jewish saints having thus defeated the allied heathen powers under Vespasian at Armageddon "the ten horns which thou sawest upon the beast, these shall hate the whore, and shall make her desolate and naked, and shall eat her flesh, and burn her with fire."[38] In other words, the ten Gentile kings will turn at last against Rome and lay her waste.

The eighteenth chapter calls upon the Jews to come out of Babylon (Rome),[39] in order to avoid her doom, and then describes her impending destruction, and the rejoicing of the Jewish saints at the divine vengeance upon that Mother of Harlots and Abominations.[40]

13. *The Messianic Reign Instituted*. Now that God has at last "judged the great whore,"[41] and "the marriage of the Lamb is come,"[42] the Messianic kingdom supervenes. The Messiah-Christ, like the Soshans, rides forth upon his

white horse: "And out of his mouth goeth a sharp sword, that with it he should smite the nations: and he shall rule them with a rod of iron . . . And he hath on his vesture and on his thigh a name written, KING OF KINGS, AND LORD OF LORDS."[43] The slaughter of kings, captains, horses, and mighty men which is to follow would provide a feast of unparalleled proportions for all the vultures and jackals of the earth.[44]

Thus, the Christ-Messiah establishes at last the imperial dictatorship of the Jews over the Gentile nations.

14. *Paul and Vespasian Thrown into Hell.* But the destruction of Israel's enemies will not yet quite have been accomplished, for the beast is still to be capable of one more battle. Rome together with her Gentile allies are to make war once more upon Christ; but the beast and the false prophet, just as in the *Bundahis*, were to be taken captive, and both "cast alive into a lake of fire burning with brimstone,"[45] which is the final disposition of these miscreants. The beast could have been no one but Vespasian, for he was the Roman emperor from 69 to 79. And we would suggest that Paul was the false prophet "that wrought miracles . . . with which he deceived them that had received the mark of the beast," [46] that is, had become Christians without first becoming Jews. The Jewish Christians hated Paul with a ferocity exceeding even that which they felt for the Romans.

15. *The Chiliastic Kingdom.* But before the kingdom of the saints could be established, "the dragon, that old serpent, which is the devil, and Satan,"[47] had to be bound and cast into the bottomless pit for a thousand years. All this, of course, is simply a re-creation of Zoroastrian eschatology; this was the millennial, that is, the chiliastic kingdom of the saints, to be established on earth, and with its capital at Jerusalem, to endure from 72 to 1072.

16. *Devil Loosed and Defeated.* At the close of this period, Satan, like Azi-Dahak, would be unloosed to deceive all nations, so that they would make war once more upon the saints; but when their armies encompass at last the beloved city, God would send down His fire to destroy them in an instant.[48] Satan is finally cast into the lake of

brimstone, where, together with the beast and the false prophet, he "shall be tormented day and night forever and ever."[49]

17. *Last Judgment.* Christ sits upon His great white throne,[50] and heaven and earth melt away.[51] The second resurrection marshals all those who have died, before Him; the books are opened, each is judged according to his works, and those not "written in the book of life are cast into the lake of fire." [52]

18. *The New Jerusalem.* As in Zoroastrianism, heaven and earth are reconstituted; and the new Jerusalem comes "down from God out of heaven."[53] This holy city, a cube fifteen hundred miles four-square, with ramparts two hundred and sixteen feet high, has twelve gates, each of precious stones and each named after one of the tribes of Israel; it has twelve foundations, named after the apostles; and it is of pure gold, incredibly opulent.

C. A ZOROASTRIAN-JEWISH CONCEPT

Thus among the Jewish Christians Jesus became the Zoroastrian Saoshyant. He was also the King of Kings, the Davidic ruler, the Star of Jacob,[54] the Christ who would conquer the Gentiles and rule them with a rod of iron. To the very end, the Jewish Christians failed to comprehend or to accept one solitary element from the Gospel which did not come directly from Zoroastrianized Judaism.

Revelation was the swan-song of Militant Jewish Christianity. When Jerusalem was destroyed, when Rome waxed greater and more powerful, when the False Prophet gained more and more followers, when the book itself was proved totally false within two years, when it became evident that the Jewish Messiah-Christ would not come, the Hebrew Christians lost their virility and their cult faded under the combined assault of orthodox Judaism and of Gentile Christianity.

CHAPTER VII

CHRISTIAN ESCHATOLOGY

A. MODERN MANIFESTATIONS

1. *Archbishop Ussher.* The eminent Archbishop Ussher predicted the exact day and hour in 1644 when the Parousia would occur; a prediction, by the way, which the author ignored during the twelve years he outlived the expected apocalyptic year.

2. *The Southern Baptists.* One recent Sunday, this writer heard a Southern Baptist delivering a fiery radio discourse, according to which Christ is due in or about 1980.

3. *The Millerites.* Intense and widespread excitement was created in Massachusetts beginning in 1831 by William Miller, a converted deist, who produced a variety of mathematical demonstrations to prove that the Parousia would occur in 1843. His disciples sold their property so that they might be pure in the sight of the Lord. On the night the great event was to occur, thousands donned ascension robes and trooped forth from Boston to meet their Redeemer. When nothing happened Prophet Miller discovered that he had made a slight miscalculation, but that Christ would certainly arrive on October 22, 1844. And even though the second error was no less than the first, his teachings serve as the basis for a numerous denomination known as the Adventists, now split into some six or seven divisions.

4. *The Mormons.* Mormonism was another cult built on the expectation of an imminent Parousia, at which the Latter-Day Saints would rule the world with Christ as their king.

5. *Edward Irving.* In 1826, Edward Irving announced

that the Parousia would occur in 1864; and on the basis of this prediction, the English Catholic Apostolic Church developed.

6. *Jehovah's Witnesses.* Founded by Charles Taze Russell in 1881, and since reorganized at least twice, this cult continues virile by preaching the imminent Parousia.

B. CHILIASM

1. *Definitions.* The Second Coming of Christ is known as the Parousia; the doctrine that He will establish an earthly kingdom to endure for a thousand years as chiliasm. There could be no millenarian kingdom without the Second Coming; but one could believe in the Parousia without being a chiliast.

2. *Confusing Contradictions.* Jesus emphasized His own imminent Parousia and an earthly kingdom of indeterminate duration; Paul taught an imminent Parousia, but rejected the Gospel Kingdom; Revelation taught an imminent chiliasm. With such contradictions in the New Testament itself, it is little wonder that a variety of doctrines sprang up in the Church; and this confusion became worse confounded as all expectations failed, and new wine had to be poured into the bottles of old prophecy by each succeeding generation.

3. *Early Chiliasm.* We know that the Ebionites, Cerinthians, and other Hebrew Christians adapted the Judaic and Essene Messianic concept into a chiliastic kingdom, which was also embraced widely by early Gentile Christianity. There is a strong trace of it in the *Epistle of Barnabas* and in the first *Clement*. Jerome tells us that Papias, who flourished around 90-135, was a millenarian.[1] Justin Martyr says that although some pious Christians did not believe in the millenarian kingdom, he himself was certain of it.[2] Irenaeus declares his belief in an earthly kingdom of saints, in which all are to live in their physical bodies and enjoy every material blessing.[3]

4. *The Montanists.* From that churning cauldron of sects and schools emerged the shrill voice of the prophet Montanus, perhaps the most influential exponent of second

century chiliasm. He was a desexed priest of Cybele in Phrygia, converted to Christianity about the year 155. He read in the scriptures that Christ was soon to return; and yet around him he saw confessing Christians going unconcernedly about their business and pleasure, as if this world were to continue indefinitely. He and his two prophetesses, Priscilla and Maximilla, declared that the Holy Ghost, which had been conferred upon the disciples at the first Pentecost, had now been revealed in them as the Paraclete; and that, so incarnate, he spoke with a voice that must be obeyed on pain of everlasting damnation. The movement was a schism rather than a heresy, since it did not seek innovation in dogma; it sought to reestablish the now moribund principles, discipline, and aspirations of pristine Christianity. It arose immediately after the Marcionite heresy had compelled the Church to organize on an empire-wide basis. The claim of the Catholics to totalitarian universality was already unmistakable; and the compromises into which they were entering that they might ultimately take over the state were scandalous. The bishops aspired to power and authority and repudiated the chiliastic hope of the Apostolic Church.

Montanus probably predicted the exact day of the Parousia. However, since his prophecies proved no more effective than those of Daniel, Revelation, or Jesus Himself, no records of these have been preserved. But we know that by 190 the churches everywhere were infested with these fanatics and that Montanus urged them to assemble at Pepuza in Phrygia, which he declared to be the "wilderness" of Revelation 16:6 and 14, there to await the advent of Christ, which, had he read his authority rationally, he would have known to be already at least a century overdue.

Violent opposition soon developed against Montanism, not only because it threatened to reduce the Church into a sect, but also because its doctrine of permanent revelation threatened the newly established episcopal authority. About 200, Bishop Serapion of Antioch demonstrated elaborately the untenability of Montanist teachings. The eradication of these, however, proved a slow and difficult process. By 230, the Church refused to recognize baptism by Montanists, and soon thereafter they were excluded from the communion. Under Constantine, severe edicts were issued against them, especially in Phrygia, where they were most numerous. Thereupon, the cult became a tenacious underground movement. In 550, Bishop John of Ephesus had the remains of Montanus and his two prophetesses exhumed and desecrated.

We need not be surprised, then, that the Church Fathers condemned the Montanists in the most violent terms. A passage in Hippolytus[4] is typical; and we find that Cyril of Jerusalem, cir. 375, repeated the same charges against the Montanists, which were those commonly made against all Christians at an earlier date: namely, that they were in the habit of "cutting the throats of wretched little children, and chopping them up into unholy food, for the purpose of their so-called mysteries."[5]

From the two thousand pages of Tertulian, 160-230, we derive our most reliable information concerning the movement, which declared about 200 that many people in Judaea had seen "the divinely-built city of Jerusalem 'let down from heaven'" and "suspended in the sky every morning for forty days . . . We may say that this city has been provided by God for receiving the saints on their resurrection," which was thought to be imminent. Then would follow the chiliastic kingdom, the second resurrection, the last judgment, and the investiture of the saints with celestial bodies.[6] Thus Tertullian engrafted Pauline metaphysics upon Jewish chiliasm. Montanism, however, became obsolete when, by the inexorable march of time, its prophecies proved without foundation.

5. *Chiliasm in Egypt*. Although the Eastern Church, involved as it was in a thousand credal disputes, showed less interest than the western in the chiliastic kingdom, there was at least one writer, Nepas, an Egyptian bishop, who made a serious attempt about the year 200 to revive the doctrines of Revelation, of which no allegorical interpretation was to be tolerated. We learn of this man from Dionysius, Bishop of Alexandria from 247 to 265,[7] who declares that some of the brethren produced a book by one Nepas which insisted "that there will be a temporal

reign of Christ upon the earth." Debate on the issue had been so intense "that schisms and apostasies took place in whole churches." Dionysius therefore called for a complete investigation of the subject. Since Revelation was extremely confusing and was by some attributed to the early heretic Cerinthus, Dionysius could only "suspect that there is some deeper sense underlying the words."

6. *Among the Greeks.* Since the Greeks had no indigenous tradition of a divinely instituted kingdom of saints, they rejected the Judaic-Zoroastrian concepts of Revelation. Following the lead of Paul and the Fourth Gospel, Origen declared: "Certain persons" believe that "after the resurrection" they will possess "such bodily structures as may never be without the power of eating and drinking . . . not following the opinion of the Apostle Paul regarding the resurrection of the spiritual body. And consequently they say, that . . . . there will be marriages, and the begetting of children, imagining to themselves that the earthly city of Jerusalem is to be rebuilt, its foundations laid in precious stones . . . Moreover, they think that the natives of other countries are to be given them as the ministers of their pleasures, whom they are to employ either as tillers of the field or builders of walls."[8]

7. *Hippolytus and Cyprian.* For the most part, it remained for the simple Latins to revive the aspirations of the Jewish Christians. Hippolytus advanced the theory about 225 that Christ was born in the year of the world 5500 and that the Second Coming would occur in the year 6000.[9] Cyprian was convinced that "the world is now dying," and that the end would come very soon, "when the Lord shall . . . set on fire our persecutors with a perpetual fire."[10]

8. *Lactantius.* Curiously enough, the elegant Lactantius embraced without reserve the chiliastic eschatology. By method all his own, he engrafted Christian millenarianism upon the pagan doctrine of the Golden Age; and he developed a political and economic philosophy which anticipated Rousseau's *Contrat Social.* Only, instead of the age of nature, man had once enjoyed a Golden Age during the reign of Saturn, which was "not to be regarded as

poetic fiction," for then "there were neither dissensions, nor enmities nor wars . . . since the storehouses of the good lay open to all . . But . . Jove . . . introduced among men hatred . . . so that they became poisonous as serpents, and rapacious as wolves . . . they even seized the property of others, drawing everything to their private gain. . . They also, under the name of justice, passed most unequal and unjust laws, by which they might defend their plunder and avarice against the force of the multitude."[11]

However, God decided not to leave the human race forever in this pitiful condition,[12] which Lactantius considered inseparable from the institution of private property; He therefore sent His only Son to redeem those who would live in communal brotherhood. The law of God inscribed in every human heart, when obeyed, makes of each man a merciful and compassionate brother of every human being; it makes him "bountiful to the blind, the feeble, the lame, the destitute, who must die unless we bestow our bounty upon them."[13] The end of the age approaches; this will be "the six thousandth year," in which "all wickedness must be abolished from the earth, and righteousness reign for a thousand years."[14] Lactantius developed an elaborate interpretation of Revelation:[15] Antichrist must first appear and perish, then Christ will be revealed, the righteous dead will be resurrected with renewed and glorified bodies, and the chiliastic millennium inaugurated,[16] in which the unrighteous shall be "subjected to perpetual slavery" under the saints.[17] All wickedness, violence, and bloodshed will cease. The saints living at the time of the Parousia "shall not die, but during those thousand years shall produce an infinite multitude, and their offspring shall be holy."

And when would all this come to pass? "All expectations," declared Lactantius, "do not exceed two hundred years."[18] Thus Christ was due in the year of the world 6000, which would be 520 A.D., a calculation which differed only slightly from that of Irenaeus. He would then establish His kingdom and rule with His saints for a thousand years. At the end of the seventh millennium, the Devil would be unchained, and make war against the saints;

but he would be defeated and driven back for the last time to his pit, precisely as in the *Bundahis* and in Revelation.[19]

9. *Constantius as Antichrist.* The conviction that Christ's second appearance was imminent and that His precursor Antichrist was already loose in the world was common during the fourth and fifth centuries, as the light of Greek culture flickered and died. Almost anyone whom the writer hated or abhorred with particular venom could qualify as Antichrist. It is probable that several hundred human menaces have been definitely identified with this fearful personage.

However, there was one candidate who surpassed all others for this dubious honor in the fourth century: Constantius, who died in 361. He was the most ardent of the Arian emperors, and he did not hesitate to use force against the Homoousians, who hated him with a perfect hatred; and they declared in chorus with Athanasius[20] that he was the Antichrist.

Cyril of Jerusalem delivered his *Catechetical Lectures* about 351-352. One of these declares that since the Gospel had now been preached to all nations, the end must be very near; [21] that the strife over Arianism must be the final tribulation; [22] and that Antichrist (Constantius), who had already seized the total Roman power, would rule for a period of three and a half years,[23] which would be the abomination of desolation, after which Christ would reappear to destroy him and establish the chiliastic kingdom, of which the sign and herald would be a luminous cross in the sky.[24] Sozomen, IV:v, states that such a sign, stretching from Golgotha to Mt. Olivet, was said to have been seen by many at Jerusalem in 350. Constantius had become sole emperor in 351; and since, according to Daniel and Revelation, Antichrist would rule for forty-two months, the Parousia and the destruction of Constantius by the Messiah must occur in 354 or 355. Constantius, however, lived until 361, when he died on a campaign against Julian the Apostate, who promptly became the new Antichrist.

About 353, Hilary of Poitiers, one of that multitude of monks who lived in constant expectation of world's end, being also a defender of the Nicene Creed, shared the general opinion concerning the Arian emperor. He declares: "Let us look for Christ's coming, for Antichrist is already in power."²⁵ This, of course, was Constantius.

10. *Sulpitius Severus.* Sulpitius Severus, writing early in the fifth century, makes St. Martin declare that the end of the world was then only a few years away; and the saint elaborates that the Antichrist, who was then already born, would set up his capital in Jerusalem, rebuild the Jewish temple there, and establish an Israeli empire, under which all people would be forced to accept the Mosaic Law and submit to circumcision.²⁶ All this was due to happen about 425.

11. *Gregory the Great.* Pope Gregory in 600 was convinced that the tribulations of his day must be the apocalyptic woes: "all the things of this world . . . we see already ruined. Cities are overthrown, camps uprooted, churches destroyed; and no tiller of the ground inhabits our land . . . View, therefore, with anxious hearts the approaching day of the eternal judge." ²⁷

The whole land was being ravaged by the Arian Lombards; the Manichaeans, Nestorians, and Montanists were eating at the vitals of the Church; and in Africa the Donatist wolves were still rending away the sheep from the fold.²⁸ Further melancholy proof of the end was evident in the East, for in Constantinople had appeared indubitably the precursor of Antichrist himself in the person of Bishop John, since he was attempting to make himself the universal head of the Catholic Church! ²⁹

C. ST. AUGUSTINE

1. *Establishes Church Doctrine to Year 1000.* It was Augustine, however, who established what was to become Church doctrine: the entire history of the world will comprise six thousand years, after which will come the Sabbath of the saints. Christ came at the end of five thousand years, and the publication of His Gospel was the inauguration of the millennial kingdom. In the year 1000, which will be the year 6000 of the world, this dispensation will come to its end, Christ will appear in the heavens, the

dead will be resurrected, judgment will take place, heaven and earth will pass away, and eternity will begin.[30]

2. *Ridicules the Chiliasts.* Augustine ridicules, first, those pagans who had predicted that Christianity would continue for only 365 years; and, next, such Church Fathers as Hippolytus and Lactantius, who thought that the Parousia would occur about 400 or 500 and who believed that there would be an earthly kingdom of saints replete with material delights, which was "fit for none but carnal men to believe." [31]

3. *Eternity Already Begun.* Augustine declared that the first thousand years of Christianity constituted not only the millennial kingdom, but was also the beginning of eternity.[32] And he continued: "Christ reigns with his saints the same thousand years . . . all the time from His first coming . . . So that the Church now on earth is both the kingdom of Christ, and the kingdom of heaven." [33] And so, through some fantastic psychosis, Augustine translated that fourth-century madhouse and that fifth-century mansion of murder into the Kingdom of God!

4. *World-End in Year 1000.* Thus the world, now under the control of the saints and the Catholic Church, shall continue until a millennium shall have passed following the publication of the Gospel; then comes World's End and Judgment.[34] Since Revelation could neither be rejected, nor accepted as written, this new pattern of eschatology became the official doctrine of the Church; and the Catholic world focused its sight on the year of the Lord, 1000.

5. *The Doom that Failed.* And so for six hundred years the world awaited Doomsday. On the first night of the second millennium, millions kept the wake, fully persuaded that at the stroke of midnight a great light would suddenly illumine the sky, and Christ would appear, surrounded by myriads of angels, to call His own, and then to judge the quick and the dead. For years, thousands had been selling their possessions or had conveyed their land, slaves, and serfs to the less believing but more practical prelates of the Church, which, as a result, became the wealthiest landowner and exploiter in the world.

D. HELL AND PURGATORY

1. *No Purgatory in Christian Scriptures.* In Brahmanic and Pythagorean eschatology, hell itself was actually a kind of purgatory, since it was a place in which perhaps a majority of all people underwent repeated refinement and punishment. Original Christianity, however, based upon Essene concepts, had nothing of this kind: hell was permanent, and there was no other place for the wicked.

2. *Concept of Hell.* The *Apocalypse of Peter*, written about 125, was one of the most popular ancient apocryphal books. The imagination of the early saints dwelt a great deal upon the vividly physical aspects of heaven, which is described as a place of infinite beauty and splendor. "This is the place of your leaders (or high priests), the righteous men," Peter is told. But their thoughts were even more preoccupied with the fate of their enemies and opponents whom they consigned without exception or mercy to infinite and everlasting torture. And so it was that Peter witnessed an endless catalogue of writhing sinners in this Brahmanic hell, each suffering in a manner appropriate to his guilt.[35]

3. *The New Ethics.* We see in the *Apocalypse of Peter* a system of ethics quite different from that of Mathew 25; for now there are many other sins far more heinous than selfish individualism. Hell is now full of harlots, adulterers, murderers, perjurers, scoffers, blasphemers, and, worst of all, those who persecute the saints.

4. *Beginnings of Purgatory.* The evolving Christian eschatology of the third and fourth centuries is thus set forth by Hippolytus: "Hades is a place . . . beneath the earth . . . destined to be as it were a guardhouse for souls, at which the angels are stationed as guards, distributing according to each one's deeds the temporary punishments for (different) characters. And in this locality there is a certain place set apart by itself, a lake of unquenchable fire. . . . And the unrighteous . . . shall be sentenced to his endless punishment. But the righteous shall obtain the incorruptible and unfading kingdom, who indeed are at

present detained in Hades, but not in the same place with the unrighteous." [36]

This doctrine of purgatory, however, progressed slowly among the Catholics although it had long been established in older religions and was an outstanding feature of Manichaeism from the beginning. Clement of Alexandria had spoken of a purifying fire in this world,[37] which Origen [38] believed continued beyond the grave. Tertullian had declared that "no one will hesitate to believe that the soul undergoes in Hades some compensatory discipline." [39] Hilary of Poitiers seems to have absorbed some Valentinian or Manichaean ideology and supposed that there were three kinds of souls: the good, the bad, and those in whom these qualities are intermixed and who, therefore, must undergo some purification between death and resurrection.

5. *Augustine and Gregory.* Augustine himself thought it not incredible that some purificatory fire might be needed to cleanse souls from unpurged sins before the Last Judgment,[40] and that, since "few are so happy as to pass their youth without taint of some damnable sin," [41] they must undergo more purification than is possible in this life. This is what Augustine and his predecessors wrote concerning purgatory; but it was the seed from which so rank a growth was to luxuriate that within less than two centuries Gregory the Great made the doctrine of purgatory a Catholic dogma in 604.

6. *Thomas Aquinas.* Medieval theologians, such as Thomas Aquinas, used the apocryphal *II Maccabees*,[42] in which Judas offers sacrifices for those who have fallen in battle, as authority for the doctrine. (This book was written about 60-50 B. C. by a Pharisee under the influence of Zoroastrianism, the *Hamestagna* of which eventually became the Catholic purgatory.) To shorten the period of eschatological purification became one of the great Catholic objectives. Candles were burned, prayers were said, masses were recited; and a large fraction of the earnings of entire nations was channeled into the coffers of the hierarchy to reduce the duration of purgatorial refinement. This, incidentally, was precisely the element in the Or

phic-Pythagorean mystery which so outraged the moral sensibilities of Plato and which made him declare that any religion which practiced any such charlatanry was guilty of the most revolting sacrilege.

CHAPTER VIII

THE FOURTH GOSPEL

A. THE HELLENIZATION OF CHRISTIANITY

1. *The Pre-Existing Christ.* Even a cursory glance at the Fourth Gospel reveals that this differs so widely from the Synoptics that it seems to proclaim a different religion, which, in fact, it does, since it is far more Gnostic than Essene and was written by a Greek or a Hellenized Jew of the Alexandrian school who flourished during the first half of the second century. The book consists primarily of theological discourses, in which the historical Jesus is obscured and lost. Jerome declares that the document was written "at the request of the bishops of Asia, against Cerinthus and other heretics and especially against the then growing dogma of the Ebionites, who assert that Christ did not exist before Mary." [1] The chief issue, then, in the first half of the second century was whether Christ came into being at His birth or at His baptism or whether He was a pre-existing divinity. The latter doctrine had been proclaimed by Paul, but denied by all Jewish factions.

2. *The Changed Conditions.* By 120-140, the hope of an imminent Parousia had well nigh vanished. The ethics and economics laid down in the early Gospels had proved impractical. People of means and position who believed in marriage, family responsibility, and private property had begun to join the Church. The doctrine that Christ would establish a kingdom in Palestine was repugnant to the Gentiles, especially if Jews were to enjoy primacy therein. The Greeks were indifferent to disputations concerning the Mosaic Law, and such verbiage must therefore be relegated to limbo.

3. *The Altered Gospel.* Thus there was a crying need for a new Gospel "written that ye might believe that Jesus is the Christ, the Son of God." [2] And, as Jerome points out, it was composed to prove that Jesus was the eternal Word; but it repudiated also the apparitional Christology of the Cerdonites, as well as the chiliasm of both Jewish sects.

B. THE NEW SYSTEM

1. *The Logos Doctrine.* The Fourth Gospel begins with the celebrated Logos doctrine, which derives from Greek philosophical sources and which makes Christ-Jesus an incarnate supernatural principle, the Word which "was made flesh and dwelt among us." Although the author takes care to show that this Christ is not equal, but subservient to, the Father, He is also at infinite pains to elevate Him above the Synoptic concept. He has now become the "only-begotten Son of God," [3] who declares: "I am the light of the world;" [4] "I proceeded forth and came from God;" [5] "Before Abraham was, I am;" [6] "I and my Father are one;" [7] "He that hath seen me hath seen the Father;" [8] "all things that the Father hath are mine." [9] And when we note in addition that the Comforter or the Holy Ghost also has undergone a decisive expansion, we realize that the doctrine of the Trinity is already present in rudimentary form.

2. *The Judaic Christ Rejected.* The Virgin Birth as well as the Synoptic genealogies are summarily rejected in John. Joseph was the father of Jesus; and His mother is distinctly portrayed.[10] He was neither born in Bethlehem nor of the seed of David, for the Greeks wanted no Judaizing Messiah.[11] In the Fourth Gospel as in Revelation Jesus is simply a human being into whom, at His baptism, the Word of God entered as an immanent power and this made Him the Christ. This was the Cerinthian-Gnostic concept, which, however, differed sharply from the purely apparitional theory of the Marcionites and the Manichees.

3. *Necessity of Faith.* Since the Church was created through the preaching of an imminent, apocalyptic world-

end, its organization and communicants now hung suspended, as it were, in midair. John therefore preached the paramount necessity for faith; "He that believeth on the Son hath everlasting life." [12] Jesus tells His disciples pointedly that to believe without seeing is the greatest blessedness.[13] Clearly, the Fourth Gospel was written to establish the complete acceptance of the pre-existing Christ as an historical reality who died for our sins, rose from the dead, and has power to confer everlasting life in heaven.

4. *New Concept of Family.* In John, we find Jesus on the best of terms with His mother and brethren: they are at the Wedding in Cana and His mother tells the servants to do whatever He commands.[14] She and His brothers are disciples who follow Him on His journeys.[15] She and an aunt are at the foot of the cross when He is crucified,[16] and He tells the disciple whom He loves to adopt His mother. It is evident that the Synoptic repudiation of mother and family was most embarrasing to the Greek Christians.

An altered concept of Heaven, the eucharist, the resurrection, and predestination is almost all that the Fourth Gospel salvages from the Synoptics.

5. *The Eucharist.* In John there is no Last Supper; but the eucharistic doctrine is developed and heavily emphasized in an early chapter in order to emancipate it entirely from the Jewish Passover.

6. *Eschatology.* An elaborate doctrine of the resurrection is repeated often.[17] Everything is totally different from the Synoptics, or Revelation. There is no Last Judgment; at death, the unredeemed simply pass into nothingness, and the Elect of Christ to life eternal in the heavenly mansions. John knows nothing of hell or torture after death, concepts emphasized only in the Jewish-Christian documents. In fact, we read categorically: "He that believeth in the Son hath everlasting life: and he that believeth not the Son shall not see life," [18] that is, he shall undergo annihilation.

The apocalypse and the Parousia have also vanished. In their place, we are told that "In my Father's house are many mansions: if it were not so, I would have told you.

I go to prepare a place for you. And if I go ... I will come again and receive you unto myself." [19] Those mansions and this vague return became the core of the new Christianity: no longer were the brethren to keep nightly vigil awaiting the return of the Christ-Messiah. Instead, life was to go on as usual under the Roman Empire; and, in due course, the saints would be translated to the celestial kingdom. Jesus declares explicitly: "My kingdom is not of this world," [20] which, of course, is a categorical repudiation of the Kingdom of God in Matthew and the chiliasm of Revelation.

7. *Ethics.* In place of the many celibate-communist precepts of the Synoptics, John has only the one "new commandment . . . that ye love one another," [21] which was far more acceptable to Greek communicants who believed in private property and lived in monogamic families.

C. REVISING THE SYNOPTICS

1. *Omissions and Additions.* And so we find that in the Fourth Gospel much has disappeared or has been drastically altered; in fact, we have here a repudiation of the Synoptics, of Revelation, and of the Catholic epistles. No longer is Jesus hailed by members of the populace as the Son of David; there are no Herodians conspiring against Him; and there is no competing sect following John the Baptist, who openly proclaims the Christhood of Jesus. The Pharisees seek His destruction, not because He denounces them, but because He openly proclaims Himself the Christ, which He never does in the Synoptics. No longer do the disciples carry on bitter disputes as to their relative importance in the Kingdom. No communism or celibacy is advocated; not a word is spoken against marriage, family, or wealth. We are no longer told that Jesus rejects His mother and His brethren or that they sought to carry Him home under duress. No longer does He flee before the Pharisees or make prophecies which are soon proved false. The Greek influence replaces the Zoroastrian in that Jesus no longer casts out devils. There is no longer a rich man condemned to eternal hell fire simply because

he had lived in luxury while Lazarus begged at his door; nor is there a sincere young man who goes away sorrowful, because his possessions are great. There is not even a demand upon communicants to perform works of charity, as in Paul. Heaven is emphasized but hell is never mentioned. The few miracles are almost entirely non-Synoptical, highly elaborated, and instinct with theological significance. At the wedding at Cana, Jesus assumes the role of Dionysus, as the maker and giver of wine, that intoxicating elixir of the Maenads and the blood of the *soters*. He deliberately delays His return to Bethany when He learns of the death of the non-Synoptical Lazarus; and the miracle by which he is raised from the grave after four days becomes a political reason why the Pharisees wish to destroy Him. When He rides into Jerusalem, it is not the disciples who hail Him with hosannas, but an enthusiastic populace.

The Synoptical eschatology was eliminated because the Greek Church did not accept these Zoroastrian-Judaic doctrines. The Buddhist-Pythagorean discourses of Jesus disappeared, because the Church was now seeking, not indigents to be saved, but donors to support it. The burgeoning priesthood was reaching out for political influence, was formulating creeds and dogmas, and was interested, not in the Parousia, but in revenue.

Most significant, perhaps, in this transformation, was the thorough deletion of the Sermon on the Mount from the Fourth Gospel. The terse pronouncements of Matthew and Luke evaporate into exhortations that the brethren love one another and into theological disquisitions concerning faith, the nature of the Son, and His relation to the Father. Instead of universal brotherhood and works of charity, the Church now demanded implicit faith in the pre-existing Christ.

2. *The Jewish Gospel Becomes Greek.* One has a feeling that this latter-day evangelist was struggling valiantly to fill up twenty-one chapters while leaving out nearly everything that had constituted Gospel Christianity. The resurrection narrative has more detail, for the obvious reason that this had now become the foundation of the Church; the eucharistic doctrine is more elaborate, be

cause this was the Orphic-Pythagorean mystery returning to its home. It is ironic that the Eleusinian ritual, which was the "abomination that maketh desolate," [22] became for all practical purposes the Christian mystery itself.

The Fourth Gospel became the practical basis for the new, the permanent, the Gentile, the worldly, the universal Church. It was its latest pristine authoritarian document and signalized the completion of the scriptures. With its acceptance, the Church could forget the four-square Jerusalem and the apocalyptic kingdom, in order to concentrate upon its more enduring, if less exciting, career of purveying mansions in the celestial realms. And it could de-emphasize and relegate to some vague future day the ever-fading Parousia, when Christ would appear on the clouds and marshal before Him the entire human race to stand in judgment.

CHAPTER IX

PRIMITIVE CHRISTOLOGY

A. THE BASIC CONCEPTS

1. *A Jungle of Heresies.* In this and the following chapters we shall consider the development of Catholic doctrine and of heterodoxy. Before 200, Irenaeus described thirty-one subversive Christian sects; in 370, in his *Panarion,* Epiphanius delineated eighty. In that bewildering world, any man, by devising a popular and acceptable theology, could achieve power and eminence; but heresy might well cost him his life.

2. *Early Concepts.* During the earliest years the Christian propagandists had only the simplest Christology; but with a new generation came theological disputes; and by 125, three principal Christologies had emerged, each claiming a monopoly on truth.

3. *The Judaic.* The earliest was the Judaizing, according to which Jesus was born of Joseph and Mary; anointed at His baptism with the Holy Spirit; thus endowed with supernatural power; and, as the descendant of David, eligible to assume the throne of Israel, where He would reign forever after the Parousia. Here the emphasis was upon communist brotherhood and material renunciation.

4. *The Gnostic.* The second was the Gnostic, in which we find two general divisions: one of these was the Cerinthian or Johanine, in which the eternal and supernatural Christ was conjoined to the human Jesus at His baptism and left Him just before or during the Passion; the other was the purely Greek Gnostic, according to which Christ was never born at all, was only a phantom or an apparition with a body which was purely celestial or of

sidereal origin who never suffered on the cross, but abandoned His apparently human body during the simulated Passion. This Christ was simply a power or a spirit which the Deity sent into the world to perform a specific task, at the completion of which He returned to the Father, the Supreme Lord of Spirits. There was never any birth or resurrection. This Christology, known as docetism, was never completely defeated by the ancient Church.

5. *The Orthodox.* The third concept, although the latest, became the orthodox; and it was modeled after the Greek mystery-*soter*. In this, we have the Christ-Jesus, the God-man, the demi-god, a dual personality, half human and half divine, begotten by the God of the universe, but born of a woman, a savior who gave His body unto death as a sacrifice for repentant sinners.

During its first fifty or sixty years, the Christian Church knew nothing of the Virgin Birth; but by 150 this doctrine had become a dogma. At some point, and not later than the year 115, it was promulgated, and appropriate interpolations were made in the Gospels; it was accepted with little question among converted pagans and became one of the central doctrines of Christianity.

B. THE BATTLE AGAINST HERESY

1. *Barnabas.* Perhaps the oldest of the apocrypha, an apostolic document written about 70, while the pristine concepts concerning Christ were developing, is the *Epistle of Barnabas*. It could not have been composed by Paul's one-time co-worker of that name; for the writer was a Gentile[1] who knew the Pauline literature and who rejected all Judaizing in the Church. He declares that the covenant has passed from the Jews to the new church; prophesies an imminent Parousia;[2] is conversant with *The Didache*,[3] but reflects no knowledge of the Synoptics.

The Christ-concept in Barnabas shows a definite development over that found in the Synoptics or even in the Pauline literature. Since both the Gnostics and the Ebiontes were already influential, we read that, appearing "in the flesh . . . he clearly manifested himself to be the Son of

God."[4] Whereas Paul had preached simply the crucified and risen Christ, Church doctrine now declared that the savior was the Son of God, so that His devotees might not fall into Ebionite heresy; but, to avoid the Gnostic error, it was also essential to understand that He was made manifest in the form of human flesh. So here we have a rudimentary god-man without divine birth.

2. *Clement of Rome.* Nor does the *First Epistle of Clement*,[5] written about 97, reveal any important advance over *Barnabas*. The writer teaches Pauline predestinarianism and declares that day and night typify the resurrection of Christ.[6] We are a peculiar people through Jesus Christ,[7] who is invoked as "our High Priest and Protector."[8] There is no mention of the miraculous birth of Jesus; and it is no wonder that Photius objected that Clement had not written worthily concerning His divinity. Nor does the *Second Epistle of Clement*, written some twenty years later, reveal any knowledge of the Virgin Birth.

3. *Ignatius.* Sometime before 117 the doctrine of the Virgin Birth was introduced and spread rapidly in the Gentile Church. Fortunately, we possess seven epistles written about that year by Bishop Ignatius of Antioch, a very old man, while he was journeying to his much-desired martyrdom in Rome. He declares: "Jesus Christ was according to the dispensation of God conceived in the womb of Mary . . . by the Holy Ghost . . . Now the virginity of Mary, and he who was born of her was kept in secret from the prince of this world."[9] There we have it! The knowledge of this miracle had long been suppressed so that Satan might not learn of it. This would account for the fact that Paul and the other apostles were equally ignorant.

4. *War on Two Fronts.* We learn from Ignatius that already the Church was being rent asunder by fierce heresies concerning the nature of Christ: "heretics confound together the doctrines of Jesus Christ with their own poison."[10] "They are beasts in the shape of men whom you must not only not receive, but if it be possible, must not meet."[11] Such was the terror which the heretics inspired and we soon become aware that the good bishop had to wage war not only against the Judaizers but also against

— 500 —

the Semitic Gnostics, represented by the Cerinthians and Simonians. "But if either the one, or the other," he declares, "do not speak of Christ-Jesus, they seem to me to be but as monuments and sepulchres of the dead." [12] The Gnostics were a greater threat at Antioch than were the Ebionites, and Ignatius therefore presses the battle against them with greater vigor: "whosoever does not confess that Jesus Christ is come in the flesh, he is Antichrist; and whoever does not confess him suffering upon the cross, is from the devil." [13]

We find in Ignatius what is possibly the first Christian creed, which emphasizes that Jesus "was of the race of David, of the Virgin Mary." [14]

5. *Repudiation of the Eucharist.* From Ignatius we learn also that the Gnostics repudiated the eucharist.[15] Inasmuch as this ritual was the very core of Christianity, Cerinthianism struck at the whole plan of Orphic-Christian redemption.

6. *Evidence of Forgery.* Thus the germs of various heresies are reflected in the Ignatian epistles, which also throw light upon the Gospel interpolations; there were some, we read, who said: "'Unless I find it written in the originals, I will not believe it to be written in the Gospel.' And when I said, 'It is written'; they answered what lay before them in their corrupted copies." [16]

This means simply that the Gospels used by the Ebionites and the Cerinthians knew nothing of the Virgin Birth; but Ignatius produced his own version which included the interpolations, unanimously rejected by the heretics. Ignatius continues, tacitly admitting the charges of the Jews and the Gnostics: "But to me Jesus Christ is instead of all the uncorrupted monuments in the world; together with those undefiled monuments, his cross, death, and resurrection, and the faith which is by him." [17] In short, he would found his faith upon the cross, the Passion, and the resurrection, even if the genealogies and the stories of His miraculous birth were palpable forgeries!

7. *The Apology of Aristides.* This was written about 125 by an Athenian philosopher, is one of the oldest authentic documents which declares the Virgin Birth, and

was the first of a long series of expositions in which Christians sought to justify their faith to pagan readers.[18]

8. *Justin Martyr and Tatian*. Twenty-five years later, Justin Martyr, who flourished in Rome, 145-160, quoted frequently from the Synoptics as if they were now invested with authority; and he spoke not apologetically, like Aristides, but positively, when he referred to the Virgin Birth, as if it had been an accepted dogma from the beginning. When his pupil, Tatian, about 170 compiled his *Diatessaron*, combining the four Gospels into a single composition, that of John had already assumed pre-eminence in the Greek world; ninety-six per cent of the repetitious Fourth Gospel is reproduced, while only half of Mark is included. The genealogies are omitted, but the Virgin Birth remains intact. By the time of Tatian, a definitely recognized New Testament canon had taken shape; and no one could ever again obtain a hearing within the Church for any Christology which did not recognize the pre-existent Christ, the Virgin Birth, and the miraculous hypostasis of the Godman Christ-Jesus.

CHAPTER X

THE SEARCH FOR AUTHORITY

A. THE EARLY PHASE

1. *Eyewitnesses.* When Jesus proclaimed His Gospel in the highways and byways of Galilee and Gaulonitis, He had no authority except His own inner persuasion. And the first apostles based their message upon the risen Christ and His imminent Parousia. But with the passing of the apostolic age came other missionaries who had never seen the Founder of their faith and who required a new source of authority in the form of written revelations.

2. *The Canon.* More than Paul, *Barnabas* reflects the *Logia* or the *Sayings of Jesus;* a development which is expanded in Ignatius and the *First Clement,* which also reproduces exact texts from Paul. There was, however, no authoritative literature in the first century. In the *Second Clement,* cir. 120, for the first time, we find quotations from the Synoptics; and Justin Martyr is studded with them, although he knows nothing of the Fourth Gospel. By the time of Tatian, however, not only the four Gospels, but Paul also, had achieved acceptance; and these scriptures were from that time onward established as divinely inspired. Thus it required well over a hundred years for the books of the New Testament to achieve this halo of sanctity and to become a fairly definite canon. Revelation and the Catholic epistles did not achieve complete status for centuries.

3. *The Prophecies and the Officers.* The Church based its authority first on the Old Testament, which was declared to be primarily a prophecy of Christ-Jesus; and second on the power He had given His disciples to bind

and loose on earth and in heaven, and that the direct
followers of the apostles, who were now the deacons, presbyters, and bishops of the churches, had inherited the same
power. Thus the Church claimed divine scriptures possessing antiquity believed to exceed that of Homer or Hesiod;
and it claimed for itself administrative and interpretive
authority deriving from God Himself through Christ.

4. *Far-Fetched Interpretations.* We stand amazed at
the fantastic meanings which early propagandists wrung
from the Jewish scripture. *Barnabas* does not adduce Isaiah
7:14, because in 70 there was no Virgin Birth to defend;
nevertheless, the prophecies described are wonderful to
contemplate. For example, when Moses invited the Hebrews into a land flowing with milk and honey, "It is as if
it had been said, Put your trust in Jesus, who shall be
manifested to you in the flesh."[1] The red heifer of Numbers[2] "is Jesus Christ."[3] When Moses stood with arms
outstretched, he was making the sign of the cross.[4]

5. *Justin Martyr.* Creating such evidence became an
industry. Justin Martyr declared that the very foundation
of the human countenance, with a nose set in the center,
prefigures the cross by which the human race would gain
redemption.[5] The "horns of the unicorn," of Psalm 92:10
also "are the figure of the cross,"[6] he declares solemnly.
In the persons of Jacob's two wives he read a prophecy
of all future ages; the weak-eyed Leah prefigured the
blinded Jews; the sharp-sighted Rachel the Gentile Church.[7]
Plato learned his metaphysics and Homer his anthropology
from the Pentateuch.[8]

6. *Clement of Alexandria.* This priority in time and
quality of Moses over all other sages was proclaimed in
unison by the Christian apologists. Even Clement of
Alexandria, cir. 200, who considered Greek philosophers
divinely inspired, nevertheless declared that "the epoch
of Moses" and "the philosophy of the Hebrews" was "the
most ancient of all wisdom."[9]

7. *Completion of the Canon.* By 175, the Church
possessed its complete canon. This consisted of many diverse documents, which are full of discrepancies and express a variety of viewpoints. In the face of these facts

Justin Martyr laid down the rule which was to become the dogma of Catholic as well as of Protestant Christianity: "no scripture contradicts another." [10]

B. THE STRUGGLE AGAINST HERESY

1. *Heretics Buried under Abuse.* Countless heretics are embalmed in abuse and libel simply because they did not survive to write the histories. Not only were they sincere men who led exemplary lives: many of them also produced systems which were, by and large, more rational, more elevated, and more in accordance with the Gospel Jesus than those of the Church. The essential difference between the heretics and the Catholics lay, not in the moral or intellectual superiority but rather in the doctrinal expediency of the latter. Whatever doctrines were more popular and more capable of establishing the authority of the hierarchy finally prevailed, quite irrespective of reason, truth, or ethics. Catholic success lay in its eclectic method: it accepted from every important group the minimum ideology necessary to insure its allegiance without alienating others equally powerful.

2. *Aberrations among the Fathers.* If there was a great and revealed Christian truth, it certainly required centuries to discover it. Justin Martyr was a chiliast.[11] His pupil, Tatian, became an uncompromising celibate Gnostic. Irenaeus was a literal chiliast who said that Jesus continued His ministry for more than twenty years. Tertullian was still another chiliast who became one of the great schismatics. Arnobius was a Marcionite Gnostic, and his work escaped destruction only because it was a powerful polemic against the pagans. *The Clementine Homilies* are Ebionite. Hippolytus, excommunicated by Pope Callixtus, depicted this prelate as a common criminal. Cyprian and his colleagues were excommunicated by a Roman Council headed by "Pope" Stephen, who, in turn, was anathematized by the Seventh Council of Carthage under Cyprian's leadership in 256. "Pope" Novatian was driven from Rome because he decreed the permanent exclusion of Christian traitors. Paul of Samosata was driven from the Church for

teaching a form of the Homoousian prematurely. As late as the fourth century, Lactantius returned to the ethics and the chiliasm of the Ebionites. Even though Constantine the Great was a paranoiac who murdered many of his nearest relatives, the fulsome Eusebius declared that he exercised "divine sovereignty" over the world "in imitation of God Himself"; [12] and, in return for material benefits, the Church beatified this royal ogre. Cyril of Jerusalem was a Semi-Arian who was banished for embezzlement. Ambrose was a Stoic, who burned Jewish synagogues and Valentinian churches. Eusebius of Caesarea as well as almost the whole Eastern Church was Arian or Semi-Arian after the Council of Nicea. Augustine was first a Manichaean, later almost a Pelagian, and he gave final form to Western Christianity by making it essentially Manichaean and by repudiating the unanimous teachings of the Greek Fathers. Theodoret was a Nestorian, as were many other influential bishops of the day. Many, like Jerome, Antony, and St. Martin, were definitely psychotic. In fact, there was scarcely a single Father in the ancient Church who was not tainted with heresy, mental aberration, or moral enormity. Oddly enough, it was such arch-heretics as Tertullian and Origen who contributed most to the evolution of Catholic dogma.

3. *Twisting the Scriptures.* The battle with heresy and the search for authority became the dominant obsession of the Church. Clement of Alexandria said of the heretics that, "selecting ambiguous expressions, they wrest them to their own opinions . . . not looking for the sense, but making use of the mere words." [13] The heretics may well have been guilty as charged; but we *know* that the orthodox Fathers did these very things, because we have their books, and he who runs may read.

These men, whether orthodox or heretical, were neither liars nor hypocrites: on the contrary, they were, by and large, intensely earnest and sincere. But they were possessed by a blinding psychosis. The devout, acute, and infinitely energetic Tertullian, who sought neither wealth nor position, who spent most of his life combating heresy, and whose writings were therefore preserved by the Church, himself died accursed and separate from the Church. In his polemics, however, both with heretics and with the orthodox, he used a method of argumentation which would bring expulsion from any current college debating team.

That various passages were deleted, altered, or interpolated into the Gospels and even more in the Pauline epistles is true beyond all doubt. The miracle is that so much of the original remains; and this was because the authentic Gospel doctrine continued the hope of the Church until the third century and because the rapid multiplication of copies made further revision exceedingly difficult thereafter.

4. *Doctrine for Defeating the Heretics.* The Church soon found that it could not defeat the heretics by reason, moral persuasion, or scriptural authority. Some other weapon soon became imperative; and this was found in the indivisible authority of the Apostolic Church, descending through the bishops from generation to generation, and in their exclusive right to administer the sacraments and interpret the scripture.

We trace the beginning of this doctrine in the epistles of Ignatius. While declaring himself most unworthy, he says, nevertheless, that all members of the Church must be "subject to your bishop as to the command of God." [14] And again: "As therefore the Lord did nothing without the Father, being united to him; neither by himself nor yet by His apostles, so neither do ye anything without your bishops and presbyters." [15] "It is evident that one ought to look upon the bishop even as we would do upon the Lord himself." [16]

5. *Tertullian.* It was, however, the formidable Tertullian who contributed most to the doctrine. He admits that often those members of the Church who are most prudent, faithful, and approved go over to the heretics. Then they put forward the scripture to support their insolent and subversive views, and by their arguments many innocent lambs are seduced. (Ironically enough, this was precisely what Tertullian himself later did.) We must oppose them, he declares, by "not admitting them to any discussion of the Scriptures . . . nor must controversy be

admitted on points in which victory will either be impossible or uncertain . . . As they are heretics, they cannot be Christians; and they have acquired no right to the Christian Scriptures." [17] Truth, he declares, is "all doctrine which agrees with the apostolic churches," which they "received from the Apostles, the Apostles from Christ, and Christ from God." [18] Truth and authority, then, are to be found in that unbroken stream of doctrine which flows directly from God through the Catholic churches, generation after generation.

6. *Cyprian.* Cyprian, 200-256, Bishop of Carthage during the last ten years of his life, declared that heresies had arisen because "God's priest is not obeyed . . . the church is founded upon the bishops, and every act of the church is controlled by these same rulers." [19]

Cyprian continues: "Whoever is separated from the church is joined to an adulteress . . . nor can he who forsakes the church of Christ attain to the rewards of Christ."[20] And again: "Whoever . . . has not maintained . . . ecclesiastical unity has lost even what he previously had been." [21]

It is evident from this that in 255, the Church was still far from centralized authority. Cyprian considered each bishop an independent ruler, who, nevertheless, was bound to work harmoniously in democratic union with all his colleagues to maintain the pure stream of apostolic doctrine and church practice.

7. *Summary.* The ecclesiastical doctrines enunciated by Tertullian and elaborated by Cyprian may be summarized as follows: the unity of the Church must never be broken; anyone who violates it by abandoning the communion is an antichrist; only the officers of the one true Church can administer the sacraments; there is no salvation outside the Catholic Church; all its congregations are equal but united; each new bishop is to be chosen by a convocation of his peers; he then becomes the supreme ruler of his own episcopate; heretics and lapsed persons are eligible to readmission after proper penitence; baptism must be administered immediately after birth; any one coming to the Catholic Church from a heretical

communion must be rebaptized, like a new convert from paganism.

C. THE DRIVE FOR UNITY

1. *The Pretensions of Rome.* In the third century, the Roman bishops began insisting that the entire apostolic authority had been transmitted through Peter to the Roman See. Thus, the stream of pure doctrine and ultimate authority descended, not through the apostolic tradition, as with Tertullian, or through the bishops, as with Cyprian, but through a single church.

2. *Church Authoritarian and Intolerant.* The Catholic Church was something new and different in the occidental world. First, it was authoritarian: that is, it appealed to a revelation which was both final and infallible; second, it sought to become the state; and, third, it was completely intolerant.

3. *Ethical Schools.* There had long been in the pagan world a variety of philosophical schools, each seeking a rational solution for the ethical problem. The proponents of these disagreed vehemently among themselves, but their appeal was to the intelligence and the moral sense; none claimed divine or civil authority or wished to impose their speculative doctrines on others.

4. *The State Religion.* Secondly, there was the state religion in which the conventional pagan pantheon was worshiped. When Christianity arrived very few had for centuries believed seriously in the literal existence of these gods. Tertullian tells us that philosophers earned large fees ridiculing these deities.[22]

5. *The Mysteries.* Thirdly, there were the mysteries, whose gods were no anthropological concepts; but more disturbing was the fact that their soteriology was essentially that of the Christians. And yet there was a vast difference. The mysteries had existed for many centuries without conflict either with the authorities or with each other. And this was because they were exclusive, had a purely redemptive function, and never sought temporal power or influence, but only the salva-

tion of their own elect. They never dreamed of forcing anyone to enter their communions: on the contrary, they made it a great privilege to belong, and one which a member could renounce at will, or might lose by expulsion.

6. *The Basic Difference.* The characteristic of Catholic Christianity consisted in its drive to become the state, a force inherited from the Orient, particularly from Judaism and Brahmanism. Since this urge is scarcely present in the Gospel Jesus, it must have entered Christianity at least in part as a theocratic predilection from the Old Testament.

7. *Fanatical Intolerance.* From the beginning Christianity was fanatically intolerant. The Church claimed a monopoly on truth; all other gods and deities were devils; heretics were subverters planted among men by Satan. Actually, heresies were attempts to limit membership by teaching the real Gospel Jesus, by establishing moral prerequisites, or by introducing rational doctrines. Beginning in the second century, the Church sought to create an institution in which every human being, no matter how debased, might find his home; in which ethics and morality were discounted in favor of assent to irrational creeds; in which all might find salvation in return for submission and obedience to authority; in which heresy alone became the offense for which there could be no forgiveness.

8. *Place for All in the Church.* When the Decian persecution broke out in 249, Cyprian of Carthage "retired" to the safety of his country seat; but his subordinate Novatus braved the onslaught, and exhorted his fellows to do the same. When the persecution was over, Novatian, the bishop of Rome, wished to exclude those who had willingly sacrificed to idols or had voluntarily blasphemed in order to avoid confiscation, exile, or imprisonment. In this, he was supported by Novatus. But since their policy erected a barrier against weaklings who were now ready again to acknowledge the authority of the Church, Cyprian described Novatus as one "raging with the rapacity of insatiable avarice, inflated with arrogance; . . . . a torch and a fire to blow up the flame of sedition, a whirlwind

and a tempest to make shipwrecks of the faith."[23] When the irreproachable Novatian himself, thrown headlong from his primacy, attempted to set up a purer communion, he was characterized as "a deserter of the Church, a foe to mercy, a destroyer of repentance, a teacher of arrogance, a corrupter of truth, a murderer of love."[24] Such was the language used by the third-century Christian saints to describe each other.

9. *The Cardinal Sin*. And so it was established that the one cardinal sin was to disregard the authority of the Church, break its unity, or deny its dogmas. Every moral turpitude became venial, and could be forgiven after prescribed penance.

10. *Salvation Externalized*. And so arose the congenital and irrepressible drive toward intolerant and all-inclusive authority which shaped the destiny of the Church. All must belong and conform; the line dividing civil from ecclesiastical authority gradually faded away; Church and society became co-extensive. Jesus had invited into His kingdom the disinherited of the earth, provided they were of the Elect and thus endowed with power to become regenerate. The gates of the Church, however, were thrown open to all who would accept its creed and authority; those who would not must be erased from the earth. It was therefore no accident that in time all emphasis upon ethics was replaced by a search for a magical and incomprehensible formula, the implicit acceptance of which would, it was proclaimed, assure the redemption of all believers. The externalism of the Pharisees, which Jesus attacked with such virulence, was certainly no greater than that very soon erected by the Church He founded.

But we must now return to apostolic times and investigate the nature of Jewish Christianity.

CHAPTER XI

SEMITIC CHRISTIANITY

A. THE CERINTHIANS

We have already noted the two types of Semitic Christianity which confronted Ignatius at Antioch: first, the Judaizing Ebionites; and, second, the Gnostic Simonians and Cerinthians. These had certain features in common, but in other respects stood at opposite poles. Cerinthus was a Jew who flourished during the first century and who organized a splinter-sect which combined some of the characteristics of Judaism with those of Gnosticism. According to Irenaeus, Cerinthus taught that the world was made by a certain power, far inferior to the Supreme God, who had always been entirely unknown in the universe. Jesus was the son of Mary and Joseph; at His baptism, the Christ, sent by the Supreme God, entered Him, so that He could perform miracles and proclaim the Unknown Father. But at the Passion, "Christ departed from Jesus" who then "suffered and rose again, while Christ remained impassible, inasmuch as he was a spiritual being."[1]

Regarding Cerinthus, Hippolytus[2] and Tertullian[3] follow Irenaeus closely. We have already noted that Eusebius preserves a fragment from Dionysius according to which Cerinthus was the author of Revelation,[4] which certainly is in detailed agreement with his ideology. Whether or not this apocalypse was actually written by him, it is certain that he, like the Ebionites, predicted an imminent kingdom of saints upon earth in which the Jews would occupy a position of pre-eminence, although he rejected the Old Testament and the Jewish God.

— 512 —

Cerinthus projected a Zoroastrian-Danielic Jesus who was entirely independent of Jewish tradition and prophecy and who was unaware of His destiny until the day of His baptism, when He was filled with the Logos of the Supreme God and given the power to compel angels and demons to obey Him. This Christ would shortly return on the clouds, again to occupy the body of Jesus; He would then defeat the heathen, judge the wicked and the righteous, and rule for a thousand years with His saints in Palestine, where all would enjoy every physical delight which it was possible to imagine.

B. THE EBIONITES

1. *The Clementines.* Two remarkable documents have survived in which Peter appears as the protagonist and Simon Magus as the adversary. We conclude that the character and doctrines attributed to the latter must bear some resemblance to the original, since the portrait of him by two different authors is quite similar. In the *Recognitions of Clement,* Peter appears as a Catholic, whereas in the *Clementine Homilies* he is an Ebionite, and this book is a mine of information concerning Jewish Christianity. It reflects the bitter polemics carried on by Judaizing Christians (Ebionites) and Syrian Gnostics (Simonians) of the second century.

2. *The Mosaic Law.* According to the Ebionites, the Mosaic Law had not been reduced by Jesus, but made more refined and severe. The Law declared that we must not commit adultery; but Jesus said that a lustful look constitutes this sin. The Law declared that we must not commit murder; but Jesus said that we must not even harbor a hostile thought. The Law declared that a divorce could be had by giving the wife a bill of divorcement; but Jesus permits it only in the case of adultery. This, said the Ebionites, was what Jesus meant when He said that He came, not to destroy, but to fulfill the Law. As for circumcision, Sabbath regulations, etc.,—these were to be rigorously enforced, and those who disregarded them could in no wise enter the Kingdom of Heaven.

3. *Theology.* According to the Ebionites, the Jews were the chosen people under the new covenant as under the old, and Gentile proselytes were like whining dogs receiving a crumb from the table of their Lord. Jesus, born of Mary and Joseph, was of the line of David, and destined to occupy the throne of Israel. He was distinguished by His purity and wisdom, and was therefore chosen by the God of Moses, Abraham, and Jacob to reveal in its entirety to the Jewish nation the new covenant announced several centuries before by Jeremiah. This theory is reflected in the canonical Epistle to the Hebrews. At the baptism, God declared the anointment of the new Messiah by infusing into Him the Christ-power in the form of a dove, a symbol familiar in connection with Noah. It was necessary for the Christ to die as the perfect and final sacrifice for the sins of His people; and because of His death, the blood offerings in the Temple were thereafter abolished. After His death and resurrection, Christ-Jesus was elevated to sit at the right hand of the Father, whence He will very soon return in power to judge mankind and to establish the Kingdom of God in the Pleasant Land, which is Palestine.

4. *Ebionite Doctrine and Practice.* Irenaeus states that, according to the Ebionites, "the world was made by the Jewish God. They use the Gospel according to Matthew only, and repudiate the Apostle Paul, maintaining that he was an apostate from the law."[5] Hippolytus, writing about 225, some fifty years after Irenaeus, indicates that the Ebionites were still active; and that, according to them, "Jesus was named the Christ of God" because He had fulfilled every jot and tittle of the Mosaic Law. "And the Ebionites allege that they themselves also, when in like manner they fulfill the law, are able to become Christs; for they assert that our Lord Himself was a man in like sense with all humanity."[6]

C. AS REVEALED IN THE HOMILIES

1. *A Polemic against the Simonians.* We are compelled to glean our knowledge concerning most heretics from the

garbled and defamatory accounts of their enemies. We possess, however, a less biased portrait of the Ebionites, because the *Clementine Homilies,* written about 300, contains probably complete and with little alteration, a previous book called *The Circuits of Peter,* written about 200. It survived because it contained a bitter polemic against the Simonians, who were still active in the fourth century.

2. *Debates.* In the debates with Simon, he and Peter in their inimitable manner accuse each other as sorcerers, jugglers, magicians, murderers, and enemies of God. Peter refers to Jesus with such Essene epithets as Teacher, Master, True Prophet, Unlying One, the Prophet of the Truth, the Unerring Teacher, the Teacher of Righteousness, etc. Simon maintains that Jesus was a supernatural apparition and Peter that He was human flesh and blood;[7] neither knows of any Virgin Birth.

3. *Jewish Smugness.* The smug superiority of the Christian Jew, which necessitated the Pauline approach in the Gentile world, is amply demonstrated in the *Homilies.* The Ebionites could not conceive of any redemption for Gentiles unless they first became practicing Jews, since it was by this means that Jesus became the Christ; and proselytes were regarded as whining dogs. This Ebionite Peter therefore tells the Gentiles: "We are of the same nature, but not of the same worship. Wherefore, being altogether superior to you, we nevertheless do not grudge you becoming such as we are . . . the Jew believes God and keeps the law . . . But he who keeps not the law, is manifestly no Jew, but a sinner; and he is on account of his sin brought into subjection to those sufferings which are ordained for the punishment of sinners."[8]

4. *Four Versions of One Incident.* The Ebionite attitude is accurately expressed in the Aramaic version dealing with the incident involving the Syro-Phoenician woman, upon which the Matthean account of the same event is based.[9] When she entreated our Lord to heal her daughter, "He said, 'It is not lawful to heal the Gentiles, who are like to dogs on account of their using various meats and practices, while the table in the kingdom has been

given to the sons of Israel.'" Only when the woman became a Jewish proselyte did Jesus effect the begged-for cure. "For she being a Gentile, and remaining in the same course of life, He would not have healed her."[10]

This Ebionite story is retold, first in Matthew, and then in Mark and John. No other scriptural sequence demonstrates so graphically the process by which a narrowly Judaistic Christianity was Hellenized. Although the canonical Matthew edits the Aramaic version drastically, it was obviously drawn from this original; for Jesus declares that He is "not sent but unto the lost sheep of the house of Israel," and that "It is not meet to take the children's bread and cast it to the dogs."[11] However, He grants the woman's request without the prerequisite of proselytization, for which "faith" is substituted.

Mark[12] deletes entirely the Judaistic element of Matthew. Here Jesus says nothing about being sent to save the lost of Israel only; and it is not the Jews who have priority, but only the "children," or the Elect; and the woman's daughter is cured because of her humility rather than her faith.

Let us now turn to John, who declares: "Other sheep I have, which are not of this fold,"[13] which, of course, is a direct repudiation of Matthew.[14] John's completion of the sequence[15] is most revealing. Jesus declares that He is Himself the awaited Christ and Messiah; and that in the future the Father will be worshiped neither in Samaria nor in Jerusalem, but "in spirit and in truth." In short, Jesus emerges in the Fourth Gospel as the universal savior who takes no cognizance of race or previous creed.

According to the Ebionite Matthew, Jesus could neither heal nor accept any one except a Jew or a Jewish proselyte; according to the canonical Matthew, the Jews are the Children, the Gentiles are dogs, and He was sent only to the lost of Israel; He was, however, able to heal an outsider without proselytization because of faith; according to Mark, He was sent to all, and would redeem those of every nation who accept Him humbly; in John, neither Judaea nor Samaria possesses the slightest priority; Christ emerges as the Hellenic god-man. It is significant that Luke, the most Hellenized Synoptic, ignores the incident entirely.

5. *Dietary Law.* The reason the Ebionites insisted with such severity upon certain dietary regulations is explained by Peter. Any flesh offered to idols, as well as certain birds and animals, like hawks, eagles, and swine, are filled with demons or devils, and when you eat these foods "the demons . . . are admitted into your bodies by your own hands; and lying hid there a long time, they become blended with your souls . . . And . . . upon the dissolution of your bodies, your souls being united to the demon, are of necessity borne by it"[16] into hell fire, which is salubrious to these fiends. This, incidentally, explains a passage in Acts[17] which permits Gentile Christians to ignore the Mosaic Law but forbids the eating of meats offered to idols.

6. *The Law of Love.* Further study of the *Homilies* reveals the moral-metaphysical basis for Gospel and Ebionite communism. The young Clement, learning at the feet of Peter, could understand that it is our moral duty to feed the hungry, heal the sick, clothe the naked, and rescue those in prison; but he could not comprehend why we must bless those who curse us, turn the other cheek when we are smitten, surrender our tunics also when our coats are demanded, or lend our money without security. In reply, Peter explains that there are two kinds of love.[18] The first is that which relieves human distress; this we call compassion. It is *a* good, but not the highest good. The second we call philanthropy, which is the efficient cause of immortality: when the reward is great, the price is high. Those who aspire to the Kingdom of Heaven must love their enemies; and this is not so difficult, when we realize that these are the very persons who, by abusing us in this world, make possible our election to an eternity in paradise.

7. *The Two Ways.* Peter declares that the Prophet of Truth has taught us (as we saw in *The Didache* and in the *Manual of Discipline*) that there are two kings, two kingdoms, two kinds of people, and two ways of life. On the one hand, there is Satan who is the ruler of this world and who carries on his work in order that the Elect may

become manifest; and, on the other, there is the God of the universe who will ultimately take unto Himself those whom He now calls. On the one hand, there is the present brief life, in which Satan gives all good things to his servants at the price of eternal damnation; but there are also the Sons of God who renounce this world and all its goods in favor of everlasting life.[19] As the children of the kingdom are not entitled even to bread, water, or a single garment in this world, which belongs entirely to the Evil One, and are literally aliens living in the land of the enemy, they have no right to anything, but must surrender every possession to the Children of Darkness. Actually, when we surrender any of our material goods to our enemies, we are loading them down with sin and guilt.[20]

8. *The Damnation of Property.* This was the philosophy which actuated Essene communism, which served as a means by which the brethren could enjoy their own wealth without incurring the damnation consequent upon its possession. According to the commandment of Jesus, we must sell our possessions and give them to the poor; but the poor (the Ebionites) could thus enjoy their own former goods by having them placed in a common storehouse; and no longer could they be asked to give what they did not possess. Their communism was, therefore, the means by which to enjoy the wealth they had renounced.

Peter elaborates that the possession of clothing, food, drink, or any other thing is sin. "The deprivation of these in whatsoever way it takes place, is the removal of sins . . For the boundary line of the saved is, as I said, that no one should possess anything." [21]

One last difficulty, however, remains for Clement: Are all the poor automatically virtuous and therefore redeemed To this Peter replies, "that, since the sinful deed is no more reprehensible" than the moral impulse which inspire it, therefore the poor man who yearns for wealth will fr in hell alongside his more affluent brethren.[22]

This philosophy assumes that wealth can be accumulate only through wickedness; and that the heir who inherits is burdened with the same guilt. Thus all who own prop erty are irrevocably doomed to hell fire. This reveals the moral axioms on which the Gospel stories of the Rich Young Man and of Lazarus and the Rich Man are based. The indigent are holy: the industrious and the successful have sold their souls to Satan.

And now we move to a larger stage, that occupied by Greek Gnostic Christianity and its principal protagonists.

CHAPTER XII

HELLENIC GNOSTICISM: MARCION

A. BACKGROUND

1. *Sources.* The ancient Fathers are studded with references to the Gnostics, particularily Marcion; and many polemics were written against him, of which Tertullian's *Against Marcion,* which is extant, is our best source of information concerning the heresy.

2. *Influence upon Paul.* Of all the ancient heresies, Greek Gnosticism seems to us the most intriguing; its principal protagonist was Marcion, "the wolf of Pontus," as Eusebius calls him.[1] He taught in Rome about 140-150, where he established his first church, and whence he carried his gospel to all portions of the empire.

The Gnostics considered themselves superior, since their doctrine was anchored in *gnosis,* or science, which meant simply knowledge and revelation. The dualism, predestinarianism, and Christology of Paul, his repudiation of the Parousia and of chiliasm, his doctrine concerning the flesh and the resurrection, his indifference to the Sabbath, his rejection of penal eschatology, are all Gnostic.

3. *Simon Magus.* Irenaeus states that Simon Magus was the founder of Gnosticism.[2] And that Acts 8:9-24 is completely misleading we learn from indisputable testimony. The Simonian was an independent Samarian cult competing with Christianity as early as 40-50. Tertullian declares that Dositheus and Simon were the first who repudiated the Jewish scriptures, the prophets, and the God of the Old Testament;[3] and he added that Simon Magus "had the hardihood to call himself . . . the Supreme God

and to say that Christ was simply a phantom who appeared among the Jews.

The *Clementine Homilies* and *Recognitions* are the best sources concerning Simon. In the latter, we are told that John the Baptist had thirty disciples, of whom the chief were Dositheus and Simon, and of whom Helena, the later companion of Magus, was another.[4] The evidence is, therefore, quite conclusive that John the Baptist was the founder of a new religion and that he would never have proclaimed a competitor as the Christ. When John died, according to the *Homilies*, Simon was studying in Egypt and Dositheus usurped the leadership; but, upon his return, Simon captured control. Christ was the Word sent to the Jews, Helena the Holy Spirit sent to the Gentiles, and Simon the Standing One, or the Supreme God, sent to the Samarians. According to Irenaeus, however, Simon "taught that it was himself who appeared among the Jews as the Son, but descended in Samaria as the Father, while he came to other nations in the character of the Holy Spirit."[5] Here, then, we find the first concept of a modal Trinity.

4. *Corruption of the Scripture.* In the *Clementines*, Simon delivers such an overwhelming indictment of the Old Testament and its God that Peter can justify the Jewish scriptures only by the rather startling admission that quite a number of its chapters have been interpolated by the devil.[6] And he declares that since it would not do to admit this publicly, he must defeat Simon by drawing "him into a strait." Only later would he explain the evil chapters in private to the faithful.[7]

Peter declares that heresies proliferate from Holy Writ because "if any one . . . forms a dogma agreeable to himself, and then carefully searches the Scriptures, he will be able to produce many testimonies from them in favour of that dogma which he has formed."[8] Peter's disciples ask him what then can be the criterion of truth? And he replies that this can be found only "in the word of Jesus."[9] Only the Prophet of Truth, like the Teacher of Righteousness, could interpret the word of God correctly.

5. *Cerdo.* Saturninus (or Saturnilius), who seems to

have formed the link between Simon and Hellenic Gnosticism, taught a variant doctrine before the time of Cerdo, a Syrian, who was the mentor of Marcion and who, according to Tertullian, taught that there are "two Gods—one good, the other cruel" and also the "creator of the world. He repudiates the prophecies and the Law; renounces God the Creator; maintains that Christ was the Son of the superior God; affirms that He was not in the substance of the flesh; states Him to have been only in a phantasmal shape, to have not really suffered, but undergone a quasi-passion, and not to have been born of a virgin, nay, really not to have been born at all. A resurrection of the soul merely does he approve, denying that of the body. The Gospel of Luke alone, and that not entire, does he receive. Of the Apostle Paul he takes neither all the epistles, nor in their integrity. The Acts of the Apostles and the Apocalypse he rejects as false." [10]

In Cerdo, then, 120-140, we find the basic doctrines of Marcion, who, according to Irenaeus, altered Luke by "removing all that is written respecting the generation of the Lord . . . also those passages from the prophetical writings which announced" His coming "beforehand." [11]

B. THE SYSTEM OF MARCION

1. *The Power of the Movement.* The powerful Marcionite communion had congregations in Asia Minor, Greece, and Africa, in addition to the large and dynamic Mother-Church at Rome. When the Catholics assumed power in 325, they persecuted all Christian dissidents: but for the Marcionites and other Gnostics, they reserved a peculiar ferocity. In the Eastern provinces, nevertheless, the sect persisted; and it experienced a renaissance in the seventh-century heresy of the Paulicians, who flourished for hundreds of years in spite of every persecution, and who condemned relics, altars, and shrines. Their pastors, finally, were their servants and ministers, never their masters.

2. *The Marcionite Canon.* Decades before the Catholic had either, the Marcionites possessed an international communion and a well-recognized canon. This, as we have

noted, consisted of the Gospel according to Luke and ten Pauline epistles: in addition, there was an *Acts of Paul,* and a book entitled *The Antitheses,* which contrasted passages in the Old Testament with others in Luke and Paul. Luke was chosen, since it was the most Hellenized of the Synoptics and since it expressed most clearly the celibate and economic doctrines of Jesus. Whatever was held to be a Judaizing interpolation was removed in order that the "original purity" might be restored. These alterations, though sometimes decisive, were not extensive: for example, all passages linking Jesus to a human family or to the Old Testament were expunged.

The Gnostic movement produced an extensive literature of its own during the second and third century.[12]

3. *Editing Luke.* Marcion, and probably Cerdo before him, began by deleting Chapters 1 and 2 of Luke and the genealogy from Chapter 3. There can be little doubt that he possessed early copies in which these portions and perhaps other passages did not appear. However, this cannot be said concerning all his excisions, some of which, according to Tertullian, were the following: 4:17-21, in which Jesus reads from Isaiah in the synagogue at Nazareth; 8:19-21, which refers to his mother and brethren; 11:29-31, where Jonah is mentioned; 11:47-51, in which Jesus says that the blood of the Jewish prophets shall be required of "this generation"; 13:1-5, which makes an obscure reference to some Galileans who were killed; 15:11-32, which is the Parable of the Prodigal Son, considered by Marcion a Judaizing fable; 18:31-34, in which Jesus declares that the prophets had foretold His suffering; 19:29-40, in which Jesus procures an ass and rides into Jerusalem like a Jewish king; 20:9-19, which is the parable of the husbandman, who sent his son to care for his vineyard, here represented as the Jewish nation.

Not counting the two first chapters and the genealogy, the portions removed constitute less than five per cent; yet Luke was thereby so transformed that it became the authority for a system of Platonic Gnosticism. Since Tertullian did not charge Marcion with any interpolations, we conclude that he inserted nothing of his own.

4. *Paul.* We have already noted in some detail that Marcion accepted only ten Pauline epistles and that his version did not contain many of the passages found in our canonical. There can be no reasonable doubt that this was the actual corpus of Pauline literature as it existed late in the first century. We have pointed out that since the Gnostics revered Paul before he was accepted by the Catholics, it is simply incredible that the original Paul could have been seriously at variance with Cerdo and Marcion.

C. SPECIFIC DOCTRINES

Let us sketch briefly Marcion's salient doctrines:

1. The Good or Supreme God, who is the incorporeal, infinite, eternal, passionless, and unnameable ruler of the universe, created by fiat the artificer or Demiurge, who is the god of the Jews, who fashioned this world, and who brought angels, demons, and mankind into existence, without knowing anything about his own creator or of the Christ who would be sent in the fullness of time.

2. Co-existing with the Supreme God, matter is an eternal and uncreated principle, which whirled about in chaotic form, until the Demiurge reduced a portion of it to form and order, as described in Plato's *Timaeus*. Since this agent is only just and since matter possesses no ethical imperative, this world cannot be flawless. Man, likewise formed of the dust and infused with the breath of the Demiurge, is physically and spiritually imperfect.

3. Standing between the Supreme God and formless matter, there is a divine force, the energizing aspect of God, the *Nous,* a divine effluence by which he transmits his will. And, though God and matter are not in basic conflict, there is, nevertheless, a definite and eternal dualism, which can be bridged only by the agency of the Word.

4. Realizing that the human creature can never attain salvation by his own efforts, the Supreme God interferes for the first time in the affairs of the Demiurge by sending His Word into Judaea in the fifteenth year of Tiberias. This Christ was a supernatural apparition which assumed

the appearance of humanity. At the baptism, the Supreme God set His seal of approval publicly upon His Christ. At the crucifixion the Word left the apparition which had contained it for a few months; consequently, nothing was nailed to the cross except a lifeless form, which contained not blood but ichor.

5. The Supreme God determined before the foundation of the world who the Elect would be; that is, who would be given the power to accept the Gospel. These must always be a very small percentage of the human race.

6. The community of these saints constitutes a highly dedicated group of men and women, who separate themselves from the world of the Demiurge, and devote themselves without reservation to the Supreme God and to their high, spiritual destiny. Marriage must be avoided because sexual desire and intercourse constitute irremediable pollution.

7. All flesh diets must similarly be rejected.

8. The Old Testament was produced entirely under the inspiration of the Demiurge. And, since the Gospel was an absolutely original revelation never predicted or foreshadowed, anything found therein which ties it to the Hebrew scriptures must be a Jewish forgery. Judaizing corruptions have so obscured our view of Christ that before we can understand His nature or His plan of redemption, these must be removed. Acts, Revelation, the Catholic epistles, and the Gospels of Mark and Matthew must be rejected, since they are Jewish perversions. (The Fourth Gospel had not achieved currency or authority when Cerdo and Marcion flourished.) Among the apostles, Paul alone understood the Gospel, and Peter, James and John were the worst of the false prophets. Thus, at a single stroke, the Christian faith was severed from its moorings in the Old Testament.

9. The Demiurge had long planned a Messiah who was to gather his favorites from the Diaspora and establish a world-wide empire under their dominion. This project, however, has now been countermanded by the Good God, who has also through Christ abolished the Law and the Prophets. This anticipated Jewish Messiah has nothing in

common with the exalted Gnostic Christ, who was sent by the Supreme God to every tribe and nation.

10. Since matter, an eternal principle, though not actively evil, is an inferior essence, the body can never be immortal. "Flesh and blood can not inherit the kingdom of God." At the resurrection, therefore, only the spiritual portion of the Elect will ascend to the celestial realms. Human souls are not by nature immortal: only the Elect can live forever.

11. Since God is infinite and indivisible, He must be unitarian: the Word and the Spirit are merely agents, effluences, or manifestations of the Supreme Deity.

12. Since the Supreme God is a God of love and since those who are not of the Elect are not responsible for their nature, they are not morally culpable and will not be tortured after death. They will, therefore, simply be consigned to instant and merciful annihilation at the hands of the Demiurge. For the Elect, there is no judgment; they exist always in the beneficent grace of God and nothing could be more absurd than that Christ should one day return to judge all men and to send the reprobates with imprecations into eternal torture, as we read in the Judaizing Gospel of Matthew.

13. It is a perversion of the Old Testament to allegorize it: we must accept it as written, or reject it altogether. Furthermore, we must accept the Gospel as Christ delivered it, divested, however, of its Jewish corruptions.

14. The entire soteriological doctrine of the Catholics is an utter perversion; Christ is not an atonement, who died for sinners, but a guide and a teacher for the Elect, who require neither redemption nor conversion. Christ was never born and He never died; nor was He ever in a grave. Baptism is only an initiatory rite; the eucharist is merely symbolic. Eating the flesh and drinking the blood of the god-man is an ugly, cannibalistic ritual, and could never refer to Christ, a purely spiritual being, who possessed neither flesh nor blood.

15. Although Jesus adapted Himself to Jewish conditions, He always opposed the Demiurge. While that creator approved just and clean persons only, Christ called to

Himself publicans, sinners, harlots, murderers, and lepers; and He bade children come unto Him. The Messiah of the Demiurge was to redeem only the Jews: but Christ came to all nations. Jewish hopes are concentrated upon an earthly kingdom: but Christ promises a heavenly realm. The Messiah of the Demiurge is still to appear and will one day establish the Jews in a mundane state to endure for a thousand years; but this will not be the universal empire which *they* anticipate and it will stand in direct contrast to the celestial kingdom of Christ, where those who have died in Him will live and reign, forever released from the impediment of flesh.

D. GENERAL CHARACTERISTICS OF GNOSTICISM

1. *Its Strength.* The soteriology of the mystery-religions vanishes from Gnosticism; the Essene eschatology is abolished; there are no creeds or contradictory scriptures; there is little margin for theological controversy; there is mercy, brotherhood, and Hellenic universality; there is neither intolerance nor any potential for persecution; since it repudiated the Old Testament, it freed the Church at once from the immorality and the discrepancies of the Jewish scriptures. Finally, Marcion gave women complete equality; they baptized, and acted as full-fledged ministers. Rejected as wives, they became equals as saints.

2. *Its Weaknesses.* The weakness of Gnosticism lay in the fact that it attempted to divorce its Christ from a Judaic background which He Himself acknowledged. When Peter demanded that Simon reveal by what authority he declared that Jesus was sent by a God other than that of the Old Testament,[13] he could only reply that the god of the Jews and the god of Christ *must* be different because they are antithetical. Peter thereupon calls his opponent a liar and an enemy of God. The truth is that the chain which binds Jesus to the Jewish prophets could not be severed. And so, even though the Gospel was a synthesis of Greek, Buddhist, and Zoroastrian ideology, it was also

Jewish because it had enmeshed itself in Hebrew history, prophecy, and literature.

E. TERTULLIAN'S ANALYSIS OF MARCION

1. *The Phantom Christ.* Tertullian realized that Marcion's Christianity removed from the Gospel its most powerful hold upon the masses: this heretic was therefore a "viper" borrowing poison from "the asp," [14] that is, the Jew, who said also that Jesus was never foretold in the scriptures. And if Christ came not in the flesh, how can he have been resurrected? And if not, then is the Christian hope a sheer delusion.[15]

2. *Celibacy.* Since the question of celibacy was fundamental, it was imperative that Tertullian turn aside the meaning of Luke 20:34-35, which states: "they whom God shall account worthy of the possession of that world and the resurrection from the dead, neither marry nor are given in marriage." Tertullian explains that, since the Sadducees had posed a question dealing not with this life but with the next, therefore, the state in which there will be no marrying could only be that following the resurrection.[16] When Mark 12:25 and Matthew 22:30 were corrupted to read: "In the resurrection they neither marry nor are given in marriage," the celibacy taught by Jesus was stricken from those Gospels. Luke, however, somehow escaped the revisionists in this detail; yet we believe that even this Gospel had been edited between the time of Marcion and Tertullian; for in Tatian's *Diatessaron* the disputed passage appeared as follows in 170: "the sons of this world take wives and the women become the men's; but those that have become worthy of that world, and the resurrection from the dead, do not take wives, and the women also do not become the men's." [17] This was unquestionably the doctrine of pristine Christianity.

3. *The Resurrection.* Tertullian performed an ever more extraordinary feat of mental gymnastics, while attempting to refute Marcion's doctrine based on Paul, that the soul only is resurrected into heaven. His argument is ingenious: [18] since we know that there will be a resur

rection, it is certain that the body alone rises: "for, as we have shown, it is the *body* only which becomes dead." [19] Tertullian admits that Paul wrote that "flesh and blood cannot inherit the kingdom of God." [20] Unable to escape this categorical statement, he attempts to circumvent it. Our resurrection, he says, must necessarily be like that of Jesus; and, as we know that He was raised in the flesh, therefore, we too must be resurrected with our own bodies. In this, however, Tertullian begs the question: for Marcion denied that Christ was ever born, or arose from the dead, or appeared in a human body.

F. NATURE AND DEVELOPMENT OF MARCIONISM

1. *No Consistent Doctrine Possible.* The fact is, of course, that no one, orthodox or heretic, could construct any completely consistent system based on the entire scripture or even on the four Gospels, because these contain elements that will not harmonize with any general conception. Any one who accepts the Old Testament will face countless contradictions; any one who does not, will be refuted by the Gospel, which admits dependence upon it. Concerning Christ or the godhead, no one could devise an invulnerable theory. Cerdo and Marcion alone followed a method which could lead to theological consistency: they limited their canon and then edited Luke to conform with their preconceived pattern.

2. *An Admirable Failure.* Taken altogether, however, the rational attempt by Cerdo and Marcion to establish a consistent canon, to organize a church of devoted communicants, to combine what was best in the Gospel with Greek philosophy, to inspire a brotherhood based upon love, mercy, toleration, and intellectual integrity constituted one of the most admirable developments of ancient Chrisianity.

3. *Celibacy.* Tertullian exclaims in horror that, by forbidding marriage, Marcion threatened "to put a complete stop . . . to the sowing of the human race." [21] As a Montanist, however, who permitted one marriage only, he

declared: "we do not reject marriage, but simply refrain from it," [22] which seems to be only an academic difference. And in another passage he says that if we should prohibit the first as well as the second marriage, it would be "not without reason; inasmuch as it, too, consists of that which is the essence of fornication." [23] According to Eusebius, one Apollonius had written that Montanus "taught the annulment of marriage." [24] So we see that, after all, Tertullian and Marcion were not very far apart from each other or from the Gospel Jesus on the question of wedlock.

4. *A Dedicated Communion*. And this brings us to another question: Had Marcionism become the one Christian Church, would this have meant race-suicide on a broad scale? Not at all: for in that case, the religion of Jesus Christ would simply have become a strictly limited and highly dedicated communion, with fewer celibates than were actually found in the Catholic Church at a subsequent date. The number of pneumatic or spiritual men and women would always remain an insignificant minority compared to that vast multitude, the children of the Demiurge, who, yearning for material things, dance their heedless way into annihilation. And should Marcionism have found popular acceptance, its marriage-dogmas would inevitably have been revised and rationalized, even as they were in Buddhism: for the race never commits voluntary suicide.

5. *Tatian*. It is worth noting that Tatian, the disciple of Justin Martyr, later established the Encratites, who, although they seem to have accepted the orthodox Christology, followed Marcion in various doctrines and practices. They declared that sex was an evil thing, that marriage was a corruption introduced by the Jewish creator-God, and that animal food was destructive to the spiritual man.[25]

6. *Apelles*. Apelles revised the teaching of Marcion by returning in part to the emanational hypotheses rejected by his master and by declaring that Christ had a material body, but of sidereal origin. He showed definite Mithraic antecedents, but agreed with Marcion concerning the Jews and the Old Testament, and wrote a book pointing out

the mistakes of Moses,[26] somewhat in the spirit of Ingersoll.

7. *Return to Renunciation.* And thus we find various communions returning again and again to the fundamental teachings of the Essenes: holiness, they said, is impossible without self-imposed poverty, communism, and celibacy.

8. *Marcion's Method.* We must understand that when Marcion chose only a portion of the books now in our canon, he did not commit any serious violence: because none of these New Testament documents had then attained authority or sanctity. And when he made certain deletions, he merely pursued a practice then quite common. Furthermore, when he drew heavily upon Plato, he set a precedent which all the Greek Fathers were to follow; and when he rejected the Old Testament in its entirety, he was simply more consistent than the Catholics, who certainly repudiated the practices of Judaism. And when he taught celibacy and predestination, he stood on solid Gospel foundations. He was not hated and maligned because he selected and edited the sacred books; it was because the Church he established was in competition with the Catholic and because he sought to create a limited communion which could never become the state.

9. *Marcion's Influence.* Marcion forced the Catholics to develop a definitive New Testament canon; to establish an empire-wide organization and discipline; and to evolve an orthodox dogma opposed to his. Thus he actually furnished an enormous impetus to the development of the universal Church.

We must now turn our attention to a system of more extreme metaphysical dualism, a Christianity based upon Zoroastrian antecedents, and filled with Pythagorean speculation.

CHAPTER XIII

MYSTICAL-PYTHAGOREAN GNOSTICISM

A. MANY DIVISIONS

1. *Zoroastrian-Pythagorean.* Clement of Alexandria declares that the heresies arose "in the times of Adrian the king." [1] And it is true that most of the great dissident movements grew up between 110 and 140. Remarkable among these were the various systems of mystical Gnosticism, based upon Zoroastrian and Pythagorean antecedents. They were filled with endless systems of eons and emanations; they postulated a positive antagonism between God and matter, light and darkness, good and evil; and they were addicted to elaborate number-symbolics, as well as other mysteries, seeking to unite religious concepts with the phenomena of nature. Tertullian declares: "The Valentinians are no doubt a large body of heretics;" [2] and adds: "this heresy fashions itself into as many shapes as a courtezan . . . Whenever they have hit upon any novelty, forthwith they call their presumption a revelation." [3]

2. *Two principal Wings.* There was an Alexandrian division which operated for the most part in lower Egypt and which was founded by Basilides early in the second century; a decade or two later, Valentinus originated the occidental form in Rome.

Irenaeus, Hippolytus, Clement, and other Fathers ridiculed the complicated eons and emanations of these mystics and the "unspeakable number of apocryphal and spurious writings which they have forged." [4] Tertullian declares that, "as in the case of the Eleusinian mysteries . . . their secrecy is their disgrace . . . they beset all access to their body with tormenting conditions; they require a long initiation." [5]

3. *An Esoteric Mystery-Cult.* We know, therefore, that the Valentinians attempted to make of Christianity an esoteric cult patterned after the pagan mysteries. Clement tells us that Valentinus was the "Coryphaeus of those who herald community," [6] that is, who established communist societies, like the Greek *thiasoi*. There is no doubt that the Valentinians and the Basilideans were celibate and communist groups, who, like the Pythagoreans, sold their property, deposited the money with the treasurer of the society, underwent long novitiates, and sought immortality through the eucharist.

4. *Emanational Theory.* Hippolytus declares that according to Pythagoras "the primary monad became a principle of numbers . . . begetting after the manner of a parent all the rest of the numbers." [7] All mystical-Gnostic systems begin with this supreme monad, which is nameless, unbegotten, infinite, omnipotent, eternal, and invisible; and from him come various eons, emanations, powers, principalities, angels, and other creatures, including the human race.

B. BASILIDEAN GNOSTICISM

1. *Saturnilius.* Saturnilius of Antioch and perhaps Menander had taught that the unknown and unbegotten God brought forth the *Nous* who created the world and all things therein through the agency of seven angels, known as the hebdomad, of whom the Demiurge, who was the God of the Jews, was one. According to Irenaeus these heretics were "the first to affirm that two kinds of men were formed by the angels,—the one wicked, the other good." [8] They taught that Christ, the Nous who entered the body of Jesus at His baptism, came for the purpose of dethroning the God of the Jews and redeeming the children of the Supreme God, who were the Elect, or the Sons of Light. They taught also that animal food and marriage, being of Satan, cause everlasting damnation.[9]

2. *Expansion of Basilides.* To this system, Irenaeus declares, "Basilides . . . gives an immense development";[10]

and continues that the *Nous,* the first-begotten of the unborn Father, brought forth the Logos, and from Logos came the great triad, Phronesia, Sophia, and Dynamisın (Providence, Wisdom, and Power), and from them came principalities and angels, until they were thirty in number, which constituted the Triacontad. These in turn created one spiritual realm after another until there were three hundred and sixty-five. The chief of the angels was the demon Jehovah, the God of the Jews, with whom, therefore, "all other nations were at enmity." But when the Supreme God perceived that all the Gentile nations "would be destroyed without his aid," He sent the Christ, "His own first-begotten Nous . . . to bestow deliverance on those that believe in Him." [11]

Tertullian and Irenaeus state that, according to Basilides, Christ-Jesus was not crucified, but changed appearances with Simon of Cyrene, who actually suffered upon the cross.[12] Like almost all Gnostics, Basilides rejected the Jewish scriptures and denied the resurrection of the body.

We are told by Clement that, according to Basilides, faith and disbelief are congenital;[13] and that one who merely wishes to commit a sin such as murder or adultery is as guilty as if the deed had been done.[14] Sin does not consist in commission, but in the moral impulse which desires it. Clement continues: "One is saved by nature, as Valentinus would have it; and a believer and an elect man by nature, as Basilides thinks." [15] We learn also that these mystics believed in Pythagorean metempsychosis: "Basilides says that the soul, having sinned before in another life, endures punishment in this—the elect soul with honour by martyrdom, the other purged by appropriate punishment." [16]

3. *Summary.* To summarize the system of Basilides: there are, as in Zoroastrianism, two uncreated and self existent principles in the world, light and darkness, spiri and matter, good and evil, originally separated from anc without knowledge of each other. At the head of th Kingdom of Light stands the unborn and unnameable God From him unfolds the divine creation in seven successiv revelations, which form the first hebdomad, until there ar

three hundred and sixty-five spirit realms. All lower substance longs to rise in the scale of being; all earthly life is part of the general process by which creation seeks to become divine and spiritual. Gradually, the rays of divine light penetrate into the mineral, vegetable, and animal kingdoms, where an eternal struggle goes on, until all things at last become wholly spiritual, or relapse into the formless abyss. Each man is torn between the two contrary natures in his members, which always strive for mastery. But this conflict cannot end in victory for the higher without direct aid from the God of Light. The advent of Christ is the historic fact which makes the triumph for the spiritual aspect possible. God's *Nous* descended upon the entirely human Jesus at His baptism; and He thereupon proclaimed salvation to all those who are spiritual or will strive to become so. Jesus, however, since He was born of human parents, was not free from His hylic nature and He too required salvation like all other men. Basilides admitted the crucifixion as an historic fact, but he never developed a soteriological theory: in his system Christ never suffered; He simply dwelt, for a few months, like an angel or a demon, in the body of the mortal Jesus.

If it is difficult for us to understand how such theories could arise, we must remember that the original, authentic Gospels began with the baptism and contained no genealogies.

C. THE VALENTINIAN SYSTEM

1. *Nearer to the Catholic.* With the Valentinian mystics, we are confronted by a bewildering variety of systems and doctrines, put forth by their founder and by his various disciples, of whom the principal were Ptolemy, Heracleon, and Marcus. Valentinus stood midway between the Catholics and the Marcionites; he did not reject utterly the Jewish scriptures, but accepted them as an inferior revelation; he declared that, in the end, the Jewish God would become a servant and ally of Christ; and he had an ingenious doctrine concerning His generation, according to which He passed through the body of the Virgin

as water passes through a pipe, thus emancipating Him from her hylic nature.

2. *Three Kinds of Men.* We noted that the Basilideans projected two kinds of men; the Valentinians, however, "conceive . . . of three kinds of men, spiritual, animal, and material, represented by Cain, Abel, and Seth. These three natures are no longer found in one person, but constitute various kinds of men. The material" men suffer annihilation; those with an animal nature, go to a kind of purgatory, whence, after trial and purification, they pass either into destruction or redemption; the spiritual, or the Elect, attain perfection and become the brides of Christ.[17] Tertullian confirms [18] that this was the eschatology of the Valentinians.

3. *The Zoroastrians* separated the souls of the departed into three divisions, one of which was placed in *Hamestagna,* which developed into the purgatory of the Valentinians and the Manichaeans. The Valentinians, like the Marcionites, declared that the human soul is not imperishable by nature, but can achieve immortality by the intervention of Christ; and they rejected the sacraments entirely, saying that, since redemption is purely spiritual, there can be no need for such physical symbolism.[19]

4. *Theology.* In the Valentinian system also God is the great Monad, who, not loving solitude, willed to produce the first duad or syzygy, Bythos and Sige, which is Depth and Silence, who produced Nous and Veritas, i. e. Mind and Truth, which constitute the first Tetrad. They, in turn, produced Sermo, Vita, Homo, and Ecclesia: i. e., Word, Life, Man, and the Church, the second Tetrad, constituting altogether the Ogdoad. This ogdoad produced a Decad, which in turn produced the Duodecad: all these formed the Triacontad, the thirty eons who occupy the Pleroma—which is the celestial region. One of these eons or emanations was the Demiurge, God of the Jews, the artist who formed the world and breathed life into man. But there was another eon, Achamoth, who, unknown to the Demiurge, placed the seed of spirituality within the human soul; and those who partake of this in full measure are the Elect.

5. *Redemption.* In the fullness of time Christ was sent by the Nameless One to redeem the Elect; becoming a Valentinian is proof *per se* that the convert belongs to this highly exclusive circle. Those who accept another form of Christianity show that they possess a portion of the spiritual seed, and can, therefore, by infinite striving, attain to the middle region (purgatory) in the after life, to be ruled by the Demiurge, who has now become the servant of Christ. In this house of cleansing and discipline, the souls of non-Valentinian Christians will be made fit for an eternal, albeit secondary, heavenly realm. Those who remain purely material and reject the redemption of Christ must be annihilated by fire.

6. *Syncretism.* In spite of its syncretism, Valentinian terminology derived from the Bible, and it strove to make the Gospel Jesus acceptable to the Greek world. According to its dualistic metaphysics, man stands precariously poised between the realms of spirit and matter, partaking of both; and he is doomed unless he can slough off the dross of his lower nature and, winging his way over the dividing chasm, rise to the celestial realm. Even Clement shows the influence of Gnosticism, declaring that "the path for souls to ascension lies through the twelve signs of the zodiac."[20]

D. LATER VALENTINIANISM

1. *Heracleon.* Heracleon was a Valentinian who declared the "Pneumatics," or the Elect, are led by the Logos to the highest wisdom, which is salvation; the "Psychics," or animal men, who can perceive only through the senses and can be convinced only by miracles, can never do more than attain right faith; the "Hylics," being purely material, will be turned over to the Demiurge, their executioner. Judaism, like the world itself, is his work, as was the Jewish Law, which results in death by annihilation.

2. *The Threat of Dualism.* The dualism of mystic Gnosticism threatened to establish ditheism; and its ascetic discipline threatened to reduce the Church into a sect. Its great contribution consisted in making Christianity a

mystery acceptable to the pagan masses. The Church seized upon the Gnostic weapons, and, by reshaping and absorbing them, eliminated this heresy as an independent cult.

3. *Permanent Contribution.* It is obvious that in this Valentinian system, we find the groundwork of that later Manichaeism, including the doctrine of purgatory, which began to penetrate the Church in the fifth century. Much of the monastic movement which became important in the fourth century and played such a large role in the Middle Ages received its initial impetus from mystical Gnosticism, as did the universal belief in demons and witchcraft, and the use of charms, amulets, magic, incense, and holy water to exorcise the evil spirits.

We must now examine briefly the first cycle of the Trinitarian heresies which were to rend the ancient Church for two centuries before their final resolution.

CHAPTER XIV

THE MONARCHIANS

A. THE PATRIPASSIANS

1. *Origin of Name.* Tertullian coined the term *Monarchians* to describe those who sought to establish Christianity as an uncompromising monotheism without in any way reducing the divinity of Christ.[1]

2. *Endless Christological Heresies.* The Christological problem generated countless formularies which became heresies because they failed in some particular to meet the practical requirements of the Church. Since Christianity claimed a supreme God, His unity must not be questioned; at the same time, however, Christ-Jesus also could be nothing less than God; otherwise, His atonement could not be sufficient for salvation. The question then posed itself: how could Christ and the Father both be God without breaking His unity? The resolution of this enigma was to constitute the Christian faith.

Christology, however, involved not merely the Oneness of Christ and the Father; there was also the conundrum of the two natures in Christ-Jesus. For in His character as Son of Man, the Savior was human, but as the Son of God He was divine. Did these two natures exist separately? Or were they so commingled in a new hypostasis that one or the other or both man and God were excluded? Were Christ and the Logos identical? Was "Son" only another name for the Word or Logos, or was He a different entity? Were Jesus and the Son one and the same? Was the body of Jesus corruptible like all flesh? If the Logos or Christ was the only-begotten Son of God, was He not created later, and therefore a creature, inferior and mutable? And if so, was He not separate and different from the Father? These and similar questions began to plague the Church about 175 and split the faith into numberless subdivisions.

3. *The Alogoi.* Scarcely had the New Testament canon and an Empire-wide organization been established, when the Alogoi, who repudiated the Logos doctrine of the Fourth Gospel, appeared in Asia Minor. Theodotus the Tanner, considered the founder of dynamistic Monarchianism, arrived in Rome from Byzantium about 190. He taught that Jesus was a man born of the Virgin through the operation of the Holy Ghost in accordance with a special decree of God; that, after a life of purity, He was endowed with divine power at His baptism; but that He became the Christ with a specifically divine essence only at His resurrection. This process was said to have conferred upon Him divinity sufficient to make His sacrifice capable of universal atonement. This Christology, known as Adoptionism, preserves the Virgin Birth, but the Christ, no longer the eternal Word or Logos, is simply a special creation, endowed with certain qualities for a specific purpose. The unity, the omnipotence, in short, the monarchy, of God remains intact.

4. *Noëtus.* Like Theodotus and the later Praxeas, Noëtus also came from Asia Minor to Rome, arriving about 200. He emphasized many passages from scripture which declare the unity of God. He did not, however, like the Alogoi repudiate the Fourth Gospel, but used it to reinforce his views. He declared that inasmuch as God is One, and inasmuch as Christ and the Father are also One,[2] these are but different names for the same identity. God is the Word, and the Holy Spirit is also God. The Father Himself came down into the Virgin, died on the cross for our sins, arose from the grave, ascended into heaven, and returned as the Holy Spirit at Pentecost. This doctrine was known as Patripassianism, since it made God the Father suffer on the cross. But it was certainly a unitarian doctrine; it maintained the integrity of God's monarchy.

Hippolytus declares: "When the blessed presbyters heard his heresy . . . they expelled him from the Church."[3] The horror aroused among the orthodox by the thought that God the Father had been nailed to a tree, approached hysteria; and this, we believe, resulted from the fact that no one ever quite accepted the doctrine that Jesus was truly God. For were He actually so, why was it less horrible for *Him* to suffer crucifixion? If He were truly Christ, did not Marcion have a far more consistent as well as less repugnant hypothesis? But the necessities not only of the Christian tradition but also of the orthodox plan of redemption required inexorably a god-man like Osiris who could save us because He is like unto us; but it required also a Christ who is divine so that His sacrifice may accomplish a miraculous atonement. In this concept of the Deity, the singleness of God could never be preserved; and every attempt to establish it led only to further confusion and contradiction.

5. *Praxeas.* Tertullian declares that, according to Praxeas, God the Father was born of the Virgin and was Himself the Jesus Christ who was crucified.[4]

6. *Tertullian's Trinitarian Concept.* It was to refute this Monarchian doctrine that Tertullian developed the first Trinitarian creed,[5] which never postulated a Trinity of equal or co-eternal members but did develop the concept of three consubstantial persons in one divine economy. He declares[6] that the Monarchians rest their case on three passages of scripture,[7] and, ignoring all other texts, teach the blasphemy that the Father was "hanged on a tree,"[8] the very words, ironically, used by Marcion to prove that Christ could never have died on the cross.

7. *Sabellius.* About 220, a prelate in the Roman Church named Sabellius developed another Monarchian concept: that of the modalistic Trinity according to which God the Father, God the Word, and God the Holy Spirit, exist, not as divisions or *persons* in the godhead, but simply as modes of activity. As Father, God manifested Himself as the creator; as Savior, He revealed Himself as the Word or Christ; and now as Comforter, He is present among us as the Holy Spirit. Throughout, God remains unaltered: we have only the differing phases of His *modus operandi.* Thus we have a trinity of successive

manifestations, which occur, not simultaneously, but in historic sequence.

8. *Servetus.* Sabellius could not adopt the ultimate modalistic concept finally promulgated in 1531 by Servetus in his *De Erroribus Trinitate,* which we note here because it is the logical development of Sabellianism. Servetus, who is considered the founder of modern Unitarianism, declared that God exists simultaneously as a Trinity of mode or aspect: God the Father is the material essence of the universe; God the Word His energizing manifestation; and the Holy Spirit the vitalizing force which animates the world. All of these are present in the universe as a whole, in every living creature, in every tree and herb and stone.

9. *The Heresy of Callixtus.* The Monarchians had entrenched themselves so thoroughly in Rome by 225 that their teachings had become official dogma. Hippolytus thereupon entered the lists against Sabellius over the question of hypostatic Christology with such vigor that the Church was torn into two factions. The practical Pope Callixtus thereupon excommunicated both disputants and devised a compromise which he hoped would pacify all factions. On the one hand, he denied that the Father had suffered on the cross; but on the other he rejected the separate personality of Christ. Hippolytus states[9] that, according to Callixtus, the Logos is both Father and Son, an invisible spirit permeating all existence: otherwise, how can we deny that there are two gods? This Logos united with human flesh and so raised it to the nature of deity. Thus the Father was not actually crucified; He only suffered in spirit along with His Son.

B. PAUL OF SAMOSATA

1. *Greek Monarchianism.* Theologians sought on the one hand to avoid the Charybdis of Monarchianism only to be devoured by the Scylla of Arianism. Some conceived of Christ as the monotheistic God, while others believed Him to be only a divinely commissioned creature; and to express all the concepts lying between these two extremes,

a vast diversity of formulas were invented. The divine truth of one synod became the blasphemy of the next. As a prelude to the Trinitarian disputes of the fourth century, we contemplate the doctrines of Paul of Samosata, bishop of Antioch, 260-272, the last of the Monarchians, who laid the groundwork for the Arian heresy.

2. *His Christology.* The Gnostic heresy had its roots in the concept that Christ had existed as a separate power since before the creation of the world; and it was this doctrine that Paul of Samosata set out to demolish. He taught that Father, Word, and Holy Ghost are simply three qualities of the Deity. As God sent forth the Logos from Himself, we may say that He was a begotten Son; nevertheless, He remains only an impersonal power. In this theology, Logos, Word, Son, are interchangeable titles for the second aspect of the Deity, while Jesus is simply a human being, and Christ is the Gospel manifestation of the Redeemer. The Logos was made manifest in Moses, in the prophets, and pre-eminently in that Son of David, who was born of the Virgin Mary. The Redeemer is therefore of the human race. But the Logos comes from above, and its union with Jesus was like an "inner man," without, however, dwelling essentially in Jesus; the Virgin did not give birth to the Logos, but to a human being, endowed with extraordinary power. At the baptism, the Redeemer, not the Logos, was anointed. As a result of His sinless perfection, Jesus progressed ethically and became more and more like God; the Father therefore endowed Him with miraculous powers, so that He was able to become the Savior of mankind and achieve complete union with God. This, like the doctrine of Theodotus, is Adoptionism. Paul argued that to make Jesus consubstantially the Son of God was to proclaim ditheism. He postulated instead an eternal Word and an in-dwelling of this Logos in Jesus; he taught that the Father, Word, and Holy Spirit are consubstantial, *homoousia*, which was in time to constitute the basis for orthodox Trinitarianism. But, since he denied that Jesus was Himself eternal God by birth and essence, he separated Him from the Word, and became one of the great heresiarchs. One of the principal

charges brought against him at the three councils which tried him was that he made the Son and the Father of an identical essence which placed them rather in the relationship of brothers than of universal Father-Creator and begotten Son.

Paul of Samosata was not easily defeated. A great synod was called at Antioch in 264 to condemn his heresy; but it was not until a third synod was convened in 268 that the metropolitan was excommunicated; and even so he could not be driven from the Church until four years later.

Lucian of Samosata developed a variation upon Paul's doctrine; and this it was which led directly to Arianism, a heresy which so corroded the whole eastern and African Church that it fell an easy prey to Islam in the middle of the seventh century.

CHAPTER XV

MANICHAEISM:

THE GREAT GNOSTIC SYNTHESIS

A. ORIGIN

1. *An Independent Cult.* Despite the fact that Manichaeism had its inception in the third century and that quite soon it claimed to be the only true Christianity, it was originally a separate synthesis based primarily upon Zoroastrian-Mithraic antecedents and was wholly independent of the Gospel Jesus, which it simply absorbed during its development.

2. *The Founder.* Manes was born near Susa, Persia, in 216 and was crucified by Bahram I in 276 at the instigation of the Zoroastrian priesthood. In his early life, he traveled widely in Egypt, Asia Minor, Mesopotamia, and India, absorbing everywhere the prevalent religious ideologies. Combining Persian ideology with elements drawn from Buddhism, the mystery-cults, and the religion of ancient Chaldea, he constructed a system strikingly similar to that of Christianity.

3. *The Manichaean Synthesis.* Mithraism was the fountainhead of Manichaean soteriology and metaphysics. Archelaus calls Manes the "Barbarian priest and crafty coadjutor of Mithras." [1] This was natural, since he was a Persian, his mind filled with Zoroastrian concepts. But by this time, Iranian ideology had commingled with that of Semitic Babylon, and we find important elements of both in the Manichaean creation-myth. We discover also another, completely absent from the cult of Mithra: the ethics and the eschatology of Buddhism, from which Manes absorbed the doctrines of metempsychosis and the

multiple hells, as well as the practice of celibacy, monachism, vegetarianism, and communism. Thus, much of what we find in the Gospel Jesus the Manichees obtained directly from its original source.

4. *Incorporated the Gospel Jesus.* Preaching this gospel, Manes began his ministry in his native land. But, like many another prophet, he encountered bitter persecution, and was thrown into prison. While there, his disciples obtained for him copies of the Christian Gospels,[2] which he studied intently, and upon which he engrafted his own "impious inventions." Manes concluded that Jesus was the true Christ, and that he himself was the New Testament Paraclete, the greatest and final prophet, whose revelations from the God of Light were definitive. Escaping from prison, he incorporated the authentic Pauline epistles into his sacred literature as well as the four Gospels, which he re-edited in the spirit of Marcion. He rejected the Old Testament entirely, as well as the Judaizing books of the New.

5. *A Dynamic Cult.* The system of Manes was dynamic, because it combined science and philosophy with an international religious synthesis. Although it claimed the authority of revelaton, it paid the highest deference to reason, as did all Gnostics. The Manichees had a consistent metaphysical and ethical system which freed the God of Light from any imputation of evil. Manes expressed outrage and amazement because the Catholics "call God the maker and contriver of Satan . . . and . . . declare that the only-begotten Christ . . . is the son of a certain Jewish woman, Mary, and born of blood and flesh." [3]

B. HISTORY

By the time of Manes' death, his followers were spread far and wide; and the history of the cult spanned a millennium. Perhaps no faith has ever endured more fearful persecution. It was pursued with fire and sword from the very beginning in its native Persia, and driven into exile and underground. Originally, Manes had no thought of opposing the Catholic Church, which he simply expected to come over to him; but the moment his followers appeared in the Roman world, they encountered frenzied abuse and hostility. And when Christianity came to power, it slaughtered the Manichees wholesale, or confiscated their goods and exiled them to barren islands,[4] as a gesture of gratuitous mercy. In spite of universal persecution, however, we find them returning in force to Zoroastrian Persia in 661, whence they were again driven by the Mohammedans. They were still numerous in Transoxiana and elsewhere in the year 1000, where, for centuries, they retained their beliefs while pretending to be devotees of the *Koran*.

The European history of Manichaeism is curious and interesting. The movement founded in Spain by Priscillian (beheaded 385), is described in detail by Leo the Great.[5] The doctrines of this group seem to have been a synthesis of Origenism, various Gnostic theologies, and concepts drawn from pagan sources. Leo accuses them of denying the Trinity, destroying the bond of marriage, forbidding the propagation of children, condemning the nature of the flesh, declaring the human soul to be the divine essence enclosed in a devilish body-prison, teaching that Christ was a phantasm who never experienced a true passion, and proclaiming that the flesh of the resurrected Christ was fictitious. The sect persisted for generations, weakened Spanish Christianity, and simplified the conquest of Spain by Islam in the eighth century.

In the succeeding centuries, in spite of constant persecution, Manichaean sectarians spread over large areas of Europe. In the East, after the eighth and ninth centuries, we find Euchites and Bogomiles wandering about the Balkans teaching the most extraordinary doctrines concerning creation, redemption, and predestination, all hearkening back to the dualistic principles of Manes. In the West, the Cathari had grown to enormous numbers in northern Italy by 1200, and in 1228 they were one-third of the population of Florence. Thereafter, they spread northward and westward. They permitted the eating of fish, because this form of life does not originate from sexual intercourse; all flesh derived from mammals was forbidden. In southern France, the Manichaean Albigenses became numerous and politically powerful by 1200, laughed derisively at the pope, and, because of their prosperity, were the envy of Catholics everywhere. They taught the transmigration of souls and extended docetism to Mary, Joseph, and St. John the Divine; they declared that Moses and John the Baptist were the principal tools of Satan, who is also the God of the Jews. The crusade instigated by Innocent III and led by Simon de Montfort against them about 1210 drowned the first European renaissance in blood; several hundred thousands of these Manichees were murdered. The Catholic theory was that the Albigenses were a gangrenous growth upon the Church-politic which must be cut away to save the rest from corruption and damnation. The revolt was crushed, but it served as a prelude for the Teutonic revolution three centuries later.

C. LITERATURE AND EXTANT SOURCE-MATERIAL

The Manichees were convinced that theirs was an immensely superior communion; nor were they deficient in numbers, leaders, doctrines, or literature. Especially elaborate were their books, which consisted, in addition to the four Christian Gospels and the Epistles of Paul, of commentaries, and revelations to Manes. Very interesting is a corpus of romances, known as the *Acts of John,* written about 140, *of Paul,* 165, *of Peter,* 200, *of Andrew,* 250, and *of Thomas,* cir. 275. These were composed by the Marcionite or some other Gnostic communion: all five, however, were edited and used by the Manichees; all relate what purport to be the missionary labors and the final martyrdom of the various apostles. It is these Gnostic documents which serve as authority for the stories that Paul and Peter were executed in Rome, the latter head downward; and that John was boiled in oil, as well as other tales which have passed into the popular folklore of Christian legend.

A single idea runs like a scarlet thread through these *Acts,* namely that all the apostles insisted upon celibacy from their converts and suffered martyrdom because they persuaded saintly women to abandon their husbands and repudiate the connubial relationship. It is incredible that all this should have been without some authentic foundation. The Manichean *Acts* taught also the docetic Christ and required that all converts sell their goods and give their wealth to the poor.

Our most authentic source of knowledge concerning Manichaeism is the Arabian *Fihrist,* published by Gustav Flugel in Germany about 1860. The best Christian sources are *The Disputation of Archelaus,* already cited; a book by Alexander of Lycopolis;[6] and the voluminous polemics of St. Augustine against the Manicheans, which monopolized much of his time and energy during the first twenty years of his Christian ministry.

Manichaeism became the successor to Marcionism and was feared and hated even more. The Church declared with Leo the Great that "In the detestable dogma of the Manichaeans there is absolutely nothing that can be adjudged tolerable in any degree."[7]

D. THE MANICHAEAN SYSTEM

1. *Metaphysical Dualism.* Manes appropriated from the Zoroastrian and Mithraic cosmology a universe which is divided into two pantheistic portions, the kingdoms of Light and Darkness, which are in juxtaposition, the former placed immediately above the latter, and each reaching out into infinity. At the beginning, these two realms existed without intermingling. The Supreme God was ungenerated: "The God of Light," says the *Fihrist,* "is without beginning."[8] His, the celestial realm, is essentially spiritual and abhors everything from below. Although Manes never calls Darkness itself God and his followers vehemently denied that it was so conceived,[9] Light and Darkness

are both eternal and uncreated powers in everlasting opposition and conflict. Even if the God of Light is alone prescient and can therefore eventually defeat the Power of Darkness, neither is omnipotent; neither can destroy the other at will; and the ultimate victory of Light depends upon its complete withdrawal from the nether Darkness.

2. *The Inception of the Cosmic Conflict.* The cycle of mundane history consists of the original commingling of Darkness and Light, the emancipation of the latter, and the final reconstitution of all things. The first step in this cosmic process occurred when Satan was formed out of the lower elements and strove to conquer the celestial realm.[10]

3. *The Creation.* The God of Light then sent His Word into the universe to create this earth, the moon, the sun, the planets, and the twelve elements or creative eons, and Primordial Man, whose seat is in the sun. This Man went forth to do battle with Satan; but he was defeated by the Prince of Darkness, and imprisoned in the nether universe. According to Alexander, Satan had actually attempted "to remove God from His position."[11] In order to curb the power of Darkness, the God of Light "sent the power which we call the soul into matter." When this is removed or rises above it, matter dies.

Here is the ultimate source of Rev. 12:7 and of *Paradise Lost.*

The King of Light was in this manner, as in Zoroastrianism, drawn into a long conflict with the Prince of Darkness, who, now in control of the Nether Universe, continued extremely active, seeking to retain his power over the light which he had imprisoned. The chief Archon joined himself to five evil feminine powers, and thus begot the first man, who was Adam and who combined the natures of Light and Darkness: his body was unavoidably of the nether elements; nevertheless, his soul, or spiritual aspect, was in the ascendant. The Archon next begot Eve, in whom, on the contrary, the lower elements were predominant. As a result, their descendants are torn by the everlasting war in their members and can rise to spirituality only by mortifying the flesh. In all this, of course, we find Persian cosmology combined with the same primitive Chaldean myth which is reproduced in Genesis and which Manes obtained directly from the Assyrian-Babylonian sources.

Adam and Eve, recognizing their miserable fate, begged help from the higher eons. The God of Light thereupon sent Jesus, the Incarnate Word, to warn Adam that Eve was the tool of the Prince of Darkness. He therefore rejected her blandishments. But now the earth Archon copulated with Eve, and she bore him first the terrible red-haired Cain; and later the fair-haired Abel, and two daughters, whom the two young men married. The wife of Abel was akin to light, and bore two daughters to the spiritual angel. Knowing that he had not cohabited with his own wife, Abel accused Cain of adultery, who, enraged, slew his brother and married the widow. To offset the loss of Abel, the Archon taught Eve witchcraft, by which she seduced Adam so that he became her husband and begot Seth, who was so filled with light-elements that the Archon conspired with Eve to destroy him. But Adam foiled them by taking the child away.

4. *The Advent of Christ.* In due course, the God of Light again sent His Word, the Christ, this time to accomplish the redemption of the Elect. The Manichaeans, according to Archelaus, taught that "the living Father . . . sent His own beloved Son" who "transformed Himself into the likeness of a man," [12] a concept similar to Paul's.

5. *The Three Classes among Mankind.* The purpose of all useful mundane activity is to release imprisoned light or soul from the clutches of matter. As with the Valentinians, the human race divides into three classes. First, there are the Adepts, the Elect, who renounce private property, practice celibacy, observe strict vegetarianism, and never engage in trade. Second, there are the hearers, men and women of good will, who, however, cannot contain themselves, and who must, therefore, earn money, own property, eat flesh, and marry; these will ultimately earn high reward by serving and supporting the Elect in this life. And, finally, there are the completely sensual members of the human race, totally lost in wickedness, who reject the

gospel of Manes. At death, the Elect go directly to the Paradise of Light; the hearers must spend a period of purification in purgatory, after which they also ascend into the celestial realm; the wicked are doomed to eternal and irrevocable suffering in the three Manichaean hells. The bodies of all return to the dust whence they came.

6. *Metempsychosis.* Originally, the Manichaeans believed in the transmigration of the soul; and the fate of each was to be determined by his conduct.[13] In the next life, furthermore, each would become whatever he eats, —a dog, a camel, a chicken, or a mouse. However, when Manichaeism appeared as a full-blown competitor of Christianity in the West, it had discarded this reconstructed Buddhist eschatology in favor of the Zoroastrian purgatory.

7. *Eschatology.* The eschatology of Manes was simple and popular. At the death of an Adept, the Light-God, as in Zoroastrianism, sends a guide, who is one of Ishtar's light-maidens, to escort him. The devils approach to seize the dying soul, but the supernatural protector drives them away; on the way heavenward, the soul rests a while in the moon, then in the sun, and finally attains the Paradise of Light. When a hearer dies, the devils approach likewise; the soul, its light not quenched but burdened with nether elements, is conducted to purgatory, where all its dross is burned away, so that it too may proceed on its celestial journey. The souls of those who have rejected Manichaeism are left to the tender mercies of the devils, and they burn forever in hell, but are never consumed; their wailing is met throughout eternity with cold reproaches from the saints.

8. *The Final Holocaust.* According to Manes, the process of freeing the light-elements must be completed before the restitution of the world can take place. The signal will be given by "The Third Ancient One"; the angels who sustain the heavens and the earth will let go, and matter will return to its original chaos. An immense holocaust will break out and burn for 1468 years, which is almost the exact duration of the sothic year; all remaining light will be released and primordial darkness will supervene.

9. *Sacraments and Practices.* The Manichees administered baptism and the eucharist, but only as symbolic rites.

10. *Christology.* In his original system, Manes projected a novel Christology, according to which the prophets of the Old Testament were the lying and deceitful servants of the Prince of this World, who, through them, constantly foretold a Messiah who would establish a world-wide Jewish empire. The historical Jesus was intended by Yahweh as the leader who would implement this nefarious conspiracy. But the God of Light frustrated the plot by making His Christ incarnate in the very person chosen to become the Jewish Messiah when this personage was only seven years old.[14] Thus, when Christ-Jesus taught celibacy, brotherhood, self-denial, dualism, repudiation of family, predestination and election by grace, and the renunciation of property, it was the incarnate Christ who spoke; but when He accepted passages in the Old Testament as prophecies of Himself, it was the Jewish Messiah speaking. Since, however, the Christ in Jesus predominated over the Messiah, He proved so repulsive to the Jews that, ironically, they murdered their own intended king.

This concept, however, was later altered for another, similar to that of Marcion. The apparent passion of this revised Christ was a symbol of the universal process by which light is released from matter.

11. *Soteriology.* The Manichaean doctrine of grace and predestination was more extreme than Paul's. There is no atonement, since the purpose of the Manichaean Christ is not to immortalize, but simply to reveal, to instruct, and to erect the machinery by which the souls of the Elect are translated to Paradise. Their redemptive capacities are congenital. When the light-elements predominate, as in Adam and Seth, men automatically reject all sensual impulses. If they are constituted with partial spirituality, they will serve the Elect throughout their lives and become eligible to the purification of purgatory. But if Satan, matter, and darkness are in the ascendant, they must be consigned to the everlasting flames.

12. *Indulgences and Purgatory*. The Manichaean was a dedicated but practical communion offering salvation but never seeking to become the state. The straight and narrow path was for the Elect: but provision was made for those who could not renounce property, family, and a career in the world. We must not, however, mistake the nature of this indulgence: the Manichees never conceded that marriage, trade, or the possession of property was anything but evil. Yet under certain conditions, it was possible to obtain indulgence (an idea which Catholics later translated into a scandalous commercialism), the consideration being that sinners must spend their lives serving the saints and must undergo subsequent purification in purgatory. This naturally created a clerical bureaucracy, which was relieved of all necessity to perform productive labor. Permission to commit a specific sin or crime, however, was never granted for a material consideration; nor was the indulgence to live as hearers placed on a commercial basis.

13. *Became the Model for the Catholic Church*. Even among the subtle and libertarian Greeks, Manichaeism made considerable progress; and in the West, setting itself up as the only true Christianity, it reached the zenith of its virility somewhat more than a century after the death of Manes. As we shall see, the victory of Augustine over the Manichees was of a Pyrrhic nature, because at the close of his career he again became, as his Pelagian opponents emphasized, essentially a Manichee. He placed the Original Sin of Paul and Manes at the center of his system, which became the basis for European life for a thousand years. In the medieval Church, the celibates became the first-class Catholics; the lay members, who must receive constant indulgences to commit sin, the inferior orders; and purgatory, in time, one of the most important elements in the Catholic faith.

E. MANICHAEISM AS REVEALED IN THE POLEMICS OF AUGUSTINE

1. *Quotations*. It is indeed fortunate that Augustine like Origen, reproduces in his controversial works ke

passages from his opponents, which reveal their doctrines with substantial accuracy.

2. *Concerning Sex.* In Augustine's *Morals of the Manichees*, we discern the metaphysics by which these heretics condemned the sex relationship. The soul of God is constantly being freed from its physical fetters in the process of natural growth and death; but in the act of sexual intercourse, that spirit is encumbered by the dregs of creation. The joining of male to female, therefore, is the means by which the soul is chained to Satan and prevents its progress into the Kingdom of Light.

3. *The Nature of Evil.* Fortunatus declares that since God can bring "forth from Himself nothing evil . . . the things that are His remain incorrupt." Therefore all evil things in the world have an origin and a creator other than the God of Light.[15] But Augustine, following at that time the Greek Fathers, declares: "Neither is that . . . which the ancients called Hyle . . . an evil."[16] Evil is not an essence, but only the absence of good, or the corruption of nature.[17]

4. *Jewish Forgeries.* Augustine tells us in his *Confessions* that while he was a Manichee, he was under the influence of Faustus. And from his *Reply* to this former mentor, we find passages, which we reproduce below, similar to statements by Thomas Paine, which express his own conviction, the words of a fierce belligerent contending for the destiny of Europe. Faustus declared that the Bible is filled with contradictions and forgeries. "But," he exclaimed, "what escape from this difficulty can there be for you," since you condemn "the use of reason, which is the prerogative of human nature?"[18] "By examining everything," he declared, "we determine which scriptures contain Christ's actual words . . . your predecessors have made many interpolations in the words of our Lord, which thus appear under His name, while they disagree with His doctrine. Besides . . . the writings are not the production of Christ and His apostles, but a compilation of rumors and beliefs, made long after their departure, by some obscure semi-Jews, not in harmony

even with one another, and published by them under the name of the apostles, or of those considered the followers of the apostles, so as to give the appearance of apostolic authority to all these blunders and falsehoods."[19] The Gospels must "be tested to find whether they are true and genuine; for the enemy who comes by night has corrupted almost every passage by sowing tares among the wheat."[20] No wonder the Church pursued the Manichees with ferocious violence!

5. *Rejects the Incarnation.* Faustus denies that Christ ever had a human birth; for in the authentic Gospels His life begins at the baptism. As for the genealogies and the story of the Magi, all these are obvious forgeries and interpolations. He declares[21] that once he had tried seriously to believe in the incarnation; but when he found the accounts of Luke and Matthew in such hopeless disagreement, he betook himself to Mark and John, who say nothing of the birth of Jesus or of His descent from David. Jesus Himself never claimed any earthly parents [22] but said, on the contrary, that He was not of this world and that He came forth from God the Father.

6. *Repudiates the Old Testament.* Faustus declares that neither Catholics nor Manichees expect the Messianic kingdom prophesied by or among the Jews, the purpose of which was to make of them imperial masters;[23] and since both reject their ambitions and their ceremonials, the Catholics should be honest enough to reject their scriptures also.[24] In reply, Augustine declares that the Old Testament must be interpreted allegorically and symbolically.[25]

7. *Declares Belief in Genuine Gospel.* Augustine condemns Faustus for not accepting the Gospels *in toto;* to which the latter retorts: "I should rather ask *you* if you believe, since you give no proof of your belief. I have left my father, mother, wife, and children, and all else that the Gospel requires . . . I have parted with all gold and silver and have left off carrying money in my purse; content with daily bread; without anxiety for the morrow and without solicitude about how I shall be fed, o

wherewithal I shall be clothed; and can you ask if *I* believe the Gospel!"[26]

8. *Is Paul in Contradiction?* Augustine cites Paul[27] to prove that Christ was of the seed of David.[28] Faustus denies that the Son of God was so descended;[29] for if Paul ever maintained such a doctrine, he contradicted himself;[30] and thus he either changed his opinion with greater knowledge, or the first text is a forgery,—which is the only reasonable hypothesis. Augustine replies that Paul never changed his mind; that we must accept as true whatever the canon states; and that, if anyone is "perplexed by apparent contradictions, the only conclusion is that he does not understand."[31]

9. *No Jewish Prophecies of Christ.* Faustus now turns to the prophecies and the prophets. They are accepted by the orthodox, he says, because they are believed to have prophesied the coming of Christ. "For my part," he asserts, "I have read the prophets with the most eager attention, and have found no such prophecies."[32]

Augustine does not invoke the prophetic texts cited by Matthew. Instead, he declares: "The whole contents of the Scriptures are either directly or indirectly about Christ."[33] He continues with a series of interpretations, of which the following are typical:[34] God set His mark on Cain: this means that the Jewish race will never lose the Sign of the Law; Noah was saved by water and wood: this prefigures our salvation through Christ by baptism and the cross; the Ark contained all kinds of animals: this signifies that the Catholic Church would embrace all nations. Even the Jews must now come to the Catholics to understand their own scriptures, which, without this allegorical interpretation, "must appear trifling and ridiculous."[35] The literalist Faustus, says Augustine, cannot understand these profound truths, because he is full of levity and skepticism.

10. *Moses Condemned.* Faustus now delivers an excoriation of Moses, who cursed Him who was to hang on a tree, and who taught in all things the reverse of the Gospel Jesus.[36] For while Moses commanded the Jews

to increase and multiply, Jesus took His disciples away from their wives, and forbade them to marry. "Moses hurled his maledictions against Christ, against light, against chastity, against everything divine."[36] Faustus reproaches the Catholics bitterly for deluding themselves with the materialistic promises of the Old Testament God, whose lures are not merely wicked and contemptible, but completely false as well.[37] Since He is unable to rescue His own chosen people from their universal misery, certainly Christians are fools to seek redemption from him. Those who are converted from heathenism to Christ but who still run after the dead Adonai of the Jews, are "like an abandoned woman who, after the death of her husband, marries two others." Faustus cites the passage in which Christ says that Moses wrote of Him; and he continues: "I have searched the Scriptures . . . and have found no prophecies of Christ . . . Either the verse must be spurious, or Jesus is a liar."[38]

11. *Christ Unlike Moses.* Faustus warns the Catholics not to cite Deut. 18:15: "I will raise up unto them from among their brethren a prophet like unto thee." For this could not refer to Christ, who was as unlike Moses as possible. Furthermore, Jesus could never have made this statement to the Jews, for had He done so, they would have demanded the texts to which He referred. "The most obvious reply" to this, said Augustine, "is that Faustus does not understand . . . he reads with a hostile, unbelieving mind; . . . You are aware that if you refuse to believe the Gospel . . . you must fail utterly in the attempt to substitute for it any trustworthy record of the sayings and doings of Christ."[39]

12. *Jesus Destroyed the Jewish Law.* Faustus now turns to Matt. 5:17, in which Jesus says: "Think not that I am come to destroy the law and the prophets."[40] Since this text occurs only in Matthew, which was not even written by the apostle, we can only conclude that it is a forgery. The fact is, continues Faustus,[41] that Jesus *was* destroying the Law and that the Jews had the best possible reason for believing that He *had* come for that very purpose; and therefore, from their point of view, they

were justified in putting Him to death. It is absurd for Catholics to quote this text against the Manichaeans;[42] for if Christ really made such a declaration, then there are no Christians in the world, for all of them reject the Jewish law, and, in fact, the Jewish god himself, who pronounced the irrevocable penalty of death against every sabbath-breaker, which all Christians certainly are.

13. *We Must Believe.* In Chapter V we summarized the arguments of Faustus against the Virgin Birth and the genealogies. To this Augustine replies that we *must* believe the scriptures when they say that Christ was of the seed of David after the flesh, and that His mother was the Virgin Mary: ". . . whoever denies the relationship of Mary to David, evidently opposes the pre-eminent authority of . . . Scripture."[43] Augustine declares grimly that, in obedience to Moses, "the Catholic Church, as with the spiritual two-edged sword of both Testaments, puts to death all who try to turn us away from God."[44]

14. *The Catholic and the Docetic Christ.* "It is not," declares Faustus, "in accordance with the law of nature that a virgin should bring forth, and still less that she should still be a virgin after bringing forth. Why, then, do you refuse to admit that Christ, in a preternatural manner, suffered without submitting to the condition of birth? Believe me: in substance, both our beliefs are contrary to nature; but our belief is decent, and yours is not . . . we hold that He suffered in appearance, but did not really die . . . you have only to acknowledge that the birth too was a delusion, and our whole dispute will be at an end."[45]

15. *Devil-Doctrine.* Faustus declares[46] that when the Catholics cite Paul[47] to the effect that forbidding to marry and abstinence from meats is devil-doctrine, they must first acknowledge that Moses was equally guilty in prohibiting swine's flesh and other meats; and when they degrade matrons in contrast to virgins, they fall under the same condemnation.[48] The Manichees, says Faustus, use no moral suasion to reject marriage, and limit only their clergy to celibacy and a vegetarian diet. They permit

all their communicants to follow their natural inclinations: they may, therefore, with equal approbation, marry or remain celibate. Christ is the truth, the light, and the way: He does not attempt to coerce; He only leads and instructs. As sin does not consist in an overt act, but in a moral impulse, marriage itself is no greater offense than the desire for it. And, since every Manichee knows full well that the punishment for this concession to his lower nature is a period of purification in purgatory, he incurs no moral onus in living according to impulses over which he has no control. The Catholics, says Faustus, "are the functionaries of the devils in your constant endeavors to induce virgins to make this profession, so that in all your churches they nearly outnumber the married women . . . Why do you ensnare wretched young women, if it is the will of devils, and not Christ, that they fulfill?" [49]

Faustus denied that Paul wrote the disputed passage in First Timothy, and cites the *Acts of Paul and Thecla* to prove that this apostle glorified celibacy. Faustus then cites the passage from Matthew concerning those who make "themselves eunuchs for the kingdom of heaven," and asks: "Is this also the doctrine of devils? . . . and are Paul and Christ thereby proved to be the priests of devils?"

16. *Jews Had No Belief in Heaven*. Faustus expresses doubt that Moses wrote the books attributed to him. As to the patriarchs, whose conduct was "shocking and detestable," he declares that they never believed in hell, and if they go there this will only prove that the worship of the Jewish God "is the one sure way to go to hell."[50]

F. PERMANENT INFLUENCE

Manichaeism was the last great attempt in the ancient world to make Christianity an exclusive and dedicated community; to free the Gospel from its Jewish integument; to supply a logical basis for its doctrine in philosophy and metaphysics; to render it acceptable to human reason; to separate the Church from the state; to abolish belief in the Virgin Birth in favor of a single-natured, supernatural Christ; and to set free the mind of man from dogmas and doctrines derived from contradictory and inadequate revelations. All of this was rejected by the Church. On the other hand, it was the Manichees who established in Western Europe the ideas of human depravity, prevenient grace, absolute predestination, purgatory, lay indulgences, an unmarried priesthood, and holy monachist orders, all of which were absorbed by the Church, which made them the basis for its practical life and discipline.

CHAPTER XVI

THE TRINITARIAN CONTROVERSY

A. ITS GENESIS

1. *Inevitable Development from the Gospels.* In the history of speculation, there have, perhaps, never been any controversies comparable to those which raged over the Trinity and which stemmed from the Gospel itself. There were many other powerful cults and religions which had virgin births and savior-gods; but there was no other which had an historic founder who, in His lifetime, proclaimed Himself a divinity who must die as an atonement for mankind, whose body and blood must be consumed as a eucharist, and who would return shortly as the universal moral judge. Almost all controversy resulted from the necessity of determining the precise nature of this Savior and His position in the godhead, a problem upon which the Synoptics shed very little light indeed.

2. *The Christology of Paul.* Paul was the first who attempted to resolve the enigma; and though his writings contain no hint of a Virgin Birth or any explanation as to how the godhead was joined to humanity in Jesus, the concept of the pre-existing Christ is central in his theology. He declares: ". . . there is but one God, the Father, of whom are all things, and we in him; and one Lord Jesus Christ, by whom are all things, and we by him."[1] Here Christ, like the *Nous* of Anaxagoras and the *Demiurgos* of Plato, emerges as the divine agency who fashioned the universe out of the pre-existing chaos. Again Christ is revealed as "the image of the invisible God," and as His agent who created all things "that are in heaven . . and earth, visible and invisible."[2]

3. *The Logos Doctrine.* The Fourth Gospel elaborated the Pauline Christology in the Logos Doctrine, which made the metaphysics of Plato and Zeno forever a central concept of Christianity:

> In the beginning was the Word, and the Word was with God, and the Word was God . . .
> All things were made by him; and without him was not anything made that was made . . .
> And the Word was made flesh, and dwelt among us . . .
> And I saw and bare record that this is the Son of God.

Some three centuries later, Augustine wrote that, having obtained "certain books of the Platonists," he found the same doctrine. "But that the Word was made flesh and dwelt among us, I read not there." [3]

In fact, a cursory knowledge of Greek metaphysics establishes that the central dogma of Christianity is a Greek philosophic concept.

4. *Slow Growth.* The growth of Trinitarianism in the ancient Church was slow and gradual. Since I John 5:7 is a late forgery, the nearest to a Trinitarian text in the New Testament is Matt. 28:19: "Go ye therefore, and teach all nations, baptizing them in the name of the Father, and of the Son, and of the Holy Ghost."

5. *Reaction against Heresy.* The heresies were unacceptable attempts to render the Christian faith consistent or comprehensible: and every clause in the official creeds was a weapon to outlaw some heresy. The necessities of the Church were inexorable: a Savior, a God, a redemptive machinery had to be erected which would be not merely effective but which would be popular with the masses and which would make the hierarchy supreme. To meet these requirements, a doctrine totally repugnant to reason became imperative at every turn.

6. *The Apostles' Creed.* The simple Apostles' Creed[4] was designed especially to defeat the Ebionites, the Marcionites, and the Sabellians; essentially it is only an elabora-

tion of the creed of Ignatius, to which we referred in a previous chapter. Almost every phrase is a direct denial of some doctrine maintained by one or another of these sects:

1. I believe in God the Father Almighty, invisible and impassible.
2. And in Jesus Christ, His only Son, our Lord;
3. Who was born from the Holy Ghost, of the Virgin Mary;
4. Was crucified under Pontius Pilate, and buried;
5. He descended to hell; on the third day he rose again from the dead.
6. He ascended to the heavens; he sitteth at the right hand of the Father;
7. Whence he is to come to judge the quick and the dead.
8. And in the Holy Ghost;
9. The Holy Church.
10. The remission of sins.
11. The resurrection of *this* flesh.

After the Gnostic Paul and the Platonic-Stoic Fourth Gospel gained currency among the orthodox, no hearing could ever be had in the Church for any other than a pre-existing Christ. But this development only created new difficulties. For the question arose: What is the relation between the Word and the Son? between both of these and Christ? between them and Jesus? and between all these and the godhead?

7. *Rudimentary Trinitarianism.* An examination of the works of Athenagoras, Tatian, Theophilus, Hippolytus, Novatian, and Dionysius of Alexandria, all written between 170 and 250, reveals that their concept of the Christ was substantially Arian: that is, the same as expressed in Col 1:15, "the image of God, the first-born of every creature." Thus, the Son was created by the Word, was the first of all creatures, and was brought into existence for the express purpose of fashioning the universe and its inhabitants.

The elaborate formulary written by Irenaeus about 175 was simply another Christological creed; it could scarce have been Trinitarian, since the conflict over this concept broke out only after the Patripassian heresy.

B. TERTULLIAN

Tertullian was the first spokesman for the Church who wrestled consciously and elaborately with the Trinitarian problem. In his zeal to combat Praxean modalism, he was intent primarily on establishing the separation of the divine persons. In so doing, he denied not only their equality, but also their co-eternity. These heretics, he says, declare "that the Father, the Son, and the Holy Ghost are the very self-same Person."[6] And he continues that the Son derives from the Father, who "is distinct from the Son," and "greater than the Son."[7] And in another passage, we read: "God . . . has not always been Father . . . For He could not have been Father previous to the Son."[8]

Thus the Son becomes a subordinate derivative, neither co-extensive nor co-eternal with the Father. Nevertheless, Tertullian anticipated the theology of Basil, who declared two centuries later that we must preserve "the community of essence" as well as "the distinction of the hypostases."[9]

Tertullian originated an even more significant element in the Nicene theology by declaring that Son is only another name for Word. He declared that in our understanding of the Trinity, we must leave intact its *monarchia*, that is, its unity; but we must also preserve its *economy*, that is, the distinction of its personalities.[10]

Unaware that later theology would make the Son co-infinite and co-eternal with the Father, Tertullian nevertheless sought to establish an identity of essence and indivisibility of operation among the persons of the godhead. God, he declared, "sent forth the Word . . . just as the root puts forth the tree, and the fountain the river, and the sun the ray . . . the Word of God has actually received as His own peculiar designation the name of *Son*. But still the tree is not severed from the root, nor the river from the fountain, nor the ray from the sun; nor, indeed, is the Word separated from God" in the "dispensation of the divine tripersonality."[11]

Tertullian wrote an early Trinitarian formulary to combat Marcionism and other heresies which denied the Virgin Birth and the resurrection of the body or repudiated the Old Testament and the Jewish God.[12] Another, to refute the Patripassians, shows a distinct development: "We believe" in "one God, but under the following dispensation or *oikonomia* . . . that this one only God has also a Son, His Word, who proceeded from Himself, by whom all things were made . . . Him we believe to have been sent by the Father into the Virgin . . . being both Man and God, the Son of Man and the Son of God . . . we believe Him to have suffered, died, and been buried, according to the Scriptures, and . . . to be sitting at the right hand of the Father, and that He will come to judge the quick and the dead; who sent also . . . from the Father . . . the Holy Ghost, the Paraclete, the sanctifier of the faith of those who believe in the Father, and in the Son, and in the Holy Ghost." [13]

This was the most advanced Trinitarian formula extant before 225.

C. ORIGEN

The next great contributor to the Trinitarian concept was the Greek Alexandrian eunuch, Origen, 185-254. He was said to have written six thousand books; and, though this is an obvious exaggeration, his scholarship and literary industry were certainly prodigious. In spite of all this, however, he had the misfortune of becoming an almost universal heretic; and one of the principal acts of the Fifth Ecumenical Council [14] was his official anathematization.

Origen is now best remembered for his *Contra Celsum*. But it was in the *De Principiis* that he revealed most of his theology; and in the preface to this he developed a Trinitarian concept designed to refute the Marcionites and the Sabellians. At this point of the controversy, the Son-Word had advanced enormously; but the position of the Holy Spirit was still fluid. According to Origen, the three persons are co-eternal and consubstantial but not co-equal. In answer to an accusation by Celsus that the Christians made Jesus greater than God Himself, Origen declares specifically: "The Son is not mightier than the Father, but inferior to Him." [15]

Nevertheless, Origen represents a midway position between Tertullian and Athanasius, because he declares for the timeless and eternal generation of the Son. The Father is the primal essence from which both the Word and the Holy Spirit derive. In the sense, then, that all three are of the same substance and in their operations timeless, there are no degrees of priority among the persons. The Father is the primal infinity which bestows subsistence upon all creation; the Word bestows the rational faculty on the soul; the Holy Spirit sanctifies, and is given only to those who receive salvation through Christ. Thus, God the Father exists first, not in time, but as a derivative source; the Word issues from the Father as His image; and the Holy Spirit proceeds as a vital and sanctifying force. Thus each person is a separate hypostasis in a trinal unity, the second deriving from the Father, and the third proceeding from the other two.[16]

Thus Origen, like Tertullian, conceives of the Word and Son as identical to each other and consubstantial with the Father; however, he does what Tertullian did not: he makes them also co-eternal, and he calls them *hypostases*. The subordinationism of Tertullian was one of potency as well as succession. In Origen it is one of *extent* only. Suppose, says Origen, that there were a statue so great as to fill the entire world, so huge that it could not be seen; then suppose another generated simultaneously in its image, of the same form and substance, but smaller; this would illustrate the relationship of the Son to the Father.[17] Since the Father is called omnipotent, the same quality must belong to the Son;[18] for the same primal goodness which resides forever in the Father is likewise shared by the Son.[19] Origen continues: "Nothing in the Trinity can be called greater or less since the fountain of divinity contains all things by His Word and Reason." [20] All created things derive "existence from God the Father; . . . their rational nature from the Word; . . . their holiness from the Holy Spirit."[21]

In Origen, however, we note a lack of precision, resulting from his uncertainty as to the identity of Word and Son: he could not admit full equality among his Trinitarian hypostases. His works therefore became a battleground, in which both Arians and Athanasians claimed his support. Among his devoted students, we find Jerome, Rufinus, Gregory Nazianzen, the two Eusebii, Basil the Great, St. John Chrysostom, and many others.

To summarize: Origen's advance over Tertullian consists in the fact that he conceived of the three persons as eternal and incorporeal hypostases, of whom the second and third possess by derivation and procession the same essence, goodness, and omnipotence as the Father, but who do not, like Him, possess infinity and are, therefore, not co-equal. In order to establish the equality of the three hypostatic persons of the godhead, it now remained only to proclaim the identity of Son and Word, the infinity of the Son and the Holy Spirit, and their consubstantiality with the Father.

D. PAUL OF SAMOSATA

The Eastern Church struggled desperately with this problem, especially after the death of Origen; and when Paul of Samosata became an heresiarch by separating Jesus-Christ from the Word, and making the Trinity a consubstantial monarchy, the whole controversy was bitterly intensified. Gregory Thaumaturgos was one of the leaders who condemned Paul at the Council of Antioch in 265 because his consubstantialism seemed to reek of Sabellianism. And so we find, ironically enough, that the groundwork for Athanasian-Nicene Trinitarianism was created by three great heretics: Tertullian, Origen, and Paul of Samosata.

E. THE ARIAN CONTROVERSY

1. *The "Blasphemy" of Arius.* The Origenist Trinitarian concept was challenged both from the left and

from the right when the Arian heresy exploded about 320, compelling the Church to establish more precise concepts about God, the Trinity, the Word, the Son, the Christ, and Jesus, since it was now obvious that many heresies could luxuriate under the general banner of the Apostles' Creed. Everywhere theologians were seeking some formula which would make the Father into the Supreme God, and yet provide a Christ whose atonement would be efficacious for redemption, which was believed impossible unless He was separated from, yet equal to, and consubstantial and co-eternal with, the Father in an indivisible Trinity.

The eruption began when the presbyter Arius declared his position to Alexander, then metropolitan of Alexandria. Hilary of Poitiers reports that Arius made the following "blasphemous" address to his bishop: "We confess one God, alone unmade, alone eternal, alone unoriginate . . . The Son is neither eternal, nor co-eternal, nor co-uncreate with the Father, nor has He an existence collateral with the Father, as some say, who postulate two unborn principles . . ." [22]

2. *Arius Deposed and Excommunicated.* Although this statement was undoubtedly in harmony with Pauline as well as second-century theology, it had now become blasphemy. Alexander therefore convened a synod in 324 at which Arius and some of his fellows were violently anathematized; and, in a letter, the bishop falsely accused Arius of saying that the Word of God is a creature, who, therefore, could not be of the same essence with the Father; that, according to this heretic, "there was a time when God was not the Father. The Word of God was not always, but was made 'from things that are not'; . . . For the Son is a thing created . . . nor is He like to the Father in substance; nor is he the true and natural Word of the Father . . . He is by His very nature changeable and mutable . . . The Father also is ineffable to the Son; neither does the Word perfectly and accurately know the Father." [23]

The nexus of the controversy was whether Son and Word are identical. Arius denied this, although he declared that the Word, which created the Son, was a member of the godhead. In his confusion, Alexander did not distinguish between Word and Son. Arius wrote to Lucian of Samosata that he was persecuted by Alexander because he could not consent to the doctrine of "God always, the Son always; as the Father, so the Son; the Son co-exists unbegotten with God . . . These are impieties to which we cannot listen." [24]

3. *The Church Split in Twain.* Only a scant decade before had the Church achieved toleration, and already it was splitting into two hostile camps, with thousands of the saints literally ready to spring at each others' throats over the question as to whether the Son and Word are different beings or two names for one. Arianism fell into fertile ground, and spread like wildfire throughout the Greek Church: and the Catholic world stood aghast at the implications of the heresy. It is true that Arius wished to reduce only the Son to creature-status, and never questioned the nature of the Word; but, because he wished to separate the Son from the Trinity, the victory of his heresy would eventually have made of Jesus simply a Great Examplar, a divinely-endowed ethical teacher, as He is in many modern Unitarian churches. Under such a doctrine, there would probably have been no priest-state and no Dark Ages.

4. *Constantine Intervenes.* Constantine had made Christianity the state-religion to consolidate his power. When, therefore, he found the Church thus rent in twain, he sent Hosius of Spain to Alexandria[25] to reconcile the contending factions. But when the rupture only widened, the emperor commanded the bishops to meet in a council to devise a formula by which to attain peace and unity. Constantine knew little and cared less about the metaphysics of theology; but it was imperative that some kind of ecclesiastical harmony be achieved so that he could continue the administration of the empire. He wrote, therefore, to Alexander and Arius that they must resolve their differences "by the uniting power of their common doctrines," just as contending disputants in the philosophic school were wont to do.[26]

5. *The Council of Nicaea.* And so, by imperial com

mand, in the city of Nicaea in Bithynia near the Black Sea, in the year 325, the First Ecumenical Council convened 318 bishops, to resolve the "small and very insignificant questions" raised by Arius.[26] The emperor himself opened the proceedings with an exhortation to unity.[27] The position of the Lucianist-Arians was first presented by some half dozen bishops;[28] but the uproar against their formulary was so great that it was instantly repudiated and Arius denounced.

With an eye on the weather-vane, the opportunistic and half-Arian historian, Eusebius Pamphylius, thereupon presented a creed intended to serve as a compromise. This, the Arians were willing to accept,[29] since it left the road open to a construction which would not completely invalidate their position; the emperor, however,[30] perhaps at the suggestion of Hosius, suggested that the word *homoousian*, "of one substance," should be added to the description of the Son, which, translated into Latin, reads "consubstantial." After much assurance that this would not involve the faith in Sabellianism, the Council accepted what is known as the Nicene Creed: [30]

> "We believe in One God, the Father Almighty, Maker of all things . . .
> "And in One Lord Jesus Christ, the Son of God, begotten of the Father, Only-begotten, that is, from the essence of the Father; God from God, Light from Light, Very God from Very God, begotten, not made, one in essence with the Father, by Whom all things were made, both things in heaven and things in earth; Who for us men and for our salvation came down and was made flesh, was made man, suffered and rose again the third day, ascending into heaven, and cometh to judge the quick and the dead.
> "And in the Holy Ghost.
> "And those who say, 'Once He was not,' and 'Before His generation He was not,' and 'He came to be from nothing,' or those who pretend that the Son of God is 'Of other subsistence or essence,' or 'created,'

or 'alterable,' or 'mutable,' the Catholic Church anathematizes."

The formula suggested by Eusebius had read instead: 30

"And in one Lord Jesus Christ, the Word of God, God from God, Light from Light, Life from Life, Son Only-begotten, first-born of every creature, before all the ages, begotten from the Father, by whom also all things were made."

By substituting *Son* for *Word,* so that there could be no confusion, the Nicene Creed condemned the doctrines of both Arius and Paul of Samosata; and, to make the faith forever secure, it added the words *Very God of Very God* and twice declared that the Son is consubstantial with the Father. Whereas the Arians declared that Christ is identical with the Son and therefore a creature, the Athanasians asserted that Word and Son are identical, and Christ-Jesus the dual-natured incarnation of the second person of the Trinity.

6. *Conflict and Violence.* Constantine considered all this an insignificant dispute; but to the Greek theologians of the fourth century, it was a matter of eternal life and death. This *Homoousian* let loose a fury among mankind that has rarely been paralleled. Millions suffered violence or death in the pursuant wars and persecutions. Hundreds of bishops were exiled or murdered at the command of other bishops who, when the tide turned, visited the same treatment upon their rivals. The great Athanasius was driven from his see five times, and on at least two occasions barely escaped with his life. His Arian enemies, seated in his place of power, were not so fortunate: two of them were lynched, and another was barely saved from the bloodthirsty mobs by the police. Arians and Athanasians alike sought to use the secular arm to terrify and assassinate their opponents, and to seize their congregations, churches, and revenues by force.

7. *The Succession of Emperors.* At his death in 337, Constantine divided his empire among his three sons, Con-

stantine, Constans, and Constantius. Constantine was killed in 340 invading the territory of Constans, who thereupon became sole emperor of the West. Constantius, an Arian, remained in control of the East. After Constans was murdered in 350, Constantius began an aggressive campaign to establish Arianism everywhere, a step from which he had previously desisted in 343, only because Constans threatened a general war if he did so. Upon the death of Constantius in 361, the pagan Julian, who had secretly been initiated into the Eleusinian mystery ten years before, became emperor; and he established universal toleration, recalled the expropriated bishops from exile, and restored their churches. Yet the orthodox hated him for extending amnesty to their Christian rivals more than they hated Diocletian for persecuting all varieties of their faith. For his part, Julian amused himself by listening to Arian and orthodox bishops castigate each other, and he said the saints fought for episcopal power and revenue like wild beasts in an arena. The Christians were highly incensed because Julian expelled them from the army and forbade them to study poetry, rhetoric, or philosophy.[31] They should scarcely have resented the latter privation, because they themselves soon outlawed all such learning; and the wisdom of the former was soon demonstrated for, as Sozomen candidly admits,[32] after a reign of two years, the philosophic Julian was assassinated by a Christian soldier on the field of battle. Jovian then succeeded; but upon his death a few months later, Valens, an enlightened Arian, came to the Eastern throne, and ruled until 378, when he was killed in battle against the Goths. Finally, the orthodox Theodosius became emperor, and with him the Nicene Creed was at last victorious.

8. *Little Arianism in the West*. It is interesting to note that no western emperor and few Latin bishops succumbed to the Arian heresy. The Roman mind in theology as in politics and philosophy was more practical and pedestrian than was that of the subtle and intellectual Greeks. "The bishops . . . of the Western Empire," says Theodoret, "were men of simple and unsophisticated

ways." [33] Pope Gregory the Great was later to throw this in the face of the Greeks: "As we have not your cleverness, so neither have we your impostures." [34]

9. *Homoiousians.* After Nicea, desperate efforts were made to revise the creed, first by the Arians and later by the Semi-Arians, the *Homoiousians,* who declared with an iota that the Son was *like* the Father in essence. Between 325 and 367, twenty-eight synods were held—all but two in the East—of which only four were orthodox and at which a great number of creeds were adopted. Only two Eastern synods were Athanasian: that held at Sardica in 343, while Constans was threatening Constantius with war, and that of 363 at Antioch while the orthodox Jovian was emperor.

10. *The Heteroousians.* Three important exponents of post-Nicene Arianism were Aëtius, called the Ungodly, a Syrian who became an influential teacher in Alexandria and who flourished after 300; Eudoxius, called the Impious, pupil of Aëtius, whose great achievement consisted in converting the Goths to Arianism; and finally Eunomius, another student of Aëtius, who far surpassed his master in dialectics and who became the most feared and hated of the Arian theoreticians.

These men drew the ultimate conclusions from their premises and emphasized the *unlikeness* of Father and Son. Starting with the concept of God as Absolute Being, of whom no generation can be predicated, they concluded that eternal generation is simply inconceivable, since it is a contradiction in terms; therefore the Son must have had a beginning and is simply the First Creation of the Divine Energy. In this sense only may He be called the image and likeness of the Father.

During the last years of Constantius, the Eudoxians and Eunomians, called Anomoeans or *Heteroousians,* came into control of the Eastern Church. The Synod of Sirmium III, held in 357, adopted a creed which became known as the Blasphemia and which declares that such words as *ousia* and *homoousian* do not occur in scripture and should, therefore, never be used at all.[35]

The Synod of Antioch, 363, at which Athanasius was again momentarily in the saddle, anathematized Eunomius, who was thereupon driven into exile, where he soon died.

11. *The Barbarians Become Arians.* The Arians were such zealous and effective missionaries that they converted the Goths, Visigoths, Ostrogoths, Decians, Huns, Vandals, and Lombards. This was to have fateful results. Valens had given the Goths a foothold in Thrace; and, as these vigorous tribesmen multiplied, they sought new territories. It was these, under the leadership of Alaric, who sacked Rome in 410; and Attila the Hun followed him into Italy some forty years later. St. Augustine died in 430 at Hippo, beleagured by Arian Vandals, who soon thereafter captured and looted the city. We read in Gregory the Great that, at the close of the sixth century, the Arian Lombards were carrying fire and sword throughout Italy and making life for the Catholics well-nigh insupportable.[36] To the simple and straightforward barbarian mind, there was something satisfying in the Arian creed: after all, it seemed logical to an intellect untutored in Greek metaphysics that the Father should have existed before His Son!

12. *The World Goes Mad.* It is difficult for us now to realize what madness these theological controversies created, not only within the clerical orders, but among whole populations. One faction consisting of thousands of wild-eyed fanatics stood ready at any moment to engage in civil war any other faction adhering to a variant formulary, the meaning of which neither could comprehend. Nevertheless, they were convinced that their temporal as well as their eternal welfare depended upon the adoption or rejection of the precise term for which they fought. Mobs consisting of metropolitan populations, or hordes of monks, could be inflamed by a slogan to go forth to loot, burn, desecrate, kill, and destroy. The great cities of the East, such as Alexandria, Antioch, and Constantinople were in an almost perpetual state of mob-violence. Eusebius states that such rage took possession of bishops and congregations alike that the war spread from

Alexandria and Egypt into all parts of the empire. Conditions became so scandalous, he adds, "that the sacred matters of inspired teaching were exposed to the most shameful ridicule in the very theatres of the unbelievers." [37]

Basil declares that bishops were convicted upon calumny alone; many did not know who had accused them or what the charges were. Some were seized at night and exiled into remote wastes, where they died.[38] All factions, he admits, were equally ferocious and "more brutish than wild beasts." [39] The bishops "roused the strife," which was like "a contest in the dark"; for no one understood the controversy.[40] When the ascetic Eustathius was deposed as bishop of Antioch, there arose "so fierce a dissension as to threaten the whole city with destruction. The populace was divided into two factions." [41] When the Arian Constantius sent his troops to install Macedonius as bishop of Constantinople in 341 and to drive out the orthodox Paul, "3150 persons were massacred." [42] Under threat of war from his brother Constans, Constantius reinstated Paul in 348;[43] but when Constans was murdered in 350, Paul, Athanasius, and all other orthodox bishops fled for their lives or were lynched. The venerable Paul was strangled. We are told that conversions were effected by forcing the sacramental elements down the throats of fiercely resisting communicants.[44] When Macedonius sent soldiers into Paphlagonia to force the Novatians to accept his creed, civil war broke out and casualties on both sides were extremely heavy.[45] On the slightest pretext, violence erupted in Constantinople and elsewhere on an unprecedented scale. One day, two mobs, one of *Homoousians* and the other of Arians, converged upon the Church of the Apostles "in two hostile divisions, which attacked one another with great fury, and great loss of life was occasioned, so that the churchyard was covered with blood, which ran into the adjacent portico, and thence even into the very street." [46]

Such was that world, now bereft of sanity.

13. *Arianism Fostered One-World Culture.* It is interesting to note that wherever the Arian creed triumphed,

there was a tremendous outpouring of constructive energy: among the barbarians for conquest; among the civilized, for civic improvements. Constantius and his enlightened successor Valens both sponsored and promoted great public works and municipal buildings, especially in the imperial city of Constantine. [47]

The struggle between Arianism and orthodoxy was ultimately to determine whether renunciation or the one-world concept of life should gain the mastery. However, since the forces which had created the Church were still too powerful to be denied, no secular philosophy could yet be tolerated. Arianism was doomed to defeat.

Except for two brief intervals, the Arians or Semi-Arians had been in control of the Eastern Church from 335 to 381; we may call their limited rationalism the death-gasp of Hellenism. Since the Church of Rome and the Western bishops regarded any form of Arianism as a personal insult, Latin and Greek Christianity scarcely communicated at all for forty years after the Synod of Antioch in 341.[48] This was the beginning of the schism between the Roman and Byzantine churches, which deepened progressively and became final in the ninth century.

14. *The Pneumatomachi.* We have already mentioned Macedonius, whom the Arians made bishop of Constantinople at the point of the sword and who later became known as the Enemy of the Holy Ghost. He was excommunicated by the Arians themselves because he declared that the Holy Spirit was simply a divine energy diffused throughout the entire universe and not a distinct person.[49] After his deposition, Macedonius established a sect which was known by his name and sometimes as the Pneumatomachi (Those Who Make War upon the Holy Spirit).

When the orthodox Theodosius became emperor of the East in 379, the Athanasians lost little time in regaining and consolidating their position. In 381 the Second Ecumenical Council was convened in Constantinople to accomplish three objectives: first, to reaffirm the Nicene Creed, second, to condemn the Eunomians; and, third, to anathematize the Macedonians and establish the position of the Holy Spirit as an equal member of the Trinity. The creed adopted here contained also the germ of the celebrated Filioque Clause, on which the Greek and Latin churches divided forever. Epiphanius has preserved the creed of that Council.[50]

15. *The Filioque Clause.* So far as the Catholic Church was concerned, and, indeed, all orthodox Christianity, this closed the Trinitarian controversy forever. It was now established that the Son and the Word were not merely identical, but also co-equal, co-eternal, and consubstantial with the Father; and exactly the same status was accorded the Holy Spirit. The Filioque Clause, according to which the Holy Spirit proceeded from the Father *and the Son*, was gradually adopted by the Roman Church, but always rejected by the Greek Orthodox; and as late as 1870, the latter refused to attend a conference at the Vatican on the ground that the Roman Catholics are heretics because they proclaim the double procession of the Holy Spirit.

F. AUGUSTINE ON THE TRINITY

Although the great controversies concerning the godhead were almost the monopoly of the Greek theologians, it was, oddly enough, as we have seen, the Latin Tertullian who developed the first definite formularies and it remained for his African successor Augustine to make the ultimate exposition of the Trinitarian concept. For thirty years he labored, revising and perfecting it. He bent his immense energies to establish it conclusively, both from the scriptures and from logic. Like Origen, he based his reasoning upon the metaphysics of Plato, who declared that man is a trichotomy consisting of body, mind, soul. Using this as the point of departure, Augustine found in it a reflection of the trinal unity of the godhead. If man is made in the image of God, he must bear the natural imprint of his Maker. There is never a Monad; from the beginning, there is only a a divine Trinity. God is never One *and* Three, but a Three-in-One, whose essence does not exist prior to the persons, either in the order of nature or of time, but exists simultaneously and eternally in and with them.

Although Augustine declared the scriptures to be an absolutely harmonious authority, he felt the necessity and maintained the possibility of establishing their truth by reason, which is itself the image of God's Word. Some, he says, "find a difficulty . . . when they hear that the Father is God, and the Son God, and the Holy Spirit God, and yet that this Trinity is not three Gods, but one God."[51] How can the Son, sent by the Father, be co-eternal and consubstantial with Him? Augustine replies that what "issues and that from which it issues, is of one and the same substance. For it does not issue as water issues from an aperture . . . but as light from light."[52] It is true, he says, that we cannot name Father, Son, and Holy Spirit without separating these in the words we employ; yet they are interrelated like human faculties which are inseparable like "memory and intellect and will . . . for there is no one of these three names that is not uttered by my memory and my intellect and my will together."[53]

Man reflects the image of his Trinitarian Creator: "Since, then, these three, memory, understanding, and will are not three lives, but one life; not three minds, but one mind; it follows certainly that neither are they three substances, but one substance. . . therefore, while all are mutually comprehended by each, and as wholes, each as a whole is equal to each as a whole, and each as a whole at the same time to all as wholes; and these three are one, one life, one mind, one essence."[54]

And so, even as the author of John took the doctrine of the Word from Plato, Zeno, and Philo, so also Augustine found his ultimate demonstration of the Trinity in pagan philosophy. The cycle was complete.

G. THE ATHANASIAN CREED

1. *A Congeries of Contradictions.* The Athanasian Creed, here reproduced in its entirety, was completed about 600, that is, several centuries after its purported

author died. It reflects in the baldest terms the mutually contradictory elements constituting Catholic doctrine:[55]

1. Whosoever would be saved: before all things it is needful that he hold fast the Catholic Faith.
2. Which Faith except a man has kept whole and undefiled: without doubt he will perish eternally.
3. Now the Catholic Faith is this: that we worship the one God as a Trinity, and the Trinity as a Unity.
4. Neither confusing the Persons: nor dividing the Substance.
5. For there is a Person of the Father, another of the Son; another of the Holy Ghost.
6. But the Godhead of the Father, the Son, and the Holy Ghost is one: their glory is equal, their majesty co-eternal.
7. Such as the Father is, such is the Son: and such is the Holy Ghost;
8. The Father uncreated, the Son uncreated; the Holy Ghost uncreated.
9. The Father infinite, the Son infinite: the Holy Ghost infinite;
10. The Father eternal, the Son eternal: the Holy Ghost eternal;
12. As also they are not three uncreated, nor three infinities: but one infinite, and one uncreated.
13. So likewise the Father is almighty, the Son almighty; the Holy Ghost almighty;
14. And yet they are not three almighties: but one almighty.
15. So the Father is God, the Son is God, the Holy Ghost God;
16. And yet they are not three Gods, but one God. . . .
17. So the Father is Lord, the Son Lord: the Holy Ghost Lord;
18. And yet they are not three Lords: but one Lord.
19. For like as we are compelled by the Christian

verity to confess each of the Persons by himself to be both God and Lord;

20. So are we forbidden by the Catholic religion: to speak of three Gods or three Lords.

21. The Father is of none: not made, nor created, nor begotten.

22. The Son is of the Father alone: not made, nor created, but begotten.

23. The Holy Ghost is of the Father and the Son: not made, nor begotten, nor created, but proceeding.

24. There is therefore one Father, not three Fathers; one Son, not three sons: one Holy Ghost, not three Holy Ghosts.

25. And in this Trinity none is before or after: none is greater or less;

26. But all three Persons are co-eternal one with another: and co-equal.

27. So that in all ways, as is aforesaid: both the Trinity is to be worshiped as an Unity, and the Unity as a Trinity.

28. Let him therefore that would be saved: think thus of the Trinity.

29. Furthermore, it is necessary to eternal salvation: that he also believe faithfully the Incarnation of our Lord Jesus Christ.

30. The right Faith therefore is that we believe and confess: that our Lord Jesus Christ, the Son of God, is at once both God, and Man;

31. He is God of the Substance of the Father, begotten before the Worlds: and He is Man, of the Substance of his Mother, born in the world;

32. Perfect God: perfect Man, of reasoning soul and human flesh consisting;

33. Equal to the Father as touching his Godhead: less than the Father as touching his Manhood.

34. Who, although he be God and Man; yet he is not two, but is one Christ;

35. One, however, not by change of Godhead into flesh: but by taking of manhood into God;

36. One altogether: not by confusion of substance, but by unity of person.

37. For as a reasoning soul and flesh is one man: so God and man is one Christ.

38. Who suffered for our salvation: descended to the world below, rose again, from the dead;

39. Ascended into heaven, sat down at the right hand of the Father: to come from thence to judge the quick and the dead.

40. At whose coming all men shall rise again with their bodies; and shall give account for their own deeds.

41. And they that have done good will go into life eternal; they that have done evil into eternal fire.

42. This is the Catholic Faith: which except a man have faithfully and steadfastly believed, he cannot be saved.

So, after five centuries of controversy, this was the magical formula constructed by the Church to enable the soul of the believer to enter the heavenly mansions. The smallest skepticism entailed not only eternal damnation, but, what was more to the point, temporal destruction as well. "The Father is God, the Son is God, the Holy Ghost God; and yet they are not three Gods, but one God." Whosoever could not comprehend this mystery and who dared to express any doubt concerning it was doomed to eternal hell; nor could he escape the terrible fate of the heretic.

2. *Creeds vs. Ethics.* And what had become of the declaration of Jesus[56] that those on His left hand are accursed because they did not give meat to the hungry, drink to the thirsty, lodging to the homeless, comfort to the sick, or fellowship to those in prison, but in which He said not one word concerning creed, belief, or dogma? All this was now dust unto dust and under dust to lie.

CHAPTER XVII

CHRISTOLOGICAL HERESIES

A. MARCELLUS AND PHOTINUS

The first two ecumenical councils settled the Trinitarian controversy; the Third, Fourth, and Fifth dealt with the equally corrosive Christological heresies, which continued with little abatement until the Eastern Church was overwhelmed by Islam.

A highly persistent heresy was developed by Marcellus[1] and propagated by his energetic pupil Photinus.[2] Opponents accused them of reducing Christ into a mere man; but their purpose was simply to unravel the mystery of the Christ-Logos. Perceiving the Platonic base of Origen's doctrine of the three hypostases, which had been adopted by the Eusebian Arians, they declared in favor of triune monotheism. From eternity, they said, God had existed as a Monad who, by dilating Himself into a Duad, introduced Himself as the Logos or the Word into the universe by procession from Himself as His creative activity. When the Holy Spirit was conferred upon the apostles after the ascension, the Monad dilated into a Triad. The Logos became humanly operative as the Son, was knowable only from His appearance in the flesh. At the Parousia Christ will reappear upon the earth in the same flesh as He had before, to reign for a thousand years, after which both the Logos and the Spirit will be reunited with the Monad and God will again be all in all. In this Godhead there are no persons or hypostases, and the Father, Word, and Holy Spirit are simply operational modes. Christ-Jesus, the Son, having no pre-existence, is simply a man, though born of a virgin and inspired by the indwelling Logos in the same manner as the Hebrew prophets.³

The synod which met in Constantinople in 336 condemned Marcellus because he declared that the existence of the Son began with His human birth and that He would rule on earth in a millenarian kingdom. Nevertheless, Photinus popularized the Marcellian Christology and modal unitarianism with industry and pertinacity. He was condemned by one council after another and finally disappeared about 370; but his followers continued to plague the Church for centuries.

B. THE APOLLONARII

The Marcellian Christology stands in sharp contrast to that of the two Apollonarii, father and son.⁴ The latter was a great scholar,⁵ who composed a version of the scriptures in lofty Greek hexameters. He was anathematized by the Second Ecumenical Council in 381; and Theodosius confirmed this action with his Great Seal in 388.

The Apollonarii accentuated the tendency in the Church to deify Jesus; they rejected the dual nature of Christ and the implications of His sinful humanity, which, they declared, made of Him a man-God, or a goat-stag, like some monster out of pagan fable. They therefore declared that in Christ-Jesus the Word displaced the human soul and will. There was thus but a single divine mind in Jesus, His humanity being only apparent. Sometimes, the Apollinarians declared that if Jesus did have a human soul, it was not a rational one, "God the Word himself being in place of a mind";⁶ and that the physical as well as the spiritual Jesus came down from heaven, was placed miraculously within the body of His "mother," and "passed through the Virgin as through a channel."⁷ We recall that the Valentinians had proclaimed a similar doctrine and that the Buddhists and the Gainas taught parallel dogmas concerning their founders.

The heresy of the Apollonarians centered in their denial of Christ's humanity, necessary to the atonement, because in order to redeem us, He must share our nature. But this was precisely why they attacked the doctrine of the two natures: if Christ were human at all, they said, He could not be perfect because then He would, like all others, be subject to sin and incapable of perfection or redemptive power. According to Gregory Nazianzen, the heresy held "that that man who came down from above is without a mind . . . the place of which is taken by God the Word."[8] Apollinarianism was condemned and anathematized over and over, yet this assault upon Christ's dual nature remained unexorcised for centuries.

C. NESTORIANISM

1. *A Heresy Hunter.* Nestorius, who became bishop of Constantinople in 428, soon found himself pitted against Cyril of Alexandria and other bishops in a controversy which split the Eastern Church into two factions as nearly equal and fiercely hostile as had been the case over Arianism a century before. Nestorius was pious, able, influential; and his party was thoroughly intrenched at the imperial court. He had distinguished himself immediately upon ordination as the inexorable foe of all heresies, and had instituted a war of extermination against Arians, Novatians, Marcellians, Macedonians, Eunomians, and others the moment he came into power. Ironically enough, this fierce heresy-hunter was himself destined to become one of the great heresiarchs.

2. *The Theotokos.* The Second Ecumenical Council, which met at Constantinople in 381, had declared that henceforth the bishop of that city should be second only to the Roman, which meant that he was to be the arbiter of the East. This angered the metropolitans of Antioch, Alexandria, and Jerusalem, all of whom had long called themselves popes. It was therefore natural that these apostolic sees should combine against the upstart usurper at the first opportunity. Ecclesiastical war to the knife broke out when Nestorius declared that he could not call Mary *Theotokos,* Mother of God, but only *Christotokos,* Mother

of Christ. The heresy was occasioned by the then already growing tendency toward Mariolatry, which, however, was as yet unofficial. Nestorius reacted against a popular movement, based on pagan antecedents, already on foot within the Church, to make of Mary substantially a fourth deity.

Nestorius maintained that, since the Word or Son was a member of the Trinity, surely the Virgin could not be called His mother. That which she bore was an incarnation, a human Jesus, possessing, contrary to the blasphemy of Apollinaris, a body, a soul, a spirit, and a will all derived from the flesh-and-blood mother. The crux of the Nestorian heresy was the idea that after the incarnation Christ was no longer the person of the Logos, but a dual personality, one part human, the other divine. Reacting against the one-natured Christ of the Apollinarians, Nestorius so emphasized the two natures that he was accused of postulating two persons in Christ: actually he taught that the human Jesus was conjoined to the Son in a dyophysite Christ.

3. *The Dual-Natured Christ*. Nestorius based his doctrine upon two classes of Gospel texts of which one attributes to Jesus the infirmities of humanity and the other the powers of divinity; it seemed to him that these can be understood only if we accept the doctrine of Christ's dual personality, and he condemned those who believed that the human Jesus and the divine Word constitute "a common sonship."[9] Nestorius declared his position in twelve statements, in the last of which we read: "If any one, in confessing the sufferings of the flesh, ascribes these also to the Word of God . . . let him be anathema." Cyril of Alexandria replied with twelve opposing anathemas,[10] one for each of Nestorius' *Twelve Statements,* of which the last condemns "Whosoever shall not recognize that the Word of God suffered in the flesh . . . and that likewise in that same flesh he tasted death and that he is become the first-born of the dead."

4. *Rome against Nestorius*. Cyril now launched a war of extermination; knowing that he was in disfavor at the Eastern Imperial Court, he wrote cleverly to Pope Celes

tine at Rome, enclosing a copy of his own anathemas: "Condescend, therefore, to unfold your judgment, that we may clearly know whether we ought to communicate with him who cherishes such erroneous doctrine." [11] Much impressed, the Roman prelate declared that the opinions of Nestorius were blasphemous.

5. *Nestorius Finally Condemned.* Emperor Theodosius suddenly realized that the whole Eastern Church was aflame over the *Theotokos.* He therefore convened what was to become the Third Ecumenical Council at Ephesus. This opened on June 22, 431, with 198 bishops present, of whom one hundred and two were partisans or supporters of Cyril. The Roman representatives and the Nestorian delegation from Antioch were still on the road. The agents of Theodosius pleaded in vain that decisions be delayed until all delegates were present; instead, they anathematized Nestorius and proclaimed his deposition on the first day. On June 7, the Antiochian bishops arrived, who thereupon joined the other Nestorians, convened their own council, excommunicated Cyril, and declared him and his chief supporters deposed. Both parties now sought the favor of the Imperial Court. In July, the Cyrillian faction, with the support of the newly arrived Roman envoys, again condemned Nestorius. The Court now confirmed the deposition of both factions and persuaded Cyril to accept a formula differing little from the Nestorian and therefore acceptable to Theodoret, and to John of Antioch. Nestorius retired from his episcopate and lived in exile until his death twenty years later. Meanwhile, the crafty Cyril augmented his influence at Court, and in 453 Theodosius branded Nestorius a Simonian, which he certainly was not, and ordered his writings burned. Thereupon, the Nestorians became a separate cult which spread far and wide across Persia, Kurdistan, India, and as far as China. To this day, it numbers some half a million communicants, possessing hundreds of priests and churches.

6. *The Growth of Mariolatry.* After the exile of Nestorius, the woman to whom Jesus would not even speak,[12] began more and more to fill the vacuum created

in the popular imagination by the loss of Isis, Demeter, Athena, and Cybele; and by the time of the Seventh Ecumenical Council in 787, her position could no longer be challenged in the Catholic Church. The first step in this process, as we have noted, occurred in the Fourth Gospel, where Mary is placed with John at the foot of the cross during the crucifixion, addressed reverentially by the Savior, and consigned to the care of the disciple whom Jesus loved; the second was the dogma of the Virgin Birth; the third, that she remained a virgin *after* the birth of Jesus and never bore any other children; the fourth, that she was generated through an *immaculate conception* (the doctrine made a dogma in 1854, that she was born without taint of original sin); the fifth, that she never died at all, but ascended to heaven in a miraculous assumption where she sits at the side of Christ and, like Isis, makes constant intercession for sinners. Finally, in 1954, the pope crowned her Queen of Heaven, in an elaborate ceremony at the Basilica of St. Peter.

When the theologians began calling Mary *Theotokos,* she also began to assume vast powers and perquisites; and apocryphal literature began attributing to her a multitude of characteristics and activities wholly unknown to pristine Christianity. Nestorianism was simply an attempt to stem this tide of Mariolatry and reconstitute the pristine Gospel, which was of course impossible, in the fifth century; this could be done only, after more than a millennium had elapsed, by that vast Nordic European upheaval known as the Reformation. The Teutons could accomplish this revolution, at least in part, because they had never been under the spell of Isis, or others similar to her.

D. THE MONOPHYSITE HERESY

The next great Christological heresy was a reaction against Nestorianism, instigated by the presbyter Eutyches, superior of a monastery near Constantinople. In 447, this venerable ascetic had simply declared that he could not assert as a dogma that Christ has two natures. Although he made no attempt to propagate his heresy, it spread rap idly among the Eastern bishops, monks, and laity; and soon the whole Church was in a frenzied uproar. Eusebius of Dorylaeum preferred charges against Eutyches, who, after twice refusing to appear, was finally forced before a local synod in Constantinople, where he arrived with a large retinue of unruly monks. He tried to evade any direct answer, declaring that he subscribed in every way to the creeds of Nicaea and Constantinople. Finally, however, he reluctantly admitted that he doubted the existence of the two natures. He was therefore promptly excommunicated and consigned to the tender mercies of the secular arm.

The core of the Eutychian heresy was that before the incarnation there were indeed the two natures; but after it, they coalesced into a single essence which was something new and different, consubstantial neither with the godhead nor with the manhood. There exists, therefore, in Christ-Jesus only one nature, one will, one Savior, else how can we say that Christ was crucified? Eutyches thought that only in this way could docetism be banished, Apollinarianism avoided, and Nestorianism destroyed.

In Alexandria, Eutyches met a reception completely different from that accorded him in Rome, Antioch, and Constantinople. Bishop Dioscurus, who had inherited from Cyril a violent antipathy both toward Nestorianism and Constantinople and who saw perhaps in this controversy a means of gaining ecclesiastical control of the Eastern Church, immediately embraced Monophysitism.

As the whole East was now again sharply divided into hostile camps, the weak Emperor Theodosius II convened a general council at Ephesus in 449, intended as the fourth ecumenical council. Since the emperor was under the influence of the Monophysite eunuch Chrysaphius, he favored that faction, and designated Dioscurus as president. As usual, Eutyches arrived with a large and noisy following of monks. Only one hundred and fifty bishops participated. The Roman delegates were not seated and the *Tome of Leo,* which condemned Eutychianism, was not even read or mentioned. Bishops Flavian and Eusebius were forthwith deposed and excommunicated as were Ibas, Theodoret, and Domnus of Tyre, all charged with Nestorianism. This Council has ever since been known as the Robber Synod. Dioscurus was now riding high and enjoyed the favor of the Imperial Court.

Theodoret and Flavian, who had previously been somewhat cool toward Leo, now turned to him in desperation. The Roman bishop had already won over Queen Pulcheria, and when her brother Theodosius died, kaleidoscopic changes ensued. Chrysaphius was promptly executed, and Marcian, who had just become consort-emperor, quickly made plans for a new council to repudiate the Robber Synod. The Fourth Ecumenical Council, which convened some six hundred bishops at Chalcedon on October 8, 451, was marked by scenes of the wildest turmoil, in which nearly all the bishops screamed at each other that they were murderers, Christ-haters, and enemies of God, and at the end of which the venerable Theodoret was compelled to anathematize not only what was known as Nestorianism, but also his old friend Nestorius, on pain of excommunication and death. In that assembly reeking with sweat and blood, with the cries of "Nestorian heretic" ringing in his ears, the trembling Theodoret anathematized Nestorius in a ritual replete with mental and physical agony.[13]

The creeds of Nice and Constantinople were read and reaffirmed; then the anathemas of Cyril against Nestorius were read and approved. Finally, the *Tome of Leo* was received with wild acclamations. The Council then anathematized Nestorians and Eutychians alike,[14] after which the emperor voiced the age-old desire of secular rulers that "all profane contentions cease." [14]

Although this action wounded the Monophysite serpent in the head, its long body still coiled and quivered. The monks, particularly those of Palestine and Egypt, were in no mood for trifling; they promptly murdered all bishops who taught the Christology of Chalcedon and even the armies of the emperor failed to convince them of the Ecumenical Truth. Eutychianism continued century after century throughout the East and gradually spread west ward throughout the Roman Empire. In time it split into various subdivisions, united only in their common hatred for the Church.

E. THE HERESY OF THE THREE CHAPTERS

The Fifth Ecumenical Council, which met in 553 in Constantinople, was convened to anathematize Origen and to lay at rest forever the ghost of Nestorianism. During the century succeeding the Council of Chalcedon, no new heresy had arisen. But because, in its zeal in condemning Eutyches, that Council seemed to have rehabilitated Ibas, Theodore of Mopsuestia, and the historian Theodoret, all accused of Nestorianism, it now became necessary to determine the orthodoxy of certain writings of theirs known as the Three Chapters.

The Emperor Justinian told the assembled prelates that after Chalcedon the adherents of both Nestorius and Eutyches had "caused great divisions," which he wished to heal, "so that many churches had broken off communion with one another." The writings known as the Three Chapters were all duly anathematized, and Cyril of Alexandria was declared perfect in the faith. It is also interesting to note that the reigning Pope Vigilius of Rome, an adherent of the Three Chapters, was condemned to have his name removed from the diptychs of the Church.

F. THE MONOTHELITE HERESY

There remained just enough vitality in the Church to produce one more heresy: the Monothelite. This was a belated outgrowth of and reaction against the Monophysitism of Eutyches. Just as this had emphasized the single-natured physical Christ, so the Monothelites conferred upon Him exclusive spirituality; they taught that in Jesus Christ there is but one will, energy, or theandric operation. This was an idea first advanced by Apollinaris three hundred years earlier, and now resurrected by the

Alexandrian school and by Sergius, Metropolitan of Constantinople, in hope that this formula could unite the hopelessly divided Church. The situation was desperate, since all Eastern Christianity was not merely torn by internal dissensions but was also under military siege by the Moslems. Jerusalem and Alexandria were already in their hands, and every other Eastern capital was in imminent danger. Honorius, recently deceased Pope of Old Rome, had become a Monothelite.

The Sixth Ecumenical Council was therefore convened at Constantinople in 680-681 to settle forever the question of Christ's will, energy, and operation. The convocation, consisting of some two hundred bishops, was opened by reading a letter from Pope Agatho of Rome, in which he declared that it was now necessary to establish the true faith, because certain bishops had introduced a novelty by teaching dogmatically that there is only a single will and operation in the dispensation of the incarnation of the Lord Jesus Christ.

The Monothelites thereupon defended themselves by saying that they had not introduced any new method of speech but had taught only what had been handed down by the Apostolic Fathers and by the ecumenical synods, and was preached by such great and orthodox teachers as Sergius, Paul, Pyrrhus, and Peter of Constantinople, and by Honorius, Pope of Rome, and by Cyrus, Pope of Alexandria.

The letter of Agatho declared that the two natures of Christ exist "in Him unconfusedly, inseparably, and unchangeably . . . we say that as the same Lord Jesus has two natures so also he has two natural wills and operations, to wit, the divine and the human." [15]

When the emperor demanded of the patriarchs whether they agreed with this, all did so except Macarius, Archbishop of Antioch.[16]

And so the great controversy was settled by saying that in Christ there is but one person, but that there are two natures, two wills, and two operations, which, though distinct, exist inseparably and without confusion or commixture. This attempt to refute and yet to incorporate all heresies was the final word of the Church on the Christological problem.

And this marked the end of Catholic theological controversy. As we have already noted, the hotbed of heresy had always been the Greek and Oriental Eastern churches, and, to a lesser degree, the Latin African; but all these were shortly to be inundated by the Moslem tide. Rome, which had never generated a single heresy, and which always accepted whatever was established by others, finally became supreme when there remained to her only substantially the same nucleus of territory which belonged to the Roman bishop in the beginning. The Reformation stripped from him those areas in which the cults of Isis, Cybele, and Demeter had never paved the way for the cult of Mary.

G. SUMMARY

In addition to a great many regional convocations, there were nine great synods which shaped the destiny of the Catholic Church. It may be helpful to the reader if we summarize these briefly. Seven were ecumenical, that is, all-inclusive and universally accepted:

1. THE COUNCIL OF NICAEA I (Ecumenical), 325. Formulated the *homoousian* creed, placed the passion of Christ on March 22-25, and settled the date on which Easter is still celebrated.

2. CONSTANTINOPLE I (Ecumenical), 381. Reaffirmed the Nicene Creed, condemned Macedonius and the *Pneumatomachi,* adopted the *Filioque* theology, and formally elevated the Holy Ghost to equality in the Trinity.

3. EPHESUS (Ecumenical), 431. Condemned Nestorius and Nestorianism and formally established the Virgin Mary as *Theotokos.*

4. THE ROBBER SYNOD (Ephesus), 449. Made the Monophysitism of Eutyches and Dioscurus the official Christology of the Church.

5. CHALCEDON (Ecumenical), 451. Reversed the

Robber Synod and condemned Monophysitism. It also anathematized all vestiges of Nestorianism.

6. CONSTANTINOPLE II (Ecumenical), 553. Origen anathematized in detail. Nestorianism again condemned.

7. CONSTANTINOPLE III (Ecumenical), 680-1. Condemned the Monothelite heresy.

8. CONCILIABULUM (Constantinople), 754. Under the direction of Constantine V, this synod condemned all use of relics, images, and statues of saints and especially those pertaining to or depicting God, the Virgin, or Jesus Christ. It also denounced monachism and many other practices which had developed in the Church since Apostolic times.

9. NICAEA II (Ecumenical), 787. Reversed the Conciliabulum utterly and established the Catholic Church as it continued through the Middle Ages.

With this, the Roman pope became the supreme head of the occidental Church; there were no more councils; by this time almost all of oriental Christendom had been lost to Islam.

CHAPTER XVIII

PERSECUTION

A. DEFINITION

Persecution may now be defined as punishment inflicted by authority upon groups or persons simply because of beliefs which do not involve any direct threat against the civil, economic, or political security of others. However, the Catholic Church placed another security far above these: namely, the religious; and it inflicted violence upon all who doubted its dogmas, on the premise that all deviationists were the minions of the devil and that there could be no eternal salvation outside the framework of its discipline. It was therefore mandatory that any one who broke the unity, willfully violated the canons, or rejected the teachings of the hierarchy must be removed from society so that others might not be contaminated.

It is obvious that only a priest-state can confer the power to inflict unlimited persecution: but the doctrine of exclusive salvation will always supply the motive-force to do so, as Lecky points out.[1]

B. PERSECUTION AS ENDURED BY THE CHRISTIANS

1. *There Were to Be Ten Persecutions.* According to tradition, the Christians, like the Hebrews in Egypt, were destined to endure ten plagues or persecutions. Sulpitius Severus, writing early in the fifth century, informs us that nine had already occurred. The first was under Nero in 66, the second under Domitian, 95, the third under

Trajan, 115, the fourth under Hadrian, 135, the fifth under Marcus Aurelius, 175, the sixth under Severus, 205, the seventh under Decius, 250, the eighth under Valerian, 259, and the ninth under Maximian and Diocletian, 303-305. "From that time," he says, "we have continued to enjoy tranquility; nor do I believe that there will be any further persecutions, except that which Antichrist will carry on just before the end of the world." [2]

We note that this list includes some of the noblest Roman emperors, such as Trajan, Hadrian, and Marcus Aurelius. And neither Septimus Serverus nor Diocletian would knowingly have persecuted innocent men. Not even Nero persecuted the Christians because of religious zeal: they were simply a convenient scapegoat, since they were already the object of popular execration.

2. *Cause of Persecution.* We find, first, that the persecutions against the Christians were brief, and were followed by long periods of tranquillity; and, second, that they were the result of popular hatred or the official conviction that they were dangerous subversives, whose objective was to destroy the state and all the civil and religious liberties of others. Countless other cults had existed since time immemorial without friction either with each other or with the authorities; but almost from the beginning Christianity was involved in bitter conflict.

3. *Christians Sought a Priest-State.* It is therefore pertinent to inquire why Catholic Christianity became involved in strife, when the Eleusinian and other mysteries could continue for centuries without friction or interference. The truth is that the new cult provoked persecution because, finding inspiration in Judaism, Zoroastrianism, and Brahmanism, it mounted a drive to establish itself as a priest-state, in which every ideology but its own would be extirpated, and in which *the entire human race must be included, on pain of exile or death.* In short, the Church provoked persecution because, from its inception, it could not avoid revealing its ultimate objectives.

4. *Christian Demand for Toleration.* Many of the

early Fathers, like modern communists, made strong pleas for a toleration which they had no intention of extending to their own ideological opponents. Justin Martyr maintained that the beliefs of Christians were no more irrational or immoral than those of the pagans; that they should be judged, not for opinions held by them as a group, but as individuals guilty or innocent of crime under the existing civil code.[3] Athenagoras pursued the same line, and demanded that the charges of atheism, Thyestean feasting, and Oedipean intercourse be fully established or else abandoned.[4] Tertullian elaborated this thesis: "When the charges made against us are made against others, they . . . have full opportunity of answer and debate . . . Christians alone are forbidden to say anything in exculpation of themselves . . . all that is cared about is . . . the confession of a name, not the examination of a charge."[5]

Quite sincerely, Tertullian proclaimed a doctrine of universal toleration and liberty of conscience: "It is a fundamental human right, a privilege of nature, that every man should worship according to his own convictions: since one man's religion neither harms nor helps another man, it is assuredly no part of religion to compel religion."[6] He pays involuntary tribute to the toleration practiced by the pagans, who regarded the Christians alone as subversive: "For who compels a philosopher to sacrifice or take an oath? . . . Nay, they openly ridicule your gods, and in their writings they attack your superstitions; and you applaud them for it."[7] But, since the pagans were convinced that the Christians were seditious, Tertullian protested vehemently that they were the enemies of no one; and he declared that they prayed for the continuation of the Roman Empire because they knew that when that ended, the world would end.[8]

5. *Origen.* Origen reveals that Christians were charged with undermining the security of the state, and that, unless they would become loyal citizens, society would crumble. Celsus had jeered that surely the Romans could not neglect their duties and defenses on the theory

that the Christian God would fight for them if they worshiped Him, since the Jews, whom He had promised so much, now "are left with not so much as a patch of ground." [9] Celsus obviously regarded the new cult as a deadly corrosive which could only bring internal collapse and make the Empire an easy prey to external enemies. Celsus was sounding the tocsin of patriotism; he was calling upon the Christians to abandon their misguided loyalty. Origen continues: "Celsus says that 'we shrink from raising altars, statues, and temples; and this,' he thinks, 'has been agreed upon among us as the badge or distinctive mark of a secret and forbidden society.'" [10] Celsus also charged that Christians "'utter against one another dreadful blasphemies, saying all manner of things shameful to be spoken; nor will they yield in the slightest point for the sake of harmony, hating each other with a perfect hatred.'" [11] All of this, Origen vehemently denies, and continues that he would not revile "those who have adopted different opinions from ours . . . We who know the maxim, 'Blessed are the peacemakers' . . . would not regard with hatred the corrupters of Christianity nor term those who had fallen into error Circes and flattering deceivers." [12]

6. *Lactantius*. Lactantius, versed in the ethics of Plato and Cicero, was a sincere tolerationist: "There is no occasion for violence and injury, for religion cannot be imposed by force; . . . And no one is detained by us against his will . . . For nothing is so much a matter of free will as religion; in which, if the mind of the worshiper is disinclined to it, religion is at once taken away, and ceases to exist." [13]

7. *The Case of Cyprian*. However, we need not go far in patristic literature to confirm the charges of Celsus: the fact is that the Church could not even wait until it achieved power to inflict violence on its rivals. A case in point is Cyprian, who was elevated to the episcopal dignity almost immediately after conversion and who was beheaded during the Valerian persecution.

Although Tertullian gives the impression[14] that Chris

tian martyrs were dying by the thousands on every hand, we learn from the biographer of Cyprian that this bishop was the first Christian priest ever to suffer death in Africa, and the first of any status so glorified in Carthage.[15] We learn also[16] that after sentence was imposed, its execution was delayed a full year, so that he would carry on the administration of his church and put all his affairs in order, which emphasizes the fact that no persecution was intended against the Christ-cult as such but only the punishment of an individual offender. And lastly, we are told [17] that his condemnation resulted from inciting and ordering his fanatical followers to desecrate, vandalize, and destroy the pagan altars and temples. When questioned on these matters, Cyprian contemptuously refused to reply, and his biographer boasts that the charges were completely true.

We can scarcely say, therefore, that the persecution against the Christians was either widespread or brutal. A more relevant question is whether Cyprian suffered as a Christian or as a malicious desecrator and destroyer of sacred property. His biographer states that he "was the officer of Christ . . . who commanded the idols to be destroyed."[18]

8. *The Diocletian Persecution.* Early persecutions were brief and sporadic; however, the evidence is conclusive that the repression initiated by Diocletian was widespread, systematic, carefully planned, and definitely political. The facts to be gleaned from Eusebius[19] and other sources are as follows: Galerius was the heir-apparent to the throne, which he expected to inherit within a year or two at most. Diocletian had never persecuted anyone, had already admitted Christians in large numbers to important official positions. Galerius, however, had always been their bitter foe and they wished to drive a wedge between the emperor and him so that he might be barred from the succession. They therefore set two fires in the palace in 303, and attempted to fix the blame upon Galerius. This was a crude maneuver, since he had no possible motive for the crime. When the guilt of the Chris-

tians was established, Diocletian took severe measures against them. Discovering the enormity of the conspiracy, and concluding that Christianity was a highly organized, international conspiratorial subversion, which must be eradicated if the empire was to survive, he published decrees instituting actual persecution; that is, he punished many as *Christians,* not merely as criminals and arsonists. Gibbon estimates[20] that the total number of martyrs who died during a two-year period approximated eighteen hundred.

9. *Constantine the Great.* Events were soon to reveal how serious was the Christian threat. For the next emperor, Constantine the Great, son of Constantius, who had also favored the Christians, found that he could no longer regard the cult simply as a religion. He faced the same alternative as Diocletian: to destroy it or to give it power.

Sozomen states that when Constantine repented the murder of his wife, his son, and "some of his nearest relatives," he was told by Sopater, of the school of Plotinus, that such guilt as his could not be eradicated. When some Christian bishops, however, informed him that he could be purified by baptism, he was delighted, and became a Christian.[21] And we believe that his conversion was something more than a political device by which he hoped to consolidate and unify his empire; for he always carried a priest with him and accepted baptism only on his deathbed so that he might commit sin with impunity to the very end. Cf. Eusebius, *Life* IV lxi.

One of his first acts as emperor was the celebrated Edict of Toleration at Milan in 313, which gave freedom of conscience to all.[22]

C. PERSECUTION AS INFLICTED BY THE CHRISTIANS

1. *The Catholic Theory.* In 383, which was just two years after the eastern triumph of the *Homoousian,* Gregory Nazianzen formulated the theory of suppression by secular force which has always been that of the Catholic Church;

speaking of the Apollinarians, he says: "any permission of assembly granted to them is nothing less than a declaration that their view is more true than ours. For if they are permitted to teach . . . it is manifest that the doctrine of the Church has been condemned."[23] Leo the Great, writing in 450, declared that the Roman Empire, which tolerated and fostered every species of religious falsehood, had been established by God's providence so that "the preaching of the word might quickly reach all people. . . . The most blessed Peter, chief of the Apostolic band, was appointed to the citadel of the Roman empire. . . . Here the tenets of philosophy must be crushed, here the follies of earthly wisdom must be dispelled, here the cult of demons must be refuted, here the blasphemy of all idolatries must be rooted out." [24]

In short, it was the peculiar mission of the Petrine succession to assume the throne of the Caesars and use its power to extirpate all philosophy, all learning, all secular science, and all competing religions or devil-worship from the face of the earth. Leo regarded the heretic in exactly the same light as we would the poisoner of our water supply. The devil was busily engaged in contaminating the Christian mind: "there is no doubt that our enemy, Satan. . . . is aroused . . . that under a false profession of the Christian name he may corrupt those whom he is no longer allowed to attack with open and bloody persecution, and for this work he has heretics in his service whom he has led astray from the Catholic Faith." [25]

Leo correctly estimated the role of the Roman Empire in the development of Catholic Christianity; for had not the empire reduced so much of the world into a single political entity, each sovereignty would have developed its own national religion and there could never have been an international priest-state.

2. *Constantine Turns to Persecution.* In 325, Constantine rescinded the Edict of Toleration and made Christianity the imperial religion. Thereafter in rapid succession at the instigation of the clergy, he issued a series of rescripts which gave them universal preference:

they were granted tax-exemption and immunity from military service; the wealth of all those dying without direct heirs became the property of the Church, which was also empowered to receive gifts and legacies; Christians were given all posts of influence and importance in the government; provision was made to repair old churches and build new ones at public expense; and generous support for the hierarchy was provided from state revenues. Obviously, the gaze of the clergy had shifted from the next world to the present.

But this was only the beginning: and the compliant Constantine quickly outlawed every cult and communion except the Catholic. He ordered the destruction of all idols and the demolition of pagan altars and temples.[26] Eusebius, himself an Origenist Semi-Arian, wrote exultingly: "he used every means to rebuke the superstitious errors of the heathen . . . their temples in the several cities were left exposed to the weather . . . and their roofs were destroyed." [27] The Cilician temple of "the demon Aesculapius" was "razed to the ground . . . a band of soldiers laid this building, the admiration of noble philosophers, prostrate in the dust." [28]

3. *Proscription of All Christian Dissidents.* The measures taken against the pagans, however, were mild compared to those visited upon Christian deviationists. Previously "all who worshipped Christ, however they might have differed, received the same treatment from the pagans."[29] But, bereft of Roman protection from each other, the unorthodox "could no longer assemble in public, because it was forbidden; nor could they hold their assemblies in secret, for they were watched by the bishops and the clergy of their city." [30]

Thus began the millennial terror under the Catholic hierarchy, who induced Constantine to issue the following decree:[31]

"Understand now, by this present statute, ye Novatians, Valentinians, Marcionites, Paulians, ye who are called Cataphrygians [Montanists], and all ye . . .

haters and enemies of the truth and life, in league with the devil and destruction.

"Forasmuch, then, as it is no longer possible to bear with your pernicious errors, we give warning by this present statute that none of you henceforth presume to assemble yourselves together. We have directed, accordingly, that you be deprived of all the houses in which you are accustomed to hold your assemblies; and our case in this respect extends so far as to forbid the holding of your superstitious and senseless meetings not in public merely, but in any private house or place whatsoever... And in order that this remedy may be applied with effectual power, we have commanded ... all the houses of prayer ... which belong to heretics ... be made over without delay to the Catholic Church; that no facility whatever be left for any future gathering."

Ironically, scarcely was the signet dry on this edict when Arianism erupted in the East, Donatism split the northwestern African churches into warring camps, and Manichaeism began to spread throughout Christendom to corrode its very foundations. None of these developments, however, deterred Eusebius from painting this idyllic picture: "Thus were the lurking-places of the heretics broken up ... and the one Catholic Church, at unity with itself, shone with full luster, while no heretical or schismatic body anywhere continued to exist."[32]

4. *The Arian Inter-Persecution.* There is only one phase of ancient Christian persecution which remains fully recorded: that inflicted on the orthodox by the Arians during the five decades in which they contended for supremacy and in which several hundreds of thousands must have perished while millions suffered distress or exile. The Athanasians probably approximated the truth about the Arians; but they neglected to record their own persecutions, which were infinitely more barbarous.

The Arian Council of Antioch appointed Gregory to the episcopal throne in Alexandria when Athanasius was driven out the second time. We gather that it was no simple matter for the new bishop to assume his sacred duties, for Athanasius thus describes the intrusion of Gregory on Easter day, 339: "The Church and the holy baptistery were set on fire, and straightway groans, shrieks, and lamentations, were heard throughout the city: . . . holy and undefiled virgins were being stripped naked, and . . .if they resisted, they were in danger of their lives."[33]

Athanasius never sees fit to mention the violence done to his Arian rivals, of whom two were lynched. Concerning Gregorius, Theodoret declares, quite innocently: "at the expiration of six years he was destroyed by the sheep themselves."[34] In 357, George took the place of his murdered predecessor. In 361, the Athanasian mob "attacked George with shouts and reproaches . . . killed him, flung the corpse upon a camel, and after exposing it to every insult during the day, burnt it at nightfall."[35]

The murder of George followed immediately the death of Constantius, when his soldiers were no longer on hand to protect the Arian bishop. This act of violence so angered the philosophic Julian, who thereupon came to power,[36] that he ordered Athanasius into his fourth exile.[37]

The fiendish lynching of the beautiful and learned Hypatia no one could possibly blame upon the pagans; the mad and cruel monks, nurtured in the discipline of Antony, "after tearing her body in pieces, took her mangled limbs . . . and burnt them."[38]

Athanasius condemned the Arians as worse than wild beasts and "more worthless than public hangmen." And he wrote that Constantius was worse than Pilate, "the murderer of Christ."[39] In the classic phrase of St. Basil those who deny the community of essence are "shrieking drunken scum."[40]

5. *Toleration under Julian.* When Julian became emperor in 361, he issued an edict of universal toleration; and the Christians hated him with particular venom because he gave religious freedom to the Jews and relieved them of discriminatory taxation. He even encour

aged them to rebuild the Temple at Jerusalem, a task
which they undertook with immense zeal; and for this
they returned such extravagant gratitude that some even
declared Julian to be their long-delayed Messiah. The
Christian historians tell many strange tales of how divine
interference frustrated this impious project, which came
to a sudden halt when Julian was assassinated.[41] His
death brought the orthodox Jovian to the eastern throne,
who was soon succeeded by the Arian Valens, a man
more interested in building a magnificent city than in
exiling or executing *Homoousians*.

6. *Terror under Theodosius.* With the accession of
Theodosius, every vestige of toleration ceased. The Catholics began a campaign of violent suppression and destruction which was soon to encompass all ideological
opponents. The Mithraeum of Alexandria had been destroyed during the Arian episcopate of George; and in
390, Bishop Theophilus decreed the razing of the Serapeum, the most magnificent temple still remaining in
the city. The pagans, however, defended their shrine with
courage and fanaticism; and the number of slain and
wounded "on each side was almost innumerable."[42]

7. *Terror against the Jews.* Undoubtedly the tension
between the Christians and the numerous Jews of Alexandria had been building up ever since the new religion
came to power; and early in the fifth century, over an
untoward incident, civil war broke out. The Christians
"drove the Jews out of the city, permitting the multitude to plunder their goods."[43]

8. *Terror against the Manichaeans.* Meanwhile the
campaign against the Manichaeans had degenerated into
perpetual warfare. In 443, Pope Leo sent a circular to
all the Italian bishops, which stated that those Manichaeans who would not make public confession of their
error in church "have been banished into perpetual exile
by public judges."[44]

Every cleft and crevice in which a heretic could hide
was searched; those who fled were pursued wherever
they went. If they would not anathematize their faith,
they were "subjected to the laws in accordance with the

constitution of our Christian princes"; [45] that is, their goods were confiscated and they were executed, for the death penalty was established early as the only possible method of convincing the Manichees. And this was done against individuals who had no desire to establish a rival state, but asked only to worship in accordance with their own conscience.

9. *The First Index.* Intellectual suppression had become so thoroughly integrated with the Catholic way of life that Pope Gelasius in 496 published a special decree containing a list of forbidden books. This was the first such catalogue, the first time in history that some one in authority presumed to decree that no longer was any one permitted to prove all things so that they might in the end retain the good.

10. *Catholic Doctrines Indefensible.* And there was a still more important development. As the Church rapidly destroyed Greek culture and carried the world deeper into medieval ignorance, it absorbed more and more popular superstitions, including Mariolatry, belief in magic, the use of charms, amulets, etc.; partly in order to win over the Manichaean communicants, the Church adopted their doctrine of purgatory, their concept of a celibate priesthood, and a commercialized perversion of their grants of indulgence. As the clergy became more and more like the Brahmanas of India, a great celibate-monastic movement arose also, patterned after the Buddhism of the same tortured land. Above and beyond all this, the priesthood became corrupt, avaricious, immoral, worldly, and power-hungry to a degree which beggars all description. In short, with the passage of the centuries, the Church and its clergy became so utterly different from and contrary to the principles expressed in the Synoptics that it was necessary to make of the Bible the foremost among all proscribed books. And so the Church which began by making every word of its scriptures divine authority was forced to make it a crime punishable by death to possess a copy of the Gospel.

CHAPTER XIX
ST. AUGUSTINE

A. APPRAISAL

Augustine, 354-430, the most towering figure in the history of the Catholic Church, was an African, well versed in pagan literature, who spent a long life of infinite toil dealing with every current controversy. Had it been his fortune to live in another era he might have been a great secular thinker. During his early years, he developed a theory of cognition which anticipated Locke.[1] He wrote as profoundly concerning the nature of space and time as did Henri Bergson.[2] He was deeply versed in astronomy and medical science. Ranging far and wide, his mind encompassed many fields of knowledge.

Augustine was the great architect of western Christianity. His obsession to aggrandize the Church directed him into the pathway it was to follow. In this he differed from Tertullian and Origen, although he was no less sincere. He strove for greatness, but not for personal power: he aspired to be the universal philosopher-theologian. When very old, he begged relief from routine duties, so that he might devote himself to study and writing to consummate his literary labors and communicate his wisdom to posterity.[3]

The sheer bulk of his literary work is staggering. And his were no rapidly dictated treatises; on some of them he worked for decades, for he was a perfectionist. No man then living could withstand him in argument, and few attempted to do so. The older, forthright, and cantankerous Jerome, with whom at one time he exchanged some vitriolic correspondence, late in life deferred to Augustine as to a master "renowned throughout the whole world."[4]

B. THE DOCTRINE OF FREE WILL BEFORE AUGUSTINE

1. *The New Testament and the Fathers.* Paul and the Gospel Jesus teach predestination and election by grace; and in the former, original sin is certainly at least implied. It is extraordinary that in hundreds of books composed by Greek and Latin Fathers not even one ever noticed this doctrine: all proclaimed the congenital freedom of will. Possibly, the reason for this was that the Marcionites and subsequently the Manichees were uncompromising predestinarians. The orthodox doctrine was simply that God had created man good and with the power so to remain; but when Adam, tempted by Eve, fell into the sin of disobedience, the entire human race was involved in ruin, from which it could be saved only by the perfect sacrifice and atonement of Christ; this redemption, however, was conceived of as offered to all on the same terms. This comfortable doctrine remained undisturbed until demolished by Augustine.

2. *Origen.* Origen had declared[5] that all living creatures, even animals and fishes, have souls; and he continued: "According to our view, there is no rational creature which is not capable of both good and evil";[6] and again: "A soul is always in possession of free will . . . and freedom of will is always directed either to good or to evil."[7]

The problem of evil weighed heavily upon Origen: and, since he could not, like the Gnostics, find the source in metaphysical dualism, he linked it to the doctrine of metempsychosis. He declared that the obvious inequities and apparent injustices which exist on all sides are due to sins committed in previous incarnations, for only so can it be shown "that no shadow of injustice rests upon the divine government."[8] According to this Brahmanic-Buddhist-Pythagorean assumption, each human soul suffers or is rewarded in its current prison-house, for acts committed before: in universe after universe, all souls have life and, by their free will, rise toward greater purity and spirituality, or fall lower into sin and degradation.[9] Thus, "even the devil himself,"[10] who fell by voluntary choice, is capable of good and may achieve salvation. Every soul may rise to "the highest good" or descend "to the lowest evil" during the "endless periods of duration in the immeasurable and different worlds."[11]

C. AUGUSTINE ON HUMAN NATURE AND PREDESTINATION

1. *A Manichee for Nine Years.* As we have noted, Augustine was a Manichee from the age of twenty-three to thirty-two. He was converted to Christianity and baptized by Ambrose at Milan in 386, whereupon, returning to Africa, he began to polemise against the Manichees, who were his natural enemies, since he was so recently an apostate from their ranks. Since one of their principal doctrines was eternal predestination, it was natural that he should, at this point, have proclaimed the freedom of the will.

2. *A Libertarian.* Since the ethical system of the Manichees was based upon their cosmology, Augustine answered them with an opposing metaphysical theory;[12] and he continues with an argument borrowed from Origen that darkness or evil can be nothing but the absence of light or good.[13] And he maintained stoutly that no act can be sinful unless committed voluntarily by the dictate of a will that is morally free.[14]

This was essentially the argument of Arminius, who declared in 1605 that since God cannot be guilty of injustice, the eternal predestination of rational creatures to hell fire without sin of their own is incompatible with the concept of a just God.

3. *Pelagius.* This seemed reasonable enough to the young theologian seeking to defeat the Manichees. But soon after 400 the British monk Pelagius arrived in Rome. He was neither aggressive nor argumentative; but he possessed a keen, analytical mind, which plumbed with ease

the furthest reaches of speculative thought.

4. *The Pelagian Theses.* For centuries the theory of free will as well as the contradictory doctrine of human depravity had been proclaimed by the Church; Pelagius compelled it to choose between the two. When he began disseminating his rationalism in Rome before 410, he met with ready acceptance, for no one realized what an explosive train he was laying. He declared that we derive our bodies only from Adam, that each soul is a new creation endowed with pristine purity; that infants who die are without sin and will therefore attain paradise without baptism; that human nature, being the creation of God, is basically good; that the will always possesses an inalienable freedom which cannot be destroyed even by the force of habit; that the grace of Christ is universal; that Jesus was a teacher and exemplar, rather than a sacrifice or an atonement; that man can attain perfection through the practice of the Gospel ethics as well as through faith; and that salvation, therefore, is within the power of the human will and can be attained by practical works. Although Pelagius was himself a celibate, who declared that we must obey the command of Christ to renounce all material possessions and confer these upon the poor, he and his followers always held marriage and all normal human appetites in the highest esteem.

5. *History.* The first important convert of Pelagius was the Roman advocate Coelestius; and in 411 these two men arrived in Africa, where they had the misfortune of arousing the implacable enmity of Augustine. Pelagius himself went on to Palestine, where he had lived before in a monastic community; and Coelestius applied for ordination as a presbyter at Carthage. But a deacon from Milan by the name of Paulinus opposed his advancement and accused him of these seven heresies: that Adam was created mortal; that his sin injured no one but himself; that new-born infants are in the same condition as Adam upon creation; that the human race neither dies in Adam nor is resurrected in Christ; that unbaptized infants have eternal salvation; that both the law and the Gospel lead to

redemption; and that sinless men existed before Christ. Augustine charged him also with these heresies:[15] that no one, even if baptized and most diligent in good works, can attain the kingdom of God while retaining any material possessions; that God's grace and assistance are not given for single actions, but reside always in the will of all mankind; that the grace of God is bestowed according to our merits, in proportion as we are worthy; that men can never properly be called children of God, unless they are free from sin; that if the will needs the help of God, it cannot be called free; and, even as "we are partakers of the divine nature," it must follow that the soul has the power of being sinless. Since Coelestius would neither recant nor deny the charges, he was excommunicated and driven from Africa.

Meanwhile, Pelagius was living quietly in Palestine, when a young man by the name of Orosius arrived there with a message from Augustine to Jerome dealing with the heresy of Coelestius and Pelagius, who was called before a local synod of fourteen bishops who, when Pelagius evaded the charges and minimized his heresies, found him innocent.

6. *Augustine Outmaneuvers the Roman Pontiff.* Pelagius thereupon published a document called *In Defense of Free Will,* which soon reached Africa. Again St. Augustine went into action; Pelagius and his doctrine were condemned by two synods in 416. Pelagius and Coelestius appealed to the Roman pontiff, Zosimus, who, being a Greek, was inclined toward libertarianism; and as a result of their skillful pleading, he went over to their side on condition that they abide by any decision he might render. Zosimus immediately wrote peremptory letters to the African bishops ordering them to appear at Rome within two months to substantiate their charges, or abandon them; he also wrote an encyclical declaring both Pelagius and Coelestius orthodox. Zosimus, however, was no match for Augustine; for two hundred bishops quickly assembled at Carthage and again anathematized Pelagius in the most unequivocal terms. Zosimus wavered and declared pompously but timidly that he would make further investigation

in preparation for final judgment. But before Zosimus
could take the next step, Augustine and his friends prevailed
upon the Emperor Honorius to issue a rescript from
Ravenna ordering Pelagius, Coelestius, and all their followers
banished from Rome. From this, there was no
appeal; and Pelagianism became an outlaw without a
hearing.

7. *Zosimus Capitulates.* Zosimus made the best of a
bad situation by a quick reversal. He excommunicated
Coelestius and Pelagius, and issued a rigid Test Act, which
upheld the African anathemas and which all bishops must
sign on pain of excommunication. Eighteen of the Italian
bishops refused to subscribe, including Julian of Eclanum,
an acute dialectician, who thenceforth became the spokesman
for the libertarians. The Test Act was imposed in
Africa in 419; the exiled bishops were driven from Constantinople
in 424; and as they formed a coalition with the
Nestorians in 429, they too were condemned at the Ecumenical
Council of Ephesus in 431.

8. *Augustine Driven into Predestinarianism.* During
the course of the Pelagian controversy, Augustine was
gradually forced to abandon his previous libertarianism,
take final refuge in the stark predestinarianism of Paul,
and conclude that human nature must never be assigned
the smallest vestige of congenital goodness. In this system
election has no dependence upon merit, since there is no
such thing; it is simply gratuitous mercy, given to those
chosen at random from the mass of perdition by the inscrutable
mercy of God.

9. *No Ultimate Answer.* The Pelagians and the later
Semi-Pelagians, however, were constantly hammering Augustine
with this question: Since God cannot cause evil
or inflict undeserved punishment, how can we justify the
fact that of two similar persons, one is given grace and
the other is consigned to damnation? To this, Augustine
could only reply "that there is no unrighteousness with
God." [16]

10. *Doctrine Concerning Baptism.* When Pelagius denied
the existence of original sin and, consequently, the

necessity of paedobaptism, he struck at the foundation of the Church; and had he not proclaimed *these* heresies, he might have avoided the fearful condemnation he incurred. For if it be true that all deceased infants, whether baptized or not, receive salvation, what becomes of Catholic priority? Heaven would then be peopled with myriads of children born to heretics or heathen. Since the salvation of infants was impossible except through Christian cleansing and initiation, it was imperative that all receive immediately the laver of regeneration. This was the doctrine as stated by Augustine and it remains essentially unchanged in the Catholic Church to this day.

Augustine declared that any person, pagan or Christian, infant or adult, dying immediately after baptism goes to heaven.[17] Under this doctrine, it would seem that the whole human race could be transformed into elect saints by the simple if grisly procedure of first baptizing and then slaughtering them all without delay.

11. *Doubts.* We know, however, from a private letter to Jerome which Augustine wrote in 415 and in which he reveals himself as a traducianist,[18] a doctrine he never maintained openly, that he found the arguments of the Pelagians morally impregnable; and he concluded: "When we come to the penal sufferings of infants, I am embarrassed, believe me, by great difficulties, and am wholly at a loss to find an answer by which they are resolved."[19] Evidently, Jerome was equally embarrassed, for he replied after a long delay that he had no time for this controversy.

12. *Sex-Desire the Indwelling Devil.* Nevertheless, in the end, Augustine embraced without compromise the doctrine of original sin; and this he propagated with such force that it became an essential element in the philosophy of Catholics and Protestants alike for more than twelve hundred years. Because he embraced the belief so tenaciously, Julian of Eclanum accused Augustine of outright Manichaeism, which also maintained "that the sexual impulse and the intercourse of married people were devised by the devil, and that . . . it is the work of the devil,

not of God, that they are born of this diabolical intercourse." [20] Julian declared further: "if through their birth it happens that evil is in men, and through this evil the devil has power over men, so in fact you declare the devil to be the author of man, from whom comes their origin at birth." "He is completely a Manichaean who maintains original sin." [21]

Augustine vehemently denied these allegations[22] and never wearied of detailing his opposition both to Pelagius and to the Manichees. But when we compare his concept of human nature to that of Manichaeism, we find them substantially alike. In the one case, man is depraved in essence because he was created by Satan; in the other, we have an identical result because man was plunged by the Fall into original sin, which made his physical nature irretrievably corrupt; and with both the essential depravity consists in sexual desire, known as concupiscence.

13. *Truth of Pelagian Charges.* The fact is that the Pelagian charges against Augustine can be substantiated from his own writings, for he agreed with Manes and Paul that sex-desire is the indwelling Satan, by which man is "carnal, sold under sin." Augustine declares that exorcism or exsufflation of infants was a universal necessity because in no other way could "the prince of this world . . . be cast out of them." [23] "Original sin," says Augustine, "is transmitted to infants through sexual union"; they "are in the devil's power" because "they are born of the union of the sexes, which cannot accomplish its own honourable function without the incident of shameful lust." [24] Augustine adds that all men are by nature " 'children of wrath,' inasmuch as they are children of the concupiscence of the flesh." [25]

14. *Original Sin.* The fall of Adam and Eve, and consequently that of their descendants, into depravity, was marked by the sudden advent of sexual desire or lust, so that they became ashamed of their private members, which are "on this account . . . rightly called 'pudenda,' because they excite themselves just as they like . . . Such disobedience . . . is called 'the sin which dwelleth in our members.' "[26]

15. *Original Sin Universal.* Concupiscence is the "wound which the Devil has inflicted upon the human race";[27] and the guilt of that corruption will always be transmitted to every infant, whether born of regenerate or unregenerate parents.[28]

16. *Pelagian Doctrine.* In direct contradiction, the Pelagians declared that "the use of the woman is both natural and laudable";[29] and "from the intercourse of male and female those who are born derive no sin to be put away by the laver of regeneration."[30] And "this sexual connection of bodies . . . together with the ardour, with the pleasure, with the emission of seed, was made by God, and is praiseworthy on its own account."[31]

17. *Augustine's Compromise.* As Augustine inferred, Manichaeism makes all reprobates so depraved that for them the atonement of Christ is useless;[32] but Pelagianism renders humanity so excellent "that the Saviour is superfluous."[33] According to the Manichaean heresy, only the Elect, who require no atonement, can be redeemed; according to the Pelagian, the Church was shorn of its supreme function, since all men possesss not only the freedom to choose salvation but also the power to achieve it. The Gnostics held that the doctrines of predestination and atonement are mutually exclusive; to them, therefore, Christ was never the divine eucharist, but only the Great Instructor.

18. *Augustine's Drift toward Predestinarianism.* During the earlier years of the Pelagian controversy, Augustine continued to give lip-service to the doctrine of free will;[34] by 415, however, he believed that the grace by which men are saved is given gratis and cannot be rendered for human merit, since this is non-existent.[35] He expands his concept, which became the Calvinist doctrine of reprobation: the mass of humanity is corrupt, and therefore deserves damnation. "They, therefore, who are delivered therefrom by grace are called, not vessels of their own merits, but 'vessels of mercy'." Free will enabled man to fall from grace by his own volition, but he can return to righteousness only through the redemption of Christ.[36]

19. *Pelagian Doctrine*. Pelagius declared that "whatever is fettered by natural necessity is deprived of determination of will and deliberation,"[37] which is almost what Augustine himself had declared in earlier years. The Pelagians asserted that any act performed from necessity could not be imputed as sin, a concept which Augustine had proclaimed against the Manichees.

Pelagius declared that since body as well as soul were created by God, both must be good;[38] and dualism or hostility between them is impossible. He then cited a great many quotations from Catholic writers, including Jerome and Augustine himself, to prove that all of them taught or had at one time believed, in the freedom of the will.[39]

In 415, Coelestius presented his thesis in the form of a syllogism: If man is plunged into sin "by the necessity of nature ... he is blameless; if by the freedom of a choice," which was the gift of God but which is more prone to evil than to good, how can we avoid the conclusion that God is the author of evil?[40] To this Augustine replied: Man is in his present miserable condition because, by misusing his original free will, he placed himself in bonds which he is now powerless to escape.[41]

The Pelagians, like Origen, declared that man is inalienably endowed with the choice to do either good or evil: "This capacity is inherent in me, whether I will or no."[42] To this Augustine replied that it is by grace alone "not only that we discover what ought to be done, but also that we do what we have discovered."[43] And he continues: "the possibility of coming, Pelagius places in nature ... whereas the actual coming, he says, lies in the free will and act."[44]

Indignant at such impiety, Augustine exclaims: "How can this arrogant asserter of free will say, 'That we are able to think a good thought,—this comes from God; but that we actually *do* think a good thought proceeds from ourselves?'"[45]

Augustine finally conceded that he could never defeat Pelagius as long as he admitted the slightest vestige of freedom in the will.[46]

20. *Semi-Pelagianism and Prevenient Grace.* After 420, Pelagianism itself was dead: but then arose its child, Semi-Pelagianism, which Augustine confesses had once been his own doctrine,[47] but which he now attacked with renewed virility. And so, in the last year of his life, he took up the cudgels against Vitalis, who had been brought to trial for saying that the capacity for faith is universally innate.[48]

Here Augustine develops the Doctrine of Prevenient Grace, which holds there are two kinds of sinners who hear the voice of the preacher:[49] those who are moved to believe, and those who are not so moved. In the former, the Father speaks from within, and incites them with a prevenient grace; those whom the Father does not so actuate, remain cold, and never respond to the call since they are not of the Elect.[50]

That this congenital impulse is also irresistible is developed in detail. Each saint chosen from the foundation of the world, and no one else, possesses this grace, "which is the effect of that predestination."[51]

21. *The Final Perseverance.* In his last treatise, Augustine declares that no one can be sure of possessing final perseverance "so long as he is still alive."[52] The gift itself is impossible without hourly divine support, which may be withdrawn at any moment, revealing the false saint as a child of perdition. On the other hand, at any moment the most brazen heretic or the most hardened sinner may be filled with grace. This doctrine had the advantage of keeping every saint forever on the alert.

22. *A Fantastic Incongruity.* The incongruity of this doctrine when maintained by a priest-state becomes painfully obvious. It was preached logically enough by Pythagoras, the Essenes, Jesus, Paul, Marcion, and the Manichees: for all of these wished only to establish dedicated communions, which had no pretension to civil power and from which the multitude was to be systematically excluded. What Augustine and the Catholic Church demanded was the power to control and discipline, not

merely those whom it would usher into Paradise, but also that great majority who must remain forever the children of the devil. The Ebionites conceded that this world belonged to the wicked; the Catholics declared that it belongs to the Church.

23. *Practical Effects of Doctrine.* It is impossible to overestimate the practical effect of the doctrine of original sin. No speculative opinion has ever made one portion of humanity so cold, so cruel, so merciless in its treatment of the rest. Once the Church attained unchallenged power, it was only necessary to say of any person who did not conform that he was possessed by Satan and acted in accordance with his congenital, Adamic nature. The property of this "criminal" could then be confiscated, and he could be tortured, imprisoned, exiled, burned, or whatever else the ecclesiastical judges might determine; and the sentence when executed by the "secular arm," was received with complete public approbation. It is an historical fact that at *auto-da-fés* thousands of people watched and listened without the smallest twinge of sympathy while hundreds of victims, including members of their own families, writhed and shrieked in the flames. After all, those who were to suffer in hell might as well endure at once a small foretaste of their eternal fate! And, since no one could escape the damnation consequent upon original sin outside the Catholic communion, this made moral lepers of all others, who must always be feared and hated and with whom there must never be the slightest communication. The segregation of Catholics from non-Catholics must be absolute.

24. *Doctrine Concerning Sex and Marriage.* In the course of the Pelagian controversy, St. Augustine developed doctrines concerning sex and marriage which became embedded in the permanent Catholic code. He declares that wedlock is a "sacramental bond," [53] and, as such, can never be abrogated by crime, adultery, separation, impotence, childlessness, frigidity, union with another, or by any other cause whatsoever.[54] All sexual intercourse, except that which occurs in a Church-blessed union and the purpose of which is to beget children, especi-

ally if a contraceptive is used, makes of the wife a harlot and of the husband an adulterer.55

In the Catholic Church, it is a mortal sin to preserve the mother instead of the child, when either but only one can be saved, because this would deprive an immortal soul of Catholic baptism, without which the infant must be damned.

25. *Had Pelagianism Been Victorious?* The Pelagian heresy was a brave, though futile, struggle for freedom. We believe that had either this or Arianism prevailed, there would have been no Dark Ages, for then there would have been no priest-state, no renunciation, no destruction of learning and philosophy, no persecution for differing convictions concerning speculative doctrines. The world would have progressed under Christianity as it had under Hellenism and as it has under Protestantism. So overwhelming are the values by which men live.

However, Pelagianism was destined for defeat. The Council of Orange in 539 made the whole of Augustinianism, except the irresistibility of prevenient grace, a dogma. Yet neither Pelagianism nor Semi-Pelagianism were ever completely eradicated, and were to emerge as an enormous influence during the Reformation.

D. DONATISM: THE STRUGGLE FOR PURITY vs. CONFORMITY

1. *A Schism, not a Heresy.* The Donatist dispute occupied in Augustine's life a middle position between the Manichaean and Pelagian controversies. It was not properly a heresy, but a schism; that is, it did not challenge orthodox dogma. Instead, it attempted to set up a separate discipline in opposition to the Catholic, but based upon the same doctrine.

2. *Like the Novatian Schism.* It was very similar to the Novatian schism which had arisen in the time of Cyprian, and it had identical causes. During long periods of tranquillity under the pagan emperors, many, who were something less than saints, joined the Church; and,

as they achieved various degrees of prosperity and worldly success, their appetite for suffering and renunciation waned. Consequently, during the persecution of Decian, 249, and of Valerian, 258, large numbers of such comfortable Christians hastened to preserve their property and security by renouncing the faith. As soon as the danger passed, many of these backsliders clamored for readmission; but, quite naturally, those who had not succumbed resented the presence of these apostates.

3. *Defections during the Diocletian Persecution.* The persecution of Diocletian carried in its wake a still greater reaction, the Donatist schism of Africa which excluded from its ranks all Traditors, that is, Christians who had surrendered the sacred books to the authorities. Meanwhile, the Catholics established the confessional to enable those of little fortitude to purge their conscience and perform appropriate penance. The African defections had been enormous; and when the Edict of Toleration was issued in 313, the Donatists appealed to Constantine to establish their right to all revenues, edifices, and other properties. The emperor, however, realizing that Donatism constitiuted only a local schism, ruled in favor of the African Catholics, led by Cecaelianus, who was himself a Traditor. At the Council of Arles, 314, the schismatics presented an appeal, which was rejected. Thereafter, we find internecine Christian warfare in Africa until all were overwhelmed by the Moslem catastrophe of the seventh century.

4. *Wild Anarchy.* It is not easy to imagine the anarchy which took possession of almost the whole Roman world after the accession of Christianity. The various factions which had been constrained to keep the peace under the pagan emperors, now broke out into universal violence. Creed made war upon creed; and one schism upon another. Wild hordes of fanatical monks roamed the countryside and made life almost insupportable. Religious controversies raged not only in the churches and the synods, but in the market place, the streets, and in almost every private dwelling. Christianity

had indeed set father against son, and mother against daughter-in-law. Countless men with strident voices ran hither and yon declaring their doctrines and threatening their opponents with eternal damnation, as well as with immediate destruction. It was a tribulation such as the world had never seen.

When Julian became emperor, he permitted the Donatists to repossess the churches which they had themselves built; but the moment he died, the war broke out anew with redoubled fury. Two or three generations had passed since the original lapse took place; but the festering wounds only grew larger and became immedicable. The Donatists accused the Catholic Church as a traitor to the faith, of harboring countless criminals in its bosom, of being guilty of all manner of anti-Christian bestiality.

5. *Separation of Church and State.* The struggle developed into something far afield from the original controversy. The Donatists sought only to erect a dedicated communion; they did not wish to compel any one to join them: instead, they expelled those who were guilty of overt moral turpitude. Since they had little motive for persecution, they repudiated it on principle. And, since Augustine quotes his opponents extensively, we learn first-hand the opinions of these recalcitrants.

6. *Origin of Controversy.* Oddly enough, the Donatist controversy, like the Pelagian, exploded over the question of baptism, although in an entirely different manner. The Donatists declared that traitors to the Gospel, such as all Catholics were, could not possibly administer this holy sacrament; and therefore they rebaptized all their converts, whether they came from the pagans, from heretical communions, or from the Church itself. This aroused the fury of Augustine, who, repudiating the teachings of Cyprian, declared that the sacrament of baptism belongs to no church, but to the Trinity alone, and is always completely effective when given in Its name, no matter who administers or receives it.

In the controversy which ensued, both sides accused the other of murder, violence, lying, hypocrisy, fraud, the forging of documents, and many other crimes. Both claimed to be the historic and Apostolic Church. The Catholics enjoyed the immense advantage of support from the emperor. The Donatists, on the other hand, commanded the allegiance of the great majority of tried and sincere Christians, who stood ready at all times to suffer for their convictions; and especially of the Circumcelliones—monks corresponding to the Egyptian followers of Antony—who were always prepared to die for their faith, or to kill.

7. *The Council of Carthage.* In 411 occurred the great Council of Carthage, engineered largely by Augustine, to explore the possibility of peace and unity. Present were 287 Donatist and 276 Catholic bishops, who debated for three days on two issues: first, Does the Universal apostolic succession reside with the Donatists or with the Catholics? and, second, Does the efficacy of baptism belong to Christ or does it depend on the purity and the authority of the ministrant? It was agreed that if the Donatists proved victorious the Catholics would resign their sees; but if the Catholics should prevail, the Donatists were to re-enter the Church and receive ordination in it. Augustine led the debate; but since the disputants were also the judges, the decision remained in doubt; and the war did not abate.

8. *Philosophy of Compulsion.* Augustine persuaded the western Emperor Honorius to issue the most drastic rescripts against his opponents, calling for the seizure of all their churches, the confiscation of their private property, and the exile or death of their leaders. These measures brought over some of the less determined; but more of them were simply driven to acts of extreme fanaticism.

During this controversy, Augustine formulated many of the administrative and political theories which still govern the Catholic Church. These we may summarize and briefly discuss under the following headings: first, the unity and universality of the Church; second, the impossibility of separating the good from the bad in this world; third, the nature of baptism and other sacraments; fourth, the necessity of coercion and persecution; and, fifth, the use and purpose of the secular power.

E. THE GREAT AUGUSTINIAN FORMULARIES

1. *The Unity and Universality of the Church.* To Augustine it was incomprehensible that religious truth could reside in any man who has broken with the Catholic communion. Although Cyprian, according to Augustine, may have erred in his day on the question of rebaptism, he "yet remained most firm in the unity of the church that it might be shown more clearly to heretics what a sacrilegious crime it was to break the bond of peace."[56] The Donatists, said Augustine, "charge us with betrayal of the sacred books . . . but . . . *they* have received with unimpaired honors those who were stained with the sacrilege of schism."[57] It was this conviction on the part of Augustine which made of him the perfect protagonist for a church that should become supreme, intolerant, totalitarian, morally lax, and co-extensive with society itself.

Stemming directly from his theory that there could be no Christian life except in the universal Church, Augustine developed the concomitant, that no dissident group has any right to its own property: "All things of which unity was in possession belong to no other than ourselves, who remain in unity."[58] Furthermore, "since every earthly possession can be rightly retained only on the ground of divine right," heretics and schismatics have no title to the property they have themselves gathered, since it is written, "The wealth of the sinner is laid up for the just."[59] Accordingly, the most Christian emperor piously decreed the confiscation of all Donatist properties,[60] an action which drove the schismatics to indescribable frenzy.

2. *Separating the Chaff from the Grain.* Inseparably joined to the concept of all-inclusive Catholic unity was the doctrine that the chaff cannot be separated from the grain, or the tares from the wheat, in this world. The Gospel parables which used these metaphors were pressed

into service by Augustine to show that all human beings must remain in the Church. This was of course a gross misinterpretation: for Jesus meant that many who only seem to be of the Elect go through the form of conversion, and are, to all appearances, actual saints. He specifically excluded all who do not yearn for communion; and He, as well as Paul, made ample provision to expel those who did not submit to Church discipline or observe its moral code, with no punishment other than the eschatological.

Various heretical groups understood the Gospel correctly; but it was necessarily ignored by the Catholics in their drive to become the state; and they declared that the tares and the chaff were simply the cold, the skeptical, the indifferent, the irreligious, the criminal, and those guilty of moral turpitude, none of whom were ever to be denied membership in the Church. Quite the contrary: they were to be forced to enter, on pain of exile or death.

Both Donatists and Catholics set up certain credal tests as a prerequisite for membership. In addition, however, the former established moral standards unknown among the Catholics. "Nor," says Augustine, "do we separate ourselves from the society of the . . . unrighteous men whom we cannot separate from the wheat of the Lord before the winnowing at the judgment."[61] He declares that the Catholics must nurture "all who . . . profess that they know God" even though they be "covetous and envious, murderers, faithless, liars, possessed of devils, those whose words work corruption, infidels, accursed, antichrists, blasphemous, sacrilegious, servants of the devil." [62] Under the discipline instituted by Paul, all such sinners were either washed and sanctified, or else expelled.[63] Cyprian, on the other hand, like Augustine, demanded their retention: murderers, infidels, the sacrilegious, and the blasphemous, all, all were welcome in the bosom of the Church, so long as they "profess that they know God," that is, so long as they mumble the creed and submit to the hierarchy. Penance might be required for robbery, rape, and murder; but there must be no expulsion for these or any other moral enormities, no matter how numerous or flagitious, so long as the communicant accepted the authority of the Church. And this in spite of the fact that Paul had declared explicitly that fornicators, covetous, idolators, railers, drunkards, and extortioners must be expelled.[64] In another passage he extends the list of those who "shall not inherit the kingdom of God," to include those guilty of "strife, seditions, heresies,"[65] which would certainly include schismatics. Equally definite was Jesus Himself, who declared that, through moral transgressions, brethren become as heathen and must be loosed from the earthly brotherhood with a loosing that will be effective also in heaven.[66] But since all these injunctions ran directly counter to the central purpose of the Church, which was to become the universal state, Augustine could not find the texts in which they are proclaimed.

The Donatists charged that when they expelled adulterers or other criminals, these were promptly accepted by the Catholics and accorded full rank. A case in point was that of a certain Quodvulteus, probably a bishop, who had been convicted of two adulteries. Petilian reproached Augustine because this wicked man had been ordained in the Catholic Church. Augustine admitted the charge, but countered by saying that this very case proved the Donatist theory of baptism wrong; because, if this sacrament is effective only where administered by pure and undefiled priests, what then is the condition of all those who, as Donatists, had been baptized by this same Quodvulteus?[67]

3. *Concerning Baptism.* And this brings us to the bitter controversy over baptism. To refute the doctrine of the Donatists, Augustine laid the foundation for the Protestant Reformation. He declared that if their baptismal theory were correct, the whole Church had been ruined for centuries;[68] for even before the time of Cyp-

rian, heretical baptisms were accepted; and furthermore, even as Cyprian communicated with traitors at least as much as Augustine with Traditors, therefore according to the Donatists, the whole Catholic Church, including the Donatists themselves, had long been lost. But, since this is impossible, we know that the sacrilege does not consist in baptism at the hands of the heretical or the unsanctified, but in rebaptism. The sacraments do not cease to be valid merely because they are usurped,[69] for they belong to Christ alone.[70] Consecrated baptism "is not affected by the error of any man, whether ministrant or recipient, whether or not he hold views contrary to the revelation of divine teaching on the subject of the Father, or the Son, or the Holy Ghost." [71] In other words, if an infidel baptizes a heretic, the recipient is entirely cleansed of all sin, original or personal.

4. *Doctrines Concerning Persecution.* But if Augustine adopted a liberal position on the sacraments, he did quite otherwise concerning persecution. In the bitter conflict with the Donatists, the latter took the position that compulsion and violence were condemned by the Gospel. Petilian urges Augustine to read John 18:10-11 and Matt. 26:52-55, in which Jesus repudiates the use of force: "If innocence is on our side, why do you persecute us with the sword? Or if you call us guilty, why do you seek our company?"[72] Petilian continues: "Jesus Christ never persecuted any one . . . But far be it, far be it from our conscience to compel any one to embrace our faith." [73]

Petilian charges the Catholics with using even the military forces of heathen emperors, which should be employed only against an external enemy, to destroy the true Christians; and he implies the necessity of separating church and state.[74] Augustine replies that the direct command of Christ was simply being enforced; and, by a ghastly perversion, appeals to a Gospel parable: "You are of the opinion that no one should be compelled to follow righteousness; and yet you read that the householder said to his servants, 'Whomsoever ye shall find, compel them to come in.' "[75]

Throughout, Augustine assumes that Catholic violence constitutes the tenderest love and affection. "No capital punishment was imposed," he says unctuously, "that Christian gentleness might be observed." [76] The Donatists are like wounded mules or horses who kick and bite the doctors who wish to heal them.[77] And again the secular power, being a subsidiary to that of God, exists for the very purpose of enforcing ecclesiastical judgment, "for to this end their power has been ordained by God." [78]

Augustine makes it clear that no act of the Church can possibly be construed as persecution; and dissidents who are put to death by no means achieve martyrdom. And he does not hesitate to pervert the Gospel by commanding civil disobedience: "Whosoever refuses to obey the laws of the emperors which are enacted against the truth of God wins for himself a great reward." [79] The true purpose of the Catholic Church could scarcely be stated more baldly. When the civil government is the creature of the Church, the violence it inflicts is never persecution; but when it is not, disobedience becomes a sacred duty. And we are told that when heretics, pagans, or schismatics defend themselves, this is treason.[80] For Donatists, Catholics seek only "their deliverance from error . . . by the help of terror, of judges and of law, whereby they may be preserved from falling under the penalty of eternal judgment." [81]

It is apparent, however, that neither the Donatists nor their Circumcellionist monks accepted this solicitous love with equanimity. They defended their communion, churches, monasteries, and other assets with wild fanaticism. Augustine was outraged by their militancy and accused them of throwing "lime mixed with acid into" the eyes of those sent to confiscate their properties.[82]

However, the imperial soldiers were too much even for these monks, who were often compelled to choose between death and re-entry into the Church. They were the spiritual descendants of the Novatians and the Montanists, who sought the crown of martyrdom, whether at the hands of idolatrous pagans or Christian persecutors. For them, Augustine had only the most withering contempt; and his heart was no more moved by their suffering than if they had been outright infidels. For they were guilty of the crime which to him was heinous beyond all others: they had broken the unity of the Church, and they challenged its claim to be the totalitarian state.[83]

Out of this Donatist controversy, Augustine developed the philosophy embraced by the medieval Church. Full authority for all the horrors committed by the Inquisition can be found in this father, whose doctrine was consistent with his practice: any persons who, or groups which, will not submit completely and unquestioningly to the Catholic hierarchy must be extirpated like mad dogs.

5. *The Function of the Secular Arm.* The Church conferred total primacy upon itself; but this did not deprive the "secular arm" of all function. This consisted, however, only in performing certain inferior duties, among which the principal was to escort heretics beyond the pale of human society. The Church must reign supreme in all matters concerning faith, morals, and education; the state was to be the policeman, the jailor, and the executioner which would implement the decisions of ecclesiastical authority, since it is the power "ordained for that very purpose." The emperors "are the ministers of God who execute wrath upon those who do evil." [84]

The role of the civil power is sometimes like that of Elijah when he slew the eight hundred prophets of Baal; [85] and sometimes it is to force schismatics into the fold; kings are "the instruments by which those who are found in the highways and the hedges—that is, in heresies and schisms—are compelled to come in to the supper of the Lord." [86]

F. AUGUSTINE'S INFLUENCE UPON MEDIEVAL EUROPE AND THE REFORMATION

The real triumph of Catholicism came, not with Constantine, but with the Bishop of Hippo. Although the doctrine of purgatory, which was made official dogma by Gregory the Great in 604, is faintly recognized in *De Civitate Dei*, it plays no significant role there. Nor were the other developments, such as the use of relics, amulets, charms, indulgences, etc., present in Augustine. He represented to the great Protestant reformers the acme of pristine Christianity, with a theology based upon Paul and unencumbered by medieval abuses. Calvin and Luther could point to him, and thereby convict their opponents a thousand times of repudiating Paul and the Gospel, and "teaching for doctrines the commandments of men." The Manichaean rationalism of Augustine made him the perfect mentor of the Teutonic Reformation.

And so Luther, Calvin, Knox, and many others went back to Augustine. Here they found a vast treasury of philosophy, interpretation, and practical theory which they could put to effective use. The Catholics could indeed point to Augustine's insistence upon universal unity; but he never cited the creeds; nor did he appeal to ecumenical authority or pay the slightest reverence to the Roman See: throughout, he appealed to the scriptures, as interpreted by logic, and declared that in them neither error nor contradiction is possible. Thereby he established the *ipsissima verba* of the Bible as the basis for the Reformation and repudiated all other authority.

Augustine carried Christian theology to the point most acceptable to the Protestant revolutionaries: what was added after him was medieval excrescence. Even his doctrine concerning persecution was welcome to the stern reformers, and became an integral portion of their philosophy. Augustine, therefore, became the mentor of Protestantism; and his central doctrine, that of original sin, with its concomitant predestinarianism, became the foundation of Lutheran and Calvinist doctrine.

The secret of Augustine's unintentional libertarianism was twofold: first, his declaration that the scriptures remain forever the ultimate authority and his implied dictum that their meaning must be determined by individual reason, not by councils or by a priesthood; and, second, his determination to take the sacraments from the Church and give them to Christ. Augustine thereby laid the foundation for a religion in which every man could appeal directly to the Bible and in which men could receive the sacraments in a thousand competing communions.

There was present, therefore, a dual and contradictory dynamic in St. Augustine: the first conscious, by which he sought to establish the unified and universal Church, and thus he laid the foundation for medieval life; the second, a latent libertarianism, by which he made the written word the supreme authority as understood and interpreted by human reason and logic and Christ the sole source of salvation, and thus laid the foundation for the Protestant philosophy and prepared the climate for republican civilization.

CHAPTER XX

LIFE UNDER THE CATHOLIC CHURCH

A. THE GOSPEL DOCTRINE OF REGENERATION

1. *A Moral Transformation.* When Jesus broke away from the exclusive circle of the Essenes and offered His salvation to all who could receive it, He certainly expected each and every disciple to achieve a thorough reconstitution of his inner nature which would make him a celibate without erotic desire and cause him to renounce all worldly possessions without regret.

And so Jesus called to Him publicans, harlots, thieves, and every species of wrongdoer, the very dregs of society, certain that they would achieve a cataclysmic moral transformation which would make them into sons of God. Paul must have attracted similar converts, for he wrote that many of them, now washed and sanctified, had formerly been idolaters, adulterers, effeminate, abusers of themselves with mankind, thieves, covetous, revilers, and extortioners.[1]

2. *Widespread Failure.* That the Gospel was not always successful, however, we learn from Paul, who reported "such fornication as is not so much as named among the Gentiles, that one should have his father's wife." [2] We can only conclude that many converts, having renounced the normal solace of marriage, took refuge in one of the most revolting of all relationships; and the probably genuine first *Epistle of Clement,* also to the Corinthians and written about 95, supports the Pauline excoriation.

3. *Appeal to the Poor and the Lost.* Jesus declared "I am not come to call the righteous, but sinners"; and

— 631 —

in another passage He thanks His Father that His gospel had been revealed to babes, but hidden from the wise and the prudent. And this was a characteristic of the new religion which the Neo-Platonist Celsus did not fail to notice; "Other mysteries," he said, invite those with "clean hands, and a prudent tongue ... But ... these Christians invite every one ... who is a sinner, who is devoid of understanding, who is a child, and to speak generally, whosoever is unfortunate."[3]

In this appeal to the enslaved, the poor, the ignorant, the downtrodden, and the morally debased, lay the secret of Christian power, even as was the case with Buddhism: for it gave to social outcasts a sense of significance. The countless millions who had for centuries been controlled, exploited, and reduced to psychological non-entity sought avidly some compensation for their frustration. They could neither find their place in the sun nor attack their exploiters directly: nevertheless, they attained revenge by transferring their allegiance to a world beyond the grave. Rome, therefore, defeated herself by destroying the will to live among her tributaries. For millions of men and women, checkmated in this life, there was to be a heaven of gold and precious jewels, and for their rulers hell fire eternal.

4. *Complications Arise.* The process of regeneration, however, was soon enmeshed in complications. The doctrine of the pristine Church was overwhelmingly eschatological: and only as long as this was accepted without question, could there be a high degree of fervor and personal sacrifice among the saints. Furthermore, the gospel was intended for those who were called and predestinated; but when the Catholics made the Church the totalitarian state, it also assumed the impossible task of beatifying the human race.

5. *Mass-Regeneration Impossible.* Patristic literature bears melancholy witness to the failure of Christianity to accomplish such a transformation. And when Origen maintained that moral regenerations *did* occur among Christians, he certainly never implied that these were accomplished *en masse*.[4]

B. EFFECT OF ROMAN PROSPERITY

1. *Moral Laxity.* The freedom and prosperity under the Antonines were such that a great many could live in comparative security and comfort. As a result, the Church became quite worldly, its members almost indistinguishable from their pagan neighbors. This condition created havoc among the Christians on those occasions when brief but sharp persecutions broke out against them. We learn of the moral laxity in the Church from no less an authority than Cyprian, who declares that "among the priests there was no devotion to religion; among the ministers there was no sound faith: . . . bishops . . . forsook their thrones, deserted their people, wandered about over foreign provinces, hunted the markets for gainful merchandise, while brethren were starving in the church." 5

2. *Gospel Already Sacrificed.* We need not be surprised at this condition: for the Church had already sacrificed the Gospel to expediency. In its drive for membership, power, and affluence, it had minimized a life of sanctity and brotherhood in favor of an externalized ritual and blind obedience.

3. *Contradiction between Fact and Gospel.* When the Church seized the public power, the painful disparity between the Gospel and the character of its communicants became obvious. The moral conditions existing in Jerusalem are thus depicted by Gregory of Nyssa: "rascality, adultery, theft, idolatry, poisoning, quarrelling, murder, are rife; . . . nowhere in the world are people so ready to kill each other as there . . . merely for the sake of lifeless plunder." 6

C. THE CELIBATE MOVEMENT

1. *The Triumph of Asceticism.* Once the Christian Church became triumphant, the Buddhist concept of renunciation gained enormous momentum. The anchor-

ites of John Cassian found peace for their tortured souls when they renounced property and adopted celibacy as their way of life.[7] He declared that it is not enough to be without money or wealth: one must also be free from all desire to possess them.[8] Basil and Jerome, like countless others, sold their property, gave everything to the poor, lived in celibacy, and mortified their flesh. After wrestling for years with his congenital impulses, Augustine wrenched victory at last from the Enemy by realizing that he must sell his goods and give the money derived from them to the poor.[9] Methodius, bishop of Tyre, about 300, wrote that "virginity is something supernaturally great, wonderful, and glorious . . . . this best and noblest manner of life is the root of immortality." [10] Jerome declared that "Christ Himself is a virgin; and His mother is also a virgin; yea, though she is His mother, she is a virgin still . . . The apostles have either been virgins, or . . . have lived celibate lives . . . bishops, priests, and deacons are vowed to perpetual chastity." [11]

2. *Derived from Manichaeism.* Such was the tone, at least of western orthodoxy, in the fourth and fifth centuries. However, despite the fact that this philosophy had deep roots in Paul and the Gospel Jesus, it never received implementation until the fifth century, when the Manichaean influence became irresistible. In the second century, Paul had been revised to declare that a bishop should be the husband of one wife and should rule his children and his household "with all gravity." [12]

3. *Celibacy after the Third Century.* Except during the earliest years, ministerial celibacy was neither required nor recommended during the first two centuries of Church history. Tertullian, a presbyter at Carthage, writing about 200, had a wife; and although he strenuously opposed a second marriage for widows and widowers as if polygamous, he never recognized any difference between marital regulations for clerics and laity.

However, it is clear from a passage in Hippolytus,[13] written about twenty-five years later, that a change had already begun; for this writer bitterly accused his personal enemy, Pope Callixtus, of permitting twice-married bishops to retain their posts and even to marry after ordination, as if this were a practice now proscribed.

We have seen that various heretical communions, such as the Marcionite, required uncompromising celibacy from clergy and laity alike. It is worth noting that Novatian, the first anti-pope, rigorously condemned the concept of a celibate priesthood in 250. And we learn that as late as the Council of Nicaea, when certain bishops wished to make clerical celibacy mandatory, the venerable Paphnutius argued against it so forcibly that his view prevailed; it was therefore established that bishops, presbyters, and deacons who were married at the time of their ordination were required to continue in cohabitation with their wives; that such functionaries, if single, at the time of ordination, were not to enter upon matrimony thereafter; and that all must be barred from Church office who had been married twice *after* baptism or had ever been married to a divorcee, a harlot, a servant-maid, or an actress.[14] In this manner, creeping celibacy infiltrated the Church in the fourth century.

4. *Celibacy Condemned in Eastern Church.* In its reaction against the Gnostics, so far was the Eastern Church from celibacy that in 340 the Council of Gangra met particularly to condemn the celibate and ascetic opinions of Eustathius of Antioch. The canons of that Council anathematize those who condemn legitimate marriage; who teach vegetarianism; who hesitate to receive communion from married presbyters; who preserve virginity because they abhor matrimony; who treat those who are married with contempt; and who refuse their husbands because they abominate the connubial relationship.

5. *Influence of Augustine.* It is in the African Code, adopted by the Council of Carthage in 419 under the influence of Augustine, that we find for the first time an expression of the drastic celibate views which permeated the Western Church in the fifth century. Those who pray, must abstain from their wives,[15] as must all communicants during periods when the eucharist is to be received.[16] Every bishop, presbyter, or deacon must renounce his wife or his office.[17]

6. *Late Development in the Eastern Church.* Clerical celibacy developed much more slowly in the Eastern than in the Western Church. Thus the canons of the Council of Chalcedon, 451, provide that neither monks nor nuns may marry; and that clergymen may do so but may not elope.[18] The Council of Trullo finally settled the question of marriage and celibacy for the Eastern clergy in 692. It was decreed that any priest who has contracted a second marriage or who has married after ordination must break off such a relationship.[19] Celibacy, however, was required only from bishops, and not from presbyters or deacons.

D. CANON LAW

1. *Displaced the Civil Law.* The practical results of Church philosophy are revealed in its canons, which very early replaced the civil code. Ecclesiastical penance replaced the secular penal system. The chief remaining domestic function of the civil government was to eliminate heretics from society by exile or execution. Canon law assumed that every criminal yearned for the life-giving sacrament as if he were a saint; and anyone not possessed of this desire was simply a heretic. Under such a regime, there was no need for secular jurisprudence, since all unrepentant sinners were merely escorted from the world.

We learn from the Council of Ancyra, 314,[20] how tolerant the Church was in certain matters: for example, harlots were permitted to continue in their profession; but they were required to do penance for taking drugs to induce abortion.

That the Canon Law had substantially replaced the civil code by 375[21] we learn from St. Basil. An intentional homicide, we read, was to be excluded from the sacrament for twenty years, of which he will weep during four, remain among the hearers for five, pray among the kneelers for seven, and remain standing among the faithful during four.[22]

2. *Complicated Code.* There were hundreds of canons prescribing the punishment for every transgression: the unintentional homicide was to be excluded from the sacra-

ment for ten years;[23] the adulterer for fifteen;[24] the thief for one or two.[25] Incest with a sister or stepmother drew the same punishment as murder.[26] Anyone who repents after once denying Christ must weep throughout life, and can receive the sacrament only "in the hour of death."[27]

E. PRIESTS AND ASCETICS

1. *Enmity.* We have already noted that the regular priesthood was modeled upon Brahmana originals, and the monachist movement upon the Buddhist orders; and the enmity between the two, inherited from India, carried over, almost unabated, into the Catholic world. We learn something of the strained relations existing between the fanatical monks and the luxuriating bishops from the famous anchorite, Sulpitius Severus, 363-420, who accused the priests of every moral depravity conceivable.[28]

A contemporary monk, John Cassian, declared that only among the monastic orders did Christians still practice communist Gospel principles, which had been rejected as a concession to the Gentiles when they forced their way into the Christian communion.[29]

2. *Bishops Were Opulent Potentates.* That even the early bishops were powerful potentates who luxuriated in regal splendor and who received enormous revenues over which they exercised irresponsible control while many in their flocks subsisted at an animal level, we learn from many sources. Informative is the case of the historian Theodoret, who, after selling his goods and giving the money to the poor, became a monk at the age of twenty-three. At thirty, he became bishop of Cyprus, a minor see. He boasted that he never accepted any personal remuneration for his tireless labors in the Church;[30] but he must have had an immense income because he boasted also that he built many public works and even constructed an aqueduct at his own expense.[30] Truly, episcopal power and revenues were sufficient to tempt ambitious men to any extremity of intrigue and violence.

3. *Jerome.* As a guilt-ridden conscience spread in the ancient world, the more sincere and fanatical among the

Catholics became ascetics, seeking redemption through the mortification of the flesh. Such was Jerome, the translator of the *Vulgate,* and a fierce, pugnacious controversialist, who spent most of his adult life laboring in a tiny cell in the wilderness of Palestine. In his *Letter to Eustochium,* he reveals his psychotic condition: [31]

> 8. I used to sit alone because I was filled with bitterness; sack-cloth disfigured my unshapely limbs and my skin from long neglect had become as black as an Ethiopian's. Tears and groans were every day my portion; and . . . my bare bones, which hardly held together, clashed against the ground . . . Now, although in my fear of hell I had consigned myself to this prison, where I had no companions but scorpions and wild beasts, I often found myself amid bevies of girls. My face was pale and my frame chilled with fasting; yet my mind was burning with desire, and the fires of lust kept bubbling up before me when my flesh was as good as dead. . . .
>
> 30. Many years ago, for the kingdom of heaven's sake, I cut myself off from home, parents, sister, relations, and . . . from daily food . . . And so, miserable man that I was, I would fast only that I might afterwards read Cicero . . . And when at times I returned to my right mind, and began to read the prophets, their style seemed rude and repellant . . . a deep-seated fever fell upon my weakened body, and while it seems hardly credible—it so wasted my unhappy frame that scarcely anything was left of me but skin and bone. Meantime preparations for my funeral went on; my body grew gradually colder . . . Suddenly I was caught up in the spirit and dragged before the judgment seat . . . Asked who and what I was I replied: "I am a Christian." But He who presided said: "Thou liest, thou art a follower of Cicero and not of Christ. For 'where thy treasure is, there will thy heart be also.' " . . . I began to cry and to bewail myself, saying: "Have mercy upon me, O Lord: have mercy upon me." . . . At last the bystanders, falling down

before the knees of Him who presided, prayed that He would have pity on my youth, and that He would give me space to repent of my error. He might still, they urged, inflict torture on me, should I ever again read the works of the Gentiles . . . Accordingly, I made oath and called upon His name, saying: "Lord, if ever again I possess worldly books, or if ever again I read such, I have denied Thee." Dismissed, then, on taking this oath, I returned to the upper world, and, to the surprise of all, I opened upon them eyes so drenched with tears that my distress served to convince even the incredulous.

Every wilderness teemed with male celibates who escaped woman by taking refuge in caves, cells, or the top of stones. They spent their lives mortifying their flesh and condemning every desire for comfort, pleasure, or beauty; they were particularly hostile toward anyone who embraced the Gospel on less stringent terms.

4. *St. Antony.* *The Life of Antony,* written by Athanasius, reveals the demonology and superstition of Catholic Europe. The mad, emaciated monks saw supernatural apparitions on every hand. Early in life, the Gospel communism seized upon Antony's mind; as a result, he gave his land to the villagers and his money to the poor, so that no clog of sin might burden his soul. Going to the desert for purification, he was tempted by the devil in the form of a beautiful woman who lavished every seductive wile upon him. Fearful was the battle waged within his soul by the Powers of Darkness against the Powers of Light. But thinking of the hell that awaits those who look upon woman with lust in heart, Antony spurned the "adversary, and passed through the temptation unscathed." [32] He fasted constantly, and dressed in a hair shirt; like a Gaina ascetic, "he neither bathed his body with water to free himself from filth, nor did he ever wash his feet, nor even endure to put them into water." [33] He reeked with the odor of sanctity. His nights were filled with dreadful visions of Satan grasping those souls who had served him during their lives on earth,[34] but unable to

prevent the righteous from winging their way to heaven.

5. *Superstition and Demonology.* Sulpitius Severus declares that a fierce cow had long been in the habit of attacking and goring people; but when St. Martin ordered the demon sitting on her back to the pit "the evil spirit obeyed and departed." [35] Although this saint was the bishop of Tours, he lived as an anchorite in a cell on the top of a precipitous rock; around him he had gathered some eighty brethren "disciplined after the example of the saintly master. No one there had anything which was called his own; all things were possessed in common." Holy idleness was the rule, since "no art was practised there." [36]

The devil was always at hand, and St. Martin saw him in a thousand shapes and disguises. Sometimes, like a Montanist, a Novatian, or a Donatist, he would whisper that those who had once lapsed could never be redeemed; [37] sometimes he caused men to declare themselves to be the prophet Elias, or John the Baptist, or the reincarnation of Christ. From all this, it was obvious that Antichrist was at hand. Whenever the saint rebuked the devil possessing such persons, the fiend fled instantly.[38]

Such tales could be multiplied *ad infinitum*.

F. THE WAR AGAINST SATAN

1. *A World Full of Devils.* It was indeed a world full of devils; and in spite of the Church and the Cross they seemed to multiply in geometrical progression. In the forest glens and ravines, in streams and brooks, behind every tree and bush, under the bed and in the hearth, in highways and byways, in the air and on the clouds, all through the night and the gloaming, but especially within the human heart—devils were omnipresent! With the coming of original sin into the world, the human body became the habitation of the Evil One, and there he lived and moved and had his being. Each new soul occupying its infant body shared this frail abode with a fiend, or with a troop of fiends, who, by exorcism and baptism, were driven from the child, but alas! not for long. Soon the evicted demon came slithering back with seven others worse than

himself, and again original sin took over. Only by ceaseless rebuke from the ministers of Christ, by the exorcism of holy water and the Cross, could Satan be held at bay.

2. *The Heretic.* But the worst enemies were always the heretics, who were most difficult to deal with, because they used logic and the scriptures so effectively; of their writings, says Vincent of Lerins, there is "hardly a single page which does not bristle with plausible quotations from the New Testament or the Old." [39]

G. GREGORY THE GREAT

1. *Civilization Dead.* The sixth century was an age of decline, ignorance, and illiteracy. Learning fell so low that Pope Gregory, 590-604, admonished certain monks for not reading enough even to know the Commandments.[40] He wrote that a man who cannot read or who has been married to a widow should not be ordained to the priesthood.[41] Gregory was the last Catholic intellect of any consequence before the Dark Ages set in; yet he was so ignorant that he did not know who Eudoxius was;[42] he was so superstitious that he was constantly giving people keys and other amulets, allegedly made from the chains of Peter and possessing magical power to preserve the wearers from harm.[43] Of pagan philosophy he knew nothing; in fact, he knew little of Christian theology either. With him we are already in the Middle Ages. Civilization was dying or dead.

2. *The Growth of Ecclesiastical Abuses.* Most of the abuses which were to bring on the Protestant revolution were already well developed by the time of Gregory. The Church had become a vast landowner and large-scale exploiter of slave, serf, and peasant labor. Gregory made no protest against these conditions, but sought to ameliorate the harsh oppression of the toilers. His epistles contain many references to aggressions committed by the slave-owning, landlord priests.[44] He declared that the peasants of the Church were compelled to pay an inflated price for corn; that onerous contributions were exacted from the share-croppers; and that the ecclesiastical overseers compelled the serf to pay their imposts by measures of excessive size.[45] Immoderate fees were charged the peasants

for clerical services in marriages and burials. In a letter to Constantina Augusta, Gregory was moved to reprove ecclesiastical rapacity because it drove the Catholics into the arms of the Arian Lombards.[46]

3. *Simony*. In the letters to Gregory, we hear often of the "Simonical heresy,"—that is, the practice of selling places, offices, bishoprics, and preferment in the Church to the highest bidder. To the bishops of Helladia (Greece) he complained "that in those parts no one attains any sacred order without the giving of a consideration." [47]

4. *Financial Maneuvers*. The Epistles of Gregory reveal a number of interesting financial maneuvers. He offered the Jews a reduction "of some little of their dues" [48] if they would only see the Catholic truth and embrace it. He promises that whosoever from among them is "converted to our true Lord God Jesus Christ shall have the burdens of his holding lightened." [49] The Hebrew slaves of the Jews were offered an even more powerful incentive and inducement, namely, full emancipation "from the time of declaring" their conversion to Christianity.[50]

On the other hand, opposite sanctions were to be enforced upon recalcitrants: "if any peasant should be found so perfidious and obstinate as to refuse to come to the Lord God, he must be weighted down with so great a burden of payment as to be compelled by the very pain of the taxation to hasten to the right way." [51]

5. *Permitted Pagan Sacrifices*. In his zeal to win all and sundry for Christ, Gregory stood ready to offer various inducements and concessions. For example, when it was discovered that the Britons had an inordinate love for their temples, he wrote that these buildings should not be destroyed, but simply converted to Christian use. And they should be permitted to continue their pagan sacrifices, but should now offer them to the Christian God.[52]

H. STATUES AND IMAGES

1. *Their Early Proscription*. A great controversy concerning the use of pictures and statues erupted during the reign of Gregory. The early Church had smashed the statues of all pagan gods and had strictly forbidden the

making of any likeness of anything whatever, in strict conformity with the Mosaic Law. Minucius Felix, a contemporary of Tertullian, asserts that, inasmuch as man is himself the image of God, he assuredly needs neither statues, temples, nor altars.[53] Throughout the writings of Origen it is emphasized that Christians "impress upon the minds of our first converts a contempt for idols and images of all kinds."[54] Even after 300, Arnobius wrote: "We do not rear temples for the ceremonies of worship, do not set up statues or images . . . do not build altars."[55] One of the first edicts issued by Constantine "provided that no one should erect images or practice divination."[56] Christian churches were first built around 285.

2. *The Iconoclasts.* But the developing Church found it expedient to ignore not only the Second Commandment but also the dictates of the Fathers. The Iconoclasts of the sixth and seventh centuries attempted to stem the tide by declaring that in using images the Church was actually reverting to pagan idolatry. Gregory replied that so long as pictures and statues were not adored, they were harmless; and they were necessary because they served the ignorant, which almost everyone now was, in the same manner as writing serves the learned.[57] Anyone who could decipher words was now considered "learned."

3. *The Conciliabulum.* As illiteracy became almost universal, even among the upper clergy, the Church was compelled to depend more and more upon the plastic and pictorial arts to implement its message. Nevertheless, the iconoclasts, who smashed and destroyed pictures and statues as devices of the devil, were not easily defeated. Constantine V, known as the Iconoclast, became the Eastern emperor in 741. In 754, he convened at Constantinople a general synod of bishops which declared itself to be an ecumenical council but which became known as the Conciliabulum. It met under trying conditions, since the Islamites had already overwhelmed the African and almost the whole Eastern world of Christianity, which still retained only Constantinople and a few Bithynian cities across the Bosphorus from Europe.

In this tense atmosphere, Constantine V attempted to roll back the clock. The Conciliabulum, consisting of 338 bishops, declared that it was blasphemous to depict Christ in a painting or make a stone image of Him, who was actually God. The Council declared that "Christianity has rejected the *whole* of heathenism, and so not merely heathen sacrifices, but also the heathen worship of images."[58]

The ultimate purpose of Constantine V was to abolish not only monasticism but also the use of relics, magic, amulets, and charms, together with the veneration of saints, martyrs, images, and statues. Monks were dragged through the streets; they were subjected to the utmost derision and degradation, and treated as if they were the scum of humanity. But when the emperor attempted to eliminate these things, he was actually trying to abolish the Church, for these symbols had now become inseparable from its worship.

4. *The Seventh Ecumenical Council.* The reaction to the Conciliabulum was swift and terrible. Constantine V was succeeded by Constantine VI and his empress-mother, Irene, who encouraged every superstition that had grown up in the Church. The Seventh Ecumenical Council convened 350 bishops at Nicaea in 787, and proceeded at once to rescind and reverse the decisions of the Conciliabulum. Such texts as "Thou shalt not make thee any graven image, or any likeness of anything that is in the heavens above, or that is in the earth beneath," were brushed aside as wholly irrelevant. On the other hand, the text, "Comfort ye, comfort ye, my people, ye priests, saith the Lord," was cited as irrefragable authority for "the confirmation and establishment of the ancient tradition of venerable images."

I. DEATH AND RESURRECTION

This signalized the intellectual death of Europe; henceforward, for five centuries, life was to consist of a morass of ignorance, superstition, suppression, and barbaric savagery. The bishops and the lay lords lived in such luxury as was by any means attainable, the monks in idleness, and the serfs and slaves in ultimate ignorance, filth, poverty, and degradation. There were no more heresies, councils, or theological controversies. The Church had finally accomplished the objective of Leo to crush the tenets of philosophy, to dispel the fallacies of earthly wisdom and to root out the cults of the demon-worshipers. Greek learning and science having been extirpated, utter darkness hovered over this deep until life revived again in the Italian renaissance at the magic touch of Hellenic culture.

Servitude under the Romans had driven millions to seek solace in another world. Nor was it either the luxurious and immoral life of the upper-class Romans or the poverty of the toilers that brought civic disintegration: rather it was the general frustration among those who might otherwise have had significant careers of their own but for whom the Roman administration provided no place in the sun. The aspirations of Christianity filled the vacuum thus created; and when its philosophy conquered, the desire for knowledge, the capacity for national defense, all interest in progress or construction, vanished. A universal lethargy seized upon human emotion; whatever intellectual activity remained was consumed in bitter disputes over meaningless speculative doctrines. It was a fantastic neurosis, a monstrous disease which destroyed every creative impulse. Life fell into ruin and decay on every hand. And had it not been for the vitality absorbed by the Catholic world from the Arian barbarians and later from Teutonic Europe, the devastation wrought by the Christian-oriental conquest over the human mind might well have accomplished the practical extirpation of the human species in the occident. Celsus and others had implied that the Empire would disintegrate unless the Catholics would become loyal citizens; and within a few decades after the Church assumed the public power, its entire domain was ravaged at will by various barbarian nations. Yet the new victors infused the conquered, albeit in an illiterate world, with a new will to life and enabled the ancient culture of Greece to be reborn after a millennial slumber.

CHAPTER XXI

THE DEVELOPMENT OF THE PAPACY

A. BEFORE LEO THE GREAT

1. *Catholic Theory.* When the American tourist is in Rome, he is likely to visit the celebrated Church of St. Paul; and there he will see depicted two hundred and sixty-two "popes" running in unbroken succession from Peter to the current incumbent. This would seem to infer that the papacy was established by Peter himself fully endowed with all its present authority, and that it has remained essentially unchanged during these nineteen hundred years. No impression, however, could be more contrary to fact.

2. *Scriptural Authority.* We have noted that the Catholic Church has ignored Matt. 23:9; however, there was another text, Matt. 16:18-19, which made Peter the rock upon which the Church would be built and which gave him the power to loose and bind; this the Roman See has magnified beyond all others in order to make of itself the head of a totalitarian priest-state. In contravention of this claim, however, it must be admitted, first, that Peter was certainly the founder of various other churches, especially that of Antioch, which, Theodoret declared, "possesses the throne of Peter";[1] second, that there is no evidence that this apostle died at or was ever in Rome at all except in the Gnostic *Acts of Peter*, composed about 200, and otherwise completely rejected by the Catholic Church; third, that even these *Acts* do not claim that Peter founded the Roman Church, much less that he gave it primacy; fourth, that in Matthew 18:15-18 the same power to loose and bind is given equally to all

Christian administrators; fifth, that the obvious purpose of this passage was to provide specifically that for moral transgression fully established, members must be expelled; and, finally, that nothing could have been more repugnant to Jesus than the use of force to compel unbelievers to remain in His communion.

3. *Scorned by Tertullian.* We need not be surprised that the bishops in the capital of the Roman Empire advanced claims to Church primacy almost from the beginning. How unfavorably these were regarded, we learn from Tertullian, who refers satirically to Pope Zephyrinus, as that "Sovereign Pontiff, that is, the bishop of bishops," whose absurd pretensions he ridicules and whose church he describes as a den of adulterers and fornicators.[2]

4. *Condemned by Cyprian.* How little authority the Roman bishop had beyond his own see in the middle of the third century we learn from Cyprian. Pope Cornelius and his successor Stephen both declared that any one previously baptized in the name of the Trinity was eligible to full membership in the Church simply by the laying on of hands; but Cyprian considered this opinion heretical and declared that every one coming into the Catholic communion must be baptized by an orthodox priest. The battle between Carthage and Rome burned fiercely after Stephen became pope in 254. Cyprian sneered at the pretensions of Bishop Stephen who "contends that he holds the succession from Peter."[3] And he declared that no one has authority to "set himself up as a bishop of bishops . . . since every bishop . . . has his own proper right of judgment, and can not be judged by another."[4]

Cyprian was not content with mere railing. He proclaimed his baptismal doctrine to his colleagues, who re-replied with fierce denunciations of Stephen. Cyprian called three councils at Carthage, 255-256, which anathematized Stephen in the most violent terms. Shortly thereafter, "Pope" Novatian of Rome was dethroned, because he wished to exclude the lapsed from readmission.

5. *Insignificant Role.* Throughout the Arian and Semi-Arian controversies of the fourth century, the Roman

pontiff was only another bishop, and usually an insignificant one. When the fierce dispute first broke out in Alexandria, Pope Sylvester was not even consulted. It was Constantine who called the general council, not in Rome, but in the Bithynian city of Nicaea near the Black Sea. This council apportioned authority in the Catholic World[5] among various metropolitans, among whom the Roman prelate was an equal among several.

6. *East and West*. The limited influence of the Roman pontiff declined when Constantine moved the imperial capital from Rome to Constantinople about 330. When the Empire split into eastern and western divisions in 337, however, the sphere of the Roman bishop became more distinct. With the accession of Zeno the Isaurian in 474 in the Eastern Empire, the Latin monarchy was abolished, but the Church was divided more sharply than ever into its Greek and Latin wings. When the Frankish kings assumed the rule of the Western, or "Holy Roman" Empire, the Church of Rome was closely identified with it. The Church tried to operate as a unit until 800, but then the separation became irrevocable. After 474, the bishops of Constantinople put forth more and more strident claims to universal dominion, against which the Roman bishops objected most strenuously.

7. *Novel Source of Influence*. Nevertheless, the Roman Church was to reinforce its claims to universal dominion from an unusual source—its very lack of fertility. In the early days, there had been heretics in Rome, such as Cerdo, Marcion, Praxeas, and Sabellius; but not one of them was a Roman, or an Italian, or even a Latin: all had come from the East, where heretics proliferated like jungle growths. Even Pelagius came originally from Britain and gained his intellectual nurture in Greek Palestine. The great Latin theoreticians, like Tertullian and Augustine were Africans, as was also the influential Cyprian.

8. *Wielded Balance of Power*. Since the rest of the Christian world was almost always evenly divided in the great theological disputes, Rome could often wield the balance of power as a disinterested arbiter. The clever and capable Julius was not slow to realize this fact; and

when Athanasius, driven from Alexandria by the Arians in 335 and again in 339, appealed to this Roman bishop for support, the Arians did likewise; and this did much to enhance his authority. Since the Romans never developed a theology of their own, they were always ready to strengthen themselves by supporting whatever combatant expediency might dictate. Although appeals to Rome were made without any thought of acknowledging Roman supremacy, they created significant precedents. A generation later, we find Pope Damasus filling a similar role. The practice of calling upon the Roman bishop to referee disputes became more and more common.[6]

9. *Roman Popes Remain Obscure.* We have noted how Augustine defeated Pope Zosimus. Innocent I had nothing to do with the great synod which met in 411 to solve the Donatist schism. Nor did his successor, Boniface I, have any part in calling the Great Council of Carthage in 419, at which the African canon law was established. This carries us well into the fifth century, and up to this time, despite their grandiose claims, the Roman pontiffs were no more than other bishops in the Church.

B. LEO THE GREAT

1. *The Eutychian Heresy.* Leo the Great, 440-461, was, however, a more powerful personality, one of the most capable and aggressive who ever sat upon the papal throne. Following well-established precedent, the monk Eutyches appealed his case to him, and agreed to "follow your ruling."[7] Theodoret shortly thereafter did the same, declaring "for every reason it is fitting for you to hold the first place."[8] Leo assumed the posture of impartial authority; he wrote to Flavian, bishop of Constantinople, as to a subordinate, demanding full particulars, and took the case under advisement. Eutyches and Theodoret appealed to Leo only after they had been anathematized, and therefore had nothing to lose; Flavian responded, because, as he surmised, and as the event was soon to demonstrate, he needed all the help he could obtain. At this point, Dioscurus of Alexandria, being a bitter enemy of Flavian,

came to the aid of Eutyches and his monks, who had also the support of the Emperor Theodosius.

2. *Defeated at Ephesus.* This set the stage for a dramatic contest. Leo wished to anathematize the Eutychian heresy without a hearing. His wishes, however, were ignored, and the emperor convened the council of Ephesus in 449, at which Eutyches was victorious, at which the celebrated *Tome of Leo* was not even mentioned, and which was ever after known as the "Robber Synod." Dioscurus of Alexandria now rode supreme, and Flavian was deposed and excommunicated together with Theodoret and others suspected of Nestorian tendencies. Dioscurus even "purposed excommunication" against Leo the Great himself, because he "had at heart the unifying of the Church";[9] that is, he wished to subordinate all other bishops to his own authority, which even as late as the fifth century was considered treason in the Church.

3. *Victorious at Chalcedon.* Theodosius II, however, died the next year, and his sister, Pulcheria, who became empress at his death, was orthodox, as was her new consort, Marcian. Leo now began to agitate for a new council to reverse the decrees of Ephesus II. To this, Marcian agreed. When the new synod met at Chalcedon in 451, the Council declared him the chief among five hundred and twenty bishops.[10] The sees of Rome and Constantinople were given precedence over all others, the former being accorded a purely formal priority only.[11] Never before had a Roman prelate received such honor.

C. STRUGGLE AND HUMILIATION

1. *Vigilius.* One of the more humiliating experiences of the Roman prelates was suffered by Pope Vigilius, 553-554. The Emperor Justinian, seeking to reconcile the factions in the Eastern Church, sought his aid in calling the Fifth Ecumenical Council to exorcise forever the remnants of the Nestorian heresy; but since he was himself infected with the subtle Semi-Nestorianism of Ibas, Theodoret, and Theodore of Mopsuestia, he ignored the request. "In vain," complains Justinian, "we sent several commands to him to take part in the synod." [12]

From the *Acts* of the Council[13] we learn that "the name of Vigilius . . . be no more inserted in the holy diptychs of the Church, on account of the impiety he defended." However, Vigilius was not to die a heretic. Within six months, this infallible pontiff wrote a Decretal Epistle, in which he recanted abjectly.

2. *Gregory Claims Universal Priority*. When Gregory the Great came to power in 590, the Christian world was still intact, wholly unaware of the Moslem hurricane destined soon to tear away its choicest portions. The ecumenical council held in 381 had declared Constantinople second only to the Roman See; and at Chalcedon, 451, to the bitter chagrin of Leo the Great, it had been decreed that these two sees should henceforth be of substantially equal authority. When the western division of the Empire was abolished in 474 as a political entity, the patriarchs of Constantinople, no longer content with simple parity, began to agitate for universal dominion. What is more, they were winning the battle; and had it not been for Islam, the pope of Rome would unquestionaby have been reduced into a mere subordinate.

Gregory was intensely aware of the tradition he had inherited from Leo, and he labored feverishly to equal or surpass his predecessor. He declared that "the care of the whole Church was committed to the holy prince of the Apostles, Peter."[14] It was therefore obvious "that the Apostolic Roman See is, by the ordering of God, set over all churches."[15]

3. *Priority is Profanation*. In spite of his own claims to primacy, however, Gregory regarded the identical pretensions of his Byzantine rival as sheer impiety, and therefore wrote: "What wilt thou say to Christ, who is the Head of the universal Church, in the scrutiny of the last judgment, having attempted to put all his members under thyself by the appellation of Universal?"[16]

The Council of Chalcedon had *not* in fact offered authority over the whole Church to anyone, although various Roman pontiffs had repeatedly claimed it as their sovereign right. This, however, did not prevent Gregory from asserting that "this name of Universality was offered by the holy synod of Chalcedon to the pontiff of the Apostolic See which by the providence of God I serve. But no one of my predecessors has ever consented to use this so profane a title." [17]

Thus, by a curious ambivalence, Gregory condemned as profane the very title he himself sought with fierce avidity. Nor did he fail to emphasize that Constantinople had always been a hotbed of heresy and that, therefore, it should never be entrusted with authority.[18]

4. *Rival is Antichrist.* John died about 596, but his successor Cyriacus proved no less obnoxious. Gregory therefore warned him "to discard that word of pride" since it was imperative that the imminent Antichrist find no impiety in the Churches.[19] In a letter to the emperor, Gregory did not merely imply but stated flatly that his eastern rival was the precursor of Antichrist, since he aspired to be the universal head of the Church.[20] When the Protestant Reformation called the pope Antichrist, therefore, it found ample authority in Gregory for so doing.

5. *Two Sees Equal.* When the Sixth Ecumenical Council convened three hundred bishops at Constantinople in 680, the star of the East was already setting as a result of the Moslem conquests. The Council was therefore meticulous in according even-handed reverence to the magnificent prelates of Constantinople and Rome, the former of whom it addressed as "The Most Holy and Blessed Archbishop of Constantinople and Ecumenical Patriarch," and the latter as "The Most Holy and Blessed Archbishop of Old Rome and Ecumenical Pope." [21]

6. *Post-Mortem Excommunication of Honorius.* The Council found that some years before, Pope Honorius of Rome had written a letter to Patriarch Sergius of Constantinople which implicated these men in the Monothelite heresy. Both prelates, though now deceased, were therefore "expelled from the holy Church of God and anathematized." [22] And so an ecumenical council damned a pope of Rome and a patriarch of Constantinople already deceased, the result presumably being that these

infallible prelates were transferred from the bliss of heaven to the tortures of hell.

7. *Roman Pope Supreme at Last.* By 787, a decided change had overtaken the Church, as we learn from a *Sacra* sent by Constantine VI and Irene to "Hadrian, Pope of Old Rome." [23] By this time, none of African and little of Greek oriental Christianity remained. Although Constantinople itself was to remain Christian until 1453, it retained very little of the eastern world. In Europe, Latin Christianity, except for the loss of Spain to Islam, remained substantially intact. Yet, even so, it was not the Roman pope but the Byzantine emperor who convened the Seventh Ecumenical Council.

Thus, when Christian territory had been so reduced that it hardly exceeded that originally given the Roman See by the Council of Nicaea, the pope of Rome became by sheer default the universal head of the Church. Constantine VI wrote in 787 that to him belonged "the dignity of the chief priesthood." [24]

8. *East and West Forever Divided.* This was the first official acknowledgment by an eastern authority that the Roman pope was the head of the Church. But this supremacy was to be of brief duration; for in 800, East and West were severed politically; and at the same time the Latin Roman Catholic and Greek Orthodox churches became two separate communions. The Holy Roman Empire was established in the West with the Frankish kings in charge of the armies and the Roman popes at the head of the ecclesiastical polity. Gibbon remarked caustically that this conglomeration "was neither holy, nor Roman, nor yet an empire."

D. ROME TRIUMPHANT

The first ecumenical council which admitted the general authority of the pope thereby signed the death-warrant for such convocations; almost twelve centuries have now elapsed since the last was convened. The Roman Church since 787 has been governed by an irresponsible and totalitarian ruler, whose edicts and morals cannot be questioned within his communion, and whose removal, except through assassination, is impossible. All power in the Catholic Church is vested in him who sits on the throne of Peter; and thence it flows downward through a hierarchy which consists of cardinals, legates, archbishops, bishops, priests, etc., to the monastic orders and the laity, who enjoy no title in the ecclesiastical property for which they have paid, and who have no rights in their organization. Every priest, bishop, and cardinal is an absolute ruler over those below him, but he grovels at the feet of his own superior. This system is the absolute negation of democracy: a more thoroughgoing dictatorship the world has never known. And should the Catholic Church achieve its objectives, this would be the form of our society in its entire structure.

E. CONQUEST OF ISLAM

1. *Easy Victory over Christianity.* One of the most extraordinary events of history was the conquest by which, in a few short decades, the followers of Mohammed ripped from the Catholic Church nearly three-quarters of its territory, and made of its communicants, with apparent ease, such faithful Moslems that their descendants have never again desired to become Christians. How could this be? We would say that, in the first place, Arianism, which, in its extreme form, certainly sought to establish a unitarian God, had laid the groundwork for the monotheism of Islam. But beyond all this, we believe that by 650 the ancient world was so exhausted with five centuries of theological controversy that the human mind sought respite at any price in some simple and comprehensible creed.

2. *Christians Disillusioned.* Nor was this all. Over and over, the Christians had been disappointed in their expectation of the Parousia. There must be something wrong with prophecies which are never fulfilled, with a God who does nothing for men nor encourages them to do anything for themselves. It was obvious that no one practiced and few even remembered the ethics of Jesus: only

a perverted religion could so utterly ignore the central teachings of its founder, and find escape in creeds, persecution, and suppression.

The fact is, that many had become tired of the two-world religion of Pythagoras. They were tired of renunciation, poverty, celibacy, and inactivity; they were sick of a clergy which distinguished itself chiefly by its flagrant disregard for the teachings of Jesus, which monopolized wealth for itself, and which gave nothing but empty promises to the masses. They were weary of a Gospel which denied the validity of every natural and physical impulse. In short, a new frustration had developed, which gave impetus to a new mass-movement.

3. *A Reaction against Christianity.* It is significant that Islamism, which was, in large part, a synthesis of Judaism and Zoroastrianism, is to be contrasted with, rather than compared to, Christianity. Instead of teaching humility and renunciation, it preached a militant aggressiveness; instead of celibacy, it encouraged polygamy; instead of human virgins, it worshiped houris; instead of waiting for a supernatural kingdom of saints, it set out to establish a great temporal empire by force and violence; instead of teaching that we must do unto others as we would have others do unto us, it taught openly and proudly that all opponents must be extirpated; instead of waiting patiently for salvation after death, it offered something tangible in the here and now; instead of awaiting a contemplative heaven of song and adoration, it promised a paradise of physical luxury and sensual pleasure; instead of waiting endlessly for God to give them victory, it filled them with an irrepressible desire to win glory by their own deeds; instead of offering redemption through a god-man concerning whose nature no one could agree, it offered a prophet who claimed only to be a man but through whom flowed a constant stream of revelation; instead of a God who is an incomprehensible One-in-Three and Three-in-One, it gave them a single and universal divine unity; instead of an all-powerful clerical bureaucracy, it abolished the regular priesthood entirely, and replaced it with a caliph-

ate which embraced the functions of the Prophet. In short, it was a complete repudiation of Buddhist-Pythagorean-Essene ethics, of Osirian soteriology, and of Greek theological metaphysics.

4. *Area of Similarity.* Yet in one fundamental phase, Mohammedanism and Catholicism were very much alike: for both were substantially priest-states, that is, social organizations in which authoritarian control was vested in men who ruled by divine fiat, who would tolerate no competing or dissident ideology, who could not differentiate between civil and ecclesiastical law, and who must, by their very nature, stifle every democratic aspiration, every stirring of the human spirit for freedom. And so it was that, in spite of the renaissance which followed its great military conquests and in which a powerful skeptical movement produced a marvelous culture and such classics as the *Rubaiyat,* the whole Islamic world in time settled down to the filth, poverty, ignorance, repression, exploitation, injustice, reaction, and barbaric backwardness which characterize all priest-states and which can be swept away only by the prior elimination of the authoritarian beliefs, doctrines, and institutions on which they are based.

5. *Not Friendship, but Peace.* The Catholic Church suffered a vast defeat at the hands of Islam. Nevertheless, after two or three centuries, the medieval world stabilized itself; and the Christian and Moslem spheres continued, not indeed in friendship, but substantially at peace. Between 1300 and 1600, Europe experienced its Renaissance, which shook the Church to its foundations, but did not topple its superstructure. Then, beginning in Germany in 1517, after powerful, previous rumblings especially in England and Hungary, a mighty surge toward freedom wrenched much of what had once been barbarian Europe from the Catholic Church and laid the foundations on which modern civilization and our secular republics have been erected.

CHAPTER XXII

THE CHRISTIAN MYSTERIES

A. THE EUCHARISTIC SACRAMENT

1. *Based on the Pagan Mystery.* We have analyzed in some detail the esoteric pagan mysteries, in which a god-man was ceremonially slain and symbolically eaten as a mystical sacrifice; and, as the Catholic Church developed, its service came more and more to consist of the Blessed Sacrament, called the liturgy or the Mass, which was substantially a re-creation of the mysteries of Osiris, Demeter, and Dionysus.

2. *Seven Sacraments.* While some intellectual vitality still remained in Catholic society, the religious service consisted of scripture readings and hortatory sermons, known as homilies. During this period, there were only two sacraments: baptism and the eucharist; and these, although crucial to salvation, were incidental to religious activity as a whole. In time, however, the sacraments were expanded to seven and designed to control every basic human relationship.

3. *The Oft-Repeated Eucharist.* The pagan mysteries, usually celebrated once a year, were elaborate festivals redolent of harvest-symbolism. But in the Catholic Church, as among the Essenes, the eucharistic ritual was repeated often, in some places daily, and never less than once a week. Cyprian and others understood that the daily bread of the Lord's Prayer is the sacrament.

B. MYSTAGOGICAL LECTURES OF CYRIL

1. *Initiation.* In the works of Cyril of Jerusalem, 315-386, there is a series of catechetical lectures called

mystagogical, which describe the rituals of the fourth-century Eastern Church in detail. Exactly as was the case in the Eleusinian ritual, the ceremonies are named mysteries and the initiates *mystagogues*. There is a prologue followed by twenty-three lectures, designed for the initiation of new converts. After the applicants were duly listed in the sacred book, they were given the "torches of the bridal train," which, like the Eleusinians, they carried in a grand processional to the chapel, where, step by step, they learned the secrets of the cult. Now wedded to Christ, as Orphic initiates were to Dionysus, they proceeded to their more esoteric study and initiation.

2. *On the Faith.* Eighteen of the lectures enlightened the catechumens concerning the fundamentals of the faith. They were warned against the devil and his machinations; told why water is used in baptism; given a detailed explanation of the creed; warned against the various heresies, especially the Montanist and the Manichaean; told of the approaching and imminent world-end; and taught the secrets of hell, heaven, and the resurrection.

3. *Baptism.* After all this and more was fully covered, the catechumens were inducted into the esoteric mysteries. And first, elaborate preparations were made for baptism, where the neophyte, facing the west, was "to stretch forth your hand, and as in the presence of Satan ye renounced him." [1]

After thus renouncing the powers of darkness, the *mystagogue* turned, like the Zoroastrian and the Essene, toward the east, which symbolized the God of Light, and declared: "I associate myself with Christ." Then, still facing the east, he repeated: "I believe in the Father, and in the Son, and in the Holy Ghost, and in one baptism of repentance." The Nicene Creed was then repeated.

4. *Exorcism.* Then came the third portion of the ceremony, called the chrism. The candidate was stripped, and his body anointed with holy oil in a ceremony known as the unction of exorcism.[2] Thus protected from the demons, the candidate was baptized by being thrice immersed in the holy water, as a "symbol of the three days

burial of Christ." ³ As in all the pagan mysteries, the divine drama re-enacted the passion of its *soter*.

5. *The Eucharist*. Their baptism completed, the *mystagogues*, still bearing torches and now clad in white robes —again like the Essenes, the Pythagoreans, and the Eleusinians—marched in procession to the great church, where they partook of their first eucharist. This was a long and intricate ceremony in which the essential spiritual and physical unity of all Christians with Christ was emphasized and through which the Church became simply a mystical union of all its human but immortal members. Even as the elements of the eucharist, according to the doctrine of Transubstantiation, which was the center of the Catholic mystery, were transformed literally into the body and blood of Christ during the celebration of the Mass, so, by an identical and equally miraculous transmutation, the flesh and blood of the communicant became those of Christ. In the words of Cyril: "Thus we come to bear Christ in us, because His Body and Blood are distributed through our members; thus it is that, according to the blessed Peter, we become partakers of the divine nature." ⁴

C. THE MASS OR LITURGY

1. *An unintelligible Spectacle*. As the centuries wore on, there was less of reading and homily; but the Mass grew more elaborate. In the west it continued, as it is to this day, to be said in Latin, no matter what the vernacular of the communicants may be. It was an impressive but unintelligible spectacle, a mumbo-jumbo of which the laity understood not one word.

2. *Worship Becomes the Mass*. By the sixth or seventh century, the standardized Masses had become a sort of theatrical performance. In the *Ante-Nicene Library*,⁵ we have reprints of several of these, of which the most elaborate are the *Divine Liturgy of James* and the *Divine Liturgy of the Holy Apostle and Evangelist Mark,* in which the Athanasian Creed and Mariolatry are inextricably intermingled with the eucharistic sacrament. These long and intricate services were repeated millions of times without

variation in countless churches. The bishops, presbyters, deacons, and laity, all had their proper functions to perform; once learned, the sacred rite could be repeated *ad infinitum.*

This spectacle became the Christian worship. Even the Creeds were forgotten in the reiteration of the Mass. The Gospel Jesus was dissolved in the overwhelming adoration of the mystical Real Presence of Christ in the holy bread and wine, which were believed to be miraculously transubstantiated into His actual flesh and blood during the performance of the ritual.

3. *The Ritual.* In imagination we can see the priest beginning his solemn chant; the magnificent spectacle proceeds, and each communicant feels himself transported in spirit to the blessed realms of light. The priest invokes the favor of the holy God-Mother; then he breaks the bread and dips it into the wine, and each takes some of the blood-soaked body of Christ and eats with reverence and humility, thus assured that his soul achieves eternal bliss. All this is done slowly, deliberately, for every portion of the sacred ceremony must be duly emphasized. At last, however, all is done, and the sanctified worshiper goes home, persuaded that he is protected from the onslaughts of the devil until it is time again for Mass.

We reproduce in part the *Liturgy of James*. The priest intones:

> Thy only-begotten Son, and our Lord Jesus Christ, is mystically set forth as a sacrifice for me, a sinner, stained with every spot. . . .
>
> Glory to the Father, and to the Son, and to the Holy Ghost, the triune light of the Godhead, which is unity subsisting in trinity, divided yet indivisible: for the Trinity is the one God Almighty, whose glory the heavens declare, for the earth His dominion, and the sea His might. . . .
>
> Thou art the only-begotten Son and Word of God, immortal; who didst submit for our salvation to become flesh of the holy God-Mother, and ever-virgin Mary; . . .

That we may become servants of Thy new testament, ministers of Thy pure mysteries, receive us as we draw near to Thy holy altar . . . . and grant to us, O Lord, with all fear and a pure conscience to offer to Thee this spiritual and bloodless sacrifice . . . .

Hail, Mary, highly favoured: the Lord is with Thee: blessed art thou among women, and blessed the fruit of thy womb, for thou didst bear the Saviour of our souls . . .

At this point the priest breaks the bread, which he dips into the chalice, saying: "The union of the all-holy and precious blood of our Lord and God and Saviour, Jesus Christ." He then makes the sign of the cross over the bread, and declares: "Behold the Lamb of God, the Son of the Father, that taketh away the sin of the world, sacrificed for the life and salvation of the world." The priest gives each communicant a piece of wine-soaked bread, which he declares to be "A holy portion of Christ, full of grace and truth, of the Father, and of the Holy Spirit, to whom be the glory and the power to all eternity."

The priest now says this prayer before the altar:

O Lord our God, the heavenly bread, the life of the universe, I have sinned against heaven, and before Thee, and am not worthy to partake of Thy pure mysteries; but as a merciful God, make me worthy by Thy grace, without condemnation to partake of Thy holy body and precious blood, for the remission of sin, and life everlasting.

Thou hast given unto us, O Lord, sanctification in the communion of the all-holy body and precious blood of Thy only-begotten Son, our Lord Jesus Christ . . . .

Blessed is God, who blesseth and sanctifieth through the communion of the body, and through thy quickening and pure mysteries, now and forever, and to all eternity. Amen.

4. *Replica of the Immemorial Mystery.* It is true that

the eucharistic mystery was an integral portion of the Gospel Jesus, and not something later engrafted upon it by the pagans, as were the Virgin Birth, the Logos Doctrine, Mariolatry, purgatory, etc. Yet both baptism and the eucharist, like the ethics of the New Testament, were all of pagan origin. And so after six hundred years, the Catholic Church reduced its worship into a ritual very similar to one which had been practiced in Egypt for more than three thousand years before the advent of Christianity; in Thrace for two thousand; at Eleusis for fifteen hundred; by the Orphic-Pythagorean societies for six hundred; by the devotees of Mithra for two hundred; and by the Essenes for a hundred and fifty. And so the religion of Jesus-Christ became an almost exact replica of the universal pagan mystery by which the communicant became divine and immortal by essential union with his savior-god.

And so we note again that as it was in the beginning, so is it now: the consolation craved by the poor and the ignorant of ancient Egypt is still desired by their counterparts today in the United States and Europe. The freedom and enlightenment offered by Ikhnaton, Epicurus, and Marcus Aurelius is not yet for the masses. Nevertheless, the struggle is not hopeless: the human race is still in its infancy. Less than twenty thousand years ago, a great ice-cap covered the northern hemisphere and destroyed all animal life. Six or eight thousand years ago, all Europeans were still savages and cannibals. Civilization was created by Iranian-Sumerians, who carried it to Egypt, which then gave us Osiris, the first savior-god, whose mystery still reigns in the Christian churches. It is fitting that this study should end with him, even as it began: our cycle comes full turn. And when the human race outgrows its need for Osiris by finding its resources within itself, it will achieve its first great plateau of maturity.

GLOSSARY

Abhisasta: in Brahmanism, one who must commit long penance as an extreme social outcast.

Alogoi: second-century heretics who denied the eternal pre-existence of the Logos.

Apocalypse: a writing depicting impending eschatological conditions; primarily a Zoroastrian type, but used in a somewhat different manner by the Old Testament prophets.

Apocrypha: Christian forgeries of the early centuries which enjoyed considerable vogue but almost all of which were later than the canonical New Testament scriptures.

Apollonarianism: a heresy originating in the fourth century which declared that the divine incarnation in Jesus was His only soul and mind; it denied His essential humanity and His dual nature, thus making Him a simple divine personage.

Arhats: Buddhist saints.

Arianism: the doctrine that Father, Word, and Holy Spirit are consubstantial and co-eternal, but that the Son was created through the Word in time and is therefore mutable and a creature.

Asmoneans: dynasty of Jewish priest-kings descended from Mattathias, who precipitated the Maccabaean revolt.

Athanasianism: the doctrine that Word and Son are identical, that the three persons of the Trinity are consubstantial and co-eternal, of one essence, *homoousian*.

Bacchanalia: omophagic and drunken Dionysiac rituals celebrating the mystery of the god, called, in Latin, Bacchus, or Father Bacchus, or Liber.

Basilideans: a branch of the Pythagorean-Gnostic Christian heresy.

Bhikkhus and Bhikkhunis: Buddhist monks and nuns, the prototypes of the Christian.

Canon: the established scriptures of any religion.

Chasidim: an ancient order of Jewish priests who preceded and sparked the Maccabean revolt, also known as Chasids or Hasidaeans.

Chiliasm: the doctrine that following the Parousia Christ will reign on earth a thousand years with His saints.

Consubstantiation: the doctrine that the body and blood of Christ are actually combined with the eucharistic elements, as heat may combine temporarily with iron.

Cosmogony: doctrine or theory concerning the origin or creation of the universe.

Creed: a dogmatic statement concerning the composition of the Godhead.

Demiurge: in Platonic philosophy, the creator-god, who fashioned order out of chaos. A term used widely by the Hellenic Gnostics.

Diaspora: the scattering of the Jews among the Gentiles.

Docetism: the Gnostic concept of Christ, according to which He was simply a spiritual phantom appearing in the form of a human being; He was therefore never born or actually crucified. He was an emanation of the Supreme God and was unknown and hostile to Yahweh.

Dogma: in theology, a doctrine taught as authoritative truth, because based on revelation.

Dualism: in the cosmology of Zoroastrianism, the doctrine that the universe is divided into two antithetical portions: evil vs. good, matter vs. spirit, darkness vs. light, cold vs. warmth, the God of Light vs. the Power of Darkness.

Ecumenical, or Ecumenical Council: world-wide or universal.

Elect, The: those predestined for redemption by the deity from eternity, often called the Children of Light, as contrasted with the Children of Darkness, i. e., the creatures of Ahriman.

Epiphany: reputed birthday of Jesus, celebrated for centuries on January 6.
Eschatology: doctrines dealing with final things, such as the after-life, the last judgment, soul-sleeping, metempsychosis, hell, heaven, and purgatory, etc.
Essenes: literally, the Holy Ones.
Eucharist: the elements consumed as food and drink in the sacrament, symbolizing the body and blood of the *soter*.
Eunomius: the most feared and powerful heretical theoretician of the fourth century, whose theology gave rise to the *heteroousians*.
Excommunication: literally the official act by which one so punished was excluded from all social intercourse or economic activity.
Exufflation: ritual performed over infants to exorcise the evil spirit, or the derivative original sin.
Gnostics: these were various types of early heretical Christians who taught the docetic Christ, insisted on celibacy and vegetarianism, rejected the Old Testament and Yahweh, and maintained that their doctrines rested upon *gnosis*, or certain scientific knowledge.
Hamestagna: Zoroastrian purgatory.
Heteroousians: those who maintained that Son and Father are completely *unlike*; followers of Eunomius.
Hieroglyphs: holy picture-words; the writings of the Egyptians.
Hierophant: a priest; literally, one who speaks things which are holy, divine, inspired, or revealed by God.
Homoiousians: those who maintained that Father and Son are of *like* but not *identical* essence.
Homoousians: those who maintained that Father, Word, and Son are of identical essence, and also consubstantial and co-eternal. They were the orthodox.
Hypostasis: the unique essence of the godhead and of each of the persons in the Trinity.
Iconoclasts: image-breakers.
Immaculate Conception: the Catholic doctrine that Mary, the mother of Jesus, was herself miraculously born without taint of original sin; a doctrine very similar to that held by the Zoroastrians concerning the mother of their founder.
Incarnation: the doctrine that a pre-existing divinity has entered and dwelt in a human being.
Iranians: the ancient Aryan inhabitants of what became Persia.
Kharma: in Brahmanic doctrine, the concept that accumulated moral merit or demerit determines social position in each successive earthly appearance.
Logos doctrine: the concept of the savior god-man as also the eternally pre-existing Word, the creative agency of the godhead, an ancient pagan doctrine appropriated by the Fourth Gospel.
Maenads: a name for female Bacchanalians.
Manichæism: a mystery-synthesis based primarily upon a Zoroastrianized Gnosticism.
Mara: nearest approximation to the Christian devil or the Zoroastrian Ahriman to be found in Buddhist ideology.
Marcellus and his pupil Photinus: two heretics of the fourth century who developed a triune monotheism or a modal unitarianism, in which the Son becomes a divine manifestation concurrent only with the human Jesus.
Marcionites: heretics inspired by the great theologian Marcion; Greek or Platonic Gnostics.
Mass: the name used by the Catholic Church for its eucharistic ritual, based on the doctrine of Transubstantiation.
Mazdeism: the prehistoric religion out of which Zoroastrianism developed.
Messiah: a Jewish concept; a supernatural or a supernaturally supported personage who would establish a great Jewish empire on earth which would rule over all Gentile nations.

Metaphysical: dealing with concepts transcending matter.
Metaphysical Dualism: an anthropological doctrine based upon the Zoroastrian concept that matter and the flesh of mankind derive from Ahriman (the devil) and that the spirit or soul derives from the Supreme God.
Monachism: life as organized in ascetic religious communities.
Monarchians: second and third century Christian heretics who maintained the identity of Father, Son, and Holy Spirit, not only as to essence, but also as to person.
Monophysitism: a fifth-century heresy which not only denied that Jesus had two natures, but made Him substantially human.
Monothelitism: a sixth-century heresy which also denied that Jesus had two natures, but made Him substantially spiritual.
Mystagogue: an initiate into the mysteries, especially the Eleusinian; a name also given to Christian neophytes in the fourth century.
Mysteries: the ancient pagan cults based upon ritualistic soteriology.
Nestorianism: a fifth-century heresy which repudiated the *Theotokos* and which so accentuated the dual nature of Jesus-Christ that in reality He became two persons.
Nirvana: a Brahmanic concept; the state of personal extinction, in which the human soul, having escaped the Wheel of Life, that is, the otherwise endless cycle of metempsychosis, is absorbed by the Universal Soul and thus escapes consciousness forever.
Nous: a Platonic concept parallel in part to the idea of the Logos doctrine.
Omophagia: the ritualistic eating of raw flesh, as a eucharist.
Original Sin: the doctrine that by his fall Adam became irrevocably corrupt and transmitted his degeneracy to all mankind.
Pantheism: the doctrine that God and the universe are co-extensive and identical.
Pantheon: company of the gods.
Parousia: the second appearance of the sacrificial savior god-man, at which time he is to establish the saintly kingdom, or bring in the eschatological conditions.
Parsees: the Zoroastrians who emigrated to India about 1000 A.D. and established themselves around Bombay.
Passion, The: the ritualistic death of the *soter*, by which redemption becomes possible.
Pelagianism: the doctrines taught in the fifth century by Pelagius and his followers; they rejected the dogma of original sin, the need of paedobaptism, and the whole concept of reprobation. To them, Jesus was only a great teacher and exemplar, and not an atonement.
Pharisees: literally, the separated ones.
Pneumatomachi: literally, those who fight against the Holy Spirit. The fourth- and fifth-century followers of Macedonius, who declared that the Holy Spirit is not equal to the Father and the Son.
Pseudepigrapha: apocalyptic writings attributed to an author already long dead. Daniel is an example.
Sabellians: third-century heretics who maintained a trinity of successive manifestation.
Sacrifice: killing or eating of a divine animal or god-man substitute. Mass called a sacrifice in the early Christian Church. Concept found in almost all ancient religions.
Samgha: celibate Buddhist brotherhood.
Samosatenism: the third-century heresy that the persons of the Trinity are consubstantial and co-eternal, but that Jesus became the Christ by adoption.
Sheol: Old Testament Jewish concept of after life; a cold, dark, dank prison-house, in which all souls were condemned to an eternal equalitarian existence, without joy or hope, or even perhaps of consciousness. This ideology was derived from

the religions of Babylonia and Assyria; it reappears in the Homeric poems and the classic drama of Greece.

Simon Magus: a Syrian pretender to divine incarnation, a contemporary of the apostles and the reputed founder of Semitic Gnosticism.

Soshans or Saoshyant: a Persian, Zoroastrian concept; a divinely generated personage who was to appear 3000 years after Zoroaster and then to establish the universal kingdom of righteousness. The prototype of the Son of Man in Daniel and in *The Book of Enoch*.

Soter: the incarnate god-man savior who dies as an atonement for sinful humanity and whose body and blood must be consumed by the communicant so that he may become divine and immortal by absorbing the essence of the god.

Sumerians: the ancient Aryans who ruled the Iranian-Euphrates region before the Semitic-Babylonian Empire, which began cir. 2500 B. C.

Syncretism: a less unified combination of elements than in a synthesis.

Synoptics: Gospels of Matthew, Mark, and Luke, so called because of their parallelism.

Synthesis: a combination of different ideological elements, as in a new religion, into an harmonious unity.

Taurobolium: baptismal bath in the blood of a bull, sacred to, or symbolic of, Osiris, Dionysus, and Attis.

Theogony: the genealogy or generation according to which God or the pantheon originated.

Theotokos: the Catholic doctrine which became prevalent in the fourth century and which declared that Mary was literally the Mother of God. This occasioned the Nestorian heresy, which still exists and which commands some half million communicants.

Thiasoi: name used by the Pythagoreans to designate their celibate communities.

Torah: in Judaism, the five books of Moses.

Traditors: Christian African traitors who had turned over sacred writings to the authorities during the Diocletian persecution.

Transmigration: metempsychosis.

Transubstantiation: the doctrine that during the celebration of the eucharist, the elements symbolizing the body and blood of the god-man become literally transformed into his essence before the eyes of the celebrants.

Valentinians: a branch of the Pythagorean-Gnostic movement.

Vedas: the ancient psalm-like utterances of the *rishis,* the primitive priests of the Iranian conquerors of India.

Yahweh: more accurate name of Jewish creator-god, better known as Jehovah.

BIBLIOGRAPHY OF RELIGIOUS SOURCE MATERIAL

1. Egyptian Literature: *The Book of the Dead*, Edited by E. A. Budge.
2. Zoroastrian Literature:
   a. From the *Sacred Books of the East*, Parke, Austin, Lipscomb.
      The Inscription of Behistan, VII.
      The Book of Arda Viraf, VII.
      The Shah-Namah, VII.
      The Records of Artakshir, VII.
   b. From Max Muller's *Sacred Books of the East*:
      The Zend-Avesta:
         The Vendidad, IV.
         The Yasts, XXIII.
         The Gathas, XXXI.
      The Bundahis, or *The Original Creation*, V.
      The Bahman Yast, V.
      The Shayast La-Shayast, V.
      Dadistan-i Dinik and the *Epistles of Manuskihar*, XVIII.
      The Dinkard, XXXVII and XLVII.
      Zad-Sparam, V and XLVII.
      Dina-i Mainog-i Khirad; Sikand Gumanik Vigar; and *Sad Dar*, XXIV.
3. Brahmana Literature: From the *SBE*:
   The Apastamba, II.
   Gautama, or *Institutes of the Sacred Law*, II.
   The Upanishads, or *The Doctrine*, I and XV.
   The Institutes of Vishnu, VII.
   Bhagavadgita, VIII.
   The Anugita, VIII.
   The Satapatha-Brahmana, XII, XXVI, XLI, XLIII, XLIV.
   The Vasishtha Dharmasastra, XIV.
   The Laws of Manu, XXV.
   The Sutras, Discourses dealing with sacrifices and the nature of the soul. XXIX, XXX, XXXIV, XLVIII.
   The Vedic Hymns, XXXII, XLII, XLVI.
   The *Narada*, or Minor Law-Books, XXXIII.
4. Gaina Literature: From *SBE*:
   The Akaranga Sutra, XXII.
   The Kalpa Sutra, XXII.
   The Uttaradhyana Sutra, XLV.
   The Sutrakritanga, XLV.
5. Buddhist Literature: From the *SBE*:
   The Book of the Great Decease, XI.
   Dhammakakkappavattana-Sutta, or *The Foundation of the Kingdom of Righteousness*, XI.
   The Tevigga Sutta, XI.
   The Dhammapada and the *Sutta-Nipata*, XII.
   The Patimoka, XIII.
   The Mahavagga, XIII and XVII.

       The Kullavagga, XVII and XX.
       The Fo-Sho-Hing-Tsan-King, a life of Buddha, XIX.
       The Saddharma-Pundarika, XXI.
       The Questions of Melinda, XXXV and XXXVI.
       The Buddha-Karita of Asvaghosha, another life of Buddha, XLIX.

6. Mohammedan Literature: *The Koran* (many editions).
7. Classical Jewish Writings:
       Philo Judaeus, died cir. 40 A. D., *Works,* Bohn 4 vols.
       Josephus, Flavius, 37-100; *Works,* translated by William Whiston:
       History of the Jewish War.
       Antiquities of the Jews.
       Autobiography or *Life.*
       Against Apion.
8. Essene Literature, cir. 170-60 B.C.
       The Testaments of the Twelve Patriarchs.
       The Book of Enoch.
       The Habakkuk Commentary.
       The Thanksgiving Psalms.
       The War of the Sons of Light against the Sons of Darkness.
       The Manual of Discipline.
       The Damascus Document.
       The Book of the Jubilees.
9. Selected Titles from Other Jewish Literature Showing Zoroastrian Influence:
       The Assumption of Moses.
       The Ascension of Isaiah.
       The Apocalypse of Abraham.
       The Apocalypse of Baruch.
       The Fourth Esdras.
       The Secrets of Enoch.
       The Psalms of Solomon.
       The Second Book of Maccabees.
10. Apostolic Literature:
       (With approximate date of composition)
       The Didache, 40-55. *The Epistle of Barnabas,* 70.
       The First Epistle of Clement, 97.
       The Second Epistle of Clement, 120.
       The Epistle of Polycarp, 115.
       The Epistles of Ignatius (seven letters), 115.
       The Pastor of Hermas, 150.
11. Principal Early Christian Apocrypha:
       The Protevangelium of James, 80-100.
       The Acts of Pilate, 100-125.
       The Gospel of Nicodemus, early.
       The Gospel of Thomas, early.
       The Gospel of Pseudo-Matthew, early.
       The Apocalypse of Peter, 125.
       The Acts of John, 140 (Gnostic).
       The Acts of Paul and Thecla, 150 (Gnostic).
       The Acts of Peter, 190 (Gnostic).
       The Acts of Thomas, 250 (Gnostic).
       The Apocalypse of Paul, 380.
12. The Christian Fathers: From the *Ante-Nicene Fathers,* 24 vols., edited by Roberts and Donaldson, and the *Nicene and Post-Nicene Fathers,* 28 vols., edited by Schaff and Wace.

a. *The Ante-Nicene Fathers*:
   Justin Martyr, cir. 100-165.
   First Apology.
   Second Apology.
   Dialogue with Trypho.
   A Discourse to the Greeks.
   Hortatory Address to the Greeks.
   On the Sole Government of God.
   Athenagoras, wrote cir. 177.
   Plea for the Christians.
   On the Resurrection of the Dead.
   Tatian, cir. 110-180.
   Oration to the Greeks.
   Diatessaron.
   Theophilus of Antioch, cir. 170.
   Three Books to Autolycus.
   Aristides, wrote cir. 125.
   The Apology.
   Irenaeus, Bishop of Lyon in 177.
   Against Heresies.
   Clement of Alexandria (Clemens Alexandrinus), 150-220.
   Exhortation to the Heathen.
   The Instructor.
   The Miscellanies (the *Stromata*).
   Who Is the Rich Man That Shall Be Saved?
   Hippolytus, died, cir. 235.
   Refutation of All Heresies.
   Fragments.
   Treatise on Christ and Antichrist.
   Treatise against the Jews.
   Against the Heresy of Noetus.
   Julius Africanus, cir. 238.
   Epistle to Aristides on the Genealogy in the Holy Gospels.
   Chronography.
   Pope Callixtus, 217-222.
   Epistles.
   Tertullian, 160-230.
   Against Marcion; On the Martyrs; On the Spectacles; On the Testimony of the Soul; To Scapula; Apology; On Idolatry; On Prayer; To His Wife; On Female Dress; On Flight in Persecution; The Antidote to the Scorpions's Bite; To the Nations; Prescription against Heretics; Against Hermogenes; Against the Valentinians; On the Flesh of Christ; On the Resurrection of the Body; Against Praxeas; On the Soul; On Exhortation to Chastity; On Monogamy; Of Modesty; On the Veiling of the Virgins; On the Ascetics' Mantle; An Answer to the Jews; Against All Heresies.
   Clementine Forgeries, cir. 200 and 300.
   The Clementine Homilies.
   The Clementine Recognitions.
   The Clementine Constitutions.
   Methodius, died, cir. 312.
   The Banquet of the Virgins.
   Discourses and Fragments.
   Minucius Felix, cir. 170-200.
   The Octavius.
   Novatian, Anti-Pope, 251-258.

Concerning the Trinity.
On the Jewish Meats.

Cyprian, Bishop of Carthage, 200-258.
Epistles (82 in number).
On the Dress of Virgins; On the Lapsed; On the Unity of the Church; On the Lord's Prayer; On the Vanity of Idols; On the Mortality; On Works and Alms; On Patience; On Jealousy and Envy; Exhortation to Martyrdom; Against the Jews; Address to the Seventh Council of Carthage.

Origen, 185-254.
De Principiis.
Contra Celsum.
Commentaries on John and Matthew.

Dionysius, Bishop of Alexandria, 247-265.
On the Promises.
Against the Epicureans.
Epistles to Dionysius of Rome.

Gregory Thaumaturgos. died, cir. 270.
A Declaration of Faith.
Panegyric to Origen.

Archelaus, cir. 275.
The Disputation with Manes.

Alexander of Lycopolis, cir. 275-300.
On the Tenets of the Manichaeans.

Alexander of Alexandria, cir. 320-325.
Epistles on the Arian Heresy.

Lactantius, flourished cir. 310.
The Divine Institutes.
On the Anger of God.
Of the Manner in Which the Persecutors Died.
The Phoenix.

Peter, Bishop of Alexandria, 299-300.
Genuine Acts.

Arnobius, cir. 320.
Adversus Gentes.

b. The Nicene and Post-Nicene Fathers:
Eusebius of Caesarea, 260-340.
Ecclesiastical History.
The Preparation for the Gospel.
Life of Constantine.
Oration of Constantine.

St. Athanasius the Great, 293-373.
Contra Gentes; On the Incarnation; Deposition of Arius; Council of Nicea; Statement of Faith; Defense of the Nicene Council; Defense of Dionysius; Life of Antony; Apology to the Emperor; Defense of His Flight; History of the Arians; Four Discourses against the Arians; Council of Ariminum and Seleucis; Synodal Letter; Letters.

Hilary of Poitiers, died 367.
On the Trinity.
On the Synods.

Cyril of Jerusalem, 315-386.
Catechetical Lectures.

Gregory Nazianzen, 329-389.
On the Great Athanasius.
Theological Orations.
Sermons; Letters; Prolegomena.

Basil the Great, 330-379.
> *Treatise against Eunomius.*
> *On the Holy Spirit.*
> *Hexaemeron.*
> *Homilies.*
> *Letters* (366 in number).

Gregory of Nyssa, 331-396.
> *Against Eunomius; Epinoia; Answer to Eunomius; On the Holy Spirit; On the Holy Trinity; On Pilgrimages; On the Soul and Resurrection; The Great Catechism.*

Sozomen, 324-415.
> *Ecclesiastical History*

Socrates Scholasticus, 379-440.
> *Ecclesiastical History*

Theodoret, 390-457.
> *Ecclesiastical History.*
> *Answers to Anathemas of Cyril.*
> *Dialogues; Letters.*

St. Ambrose, 340-397.
> *On the Duties of the Clergy; On the Holy Spirit; Exposition of the Christian Faith; Concerning the Mysteries; Concerning Repentance; Sermon against Auxentius; Letters; Homilies.*

St. John Chrysostom, 345-407.
> *Homilies.*

Rufinus, 345-410.
> *Apology against Jerome.*
> *Commentary on the Apostles' Creed.*

St. Jerome, 340-420: Translator of the *Vulgate.*
> *Letters,* 150 in number.
> *Life of St. Paul the Hermit.*
> *Life of Hilarion.*
> *Dialogue against the Luciferians.*
> *Dialogue against Helvidius on the Perpetual Virginity of the Blessed Mary.*
> *Dialogue against Jovianus.*
> *Dialogue against the Pelagians.*
> *Dialogue against Vigilantius.*
> *Dialogue against John of Jerusalem.*
> *Apology.*
> *Lives of Illustrious Men.*

St. Augustine, 354-430.
> General Treatises:
>> *Confessions.*
>> *De Civitate Dei.*
>> *Letters,* 238 in number.
>> *De Doctrina Christiana.*
>> *Enchiridion.*
>> *On Catechising the Uninstructed.*
>> *On Holy Virginity.*
>> *To Consentius; The Work of Monks; Letter to Jerome.*
>> *De Trinitate.*
>
> On the Manichaean Controversy:
>> *Morals of the Catholic Church.*
>> *Concerning Two Souls: Against the Manicheans.*
>> *Disputation against Fortunatus.*
>> *Against the Epistle of Manichaeus Called Fundamental.*

      Reply to Faustus the Manichaean.
      Concerning the Nature of God.
   On the Donatist Controversy:
      Seven Books on Baptism against the Donatists.
      Three Books in Answer to Petilian.
      A Treatise Concerning the Correction of the Donatists.
   On the Pelagian Controversy:
      A Treatise on the Merits and Forgiveness of Sins.
      A Treatise on the Spirit and the Letter.
      A Treatise on Nature and Grace.
      A Treatise Concerning Man's Perfection.
      On the Proceedings of Pelagius.
      A Treatise on the Grace of Christ and Original Sin.
      On Marriage and Concupiscence.
      A Treatise on the Soul and Its Origin.
      A Treatise against Two Letters of the Pelagians.
      A Treatise on Grace and Free Will.
      A Treatise on Rebuke and Grace.
      On the Predestination of the Saints.
      On the Gift of Perseverance.
Vincent of Lerins, wrote cir. 435.
   The Commonitory.
John Cassian, 360-435.
   The Institutes of the Coenobia.
   The Conferences.
   On the Incarnation.
Sulpitius Severus, 363-420.
   Life of St. Martin.
   Dialogues.
   The Sacred History.
Leo the Great, 390-461.
   Letters; Sermons.
Gregory the Great, 540-604.
   Pastoral Rule; Epistles.
John of Damascus, 700-754.
   The Exposition of the Orthodox Faith.

c. Liturgies and Decrees:
Liturgies: Vol. XXIV *ANF.*
   Divine Liturgy of James.
   Divine Liturgy of Mark.
Ecumenical Councils, The Seven:
   Decrees and Canons: Vol. XIV, *N&PNF*, Second Series.

d. Not Included in *ANF* or *N&PNF*:
Epiphanius, 315-403: *Panarion.*
Maternus, Julius Firmicus, fourth century: *De Errore Profanorem Religionem.*

NOTES

CHAPTER I: 1

THE ORIGINAL SAVIOR-GOD OSIRIS

1. *Persian War* II 14.
2. *Library of History* I 10.
3. Cf. *Egyptian Ideas of the Future Life* I.
4. Line 465 of the Pyramid Text of Pepi II, cir. 2500 B.C.
5. Cf. the *Hymn to Osiris Un-nefer*, from the Papyrus of Ani.
6. In the rubric accompanying Ch. CXXXVIIa of *The Book of the Dead*.
7. *Isis and Osiris* 35.
8. *Description of Greece* I 14.
9. *Isis and Osiris* 12-20.
10. *Library of History* I 11-27.
11. Cf. Diodorus I 73.
12. Cf. *Hymn to Ra* in the Papyrus of Nekht.
13. Diodorus I 11.
14. The Pyramid Text of Pepi I.
15. Plutarch, *Isis and Osiris* 52.
16. *Ib.* 20.
17. Budge, *Osiris and the Egyptian Resurrection* II p. 15.
18. *The Book of the Dead* CLXVIII 15.
19. Pausanias X 32.
20. *Isis and Osiris* 39.
21. *Hymn to Osiris Un-nefer*.
22. From the Papyri of Ani, Nu, and Nebseni, all from cir. 1550 B.C.
23. *The Book of the Dead* CXXVI.
24. Cf. *ib.* LXXI; XVII; and XIX.
25. Cf. *ib.* CIX, the Papyrus of Nu.
26. *Ib.* XCVIII.
27. *Ib.* CX.
28. *History* II 86-89.
29. After Ch. LXXII, *The Book of the Dead*, Papyrus of Nebseni.
30. *Ib.* CXVII.
31. *Ib.* XLV.
32. *Ib.* X.
33. *Ib.* XLIII.
34. *Isis and Osiris* 69.
35. *De Errore Profanorem.*
36. *History* II 63.
37. *Isis and Osiris* 39.
38. Translated, Ch. XV, Budge, *Osiris and the Egyptian Resurrection*.
39. Cf. *The Book of the Dead* XVII.
40. *Isis and Osiris* 21.
41. Cf. *Typee* XXXI.
42. Line 531 ff.
43. *The Book of the Dead* CLXXXI.
44. *Ib.* LXXII.
45. *Ib.* LXXVII.
46. *Ib.* LXXXV.
47. *Ib.* LXXVIII 53.
48. *Ib.* CXXX 40.
49. *Ib.* XCIX.
50. Line 390.

CHAPTER II: 24

ADONIS AND APHRODITE

1. *History* I 199.
2. *Geography* XVI i 20.
3. *History* I 196.
4. *Geography* XI xiv 16.
5. *Golden Bough* IV: I iii.
6. *Isis and Osiris* 15-16.
7. *De Dea Syria* 7.
8. Cf. Ovid, *Metamorphosis* X vii.
9. Pausanias, *History* I xiv.
10. *History* I 105.
11. Thucydides, *History* VI 30.
12. Plutarch, *Nicias* and *Alcibiades*.
13. Ammianus Marcellinus, XXII 9:15.
14. *Exhortation* II.

CHAPTER III: 32

THE PRIMITIVE GREEK DIONYSUS

1. *Library of History* II 29.
2. *Ib.* I 94.
3. *Geography* X iv 8.
4. Cf. Diodorus I 73.

5. *Ib.* III 61, 73; V 46. Also Clement of Alexandria, *Exhortation* II.
6. *De Rerum Natura.*
7. *Geography* IX iii 4.
8. *Description of Greece* VIII **xxv.**
9. *Cessation of the Oracles* 5.
10. *The Dialogues.*
11. Diodorus V 77.
12. By Apollonius Rhodius, IV 263.
13. *Persian War* II 102-110.
14. I 53-58.
15. *Persian War* I 150.
16. *Ib.* IV 78-80.
17. *Ib.* IV 87.
18. *Ib.* IV 108.
19. *Ib.* IV 93-96.
20. *Ib.* V 7.
21. *Ib.* VII 111.
22. *Ib.* II 144.
23. *Ib.* II 146.
24. Diodorus III 66-70.
25. *Isis and Osiris* 28.
26. I 96.
27. *Ib.* IV 1.
28. *Isis and Osiris* 34.
29. *Ib.* 35.
30. Diodorus III 62.
31. *Persian War* II 49.
32. *Odyssey* XI 353, Cowper's translation.
33. Diodorus I 97.
34. *Ib.* I 22.
35. *Persian War* II 49.
36. *Ib.* 48.
37. *History* II ii.
38. *History* III 63-65.
39. *History* III iv-v.
40. *History* IV 3.
41. *Ib.* I 23.
42. *Geography* X iii 13.
43. *Description of Greece* V:I xxvi.
44. *Iliad* VI.
45. Line 377.
46. *De Abstinentia* 4:19.
47. *On the Cessation of the Oracles* 14.
48. *Exhortation* II.
49. *Ib.* III.
50. *Adversus Gentes* V 19.
51. *Metamorphoses* IV vii.
52. *History* IX 34.
53. *History* II ii.
54. *Ib.* III v.
55. *Orpheus and the Greek Religion* p. 131.
56. *Diodorus* I 85.
57. *Isis and Osiris* 64.

CHAPTER IV: 51

ATTIS AND CYBELE

1. *Geography* X iii 16, 15.
2. Diodorus V 49.
3. *Ib.* III 58-59.
4. *Ib.*
5. *Adversus Gentes* V 5-7, 13-17.
6. *Geography* X iii 18.
7. *Description of Greece* II iv; VIII xxxvii.
8. *Dithyramb for the Thebans.*
9. *History* XXIX 10, 11, 14.
10. *The Golden Ass* VIII.
11. *Adversus Gentes* V 16-17.
12. *Refutation of All Heresies* V i-v.
13. *Ib.* V iv.
14. *The Golden Bough* IV: II i.
15. Plutarch, *Isis and Osiris* 69.
16. *Adversus Gentes* V 17.
17. Clement of Alexandria, *Exhortation* II.
18. *Fragments* III.
19. *The Manner In Which the Persecutors Died* II.

CHAPTER V: 60

DEMETER-PERSEPHONE

1. Cf. Diodorus Siculus V 69.
2. *Isis and Osiris* 66.
3. *Ib.* 69.
4. *History* V 4.
5. Strabo, *Geography* IX i 12.
6. Pausanias, *Description of Greece* I xxxvi.
7. *Golden Bough* IV:I iv 8.
8. *Works and Days.*
9. *History* IV 25.
10. *Description of Greece* V:I x.
11. *Ib.* VIII xlii.
12. *The Dirges.*
13. *Fragments* 137.
14. *Panegyrics* 27.
15. *Description of Greece* I xxxviii.
16. *History* V 2-5.
17. *Isis and Osiris* 15-16.
18. Cf. Diodorus V 4.
19. Cf. Schaff-Herzog, "Tribal Mysteries" II 5-7.
20. *Refutation* V iii.
21. Reproduced by Macchioro in *From Orpheus to Paul.*
22. Cf. Apollodorus III iv. According to the myth, Zeus transformed Dio-

nysus into a kid, in order to escape the wrath of Hera.
23. *Exhortation* II.
24. *Adversus Gentes* V 24.
25. *Ib.* 25.
26. *Ib.* 26.
27. *Exhortation* II.
28. *Parallel Lives.*
29. Cf. Aristotle, *Nichomachean Ethics* 1111a.

CHAPTER VI: 72

THE ORPHEAN RECONSTRUCTION OF DIONYSUS

1. *Description of Greece* X xxx.
2. *History* IV 25.
3. *Description of Greece* IX xxx.
4. By Apollonius Rhodius.
5. *Metamorphoses* XI i.
6. Pausanias, *Description* IX xxx.
7. *Stromata* VI ii.
8. *Description* I xxxvii.
9. *Adversus Gentes* V 26.
10. *Persian War* VII 6.
11. *Description of Greece* VIII xxxvii.
12. *Isis annd Osiris* 35.
13. *History* III 62.
14. *Ib.* IV 4.
15. Eminent scholar, 1758-1835; cf. his note to Number XXXVII of *The Mystical Hymns of Orpheus*, "To the Titans."
16. *Geography* X iii 10.
17. *Description* VIII xxv.
18. *Ib.* II xxxvii.

CHAPTER VII: 83

THE ZOROASTRIANS

1. *Dinkard* VII ii 14.
2. *Ib.* VII ii 2-3; *Zad-Sparam* XIII 1.
3. *Dinkard* VII ii 6.
4. *Ib.* 10.
5. *Ib.* VII ii 10-51; Zad-Sparam XIII 4.
6. *Zad-Sparam* XX 7.
7. *Ib.* XXI 1-6; *Dinkard* IX xiii I.
8. *Zad-Sparam* XXI 8-11.
9. *Ib.* XXII 1.
10. *Ib.* XXIII 1.
11. *Zad-Sparam* XXI 11-19; *Dinkard* VII i 41-42; VIII xiv 3-9.
12. *Vendidad* XIX.
13. *Dinkard* VII v 1.
14. Cf. *Aban-Yast.*
15. *Vendidad* VIII 246.
16. Matt. 3:11.
17. Herodotus I 140.
18. *Vendidad* II.
19. *Ib.* I 3.
20. *Yasts, SBE* XXIII.
21. *Bundahis* XXVII 4.
22. *Persian War* I 131.
23. *Sikand-Gumanik-Vigar* I 1-3.
24. *Bundahis* I 1 ff.
25. *Ib.* 9.
26. *Dina-i Mainog-i Khirad* VIII 7.
27. *Yasna* LI 7.
28. *Yasna* XLVII 3.
29. *Srosh Yast.*
30. Cf. Gathas, *Yasna* XXX 4-5.
31. I Cor. 15:28.
32. In the *Sikand-Gumanik-Vigar.*
33. *Ib.* XV 142.
34. *Ib.* 144-145.
35. *Ib.* III 14-16.
36. *Ib.* 18.
37. *Ib.* IV 55-59.
38. Cf. the *Bundahis, Dina-i Mainog-i Khirad*, the *Dinkard*, and the *Dadistan-i Dinik.*
39. *Bahman Yast* II 15-22.
40. *Ib.* II 24.
41. *Ib.* 30.
42. *Ib.* II 37.
43. *Ib.* III 4.
44. *Ib.* III 21-22.
45. *Ib.* III 36.
46. *Ib.* III 43-44.
47. Cf. Matt. 10:5-23, 24:6-31; **Mark** 13.
48. *Dinkard* VII viii 55-60.
49. *Ib.* VII ix 18-20.
50. *Dinkard* VII xi 4.
51. *Ib.* 4, 6.
52. *Bahman Yast* III 18-21.
53. *Dinkard* IX xxi 10-11.
54. *Bahman Yast* III 56.
55. *Ib.* III 57-58.
56. *Yast* XXII.
57. *Sad Dar* II 3.
58. *Dadistan-i Dinik* XXVII **2.**
59. XXX.
60. *Bundahis* XXX **14.**
61. *Ib.* XXX 26.
62. *Ib.* XXX 23.
63. *Ib.* XXX 26.
64. *Ib.* XXX 29.
65. *Ib.* XXX 30.

66. *Ib.* XXX 32.
67. *Ib.* XXX 33.
68. *Gathas, Yasna* XLIV 11.
69. *Yasna* XLV 3.
70. *Vendidad* IX 56.
71. *Dinkard* IX liii 2.
72. *Dadistan-i Dinik* XLI 3.
73. *Dinkard* IX xxxvii.
74. *Dina-i Mainog-i Khirad* XIII 17.
75. *Dinkard* IX xxviii 3.

CHAPTER VIII: 107

BRAHMANISM

1. *Rig-Veda* VII 56.
2. *Institutes of Gautama* I 1.
3. As outlined in the *Laws of Manu*, I 5-31.
4. *Ib.* I 5-11.
5. *Manu* I 31, 87-91; *Inst. of Vishnu* II 1-14; *Vasishtha* II 1-20.
6. *Apastamba* II i 10:4-8.
7. *Inst. of Gautama* VIII 1-3.
8. *Manu* IX 320.
9. *Ib.* VIII 418.
10. *Vasishtha* II 1-4.
11. *Manu* IV 81.
12. *Vasishtha* XVIII 12.
13. *Ib.* 10.
14. *Ib.* IV 30.
15. *Inst. of Vishnu* XXIV 10-27.
16. *Baudhayana* I xi 21:1.
17. *Inst. of Vishnu* XXIV 1-4.
18. *Ib.* XXVI 6.
19. *Ib.* XLV 2-17.
20. *Vasishtha* I 4; *Apastamba* I i 1:1-2.
21. *Inst. of Vishnu* XIX 22-23.
22. *Ib.* 20-21.
23. *Inst. of Vishnu* III 26-27; *Vasishtha* II 42-43.
24. *Manu* VII 133.
25. *Inst. of Vishnu* V 2, 8.
26. *Inst. of Gautama* VIII 13.
27. *Ib.* XII 4-6.
28. *Visishtha* XXI 1.
29. *Manu* VIII 271.
30. *Ib.* 272.
31. *Ib.* XI 56.
32. *Inst. of Vishnu* V 19-23.
33. *Apastamba* II i 28:2.
34. *Inst. of Gautama* XVIII 24-27.
35. *Inst. of Gautama* XXIII 8-11; *Vasishtha* XX 13.
36. *Apastamba* I i 25:1-2.
37. *Inst. of Gautama* XXIII 14-15.
38. *Baudhayana* II i 1:2-3.
39. *Apastamba* I i 24:1-25.
40. *Baudhayana* II i 1:8-11.
41. *Apastamba* I i 25:13.
42. *Inst. of Gautama* XXII 23.
43. *Ib.* 27.
44. *Manu* IX 325.
45. *Inst. of Vishnu* XCVI 1.
46. *Baudhayana* I i 11:7.
47. *Manu* V 148.
48. *Ib.* 156.
49. *Ib.* 157, 162.
50. *Inst. of Gautama* XIV 18.
51. *Inst. of Vishnu* XXV 14.
52. *Ib.* IX 27.
53. *Ib.* IX-XIII.
54. *Apastamba* I i 7:8-9.
55. *Inst. of Vishnu* XXVIII 1-47.
56. *Apastamba* I ii 21:1-3; *Vasishtha* VII-XIII.
57. *Inst. of Gautama* III 36.
58. *Ib.* III 3.
59. *Vasishtha* VIII 16.
60. *Apastamba* I i 22:3-6.
61. *Apastamba* II i 23:5.
62. *Apastamba* II i 21:7-13; *Inst. of Vishnu* XCVI 1-25.
63. *Inst. of Vishnu* XCVI 26-85; *Vasishtha* X 1-19; *Manu* VI 37-65.
64. *Vasishtha* XXII 12.
65. *Ib.* 13.
66. *Inst. of Vishnu* XLII 2.
67. *Ib.* XLIII.
68. *Ib.* 1-45.
69. *Ib.* XLIV i.
70. *Manu* II 103.
71. *Vasishtha* XV 11, 15.
72. *Manu* IV 30.
73. *Ib.* XII 95-96.
74. *Bhagavad-Gita* III.
75. *Vasishtha* IV 30.
76. *Katha-Upanishad* I i 2:23.
77. *Vasishtha* II 4.

CHAPTER IX: 126

BUDDHISM: REVOLUTION IN INDIA

1. *Questions of Melinda* III 1:47.
2. *Dhammapada* XX 284.
3. *Uttaradhyana* II:VIII 18.
4. *Fo-Sho-Hing-Tsan-King* 1754-1765.
5. *Questions of Melinda* IV 8:1.
6. *Ib.* IV 8:6.
7. *Sutrakritanga* I iii 2:2-14.

8. *Sutra-Nipata* I 7:135; *Uttaradhyana* II:XXV 33.
9. *Dhammapada* XXVI 394.
10. *Uttaradhyana* II:XXV 18.
11. *Ib.* 32
12. *Tevigga-Sutta* I 33-36.
13. *Ib.* 14.
14. From the *Kalpa-Sutra*.
15. *Uttaradhyana* II:XIX 86-87; *Akaranga Sutra* I viii 1:2.16
16. *Kalpa-Sutra* 119.
17. *Akaranga-Sutra* I ii 1:1-4.
18. *Ib.* I ii 3-5.
19. *Uttaradhyana* II:VI 15.
20. *Ib.* II:XII 7.
21. *Ib.* 9, 12.
22. *Ib.* 14-15.
23. *Ib.* II:VII 14-28.
24. *Dhammapada* IX 126.
25. *Uttaradhyana* II:XIV 38.
26. II Peter 2:22.
27. *Uttaradhyana* II:XIX 83-84.
28. *Sutrakritanga* II i 41.
29. *Fo-Sho-Hing* 21.
30. Cf. Luke 2:25-26.
31. *Fo-Sho-Hing* 95-96.
32. *Buddha-Karita* I 65.
33. *Ib.* 74, 77, 80.
34. *Ib.* II 26, 46.
35. *Fo-Sho-Hing* 281.
36. *Ib.* 330-331.
37. *Ib.* 765, cf. Matt. 15:14.
38. *Fo-Sho-Hing* 947-948.
39. *Ib.* 975, 977.
40. *Fo-Sho-Hing* 997; *Buddha-Karita* XII 69-86.
41. *Buddha-Karita* XII 87-101.
42. *Fo-Sho-Hing* 1036.
43. *Ib.* XV 104-105.
44. *Ib.* XV 17-18.
45. *Ib.* XIV 70-71.
46. *Fo-Sho-Hing* 1106-1108.
47. *Buddha-Karita* XIV 67-68.
48. *Fo-Sho-Hing* 1299.
49. *Ib.* 1551, 1553.
50. *Ib.* 1671.
51. *The Great Decease* II 17-24.
52. *Buddha-Karita* XVII 25, 30.
53. *Great Decease* III 45.
54. Matt 28:19.
55. *Fo-Sho-Hing* 2104-08.
56. Matt. 27:51 ff.
57. *Great Decease* II 7.
58. *Foundation of the Kingdom of Righteousness* 4.
59. *Fo-Sho-Hing* 1243.

60. *Dhammapada* X 141-142.
61. *Ib.* I 1.
62. *Kullavagga* 248.
63. *Dhammapada* VIII 103.
64. Matt. 5:45.
65. *Saddharma-Pundarika* V 45-46.
66. *Great Decease* I 11.
67. *Kullavagga* IV xiv 3.
68. *Patimokkha*, Paragika Dhamma 1-4.
69. *Sutra-Nipata* I 7:131.
70. *Dhammapada* X 133.
71. *Ib.* XVII 223.
72. *Ib.* XV 197, 199.
73. *Ib.* XVIII 252.
74. *Ib.* XXVI 389.
75. *Ib.* XV 200.
76. *Mahavagga* VIII 13:7.
77. *Dhammapada* XX 286-287.
78. *Uttaradhyana* II:XIV 39.
79. Matt. 16:26 and Mark 8:36.
80. *Mahavagga* 490.
81. *Saddharma-Pundarika* XVI 17-22.
82. *Questions of Melinda* IV 5:3.
83. *Ib.* IV 2:26.
84. *Saddharma-Pundarika* III 113-130.
85. *Ib.* XXVI.
86. *Ib.* XXI.
87. *Ib.* XXIV 11.
88. *Ib.* XIII 58.
89. *Ib.* XXVI.
90. *Ib.* V 44.
91. Matt. 13:44.
92. *Saddharma-Pundarika* VIII 36-42.
93. *Ib.* IV 2-50.
94. *Ib.* IX 18.
95. *Ib.* VIII.
96. *Maha-Sadassana Gotaka* or *The Great King of Glory*.
97. *Ib.* I 63.
98. *Questions of Melinda* I 1:22.
99. *Ib.* 23.
100. *Ib.* IV 6:24.
101. *Ib.* IV 3:35.
102. *Ib.* IV 3:36.
103. *Ib.* VI.
104. *Ib.* VI 5.
105. *Ib.* VI 22.
106. *Ib.* V 8.
107. *Ib.* VI 22.

CHAPTER X: 155

PYTHAGORAS

1. *Life of Pythagoras* I 11.
2. *Ib.* 14.

3. Cf. Tertullian, *De Anima* XXVIII.
4. *Homily* XXII.
5. *Dialogue with Trypho* II.
6. By Philostratus.
7. Clemens Alexandrinus, *Exhortation* VI.
8. *Disputation with Manes* 51.
9. Hippolytus, *Refutation* VI xx-xxi.
10. *Ib.* xxii.
11. *Ib.* I ii.
12. *Life* I 41.
13. *Oration of Constantine* IX.
14. *Life* I 6.
15. *History* I 96.
16. A quotation from the *Triagmi* of Ion of Chios reproduced by Diogenes Laertius in his *Life of Pythagoras*.
17. Diogenes Laertius, *Life* I 1.
18. Clemens Alex., *Misc.* I xv.
19. Hippolytus, *Refutation* I ii.
20. *Persian War* II 81.
21. Reproduced in Guthrie's *Orpheus and the Greek Religion*, pp. 172-3.
22. Diog. Laertius, *Life*; Clemens Alex., *Misc.*, VI ii; Tertullian, *De Anima* XXVIII-XXXI; Jerome, *Letter* LIII.
23. *Treatise against Philostratus* XI.
24. X 888c.
25. *The Republic* II.
26. *Phaedo* 69 c.
27. *Cratylus* 400 c.
28. *The Republic* I.
29. *Laws* IX 70 E.
30. Book X.
31. Quoted by Justin Martyr in *Sole Government of God* III.
32. Book VI xciv, tr. of E. Fairfax Taylor.
33. *Ib.* xcvi.
34. *Ib.* xcvii. Cf. Shakespeare, Sonnet 146.
35. *Vengeance of the Gods* 22.
36. In *Hippolytus* 952-3.
37. From *The Cretans*, reproduced by Porphyry, *De Abstinentia* IV 19.
38. Quotation from *Timaeus*, reproduced by Jerome, *Against Jovianus* I 42.
39. Hippolytus, *Refutation* I ii.
40. *Contra Celsum* III ii.
41. *Life.*
42. *The Republic* II.
43. *Ib.* X.
44. *Antiq.* XV x 4.

CHAPTER XI: 177
ISIS AND SERAPIS

1. *Eccl. Hist.* I xviii.
2. *Ib.* V xvi.

CHAPTER XII: 182
MITHRAISM

1. *First Apology* LXVI.
2. *On Baptism* V.
3. *Prescription against Heretics* XL.
4. *De Corona* 15.
5. *Trypho* LXXVIII.
6. *Life of Pompey* 24.
7. *Mihir Yast* VII 25.
8. *Mihir Nyayis.*
9. *Mihir Yast* VIII 29.
10. *Ib.* IX 35.
11. *Ib.* XIII 59.
12. *Ib.* XXII 84.
13. *Ib.* XXIII 93.
14. *Ib.* XXX 122.
15. *Texts et Monuments figures relatifs aux Mysteres de Mithra*, by Franz Cumont.
16. *Epistle* XVII 2.
17. Sozomen, *Eccl. Hist.* V vii.
18. Socrates, V xvi.

PART TWO: THE JEWISH SOURCES

CHAPTER I: 195
JUDAISM

1. *Life of Apollonius of Tyana* V xxxiii.
2. Deut. 14:2.
3. *Ib.* 28:1.
4. *Ib.* 15:6.
5. *The Haggadah of Passover.*
6. *Ency. Brit.* 12:77.
7. *Ib.* 79.
8. Gen. 46:34.
9. Ex. 1:8 ff.
10. Lev. 25:35-36; Deut. 23:20.
11. Lev. 19:18.
12. Deut. 15:12 ff.; Ex. 21:2.
13. Lev. 25:12-13.
14. See the story of Saul and Agag, I Sam. 15:8 ff.
15. I Kings 12:13-14.

16. I Kings 15:16, 32.
17. II Kings 17:6 ff.; 18:10 ff.
18. II Kings 23:29-30; *Antiq.* X v 2.
19. II Kings 24:1.
20. *Ib.* 24:10.
21. *Ib.* 24:20; 25:1 ff.; *Antiq.* X vii 1-4.
22. *Antiq.* XIII xv 5.
23. Josephus, *Wars of the Jews* I iv 6,
24. *Antiq.* XVII x 8-10.
25. *Ib.* XVIII i 1.
26. *Wars* II xiii 4.
27. Cf. Joshua 4; *Antiq.* XX v 1.
28. In Acts 5:36-37, there is a reference to Judas and Theudas, but the historical facts are completely garbled; for Judas is supposed to be subsequent; actually, he came thirty-seven years earlier. The only portion that is accurate is the statement that Judas came during the days of "the taxing."
29. *Wars* II xiii 3.
30. *Ib.* II xiv 2.
31. *History* V 10.
32. *Wars* II xvii 4.
33. *Ib.* II xvii 6.
34. I Sam. 19:20-24.
35. I Sam. 22:2.
36. Lam. 1:7.
37. II Kings 1:8.
38. I Kings 18:19 ff.
39. *Ib.* 18:22.
40. II Kings 21:3-6.
41. *Ib.* 18:14-16.
42. *Ib.* 18:4-5.
43. 7:21-23.
44. Hosea 6:6; 8:13; 9:4; Micah 6:6-8.
45. Deut 23:18.
46. II Kings 22:8; II Chron. 34:3-7; 14; 21.
47. II Kings 22:11.
48. Jer. 8:8.
49. II Chron. 34:4-5.
50. Ezra 7:6 ff.
51. Zech. 13:3-4.
52. Micah 3:3-12.
53. Jer. 34:8-12.
54. *Ib.* 34:13-17.
55. Cf. Bokser, *Wisdom of the Talmud*, p. 72.
56. Ezra 2:65.
57. I Sam. 28:7 ff.
58. *Helen.*
59. *Wars* II viii 14.
60. *Wars* III viii 5.
61. *Antiq.* XVIII i 3.
62. Milman, *Hist. of the Jews* II 178 ff.
63. Tacitus, *Hist.* V 13.
64. Deut. 18:18.
65. Isaiah 2:2-4.
66. *Ib.* 7:14-17.
67. *Ib.* 8:4.
68. *Ib.* 9:6-7.
69. *Ib.* 10:5-6.
70. *Ib.* 10:20-21.
71. *Ib.* 11:1-12.
72. *Ib.* 8:3.
73. Micah 5:2.
74. *Ib.* 7:16-17.
75. *Ib.* 4:6-7.
76. *Ib.* 4:1-3.
77. Zech. 6:12-13.
78. *Ib.* 8:7-8.
79. *Ib.* 8:23.
80. *Ib.* 9:10.
81. *Ib.* 14:1-2.
82. *Ib.* 14:14.
83. *Ib.* 14:16..
84. Lev. 24:16.
85. Isaiah 45:1.
86. *Ib.* 40:1-5.
87. *Ib.* 42:1; 45:14, 23.
88. *Ib.* 66: 15-16.
89. *Ib.* 65:17-19.
90 *Ib.* 65:25.
91. *Ib.* 66:3.
92. *Ib.* 60:19.
93. *Ib.* 60:3-12.
94. *Antiq.* X xi 7.
92. *Ib.* 60:19.
96. *Ib.* 9:24-27.
97. *Ib.* 6:3.
98. *Ib.* 2:34.
99. *Ib.* 2:35.
100. *Ib.* 2:44.
101. *Ib.* 8:23.
102. *Ib.* 7:25; 11:30-32.
103. *Ib.* 12:11-12.
104. *Ib.* 7:3-8.
105. *Ib.* 7:11.
106. *Ib.* 7:9-18.
107. *Ib.* 12:11-12.

CHAPTER II: 225

THE ESSENES: THE EXTERNAL EVIDENCE

1. Solomon Zeitlin.
2. J. L. Teicher.
3. *Nat. History,* Bohn I 430-1.
4. *Antiq.* XV x 4.
5. *Ib.* XIII v 9.
6. *Ib.* XIII x 6.
7. *Ib.* XIII x 7.
8. *Ib.* XIII ix-x.
9. *Ib.* XIV ii 1.
10. *Ib.* XV x 4-5.
11. This passage reproduced by Eusebius, *Preparation for the Gospel* VIII 8, is a quotation from Philo's lost *Apology for the Jews.*
12. *A Treatise to Prove that Every Man Who Is Virtuous Is Also Free* XIII.
13. *Life* 2, by Josephus.
14. *Antiq.* XVIII i 3-6.
15. *Wars of the Jews* II viii 2-13.

CHAPTER III: 247

THE ESSENES: THE INTERNAL EVIDENCE

1. Section VIII.
2. *Ib.* IX.
3. *Ib.*
4. Sects. X-XX.
5. *Ib.* XVI, XIX.
6. *Ib.* XVII.
7. *Ib.* XVIII.
8. *Ib.* VIII.
9. *The War* I i.
10. *Ib.*
11. *Ib.*
12. *Ib.*
13. *Ib.*
14. *Jubilees* IV.
15. *Ib.* XXX.
16. *Ib.*
17. *Ib.* XXXI.
18. *Ib.* I.
19. *The Book of Enoch* x.
20. *Ib.* PART THREE xviii.
21. *Ib.* xxv.
22. *Ib.* xc.
23. *Ib.* xciii.
24. *Ib.* xciv.
25. Luke 16:19-31.
26. *Enoch* xcvii.
27. *Ib.* xcix-cii.
28. *Ib.* xlv.
29. *Ib.* xlviii.
30. *Ib.* liii.
31. *Ib.* lxii.
32. *Yasna* xlv 2; xxx 3-5.
33. *Manual* II.
34. Cf. *Test. of the Twelve Patriarchs* I 3-32.
35. *Manual* III.
36. *Commentary* II 1.
37. *Ib.* I 12.
38. *Ib.* I 4.
39. *Ib.* II 6.
40. *Antiq.* XIII x 7.
41. *Commentary* II 8.
42. *Ib.*
43. *Antiq.* XIV ix 4-5.
44. *Life of Pompey.*
45. *Commentary* II 15.
46. "Judah" IV 2-3.
47. "Reuben" II 26.
48. "Levi" III 23-26. Josephus says, *Antiq.* XIII x 7: "Hyrcanus . . . administered the government . . . for thirty-one years . . . . He was esteemed by God worthy of three of the greatest privileges,—the government of the nation, the dignity of the high priesthood, and prophecy; for God was with him, and enabled him to know futurities."
49. "Levi" III 45.
50. "Judah" IV 12.
51. "Levi" V 1-12.
52. Cf. Dupont-Sommer, *Jewish Sect of Qumran* III.
53. *Antiq.* XIII xi.
54. "Simeon" III 9, 11.
55. "Naphtali" II 24-25.
56. "Asher" 39-41.
57. "Zebulon" II 32-35.
58. "Levi" III 44-47, version published in the *Ante-Nicene Library.*
59. "Levi" II 6:8, also from the *ANF.*
60. "Levi" IV 11-12; 27-29.
61. "Benjamin" I 21.
62. I Thess. 4:16.
63. "Benjamin" II 18-23.
64. "Judah" IV 12-31.
65. *Ib.* IV 31.
66. "Levi" V 1-12..
67. *Ib.* V 13-14.
68. *Ib.* V 14-27.

CHAPTER IV: 280
THE ESSENES: ANALYSIS AND TRADITION

1. "Joseph" II 74.
2. *Contra Celsum* VII ix.
3. *Jesus in Jewish Tradition* pp. 148-154.
4. *Essenism and Christianity.*
5. Coleridge, *Works* VIII p. 136.
6. *Dead Sea Scrolls* p. 99.
7. *The Scrolls from the Dead Sea*, pp. 97-98.

PART THREE: THE INNER MEANING OF THE GOSPEL

PREFATORY: CULTIC 295
PREPARATION FOR CHRISTIANITY

1. *First Apology* XLIX.
2. *Contra Celsum* I xxxii.
3. *First Apology* LIV.
4. *Trypho* LXIX-LXX.
5. *First Apology* VIII.
6. I Cor. 10:20-21.
7. *Trypho* X.
8. *Three Books* III 44.
9. *Apology* 39.
10. *Ib.* 7.
11. *Contra Celsum* I xxxvii.
12. *Against Jovianus* I 42.
13. *First Apology* XXI-XXII.
14. *Apology* 21.
15. *Ib.* 47.
16. *Description of Greece* VI xxvi.
17. *Ib.* VIII xxvi.
18. *Apology* 46.
19. *Ib.* 6.
20. *Ib.* 37.
21. *History of Rome* XXV i.

CHAPTER I: 304
THE HISTORICITY OF JESUS

1. *Pagan and Christian Creeds.*
2. *Jesus: A Myth.*
3. Cf. Brandes, ib. 46-47.
4. *Antiq.* XVIII iii 3.
5. *Eccl. Hist.* I xi.
6. *Ib.* XVIII v 2.
7. *Contra Celsum* I xlvii.
8. *Antiq.* XX ix 1.
9. *Commentary on Matt.* 17.
10. *Annals* 15:44.
11. In Letter 97.
12. Ch. on Nero in *Lives of the Twelve Caesars.*
13. *Jesus and Judas* p. 67.

CHAPTER II: 311
THE COMPOSITION OF THE SYNOPTIC GOSPELS

1. Cf. Matt. 7:28; 19:1; 26:1; Luke 1:65; 7:1; 9:44; etc.
2. *Eccl. Hist.* III xxxix 15.
3. *Against Heresies* I xxvi 2.
4. *Panarion* XXIX ix 4.

CHAPTER III: 316
THE APOTHEOSIS OF JESUS

1. Luke 3:8 ff.
2. *Ib.* 3:16-17.
3. Mark 1:10-11.
4. Matt. 3:17.
5. Mark 1:11.
6. Luke 3:22.
7. *Panarion* XXX.
8. *Dialogue with Trypho* CIII.
9. *Reply to Faustus the Manichean* XXIII 2.

CHAPTER IV: 319
JESUS REJECTED IN NAZARETH

1. Cf. Tertullian, *Against All Heresies* I.
2. Mark 1:14-16.
3. *Ib.* 1:16-20.
4. John 1:43-45.
5. *Ib.* 1:51.
6. Luke 4:16-30.
7. *Ib.* 4:18-19.
8. *Ib.* 4:21.
9. Mark 6:6.
10. Luke 4:25-27.
11. *Ib.* 4:29-30.

CHAPTER V: 322
MIRACLES IN GALILEE

1. *Innocents Abroad* II:XXI.
2. Mark 1:21-28.
3. *Ib.* 1:30-31.
4. *Ib.* 1:33.
5. *Ib.* 1:38.
6. *Ib.* 2:1 ff.
7. *Ib.* 2:5.
8. *Ib.* 2:14.
9. Luke 5:28.

CHAPTER VI: 327

THE STORM-CLOUDS GATHER

1. Mark 2:15; 3:6; Matt. 9:10-12:21; Luke 5:29-6:12.
2. Mark 2:16.
3. Matt. 9:12-13.
4. To Isaiah 1:11, Hosea 6:6, and Micah 6:6-8.
5. Mark 2:18.
6. *Ib.* 2:20.
7. *Ib.* 2:21-22.
8. *Ib.* 2:23-3:6.
9. Deut. 5:13-14.
10. Mark 3:4.
11. Luke 6:12.
12. Mark 3:14-15.
13. Mark 3:21.
14. *Ib.* 3:31-32.
15. *Ib.* 3:33-35.
16. *Ib.* 3:7 ff.
17. *Ib.* 3:11.

CHAPTER VII: 332

ETHICS: THE SERMON ON THE MOUNT

1. Luke 6:24-25.
2. Matt. 5:17-48.
3. *Ib.* 10:6; 15:24.
4. *Ib.* 5:25.
5. *Ib.* 19:12.
6. *Ib.* 5:31-32.
7. *Ib.* 33-37.
8. *Dialogue* X.
9. Luke 9:54.
10. As laid down in Matt. 5:43-46.
11. Matt. 6:24.
12. *Ib.* 6:25-34.
13. *Ib.* 7:6.
14. *Ib.* 7:13-14.

CHAPTER XIII: 345

ART THOU HE THAT SHOULD COME?

1. Matt. 8:10-13.
2. Luke 7:11-17.
3. Luke 7:18-30.
4. Isaiah 40:3.
5. Malachi 3:1.

CHAPTER IX: 347

APPROACHING CRISIS IN GALILEE

1. Matt. 11:16-19 and Luke 7:31-35.
2. 7:36-50.
3. Luke 8:1.
4. *Ib.* 8:2-3.
5. Mark 4:2-25.
6. *Ib.* 4:11-12.
7. Matt. 13:24-43.
8. *Ib.* 11:12.
9. *Ib.* 13:40-42.
10. Luke 17:21.
11. Matt. 13:44.
12. *Ib.* 13:45-46.
13. *Ib.* 13:47-48.
14. *Ib.* 13:49-50.
15. Mark 4:35-41.
16. *Ib.* 5:1-20.
17. *Ib.* 5:21-43.

CHAPTER X: 354

THE FIRST APOCALYPSE

1. Matt. 10:5-7.
2. *Ib.* 10:21-23.
3. *Ib.* 13:41-43, 49-50.
4. Luke 10:13-16.
5. Matt. 10:28.
6. *Ib.* 10:34.
7. Luke 12:51-53.
8. Matt. 10:37.
9. *Ib.* 19:28-29.
10. Luke 14:26.
11. *Ib.* 22:34-35.
12. *Ib.* 10:17.
13. *Ib.* 10:18-20.

CHAPTER XI: 360

INDECISION AND RE-ORIENTATION

1. Mark 6:17-29.
2. *Ib.* 6:16.
3. *Ib.* 6:31 and Luke 9:10.
4. Mark 6:33.
5. Matt. 14:23.
6. Mark 6:47-51.
7. *Ib.* 6:53-56.

8. *Ib.* 7:1 ff.
9. *Ib.* 7:13, 9.
10. *Ib.* 7:15.

CHAPTER XII: 363
THOU ART THE CHRIST!

1. Mark 7:24-30.
2. *Ib.* 7:31.
3. *Ib.* 8:10.
4. *Ib.* 8:11.
5. *Ib.* 12.
6. *Ib.* 8:13.
7. *Ib.* 8:27.
8. Matt. 16:13-17.
9. *Ib.* 16:21.
10. Mark 8:32.
11. Matt. 16:24-27.
12. Matt. 16:28; Mark 9:1; Luke 9:27.
13. *The Quest of the Historical Jesus,* p. 360.

CHAPTER XIII: 367
THE TRANSFORMED CHRIST

1. Mark 9:2.
2. *Ib.* 9:7.
3. *Ib.* 9:9.
4. *Ib.* 9:19.
5. *Ib.* 9:30-31.
6. *Ib.* 9:33-37.
7. Matt. 17:24-27.
8. Mark 9:31-42.
9. *Ib.* 9:43-48.

CHAPTER XIV: 370
INTERLUDE AT BETHANY

1. Luke 9:51.
2. *Ib.* 10:21.
3. Matt. 11:29-30.
4. Luke 10:25-37.
5. *Ib.* 10:38.
6. Matt. 12:33.
7. *Ib.* 12:38-39.
8. *Ib.* 12:33-42.
9. Mark 7:1 ff.
10. Matt. 23:14-15 and 23:33; Luke 11:47-51.
11. Luke 11:53-54.
12. *Ib.* 12:13-15.
13. *Ib.* 12:18-20.
14. *Ib.* 12:33.
15. Mark 13:32-37.
16. Mark 13:30; Matt. 24:34; 23:36; Luke 21:32.
17. Luke 12:45.

CHAPTER XV: 375
MANY ARE CALLED, BUT FEW ARE CHOSEN

1. Luke 13:11-17.
2. *Ib.* 12:23-30.
3. *Ib.* 13:31.
4. *Ib.* 13:33-35.
5. Matt. 22:1-14.
6. *Ib.* 22:14.
7. Luke 15:4-32.
8. *Ib.* 16:1-12.
9. *Ib.* 16:13.

CHAPTER XVI: 381
THE KINGDOM OF HEAVEN

1. Mark 10 and Luke 16-19.
2. Matt. 19:3 ff.
3. *Ib.* 19:9.
4. *Ib.* 19:11-12.
5. Luke 16:19-31.
6. Matt. 18:15-22.
7. Ephes. 4:26.
8. Luke 17:11-19.
9. *Ib.* 17:20.
10. *Ib.* 17:24-25.
11. *Ib.* 17:29-30.
12. *Ib.* 18:9 ff.
13. Mark 10:13.
14. Mark 10:17.
15. Mark 10:21, Matt. 19:21, and Luke 18:22.
16. Mark 10:22.
17. *Ib.* 27.
18. Matt. 19:29.
19. *Ib.* 19:28.
20. Mark 10:29-30.
21. *Ib.* 10:33-34.
22. *Ib.* 10:47.
23. Matt. 20:1-16.
24. Luke 19:1 ff.
25. *Ib.* 19:11.
26. Matt. 25:14-30.

CHAPTER XVII: 389
AT WAR WITH THE PHARISEES

1. Mark 11:2-3.
2. Matt. 21:9.

3. Luke 19:39.
4. Mark 11:15-17.
5. *Ib.* 11:18
6. *Ib.* 11:28.
7. Matt. 21:31.
8. Mark 12:1-12 and Matt. 21:33-46.
9. Matt. 21:45-46.
10. Mark 12:13.
11. *Ib.* 12:14-15.
12. Mark 12:18-27.
13. *Ib.* 12:24-26.
14. Matt. 22:28-31.
15. Luke 20:34-35.
16. Mark 12:35-37.
17. *Ib.* 12:40.
18. Matt. 23:4.

CHAPTER XVIII: 394

THE SECOND GOSPEL APOCALYPSE

1. Mark 13.
2. Mark 13:3-4.
3. Luke 19:11.
4. Mark 13:14.
5. Luke 21:20-24.
6. Mark 13:26-27.
7. Matt. 24:34; Mark 13:30; Luke 21:32.
8. Matt. 25:1-13.
9. *Ib.* 25:31-40.
10. *Ib.* 35:45-46.

CHAPTER XIX: 398

THE EUCHARISTIC MYSTERY

1. Matt. 26:3-5.
2. Mark 14:10-11.
3. Matt. 26:20-29; Mark 14:22-25; Luke 22:14-20.
4. John 6:33, 35, 51.
5. *Ib.* 6:54.
6. Luke 22:15-18.
7. Matt. 26:26-28.
8. *Ib.* 20:20-24.
9. Luke 22:33.
10. *Ib.* 22:32.

CHAPTER XX: 402

GETHSEMANE

1. Mark 14:34-36.
2. Luke 22:44.
3. Mark 14:41.

CHAPTER XXI: 404

THE TRIAL AND DEATH OF JESUS

1. Matt. 26:63.
2. Mark 14:62; Matt. 26:64.
3. Mark 14:63-64.
4. *Ib.* 14:66-72.
5. *Ib.* 15:1-5.
6. Luke 23:2.
7. *Ib.* 23:6-11.
8. *Antiq.* XVIII iii 1.
9. Mark 15:15.
10. Psalms 22:1.
11. Matt. 26:53.
12. Mark 15:43.
13. Luke 2:25, 38.
14. Mark 15:47.
15. Luke 24:3; Matt. 28:6; Mark 16:5-6.
16. Matt. 27:62-66.
17. *Ib.* 64.

CHAPTER XXII: 411

SUMMARY AND EVALUATION

PART FOUR: REDEVELOPMENT IN THE PAGAN WORLD

CHAPTER I: 425

THE EARLIEST CHRISTIANS

1. Acts 4:33.
2. *Ib.* 11:26.
3. Luke 24:21.
4. *Ib.* 19:11.
5. Acts 1:6.
6. *Ib.* 2:36-45.
7. *Ib.* 4:32-37.
8. *Ib.* 5:11.
9. *Ib.* 9:36.
10. *Ib.* 10:1-2.
11. *Ib.* 6:1.
12. Gal. 2:7.
13. Acts 6:8.
14. *Ib.* 6:11-14.
15. *Ib.* 6:12.
16. *Ib.* 7:58.
17. *Ib.* 13:46.
18. *Ib.* 10:11.
19. *Ib.* 10:15.
20. Gal. 2:11-14.

21. *Ib.* 2:3.
22. Acts 15:29.
23. *Ib.* 15:39.

CHAPTER II: 434

THE DIDACHE

CHAPTER III: 437

PAUL: JEW VS. GENTILE

1. Tertullian, *Against All Heresies* VI.
2. Rom. 10:2.
3. *Ib.* 16:25.
4. Col. 1:26.
5. Acts 3:18, 21, 22, 24; 7:37, 52.
6. I Cor. 7:1.
7. *Ib.* 7:2.
8. *Ib.* 7:9.
9. II Cor. 6:14.
10. I Cor. 7:12-15.
11. *Ib.* 7:38.
12. I Cor. 7:39; Rom. 7:3.
13. I Cor. 7:29.
14. I Tim. 1:4; Titus 1:14, 3:9.
15. Eph. 2:20, 4:11; I Cor. 12:29.
16. I Tim. 3:2-4, 3:8, 4:14; Titus 1:7.
17. I Tim. 3:2-4, 3:8.
18. I Tim. 2:4.
19. I Tim. 1:18; II Tim. 1:2.
20. II Tim. 4:1.
21. I Tim. 5:8.
22. I Tim. 6:20.
23. Titus 2:4.
24. I Tim. 2:15.
25. *Ib.* 5:14.
26. *Ib.* 4:1-3.
27. E. g., Acts 20:35; I Cor. 11: 24-25; Rom. 13:6-9; I Thess. 5:2-3.
28. Gal. 1.12; Rom. 1:1, 15:16; I Cor. 1:1, 4:16; Phil. 3:17; Eph. 3:3.
29. Gal. 1:13.
30. II Cor. 11:23-28.
31. Acts, Chas. 25-26.
32. I Cor. 9:22.
33. Acts 26:24.
34. *Ib.* 28:23-27.
35. *Ib.* 28:30-31.
36. I Thess. 2:15.
37. *Ib.* 16.
38. I Cor. 16:22.
39. Rom. 2:11.
40. I Cor. 12:13.
41. Col. 3:11.
42. Acts 15:1.
43. *Ib.* 21:20-21.
44. *Ib.* 23:12-13.
45. Acts 21:23-26.
46. Gal. 6:15.
47. Acts 13:16-43.
48. *Ib.* 13:50.
49. *Ib.* 14:19.
50. *Ib.* 18:6.
51. I Cor. 1:24.
52. Rom. 3:19.
53. *Ib.* 3:28-29.
54. *Ib.* 7:6.
55. *Ib.* 10:12.
56. *Ib.* 14:2-3.
57. Col. 2:14-16.
58. I Cor. 8:4-11.
59. Rom. 14:14-23.
60. *Ib.* 14:6.
61. Gal. 4:9-21.
62. *Ib.* 2:11-16.
63. *Ib.* 3:24-25.
64. *Ib.* 4:3-5.
65. Rom. 11:25-26.
66. Gal. 5:2-4.
67. I Cor. 11:3, 8-9.
68. Rom. 13:1-4.
69. I Cor. 6:1, 6.
70. Rom. 12:20.
71. I Cor. 4:12-13.
72. Eph. 6:5-8; I Cor. 7: 20-24.
73. I Thess. 2:9; II Cor. 11:9, 12:14-15; Acts 18:3, 20:34.
74. I Cor. 9:14.
75. II Thess. 3:10.
76. I Thess. 4:3-5.
77. Rom. 8:1-14.
78. *Ib.* 8:6, 13.
79. II Cor. 11:2.
80. I Cor. 6:13.
81. *Ib.* 6:18-19.
82. *Ib.* 7:29-33.
83. I Tim. 6:17-19.
84. *Ib.* 6:10.
85. *Ib.* 6:18.
86. I Cor. 5:1.
87. Eph. 6:12.
88. Gal. 5:17.
89. Col. 1:12-13; Eph. 2:2-3; Rom. 9:8. Etc.
90. Rom. 7:18.
91. *Ib.* 7:22-24.
92. Col. 3:5.
93. I Cor. 9:27.
94. Gal. 5:24.
95. Rom. 8:1-4.
96. *Ib.* 8:29-30.
97. *Ib.* 9:20-21.

98. *Ib.* 22-23.
99. I Cor. 1:26-27.
100. II Thess. 2:13.
101. I Thess. 5:9-10.
102. Col. 1:15-17; Eph. 3:9.
103. Rom. 1:3.
104. Gal. 4:4.
105. II Cor. 5:16.
106. Rom. 1:4.
107. I Cor. 15:20.
108. *Against All Heresies* VII xxii.
109. Eph. 5:30.
110. I Cor. 10:16-17.
111. Eph. 1:23; Rom. 12:5.
112. I Cor. 11: 23-26.
113. Rom. 13:11-12.
114. I Cor. 7:29.
115. *Ib.* 15:50-53.
116. Phil. 3:21.
117. I Cor. 11:27-29.
118. I Thess. 4:13-15.
119. I Cor. 15:16-22.
120. I Thess. 4:15-17.
121. II Thess. 2:3.
122. *Ib.* 2:4.
123. Mark 13:14.

CHAPTER IV: 453
THE CATHOLIC EPISTLES

1. James 1:9-10.
2. *Ib.* 3:1.
3. *Ib.* 5:1-6.
4. *Ib.* 5:7-8.
5. Ex. 24:8.
6. I Peter 1:19.
7. *Ib.* 2:9.
8. *Ib.* 4:7.
9. II Peter 3:3-10.
10. II Tim. 1:15.

CHAPTER V: 456
THE GREAT SYNOPTICAL ADDITIONS

1. Matt. 28:2.
2. Mark 16:9-15.
3. *Ib.* 16:7.
4. *Ib.* 16:19.
5. Matt. 28:9.
6. *Ib.* 28:17.
7. Luke 24:10.
8. *Ib.* 24:12.
9. *Ib.* 24:13-32.
10. *Ib.* 24:30-31.

11. *Ib.* 24:49.
12. *Ib.* 24:50-51.
13. John 20:1-17.
14. *Ib.* 20:18-31.
15. *Ib.* 21:1-14.
16. Matt. 27:64; 28:11-15.
17. *Ib.* 28:13.
18. I Cor. 15:6.
19. *Panarion* XXIX ix 4.
20. I Tim. 1:4; Titus 3:9.
21. Rom. 1:3; 15:12; Gal. 4:4; II Tim. 2:8.
22. I Cor. 1:24.
23. Mark 12:35-37.
24. *Acts of Pilate* II 4-5.
25. *Panarion* XXX.
26. *Eccl. Hist.* I vi 1-16.
27. *Reply to Faustus* XXIII 2, 3, 4.
28. *Ib.* III 3.
29. *Ib.* X 5.
30. XVIII 1.
31. *Trypho* LXXVIII.
32. *Contra Celsum* I li.
33. Luke 2:39.
34. Judges 13:5.
35. Matt. 2:6.
36. Luke 2:1.
37. *Ib.* 2:18-19.
38. *Ib.* 1:28-33.
39. *Ib.* 1:46-55.
40. *Ib.* 2:33.
41. *Ib.* 2:49.
42. *Ib.* 2:25.
43. *Ib.* 2:35.
44. *Ib.* 1:71.
45. *Contra Celsum* V lxi.
46. Cf. Augustine, *Letter LXXV* iv 13.
47. Luke 1:35.
48. *Ib.* 1:42-43.
49. *Ib.* 1:32-33.
50. *Ib.* 1:46-55.
51. *Trypho* LXXVIII.

CHAPTER VI: 471
REVELATION

1. Rev. 22:7, 10; 1:7.
2. Dan. 12:11.
3. Mark 13:14.
4. Rev. 1:10 ff.
5. Dan. 7:9, 13.
6. Rev. 1:13-14.
7. *Ib.* 2:9; 3:9.
8. *Ib.* 4:4-10.
9. *Ib.* 5:5-6.
10. *Ib.* 5:10.

11. *Ib.* 5:11.
12. *Ib.* 6:10.
13. *Ib.* 7:4.
14. Ezek. 9:4.
15. Rev. 7:9.
16. *Ib.* 11:2.
17. *Ib.* 11:15.
18. *Ib.* 11:18.
19. Dan. 10:1 ff.
20. Rev. 12:1 ff.
21. *Ib.* 12:4.
22. *Ib.* 12:5-6.
23. *Ib.* 12:14. Cf. Dan. 7:25.
24. Dan. 7:13.
25. Rev. 13:11.
26. *Ib.* 13:18.
27. *Ib.* 14:4.
28. *Ib.* 14:10.
29. *Ib.* 14:14.
30. *Ib.* 16:17.
31. *Ib.* 17:1-2.
32. *Ib.* 17:3.
33. *Ib.* 17:6.
34. *Ib.* 17:10.
35. *Ib.* 17:11.
36. *Ib.* 17:12.
37. *Ib.* 17:14.
38. *Ib.* 17:16.
39. *Ib.* 18:4.
40. *Ib.* 18:12-24.
41. *Ib.* 19:2.
42. *Ib.* 19:7.
43. *Ib.* 19:15-16.
44. *Ib.* 19:17-18.
45 *Ib.* 19:19-20.
46. *Ib.* 19:20.
47. *Ib.* 20:2.
48. *Ib.* 20:8-9.
49. *Ib.* 20:10.
50. *Ib.* 20:11-15.
51. *Ib.* 21:1.
52. *Ib.* 20:15.
53. *Ib.* 21:1-2.
54. *Ib.* 22:16.

CHAPTER VII: 480

CHRISTIAN ESCHATOLOGY

1. *Lives of Illustrious Men* XVIII.
2. *Trypho* LXXX.
3. *Against Heresies* V xxxii-xxxvi.
4. *Refutation of All Heresies* VIII xii.
5. *Catechetical Lectures* XVI 8.
6. *Against Marcion* III xxiv.
7. Discussion by Dionysius, preserved by Eusebius, *Eccl. Hist.* VII xxiv-xxv.
8. *De Principiis* II xi 2.
9. *Commentary on Daniel* 5, 6.
10. *Epistle* LV 1, 2, 10.
11. *Divine Institutes* V v-vi.
12. *Ib.* vii.
13. *Ib.* VI x, xi.
14. *Ib.* VII xiv.
15. *Ib.* VII xvii-xix.
16. *Ib.* xxiii.
17. *Ib.* xxiv.
18. *Ib.* xxv.
19. *Ib.* xxvi.
20. *History of the Arians* 74.
21. *Catechetical Lectures* XV 8.
22. *Ib.* XV 7.
23. *Ib.* XV 12.
24. *Ib.* XV 22.
25. *Invective against Constantius.*
26. *Dialogues* II xiv.
27. *Epistle* III xxix.
28. *Ib.* II xlviii.
29. *Epistle* VIII xxxiii.
30. Cf. Bks. XVIII-XXI of *The City of God.*
31. *Ib.* XX vii.
32. *Ib.* XX vii.
33. *Ib.* XX ix.
34. *Ib.* XX xxx.
35. *Apocalypse of Peter* B 21-24.
36. *Discourse against the Greeks* 1.
37. *Stromata* VII.
38. *Homily on Numbers* XXV.
39. *De Anima* LVIII.
40. *De Civitate Dei* XXI xiii.
41. *Ib.* xvi.
42. 12:43-45.

CHAPTER VIII: 492

THE FOURTH GOSPEL

1. *Lives of Illustrious Men* IX.
2. John 20:31.
3. *Ib.* 3:18.
4. *Ib.* 8:12.
5. *Ib.* 8:42.
6. *Ib.* 8:58.
7. *Ib.* 10:30.
8. *Ib.* 14:9.
9. *Ib.* 16:15.
10. *Ib.* 1:45; 2:1, 2.
11. *Ib.* 7:41-42.
12. *Ib.* 3:36.
13. *Ib.* 20:29.
14. *Ib.* 2:5.

15. *Ib.* 2:12.
16. *Ib.* 19:25.
17. *Ib.* 5:27-30.
18. *Ib.* 3:4.
19. *Ib.* 14:2-3.
20. *Ib.* 18:36.
21. *Ib.* 13:34.

CHAPTER IX: 498
PRIMITIVE CHRISTOLOGY

1. *Epistle of Barnabas* IV 2.
2. *Ib.* XV 10.
3. *Ib.* XIV; XV.
4. *Ib.* IV 10, 13.
5. To the Corinthians.
6. *Ib.* XXIV.
7. *Ib.* LVIII.
8. *Ib.*
9. "Ephesians" IV 9-10.
10. "Trallians" II 2-3.
11. "Smyrneans" II 2.
12. "Philadelphians" II 7.
13. "Phillipians" III 1.
14. "Trallians" II 10-12.
15. "Smyrneans" II 16.
16. "Philadelphians" II 20.
17. *Ib.* 21.
18. II.

CHAPTER X: 503
THE SEARCH FOR AUTHORITY

1. *Barnabas* V 9.
2. Numbers 19:2-7.
3. *Barnabas* VII 4-7.
4. *Ib.* XI 3.
5. *First Apology* LV.
6. *Trypho* CV.
7. *Ib.* CXXXIV.
8. *Hortatory Address to the Greeks* XXIX-XXX.
9. *Stromata* I xxi.
10. *Trypho* LXV.
11. *Ib.* LXXX.
12. *Oration of Eusebius* I 6.
13. *Stromata* VII xvi.
14. "Romans" III 7.
15. "Magnesians" II 8.
16. "Ephesians" II 4.
17. *Prescription against Heretics* XV, XIX, XXXVII.
18. *Ib.* XXI.
19. *Epistles* LIV 5; XXVI 1.
20. *The Unity of the Church* 6.

21. *Epistle* LI 24.
22. *Apology* 46.
23. *Epistle* XLVIII 2.
24. *Epistle* LVI 3.

CHAPTER XI: 512
SEMITIC CHRISTIANITY

1. *Against Heresies* I xxvi 1.
2. *Refutation of All Heresies* VII xxi.
3. *Against All Heresies* III.
4. *Eccl. Hist.* VII xxiv-xxv.
5. *Against All Heresies* I xxvi 2; III xxi 1.
6. *Refut. of All Heresies* VII xxii.
7. *Homilies* XVI xvi.
8. *Ib.* IX xx; X iv; XI xvi.
9. Matt. 15:21-28.
10. *Homilies* II xix.
11. Matt. 15:24, 26.
12. Mark 7:24-30.
13. John 10:16.
14. Matt. 15:24.
15. John 4:2-26.
16. *Homilies* IX ix.
17. Acts 15:20, 29.
18. *Homilies* XII xxxii-xxxiii.
19. *Ib.* XV vii.
20. *Ib.* XV viii.
21. *Ib.* XV ix.
22. *Ib.* XV x.

CHAPTER XII: 520
HELLENIC GNOSTICISM: MARCION

1. *Eccl. Hist.* V xiii.
2. *Against Heresies* I xxiii 1-4.
3. *Against All Heresies* I.
4. *Homilies* II xxii-xxv.
5. *Against Heresies* I xxiii.
6. *Homilies* II xxxviii.
7. *Ib.* II xxxix.
8. *Ib.* III ix.
9. *Ib.* III liv.
10. *Against All Heresies* VI.
11. *Against Heresies* I xxvii 2.
12. Edited by M. R. James, *Apocryphal New Testament*.
13. *Homilies* XVIII v.
14. *Against Marcion* III viii.
15. *Ib.*
16. *Ib.* IV xxxviii.
17. *Diatessaron* XXXIV 18.
18. *Against Marcion* V x.

19. *Ib.*
20. *On the Resurrection of the Flesh* XVIII.
21. *Against Marcion* I xxix.
22. *Ib.*
23. *Exhortation to Chastity* IX.
24. *Eccl. Hist.* V xviii.
25. Irenaeus, *Against Heresies* I xxviii.
26. Tertullian, *Against All Heresies* VI.

CHAPTER XIII: 532

MYSTICAL-PYTHAGOREAN GNOSTICISM

1. *Stromata* VII xvii.
2. *Treatise against the Valentinians* I.
3. *Ib.* IV.
4. Irenaeus, *Against Heresies* I xx 1.
5. *Against the Valentinians* I.
6. *Stromata* VI vi.
7. *Refutation* I ii.
8. *Against Heresies* I xxiv 2.
9. *Ib.*
10. *Ib.* 3. Cf. also Tertullian, *Against All Heresies* I.
11. Irenaeus, *Against Heresies* I xxiv 4.
12. *Against All Heresies* I.
13. *Stromata* II iii.
14. *Ib.* IV xii.
15. *Ib.* V i.
16. *Ib.* IV xii.
17. Irenaeus, *Against Heresies* I vii 5.
18. *Against the Valentinians* XXXII.
19. Irenaeus, *Against Heresies* I xxi 1-4.
20. *Stromata* V xiv.

CHAPTER XIV: 539

THE MONARCHIANS

1. *Against Praxeas* III.
2. *According to John* 10:30.
3. *Against the Heresy of Noetus* 1.
4. *Against Praxeas* I.
5. *Ib.* II.
6. *Ib.* XX.
7. Isaiah 45:5; John 10:30; 14:9-10.
8. *Against Praxeas* XXIX.
9. *Refutation* IX vii.

CHAPTER XV 545

MANICHAEISM: THE GREAT GNOSTIC SYNTHESIS

1. *The Acts of the Disputation with Manes* 36.
2. *Ib.* 54.
3. Archelaus, *Disputation* 5.
4. Augustine, *Reply to Faustus* V 8.
5. *Letter* XV.
6. *On the Tenets of the Manichaeans.*
7. *Sermons* XXIV v.
8. Cf. "Manichaeism" in the Schaff-Herzog *Ency. of Religious Knowledge.* For a summary of the *Fihrist,* cf. "Introductory Essay" to Augustine's writings against the Manichees, *N&PNF,* First Series, IV, whence our quotations derive. Cf. also article on Manes in Scribner's *Ency. of Religion and Ethics.*
9. *Reply to Faustus* XXI 1.
10. *Fihrist.*
11. *On the Tenets* III.
12. *Disputation* 8.
13. Archelaus, *Disputation* 9.
14. Alexander, *On the Tenets* XXIV.
15. Augustine, *Disputation against Fortunatus* 19-20.
16. *Concerning the Nature of God* 18.
17. *Ib.* 34.
18. *Reply to Faustus* XVIII 3.
19. *Ib.* XXXIII 3.
20. *Ib.* XVIII 3.
21. *Ib.* III 1.
22. *Ib.* VII 1.
23. *Ib.* IV 1.
24. *Ib.* VI 1.
25. *Ib.* VI 2.
26. *Ib.* V 1.
27. Romans 1:3.
28. *Reply* IX.
29. *Ib.* X 1.
30. II Cor. 5:16.
31. *Reply* XI.
32. *Ib.* XII 1.
33. *Ib.* VII 7.
34. *Ib.* XII 13, 14, 15.
35. *Ib.* XII 39.
36. *Ib.* XIV 1.
37. *Ib.* XV 1.
38. *Ib.* XVI 1, 2.
39. *Ib.* XVI 14.
40. *Ib.* XVII 1.
41. *Ib.* XVII 2.
42. *Ib.* XIX 6.
43. *Ib.* XXIII 9.
44. *Ib.* XVI 25.
45. *Ib.* XXIX 1.
46. *Ib.* XXX 1.
47. I Tim. 4:1-3.
48. *Reply* XXX 4.
49. *Ib.*
50. *Ib.* XXXIII 1.

CHAPTER XVI: 562
THE TRINITARIAN CONTROVERSY

1. I Cor. 8:6.
2. Col. 1:15 ff.
3. *Confessions* VII 13,14.
4. This may have become current even in the third century, but we find it reproduced for the first time by Rufinus about 408 in *A Commentary on the Apostles' Creed.*
5. *Against Heresies* I x.
6. *Against Praxeas* II.
7. *Ib.* IX.
8. *A Treatise against Hermogenes* III.
9. *Letter CCX* 5.
10. *Against Praxeas* III, IV.
11. *Ib.* VIII.
12. *In Prescription against Heretics* XIII.
13. *Against Praxeas* II.
14. II Constantinople, 553.
15. *Contra Celsum* VIII xv.
16. *De Principiis* I ii 2,3.
17. *Ib.* I ii 8.
18. *Ib.* I ii 10.
19. *Ib.* I ii 13.
20. *Ib.* I iii 7.
21. *Ib.* I iii 8.
22. *De Trinitate* IV 12, 13.
23. Arian Epistles, *Deposition of Arius* II 3.
24. Theodoret, *Eccl. Hist.* I iv.
25. Socrates, *Eccl. Hist.* I vii.
26. Eusebius, *Life of Constantine* II lxviii, lxxi.
27. *Ib.* III xii.
28. Theodoret, *Eccl. Hist.* I vi.
29. Socrates, *Eccl. Hist.* I viii.
30. Letter of Eusebius, *N&PNF* II:IV, *Council of Nicaea*, pp. 74-76.
31. Theodoret, III iv.
32. Sozomen, *Eccl. Hist.* VI ii.
33. *Eccl. Hist.* II xv.
34. *Letters*, VI xiv.
35. *De Synodis* of Hilary of Poitiers.
36. *Epistles* XIII xxxviii.
37. *Life of Constantine* II lxi.
38. *Letters* CCXLIII.
39. *The Book on the Spirit* XXX 77-78.
40. Socrates, I xxiii.
41. *Ib.* I xxiv.
42. *Ib.* II xvi.
43. *Ib.* II xxii-xxiii.
44. *Ib.* II xxxviii.
45. *Ib.* II xxviii.
46. *Ib.* Cf. also Sozomen IV xvi.
47. Gregory Nazianzen, *Oration against the Arians* XXXIII vi, vii.
48. Sozomen, III vii.
49. Sozomen IV xxvii; Theodoret II v.
50. Documents of I Constantinople, *N&PNF* II:XIV.
51. *De Trinitate* I 8.
52. *Ib.* IV 27.
53. *Ib.* IV 30.
54. *Ib.* X 18.
55. *Schaff-Herzog Ency.*: article on "Symbolics."
56. Matt. 25:42-45.

CHAPTER XVII: 583
CHRISTOLOGICAL HERESIES

1. Died in 374, was bishop of Ancyra, which is modern Angora.
2. Bishop of Sirmium, died 376.
3. Cf. Vincent of Lerin, *Commonitory* XII 33; Athanasius, *Discourses against the Arians.*
4. Bishop of Laodicea in 362.
5. Cf. Philostorgius, *Eccl. Hist.* VIII ii and VII xv.
6. Socrates II xlvi.
7. Gregory Nazianzen, *Letter to Cledonius.*
8. *Letter to Nectarius*, 383.
9. *N&PNF*, Documents of the Third Ecumenical Council, 431, Vol. XIV.
10. *N&PNF* II:III, *Works* of Theodoret.
11. *N&PNF* II:XIV: Documents of the Third Ecumenical Council.
12. Mark 3:31-35.
13. *N&PNF* II:III, *Prolegomena* V.
14. *N&PNF* II:XIV, Documents dealing with the Fourth Ecumenical Council.
15. *Ib.* Documents dealing with the Sixth Ecumenical Council.
16. *Ib.*

CHAPTER XVIII: 595
PERSECUTION

1. *History of Rationalism* II iv, Vol. II pp. 10-11.
2. *Sacred History* II xxxiii.
3. *First Apology* I-XV.
4. *Plea for the Christians* III.
5. *Apology* 2.
6. *Ad Scapulam* 2.

7. *Apology* 46.
8. *Apology* 32; *Ad Scapulam* 2.
9. *Contra Celsum* VIII lxix.
10. *Ib.* VIII xvii.
11. *Ib.* V lxiii.
12. *Ib.*
13. *Divine Institutes* V xx.
14. *Apology* 50.
15. Pontius, *Life and Passion of Cyprian* 19.
16. *Ib.* 14-15.
17. *Ib.* 17.
18. *Ib.* 16, 17, 19.
19. *Eccl. Hist.* VIII i-vi.
20. *Decline and Fall of the Roman Empire* XVI.
21. *Eccl. Hist.* I v.
22. Eusebius, *Life of Constantine* II lvi.
23. *Letter to Nectarius.*
24. *Sermons* LXXXII ii-iii.
25. *Ib.* XVI iii.
26. Eusebius, *Life of Constantine* III liv-lv.
27. *Ib.* liv.
28. *Ib.* lvi.
29. Sozomen II xxxii.
30. *Ib.*
31. Eusebius, *Life of Constantine* III lxiv-lxvi.
32. *Ib.*
33. *Circular Letter* 3.
34. *Eccl. Hist.* II iii.
35. Sozomen, V vii.
36. Socrates, III iii.
37. *Ib.* III xiii-xiv.
38. *Ib.* VII xv.
39. *History of the Arians* 64, 68.
40. *Letters* CCX 6.
41. Cf. Theodoret, III xv; Socrates, III xx; Sozomen, V xxii; and Milman, *History of the Jews* XX ii.
42. Socrates, V xvi.
43. *Ib.* VII xiii.
44. *Letter* VII.
45. St. Augustine.

CHAPTER XIX: 607
ST. AUGUSTINE

1. *Letter* VII.
2. *Confessions* XI 15 ff.
3. *Letter* CCXIII, written in 426, in which he appoints his successor to the episcopate of Hippo.
4. *Letter* CXCV.
5. *De Principiis* II viii 1.
6. *Ib.* I viii 3.
7. *Ib.* III iii 5.
8. *Ib.*
9. *Ib.* III vi 3-6.
10. *Ib.* I viii 3.
11. *Ib.* III i 21.
12. *Against the Manichaeans* 26.
13. *Ib.* 33.
14. *Against Fortunatus* 21, 15.
15. *On the Proceedings of Pelagius* 65.
16. *Against Two Letters of the Pelagians* IV 16.
17. *Ib.* III 5.
18. The doctrine that every soul derives in a direct line of descent from Adam and is therefore not an individual creation.
19. *Letter* CLXVI.
20. *Against Two Letters* I 10.
21. *On Marriage and Concupiscence* II 44, 49.
22. *Against Two Letters* II 2.
23. *On Marriage and* II 33.
24. *Ib.* II 15.
25. *On the Merits and Forgiveness of Sins* II 15.
26. *Ib.* II 36.
27. *On Marriage and* I 26.
28. *On the Grace of Christ* II 45.
29. *Ib.* II 34.
30. *Against Two Letters* I 30.
31. *On Marriage and* II 25.
32. *On the Merits and Forgiveness* II 28.
33. *On the Nature of Grace* 39.
34. *On the Spirit and the Letter* 52.
35. *On the Nature of Grace* 4.
36. *Ib.* 5, 25.
37. *Ib.* 54.
38. *Ib.* 63.
39. *Ib.* 71-80.
40. *Treatise Concerning Man's Perfection* 9, 14.
41. *Ib.* 13.
42. *On the Grace of Christ* I 5.
43. *Ib.* 13.
44. *Ib.* 15, 17.
45. *Ib.* 26.
46. *Ib.* 52.
47. *Predestination of the Saints* 7.
48. *Ib.* 3.
49. *Ib.* 11.
50. *Ib.* 14.
51. *Ib.* 19.
52. *The Gift of Perseverance* 1.

53. *On Marriage* I 19.
54. *Ib.* I 11.
55. *Ib.* I 17.
56. *Seven Books on Baptism* VI 3.
57. *Three Books in Answer to Petilian* I 27.
58. *Ib.* II 134.
59. *Letter XCIII* 50.
60. *Correction of the Donatists* 36.
61. *Three Books* II 134.
62. *Seven Books on Baptism* VI 12.
63. I Cor. 6:9.
64. I Cor. 5:11-13.
65. Gal. 5:19-20.
66. Matt. 18:15-18.
67. *Three Books* III 32.
68. *Seven Books* VII 7.
69. *Ib.* III 13.
70. *Ib.* III 16.
71. *Ib.* III 23.
72. *Ib. Three Books* II 194, 216, 220.
73. *Ib.* II 175, 177, 183.
74. *Ib.* II 202.
75. *Letter XCIII* 5; reference is to Luke 14:23.
76. *Correction of the Donatists* 26.
77. *Ib.* 7.
78. *Three Books* II 217.
79. *The Correction of the Donatists* 8.
80. *Letter XCIII* 8.
81. *Letter C* 1.
82. *Letter LXXXVIII* 8.
83. *The Correction of the Donatists* 12.
84. *Letter LXXXVII* 8.
85. *Letter XLIV* 9.
86. *The Correction of the Donatists* 24.

CHAPTER XX: 631

LIFE UNDER THE CATHOLIC CHURCH

1. I Cor. 6:9-10.
2. I Cor. 5:1.
3. *Contra Celsum* III lix.
4. *Ib.* I lvii.
5. *On the Lapsed* 6.
6. *On Pilgrimages.*
7. *Institutes of the Coenobia* II iii; IV xii; *Conferences* XVIII v.
8. *Ib.* vii.
9. *Confessions* VIII 29.
10. *Banquet of the Virgins* I 1.
11. *Letter XLVIII* 21.
12. I Tim. 3:2-4.
13. *Refutation* IX vii.
14. Sozomen, I xxiii; Socrates, I xi.

15. Canon IV.
16. Canon XXV.
17. Canon LXX.
18. *N&PNF* II:XIV.
19. Canon III.
20. Canon XXI.
21. *Letters CLXXXVIII, CXCIX,* and *CCXVII* to Amphilochius on the Canons.
22. *Letter CCXVII* lvi.
23. *Ib.* lvii.
24. *Ib.* lviii.
25. *Ib.* lxi.
26. *Ib.* lxvii, lxxix.
27. *Ib.* lxxiii.
28. *Sacred History* II li.
29. *Conferences,* Third Part XVIII v.
30. *Letter LXXXI* to the Consul Nomus.
31. XXII.
32. *Life of Antony* 5.
33. *Ib.* 47.
34. *Ib.* 66.
35. *Dialogue* II ix.
36. *Life of St. Martin* X.
37. *Ib.* XXII.
38. *Ib.* XXIV.
39. *Commonitory* 64.
40. *Epistle* III iii.
41. *Ib.* II xxxvii.
42. *Ib.* VII iv.
43. *Ib.* VII xxviii and IX cxxii.
44. *Ib.* I xxxvi.
45. *Ib.* I xliv.
46. *Ib.* V xli.
47. *Ib.* V lviii.
48. *Ib.* II xxxii.
49. *Ib.* V viii.
50. *Ib.* III xxxviii; VI xxxii.
51. *Ib.* IV xxvi.
52. *Ib.* XI lxxvi.
53. *Adversus Gentes* VI 1.
54. *Octavius* XXXII.
55. *Contra Celsum* III xv.
56. Eusebius, *Life of Constantine* II xlv.
57. *Letters,* XI xiii.
58. *N&PNF* II:XIV, Documents concerning the Concillabulum.

CHAPTER XXI: 646

THE DEVELOPMENT OF THE PAPACY

1. *Letter LXXXVI.*
2. *On Modesty* 1.
3. *Epistle LXXIV* 17.

4. *Address to the Seventh Council of Carthage.*
5. Canon VI.
6. Cf. Socrates, II xv; Sozomen, III x.
7. *Letters,* Leo the Great, XXI i.
8. *Letters,* Theodoret, CXIII.
9. Leo, *Letters* XCVIII ii, from the Council of Chalcedon to Leo
10. *Ib.* XCVIII 1.
11. *Ib.* XCVIII iv.
12. *N&PNF* II:XIV. Documents of the Fifth Ecumenical Council.
13. *Ib.* Session VI.
14. *Epistles* of Gregory, V xx.
15. *Ib.* III xxx.
16. *Ib.* V xviii.
17. *Ib.* V xliii.
18. *Ib.* V xx.
19. *Ib.* VII xxxi.
20. *Ib.* VII xxxiii.
21. *N&PNF* II:XIV. Documents of the Sixth Ecumenical Council.
22. *Ib.*
23. *Ib.* Documents of the Seventh Ecumenical Council.
24. *Ib.*

CHAPTER XXII: 657

THE CHRISTIAN MYSTERIES

1. Lectures XIX 1, 2.
2. *Ib.* XX 2, 3.
3. *Ib.* 4.
4. *Lectures* XXII 3.
5. Vol. XXIV.

INDEX

Abhisasta, 115
Abraham, 221, 315, 316, 345, 382, 461, 493, 514
Acdestis, 52, 53
Achaemenides, the 84, 186
Achamoth, con, 536
Achilles, 34, 66
Acts, 461, 522, 525
Acts of Andrew, 548
Acts of John, 548
Acts of Paul, 523, 548
Acts of Paul and Thecla, 439, 560
Acts of Peter, 548, 646
Acts of Pilate, 463
Acts of Thomas, 548
Adam, 199, 461
Adam, name for Attis, 56
Adonis, 7, 37, 44, 51, 53, 56, 63, 296 301
Adoptionism, 540, 542-3
Adoptionist Christologies, 449
Aeschylus, 5, 71
Aesculapius, 297, 322, 602
Aëtius, the Ungodly, 574
Afghanistan, Buddhism in, 141
Africanus, 463, 464
Against Marcion, 520
Agamemnon, 66
Agatho, 592
Agave, 44-5, 46
Age of Reason, 555
Agni, 108, 109
Agrippa, 206, 306
Ahab, 209
Aharman, 88, 91, 93, 94, 95, 96, 97, 98, 99, 103, 104
Ahasuerus, 195, 222
Ahriman, 88, 91, 93, 94, 95, 96, 97, 98, 99, 106, 186, 187, 190, 191, 379, 380, 403
Ahrimanic nature, 165
Ahuramazda, 83, 85, 86, 88, 89, 91, 93, 94, 95-6, 99, 186
Aidoneus, 64, 180
Akiba, Rabbi, 206
Alaric, 61, 575
Albigenses, 548
Albinus, 306
Alcibiades, 71

Alexander, Bishop, 569, 570
Alexander Jannaeus, 203-4, 260, 269, 273, 274, 282
Alexander of Lycopolis, 549
Alexander the Great, 85, 86, 180, 223, 261
Alexandria, Mithraeum of, 191
Alogoi, 540
Alpheus, 326
Amazons, 49
Ambrose, 506, 609,
Amelekites, 200
Amen, name of, expunged, 197
Amenhotep III, 197
Amenhotep IV, 197-199
Ameshapentas, 93, 186, 187, 256
Amish, 417
Ammonites, 200, 233
Amos, 212
Anahita, 108
Ananda, 141
Ananias, 206, 266
Ananias and Sapphira, 429
Ananus, 306
Anaxagoras, 562
Ancient of Days, 224
Andrew the disciple, 310, 319, 325
Angra Mainyu, 88, 89, 90, 91-2, 93
Ani, 47, 82
Anna, 408, 467
Annas, 277
Anne de Beaupre, St., 322
Anomoeans, 574
Anquetil-Duperron, 86
Ante-Nicene Library, 271, 659
Antichrist, 452, 454, 471, 476, 477, 486, 487, 501, 596, 640, 652
Antioch, Synod of, 575
Antiochus Epiphanes, 195, 203, 222, 223, 224, 230, 395, 414, 452, 473
Antitheses, The, 523
Antonia, the, 206
Antonines, the, 632
Antony, the hermit, 13, 118, 506, 604, 622, 639
Anubis, 3, 178
Anugita, 108, 121
Apastamba, 107
Apelles, 530-1
Apep, 15, 162
Aphrodite, 28, 31, 36-7, 75, 308

Aphrodite-Adonis cult, 24, 28, 29, 30
Aphrodite-cult, 53, 75
Aphrodisiacs, 31
Apis, 49, 180
Apocalypse, 211-12, 354, 394-7
Apocalypse of Abraham, 319
Apocalypse of Baruch, 426
Apocalypse of Peter, 488, 489
Apollo, 79
Apollodorus, 41, 42, 47
Apollonarii, 584-5, 586, 589, 591, 600
Apollonius of Tyana, 157
Apology of Aristides, The, 501-2
Apostolic Church, the, 123, 482, 507, 622
Apuleius, 54, 69, 179-80
Arabians, 83
Arada, 138
Archelaus, 158, 545, 551
Archigallus, 58
Archytus, 157
Ardashir, 85-6
Ardvi Sura Anahita, 89
Areopagitica, 424
Argonautica, 38, 73
Arhats, 129, 130, 139, 143, 146, 147, 152, 153
Arian, Arianism, Arians, 61, 486, 544, 568-78, 585, 603, 604, 619, 645, 649
Aridaeus, 169
Aristides, 501, 502
Aristobulus I, 273, 274
Aristobulus II, 204, 235, 267, 269, 270, 271, 273, 274, 277, 278, 282
Aristophanes, 166
Aristotle, 158, 417
Arius, 568-9, 569-70, 572
Armageddon, 96, 101, 105, 219, 476, 477
Arminius, 609
Arnobius, 46, 52, 54, 55, 57, 69, 70, 77, 505, 643
Arsaces, 84
Arsacids, 182
Artaxerxes, 222
Artemis, 53, 63
Aryan-Sumerians, 3, 4
Aryans, 83, 107, 110
Ashavahisto, 87
Ashtoreth, 209, 210
Asmoneans, 203, 204, 233, 234, 235, 252, 260, 269, 270, 272, 273, 278
Asoka, King, 141-2
Assyria, Assyrians, 83, 195, 196, 200, 201, 202, 218, 220

Astarte, 52, 63
Astarte-Adonis cult, 38
Astarte-Tammuz myth, 65
Aston of Croton, 159
Athanasian Creed, 580-2, 659
Athanasians, 568, 572, 577, 603
Athanasius, 13, 486, 567, 575, 604, 648-9
Atharva-Veda, 107, 123
Athena, 46, 63, 80, 308, 588
Athenagoras, 564, 597
Athenians, the Demeter of the, 60
Atman, 117, 121, 122
Aton, 197, 199
Attila, 575
Attis, 51-9, 75, 296, 306, 309
Attis-Cybele cult, 51-9, 182, 184, 365
Augustine, St., 171, 317, 318, 464-5, 487, 490, 506, 549, 554-5, 556, 563, 575, 578-9, 607-29, 633, 635, 648, 649
Augustus Caesar, 301, 360, 467
Auharmazd, 103
Aurelian, 185
Aurelius, Marcus, 305, 596, 662
Aushedar-Mah, 96, 100, 104
Avesta, 84, 85, 86
Azazel, 256, 319
Azi-Dahak, 94, 101, 103, 478

Baal, 209, 628
Baalim, 209
Babylon, 84, 195, 210, 213, 220, 476, 477
Babylonian, Babylonians, 83, 196, 200, 202, 222, 223, 224, 257, 259
Bacchanals, 46-8, 435
Bacchantes, 44, 45, 48, 77
Bacchoi, 46, 168, 172
Bacchus, 70, 81, 172, 297, 300
Bacon, Francis, dream of, 379
Bahman Yast, 98, 260
Bahram I, executed Manes, 545
Bahrdt, 287
Baluchistan, 141
Banus, 240, 335
Baptists, 480
Bar-Cochba, 200, 206, 207, 213, 233
Barnabas, 432, 443, 444, 500
Barnabas, The Epistle of, 481, 499, 503, 504
Bartimeus, 386
Baruch, 222
Basil, St., 156, 568, 576, 604, 634
Basilideans, 533, 537-8
Basilides, 532, 533, 534, 535

— 696 —

Baudhayana, 107
Bauer, Bruno, 304, 305-6
Beelzebub, 372
Behistun, 87
Belial, 250, 262, 279
Belshazzar, 222
Berenice, 206
Bergson, Henri, 607
Bhagavad-Gita, 108, 121, 134
Bhagavat, the, 139
Bhikkunis, 140
Bhikkhus or Bhikkshus, 139, 145, 146
Bimbasara, King, 139
Bindumati, 127
Bios, 40
"Blasphemia, The," 574
Blessed One, 146
Bodhi tree, the, 138, 139
Bodhisattva, 131
Bogomiles, 547
Boniface I, 649
Book of Enoch, The, 194, 227, 230, 252, 253-61, 271, 277, 278, 290, 318, 373, 377, 385, 389, 395, 411, 412, 413, 426, 453
Book of Noah, 254
Book of the Dead, The, 4, 9, 14, 18
Book of the Jubilees, The, 227, 251, 252, 254
Book of the Maccabees, The, 490
Brahman, 109, 110, 122
Brahmanas, 77, 101, 109, 110, 113, 117-8, 120, 123, 124, 126, 128, 135, 143, 144, 147, 150, 161, 163, 168, 171, 350, 416
Brahmanic, 109, 119, 128, 129, 132, 148, 158, 160, 489, 608, 637
Brahmanic-Buddhist eschatology, 417
Brahmanic-Pythagorean doctrine, 216
Brahmanism, 66, 91, 107-25, 127, 131, 138, 142, 154, 162, 164, 510, 596
Brandes, Georg, 304
Bromius, 37, 308
Brother Joseph, 322
Bryce, 253
Buck, Pearl, 420
Buddha, 147, 149, 213, 299, 409, 418
Buddhism, 24, 66, 86, 122, 125, 126-54, 163, 172, 412, 416, 445, 545, 606, 632
Buddhist, Buddhists, 77, 109, 124, 126-54, 156, 158, 160, 208, 241, 262, 284-6, 328, 329, 330, 331, 334, 335, 338, 339, 340, 342, 344, 347, 350, 354, 358, 362, 372, 373, 378, 398, 407, 412, 413, 415, 420, 435, 448, 527, 552, 584, 608, 633, 637
Buddhist-Pythagoreans, 417, 496
Budini, 38
Bundahis, The, 102, 260, 478, 486
Burrows, Millar, 227, 247
Byblus, 7, 28, 38
Byzantines, 38

Cadmus, 42, 43
Caiphas, 277, 404
Calliope, 75
Callixtus, 505, 542, 634
Calvin, 629
Calvinist doctrine, 615
Canaanites, 200
Canon Law of Catholic Church, 636-7
Carbon-14 Process, 227
Carchemish, battle of, 202
Carpenter, Edward, 304
Carthage, 54
Caste system of India, 110, 112
Cataphrygians, 602
Cathari, 547-8
Catholic Apostolic Church, English, 427-8
Catholic Christianity, 71, 106, 596, 601
Catholic Church, 57, 59, 92, 124, 125, 164, 192, 291, 338, 437, 487, 508, 509, 510, 511, 547, 588, 606, 613, 617, 624-5, 631-45, 653, 656, 657, 662
Catholic Epistles, The, 432, 453-5, 525
Catholic hierarchy, 113, 153
Catholicism, 192, 510, 628-9
Catholics, 47, 91, 123-4, 168, 177, 271, 482, 535
Cecaelianus, 620
Celeus, 63
Celibate movement in Catholic Church, 633-37
Celsus, 281, 296, 463, 567, 597-8, 632, 645
Cephalus, 168
Cerberus, 62
Cerdo, Cerdonites, 437, 438, 493, 522-3, 524, 525, 529, 648
Ceres, 81, 179
Ceres-Proserpina ritual, 82
Cerinthian, Cerinthians, 432, 481, 493, 501, 512-3
Cerinthus, 483, 492, 512-3
Chaldean-Jewish myth, 256
Chaldeans, 84, 94, 161, 182
Charles, R. H., 271-2, 276

— 697 —

Charops, 73
Chasid-Zadokites, 247
Chasidim, Chasids, Chasid, 203, 230, 231, 247, 248, 254, 258,
Children of Darkness, 190, 337, 338, 339, 341, 379, 380, 518
Childern of Light, 190, 341, 380, 383
Chiliasm, 481, 483
Chiliastic kingdom, 366, 432, 455, 478, 486
Christ, 55, 101, 116, 183, 184, 226, 288, 292, 296, 298, 307, 308, 310, 315, 369, 383, 391, 411, 435, 462-3, 492, 502 564, 583
Christ, the Gnostic, 524-5, 526
Christ, the Jewish, 474, 477, 479, 498
Christ, the Manichaean, 560
Christ-Jesus, 493, 501, 503, 514, 572, 584
Christ-Logos, 583
Christ-Messiah, 346, 477, 478, 495
Christian Church, 277, 385, 430-33, 499
Christian Fathers, 182-3
Christian mystery, the, 657-62
Christian Science, 322
Christian scriptures, 489
Christianity, 23, 58, 59, 69, 71, 91, 101, 105, 123-24, 128, 143, 153-4, 178, 182, 183, 184, 191-2, 207, 213, 216, 226, 287, 291, 295, 295-6, 297, 301, 302, 306, 308-9, 314, 338, 366, 368, 387, 397, 399, 416, 418, 426, 429, 432, 433, 461, 463, 489, 495, 505, 506, 510, 531, 537, 539, 547, 563, 600, 607, 619, 620-1, 629, 645, 654-5, 662
Christianity, Jewish, 334, 432, 479, 498, 501, 511, 513-4
Christians, 47, 99, 121, 124, 181, 184, 191, 226, 271, 289, 299, 308, 338, 425-33, 452, 596-7, 597-8, 599-600
Christians, the Greek, 494
Christological heresies, 539, 583-94
Christology, Ebionite, 453, 465, 498-502, 539, 540
Chronicle of the Jewish Kings, by Justus of Tiberias, 304
Chrysaphius, 589, 590
Cicero, 598, 638
Cinyras-Aphrodite myth, 51
Circe, 34
Circuits of Peter, The, 515
Circumcelliones, Donatist monks, 627, 628

Clemens Alexandrinus, 46, 69, 70, 77, 161, 306, 385, 490, 504, 506, 531, 532, 534 537
Clement, First Epistle of, 481, 500, 503, 631
Clement of Rome, 308
Clement, Recognitions of, 513, 514
Clement, Second Epistle of, 500, 513
Clement, the, of the *Homilies*, 517
Clementine Homilies, 505, 513, 514, 515, 517, 518-9, 521
Clementines, The, 513-4, 521
Coelestius, 610, 611, 616
Colossians, 439
Community of God, 250
Conciliabulum, 594, 643, 644
Confessions of St. Augustine, 555
Confucius, 160
Constans, 573, 574, 576
Constantina Augusta, 642
Constantine the Great, 178, 191, 416, 483, 506, 570, 572-3, 600, 601, 602, 603, 643
Constantine, son of Constantine the Great, 573
Constantine V, 643, 644
Constantine VI, 653
Constantinople, 23, 487, 648
Constantius, father of Constantine the Great, 600
Constantius, son of Constantine the Great, 486, 487, 573, 574, 576, 604
Contra Celsum, by Origen, 566
Contrat Social, 484
Corinthians, 439, 440, 446, 447, 450
Cornelius, 429, 431
Cornelius, pope of Rome, 647
Corybants, 51
Corybas, 37, 51, 56
Council of Ancyra, 636
Council of Arles, 620
Council of Carthage, 622, 635
Council of Chalcedon, 635
Council of Gangra, 635
Council of Orange, 619
Council of Trullo, 636
Covenanters, 250
Crati, the river, 164
Crete, 36
Cronos, 78
Croton, 155, 156, 164
Cybele, 44, 51, 55, 63, 67, 180, 189, 301, 588, 592
Cylon, 156

Cyprian, 484, 508, 510, 599, 619, 623, 624, 625-6, 633, 647, 648, 657
Cyrenius, 466, 467
Cyriacus, 652
Cyril of Alexandria, 585, 586-7, 591
Cyril of Jerusalem, 483, 486, 506, 657-9
Cyrus, 24, 83, 186, 220, 222
Cyrus, Pope, 502

Damascus, 201, 218
Damascus Document, The, 227, 247, 248, 250, 251, 257, 262, 265
Damasus, pope of Rome, 649
Daniel, 94, 99, 215, 221, 222, 223, 224, 232, 253, 256, 260, 318, 389, 395, 426, 452, 472, 473, 474, 475, 482, 486
Dardanus, attendant of Corybas, 51
Darius the Great, 83, 84, 86, 222
Das Leben Jesu, by Strauss, 305
David, 200, 208, 217, 218, 230, 231, 329, 391, 449, 461, 462, 464, 467, 468, 469, 471, 472, 493, 498, 501, 514, 557
Day of Blood, 56-57
De Civitate Dei, 629
Dead Sea Scrolls, 226, 227, 228, 246, 267, 272, 288, 341
Decius, Decian, 510, 596, 620
Deists, 366
Delight, daughter of Mara, 139
Delphian Oracle, 34, 38, 54
Demeter, 37, 39, 44, 53, 60, 61, 63, 64, 66, 67, 69, 71, 77, 78, 80, 81, 82, 178, 180, 301, 304, 308, 588, 593, 657
Demeter cult, 78
Demeter-Persephone cult, 28, 60-71, 72, 81
Demeter-Persephone mystery, 65, 66-70, 81
Demiurge, 524, 525, 525-7, 533, 536, 537, 562
Demonology, 640
Demophoon, 63
De Principiis, 566
De Quincey, Thomas, 287-8
Deutero-Isaiah, 220
Deuteronomy, 58
Devananda, 133
Devil, 184, 256
Dhamma, 145
Diaspora, 212, 473, 525

Diatessaron, 502
Didache, The, 340, 341, 401, 433, 434-6, 440, 452, 499, 517
Dindymeme, 52
Dinkard, The, 260
Diocletian, 185, 573, 596, 599-600, 620
Diodorus Siculus, 1, 5, 6-7, 33, 38, 39, 41-42, 42-3, 61, 63, 73, 75, 79, 161, 164
Diogenes Laërtius, 133, 156, 158, 159, 173
Diogenes the Cynic, 67
Dionysia, 53, 75
Dionysiac cult, 36, 37-8, 40, 42-3, 44-46, 48
Dionysiac festivals, 40, 69
Dionysiac mystery, 44, 48, 203, 435
Dionysiac myth, 72
Dionysiac sacrament, 46, 47, 163, 400
Dionysiacs, 31, 48, 49
Dionysius, Bishop, 483, 484, 512, 564
Dionysus, 32-50, 51, 52, 53, 56, 60, 61, 63, 68, 70, 72-82, 180, 184, 296, 299, 300, 301, 308, 309, 396, 463, 470, 657, 658
Dionysus, the cult of, 82, 160, 173, 297
Dionysus, the Orphic, 68
Dionysus, the Thracian, 47, 76
Dioscurus, Bishop, 589, 590, 649, 650
Disciples, the, of Jesus, 368, 370, 387, 408, 462
Disputation of Archelaus, 549
Divine Liturgy of James, 659
Divine Liturgy of the Holy Apostle and Evangelist Mark, 659
Docetism, 499
Domitian, 595
Domnus of Tyre, 690
Donatist, Donatism, Donatists, 487, 603, 619-23, 624, 640, 649
Dosidas, 46
Dositheus, 520, 521
Doukhobors, 342, 417
Doweyites, 417
Dukdaub, 87, 298
Dupont-Sommers, 227, 267, 288
Dynamism, 534

Easter, 57
Eastern Church, 59
Ebionites, 315, 317, 432, 453, 468, 469, 481, 492, 499, 500, 501, 505, 506, 512, 513, 514, 515, 516, 517, 518, 618

Ecclesiastes, 379
Ecumenical Councils, 593-4
Edict of Toleration, 600, 620
Edomites, 200, 233, 269
Egypt, 1, 201, 352
Egyptian longing for imortality, 1, 3, 4, 11-12
Egyptian-Dionysiac soteriology, 417
Egyptians, 202
Eight-Fold Path of Buddhism, 139, 141, 143
El, Phoenician god, 29
Eleazor the Zealot, 205
Eleusinia, 40, 60, 61, 62, 66, 71, 72, 77, 78, 81, 187, 500, 398
Eleusinian ritual, 223, 497
Eleusinian Orphism, 80
Eleusinians, 31, 51, 62, 67, 69, 82, 659
Eleusis, 61, 63, 64, 66, 67, 70, 77, 662
Elias, 321, 367, 640
Elijah, 196, 208-9, 212, 219, 220, 236, 316, 628
Eliseus, 326
Elisha, 212
Elizabeth, 468
Elysian Fields, 2, 15, 162
Elysium, 66, 67
Emerson, 122
Empedocles, 166
Enlightened One, 139
Enoch, 221, 232, 256
Epaminondas, 67, 157
Ephesians, 439
Epicurus, Epicureans, Epicureanism, 36, 231, 421, 662
Epiphanius, 315, 317, 461, 498
Epiphany, 184
Epistle to the Hebrews, 514
Erus, 169
Eschatology, 15-16, 24, 162-3, 214, 215, 494
Essene cult, the, 195, 468, 475
Essene-Christian faith, 413-4
Essene-Pythagorean, 286, 368, 391, 411
Essene-Zoroastrian sacrament, 277, 317, 350
Essenes, the, 105, 121, 153, 164, 176, 217, 225, 226-92, 316, 319, 325, 327, 330, 331, 332, 334, 335, 337, 338, 340, 342, 343, 344, 347, 350, 352, 355, 356, 358, 362, 365, 372, 379, 381, 383, 386, 392, 399, 400, 405, 408, 409, 411, 412, 413, 417, 420, 428, 434, 445, 489, 518, 531, 617, 631, 658, 659
Essenism, 190, 226, 232, 250, 252, 256, 259, 288, 412, 436
Ethical schools, the pagan, 509
Ethiopia, 221
Eucharist, Egyptian, 20, 21
Eucharistic mystery, 399, 400-1
Euchites, 547
Eudoxius, the Impious, 574, 641
Eudoxus, 49
Eunomius, Eunomians, 574, 585
Euripides, 41, 43-4, 46, 47, 75, 172
Eurydice, 63, 74
Eusebius, Bishop, 598-99
Eusebius of Caesarea, 506, 568
Eusebius of Dorylaeum, 588
Eusebius of Pamphylia, 159, 305, 463, 506, 512, 520, 530, 568, 571, 572, 575, 599, 602, 603
Eustathius, 576, 635
Eutyches, 588, 589, 590, 591, 649-50
Eutychian heresy, 649
Excommunication under Brahmanas, 120
Existentialist, 118
Ezekiel, 26, 160, 212, 213, 220, 248, 389, 472, 473,
Ezra, 210, 211, 222, 247

Father Bacchus, or Liber, 78
Faustus the Manichee, 318, 464, 555, 556, 559-60
Festus, 306, 442
Fifth Ecumenical Council, 591, 650
Fihrist, the Arabian, 549
Filioque Clause, 578
First Book of Esdras, 211
First Book of the Maccabees, 202-3
First Buddhist Council of Ragagriha, 141
First Ecumenical Council, 59
Flavian, Bishop, 589-90, 649, 650, 652
Florus, 205, 206
Fortunatus, 555
Fo-Sho-Hing-Tsan-King, 136, 331
Four Noble Truths of Buddhism, 139, 141, 142, 143
Fourth Ecumenical Council, 590
Fourth Esdras, 199, 426
Fourth Gospel, 310, 331, 332, 346, 352, 408, 484, 492-7, 502, 503, 516, 516, 563, 564, 588
Frahimrvana-zois, 87
Franklin, Benjamin, 37
Frashaostra, 88
Frazer, Sir John G., 26-7, 56-7, 61, 424

Fredun, 94, 101
Free Will, doctrine of, 608
Frogs, The, 166

Gabriel, 467
Gad, 208
Gainas, 112, 126-36, 143, 163, 328, 584
Galatians, 439
Galba, 475, 476, 477
Galerius, 185, 599
Ganges, 119, 127
Gathas, the, 84, 85, 93, 108
Gautama, 126, 136-41, 144, 147, 160, 290, 291, 303, 319, 369
Gayomard, 97
Ge, 77
Gelasius, Pope, Index of, 606
Genealogies, 310-11, 462
Gentiles, 199, 217, 218, 219, 225, 258, 269, 276
George, Bishop, 191, 604, 605
Getae, 38
Gförer, 287
Gibbon, 600, 653
Gnostic Christianity, Greek, 520-31
Gnostic-Zoroastrian concept, 462
Gnosticism, Hellenic, 520, 532, 538
Gnostics, 437, 449, 469, 498-9, 501, 520, 608
Gobak-Abu, 100
God of Light, 94, 96, 535, 546
God-man, the sacrificial, 280
Golden Ass, The, 69, 179
Golden Bough, The, 424
Golden Fleece, the, 73
Goldstein, Morris, 28
Good Principle, the, 96, 97
Gorgias, the, of Plato, 168
Gospel According to the Ebionites, The, 315, 317, 453
Gospel According to Matthew, the Aramaic, 315, 432, 461
Gospel Jesus, the, 92, 105, 123, 127, 133, 145, 147, 150, 154, 167, 175, 180, 192, 207, 212, 217, 223, 225, 226, 250, 259, 271, 284-6, 288-90, 292, 303, 309, 317, 322, 323, 324, 337, 345, 354, 364, 366, 375, 376, 378, 413, 415-6, 419, 420, 425, 431, 434, 453, 492, 507, 510, 525, 529, 537, 546, 608, 631-2, 602, 634, 660, 662
Gospels, Christian, the Jewish primitive, 314-5

Gospel to Hebrews, 312, 315, 334, 342
Gotama family, 136
Goths, the Arian, 575
Great Glory, the, 256
Great Goddesses, the, 65
Great Mother, the, 65
Greeks, the resourceful, 32-6
Gregory, Bishop, 603-4
Gregory Nazianzen, 568, 585, 600
Gregory of Nyssa, 633
Gregory Thaumaturgos, 568
Gregory the Great, 213, 490, 574, 575, 629, 641, 642, 643, 651-2
Guru, 110, 112, 114, 115, 116
Guthrie, W. K. C., 47

Habakkuk Commentary, The, 227, 267-9, 273-4, 475
Hades, brother of Zeus, 63, 64, 78, 79, 166, 169
Hadrian, Adrian, 195, 206, 532, 596
Hadrian, Pope, 653
Hamestagna, 101, 102, 162, 490, 536
Hannibal, 53
Haoma, 88, 92, 108, 257
Harikesa, 135
Heaven, 101, 105, 126, 164, 200, 230
Hebrew, Hebrews, 195, 199, 203, 204, 213, 221
Hebrews, Epistle to the, 453
Hecate, 301
Helen, 66
Helene, Queen, 282, 283
Heli of Luke, 463
Hell, 97, 101, 105, 111, 126, 164, 175, 200, 230
Hennel, 287
Hera, 41, 42
Heracleon, 535, 537
Heraclitus, 166
Hercules, 61, 77, 299
Heresies, 510, 600
Heretics, 600, 641
Hermes, 42, 64
Hermippus, 159
Herod Antipas, 360, 363, 376, 464
Herod the Great, 204, 236, 360, 467
Herodians, 319, 353, 368, 372, 495
Herodias, 360
Herodotus, 1, 5, 18, 36, 40, 41, 44, 46-7, 78, 93, 161, 164
Hesiod, 35, 61, 77, 78, 159, 337, 379, 417, 504
Heteroousians, 574-5

— 701 —

Hezikiah, 209, 210, 218, 219
Hilary of Poitiers, 486, 490, 569
Hilkiah, 210
Hinduism, 124, 142
Hindus, 86, 123
Hipparchus, 78
Hippo, Bishop of, 628
Hippolytus, 55, 56, 67-8, 158, 161, 449, 483, 484, 488, 505, 514, 532, 533, 540, 542, 564, 634
Hippolytus, son of Theseus, 75
Hippolytus, 75
Hitler, 195
Holy Family, 177
Holy Great One, 254, 256, 257, 258
Holy Roman Empire, 648
Hom-Eucharist, 92
Homer, 35-6, 44, 67, 75, 78, 159, 504
Homeric, 60, 66, 67, 77
Homoiousians, 574
Homoousians, 486
Honorius, Roman pope, 592, 652
Horus, the Elder, 6, 47
Horus, the Younger, 3, 9, 178, 198
Hoshea, 201
Huns, 575
Hushedar, 96, 98, 99, 100, 104
Hosius, 570, 571
Hyksos, 198
Hymn to Demeter, 60, 63
Hymns to Orpheus, 74
Hypatia, 604
Hyrcanus II, 204, 267, 269

Iacchus, 70
Ibas, 590, 591, 650
Iconoclasts, the, 643
Ictinus, 61
Ignatius, Bishop, 308, 500-1, 507, 512, 564
Ikhnaton, 197, 198, 418, 662
Ilia, 299
Iliad, 44
In defense of Free Will, 611
Index Expurgatorius, the first, 606
India, 107, 122, 124, 127, 128, 141, 148, 163, 186, 191, 295, 352
Indo-Aryans, 108
Indra, 109
I. W. W., 128, 129
Ineffable Name, the, 282
Infinite Soul, 122
Ingersoll, 531
Innocent I, Pope, 649

Inquisition, 195
Institutes of Vishnu, The, 107
Iran, 107, 108
Iranian, 104, 109
Iranian-Sumerians, 662
Irenaeus, 59, 306, 481, 485, 498, 505, 512, 514, 520, 521, 532, 533, 534, 564-5
Irene, Queen, 653
Irving, Edward, 481
Isaiah, 208, 209, 215, 218, 220, 221, 227, 232, 282, 316, 320, 346, 365, 389, 406, 459, 469, 504
Ishtar, 25, 26, 27, 29, 30, 31, 53, 65, 75, 210, 552
Isis, 2, 7-8, 9-10, 11, 15, 37, 39, 52, 53, 60, 61, 62, 63, 64, 65, 68, 177, 178, 179, 180, 183, 198, 300, 301, 588, 593
Isis-Demeter, 61, 68
Isis-Osirian symbolism, 9
Islam, 86, 122, 547, 654-6, 656
Islands of the Blest, 168
Isocrates, on Demeter, 62
Israel, 200, 201, 207, 208, 212, 213, 217, 218, 219, 220, 248, 274, 275, 321, 354, 355, 426, 468, 478, 487, 498, 514
Israelites 198, 200, 201, 210

Jacob, 199, 200, 201, 202, 261, 271, 345, 469, 504, 514
Jacob, the, of Matthew, 463
Yahweh-cult, 207, 208, 210, 211
Jairus, 352
James the Disciple, 319, 330, 338, 367, 401, 402
James, the Epistle of, 453
James the Just, 304, 306, 307, 310
Jason, 73
Jebusites, 200
Jehoiakim, puppet-king, 202
Jehovah, 534
Jehovah's Witnesses, 420, 426, 428, 481
Jehu, 202
Jeremiah, 160, 209, 210, 213, 514
Jericho, 196
Jerome, 136, 299, 468, 481, 493, 506, 568, 613, 616, 634, 637-8, 639
Jerusalem, 199, 201, 203, 204, 205, 206, 210, 212, 213, 216, 218, 219, 220, 221, 234, 248, 257, 258, 267, 270, 272, 473, 479
Jesse, 219, 223, 462, 465

— 702 —

Jesus, detailed discussion of, **419-421**
Jesus-Christ, 82, 88, 184, 662
Jewel, the Parable of the, 148
Jewish colony in China, 216
Jewish-Christian God, 95
Jewish Christians, 443, 453, 455, 463, 472, 478, 479, 484, 494, 515
Jewish-Gentile problem, 149
Jewish parties, 230
Jewish Sect of Qumran, 267
Jewish War, a, 304
Jews, 77, 95, 124, 158, 195-6, 197, 199, 200-7, 211, 213, 214, 216-25, 274, 276, 405, 413-14, 478
Jezebel, Queen of Ahab, 209, 212
Joachim, father of Mary, 464
Joanna, 348
Job, 229
Joel, 212
John, Bishop, 487
John, bishop of Ephesus, 483
John Cassian, 634, 637
John Chrysostom, St., 568
John the Baptist, 89, 138, 236, 304, 308, 316-7, 346, 360, 368, 390, 416, 468, 495, 521
John the Disciple, 310, 319, 330, 338, 367, 401, 402, 409, 443
John, the epistles of, 454-5
John, the Gospel of, 312, 313-4, 320, 345, 364, 400, 407, 457, 458, 459, 556, 579, 588
John Hyrcanus, 203, 233, 234, 251-2, 267, 271, 272, 273, 274
John of Gischala, 205
John, Pope, 652
Jonas, 372
Jonathan, the Maccabee, 230, 273
Jonathan, the high priest, 205
Jordan, John at the, 317
Joseph, father of Jesus, 320, 461, 462, 464, 465, 466, 467, 493, 498, 514
Joseph of Arimithea, 408, 461, 463, 464
Josephus, 176, 204, 205-6, 215, 221, 226, 228, 229, 230, 231, 236, 237, 239-45, 246, 261, 262, 265, 270, 274, 287, 304, 305, 306, 307, 310
Joses, 432
Joshua, 196, 205
Josiah, King, 202, 210
Jovian, 573, 574, 605
Judah, 204, 221, 272, 275
Judah Iskarito, 282
Judaic Christology, 498

Judaism, 91, 123, 154, 195-224, 199, 200, 230, 232, 253, 262, 280, 292, 342, 370, 377, 414, 416, 432, 437, 479, 510, 531, 596, 655
Judaizers, genealogies of the, 462, 470, 500, 512, 513, 525
Judas Iscariot, 284, 398, 399, 403
Judas Maccabaeus, 254, 257, 273, 490
Judas the Gaulonite, 204, 360
Jude, 253
Julian, Emperor, 29-30, 185, 191, 573, 604-5, 621
Julian of Eclanum, 612, 613-4
Julius Caesar, 308
Julius Firmicus Maternus, 17, 78
Julius, Pope, 648-9
Jupiter, 52, 297
Justin Martyr, 157, 164, 182-3, 296, 297, 298, 299, 317, 337, 463, 466, 469, 481, 502, 503, 504, 505, 530, 597
Justinian, 23, 178, 591, 650
Justus of Tiberias, 304, 310

Kasyapa, 141
Khandalas, 111, 120
Kharma, 112, 126, 132, 134, 135, 171, 350
Khirbet-Qumran, 227, 233, 236, 266, 274, 288, 399
King of Heaven, 278, 281
Kingdom, the apocalyptic, 394-5
Kingdom of God, of Heaven, of Christ, 150, 317, 324, 325, 335, 342, 345, 348, 351, 354, 355, 358, 368, 373, 376, 377, 379, 371-8, 392, 395, 396, 397, 415, 425, 426, 513, 514, 517
Kingdom of Righteousness, 150, 409
Kinvad Bridge, 101, 102, 104, 186
Kittim, 250, 267, 269
Knox, 629
Koran, 86, 547
Kore, 63, 67, 68, 69
Krishna, 121
Kshatriyas, 109, 110, 111, 118, 125, 132, 133, 144, 153
Kuretes, 46

Lactantius, 59, 484-6, 488, 506, 598
Lake of Fire, 162
Lake of Memory, 169
Last Judgment, 102-3, 396, **479**
Latter-Day Saints, 480

— 703 —

Laws, of Plato, 167
Laws of Manu, The, 107
Lazarus, resurrection of, 345, 496
Lazarus-rich-man story, 259, 382, 496, 518
Leah, 504
Lenin, 379
Leo the Great, 547, 549, 590, 600, 605-6, 644, 649, 650, 651
Lesbians, 46
Lethe, 164, 171
Leucippe, 46
Leucippus, 36
Levirate marriage, 392
Levites, 249, 262, 272, 275, 371
Leviticus, 219
Libby, W. F., 227
Libyans, 199
Licinius, 185
Life of Anthony, 639
Livy, 54, 301-2
Locke, 607
Logia, the, of Jesus, 503
Logos Doctrine, 105, 186, 237, 433, 449, 513, 534, 539, 540, 543, 563, 662
Lombards, the, 489, 575, 642
Lord of Spirits, 255, 260, 261, 499
Lord's Prayer, the, 340
Lost Books of the Bible, The, 272
Lourdes, shrine of, 322
Lucian, 36
Lucian of Samosata, 544
Lucianist-Arians, 571
Lucretius, 36
Luke, 132, 133, 136, 187, 260, 311-12, 313, 316, 317, 320, 330, 333, 345, 347, 354, 382, 383, 392, 397, 398, 404, 407, 457, 458, 462, 463, 465, 466, 467, 468, 469, 470, 498, 517, 522, 523, 528, 556
Lust, daughter of Mara, 139
Luther, 629
Lycurgus of Sparta, 34
Lycurgus of Thrace, 7, 44
Lysis, 157, 159

McPherson, Aimee Semple, 323
Maat, 3
Macarius, 592
Maccabees, 203, 251, 257, 269
Macedonians, 84, 585
Macedonius, Bishop, 577
Maenads, 43, 44, 45, 49, 74, 75, 496
Magi and Magianism, 94, 161, 469

Magna Grecia, 156
Mahavira, 133-36, 160, 299, 308
Mahendra, 142
Mahershalalhashbaz, 219
Maimonides, 216
Malachi, 207, 316
Mammon, 380
Man of the Lie, 249
Manahem, 236
Manasseh, 209, 210
Manes, 158, 308, 416, 545, 546, 549, 551
Manichaeans, 317, 464, 487, 490, 493, 536, 545-6, 547-8, 605-6, 608, 609, 629
Manichaeism, 91, 99, 101, 182, 192, 291, 416. 538, 545-61, 603, 613-14, 615, 617, 634
Manual of Discipline, The, 227, 232, 261, 262, 263, 264-7, 265, 341, 434, 517
Mara, 129, 139, 146
Marathon, 85
Marcan Hypothesis, 311
Marcellians, 585
Marcellus, 583-4
Marcian, 590, 650
Marcion, 305, 437, 520-31, 541, 546, 617, 648
Marcionism, 529, 549
Marcionites, 318, 378, 392, 438, 451, 482, 493, 522-3, 526, 535, 566, 602, 608, 635
Marcus, Valentinian Gnostic, 535
Mariolatry, 433, 587-8, 606, 659, 662
Mark, 103, 131, 148, 233, 311-12, 313, 317, 320, 330-31, 332, 345, 346, 354, 370, 382, 383, 392, 395, 397, 404, 407, 432, 436, 453, 454, 458, 459, 472, 502, 516, 525, 528, 556
Mark Twain, 323, 324, 325
Marriage, Brahmanic, 111
Mars, 299
Martha and Mary, 371
Martin, St., 487, 640
Marx, Karl, 379, 418
Mary, 87, 136, 180, 184, 464, 466, 467, 469, 492, 498, 501, 514, 588, 593
Mary, mother of James, 408
Mary-Jesus, 177
Mary Magdalene, 348, 408, 457
Master of Justice, 234, 288, 405, 409, 425

Mattathias, 203
Matthew, the Disciple, 326, 467, 470
Matthew, the Gospel of, 132, 138, 144, 169, 310, 311-12, 315, 317, 318, 332, 334, 336, 345, 350, 368, 370, 376, 382, 383, 392, 393, 394, 397, 403, 407, 409, 435, 453, 457, 458, 459, 460, 461, 463, 464, 465, 466, 469, 496, 516, 525, 526, 528, 530
Maximian, 596
Maximilla, 482
Maya, Queen, 136
Mazda, 88
Mazdeans, 184
Mazdeism, 84, 91, 94, 108
Media, 201
Median-Assyrian Empire, 224
Megiddo, battle of, 202
Meison, King, 51
Melampian cult, 40
Melampus, 40, 41, 47, 48
Melchizedek, 453
Melinda, King, 152
Menander, 533
Menelaus, 66
Mennonites, 417
Merneptah, 199
Mesopotamia, 201
Messiah, the Ebonite, 514
Messiah, the Essene, 253, 258, 266, 267, 268, 277, 278, 318, 350, 411
Messiah, the Jewish, 82, 109, 206, 218, 219, 220, 221, 222, 225, 230, 231, 313, 316, 371, 386, 408, 414, 456, 462, 469, 493
Messiah of Moral Judgment, 350, 399, 403, 408, 414, 425
Messiah-Christ, the Jewish, 474, 479, 481
Messiahs, Zoroastrian, 299
Messianic expectation, 195, 204, 212, 216-25
Messianic empire, the, 474
Messianic kingdom, the, 254, 256, 258, 259, 260, 477
Messianic pretenders, 296
Metaneira, 63
Metapontium, 156
Methodius, 634
Micah, 212, 219
Midas, 52
Miller, 480
Millerites, 480
Milo, 156

Milton, 424
Mine Elect One, 260
Mine Elect Ones, 260
Minei, 468
Minerva, 179
Minoan period, 62
Minos, 35, 36, 298
Minucius Felix, 643
Minyas, 16
Miracles, 322, 351-2
Mithra, 94, 102, 182, 184, 185-6, 188, 296, 301, 304, 308, 662
Mithraic cosmology, 549
Mithraism, 181-192, 256, 291, 400, 416, 444, 445, 466
Mitra, 99, 108, 109
Mnemosyne, 78, 164, 416
Moabites, 200, 233
Mohammedans, 91, 95, 124, 420, 547, 656
Monarchians, the, 539-44
Monophysitism, 588-91
Monothelite heresy, the, 591
Monthelites, 592
Montanism, 482, 483, 529-30
Montanists, 47, 481, 483, 487, 627, 640
Montanus, 481-2, 483, 530
Morals of the Manichees, 555
More, Thomas, 379
Mormons, 342, 417, 421, 427, 480
Morsimus, 166
Mosaic Law, 210, 211, 213, 287, 326, 327, 334, 371, 376, 378, 384, 390, 429, 443, 453, 473, 487, 492, 513, 514, 643
Moses 36, 207, 211, 215, 217, 221, 231, 320, 367, 413, 430, 443, 504, 514
Moslems, 86, 620, 651, 652
Mother Goddess, 52, 53, 56
Muller, Max, 84, 136
Musaeus, 61, 72, 73, 77, 78, 175
My Several Worlds, 420
Mycenaean era, 36, 73, 75
Mystagogues, 67, 70
Mysteries, the Greater, 61, 66-8, 70
Mysteries, the Lesser, 67
Mystery-cults, 24, 154, 300-2, 509-10

Naaman the Syrian, 321
Naasenes, 55, 68
Nagasena, 150, 152
Nana, 52
Narses, 23
Nazarenes, 325, 330, 432, 468

Nebseni, 47, 82
Nebuchadnezzar, 24, 83, 99, 202, 212, 223, 248
Negative Confession, 14-15
Nehru, 124
Neo-Dionysus, the Orphic, 67
Neo-Orphic system, 161
Neo-Platonists, 78
Nepas, 483
Nephthys, 3, 178
Nero, 185, 308, 471, 475, 476, 477, 595, 596
Neron, 475, 476
Nestorians, 487, 506, 585-8, 589, 590, 591
Nestorius, 585, 586, 587
Republic, The, of Plato, 332
Nicaea, Council of, 59, 506, 570-81, 635
Nicene Creed, 486, 565, 571-2, 573, 658
Nile, the, 1, 3
Nirvana, 82, 115, 116, 117, 118, 126, 127, 136, 137, 146, 152, 164, 289, 373
Nisan, 381
Noah, Noe, 90, 384, 514
Nous, 524, 533, 534, 562
Novatian, Pope, 505, 510, 511, 564, 585, 619-20, 627, 635, 640
Novatus, 510

Odyssey, the, 44
Oeagrus, 73
Ohm, 117
Olympian Games, 62
Onomacritus, 40, 78, 80-1, 160, 161
Origen, 281, 296, 299, 306, 307, 336, 466, 467, 484, 490, 506, 554, 566, 567, 568-9, 583, 597-8, 607, 608, 609, 643
Origenism in Spain, 547
Original Sin, 554, 614, 615, 618
Ormazd, 185, 186, 188, 190
Orosius, 611
Orphean Dionysus, 65
Orphean reform, 47, 76
Orpheans, the primitive, 158
Orpheus, 40, 43, 48, 61, 63, 72-82, 161, 175
Orpheus, the Pythagorean, 160, 166, 167, 168, 172
Orphic literature, 72, 73, 77, 80
Orphic-Bacchic mystery, 161
Orphic-Christian redemption, 501
Orphic-Dionysiac, 69, 78, 164, 400
Orphic-Eleusinian ritual, 69, 658

Orphic-Essene Jesus, 431
Orphic-Pythagoreanism, 163, 164-6, 169, 170, 171, 172-5, 232, 396, 412, 429, 490-1, 497, 662
Orphics, 77
Orphism, 49, 66, 68, 74, 76-7, 81, 160
Osirian cult, 13-15, 17-18, 19, 20, 21, 22-3, 38
Osirian-Dionysiac soteriology, 417
Osirian myth, 9, 66
Osirian ritual, 79, 400
Osirianism, 58, 66, 69, 80, 164, 412
Osiris-cult, 2-23, 38, 39, 43, 48, 49, 51, 53, 56, 60, 63, 75, 79, 81, 82, 162, 177, 178, 180, 187, 198, 281, 296, 365, 541, 657, 662
Osiris-Dionysus, 38, 39, 81, 92, 166
Ostrogoths, 575
Otho, Emperor, 477
Outcastes, 111, 125
Over-Soul, 122
Ovid, 46, 75

Padiragtaraspo, 87
Pahlavi Texts, 84, 182
Paine, 418, 555
Painful Forest, the 137
Palestine, 200, 205, 216, 220
Panarion, 498
Pandera, Panthera, 281-4
Pantheism, Brahmanic, 121
Papacy, 646-49, 650, 651, 653
Paphos, 30
Paphnutius, 635
Papias, 305, 308, 311, 481
Pappa, 52, 56, 58
Paraclete, the, 482
Parasava, 111, 139
Parousia, 82, 105, 225, 253, 274, 277, 278, 286, 310, 335, 343, 345, 350, 351, 354, 365, 373, 376, 379, 384, 385, 386, 387, 394, 396, 401, 404, 409, 411, 412, 417, 421, 425, 436, 450, 451, 452, 454, 462, 470, 472, 475, 476, 480, 481, 485, 492, 497, 499, 503, 583
Parsees, 86-7
Parthenon, 61
Parthian Empire, 84, 86, 182
Passover, the, 59, 270, 365, 368, 375, 381, 398, 406
Pataliputra, 127, 242
Patripassians, 539-42, 566
Paul, St., 105, 190, 278, 298, 305, 306,

— 706 —

308, 425, 431, 432, 436, 437-52, 454-5, 460, 462, 472, 478, 481, 484, 492, 496, 503, 520, 522-4, 525, 528-9, 548, 553, 557, 560, 562, 564, 608, 617, 624, 625, 629, 631, 634
Paul of Samosata, 505-6, 542-4, 568, 572
Paulians, 602
Paulicians, 522
Pauline, 17, 190, 437, 438, 441, 445-7, 448, 449, 453, 462, 472, 483, 499, 500, 507, 515, 546
Paulinus, 610-11
Pausanias, 5, 36, 44, 53, 61, 62, 66, 72, 73, 77, 78, 300, 301
Pelagianism, 612, 420, 617, 619
Pelagians, 609-19, 621
Pelagius, 609-11, 612-3, 648
Pella, 474-5
Pentecost, 482
Pentheus, 44-5
Pepi, 82
Periphlegethon, 103
Persecution, 594-606, 620
Persephone, 28, 60, 62-4, 74, 78, 79, 80, 81, 82, 160, 164, 168, 184, 301, 308
Persepolis, 86
Perseus, 35, 297
Persia, 186, 202, 233, 295, 352
Persian Empire, 85, 161, 220, 223, 256, 411, 414, 471, 545
Pessinus, 54, 179
Peter of Constantinople, 592
Peter, St., 54, 113, 305, 306, 308, 310, 311, 324, 330, 364, 365, 367, 385, 401, 402, 405, 408-9, 425, 428, 429, 431-2, 438, 443, 444, 457, 458, 459, 460, 513, 515, 517, 518, 527, 548, 588, 646
Petilian, 625, 626
Petrine epistles, 454
Phaedra, 75
Phanes, 78
Phanes-Eros-Dionysus, 80
Pharaoh-Necho, 202
Pharisees, 147, 203-4, 215-6, 234, 268, 269, 274, 319, 327, 338, 347, 349, 352, 353, 358, 360, 361, 362, 363, 365, 368, 370, 371, 372, 376, 381, 383, 384, 389, 391, 393, 409, 414, 425, 443, 461, 490, 495, 496, 511
Philae, 23, 178
Philemon, 170

Philip, 360
Philip the Disciple, 320
Philippians, the, 439
Philistines, the, 200
Philo Judaeus, 93, 226, 235-39, 237, 246, 247, 265, 579
Philolaus, 157, 159
Philostratus, 195
Phoenicians, 83
Photinus, 583, 583-4
Photius of Constantinople, 304, 500
Phronesia, 534
Phrygia, 51, 54, 60, 82, 179, 182
Pindar, 43-4, 53, 62
Plataea, 85
Plato, 167, 167-70, 172, 175, 176, 237, 299, 332, 379, 562, 563, 579, 598
Platonic, 103
Platonic Gnosticism, 523
Platonism, 190
Platonists, 157
Pleasant Land, 514
Pleroma, 536
Pliny the Elder, 227-8
Pliny the Younger, 306, 308, 442
Plotinus, 600
Plutarch, 5, 27, 36, 39, 46, 49, 60, 64, 71, 79, 152, 171, 185, 270
Pneumatomachi, 577
Polycrates, 155
Polygnotus, 72, 73
Pompeii, Villa of Mysteries at, 68
Pompey, 204, 234, 252, 267, 270, 272, 277
Pontius Pilate, 283, 304, 307-8, 405-6, 408, 409, 430
Porphyrios, 46
Poseidon, 75, 78
Pragapati, 109, 121
Praxeas, 541, 648
Priapus, 180, 181, 308
Primeval Ox, 97
Primordial Man, 550
Prince of Darkness, 550
Priscilla, 482
Priscillian, 547
Prodigal Son, 149
Proetus, 47
Proserpine, 81
Prosymne, 81
Protagoras, 36
Protestant Reformers, 629-30, 652
Protestant Revolution, 641, 656
Proteus, 42

Protevangelium, 464, 466
Psalms of Solomon, 252
Ptolemies, 202, 222, 223
Ptolemy, 535
Ptolemy I Soter, 177
Pulcheria, Queen, 590, 650
Purgatory, 97, 489-91
Purushaspo, 87
Pyramid Texts, 20, 47
Pyramids, 2
Pythagoras, 140, 155-76, 213, 232, 234, 237, 248, 417, 418, 420
Pythagorean, 40, 153, 189, 256, 265, 334, 336, 344, 352, 379, 411, 412, 413, 415, 489, 531, 532, 608
Pythagoreanism, 72, 155, 157, 159-60, 175, 176, 190, 232, 261, 280, 341, 399, 412, 445
Pythagoreans, 76, 77, 81, 155-6, 157-8, 169, 172-5, 241, 253, 284-6, 290, 301, 327, 330, 332, 335, 338, 340, 358, 373, 435, 533, 617, 659
Pythagoristae, 173

Questions of Melinda, The, 151
Qumran monastery, 226
Quodvulteus, 625

Ra, 2, 77
Rachel, 504
Rahab, 453
Rahula, 137
Rameses II, 199
Raphael, 256
Rashnu, 102
Reformation, 588, 619, 628-30
Rehoboam, 201
Renaissance, 656
Renan, 182
Republic, The, of Plato, 169
Revelation, 101, 105, 165, 219, 220, 256, 260, 278, 426, 432, 455, 471-9, 481, 482, 483, 484, 486, 493, 495, 503, 522
Rhadamanthus, Rhadamanthys, 35, 298
Rhea, 35, 42, 56, 78
Rich Fool, the parable of the, 134-5
Rich Young Man, the story of, 519
Rig-Veda, the, 107, 117
Rishis, 132
Robber Synod, 449, 589, 589-90, 650
Roberts, Oral, 323
Robertson, John M., 304, 309, 356
Roman Empire, 185, 226, 302, 306, 450

Roman pope supreme ruler, 594
Romans, 83, 178, 181, 195, 204, 205, 216, 217, 267, 268, 270, 277, 476, 645
Romans, The Epistle to the, 439
Rome, 55, 177, 474, 476, 477
Rousseau, 484
Rubaiyat, 656
Rufinus, 568
Russelites, 428

Sabaeans, 221
Sabazius, 37, 44
Sabbath, 231-2, 270, 329, 362, 414
Sabellians, 77, 563, 566, 568, 571
Sabellius, 541-2, 648
Sacra Via, 61, 70, 71
Sacred Books of the East, 136
Sadducees, 203, 214, 215, 230, 231, 233, 234, 252, 259, 269, 349, 392, 528
Sadvastaran, 102
Saints, the Jewish, 473, 476
Sakya, King, 136
Salamis, 85
Salome, 408
Sama-Veda, 107
Samaria, 201, 209, 218, 219
Samaritan leper, the, 383
Samgha, the, 126, 140, 144-5
Samos, 155
Samothrace, 51
Samuel, 207
Sangarius, 52
Sanhedrin, the, 306, 404-5, 431, 460
Saoshyant, 100, 103, 222, 223, 230, 232, 281, 479
Sargon II, 201, 209
Sarpedon, 35
Satan, 95, 105, 183, 256, 279, 472, 475, 476, 478, 510, 517, 518, 550, 601, 614, 618, 640-41
Saturninus, Saturnilius, 521-2, 533
Saul, King, 208
Sayings of Jesus, 312, 313, 503
Schweitzer, Albert, 332, 366
Scythia, Scythians, 38
Second Coming, 277, 397, 412, 451, 481, 484
Second Ecumenical Council, 577-8
Seleucids, Seleucidae, 202, 222, 223
Semele, 35, 41, 42, 43, 63, 76, 79, 80, 160, 297
Semi-Pelagianism, 617

Semi-Pelagians, 612, 619
Semites, 24, 200, 256, 512-19
Semjaza, 256
Sennacherib, 195, 209
Serapeum, the, 181
Serapion, Bishop, 482
Serapis, 37, 180-1, 300, 301
Sergius, 591-2, 652
Sermon on the Mount, 331, 332-44, 369, 381, 434, 496
Servetus, 542
Sesostris III, 38
Set, 6-9, 79
Seventh-Day Adventists, 427
Seventh Ecumenical Council, the, 588, 644, 645, 653
Severus, 596
Shalmaneser, 201
Shaphan, 210
Shapirabo, 100
Shayast-La-Shayast, 424
Shemig-Abu, 100
Shu, 2
Sicarii, 205
Sicily, 65
Sign of the Cross, 91
Silas, 432
Simeon, 408, 467
Simon Magus, Simonians, 308, 416, 501, 512, 515, 520-1, 527
Simon of Cyrenia, 406
Simon of Gioras, 205
Simon, the Maccabee, 203, 273
Simon, the Pharisee, 347
Sirmium III, Synod of, 574
Siva, 109
Sixth Ecumenical Council, 592, 652
Smyrneans, 38
Socrates, 156
Socrates Scholasticus, 181
Solomon, 200, 201, 204, 207, 209, 257, 372
Soma, 108
Son of David, 371, 386, 389, 392-3, 398, 398-9, 495
Son of God, 317, 318, 331, 393, 436, 500, 539
Son of Man, 204, 220, 224, 235, 253, 255, 260, 261, 279, 290, 318, 320, 328, 350, 355, 373, 383, 396, 411, 426, 472, 539
Sons of Darkness, 234, 250, 251, 261, 518
Sons of Light, 250, 251, 261, 518, 533

Sons of Zadok, 230, 248
Sopater, 600
Sophia, 534
Soshans, 96, 100, 101, 102, 103, 220, 224, 260, 396, 397, 477
Soteriology, the Essene, 281
Soul of the Universe, 121
Sower, the parable of the, 135
Sozomen, 106, 573, 600
Sraosha, 102
Srotriyas, 113
Star of Jacob, the, 206, 479
State religion, Greek and Roman, 509
Stephen, 430-1, 443
Stephen, Pope, 505, 647
Stoics, 158, 231, 237, 240
Strabo, 24, 34, 36, 43, 51, 53, 81
Strauss, 305, 322
Students in India, 116
Stylites, 118
Sudras, 110, 111, 113-4, 120, 121, 125, 127, 139, 144
Suetonius, 306, 308
Suffering Servant, the, 220, 355, 358, 407, 411, 459
Sulpitius Severus, 487, 595, 637, 640
Sumerian culture, 1, 83
Supreme God, 96, 108, 231, 471, 499, 513, 524-5, 533, 549, 569
Susanna, 348
Sylvester, Pope, 648
Synoptic Gospels, the, 105, 311-4, 317, 331, 349, 352, 364, 378, 400, 438, 440, 445, 456-69, 492, 493, 495, 499, 502, 503
Syracuse, 64
Syria, Syrian, 60, 64, 177, 201, 204
Syrian Gnostics, 513
Syro-Phoenician woman, 515-7

Tabitha, 429
Tacitus, 205, 306, 307, 308
Tammuz, 26, 29
Tarentum, 157
Tartarus, 168, 170
Tathagata, 138-9, 141, 144
Tatian, 502, 503, 505, 530, 564
Taurobolium, 57-8, 189
Taylor, Thomas, 80
Teacher of Righteousness, 234, 235, 236, 248, 268, 269, 270, 274, 275, 276, 277, 280, 281, 292, 316, 365, 386, 399, 408, 409, 412, 460, 468, 521

— 709 —

Tufnet, 2
Tem, 2, 77
Ten Tribes of Israel, 201, 209
Tertullian, 159, 182, 298, 299, 299-300, 306, 483, 490, 505, 506, 507, 512, 520, 522, 523, 528-9, 532, 534, 536, 539, 541, 565, 566, 597, 598, 607, 634, 643, 647, 648
Testaments of the Twelve Patriarchs, The, 194, 227, 252, 271, 272, 273, 274-6, 277, 278, 290, 341, 345
Teutons, 83
Thanksgiving Psalms, The, 227, 252
Thebes, Dionysus comes to, 42
Theodore of Mopsuestia, 591, 650
Theodoret, 506, 573, 587, 590, 591, 637, 646, 649, 650
Theodosius, 23, 61, 181, 191, 573, 577, 587, 605
Theodosius II, 589, 650
Theodotus the Tanner, 449, 540
Theophilus of Alexandria, 181, 605
Theopilus of Antioch, 298, 564
Theotokos, the, 587
Theseus, 75, 172, 299
Thesmophoria, 65, 69
Thessalonians, 439, 440, 446, 450
Theudas the Egyptian, 205
Thiasoi, the, 176, 189
Third Buddhist Council, 142
Thirst, daughter of Mara, 139
Thomas Aquinas, 490
Thoth, 3, 15
Thrace, 38, 40, 42, 60, 75, 82
Thracians, 38, 49, 51
Thrasymachus of Plato, 168
Three Chapters, the heresy of the, 591
Three Talents, the parable of the, 135
Thucydides, 71
Thyone, 42
Tiberias Caesar, 306
Tiglah-Pileser III, 209
Timothies, the Pauline, 437, 440
Titanic fragments, 80, 165
Titans, 35, 78, 80, 160, 435
Titus, 195, 199, 205-6, 395
Titus, friend of Paul, 432
Titus, the Pauline epistle, 437, 440
Tome of Leo, The, 590, 650
Traditors, 620, 626
Trajan, 308, 596
Transubstantiation, 659
Trappists, 337, 342
Trial by Ordeal in India, 116

Trinitarian doctrine and controversy, 59, 562-82
Trinitarianism, 564-5, 566
Trinity, doctrine of, 313, 433, 493
Trisala, 133
Trito-Isaiah, 221
Trypho, 337
Turanians, 88

Ulysses, 34
Unas, 20, 47
Unique Teacher, the, 248, 249, 267
Universal Soul, 117, 118
Upali, 141
Upanishads, 108, 121, 122, 126, 131, 138, 164
Uranos, 77
Uriel, 256
Ussher, Archibishop, 480

Vaisyas, 110, 111, 125 153
Valens, Emperor, 573, 575, 605
Valentinians, 490, 532, 533, 535-38, 602
Valentinus, 532, 533, 534, 535
Valerian, 596, 598, 620
Vandals, 575
Varuna, 108
Varus, 204
Vasishtha Darmasastra, 107
Vayu, 108, 109
Vedanta-Sutra, 108, 121
Vedas, 107-8, 109, 110, 113, 118, 121, 122, 124, 127, 132, 151
Vendidad, 85, 91
Venturini, 287
Venus of Paphos, 179
Vigilius, Pope, 650, 651
Vergil, 171, 172
Vespasian, 205, 471, 474, 475, 476, 477, 478
Vesantara, King, 131
Villa of Mysteries, 68
Vincent of Lerins, 641
Virgin Birth, 154, 312, 313, 317, 318, 413, 432, 433, 449, 456, 463, 465-73, 468, 493, 499, 501, 502, 504, 515, 535-6, 540, 558, 562, 566, 588, 662
Virgin Mary, 543
Vishnu, 109, 121
Vishtasp, King, 84, 88, 98
Visigoths, 575
Vitellius, Emperor, 477
Vohu Mano, 87, 88
von der Alm, 287

Vulgate, the, 638

War of the Sons of Light with the Sons of Darkness, 227, 250, 254, 257
Washington, George, 308
Watchers, the, 254, 256, 258
Wealth, 146
West, E. W., 84
Wheel of Life, 117, 122, 126, 137, 143
Wheel of the Law, 137, 143
Who is the Rich Man?, 385
Wilson, Edmund, 288
Wisdom Literature, Jewish, 337
Wise Men, 466
Women, 48, 115-6, 130, 185, 348, 371, 445, 527
Wood of Austerities, 137
Word, in Fourth Gospel, 492 ff., 540, 565, 579

Yagur-Veda, 107
Yahweh, 195, 196, 197, 207-11, 212, 223, 469
Yasas, 139
Yasodhara, 137
Yasts, 85
Yeshu, Yeshoshua, 281-4, 376, 459, 460, 463
Yima, 90, 96

Zacchaeus, 387
Zadokite Fragment, A, 247
Zadokites, 230, 248
Zagreus, 79, 80, 160, 365, 435
Zagreus-Titan myth, 46, 69, 78, 165

Zalmoxis, 37
Zarathustra, 83
Zaratus, 161
Zaratust, 83, 88, 97, 98, 100, 104
Zathraustes, 83
Zealots, 204, 205, 319, 390, 391
Zechariah, 207, 219, 372, 389, 459
Zecharias, 468
Zedekiah, 202
Zend, 85
Zend-Avesta, 85
Zeno the Isaurian, 648
Zeno the Stoic, 93, 237, 299, 442, 563, 579
Zephyrinus, Pope, 647
Zeus, 28, 38, 41, 63, 78, 79, 160, 180, 435
Zoroaster, 83, 84, 86, 87-8, 156, 160, 169, 186, 232, 298, 308, 319
Zoroastrian, 216, 220, 221, 222, 223, 225, 229, 247, 248, 250, 252, 256, 257, 259, 354, 370, 380, 398, 397, 411, 412, 413, 414, 415, 417, 454, 466, 471, 472, 478, 495, 527, 532, 534, 545, 547, 549, 552, 568
Zoroastrian-Danielic Jesus, a, 513
Zoroastrian-Pythagoreanism, 215, 216, 230, 255
Zoroastrianism, 24, 66, 83-106, 108-9, 123, 154, 182, 187, 188, 190, 231, 253, 255, 256, 279, 341, 412, 447, 479, 490, 596, 655
Zoroastrians, 77, 83-106, 124, 158, 162, 182, 185, 196, 286, 316, 420, 536
Zosimus, Pope, 611, 612, 649